PACIFIC NORTHWEST HIKING

FOGHORN OUTDOORS®

PACIFIC NORTHWEST HIKING

The Complete Guide to More Than
1,000 of the Best Hikes in Washington and Oregon

5th Edition

Scott Leonard & Megan McMorris

AVALON
TRAVEL

FOGHORN OUTDOORS PACIFIC NORTHWEST HIKING
The Complete Guide to More Than 1,000 of the Best Hikes in Washington and Oregon

Fifth Edition

Scott Leonard & Megan McMorris

Printing History
1st edition—1995
5th edition—May 2005
5 4 3 2 1

Avalon Travel Publishing
An Imprint of
Avalon Publishing Group, Inc.

AVALON
publishing group incorporated

ISBN: 1-56691-590-2
ISSN: 1082-0760

Editor: Elizabeth McCue
Series Manager: Ellie Behrstock
Acquisitions Editor: Rebecca K. Browning
Copy Editors: Karen Gaynor Bleske, Elizabeth Wolf
Graphics Coordinator: Justin Marler
Production Coordinator: Tabitha Lahr
Cover and Interior Designer: Darren Alessi
Map Editor: Kat Smith
Cartographers: Mike Morgenfeld, Kat Kalamaras
Indexer: May Hasso

Front cover photo: Hiker on the trail to Mason Lake © Chris Duval

Printed in United States by Worzalla

About the Author

Scott Leonard has been hiking in Washington for nearly 10 years. A Pacific Northwest native, Scott started his outdoor adventures in the forests and high deserts of Oregon before coming to Washington during college and exploring the Olympic Mountains. After years of hiking in the state for recreation, Scott spent several years at the nonprofit EarthCorps, specializing in trail construction projects. So he has not only hiked many of Washington's trails, but has built several of them as well.

While writing *Foghorn Outdoors Pacific Northwest Hiking,* Scott spent much of two summers on the trail, logging more than 1,000 miles. That much trail time is not without peril, as he escaped disaster on the Gray Wolf River by braving record rains in October 2003. Although bears have been frequent acquaintances, he fears no wildlife more than the tent-eating field mouse.

Scott's love lies first with the Olympic Mountains, but he enjoys exploring all of the Northwest's wilderness areas. He also has a strong passion for the outdoors, both in experiencing the environment and in protecting it. He is currently studying environmental law at Lewis & Clark University in Portland, Oregon.

About the Author

On a post-college road trip in 1992, Ohio native Megan McMorris and her childhood buddy, Andy, fell in love with Oregon, prompting them to write a "cool things about Oregon" list as they drove. (Included on the list: friendly, waving highway workers and Portland businessmen in suits who played Hacky Sack on their lunch break.) But in the meantime, the real world beckoned: The Indiana University graduate's goal of becoming a freelance writer led her first to New York City, where she spent eight years in cramped cubicles writing about fitness and the outdoors for magazines, before finally moving to Portland. Having run 12 marathons, she nonetheless swapped her road-running shoes for trail shoes and has never looked back. She now lives and works in northwest Portland where she hikes, runs, mountain bikes, and snowboards, often followed by a cold pint at one of the many local microbreweries.

While covering every inch of Oregon to research this book, Megan and her husky dog Corvus got a crash course in the outdoors—including hail, rain, snow, lightning, a bear sighting, and plenty of off-road car adventures. She has proudly emerged unscathed as an expert on the trails; driving on bumpy, snowy Forest Service roads without getting stuck; and setting up a tent in two minutes flat. Megan is also the author of *Foghorn Outdoors Oregon Hiking,* and her magazine articles have appeared in *Fitness, Self, Shape, Sports Illustrated Women, Glamour, Marie Claire, Runner's World, Hooked on the Outdoors, Parents,* and *Muscle & Fitness Hers.*

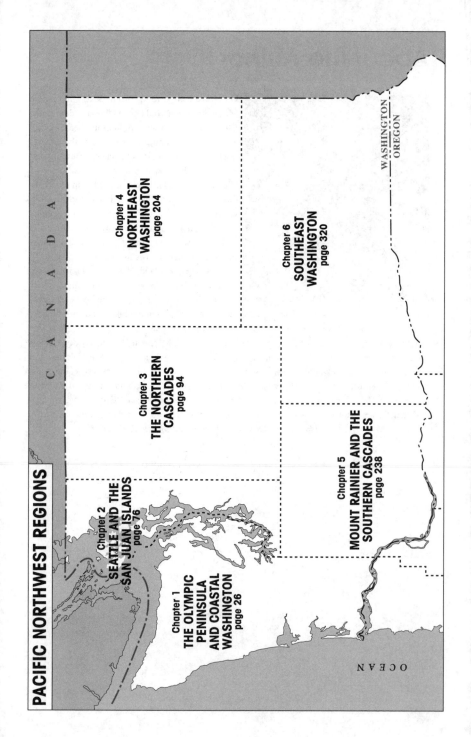

PACIFIC NORTHWEST REGIONS

CANADA

Chapter 4
NORTHEAST
WASHINGTON
page 204

Chapter 6
SOUTHEAST
WASHINGTON
page 320

Chapter 3
THE NORTHERN
CASCADES
page 94

WASHINGTON
OREGON

Chapter 2
SEATTLE AND THE
SAN JUAN ISLANDS
page 76

Chapter 5
MOUNT RAINIER AND THE
SOUTHERN CASCADES
page 238

Chapter 1
THE OLYMPIC
PENINSULA
AND COASTAL
WASHINGTON
page 26

OCEAN

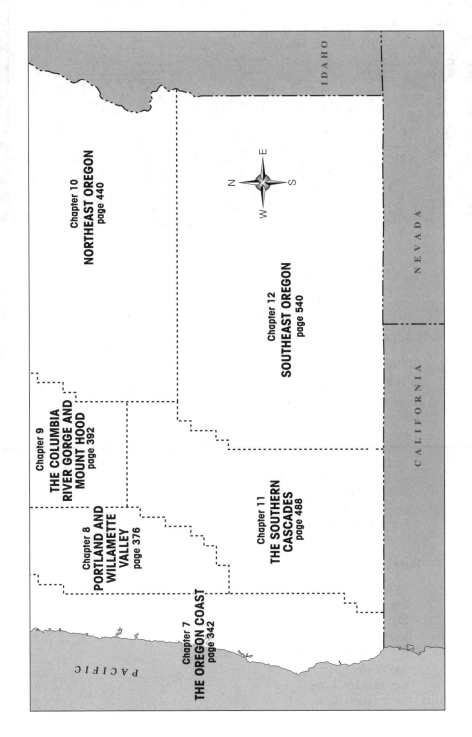

Chapter 10
NORTHEAST OREGON
page 440

Chapter 9
THE COLUMBIA
RIVER GORGE AND
MOUNT HOOD
page 392

Chapter 8
PORTLAND AND
WILLAMETTE
VALLEY
page 376

Chapter 7
THE OREGON COAST
page 342

Chapter 12
SOUTHEAST OREGON
page 540

Chapter 11
THE SOUTHERN
CASCADES
page 488

IDAHO

NEVADA

CALIFORNIA

PACIFIC

© SCOTT LEONARD

Contents

WASHINGTON

Chapter 1—The Olympic Peninsula and Coastal Washington. 23

Including:
- Brothers Wilderness
- Buckhorn Wilderness
- Colonel Bob Wilderness
- Lake Crescent
- Lake Quinault
- Makah Indian Reservation

- Mount Skokomish Wilderness
- Olympic National Forest
- Olympic National Park
- Willapa Bay
- Wonder Mountain Wilderness

Chapter 2—Seattle and the San Juan Islands 73

Including:
- Chuckanut Mountain
- Cougar Mountain Regional Park
- Deception Pass State Park
- Moran State Park
- Orcas Island

- Puget Sound
- Snohomish County
- Tennant Lake County Park
- Whidbey Island

Chapter 3—The Northern Cascades 91

Including:
- Alpine Lakes Wilderness
- Boulder River Wilderness
- Cedar River Municipal Watershed
- Clearwater Wilderness
- Diablo Lake
- Glacier Peak Wilderness
- Henry M. Jackson Wilderness
- Lake Chelan National Recreation Area
- Lake Chelan Sawtooth Wilderness
- Lake Wenatchee
- Mount Baker Wilderness
- Mount Baker-Snoqualmie National Forest
- Mount Pilchuck State Park
- Mount Si Natural Resources Conservation Area

- Noisy-Diobsud Wilderness
- Norse Peak Wilderness
- North Cascades National Park
- Okanogan National Forest
- Pasayten Wilderness
- Ross Lake National Recreation Area
- Snoqualmie Pass
- Tiger Mountain State Forest
- Twin Falls State Park
- Wallace Falls State Park
- Washington Pass
- Wenatchee National Forest

Chapter 4—Northeast Washington 201

Including:
- Colville National Forest
- Little Spokane River Natural Area
- Metaline Falls

- Okanogan National Forest
- Pasayten Wilderness
- Salmo-Priest Wilderness

- Sky Lakes Wilderness
- South Fork McKenzie River
- South Sister Summit
- Three Sisters Wilderness
- Umpqua National Forest

- Waldo Lake
- Waldo Lake Wilderness
- Willamette National Forest
- Willamette Pass Ski Area
- Winema National Forest

Our Commitment

We are committed to making *Foghorn Outdoors Pacific Northwest Hiking* the most accurate, thorough, and enjoyable hiking guide to the region. With this fifth edition you can rest assured that every hiking trail in this book has been carefully reviewed and is accompanied by the most up-to-date information. Be aware that with the passing of time some of the fees listed herein may have changed, and trails may have closed unexpectedly. If you have a specific need or concern, it's best to call the location ahead of time.

If you would like to comment on the book, whether it's to suggest a hike we overlooked or to let us know about any noteworthy experience—good or bad—that occurred while using *Foghorn Outdoors Pacific Northwest Hiking* as your guide, we would appreciate hearing from you. Please address correspondence to:

Foghorn Outdoors Pacific Northwest Hiking, fifth edition
Avalon Travel Publishing
1400 65th Street, Suite 250
Emeryville, CA 94608

email: atpfeedback@avalonpub.com
If you send us an email, please put "Pacific Northwest Hiking" in the subject line.

How to Use this Book

Foghorn Outdoors Pacific Northwest Hiking is divided into twelve chapters based on major regions. Each chapter begins with a map of the area, which is further broken down into detail maps. These detail maps show the location of all the hikes in that chapter.

This guide can be navigated easily in two ways:

1. If you know the name of the specific trail you want to hike, or the name of the surrounding geographical area or nearby feature (town, national or state park, forest, mountain, lake, river, etc.), look it up in the index and turn to the corresponding page.

2. If you know the general area you want to visit, turn to the map at the beginning of the chapter that covers the area. Each chapter map is broken down into detail maps, which show by number all the hikes in that chapter. You can then determine which trails are in or near your destination by their corresponding numbers. Hikes are listed sequentially in each chapter so you can turn to the page with the corresponding map number for the hike you're interested in.

Mount Rainier

About the Trail Profiles

Each hike in this book is listed in a consistent, easy-to-read format to help you choose the ideal hike. From a general overview of the setting to detailed driving directions, the profile will provide all the information you need. Here is an example:

Map number and hike number

Round-trip mileage (unless otherwise noted) and the approximate amount of time needed to complete the hike (actual times can vary widely, especially on longer hikes)

Map on which the trailhead can be found and page number on which the map can be found

Symbol indicating that the hike is listed among the author's top picks

The difficulty rating (boot—rated 1–5) is based on the steepness of the trail and how difficult it is to traverse; the quality rating (mountain—rated 1–10) is based largely on scenic beauty, but it also takes into account how crowded the trail is and whether noise of nearby civilization is audible

General location of the trail, named by its proximity to the nearest major town or landmark

❶ SOMEWHERE USA HIKE
9.0 mi/5.0 hrs   👢 ⛰8

At the mouth of the Somewhere River on Lake Someplace

Map 1.2, page

Each hike in Foghorn Outdoors Pacific
Ⓕ Northwest Hiking begins with a brief overview of its setting. The description typically covers what kind of terrain to expect, what might be seen, and any conditions that may make the hike difficult to navigate.

User Groups: This section notes the types of users that are permitted on the trail, including hikers, mountain bikers, horseback riders, and dogs. Wheelchair access is also noted here.

Open Seasons: This section notes the times of year the trail is accessible. Please note that the open season is not indicated for every hike in this book.

Permits: This section notes whether a permit is required for hiking, or, if the hike spans more than one day, whether one is required for camping. Any fees are also noted here. The Hiking Tips section describes passes that are commonly required.

Maps: This section provides information on how to obtain detailed trail maps of the hike and its environs. Whenever applicable, names of U.S. Geologic Survey (USGS) topographic maps and national forest maps are also included; contact information for these and other map sources are noted in the Resources section at the back of this book.

Directions: This section provides mile-by-mile driving directions to the trailhead from the nearest major town.

Contact: This section provides an address and phone number for each hike. The contact is usually the agency maintaining the trail but may also be a trail club or other organization.

About the Maps

This book is divided into chapters based on regions; an overview map of these regions precedes the table of contents and is printed on the inside of the back cover. At the start of each chapter, you'll find a map of the entire region, enhanced by a grid that divides the region into smaller sections. These sections are then enlarged into individual detail maps. Trailheads are noted on the detail maps by number.

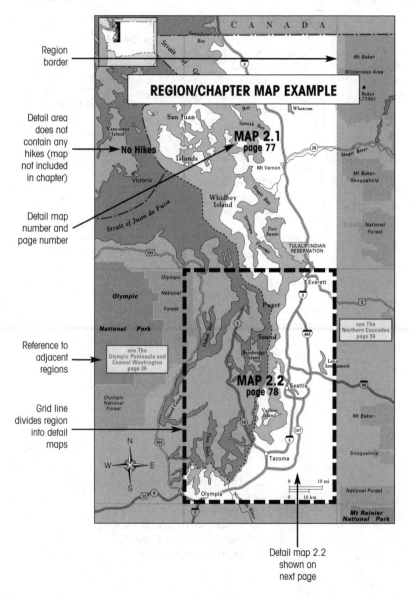

Region border

Detail area does not contain any hikes (map not included in chapter)

Detail map number and page number

Reference to adjacent regions

Grid line divides region into detail maps

Detail map 2.2 shown on next page

Indicates adjacent
detail maps
within region

Locates detail
map within
region

Map
number → **Map 2.2**

Sites shown on
detail map and
the page range
where those
sites are listed →
**Sites 11–18
Pages 564–570**

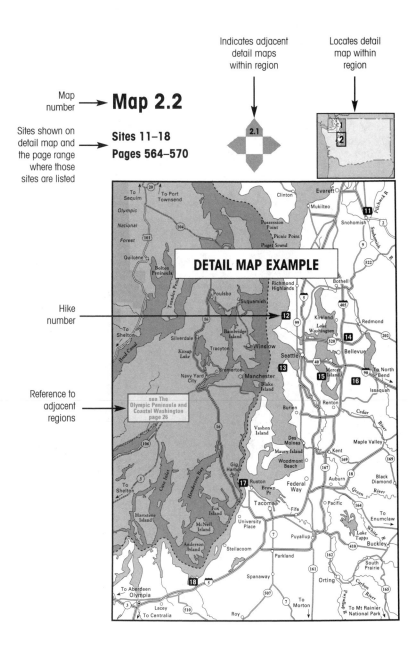

DETAIL MAP EXAMPLE

Hike
number

Reference to
adjacent
regions

Authors' Note

Here in the Pacific Northwest, life revolves around the mountains. Our infamous rainy weather is pushed out of the sky by the mountains; the dry and warm eastern portions of both Oregon and Washington have the Cascade Mountain Range to thank for that; even our renowned salmon rely on the cold, crystal clear waters that trickle from the mountains. And, of course, the mountains are where millions of Pacific Northwest dwellers choose to relax.

It's not so relaxing, however, to search endlessly for a trailhead or spend hours driving to a trail only to discover that the last road there is too rough a ride for your delicate vehicle.

Well, this book takes away all those miseries. In order to bring you this book, we set out to make *Pacific Northwest Hiking* the ultimate authority for trails in this very cool region of the United States. As they say, it was a dirty job but someone had to do it. And we did.

In doing so, we packed thousands of miles on our two trusty Subaru (while Scott was zipping across Washington, Megan was doing the same in Oregon). We literally hiked through snow, hail, wind, and yes, plenty of rain in our research. But we enjoyed it every step of the way.

The result? The most comprehensive, accurate, fun-to-read (we hope!) hiking guide to the entire Pacific Northwest region all in the cozy confines of one book. For each listing, we include not only detailed driving directions but whether the road is rough-going on the way in as well as when the snow tends to clear from higher-elevation hikes. We note areas where trails tend not to be well marked so you can arm yourself with a map before you go. Our goal is to give you as many details in each listing as are practical so you can choose whether it's the right hike for you *before* you go. If you're looking for adventure, there are plenty of remote areas to explore. If you prefer to have everything marked for you and want to just soak up the scenery, we have you covered there too. From short, paved hikes on the Oregon coast to multiday backpacking trips at Mount Rainier, and everything in between, there is something for everyone in this book.

So now that we've done the research for you, it's up to you to get out there and experience the Pacific Northwest. Thanks for letting us do the dirty work for you.

Hiking Tips

Don't Leave Home Without . . .

When it's a sunny day, it can be tempting to just head out with nothing but lightweight clothes and a Snickers bar. Hey, you're only going four miles; what's the big deal, right? Not so fast: Plenty of people have made just that mistake and have been lucky to live to tell about it. This checklist hits upon all the must-brings.

Map and Compass

Let's start with the obvious, shall we? A map is essential for those "am I supposed to take a left here?" moments. Even the seemingly obvious trails can become confusing when you're actually hiking them. Consider a map to be your security blanket, just to make sure you're on the right trail. Although this book provides many details of major trail junctions you'll come across, keep in mind that some areas can be a trail jungle out there, with many intersecting paths just begging to lead you astray. Not to mention the fact that some trails are not well marked due to fire damage, wind, or, depending on the area, the locals getting a little crazy with their BB guns.

Realize that all maps are not created alike—a AAA map may help you get to the trailhead, but it's not going to do much good once you're on the trail. It's best to get a quality topographic map (Green Trails of Seattle earns a thumbs-up from us; they cover 90 percent of Washington trails and the Southern Cascades and Columbia River Gorge areas of Oregon). Some managing agencies also produce useful maps, which you can buy online (sources are provided with each trail featured in this book, and their contact information is listed in the Resources section at the back of the book).

Of course, a compass is also a must (but only if you know how to use it), because what good is a map if you're not sure what direction you're heading? Some people also swear by GPS devices, and true tech-heads will love the features that let you track your exact route and download it to your computer. They also can be useful for figuring out elevation: If you know you're supposed to climb to 4,000 feet and then turn right, and you suddenly discover you're at 6,000 feet, you've probably missed your turn. As with any technology, though, it's a good idea not to rely on it too much, because they often don't work in a thick forest canopy, creating the ultimate catch-22: The more remote the area—and therefore the more likely you'll get disoriented—the least likely you are to get a satellite signal. And if the batteries are dead, it obviously won't do you any good either, so it's a good idea to back up any gadgets with a compass if you're out in the backcountry.

Extra Food

Isn't hiking great? What other sport allows you to exercise and eat at the same time? It's like a buffet with a view! Of course, there are other reasons to pack food other than munching on tasty morsels while you check out the scenery, the main one being this: The unexpected can happen out on the trail. You could get turned around or linger longer than you planned at a viewpoint, when suddenly your blood sugar dips to dangerous levels. Even if you gorged on an all-you-can-eat buffet before you hit the trailhead, you'd be surprised at how quickly your stomach will be crying for more once you've trekked up 2,000 feet. The best foods are those that have a little combination platter packed inside them: a mixture of salt (to replenish sodium you're losing to sweat), sugar (to boost your blood sugar levels), and carbs and/or protein (to give you sustained energy and fill you up). Trail mix has all those delicious features and more. Take it from those who have been there: It's best to leave the chocolate for after the hike, because that nice Snickers bar can be reduced to a soggy mess in your trail pack, which is a crime.

Besides packing something for the immediate future, you should also carry a little extra—the lore of backcountry is filled with tales of hikers who head out for a quick day-hike and end up spending the night (or more) in the wilderness. So don't be shy about packing a little extra—at the very least, you'll be popular with your hiking partners! When we mean "extra," we mean enough that you won't be tempted to dive into it as soon as you set off. One of our favorite tips from a grizzled old backcountry veteran is that extra food is meant for an emergency, not for noshing on just because, well, it looked good. His emergency stash? Something nutritious he'd only consider eating in a true emergency: canned dog food.

Water

More important than food is water. Dehydration can creep up on you. You may not even feel thirsty, when suddenly you become a little dizzy. Another mile of walking, and suddenly you feel as if you've just caught a bad case of the flu. Even if you're hiking just a few miles, it's better to be prepared in case you're out on the trail longer than you planned. (It happens.) You don't have to lug a water bottle along, either; many hydration packs available these days do double-duty as a pack and water carrier, without the extra weight of a bottle (and you don't have to carry anything in your hands). The whole hydration-pack concept is quite the rage now, which means that many manufacturers have leapt onto the bandwagon. Having tried many different brands, one favorite remains CamelBak, the company that first created the concept. The CamelBak Cloud is as big as a daypack to accommodate all your gear, carries 70 ounces of water, and looks cool, to boot. However you carry water, though, just do it.

Water filters are a wise investment since all wilderness water should be considered contaminated. Make sure the filter can be easily cleaned or has a replaceable cartridge. The filter pores must be 0.4 microns or less to remove bacteria.

If you're going for a longer day hike or backpacking, you don't need to carry all of your water with you—add a water filter to your pack so you can gather it from streams or rivers. Filtering water is a must if you're going to access water in the backcountry—water in the wild may look crystal clear and be ice cold, but it can also play host to nasty parasites and viruses. Not only are they not very tasty, they also wreak havoc on your intestines: Catch a case of giardia or cryptosporidia and you can be incapacitated for a full week. As

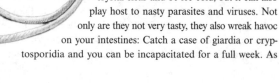

with hydration packs, the water filters available now are lighter and easier to use than ever. They also keep water cold and don't alter the water's taste. Other options for water purifying are iodine and chlorine systems, and the old-fashioned method of boiling it for one minute.

Extra Clothing

You can't judge the weather by the trailhead, especially in the Pacific Northwest, where the weather can turn at the drop of a hat (no pun intended). Rain, snow, and the occasional hailstorm are only the tip of the iceberg—even on a sunny day you can reach a gusty ridge top that will cause your body temperature to plummet. Most accidents in the wilderness are the result of or complicated by hypothermia. It can set in quickly and with little warning. Once you start to get cold, your ability to think and further protect yourself heads downhill.

Your best bet is to bring clothes that you can pull on and off accordingly as the weather—and your body temperature—changes. At the very least, bring along something warm and cozy, such as a fleece vest or pullover. Add a warm, fuzzy hat and a miserable, cold hike will turn into a fun jaunt through the wilds because most your body heat escapes from your head. Don't think you're immune to this bit of advice if it's summer, either, because we've been in enough July snowstorms to have learned this lesson. Add some type of raingear to your pack no matter what the weather or season. Even if the weather forecast calls for clear skies, keep in mind that the local weather folks often forecast for the cities, not the mountains.

Finally, we have two words for you: Cotton kills. Cotton laps up moisture like nobody's business, be it from your body (from sweat) or from the elements. Add a pair of denim jeans to that ensemble and you'll be one unhappy camper by the time you get back to the trailhead. Think light. Think breathable. Think fabrics like CoolMax or PolarTec, which wick moisture from your body and keep you toasty. Pull on a fleece over that to insulate you, top it off with a water-resistant and breathable or waterproof layer, and you're good to go. And don't forget about the drive home: Leave in your car an extra towel, a pair of socks, and comfy slip-in sandals for your trip home. Changing into a clean, dry pair of socks (and getting out of those shoes that may be hurting your feet by now) makes a big difference, as does the towel for wiping the sweat or rain from your brow.

Wristwatch

You won't find a wristwatch on any 10 Essentials list that we've ever seen. Yeah, yeah, you're supposed to be out enjoying nature and not worrying about the time, but a watch can be handy out on the trail. Time marches to the beat of a different drummer in the wilderness—what seems like two hours may really be only one (or vice versa). Why does it matter what time it is? For starters, if you're planning an out-and-back hike, it's a good way to gauge your turnaround point. If you're planning to hike a loop with several junctions, it can help you figure out how far you've hiked. Using the general rule that the average person hikes a mile in a half-hour (most experienced hikers will be much faster), you'll have a sense of when you should start looking for a turn, or if you may have missed it altogether. Of course, a watch is also good for bragging purposes ("Dude, I hiked, like, 7 hours and 42 minutes today!"). But you're way too mature for that nonsense, right?

Sunscreen and Sunglasses

Just like a sunny day can turn into a sogfest, a rainy, cloudy one can suddenly turn into a brilliant, sunshiny day. And then there you are, on the peak enjoying a view, perhaps enjoying an impromptu picnic, getting sizzled without realizing it. On the way home, you fill your tank at the gas station and notice the attendant peering at you with interest. "He must not see many true outdoors people like me," you think to yourself, feeling pretty cool. And then you arrive home to hit the shower and see yourself in the bathroom mirror: Your sun-glazed eyes peek back at you from a lobster-hued face. You're burned. Really burned. Don't let this happen to you. Bring sunscreen and sunglasses, even if it's not sunny; those pesky UV rays can filter through the clouds too, and they can really scorch at higher elevations. A hat (like a baseball cap) and lightweight clothing with long sleeves can also keep the rays at bay.

Not only can avoiding sunburn make your hike more enjoyable, but it's also helpful for warding off heat stroke, a serious condition in the backcountry.

Light Source

Time can fly when you're having fun, and so can light. You may have planned for a simple five-mile jaunt, but once you're out there, you realize that hey, you're feeling good, why not try to make it to that scenic waterfall you've been hearing so much about just two miles up the trail? And while you're at it, what's that viewpoint up there? You know the story: Before you know it, the light grows dim, and darkness creeps up on you. Trust us, it's no fun hiking by yourself (or even with a friend) in a pitch dark forest. Even if you've planned to get back in plenty of time before the sun officially sets, keep in mind the thick forest canopy can bring on night an hour or two early.

You don't need to lug along a heavy flashlight to shed some light on your hike: Headlamps (which are basically small flashlights that fit around your head) are lightweight, relatively cheap, and add the extra bonus of keeping your hands free as you negotiate the dark shadows of night. You'll be glad you have it.

Fire Starter

Starting a fire when it's cold, dark, and wet can likely save your life. Sticks don't like to start up easily, even when it's dry, so it's best to play it safe and bring some quality waterproof matches or a lighter, and keep them packed away in a safe and dry place (a sandwich baggie does the trick). Besides something to start a fire, bring along something to keep it going for a bit. Fire pellets are available at any outdoors store, and do-it-yourselfers will be glad to know that toilet paper is highly flammable, as are cotton balls dipped in Vaseline.

Footwear

Nothing stirs up a frenzy more than two hikers comparing boots. That's because there are so many styles to choose from.

The type of boot you choose depends on what type of hike you're planning. For day hikes where you don't have to carry everything and the kitchen sink on your back, you can go with a trail-running shoe. They're lightweight, they know their way around rocks, and they have the extra bonus of flexibility (read: fewer blisters). Think about it: If these guys were made to run up, over, and through obstacles, they'll be just as good for walking. Asics Gel is a good brand, as is Montrail. The price for a good trail-running shoe is about $80.

Of course, there's a downside to trail runners. They don't offer much in the way of ankle support, so you'll want to get a lightweight hiking boot if you're planning a longer day hike or a short backpacking trip. The good thing about lightweight hiking boots compared to trail runners is not only the extra ankle support but also the superior traction to power through mud and snow. They're also relatively flexible, requiring less breaking in than heavier boots. A good pair of light hiking boots will set you back about $100.

For extended backpacking trips, you'll want to take things up a notch with a true backpacking boot. A midweight or heavy backpacking boot is the full tamale in the hiking-boot world. They extend above your ankle to provide even more support when you're carrying a heavy backpack. As a result, they tend to be stiffer, so you'll want to break them in before setting out. Unless you're planning to through-hike the Pacific Crest Trail, you'll be better off with a midweight hiking boot for weekend or weeklong backpacking trips. A pair of midweight hiking boots ranges in price from $125 to over $200.

To throw a wrench into everything, there really are no hard-and-fast rules when it comes to shoes, and everyone has their little quirks about what they put on their feet (we've seen it all on the trail). The most important thing: While it's oh-so handy to click and pick online, you should definitely try on a few pairs before you sign the dotted line; something that looks pretty cool on the Internet may become the bane of your existence on the trail. A good fit is everything, and stores like REI are excellent sources for trying on a range of styles and brands (plus the store employees are at the top of their game, knowledge-wise).

Finally, a good pair of shoes is nothing without the right kind of socks. The best route to a blister-free hike is a sock that wicks moisture away from your feet. Again, the type of socks you pick depends on what type of hike you're planning. For shorter hikes, you're fine with a lightweight sock that gives you a little cushioning and wicks sweat away. Longer trips call for heavier socks with a liner underneath. SmartWool is the go-to brand for the full range of socks made from breathable yet sturdy Merino wool. You may look at the price tag and balk (about $15 per pair), but they're worth it.

First Aid/Emergency Kit

Whether it's as simple (but annoying) as a cloud of mosquitoes or as dangerous as getting lost overnight, you should always expect the unexpected out on the trail and tote along a first-aid kit. You can buy a kit at any outdoors store; they come in different sizes, depending on your use, and are stocked with the fundamentals. Besides a kit, make sure you're hiking with the following items for an emergency kit:

• Ibuprofen works well to combat swelling if you twist an ankle or suffer a nasty bruise.

• Athletic tape and gauze are helpful for treating twisted or strained joints. A firm wrap will make that three-mile hobble back to the car less of an ordeal.

• Travel-sized supplies of general medicines like Alka-Seltzer or NyQuil are multipurpose and practical, as is insect repellent.

• Space blankets are small, shiny blankets that insulate extremely well, are highly visible, and will make do in place of a tent when needed.

• Mirrors aren't for vanity when you're on the trail: They're useful when you get lost to catch the glare of the sun and signal your position to others. The small mirror that comes attached to some compasses works perfectly.

• A whistle is useful if you get lost—you'll save more energy than if you're yelling, and the sound travels well.

Finally, there are several organizations that offer medical training for backcountry situations. Courses run from one-day seminars in simple first aid to month-long classes for Wilderness EMT. We recommend a course in Wilderness First Aid (WOOFA) or Wilderness First Response (WOOFER)—you'll get so much useful information you won't believe you ever went without it.

Multipurpose Knife

A high-quality multipurpose knife will come in handy in a slew of situations, because they offer much more than just a slicing blade. Today's features include a variety of knife sizes, saws, scissors, corkscrews, bottle openers, ballpoint pens, and screwdrivers, and about 30 other fun little tools. We take ours everywhere (well, except the airport).

Trail Etiquette

You're out in the middle of the trail, free from the pressures of life and all the rules that go along with it. Right? Kinda. There are a few finer points on trail etiquette that will make for smoother sailing for yourself and fellow hikers. (Don't worry, you can still talk with your mouth full and slurp your water all you like.)

Horses, Mountain Bikers, and Fellow Hikers

Just as there are highway traffic rules (which you always follow, right?), there are rules of the "road" for dealing with other people on the trail. Here's a Trail Manners 101 checklist.

Horses: Probably the most confusing fellow trail users are the four-legged types. They can spook easily, so you'll want to take care not to cause a horse heart attack. You may have all the right intentions, but sometimes the smallest things can set off these sensitive creatures. While hikers should always yield to horses, make sure the horse has seen you before you go diving behind a tree—you don't want to startle the poor beast. Also, some horses are frightened by big backpacks; keep your distance, and never go up to pet the creature, no matter how tempting its pretty eyes are. Horseback riders usually let hikers know the quirks of their animals, but nevertheless, always yield, and make your presence known to horses. Luckily, many trails open to horses are wide enough for you to safely keep your distance and let them pass with ease.

Mountain bikers: Bikers are supposed to yield to hikers and restrain the screaming pace of descent. Why the chuckling? Well, nothing against bikers, but sometimes this doesn't happen. We don't want to get into trouble with the trail police or anything, but this is a rule that personally just doesn't make sense. After all, it's much easier for hikers to step aside than it is for bikers to slow down, stop, and move aside (without falling off said bike, no less), especially when they're going up or down hills. To avoid getting into an all-out rumble about it, what's the big deal about a quick sidestep to let a biker cruise right on through? They'll appreciate it, you'll feel cool about being such a great guy/gal, and everyone wins.

Fellow hikers: Horses aren't the only creatures who can spook easily on a trail. When you're lost in thought, feeling like you're alone in the world, having someone creep up on you from behind can give the nerves quite a jolt. Whenever you come across another hiker who is headed in the same direction (i.e., their back is turned toward you), before you pass them, say "hi," "hello," "yo"—whatever your salutation of choice (don't be shy!). When you're hiking up or down a hill and you come across a fellow hiker, the uphill hiker gets the right of way.

Hiking with Dogs

Dogs are perfect hiking companions. They keep you company but don't talk your ear off about their troubles, they never say "I told you so" when you turn the wrong way, and they're cute to boot.

Not everyone owns a dog, of course, but nearly everyone has an opinion about dogs on the trail. Please keep one thing in mind: Not everyone shares your enthusiasm for the canine species. Your friendly doggie may be running toward a fellow hiker hoping for a little pat on the head, but someone who is afraid of dogs (or maybe just isn't in a "dog mood" that day) may misread your dog's eager demeanor as an appetite for a healthy chunk out of their leg.

Also, be aware that national parks don't allow dogs on any trail (national forests and wilderness areas do allow dogs), so read the fine print before you bring your canine buddy along. Also, keep your dog on the trail at all times. Dogs are smart—they'll see a shortcut and take it, cutting switchbacks and creating erosion. Dogs and other wildlife don't mix well: They love to chase chipmunks, rabbits, deer, and anything else that moves (one of our dogs prefers butterflies). Think about a chipmunk's point of view: Having a big, slobbering beast chasing you is stressful, don't you think?

It's not only the smaller creatures you have to worry about, either—bears and cougars consider dogs Public Enemy #1, and can transform a peaceful bear into an assault of claws and teeth (not to mention, they find dogs to be especially tasty).

To recap: Keep your dog on the trail, under your control (and acquaint yourself with a leash if your little buddy has a mind of her own), and away from wildlife and other hikers, then we'll all be happy.

Dealing with the Great Outdoors

You may have some unexpected visitors on the trail. Use these tips to keep you safe (and sane) when you happen across the following Oregon creatures and plants.

Rattlesnakes, Bears, and Cougars

While some forest natives like deer are a joy to see when you're out on the trail, these three guys can make your heart skip a beat. Fortunately, most encounters with these creatures are nothing more than a memorable story, and needn't be dangerous if you follow a few tips. Be prepared before you go, so you can keep your cool and avoid confrontations.

Rattlesnakes: There are 15 species of snakes in Oregon and 12 in Washington, but the only poisonous one in is the *Crotalus viridisis,* which prefers to be called the Western rattler. The Western rattler, which looks like the more common gopher snake, are more active in spring, summer, and early fall, and are mostly found in the southern and eastern regions of both states. You don't need to be a snake expert in order to identify these slithery guys, because you'll most likely hear them before you see them: The unmistakable rattle sound will instantly freeze you in your tracks. This is actually a good thing, because rattlesnakes rarely attack a nonmoving object. Once the snake realizes you're not a threat, it will retreat.

The best way to avoid a rattler bite is to be aware of your surroundings. Walk only where you can see your next footstep; that is, resist the urge to do your Sound of Music imitation and don't go running through open grass (or around rocky outcrops). When hiking in rattler country, wear boots that extend to at least your ankles, and wear long pants if you really want to cover yourself.

In the unlikely event you are bitten—and keep in mind that 80 percent of bites are "dry bites" with no venom, and that overall the bites are rarely lethal—you need to be treated within 18 hours. Rattler bites are most serious when they're on the face, neck, or an artery. The most important thing to remember—and probably the hardest thing to do—is to remain calm and move slowly so your blood isn't racing through your body. Remember these tips:

• remove any restrictive clothing
• wrapping or constricting the area isn't necessary. If your bite is on a limb, you can tightly wrap the limb (without cutting off total blood supply) above the bite to slow circulation.
• don't cut the bite area or ice the bite
• don't take any type of medication

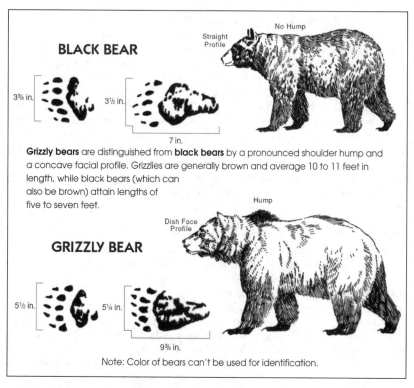

BLACK BEAR

No Hump

Straight Profile

3¾ in.

3½ in.

7 in.

Grizzly bears are distinguished from **black bears** by a pronounced shoulder hump and a concave facial profile. Grizzlies are generally brown and average 10 to 11 feet in length, while black bears (which can also be brown) attain lengths of five to seven feet.

Hump

Dish Face Profile

GRIZZLY BEAR

5½ in.

5¼ in.

9¾ in.

Note: Color of bears can't be used for identification.

- don't suck the venom by mouth; apply a Sawyer Extractor (reverse syringe) if available
- finally, calmly but immediately seek medical attention

Bears: You may have aced the bear question on the Worst-Case Scenario Survival Guide game at your family holiday gathering, but when you actually see a bear in the forest, it's amazing how all that handy knowledge can fly out of your head when adrenaline takes charge. The good news is that Oregon has only black bears—whose coats can actually range from light brown to cinnamon to black—so there's no need to identify which type of bear it is if you encounter one. There are 25,000 black bears in Oregon, and the same number in Washington—they mainly reside in mountainous and forested areas. The Evergreen State does play host to the infamous Grizzlies, but they are extremely rare—less than 50, in fact, and are mainly located along the Canadian border in the Pasayten Wilderness and Selkirk Mountains. (One super-quick way to note the difference is that Grizzlies have that distinctive and kinda spooky hump on their shoulders.)

While seeing a bear can naturally be a little scary upon first sight, keep in mind that these furry guys generally want nothing to do with people and prefer to avoid us altogether (the nerve!). As long as you don't pick up a bear cub and cuddle it, bears will nearly always leave hikers be. The most important thing to remember when you see a bear is to do the opposite of what your body tells you to do: Don't run. Bears can clock speeds of 35 mph and are more likely to go after you if you're running away. Usually bears will hear you before you even see them and will leave the area undetected. If you and a bear do spot each other, back away slowly but surely while facing the bear, reassuring it with such niceties as "nice bear, yes, aren't you sweet." It will likely move away from you. If you come across a bear who got out on the wrong side of its bear bed and decides to charge you, try to stay calm (yeah, right) and be prepared to fight back. Never look a bear in the eyes, because it will view this as aggression, but do make yourself look as big as possible by waving your arms over your head or opening your coat. If it comes close enough to attack, now is not the time to drop and play dead (that's for Grizzlies). Fight back with anything you have—sticks, rocks, your hiking guidebook. Give it what you got. If you have a backpack filled with food, throw it at the beast—a hungry bear will most likely be more interested in your trail mix than in you as an appetizer. If the bear doesn't budge, go around it in a wide circle. And if in the unlikely event that a bear does attack, curl up in a ball, cover your neck, and hit the bear's nose (they don't like being hit in their sensitive snouts).

While all this is tidy advice, everyone has a dramatically different bear story. Black bears can be unpredictable, so the best rule is to make noise when you're out alone so you don't surprise a bear, and try to remain calm if you do encounter one. If you have a dog, make sure it's leashed so it doesn't run after the bear, because that will provoke it to come after both of you. Dogs will most likely stick by you to protect you, and will be aggressive only if the bear charges. No matter what, though, you should always bring a leash to protect both of you.

If you're camping, never leave food in your tent. Leave your food in the car or secure it in a bear canister at the campsite; if backpacking, hang your food from a tree. If a bear saunters into your campsite, the main rule is to cause a scene: Bang pots and pans, blow a whistle, throw rocks. Most likely the creature will scamper away, figuring you're not worth the trouble.

Finally, on the trail is not the place to try out that new cologne or perfume. Bears are attracted to fragrances just like we are.

Cougars: Also called mountain lions, panthers, and pumas, cougars are the largest member of the cat family in the Pacific Northwest. Their habitats are as varied as their names. These highly adaptable creatures can be seen in zones ranging from high alpine areas to desert regions—you've probably hiked through mountain lion territory without knowing it. And you probably wouldn't know it, because these big cats are notoriously secretive and will usually run away at the first sign of humans. Not to mention, they're rare—at last count, there were an estimated 2,500 cougars in Washington and 4,000 in Oregon. The risk of being attacked by a mountain lion is smaller than that of being hurt by a dog, bee, or even a deer. Of course, there is always the slightest chance that a cougar will attack, so it's best to be prepared.

The rules are similar to the above bear rules: Don't run, make yourself appear as large as possible, and fight back if attacked. If you're hiking with children, pick them up—but this time ignore that "bend at the knees when lifting heavy objects" tip, because you don't ever want to crouch in front of a cougar. Face the animal, speak in a loud voice, and give it your best beady-eyed stare right in the eyes.

Poison Oak, Poison Ivy, Stinging Nettles, and Ticks

They may not be as scary as the above creatures, but you're much more likely to come across poison oak and ivy, stinging nettles, and ticks on your hike. With some simple tips, you can learn to avoid these nuisances and keep them from taking all the fun out of hiking.

Poison Oak and Ivy: The best way to avoid encounters with poison oak and ivy is to wear long pants when you hike. Poison oak thrives more in the western regions, while its counterpart, poison ivy, takes over the eastern portions. Learn to identify these plants: They have the infamous "leaves of three" and constantly change colors throughout the year (hoping to fool you into touching them, most likely). In the spring, the leaves are reddish; then they turn green in the summer, bursting into yellow, orange, or red in the fall. The berries don't change, though, so if you see the duo of three leaves with white berries, don't touch it. If you accidentally come into contact, wash with hot water and soap as soon as possible (or, if near a water source, rinse off right away); when you get home, make sure that everything that came into contact with these pesky plants is thoroughly washed, including your dog. If the oil got on your dog's fur, it can easily get on you, so treat your canine friend to a post-hike bath. Along with learning to identify and keeping away from these plants, slather on a cream with bentoquatum, like Ivy Block, before you head out, and bring along some wipes, like Tecnu, to use after you've been exposed.

Avoiding Poison Oak: Remember the old Boy Scout saying: "Leaves of three, let them be."

Stinging Nettles: Brush up against a stinging nettle and you'll know it immediately—it causes an intense sting and white bumps as the acid (the same substance that acid ants produce) is released onto your skin . Nettles thrive in the coastal range in forested areas and have heart-shaped leaves with razorlike edges. The good news is, unlike poison oak or ivy, the itch lasts only 24 hours at the most, and then you'll be good as new. To soothe the itch, spit on the site. When you get home, apply a baking soda poultice or hydrocortisone lotion, and just be thankful you're not a monk: In the Middle Ages, the brothers thrashed themselves with the sharp-toothed leaves for penance!

Ticks: There are four types of ticks in the Pacific Northwest that are commonly found on humans, but only one of them carries the dreaded Lyme disease: the Western black-legged tick. Generally, ticks are more active in the spring and summer. They thrive in tall grasses and low shrubs. Dogs are much more likely to come across a tick, so make sure to check your little guy or gal out, especially on the head, behind the ears, and on the stomach, where the fur is shorter. For humans, the best way to deter these stubborn creatures is to wear long pants and a long-sleeved shirt. Check yourself thoroughly after hiking, and if you find one burrowed in your skin, pull it out carefully with tweezers. Keep in mind that you need to remove the entire body and head, so grasp it firmly from the skin surface. Although only a small percentage of the Western black-legged ticks actually carry Lyme disease, have a doctor examine the tick if it's black; the brown types are harmless, but you may want to get it checked out just in case. See a doctor immediately if you begin to experience flu-like symptoms. Since dogs are more susceptible, you can also get a tick-prevention prescription, like FrontLine, for your four-legged friend.

Permits and Land Use
Northwest Forest Pass
The most widely used permit in the Pacific Northwest is the Northwest Forest Service Pass, accepted at 680 day-use recreation sites in Washington and Oregon. Each featured trail in this book provides information on whether you need this pass or not. You can buy an annual pass

($30) at ranger stations, outdoors stores, or with a quick and painless online transaction through Nature of the Northwest (www.naturenw.org). They're mysteriously speedy about shipping anything you order, and you can just put 'er in your windshield and never worry about it again.

There's controversy swirling around the pass-critics contend that the national forests are public lands and are therefore already paid by federal taxes-but to look on the bright side, consider this: In 2002, $3.6 million was raised from pass sales, resulting in 7,000 miles of trail maintenance.

Parks in Washington

North Cascades National Park is the easiest and cheapest park to visit in Washington. All trailheads accessing the park require Northwest Forest Passes (see "Northwest Forest Pass" paragraph below) for parking and day-use. The park limits the number of visitors at backcountry camps; thus, overnight visitors must also register for a free Wilderness Camping Permit. These permits are required for any overnight stay within the North Cascades National Park Service Complex (this includes Lake Chelan and Ross Lake National Recreation Areas). You can get a permit at the Wilderness Information Center in Marblemount, North Cascades Visitor Center in Newhalem, Methow Valley Visitor Center in Winthrop, and Golden West Visitor Center in Stehekin. Keep in mind that just because they're free doesn't mean you can bypass them; park rangers don't hesitate to hand out hefty fines.

Olympic National Park has a grab-bag of regulations. While most areas require a fee, some are accessible for free. Passes are required at the following entrances: Hoh, Sol Duc, Elwha, Hurricane Ridge, and Skokomish, while the Quinault and other river entrances are free. Visitors have several options when it comes to which permit to buy. A Single Visit Vehicle permit (good for 7 days) costs $10, or you can get an Olympic National Park Annual Pass (good for one year) for $30. They also accept a variety of National Passes, which are good for one year at all national parks in the country.

For overnight stays, you need a Wilderness Camping Permit, which you can pick up at the Wilderness Information Center in Port Angeles or at staffed ranger stations at Hoodsport, Staircase, Hurricane Ridge, Hoh, and Quinault. The permits are good for parties up to 12 people, and they cost $5 per permit plus $2 per night per person (so one person camping for three nights would pay $11). There's no charge for people 16 years of age or younger.

Mount Rainier requires fees to access some areas by car, while others are free. Trailheads along State Route 410 (from Enumclaw to Yakima) and State Route 123 (south to State Route 12 and Packwood) are free. If you access the park via Paradise-Longmire Road, Stevens Canyon Road, White River Road, Carbon River Road, or Mowich Lake Road, you'll need one of three passes: A Single Visit Vehicle permit ($10, good for 7 days), a Mount Rainier National Park Annusal Pass ($30, good for one year), or a variety of National Passes, good for one year at all national parks in the country.

Overnight stays are free-kind of. Since the park service has quotas on the number of backcountry camps, a free Wilderness Camping Permit is required for all backpackers. But here's the fine print: During the summer, a reservation is highly recommended, and the cost per reservation is $20, good for 1 or 2 people for up to 14 nights. Check out the Mount Rainier website, www.nps.gov/mora, or call the Wilderness Information Center at 360/569-2211 for availability and more information.

Parks in Oregon

Oregon is filled to capacity with parks, forests, and wilderness areas, all with different rules and managing agencies. Here's what you need to know: First of all, the National Forest Service (a division of the U.S. Department of Agriculture) manages the 13 national forests in Oregon. The national forests in Oregon include Deschutes, Fremont, Malheur, Mount Hood, Ochoco, Rogue River, Siskiyou, Siuslaw, Umatilla, Umpqua, Wallowa-Whitman, Willamette, and Winema. Some forests require a Northwest Forest Service pass at most trailheads, while others, like Fremont, Malheur, and Ochoco, are free.

Then you have your state forests, which are managed by the Oregon Department of Forestry. These include Clatsop, Elliott, Santiam, Tillamook, and Sun Pass.

Moving on down the line are the state parks, which are managed by the Oregon State Parks and Recreation Department. There are 115 state parks, 26 of which require a parking fee or pass. Still with me? Good.

Then there are the 38 designated wilderness areas, managed by the Forest Service or the Bureau of Land Management and set aside as protected areas. Typically, you'll need a wilderness permit to enter these areas.

Add in the four national monuments (Newberry Crater, Oregon Caves, John Day Fossil Beds, and Cascade-Siskiyou), one national park (Crater Lake), and one national scenic area (Columbia River Gorge)—all governed by the Bureau of Land Management, the Forest Service, the National Park Service, or other agencies—and there you have it. (Don't worry, you won't be quizzed on this.)

Leave No Trace

If you want trails to stick around for a while, follow the simple rules of Leave No Trace (for more information, go to www.lnt.org).

• Plan Ahead: A little careful planning makes your trip safer and minimizes resource damage. Find out what regulations are in place for your destination, such as group size limits or campfire regulations, before hitting the trail. Prepare for any special concerns an area may have, so you can bring along items like ice axes or water filters. Keep in mind that many places are heavily used during summer weekends, so try and schedule your trip for a weekday or off-season for more elbow room out there.

• Travel and Camp on Durable Surfaces: Alpine meadows and lakeshores are fragile, and are easily injured by footprints or camping. Travel only on the main trail, don't cut switchbacks, and avoid the "social trails" that spiderweb up high meadows. When camping, pitch your tent in already established sites, never on a meadow.

• Dispose of Waste: It goes without saying that trash doesn't belong in the great outdoors, so if you packed it in, bring it with you on your return trip. That goes for all trash, whether it's biodegradable or not. From food packaging to food itself, to toilet paper, it should all come home on your back. For human waste, dig a cathole (6 to 8 inches deep and 200 feet from any water source).

• Leave What You Find: As the saying goes, "take only photographs and leave only footprints." (Of course, if you travel on durable surfaces, you won't even leave footprints, but you get the point.) If you see cool rocks or deer antlers or wildflowers, keep in mind that you only saw them because the guy before you kept them there—so do the same for those that follow. Also, don't alter sites by digging trenches, building lean-tos or harming trees.

• Minimize Campfire Impacts: Thanks to Smokey the Bear, we all know the seriousness of forest fires. If you're going to build a fire, make sure you put it out before you go to sleep or leave camp. Many national forests and wilderness areas have campfire bans above an elevation above 3,500 feet-at these higher altitudes, trees grow slowly and depend on decomposition of downed trees. Burning those limbs robs the ecosystem of much-need nutrients, an impact that lasts for centuries to come. Carry a camp stove instead when you plan to cook while backpacking.

• Respect Wildlife: They may be cute as they look at you with sad eyes, peering at the tasty morsels in your hand, but the most important way we can respect wildlife is by not feeding them. Filling those chipmunk cheeks only makes them more dependent on humans for food. Keep a clean camp without food on the ground, and hang food anytime you're separated from it. A good "bear hang" is less about keeping bears out than it is about keeping mice and squirrels from digging in.

Best Hikes List

So many trails, so little time. Here's a guide to the best of the bunch in eight categories.

ⓕ Top 10 Waterfall Hikes

Marymere Falls, The Olympic Peninsula and Coastal Washington, page 37. If the Olympic rain isn't enough, the mist from Marymere will soak you through.

Sol Duc Falls/Lover's Lane, The Olympic Peninsula and Coastal Washington, page 42. Three parallel cascades pour into a narrow gorge among a beautiful forest.

Wallace Falls, The Northern Cascades, page 161. A great trail leads to the 265-foot falls in one of Washington's best state parks.

Denny Creek and Lake Melakwa, The Northern Cascades, page 179. A pair of big falls invite hikers to soak in the refreshment around their bases.

Comet Falls/Van Trump Park, Mount Rainier and the Southern Cascades, page 268. The 320 foot drop of Comet Falls is a welcome sight on the way to Van Trump Park at Mount Rainier.

Trail of Ten Falls/Canyon Trail, Portland and Willamette Valley, page 385. From dainty drib bles to powerful cascades, it's like walking through a waterfall museum as you pass 10 falls throughout the popular loop.

Multnomah Falls, The Columbia River Gorge and Mount Hood, page 400. The granddaddy of them all, the second-highest year-round waterfall in the country.

Eagle Creek to Tunnel Falls, The Columbia River Gorge and Mount Hood, page 405. Your reward for walking six miles down Eagle Creek trail is a tunnel that travels under this powerful falls.

Ramona Falls, The Columbia River Gorge and Mount Hood, page 412. A wall of trickling water makes up this unique water display.

Tamanawas Falls, The Columbia River Gorge and Mount Hood, page 415. Stand underneath this waterfall to experience a slice of your own private Oregon.

ⓕ Top 10 Summit Hikes

Moran State Park, Seattle and the San Juan Islands, page 80. Although it's less than 3000 feet in height, the panoramic view of Puget Sound and the San Juan Islands can't be beat.

Church Mountain, The Northern Cascades, page 99. Old-growth forest gives way to acres of meadows and incredible views of Mount Baker.

Park Butte/Railroad Grade/Scott Paul Trail, The Northerns Cascades, page 110. Miles of mead ow wandering ends up at a lookout on the south slopes of Mount Baker.

Granite Mountain (Snoqualmie), The Northern Cascades, page 177. The view from the look out site ranges from Mount Rainier to Glacier Peak.

Mount Fremont Lookout, Mount Rainier and the Southern Cascades, page 257. There is no better summit from which to gaze out upon Mount Rainier National Park.

Kings Mountain, The Oregon Coast, page 352. Elk Mountain's neighbor in the Tillamook Forest offers a good vantage point from its 2,700-foot peak.

Elk Mountain, The Oregon Coast, page 352. A tough scramble to incredible sweeping views of the Tillamook Forest and the coastal range.

Mount Defiance/Starvation Ridge, The Columbia River Gorge and Mount Hood, page 406. A renowned sweat-fest, gaining 5,000 feet in five miles en route to the tallest peak in the Gorge.

South Sister Summit, The Southern Cascades, page 507. The third-tallest peak in Oregon at 10,538 feet, South Sister offers up great views of the Southern Cascade region and boundaries beyond.

Paulina Peak, Southeast Oregon, page 547. View the Newberry Crater and Paulina Lake (plus more than eight peaks on a clear day) from the 7,985-foot summit.

Ⓕ Top 10 Hikes with Kids

Ozette Triangle, The Olympic Peninsula and Coastal Washington, page 34. Kids who love tidal pools and the beach will enjoy this loop.

Hurricane Hill, The Olympic Peninsula and Coastal Washington, page 45. A better view of the Olympic Mountains is hard to find than from this meadow ramble.

Staircase Rapids, The Olympic Peninsula and Coastal Washington, page 65. Follows the North Fork Skokomish River as it pours over numerous cascades.

Ape Cave, Mount Rainier and the Southern Cascades, page 250. Two miles of lava cave just south of Mount St. Helens.

Grove of the Patriarchs, Mount Rainier and the Southern Cascades, page 276. This stand of 1,000-year old-growth sits on a small island in the Ohanapecosh River.

Cape Meares, The Oregon Coast, page 355. Great ocean views, a lighthouse, and short trails can keep the kids busy all day.

Yaquina Head Lighthouse, The Oregon Coast, page 357. Climb up the tallest lighthouse in Oregon and watch for whales, then stroll down to see the tidepools and the cobble beach.

John Day Painted Hills, Northeast Oregon, page 468. Four short trails lead you through the colorful sand hills filled with fossils.

Flood of Fire/Story in Stone, Northeast Oregon, page 469. A touch exhibit of fossils and an overlook highlight these two super-short strolls through the John Day Fossil Beds National Monument.

Big Obsidian Flow Trail, Southeast Oregon, page 547. An interpretive trail through the youngest lava flow in Oregon.

Ⓕ Top 10 Hikes to See Wildflowers

Silver Lakes, The Olympic Peninsula and Coastal Washington, page 58. Above these lightly forested lakes lie meadowy slopes covered in aster and lupine.

Meadow Mountain, The Northern Cascades, page 123. The name says it all, a mountain aflame with wildflowers in July.

Berkeley and Grand Parks, Mount Rainier and the Southern Cascades, page 256. After the flowers and the cascading streams of Berkeley Park, prepare for the sheer size of the Grand Park.

Skyline Loop, Mount Rainier and the Southern Cascades, page 272. Located right out of Paradise Lodge at Mount Rainier, this is one for the whole family.

Yakima Rim, Southeast Washington, page 325. Early-season blooms in April and May make this trail the perfect choice to get out after the long winter.

Cascade Head Nature Conservancy Trail, The Oregon Coast, page 357. Rare wildflowers dot this protected meadow bluff overlooking the ocean.

Tom McCall Preserve, The Columbia River Gorge and Mount Hood, page 408. More than

300 plant species call this nature preserve home, with a commanding view over the eastern Columbia River Gorge.

Elk Meadows Loop, The Columbia River Gorge and Mount Hood, page 416. After a healthy climb, the wildflower meadow is your reward.

Madison Butte Lookout Trail to Tupper Butte, Northeast Oregon, page 449. Look out over northeastern Oregon on this secluded open meadow filled with flowers in the summer.

Castle Crest Wildflower Garden, The Southern Cascades, page 531. A short stroll through blooming flowers and plants in the Crater Lake National Park.

⑤ Top 10 Weekend Backpacking Trips

Ozette Triangle, The Olympic Peninsula and Coastal Washington, page 34. This is the most popular route along the coast and visits historic Wedding Rocks.

Lena Lakes, The Olympic Peninsula and Coastal Washington, page 62. A demanding hike through beautiful forests to an alpine playground.

Phelps Creek (Spider Meadow), The Northern Cascades, page 158. An easy trip to a magnificent valley topped by an easily accessed glacier to play on.

Necklace Valley, The Northern Cascades, page 165. A long valley of high lakes just 1.5 hours from Seattle.

Goat Ridge, Mount Rainier and the Southern Cascades, page 287. Miles of meadow, a great lake, and always good chances to see many goats.

Timberline Trail, The Columbia River Gorge and Mount Hood, page 422. A 40-mile ring around Mount Hood with views galore.

Bowman Trail to Chimney/Wood Lakes, Northeast Oregon, page 457. One of the many lake-filled backpacking routes in the Wallowa-Whitman National Forest.

Lakes Basin Loop, Northeast Oregon, page 461. A popular backpacking loop connecting alpine lakes where you can see why the Wallowa mountains are called the Alps of Oregon.

Eagle Creek to Echo/Traverse Lake, Northeast Oregon, page 463. Take your pick between two alpine lakes in the Wallowa-Whitman National Forest.

Camp Lake/Chambers Lake Basin, The Southern Cascades, page 506. Nestled between South and Middle Sisters peaks, the Chambers Lake Basin is a perfect overnight spot.

⑤ Top 10 Lake Day Hikes

Seven Lakes Basin Loop, The Olympic Peninsula and Coastal Washington, page 43. The loop route is best, with countless great lakes and eye-popping views of the Olympics' biggest mountains.

Lake 22, The Northern Cascades, page 126. Just an hour from Seattle, this trail enjoys old-growth forest, a cascading stream, and a beautiful lake.

Blanca Lake, The Northern Cascades, page 161. Not far off Highway 2, this is the crown jewel in the Henry M. Jackson Wilderness.

Rachel Lake, The Northern Cascades, page 183. Just east of Snoqualmie Pass, the popularity of this trail doesn't steal from its scenic appeal.

Snow and Bench Lakes, Mount Rainier and the Southern Cascades, page 274. Short, flat, and beautiful, this is one of Mount Rainier's best trails.

Mirror Lake, The Columbia River Gorge and Mount Hood, page 423. Just a gentle jaunt from the highway, this lake feels so remote and wild that you swear you just hiked in 10 miles to get there.

Strawberry Lake/Little Strawberry Lake, Northeast Oregon, page 481. How can you resist such cute names? These popular lakes are worth the trip in the Strawberry Wilderness.

Cleetwood Cove/Wizard Island, The Southern Cascades, page 527. Walk directly to the shores of the clear-blue Crater Lake, take a ferry, then walk up the cinder-cone volcano of Wizard Island, smack dab in the middle of the clearest lake in Oregon.

Paulina Lakeshore Loop, Southeast Oregon, page 546. Explore lava flows and hot springs, and witness nearby Paulina Peak along this seven-mile lakeshore loop.

Wildhorse Lake, Southeast Oregon, page 551. A picturesque alpine lake nestled under the summit of Steens Mountain.

Ⓕ Top 10 River Hikes

Hoh River, The Olympic Peninsula and Coastal Washington, page 48. The end-all, be-all destination of rain forest ecosystems, where trees dwarf skyscrapers.

Upper Big Quilcene, The Olympic Peninsula and Coastal Washington, page 58. Trace the river's path through cool old-growth forest as it flows from scenic headwaters at Marmot Pass.

Thunder Creek, The Northern Cascades, page 118. A classic trek into the wilderness of North Cascades National Park along a large, glacial-milk filled stream.

Boulder River, The Northern Cascades, page 120. Four miles of easy trail through old-growh forests, ending at great riverside camps.

Cady Creek/Little Wenatchee Loop, The Northern Cascades, page 163. An eastside take on old-growth forests, this trail reaches pictorial Meander Meadows on the Pacific Crest Trail.

Clackamas River, The Columbia River Gorge and Mount Hood, page 402. Plenty of picnic and fishing spots line the way of this scenic river for a perfect year-round weekend getaway.

South Fork Walla Walla, Northeast Oregon, page 451. Follows the popular Umatilla National Forest river, and hugs canyon walls, for nearly 20 miles.

McKenzie River National Recreation Trail, The Southern Cascades, page 497. Passing by water falls, lava flows, and hot springs, this trail follows the McKenzie River for 26.5 miles.

Upper Rogue River/Crater Rim Viewpoint, The Southern Cascades, page 516. The picturesque Rogue River whitewater rapids have plenty of hot spots—this 18-mile section hits the highlights.

Deschutes River/Dillon and Benham Falls, The Southern Cascades, page 519. A couple falls line the way in this gorgeous and popular river near Bend.

Ⓕ Top 10 Easy Hikes

Mount Townsend, The Olympic Peninsula and Coastal Washington, page 57. A popular trail to the summit of a large, meadowy butte in the Eastern Olympic Mountains.

Deception Pass State Park, Seattle and the San Juan Islands, page 82. Miles of trail along the most beautiful stretch of coastline in the Puget Sound.

Mount Pilchuck, The Northern Cascades, page 125. A popular summit hike ends at a lookout that offers historic information and views.

Middle Fork Snoqualmie River, The Northern Cascades, page 173. Old-growth forest highlights this great river hike, less than an hour from Seattle.

Snow Lake, The Northern Cascades, page 180. Old-growth forest and meadows in the Alpine Lakes Wilderness end in a spectacular lake basin.

Banks-Vernonia State Trail, The Oregon Coast, page 353. A countryside rails-to-trails hike with plenty of access points.

Cape Lookout, The Oregon Coast, page 355. Plenty of viewpoints line the way of this trail that extends along the 2.4-mile length of the cape.

Redwood Nature Loop, The Oregon Coast, page 368. An interpretive trail leads you through this homage to the rare Redwoods that stray north to Oregon.

Wahclella Falls, The Columbia River Gorge and Mount Hood, page 404. A simple hike to a stellar waterfall that will make you feel miles away from the highway.

Mosier Twin Tunnels, The Columbia River Gorge and Mount Hood, page 407. Walk through the tunnels with a windswept view of the Gorge below.

Washington

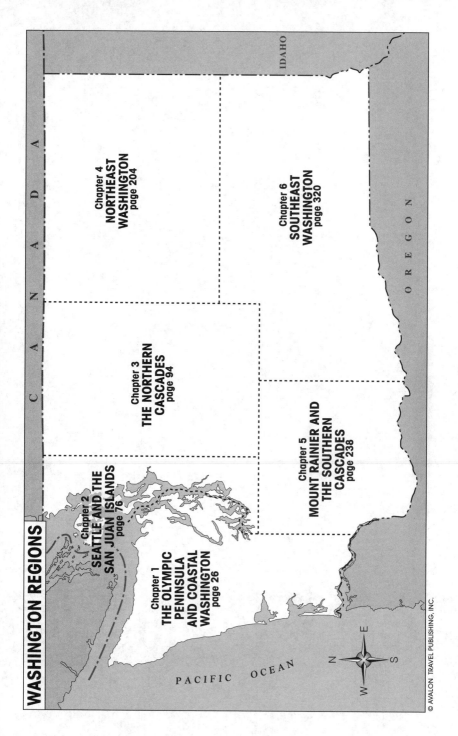

WASHINGTON REGIONS

CANADA

IDAHO

Chapter 4
NORTHEAST
WASHINGTON
page 204

Chapter 6
SOUTHEAST
WASHINGTON
page 320

Chapter 3
THE NORTHERN
CASCADES
page 94

Chapter 5
MOUNT RAINIER AND
THE SOUTHERN
CASCADES
page 238

OREGON

Chapter 2
SEATTLE AND THE
SAN JUAN ISLANDS
page 76

Chapter 1
THE OLYMPIC
PENINSULA
AND COASTAL
WASHINGTON
page 26

PACIFIC OCEAN

N E S W

© AVALON TRAVEL PUBLISHING, INC.

© SCOTT LEONARD

The Olympic Peninsula and Coastal Washington

The Olympic Peninsula and Coastal Washington

The Olympics are justifiably famous (or infamous) for the crazy amount of rain that visits the peninsula. The west-side river valleys get about 140 inches a year, and the region tops out at 200 inches a year near the crest. Yes, more than 200 inches, which amounts to more than 18 vertical feet of water. There may be other, drier regions of Washington, but the Olympic Peninsula is one of the United States' most unique places. Three distinct and highly beautiful environments grace this isolated and lightly inhabited peninsula.

On the west side is the Pacific Ocean and the Olympic Coast Wilderness, where picturesque sea stacks and tidal pools bless one of the West Coast's finest stretches of coastline. Protected by wilderness and wildlife designations, the Olympic Coast is one of the most scenic places on the peninsula. Bald eagles patrol the skies, while sea otters play in the surf. January storms roll in one after another, each giving way to welcome and frequent doses of sunshine. Luckily for hikers, trails run the length of the Olympic Coast, and Cape Flattery, Shi Shi Beach, and Ozette Triangle make good days hikes or overnighters. Longer trips can be made along the North, Central, or South Coast Trails. Regardless of the season, the coast is a special place to visit.

Farther inland are the area's famous rainforests, with trees growing to immense proportions and moss blanketing anything that will sit still for a minute (or so it seems). If you've never visited the Olympic rainforest, you're in for a treat. The home of one of the United States' few rainforests, the west side of the peninsula grows some of the earth's largest trees. Forests teeming with gargantuan specimens of western hemlock, Sitka spruce, and western red cedar cover the land. Towering some 200–300 feet overhead, these grand forests form giant canopies, beneath which grow dense understories of vine maple, elderberry, devil's club, and salmonberry. On rare spring or fall days when it's not raining, humidity hangs in the air, wetting everything it touches, even Gore-Tex. The Bogachiel, Hoh, and Quinault River Valleys are full of trails that explore this great area.

Finally, the Olympic Mountains, with their subalpine meadows and flowing glaciers, are one of Washington's wildest and most beautiful ranges. First, a little geology. The Olympics are profoundly unique in that they have a circular shape, known as a radial formation. The river drainages start in the center of the range and flow outward in all directions. The Olympics are very young, at least geologically speaking. The oldest rocks are only 55 million years old, with most rocks closer to 40 million years of age. The mountains got their start as deposits of lava and sedimentation under the Pacific Ocean. Gradually they were bent out of shape by the Juan de Fuca plate colliding offshore with the continental plate. The light sedimentary rocks, driven below the heavier continental plate, eventually broke through and sprang like a cork to the surface, creating the dome/circular shape. More recently (about 14,000 years ago), the Ice Age left its mark on the range. The Cordilleran ice sheet scraped past and around the mountains, creating the picturesque Hood Canal. Alpine glaciers spread down the valleys for miles from their starting points, producing distinctive U-shaped valleys. To say the least, the Olympics are a great place to geek out on geology.

They are also home to an abundance of wildlife. Several unique species call these forests home, including Roosevelt elk, Olympic salamanders, and Olympic marmots. The park offers some of our best chances to see black bears. Late summer in the high country is practically a bear mecca, when the sedate creatures gorge themselves into a stupor on ripe huckleberries. Wolf packs prowled these mountains before humans wiped them out in the early 20th century. While talks of reintroduction to the area have quieted down recently, wilderness lovers can only hope for such an action.

Of the Olympics' many rivers, the largest (or at least longest) of them is the Elwha River, flowing northward into the Straight of Juan de Fuca. The glacier-fed Elwha was once one of our region's most productive rivers, bearing populations of all five northwest salmon species. This came to an end when two dams were built on the river in the early 1900s, cutting off most of the spawning ground. Happily, these dams are slated for removal by the end of the decade. While full restoration may take 30 years or more, hope remains for future major runs on the river. Also on the north peninsula are trails out of Hurricane Ridge, an outstanding visitor center at 6,000 feet. After hiking, grab dinner and a beer in scenic Port Angeles.

The northeastern portion of the range is distinguishable by its relatively light rainfall, where the mountains receive as little as 20 inches of annual rainfall—an anomaly in this rainy region. Most fronts move off the Pacific in a southwest to northeast direction over the mountain range, and as wet air from the ocean crosses the range, the water is squeezed out over the western side. By the time air reaches the east side, much of the rain has fallen already, leaving the "rain shadow" dry. All of the retirees flocking to Sequim couldn't be happier. While this region is noticeably drier (tell that to someone hiking here in October), it has some extraordinary richness in landscape and forests.

Moving southward, the rest of the eastern side of the range is comprised of rivers dropping quickly from high mountain crests to the Hood Canal. This area receives its fair share of rain, certainly more than the rain shadow. Its major rivers include the Dosewallips, Duckabush, Hamma Hamma, and Skokomish Rivers.

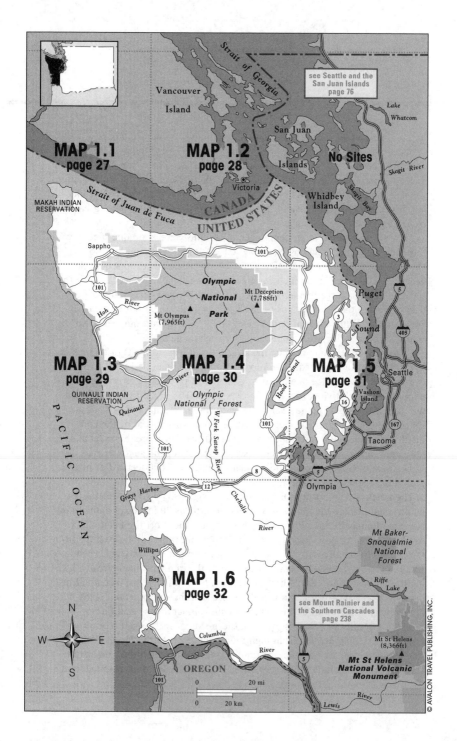

Map 1.1

Hikes 1–4
Pages 33–35

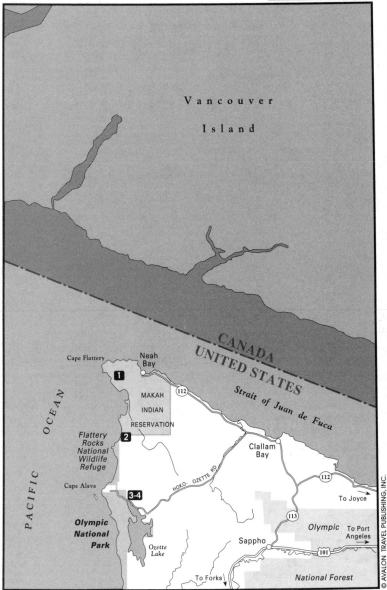

Map 1.2

Hikes 5–10
Pages 36–39

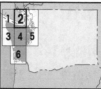

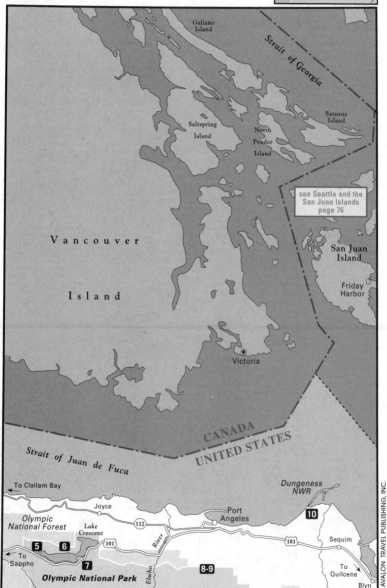

see Seattle and the
San Juan Islands
page 76

© AVALON TRAVEL PUBLISHING, INC.

Map 1.3

Hikes 11–14
Pages 40–41

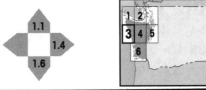

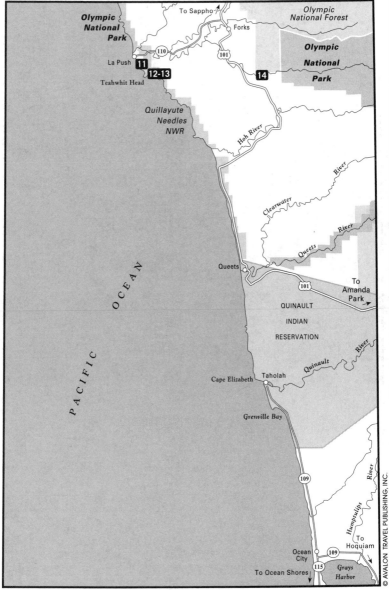

Olympic National Park

To Sappho

Olympic National Forest

Forks

Olympic National Park

La Push

110

101

11

12-13

14

Teahwhit Head

Quillayute Needles NWR

Hoh River

River

Clearwater

River

Queets

Queets

101

To Amanda Park

QUINAULT

INDIAN

RESERVATION

Quinault

River

O C E A N

Cape Elizabeth

Taholah

Grenville Bay

P A C I F I C

109

Humptulips River

To Hoquiam

Ocean City

109

To Ocean Shores

115

Grays Harbor

© AVALON TRAVEL PUBLISHING, INC.

Map 1.4

Hikes 15–57
Pages 42–69

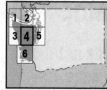

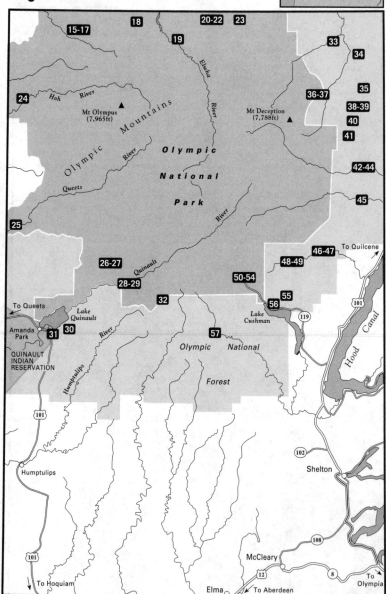

Map 1.5

Hike 58
Page 70

1.4

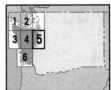

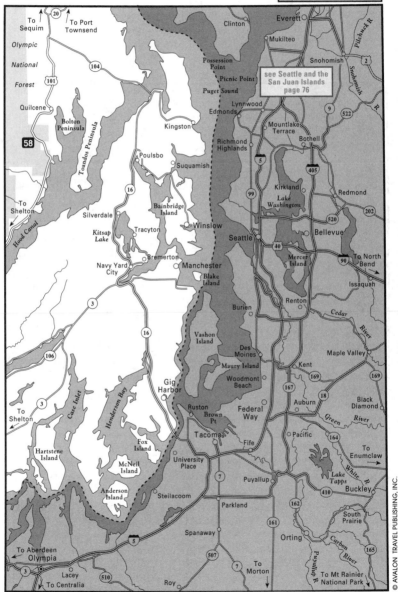

see Seattle and the San Juan Islands page 76

© AVALON TRAVEL PUBLISHING, INC.

Map 1.6

Hikes 59–61
Pages 67–68

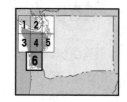

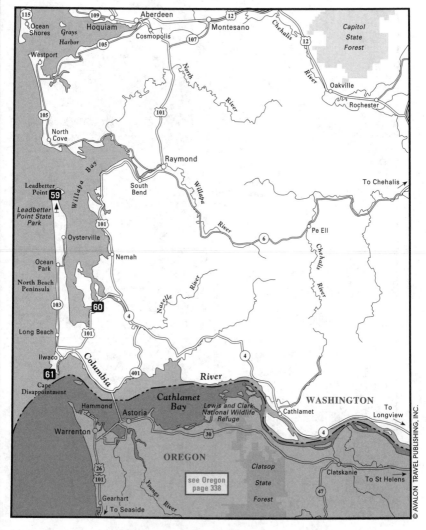

◼ CAPE FLATTERY
1.5 mi/1.0 hr

**northwest of Neah Bay on the Makah
Indian Reservation**

Map 1.1, page 27

A newly refurbished trail leads through great
coastal forest to one of the Washington coast's
most scenic places. The Makah Nation rebuilt
Cape Flattery Trail several years back, taking
a dangerous, muddy trail to near perfection.
Four observation decks hover above sea cliffs
overlooking the cape, providing views of ocean
and wildlife. Birds and sea life flock to the area
year-round. During the spring and fall, it's possible to sight gray whales.

Cape Flattery Trail works its way through
a coastal forest of large old-growth cedars and
firs. Many boardwalks and bridges along the
way keep feet dry on this once infamously
muddy trail. The trail pops out of the forest at
the cape, above the Olympic Coast National
Marine Sanctuary. The sanctuary designation
provides protection for numerous animals.
Scores of cormorants and tufted puffins make
their way in and out of homes in the sea cliffs.
Below in the water, sea lions swim from cove
to cove on the prowl for a meal. From mid-
March through mid-April, Cape Flattery is a
prime location for spotting migrating gray
whales; binoculars are a must. Cape Flattery
may be a long way from the rest of Washington, but North America's most northwestern
point is awesome.

User Groups: Hikers and leashed dogs. No
horses or mountain bikes are allowed. No wheelchair access.

Open Seasons: This trail is accessible year-round.

Permits: A Makah Recreation Pass is required
to park here. An annual pass costs $7 and is
available at most businesses in Neah Bay.

Maps: For topographic maps, ask Green Trails
for No. 98S, Cape Flattery, or ask the USGS
for Cape Flattery.

Directions: From Port Angeles, drive 5 miles
west on U.S. 101 to Highway 112. Turn right
(north) onto Highway 112 and drive 63 miles

to Neah Bay. At the west end of town, turn
left on Cape Flattery Road and drive to Cape
Loop Road. Turn right and drive to the signed
trailhead at road's end.

Contact: Makah Tribe, P.O. Box 115, Neah
Bay, WA 98357, 360/645-2201.

◻ SHI SHI BEACH
4.0–9.6 mi/2.0 hrs–2 days

**south of the Makah Indian Reservation in
Olympic National Park**

Map 1.1, page 27

Protected from development by wilderness designations, more than 75 miles of Olympic Coast
remain in pristine condition, untamed by humans. This rich habitat sustains a biodiversity that offers unparalleled opportunities for
seeing wildlife. And its most beautiful section
lies here, from the wide, sandy shores of Shi
Shi Beach to the rugged sea stacks at Point of
the Arches.

The Makah Tribe recently began rebuilding
Shi Shi Beach Trail from its reservation, providing a new and easier access to this beach.
The trail travels 2 muddy miles through forest
before breaking out onto Shi Shi Beach. Two
miles of beach stretching southward offer great
strolling, even when the weather fails to co-
operate (which is often). The beach is a good
point to turn around, for those looking for a
shorter hike.

Shi Shi Beach ends where Point of the Arches begins. Here, a large grouping of enormous
sea stacks spread out into the sea off a point.
Tidal pools abound here, offering excellent
chances for seeing starfish and urchins. Sea
otters often play in the water while bald eagles
soar overhead in perpetual wind.

The trip to Point of the Arches (4.8 miles)
can easily be done in one day, but camping is
a popular activity along Shi Shi. Permits, however, must be obtained from the park service.
Good sites are found regularly along the shore.
Water should be obtained at Petroleum Creek
(3.3 miles), which must be forded to access
Point of the Arches. It is an easy crossing

made easier by low tides. Traveling south of Point of the Arches brings hikers to Cape Alava and the Ozette Triangle, not a recommended approach.

User Groups: Hikers only. No dogs, horses, or mountain bikes are allowed. No wheelchair access.

Open Seasons: This trail is accessible year-round.

Permits: A Makah Recreation Pass is required to park here. An annual pass costs $7 and is available at most businesses in Neah Bay. Overnight stays within the national park require backcountry camping permits, which are available at the Wilderness Information Center in Port Angeles.

Maps: For a map of Olympic National Park, contact the Outdoor Recreation Information Center at the downtown Seattle REI. For topographic maps, ask Green Trails for No. 98S, Cape Flattery, or ask the USGS for Makah Bay and Ozette.

Directions: From Port Angeles, drive 5 miles west on U.S. 101 to Highway 112. Turn right (north) onto Highway 112 and drive 63 miles to Neah Bay. At the west end of town, turn left on Cape Flattery Road and drive 3 miles to Hobuck Beach Road. Turn left, cross the Waatch River, and drive to Sooes River. Here, Hobuck Beach Road becomes Sooes Beach Road. Cross the Sooes River and drive to the clearly marked trailhead on the right. The parking area here is for day use only. Overnight visitors can pay local homeowners (who have signs advertising parking) to park on their private property (where their cars will be secure).

Contact: Makah Tribe, P.O. Box 115, Neah Bay, WA 98357, 360/645-2201; Olympic Wilderness Information Center, 600 East Park Avenue, Port Angeles, WA 98362-6798, 360/565-3130.

3 OZETTE TRIANGLE
9.0 mi/1–2 days

northwest of Forks in Olympic National Park

Map 1.1, page 27

No route in Washington claims a heritage quite like the Ozette Triangle. Three trails form this triangle, with the leg along the beach home to Wedding Rocks. Wedding Rocks bear petroglyphs carved by Native Americans hun-

Wedding Rocks, along Ozette Triangle

dreds of years ago. Their illustrations depict orcas, the sun and moon, and even a ship of western explorers. Even without Wedding Rocks, this beach would be highly popular. Large sea stacks set among larger islands, countless tidepools brimming with sea life, bald eagles aplenty, and even the possible sightings of gray whales make this a pleasurable trip.

Cape Alava and Sand Point Trails lead to the beach from Lake Ozette. Each trail is three miles long, flat, and forested by big trees. Boardwalk covers most of each trail and can be slippery; watch out! Starting on the northern route (Cape Alava) will drop you off at a coastline full of sea stacks and wildlife. The numerous campsites near Cape Alava require reservations (from the Port Angeles Wilderness Information Center) because of large summer crowds.

Head south from Cape Alava among countless tidal pools, brimming with life. Wedding Rocks are one mile south from Cape Alava, scattered around a jutting point; they are above the high tide line. The site is legendary for attracting cultists and other New Age folk, but you're more likely to run across sea otters floating offshore in beds of kelp. The beach extends south two miles before intersecting Sand Point Trail. Here, a large headland juts into the sea and provides an excellent vantage point from atop it. The Ozette Triangle is rightfully one of the peninsula's most valued trails.

User Groups: Hikers only. No dogs, horses, or mountain bikes are allowed. No wheelchair access.

Open Seasons: This trail is accessible year-round.

Permits: There is a $1 daily parking fee here, payable at the trailhead. Overnight stays within the national park require backcountry camping permits, which are available at the Wilderness Information Center in Port Angeles.

Maps: For a map of Olympic National Park, contact the Outdoor Recreation Information Center at the downtown Seattle REI. For topographic maps, ask Green Trails for No. 135S, Ozette, or ask the USGS for Ozette.

Directions: From Port Angeles, drive east 5 miles on U.S. 101 to Highway 112. Turn right (west) and drive 49 miles to Hoko/Ozette Lake Road. Turn left and drive 21 miles to the well-signed trailhead at Lake Ozette.

Contact: Olympic National Park, Wilderness Information Center, 3002 Mount Angeles Road, Port Angeles, WA 98362, 360/565-3100.

4 NORTH WILDERNESS BEACH
19.7 mi one-way/2–3 days 🥾 ⏱

west of Forks in Olympic National Park

Map 1.1, page 27

This stretch of the Olympic coastline is one of the wildest and most scenic beaches anywhere in the United States. North Wilderness Beach features countless tidal pools packed with creatures crawling, swimming, or simply affixed to the rocks. Unremitting waves roll in through the fog to break apart on the sea stacks jutting into the Pacific Ocean. Sea otters, eagles, herons, cormorants, and ducks are all likely sightings.

Access to North Wilderness Beach Route is via Sandpoint Trail, three miles of virgin coastal forest. The travelway heads south along sandy beaches, but at times may test ankles with stretches of cobbles and boulders. Several times the trail is driven on land because of impassibility around a point. Circular signs (painted like bull's-eyes and visible from the shore) indicate these points. Also, it is important to carry a tide table, as 12 sections of trail require passage at low or medium tides. Green Trails maps indicate points that require passages during low tides.

The route encounters the tall cliffs of Yellow Bank (4.5 miles). A pair of memorials stand along the route; Norwegian Memorial (9.9 miles), marked by an obelisk, and Chilean Memorial (16.5 miles). The travelway crosses Cedar Creek (11.3 miles), a necessary ford, and rounds Cape Johnson (15 miles). Hole in the Wall appears south of Cape Johnson, a rock formation forming a natural arch, where hikers can capture a postcard moment. The route ends at the sea stacks of Rialto Beach.

Throughout the route, camping is plentiful, with numerous sites on the shore. Campfires are not permitted between Wedding Rocks, north of Sand Point, and Yellow Banks. Elsewhere, be sure to gather only driftwood from the beach.

User Groups: Hikers only. No dogs, horses, or mountain bikes are allowed. No wheelchair access.

Open Seasons: This trail is accessible year-round.

Permits: There is a $1 daily parking fee here, payable at the trailhead. Overnight stays within the national park require backcountry camping permits, which are available at the Wilderness Information Center in Port Angeles.

Maps: For a map of Olympic National Park, contact the Outdoor Recreation Information Center at the downtown Seattle REI. For topographic maps, ask Green Trails for No. 130S, Lake Ozette, or ask the USGS for Ozette, Allens Bay, and La Push.

Directions: From Port Angeles, drive east 5 miles on U.S. 101 to Highway 112. Turn right (west) and drive 49 miles to Hoko/Ozette Lake Road. Turn left and drive 21 miles to the well-signed trailhead at Lake Ozette.

Contact: Olympic National Park, Wilderness Information Center, 3002 Mount Angeles Road, Port Angeles, WA 98362, 360/565-3100.

5 PYRAMID MOUNTAIN
7.0 mi/3.5 hrs

north of Lake Crescent in Olympic National Park

Map 1.2, page 28

Pyramid Mountain Trail provides a good workout through old-growth forest culminating at a wonderful cabin lookout. From the top, peer out over the Strait of Juan de Fuca to Canada and over Lake Crescent to the Olympics. The lookout was built during World War II so the army could watch for incoming enemy aircraft. Fortunately none arrived but the lookout remained. The cabin on stilts perches atop the 3,100-foot peak, not high by Olympic standards, but good enough to work up a sweat and enjoy it.

Pyramid Mountain Trail starts off in a previously logged forest but soon enters old-growth forest. Mixed with the large conifers are numerous Pacific madrona, the Northwest's distinctive broadleaved evergreen. Madrona is known for its uniquely papery bark that comes off in ragged shreds to reveal fine, smooth wood. These handsome trees produce small, bell-shaped flowers in the spring. Madrona trees deserve close inspection and always garner admiration.

The trail climbs through forest, crossing June Creek, which often runs below ground at this spot. It's a good idea to bring your own water on this hike, especially on warm days. The trail eventually reaches the ridgeline, where devastating clear-cuts have revealed views of the strait. After several false summits, the trail finally reaches the lookout. Be a bit careful up here; the north side of the mountain features a precipitous drop. The views extend in every direction. Lake Crescent is a beautiful green jewel to the south, while the strait is wide and large to the north.

User Groups: Hikers only. No dogs, horses, or mountain bikes are allowed. No wheelchair access.

Open Seasons: This trail is accessible April–October.

Permits: Permits are not required. Parking and access are free.

Maps: For a map of Olympic National Park, contact the Outdoor Recreation Information Center at the downtown Seattle REI. For topographic maps, ask Green Trails for No. 101, Lake Crescent, or ask the USGS for Lake Crescent.

Directions: From Port Angeles, drive west 28 miles on U.S. 101 to North Shore Road. Turn right and drive about 3 miles to the well-signed trailhead on the left side of the road.

Contact: Olympic National Park, Wilderness Information Center, 3002 Mount Angeles Road, Port Angeles, WA 98362, 360/565-3100.

6 SPRUCE RAILROAD
8.0 mi/4.0 hrs

north shore of Lake Crescent in Olympic National Park

Map 1.2, page 28

Anyone who has ever navigated the twisty section of U.S. 101 as it passes Lake Crescent knows the beauty of the emerald lake. With lush green forests and high mountain ridges containing the waters, Lake Crescent often stands out in the memories of passing motorists. That is to say nothing of the memories it leaves in hikers who walk the shores of Lake Crescent on the Spruce Railroad Trail.

Four miles of trail edge the lake along a former railroad built by the U.S. Army. This rail route once carried high-quality spruce timber to Seattle and eastward for production of World War I airplanes. Metal eventually replaced wood in aircraft production and the army sold the route, allowing the railway to be successfully converted into a level, easy-to-walk trail. The highlight is Devil's Punchbowl, 1.1 miles from the east trailhead. Here, a small cove from the lake is encircled by cliffs of pillow basalt. The depth of this popular swimming hole is reportedly more than 300 feet. Spruce Railroad Trail continues another three miles below towering cliffs where Pacific madrona cling to the walls. Lush forest covers parts of the trail, but Lake Crescent rarely leaves your sight. A trailhead exists at the west end, also. This hike is extremely well suited for families and for the off-season. It's a local winter favorite.

User Groups: Hikers only. No dogs, horses, or mountain bikes are allowed. No wheelchair access.

Open Seasons: This trail is accessible year-round.

Permits: Permits are not required. Parking and access are free.

Maps: For a map of Olympic National Park, contact the Outdoor Recreation Information Center at the downtown Seattle REI. For topographic maps, ask Green Trails for No. 101, Lake Crescent, or ask the USGS for Lake Crescent.

Directions: From Port Angeles, drive west 28 miles on U.S. 101 to North Shore Road. Turn right and drive 5 miles to the well-signed trailhead.

Contact: Olympic National Park, Wilderness Information Center, 3002 Mount Angeles Road, Port Angeles, WA 98362, 360/565-3100.

7 MARYMERE FALLS
1.4 mi/1.0 hr

south of Lake Crescent in Olympic National Park

Map 1.2, page 28

Marymere Falls Trail offers hikers of all ages and abilities a great view of the Olympics' best waterfall. A short stroll through old forest and a climb up a large series of crib steps presents visitors with a vantage point well positioned for the showcase cascade. Falls Creek shoots over Marymere Falls and tumbles more than 100 feet. With adequate flow, the creek plummets so fiercely that surrounding trees and ferns sway. A delicate mist covers all who lean over the railing. Marymere is a beautiful spot and is popular in the summer with the many people passing by on U.S. 101. Ferns and mosses grow upon everything in the forest, a great example of what the Olympic forests are all about. The route starts at Storm King Ranger Station, follows the Barnes Creek Trail for .5 mile, then cuts off by crossing Barnes Creek and Falls Creek before ascending to the viewpoint.

User Groups: Hikers only. No dogs, horses, or mountain bikes are allowed. No wheelchair access.

Open Seasons: This trail is accessible year-round.

Permits: Permits are not required. Parking and access are free.

Maps: For a map of Olympic National Park, contact the Outdoor Recreation Information Center at the downtown Seattle REI. For topographic maps, ask Green Trails for No. 101, Lake Crescent, or ask the USGS for Lake Crescent.

Directions: From Port Angeles, drive west 20 miles on U.S. 101 to the well-signed Storm

King Ranger Station. Turn right and drive 200 yards to Lake Crescent Road. Turn right for the trailhead at Storm King Ranger Station.

Contact: Olympic National Park, Wilderness Information Center, 3002 Mount Angeles Road, Port Angeles, WA 98362, 360/565-3100.

8 HEATHER PARK/ MOUNT ANGELES
10.0 mi one-way/5.5 hrs

south of Port Angeles in Olympic National Park

Map 1.2, page 28

A popular route for Port Angeles visitors, Heather Park Trail delivers grand views into the Olympics from along windswept ridges. Meadows are the name of the game along the upper sections. An outstanding parkland basin is found at Heather Park, while several accessible peaks offer views stretching over the heart of the Olympic Range. The route can also be completed from Hurricane Ridge Visitor Center, a less strenuous but busier choice.

Heather Park Trail leaves Heart o' the Hills in pleasant but unspectacular second-growth forest and climbs steadily to timberline and Heather Park (4.1 miles). The wide open basin rests between the pinnacles of First Peak and Second Peak. Meadows of heather and lupine fill in the voids between scattered subalpine fir trees, and several campsites are to be had. This is a good turnaround.

Heather Park Trail continues, climbing below the base of Mount Angeles (6 miles), whose summit is accessible by an easy social trail. Beyond, the trail drops to a junction with Sunrise Trail (6.3 miles), a highly used route that leads west to Hurricane Ridge Visitor Center. It's 3.5 miles of ridgeline hiking through open forest and meadows. Sunrise Trail gains less elevation and has its own social trail to the top of Mount Angeles.

User Groups: Hikers and horses. No dogs or mountain bikes are allowed. No wheelchair access.

Open Seasons: This trail is accessible mid-June–October.

Permits: Permits are not required. Parking and access are free.

Maps: For a map of Olympic National Park, contact the Outdoor Recreation Information Center at the downtown Seattle REI. For topographic maps, ask Green Trails for No. 103, Port Angeles, and No. 135, Mount Angeles, or ask the USGS for Port Angeles and Mount Angeles.

Directions: From Port Angeles, drive north 2 miles on Race Street as it turns into Mount Angeles Road. Veer right at the well-signed fork and continue on Mount Angeles Road 5 miles to the trailhead immediately before the national park entrance booth. The trailhead is down a short access road.

Contact: Olympic National Park, Wilderness Information Center, 3002 Mount Angeles Road, Port Angeles, WA 98362, 360/565-3100.

9 KLAHHANE RIDGE
13.0 mi/6.5 hrs

south of Port Angeles in Olympic National Park

Map 1.2, page 28

Klahhane Ridge Trail is much more than just Klahhane Ridge. For starters, the Klahhane Ridge Trail passes Lake Angeles, one of the peninsula's larger subalpine lakes, set beneath cliffs. Talk about picturesque. Second, the trail makes an outstanding loop when combined with Mount Angeles Trail. This 12.9-mile round-trip samples all of the best of the North Olympics. And the trail leads out along Klahhane Ridge, a place where open meadows and small trees give way to sweeping views of the interior Olympics. It may well be the best sampler of the Olympics around.

Klahhane Ridge Trail leaves Heart o' the Hills and climbs steadily through forest to Lake Angeles (3.7 miles). The lake is very popular with visitors to the North Peninsula, particularly on weekends. One would think the steep trip would weed folks out, but apparently not enough. A few camps are found around the lake. The trail continues up to Klahhane Ridge (5 miles), where distant vistas make their appearance, extending in every direction. The cities of Port Angeles and Victoria are visible to the north. Klahhane Ridge Trail ends at a junction with Mount Angeles Trail (6.5 miles), where turning north takes you through spectacular Heather Park and back to Heart o' the Hills.

User Groups: Hikers and horses. No dogs or mountain bikes are allowed. No wheelchair access.

Open Seasons: This trail is accessible mid-June–October.

Permits: Permits are not required. Parking and access are free.

Maps: For a map of Olympic National Park, contact the Outdoor Recreation Information Center at the downtown Seattle REI. For topographic maps, ask Green Trails for No. 103, Port Angeles, and No. 135, Mount Angeles, or ask the USGS for Port Angeles and Mount Angeles.

Directions: From Port Angeles, drive north 2 miles on Race Street as it turns into Mount Angeles Road. Veer right at the well-signed fork and continue on Mount Angeles Road 5 miles to the trailhead immediately before the national park entrance booth. The trailhead is down a short road on the right.

Contact: Olympic National Park, Wilderness Information Center, 3002 Mount Angeles Road, Port Angeles, WA 98362, 360/565-3100.

🔟 DUNGENESS SPIT
10.0 mi/5.0 hrs

north of Sequim on the northeast tip of the Olympic Peninsula

Map 1.2, page 28

Set within Dungeness National Wildlife Refuge, Dungeness Spit is undoubtedly one of the state's premier sites to watch wildlife. The refuge hosts a rich and diverse ecosystem that is home to birds, critters by land and sea, and numerous fish and shellfish. The trail is less of a trail and more of a walk on a great beach.

Dungeness Spit juts into the Strait of Juan de Fuca 5.5 miles, creating a quiet harbor and bay of tide flats. The spit is constantly growing, being added to from nearby bluffs eroding sandy sediments into the strait. At the end of the spit stands a historic lighthouse built in 1857 and still open to the public.

The refuge sees more than 250 species of birds each year, mainly shorebirds and waterfowl, some migratory and some permanent residents—definitely a bird-watcher's dream. More than 50 mammals of both land and sea live here, too. Harbor seals occasionally use the tip of the spit as a pup-raising site. In the bay, eelgrass beds provide a nursery for young salmon and steelhead adjusting to saltwater. This is a wonderful place to enjoy the wildlife.

User Groups: Hikers and horses (horses allowed except on summer weekends). No dogs or mountains bikes are allowed. The trail is wheelchair accessible (to several lookouts, not the spit).

Open Seasons: Most of this area is accessible year-round (some parts are closed seasonally to protect wildlife feeding and nesting).

Permits: The entrance fee is $3 per family daily. Admission is free with a federal duck stamp, a Golden Eagle Pass, a Golden Age Pass, or a Golden Access passport.

Maps: For a topographic map, ask the USGS for Dungeness.

Directions: From U.S. 101, go just west of Sequim and turn north on Kitchen-Dick Road. Continue for 3 miles to the Dungeness Recreation Area. Go through the recreation area to the refuge parking lot at the end of the road. The well-marked trailhead is located immediately before the parking area.

Contact: Dungeness National Wildlife Refuge, Washington Maritime NWR Complex, 33 South Barr Road, Port Angeles, WA 98362, 360/457-8451.

11 SECOND BEACH
2.4 mi/2.0 hrs

south of La Push on the central
Olympic Coast

Map 1.3, page 29

Second Beach is a place to do some thinking. Sit and stare at the many sea stacks out
among the waves. Watch waves crash through
the large archway to the north. Spy eagles
and gulls tangling high overhead. The months
of March, April, and October may bring migrating whales past you not far offshore.
When you tire of resting, walk along the sandy
beach. It is in pristine condition, save for a
little garbage that floats in from the ocean.
Well over a mile long, Second Beach provides
lots to see: driftwood, crabs, eagles, sea otters, and who knows what else. The trail down
to the beach (.7 mile) is easy to negotiate,
being flat and wide the whole way save for
the last few hundred yards. A wide pile of
driftwood stands between the trail and beach,
requiring a bit of scrambling, but it's nothing much. Second Beach is well worth a couple of extra hours for anyone on the way to
La Push.

User Groups: Hikers and leashed dogs. No
horses or mountain bikes are allowed. No wheelchair access.

Open Seasons: This trail is accessible year-round.

Permits: Permits are not required. Parking and
access are free.

Maps: For a map of Olympic National Park,
contact the Outdoor Recreation Information
Center at the downtown Seattle REI. For topographic maps, ask Green Trails for No. 163S,
La Push, or ask the USGS for Toleak Point.

Directions: From Port Angeles, drive west 54
miles on U.S. 101 to La Push Road (Highway
110; just before the town of Forks). Turn right
and drive 8 miles to a Y, where the road splits.
Stay left, on La Push Road, and drive 4.5 miles
to the signed trailhead on the left.

Contact: Olympic National Park, Wilderness
Information Center, 3002 Mount Angeles Road,
Port Angeles, WA 98362, 360/565-3100.

12 THIRD BEACH
2.6 mi/2.0–3.0 hrs

south of La Push on the central
Olympic Coast

Map 1.3, page 29

Snaking its way through a nice lowland forest, Third Beach Trail accesses a long strip of
extravagant Olympic coast. The beach is wide
and sandy for nearly its entire length, well over
a mile, and bends inward slightly to make a
crescent. The resulting bay was named Strawberry Bay after the ubiquitous strawberry plant
in the coastal forests. Tall, rocky cliffs mark
the north end of the crescent and are impassable, no matter your skill level. As you
look to the south, beyond Taylor Point, a number of sea stacks are visible in the distance.
It's easy for hikers of all abilities to see such
great things, as the trail down to the beach
loses very little elevation and is wide and well
maintained. As you hike through the forest,
the increasing roar of the ocean signals your
progress, as does the increasing size of massive cedar trees. Although some may say that
Second Beach is more scenic, Third Beach is
a great trip as well.

User Groups: Hikers and leashed dogs. No
horses or mountain bikes are allowed. No wheelchair access.

Open Seasons: This trail is accessible year-round.

Permits: Permits are not required. Parking and
access are free.

Maps: For a map of Olympic National Park,
contact the Outdoor Recreation Information
Center at the downtown Seattle REI. For topographic maps, ask Green Trails for No. 163S,
La Push, or ask the USGS for Toleak Point.

Directions: From Port Angeles, drive west 54
miles on U.S. 101 to La Push Road (Highway
110; just before the town of Forks). Turn right
and drive 8 miles to a Y, where the road splits.
Stay left, on La Push Road, and drive 3 miles
to the signed trailhead on the left.

Contact: Olympic National Park, Wilderness
Information Center, 3002 Mount Angeles Road,
Port Angeles, WA 98362, 360/565-3100.

13 CENTRAL WILDERNESS BEACH

16.7 mi one-way/2 days

south of La Push on the central Olympic Coast

Map 1.3, page 29

As beautiful as the other long beach routes, Third Beach to Oil City provides a bit more of a hiking challenge. This is the South Coast Beach Travelway, and it requires that several overland bypasses and three creeks be crossed. Not that any of these obstacles is too much to overcome. The South Travelway has some great scenery, including Giants Graveyard, Alexander Island, and an extraordinary abundance of birds and sea life. Bald eagles and blue herons regularly sweep the shores in search of dinner, while sea otters play it cool, reclining in the water and eating shellfish off their stomachs.

Access the route via Third Beach, hiking south above Taylor's Point, impassable along the water. Many times hikers must avoid impassable coastline by hiking trails on land; it's important to carry a map to properly identify these sections. Five miles of great beach present views of Giants Graveyard (4.2 miles), Strawberry Point (6.5 miles), and Toleak Point (7.2 miles), appropriate images of the rugged coastline.

The middle section of Southern Travelway requires fords of Falls Creek (8.5 miles), Goodman Creek (9 miles), and Mosquito Creek (11.5 miles). If it's been wet recently, expect them to be difficult. The lower section of Southern Travelway uses beach, with Alexander Island offshore, and a long 3.5-mile overland route bypassing Hoh Head. This leaves you just north of the trailhead at Oil City (16.7 miles), near the mouth of the Hoh River. Campsites are spread throughout the trip, usually tucked away on shore but visible from the beach.

User Groups: Hikers only. No dogs, horses, or mountain bikes are allowed. No wheelchair access.

Open Seasons: This trail is accessible year-round.

Permits: Permits are not required. Parking and access are free.

Maps: For a map of Olympic National Park, contact the Outdoor Recreation Information Center at the downtown Seattle REI. For topographic maps, ask Green Trails for No. 163, La Push, or ask the USGS for Toleak Point and Hoh Head.

Directions: From Port Angeles, drive west 54 miles on U.S. 101 to La Push Road (Highway 110; just before the town of Forks). Turn right and drive 8 miles to a Y, where the road splits. Stay left, on La Push Road, and drive 3 miles to the signed trailhead on the left.

Contact: Olympic National Park, Wilderness Information Center, 3002 Mount Angeles Road, Port Angeles, WA 98362, 360/565-3100.

14 BOGACHIEL RIVER

41.6 mi/4 days

southeast of Forks in Olympic National Park

Map 1.3, page 29

Let the masses drive the road up the Hoh River and visit the overpopulated Hoh River Valley. Follow the wiser hikers who access the Bogachiel River for the same gargantuan trees covered in moss, the same cascading streams filled with juvenile salmon, and the same forests teeming with wildlife—but with considerably more solitude.

An OK day hike, Bogachiel River Trail makes for an outstanding river valley trek. Beginning along an old logging road, the trail soon enters the national park and virgin rainforest (2 miles). Massive trees fill the forests, awash in green from the heavy rains off the Pacific Ocean. The mostly flat trail moves in and out of the forest, regularly nearing the river and passing camps. Maintenance on the trail often fails to keep up with the regular washouts from heavy winter rains, so be ready for some route-finding along the way.

After Flapjack Camp (10 miles), Bogachiel River Trail leaves the main branch of the river and slowly climbs with North Fork Bogachiel

River toward High Divide. This is the trail's best section, where at 15 Mile Shelter (14.5 miles) the river surges through a deep gorge. After Hyak Camp (17.6 miles) and 21 Mile Camp (20.8 miles), the trail overlooks the Bogachiel and vast meadows. Those who plan for it can connect this trail to Mink Lake or Deer Lake Trails (25.5 miles) for through-hikes via the Sol Duc Valley. This route is truly wild country, where elk and ancient trees far outnumber bipeds.

User Groups: Hikers and horses. No dogs or mountain bikes are allowed. No wheelchair access.

Open Seasons: This trail is usually accessible year-round (up to about 15 Mile Camp, where the winter snowpack becomes quite deep).

Permits: A federal Northwest Forest Pass is required to park here. Overnight stays within the national park require backcountry camping permits, which are available at the Wilderness Information Center in Port Angeles.

Maps: For a map of Olympic National Park, contact the Outdoor Recreation Information Center at the downtown Seattle REI. For topographic maps, ask Green Trails for No. 132, Spruce Mountain, No. 133, Mount Tom, and No. 134, Mount Olympus, or ask the USGS for Reade Hill, Indian Pass, Hunger Mountain, Slide Peak, and Bogachiel Peak.

Directions: From Forks, drive south 6 miles on U.S. 101 to Undie Road. Turn left (east) and drive 4 miles to the trailhead at road's end.

Contact: Olympic National Park, Wilderness Information Center, 3002 Mount Angeles Road, Port Angeles, WA 98362, 360/565-3100.

15 SOL DUC FALLS/ LOVER'S LANE

5.6 mi/3.0 hrs

south of Lake Crescent in Olympic National Park

Map 1.4, page 30

This is not an exclusive trail for sweethearts. Sure, a couple in love are apt to find this the perfect stroll. But those even more likely to find this a great trail are those who love an easy hike along a great trail through the forest. That group includes couples and kids, seasoned hikers, singles, groups, and anyone between. Add to the pleasure of Lover's Lane the excitement of Sol Duc Falls, one of the Olympics' premier photo ops, and you have a widely agreed-upon fun hike.

The trail departs from the Sol Duc Hot Springs Resort, where folks can relax weary muscles in a number of springs, and starts off into an old-growth forest. The Sol Duc River is never far away and calls out with its incessant rushing. The trail crosses three streams on easy-to-negotiate footbridges, each a nice interruption in the scenery.

Before three miles are underfoot, the trail arrives at Sol Duc Falls. Here, the river makes an abrupt turn and cascades from three notches into a narrow gorge. The forest is incredibly green in these parts and moss seems omnipresent. Regardless of your romantic pursuits, Lover's Lane is a trail for all.

User Groups: Hikers only. No dogs, horses, or mountain bikes are allowed. No wheelchair access.

Open Seasons: This trail is accessible year-round.

Permits: A federal National Parks Pass is required to park here.

Maps: For a map of Olympic National Park, contact the Outdoor Recreation Information Center at the downtown Seattle REI. For topographic maps, ask Green Trails for No. 133, Mount Tom, or ask the USGS for Bogachiel Peak.

Directions: From Port Angeles, drive west 30 miles on U.S. 101 to well-signed Sol Duc Hot Springs Road. Turn left (south) and drive 14 miles to the trailhead at road's end.

Contact: Olympic National Park, Wilderness Information Center, 3002 Mount Angeles Road, Port Angeles, WA 98362, 360/565-3100.

16 SEVEN LAKES BASIN LOOP
20.1 mi/2 days

south of Lake Crescent in Olympic
National Park

Map 1.4, page 30

This is one of the peninsula's greatest hikes, a exceptional journey into one of the best lake basins in Washington. The destination is High Divide and the numerous lakes of the area. The divide is more than 5,000 feet in elevation, making this meadow territory. Views open wide to the south, revealing Mount Olympus at close range. Wildlife is plentiful in this part of the park, where regular sightings include black bear, ravens, Roosevelt elk, picas, and Olympic marmots. If you have a camera, please bring it. During July, wildflowers are prolific and difficult not to trample underfoot.

The trail makes a loop by heading up the Sol Duc River to High Divide, then coming back via Deer Lake and Canyon Creek. The trail up the Sol Duc River is a trip through pristine old-growth forests along a river making constant cascades and falls. After the Appleton Pass Trail cuts off at 4.8 miles, the Sol Duc Trail climbs vigorously up Bridge Creek to High Divide. Camps are frequent, but Sol Duc Park and Heart Lake are highly recommended.

From High Divide, Mount Olympus and the Bailey Range ring the Hoh Valley. Head north on the High Divide to the Seven Lakes Basin, a series of not seven but actually eight subalpine lakes. The lakes lie on a gentle slope facing the north, meaning snow can linger well into July. To curb overuse, campsites here must be reserved with the Wilderness Information Center. The trail leaves the basin and drops to Deer Lake. Here, one trail leads down to the trailhead via Canyon Creek, another long string of waterfalls.

User Groups: Hikers only. No dogs, horses, or mountain bikes are allowed. No wheelchair access.

Open Seasons: This trail is accessible July–October.

Permits: A National Parks Pass is required to park here. Overnight stays within the national park require backcountry camping permits, which are available at the Wilderness Information Center in Port Angeles.

Maps: For a map of Olympic National Park, contact the Outdoor Recreation Information Center at the downtown Seattle REI. For topographic maps, ask Green Trails for No. 133, Mount Tom, and No. 134, Mount Olympus, or ask the USGS for Bogachiel Peak and Mount Carrie.

Directions: From Port Angeles, drive west 30 miles on U.S. 101 to well-signed Sol Duc Hot Springs Road. Turn left (south) and drive 14 miles to the trailhead at road's end.

Contact: Olympic National Park, Wilderness Information Center, 3002 Mount Angeles Road, Port Angeles, WA 98362, 360/565-3100.

17 APPLETON PASS
14.8 mi/8.0 hrs

south of Lake Crescent in Olympic
National Park

Map 1.4, page 30

Appleton Pass Trail provides a crossing from the Sol Duc to the Elwha drainages. It's also an alternate route up to Boulder Lake and a great entry to acres of open meadows and parkland. The Sol Duc Valley is full of waterfalls, and this route passes by several of them.

From the trailhead, the route uses Sol Duc River Trail for the first 4.8 miles. Along the way is Sol Duc Falls, a popular day hike. This section of trail passes through cool forests of old-growth timber. Appleton Pass Trail climbs steeply via a tiring number of switchbacks to the pass. Just before the pass, it reaches the timberline, and spacious meadows break out in abundance.

Small Oyster Lake is a short side trail from the pass and well recommended. Mount Appleton stands to the north, cloaked in wildflowers and heather during the early summer. For through-hikers, the trail continues beyond the pass down the South Fork of Boulder Creek. Just before the trail converges with North Fork

Trail, Boulder Creek makes a tremendous leap into a deep pool, followed by several smaller cascades, a wonderful sight.

User Groups: Hikers and horses. No dogs or mountain bikes are allowed. No wheelchair access.

Open Seasons: This trail is accessible July–October.

Permits: A National Parks Pass is required to park here. Overnight stays within the national park require backcountry camping permits, which are available at the Wilderness Information Center in Port Angeles.

Maps: For a map of Olympic National Park, contact the Outdoor Recreation Information Center at the downtown Seattle REI. For topographic maps, ask Green Trails for No. 133, Mount Tom, and No. 134, Mount Olympus, or ask the USGS for Bogachiel Peak and Mount Carrie.

Directions: From Port Angeles, drive west 30 miles on U.S. 101 to well-signed Sol Duc Hot Springs Road. Turn left (south) and drive 14 miles to the trailhead at road's end.

Contact: Olympic National Park, Wilderness Information Center, 3002 Mount Angeles Road, Port Angeles, WA 98362, 360/565-3100.

18 BOULDER LAKE
11.2 mi/6.0 hrs

southwest of Port Angeles in Olympic National Park

Map 1.4, page 30

Although Boulder Lake is a great destination, it's often forgotten for the soothing water of Olympic Hot Springs. The hot springs draw the majority of visitors (understandably), but they miss out on a great hike. The hike is a relatively easy one, climbing gradually through virgin forests. At the base of Boulder Peak, small Boulder Lake sits within open forests of subalpine fir and mountain hemlock. In spite of the lake's beauty, you're more likely to remember your soak in the Olympic Hot Springs on the way back down the trail.

The first 2.2 miles of the trail are old roadbed, terminating at Boulder Creek Camp. The hot springs are just across Boulder Creek. Consisting of several pools collecting hot mineral water, the springs feel primitive and natural. Save it for your muscles on the way down, when they'll be more thankful. The trail splits .5 mile beyond the camp; the left fork goes to Appleton Pass, the right fork travels another two miles to Boulder Lake. Campsites can be found around the lake within the open forest. View seekers can scramble Boulder Peak.

At the lake, the trail turns into Happy Lake Ridge Trail, an optional return of 10 miles to Hot Springs Road, two miles below the trailhead. Most of the hike is on the ridge, within open spreads of subalpine meadows. Happy Lake sits at the midpoint of the ridge, perfect for longer stays. It's nice, but we prefer the hot springs.

User Groups: Hikers and horses. No dogs or mountain bikes are allowed. No wheelchair access.

Open Seasons: This trail is accessible June–October.

Permits: A National Parks Pass is required to park here. Overnight stays within the national park require backcountry camping permits, which are available at the Wilderness Information Center in Port Angeles.

Maps: For a map of Olympic National Park, contact the Outdoor Recreation Information Center at the downtown Seattle REI. For topographic maps, ask Green Trails for No. 134, Mount Olympus, or ask the USGS for Mount Carrie.

Directions: From Port Angeles, drive west 8 miles on U.S. 101 to Elwha Hot Springs Road. Turn left (south) and drive 10 miles, into the national park, to the road's end at a barrier with a well-signed trailhead.

Contact: Olympic National Park, Wilderness Information Center, 3002 Mount Angeles Road, Port Angeles, WA 98362, 360/565-3100.

19 ELWHA RIVER

54.2 mi/3–5 days

southwest of Port Angeles in Olympic National Park

Map 1.4, page 30

The Elwha River serves as the main artery of the Olympic Mountains. For more than 25 miles, the trail closely follows a historic and well-traveled route deep into the heart of the range. The Elwha was used for ages by local tribes to delve into the mountains for hunting and ceremonial reasons. In the late 1800s, the Press Expedition (a contingent of newspapermen and explorers) followed it on their trek across the mountain range. It has been an often-visited trail by backpackers and hikers for decades and is thought of as the spirit of the Olympics. The glacially fed waters boom through magnificent forests, a setting for many a backcountry tale. Sounds like a great place, doesn't it?

Elwha Trail travels deep into the Olympics to Low Divide. There are many campsites and shelters, and they receive heavy use in the summer. Old-growth forest breaks to reveal the river in stands of alder and maple. The trail forks at Chicago Camp (25 miles). The north fork heads to Elwha Basin, while the south fork proceeds up to Low Divide and the North Fork Quinault. It's an amazing trek for those who complete it, and especially great when done with a friend.

Day hikers will also find much to see and do within several miles of the trailhead. Side trails (1.2 miles in) lead down to Goblin's Gate (1.7 miles), where the Elwha passes through a narrow gorge. From here, a small network of trails finds the sites of old homesteads and large meadows. These are great places to see deer, elk, and even black bears.

User Groups: Hikers and horses. No dogs or mountain bikes are allowed. No wheelchair access.

Open Seasons: The lower part of this trail is usually accessible year-round (upper part is accessible June–October).

Permits: A National Parks Pass is required to park here. Overnight stays within the national park require backcountry camping permits, which are available at the Wilderness Information Center in Port Angeles.

Maps: For a map of Olympic National Park, contact the Outdoor Recreation Information Center at the downtown Seattle REI. For topographic maps, ask Green Trails for No. 134, Mount Olympus, No. 135, Mount Angeles, No. 166, Mount Christie, and No. 167, Mount Steel, or ask the USGS for Hurricane Hill, Mount Angeles, McCartney Peak, Chimney Peak, and Mount Christie.

Directions: From Port Angeles, drive west 8 miles on U.S. 101 to Elwha Hot Springs Road. Turn left (south) and drive 4 miles to the cutoff for Whiskey Bend Road. Turn left and drive 5 miles to the trailhead at road's end.

Contact: Olympic National Park, Wilderness Information Center, 3002 Mount Angeles Road, Port Angeles, WA 98362, 360/565-3100.

20 HURRICANE HILL

3.2 mi/2.0 hrs

south of Port Angeles in Olympic National Park

Map 1.4, page 30

Visitors to Hurricane Ridge should and very often do hike this trail. Why? Because no trail in the Olympics offers such easy access to such exceptional views. The trail is completely within the high country, where windswept ridges are covered in lush, green meadows. The open trail offers nonstop views to the north and south, and the summit of Hurricane Hill is one giant panoramic vista. The hike is relatively easy and can be made by hikers of all abilities at their own pace.

Hurricane Hill Trail starts off on a cleared roadbed and gently climbs for its entire length. Wildflowers are in full gear during late June, while the last vestiges of the winter's snowpack hang on. Eventually the roadbed ends, but the trail remains wide and easy to hike. At the top of Hurricane Hill are wide knolls, perfect for a picnic or extended rest before heading back to the car. It's likely you'll want to stick around for awhile, mostly for the views. Much of the Olympic interior is revealed, including the Bailey Range and most of the Elwha drainage. The views to the north include the Strait of Juan de Fuca, Vancouver Island, and to the east, the Cascades. If there is any one trail that will endear the Olympics to its visitors, this is surely it.

User Groups: Hikers only. No dogs, horses, or mountain bikes are allowed. No wheelchair access.

Open Seasons: This trail is accessible June–October.

Permits: A National Parks Pass is required to park here.

Maps: For a map of Olympic National Park, contact the Outdoor Recreation Information Center at the downtown Seattle REI. For topographic maps, ask Green Trails for No. 134, Mount Olympus, or ask the USGS for Hurricane Hill.

Directions: From Port Angeles, drive north 2 miles on Race Street as it turns into Mount Angeles Road. Veer right at the well-signed fork and continue on Mount Angeles Road 19 miles, past the lower and upper visitors centers, to the well-signed trailhead.

Contact: Olympic National Park, Wilderness Information Center, 3002 Mount Angeles Road, Port Angeles, WA 98362, 360/565-3100.

21 GRAND RIDGE
8.0 mi/4.0 hrs

south of Port Angeles in Olympic National Park

Map 1.4, page 30

The National Park Service was once crazy about cars. It hoped to build a road through the park connecting Obstruction Point to Deer Park. Fortunately, the park service realized it would be insane to destroy such a beautiful area and abandoned the idea after surveying the route. Survey markers from the Bureau of Public Roads still line the trail, the intended course. Barren, open, and windy, Grand Ridge offers views of the Gray Wolf River drainage and many northern Olympic peaks. It's a great trip for those visiting Obstruction Point and the Hurricane Ridge area.

The trail primarily follows the southern side of Grand Ridge. This area is extremely barren, where even krummholz (small, distorted trees that look more like bushes) struggle to establish a foothold. Thin soils and intense winds work together to keep this area devoid of trees and full of views. A couple of high points offer good scramble opportunities and panoramic views: Elk Mountain (1.5 miles) and Maiden Peak (4 miles). Be sure to bring water, as hot days are even hotter on this south-facing slope. And be aware that when the wind picks up, which is often, you can expect 50–60 mph gusts to knock you around. Usually the wind blows you into the mountain, a good thing, because the drop down the mountain is precipitous.

User Groups: Hikers only. No dogs, horses, or mountain bikes are allowed. No wheelchair access.

Open Seasons: This trail is usually accessible May–October.

Permits: A National Parks Pass is required to park at Hurricane Hill; parking at Deer Park is free.

Maps: For a map of Olympic National Park, contact the Outdoor Recreation Information Center at the downtown Seattle REI. For topographic maps, ask Green Trails for No. 135, Mount Angeles, or ask the USGS for Mount Angeles and Maiden Peak.

Directions: From Port Angeles, drive north 2 miles on Race Street as it turns into Mount Angeles Road. Veer right at the well-signed fork and continue on Mount Angeles Road 17 miles to Obstruction Point Road. Turn left and drive 7 miles to road's end and Obstruction Point Trailhead.

Contact: Olympic National Park, Wilderness Information Center, 3002 Mount Angeles Road, Port Angeles, WA 98362, 360/565-3100.

22 GRAND PASS
12.0 mi/1–2 days

south of Port Angeles in Olympic National Park

Map 1.4, page 30

This is one of the Olympics' most popular destinations and with good reason. Easily accessible and very beautiful, Grand and Moose Lakes are favorite campgrounds. Farther up Grand Valley are plentiful subalpine meadows and rough, rocky slopes leading to Grand Pass, where views reach for miles around. Throw in two routes to the valley from Obstruction Peak (each of which is terrific), and you have a popular and well-visited spot in the North Olympics.

Leaving Obstruction Point, you are faced with two possible routes. Grand Pass Trail traverses Lillian Ridge, well above 6,000 feet and awash in mountain views, before dropping to Grand Lake. Alternatively, Badger Valley Trail makes its way through meadows and Alaskan cedar groves before climbing to Grand Lake. The best option is to make this a small loop, along the ridge on the way in and up the valley on the way out.

Overnight guests to Grand and Moose Lakes are required to secure a permit and reservation from the Wilderness Information Center. While there are numerous sites, they often fill up in the summer. The lakes are bordered by beautiful forests and rocky valley hillsides. Beyond, Grand Pass Trail passes small Gladys Lake and climbs steeply to Grand Pass. The rocky and barren territory is a testament to the snowpacks that linger well into summer along these north-facing inclines. From Grand Pass, the Olympics are at hand and breathtaking.

User Groups: Hikers only. No dogs, horses, or mountain bikes are allowed. No wheelchair access.

Open Seasons: This trail is usually accessible June–October.

Permits: A National Parks Pass is required to park here. Overnight stays at Grand or Moose Lake require reservations and backcountry camping permits, which are available at the Wilderness Information Center in Port Angeles.

Maps: For a map of Olympic National Park, contact the Outdoor Recreation Information Center at the downtown Seattle REI. For topographic maps, ask Green Trails for No. 135, Mount Angeles, or ask the USGS for Mount Angeles, Maiden Peak, and Wellesley Peak.

Directions: From Port Angeles, drive north 2 miles on Race Street as it turns into Mount Angeles Road. Veer right at the well-signed fork and continue on Mount Angeles Road 17 miles to Obstruction Point Road. Turn left and drive 7 miles to road's end and Obstruction Point Trailhead.

Contact: Olympic National Park, Wilderness Information Center, 3002 Mount Angeles Road, Port Angeles, WA 98362, 360/565-3100.

23 CAMERON CREEK
32.0 mi/4 days

south of Sequim in Olympic National Park

Map 1.4, page 30

The best backcountry locations often require an extra bit of effort to reach. Perhaps it is that extra exertion that makes some places so special and memorable. Cameron Creek is one of those places. It requires more than a few miles of approach hiking before you even embark on the long trail itself. Don't fret, time-conscious hikers; the journey along the trail and the vast mountain meadows deep within Cameron Basin are reward enough.

Cameron Creek Trail begins at Three Forks, where the creek joins Grand Creek and Gray Wolf River. The best access is via Three Forks Trail, a steep drop from Deer Park. While it's possible to hike up from the Lower Gray Wolf, river crossings are necessary and difficult. Cameron Creek Trail heads up the valley 7 miles, passing through beautiful forests of Douglas fir. Lower Cameron Camp (4 miles from Three Forks) is the primary campground.

Cameron Trail becomes more rugged near its headwaters, sometimes blown out by the creek. The upper basin is pure parkland, where wildflowers and waterfalls cover the landscape. Although it's a tough climb, Cameron Pass rewards with deep wilderness views. Mount Claywood and Sentinel Peak beckon from across Lost River Basin, one of the wildest places on the peninsula. The trail eventually drops to Dosewallips River. Campsites for the second night are scattered along the trail and throughout Cameron Basin.

User Groups: Hikers only. No dogs, horses, or mountain bikes are allowed. No wheelchair access.

Open Seasons: This trail is accessible June–early October.

Permits: Parking and access are free. Overnight stays within the national park require backcountry camping permits, which are available at the Wilderness Information Center in Port Angeles.

Maps: For a map of Olympic National Park, contact the Outdoor Recreation Information Center at the downtown Seattle REI. For topographic maps, ask Green Trails for No. 135, Mount Angeles, and No. 136, Tyler Peak, or ask the USGS for Tyler Peak, Maiden Peak, and Wellesley Peak.

Directions: From Port Angeles, drive east 5 miles on U.S. 101 to Deer Park Road. Turn right (south) and drive 17 miles to the well-signed trailhead.

Contact: Olympic National Park, Wilderness Information Center, 3002 Mount Angeles Road, Port Angeles, WA 98362, 360/565-3100.

24 HOH RIVER
34.0 mi/1–4 days

southeast of Forks in Olympic National Park

Map 1.4, page 30

The Hoh Valley is world famous for the enormous size of its forests. Known as cathedrals, the forest canopy stands 200 feet above, filtering sunlight onto numerous ferns and draping mosses. This trail is also popular because it is the route for those seeking the pinnacle of the Olympic Mountains, Mount Olympus. Never mind the herds of people (or elk), for trees with trunks that wouldn't fit in your living room are calling from above.

The entire trail is outstanding. The first 12 miles are flat and well laid out, avoiding many ups and downs. It's a constant biology lesson in growth limits, as behemoth trees compete to outgrow each other. Many places along the trail allow for full appreciation of a river's ecology. Eagles and ravens stand atop trees looking for salmon or steelhead within the river. American dippers patrol the waterline while herds of Roosevelt elk graze along the forest floor. There are several well-interspersed campgrounds throughout. At 9.5 miles is Hoh Lake Trail cutoff, a trip for another day.

After 12 miles, the trail begins to slowly climb. The river courses through a spectacular canyon more than 100 feet deep by the time a hiker reaches the 13-mile mark. Hoh Trail crosses the canyon on a well-built bridge and begins its true ascent. Through a series of switchbacks, the trail passes through the forest and into a deep ravine. Beyond lies Glacier Meadows, where Olympus stands tall above terminating glaciers, revealing fields of blooming wildflowers among piles of glacial moraine. There are numerous camps here, all on a first-come first-served basis for the many backpackers and mountain climbers. This is the climax of the Olympics, standing beneath mighty Olympus and above miles and miles of rainforest. Enjoy your hike out.

User Groups: Hikers and horses. No dogs or mountain bikes are allowed. No wheelchair access.

Open Seasons: This trail is usually accessible April–October.

Permits: A National Parks Pass is required to park here. Overnight stays within the national park require backcountry camping permits, which are available at the Hoh Ranger Station (at the end of Hoh River Road, 360/374-6925).

Maps: For a map of Olympic National Park, contact the Outdoor Recreation Information

Center at the downtown Seattle REI. For topographic maps, ask Green Trails for No. 133, Mount Tom, and No. 134, Mount Olympus, or ask the USGS for Owl Mountain, Mount Tom, Bogachiel Peak, Mount Carrie, and Mount Olympus.

Directions: From Port Angeles, drive south 14 miles on U.S. 101 to Upper Hoh River Road. Turn left (east) and drive 18 miles to the Hoh Ranger Station and trailhead.

Contact: Olympic National Park, Wilderness Information Center, 3002 Mount Angeles Road, Port Angeles, WA 98362, 360/565-3100.

25 QUEETS RIVER
30.8 mi/2–3 days

south of Forks in Olympic National Park

Map 1.4, page 30

Queets River Trail is all about two things: forests chock-full of enormous trees and total seclusion. Trees here grow to tremendous sizes, with Sitka spruce, western hemlock, western red cedar, and Douglas fir creating a community of giants. In fact, the Queets is home to the world's largest living Douglas fir, a monster with a trunk 14.5 feet in diameter and a broken top 221 feet above the ground. While as impressive as the Hoh, this valley receives just a fraction of the visitors. That's because of a necessary river ford just beyond the trailhead. The river can be forded only during times of low water (late summer or fall) and should be undertaken with care at any time; once you're past, though, traveling is easy.

The trail travels roughly 15 miles along the river. The forest often gives way to glades of big leaf maple and the cutting river. Bears outnumber people here. The world's largest Douglas fir is two miles in, just off Kloochman Rock Trail heading north. There are three established camps along the trail, easily providing sufficient camping for the few backpackers on this trail. The first is Spruce Bottom (6 miles). Sticking on the trail will eventually take you to the Pelton Creek Shelter (15 miles), where the trail ends. It is certainly possible to carry on farther to Queets Basin, but it's a bushwhack. It's enough to sit down, enjoy the permeating quiet of the wilderness, and smile.

User Groups: Hikers and horses. No dogs or mountain bikes are allowed. No wheelchair access.

Open Seasons: This trail is usually accessible May–October.

Permits: Parking is free. Overnight stays within the national park require backcountry camping permits, which are available at the Wilderness Information Center in Port Angeles.

Maps: For a map of Olympic National Park, contact the Outdoor Recreation Information Center at the downtown Seattle REI. For topographic maps, ask Green Trails for No. 165, Kloochman Rock, or ask the USGS for Stequaleho Creek, Kloochman Rock, and Bob Creek.

Directions: From Forks, drive south on U.S. 101 to Queets River Road. Turn left (east) and drive 14 miles to the trailhead at road's end.

Contact: Olympic National Park, Wilderness Information Center, 3002 Mount Angeles Road, Port Angeles, WA 98362, 360/565-3100.

26 SKYLINE RIDGE
45.0 mi/5–6 days

northeast of Quinault in Olympic National Park

Map 1.4, page 30

Sure to test even the toughest hikers, Skyline Ridge rewards with one of the most beautiful hikes on the peninsula. The trail never leaves the high country as it follows the ridge separating the large Quinault and Queets Valleys. The views up here are unbelievable, with Mount Olympus standing just one ridge away. Watch the sun set from this high place and the fog roll in from the Pacific Ocean, visible in the distance. And stay on your toes, as this is the perfect place to spot black bears as they drunkenly wolf down huckleberries. The Quinault is said to sport some of the highest black bear concentrations in the state, so be ready for some excitement. Mile after mile, the Skyline consistently offers the best of the Olympics.

The route must be accessed by Three Lakes Trail (6.5 miles) or North Fork Quinault Trail (16 miles; see listing in this chapter). The best route is via North Fork Quinault, making a loop. Climbing out of Low Divide, Skyline Trail skirts several basins of meadows and rises to Beauty Pass (7.4 miles from Low Divide). A side trail heads to Lake Beauty and campsites with views of Olympus.

Beyond, the trail is difficult to follow and marked by rock cairns. Excellent map and route-finding skills are needed here. Skyline Trail heads for Three Prune Camp (18 miles), switching between the Quinault and Queets Valleys several times. Water can be difficult to find here until Three Prune. The trail begins its decent to Three Lakes, the last spot for camping, and Three Lakes Trail back to the trailhead. By the time you get back to the car, you'll already be planning next year's trip.

User Groups: Hikers only. No dogs, horses, or mountain bikes are allowed. No wheelchair access.

Open Seasons: This trail is usually accessible August–September (depending on the previous winter's snowpack).

Permits: Parking is free. Overnight stays within the national park require backcountry camping permits, which are available at Quinault Ranger Station.

Maps: For a map of Olympic National Park, contact the Outdoor Recreation Information Center at the downtown Seattle REI. For topographic maps, ask Green Trails for No. 166, Mount Christie, or ask the USGS for Bunch Lake, Kimta Peak, and Mount Christie.

Directions: From Forks, travel south on U.S. 101 to North Shore Road at Lake Quinault. Turn left (east) and drive 17 miles to North Fork Ranger Station at road's end.

Contact: Olympic National Park, Wilderness Information Center, 3002 Mount Angeles Road, Port Angeles, WA 98362, 360/565-3100.

27 NORTH FORK QUINAULT
31.4 mi/3–4 days

northeast of Quinault in Olympic National Park

Map 1.4, page 30

With headwaters at Low Divide, North Fork Trail provided the way for many a party of explorers. From this popular junction, used by the Press Expedition, Army Lieutenant Joseph P. O'Neil, and others, the river flows more than 30 miles to the Pacific through beautiful high country and forests of enormous size in the lowlands. Its link to Low Divide makes it a well-used route for folks coming or going to the Elwha River. It also makes a great counterpart to Skyline Trail, which skirts the North Fork's upper ridge. There's no end to things to see as the trail crosses numerous beautiful creeks and even the river itself. It passes through superb forests of trees swollen to large, rainforest dimensions, and hikers often encounter wildlife.

The trail follows the river all the way to its source at Low Divide. Campsites and shelters occur regularly throughout this section of trail, including Wolf Bar (2.5 miles), Halfway House (5.2 miles), Elip Creek, (6.5 miles), Trapper Shelter (8.5 miles), and 12 Mile (11.5 miles). Be prepared for several easy creek crossings. The ascent up the valley is modest, making these 12 miles pass quickly underfoot.

After a good day's hike, the trail crosses the North Fork at 16 Mile Camp (12.3 miles). This river crossing can be difficult if not impassable during times of high flow. If coming from the Elwha, beware. A U-turn here makes the return trip more than 40 miles. Beyond, the trail climbs to Low Divide, an open meadow surrounded by waterfalls. Low Divide Ranger Station lies just beyond the Skyline Trail junction.

User Groups: Hikers and horses. No dogs or mountain bikes are allowed. No wheelchair access.

Open Seasons: This trail is accessible June–October.

Permits: A federal Northwest Forest Pass is required to park here. Overnight stays within the national park require backcountry camping permits, which are available at Quinault Ranger Station.

Maps: For a map of Olympic National Park, contact the Outdoor Recreation Information Center at the downtown Seattle REI. For topographic maps, ask Green Trails for No. 166, Mount Christie, or ask the USGS for Bunch Lake, Kitma Peak, and Mount Christie.

Directions: From Forks, travel south on U.S. 101 to North Shore Road at Lake Quinault. Turn left (east) and drive 17 miles to North Fork Ranger Station at road's end.

Contact: Olympic National Park, Wilderness Information Center, 3002 Mount Angeles Road, Port Angeles, WA 98362, 360/565-3100.

28 ENCHANTED VALLEY
36.0 mi/4 days

east of Quinault in Olympic National Park

Map 1.4, page 30

Undoubtedly one of Washington's most beautiful places, Enchanted Valley leaves visitors reminiscing about their trip here for years to come. East Fork Quinault Trail travels through old-growth forests of giant trees to the steep cliffs and waterfalls of Enchanted Valley. The wide and wild valley offers miles of exploration and loads of views of the tall peaks enclosing the Quinault. The trail eventually finds the high-country playground of Anderson Pass, home to glaciers and acres of meadows.

East Fork Quinault Trail immediately crosses Graves Creek, where a bridge was recently blown out by heavy rains; call the Wilderness Information Center to see if a ford is required. The trail travels 13 level and easy miles among ancient trees growing in a lush and humid forest. Elk and deer roam the thick understory. The forest gives way to clearings as the trail nears Enchanted Valley. A ford of the river is required here, difficult at times of high water. Countless waterfalls cascade from the vertical cliffs on both sides of the valley. The valley is

home to a ranger station and old chalet, now closed to visitors except in emergencies.

East Quinault Trail continues out of the Enchanted Valley and finally begins climbing to reach Anderson Pass and several glaciers. This high country is home to huckleberries and their biggest fans: black bears. Good places to pitch a tent are found at O'Neil Creek Camp (6.7 miles), Enchanted Valley Camp (13.1 miles), and Anderson Pass Camp (18 miles).

User Groups: Hikers and horses. No dogs or mountain bikes are allowed. No wheelchair access.

Open Seasons: This trail is accessible June–September.

Permits: Parking is free. Overnight stays within the national park require backcountry camping permits, which are available at Quinault Ranger Station on North Shore Road.

Maps: For a map of Olympic National Park, contact the Outdoor Recreation Information Center at the downtown Seattle REI. For topographic maps, ask Green Trails for No. 166, Mount Christie, and No. 167, Mount Steel, or ask the USGS for Mount Hoquiam, Mount Olson, Mount Steel, and Chimney Peak.

Directions: From Forks, drive south on U.S. 101 to South Shore Road. Turn left (east) and drive 18.5 miles to Graves Creek Ranger Station and the signed trailhead.

Contact: Olympic National Park, Wilderness Information Center, 3002 Mount Angeles Road, Port Angeles, WA 98362, 360/565-3100.

29 GRAVES CREEK
18.0 mi/2 days

northeast of Quinault in Olympic National Park

Map 1.4, page 30

Sometimes the itch to visit the Quinault area cannot be denied. The desire to see big trees, experience high-country meadows, and hear the boom of a roaring creek must be met. Fortunately, Graves Creek Trail scratches these itches without the considerable crowds of people found in the Enchanted Valley.

Graves Creek Trail begins soon after crossing Graves Creek on Quinault River Trail. It climbs gently above Graves Creek, which roars from within a box canyon for most of its descent. The trail makes a lot of ups and downs, but the overall trend is definitely up. At 3.2 miles the trail crosses Graves Creek, which can be difficult at times of high water (fall and spring). The forest breaks as meadows take over, a place where most hikers linger to fill up on huckleberries. The trail reaches Sundown Lake, set within a small glacial cirque complete with campsites. The trail eventually winds up at Six Ridge Pass and continues as Six Ridge Trail.

User Groups: Hikers only. No dogs, horses, or mountain bikes are allowed. No wheelchair access.

Open Seasons: This trail is accessible July–October.

Permits: No permits are needed for parking. Overnight stays within the national park require backcountry camping permits, which are available at Quinault Ranger Station on North Shore Road.

Maps: For a map of Olympic National Park, contact the Outdoor Recreation Information Center at the downtown Seattle REI. For topographic maps, ask Green Trails for No. 166, Mount Christie, or ask the USGS for Mount Hoquim.

Directions: From Forks, drive south on U.S. 101 to South Shore Road. Turn left (east) and drive 18.5 miles to Graves Creek Ranger Station and the signed trailhead.

Contact: Olympic National Park, Wilderness Information Center, 3002 Mount Angeles Road, Port Angeles, WA 98362, 360/565-3100.

🗷 COLONEL BOB MOUNTAIN
14.4 mi/8.0 hrs

east of Quinault in the Colonel Bob Wilderness of Olympic National Forest

Map 1.4, page 30

It's a hard climb from the bottoms of the Quinault Valley to the peaks of the southern ridge, the home of Colonel Bob Mountain. The overall elevation gain is greater than 4,000 feet, much of it covered twice. The trail climbs out of the rainforests of the lower valley to subalpine meadows, where ridges and views seem to extend for days on end. While crowds of folks bump into each other down in the Enchanted Valley, far fewer people are to be found up here. Trips to Colonel Bob during June and July are absolutely wonderful, when the wildflowers are in full bloom and snowfields linger on distant mountains.

Colonel Bob Trail is a true scaling of the peak, starting directly from the Quinault River. The trail heads up through a forest of Douglas fir and western red cedar. Mosses, lichens, and ferns grow on anything that can support them. The trail eventually reaches the camps of Mulkey Shelter (4 miles) and Moonshine Flats (6 miles).

The trail now climbs steeply to a ridge and dishearteningly drops down the other side. Take courage in knowing that while you must give back some elevation, open meadows await you. The trail navigates between the surrounding peaks before ascending Colonel Bob. The views are grand from on top, revealing much of the southern Olympics.

User Groups: Hikers and leashed dogs. No horses or mountain bikes are allowed. No wheelchair access.

Open Seasons: This trail is accessible mid-June–October.

Permits: A federal Northwest Forest Pass is required to park here.

Maps: For a map of Olympic National Forest, contact the Outdoor Recreation Information Center at the downtown Seattle REI. For topographic maps, ask Green Trails for No. 197, Quinault Lake, and No. 198, Griswold, or ask the USGS for Lake Quinault East and Colonel Bob.

Directions: From Forks, drive south on U.S. 101 to South Shore Road. Turn left (east) and drive 6 miles to the signed trailhead on the right side of the road.

Contact: Olympic National Forest, Quilcene

Ranger Station, 295142 U.S. 101 South, Quilcene, WA 98376, 360/765-2200.

31 LAKE QUINAULT LOOP
0.6–4.0 mi/0.5–2.0 hrs

on the shores of Lake Quinault in Olympic National Forest

Map 1.4, page 30

Lake Quinault Loop is one of three trails on the south side of the lake. Built within exceptional old-growth forests, the three trails offer two loops and a creek hike. The shortest of the three is Rain Forest Trail, a loop that finds its way into a stand of 500 year-old Douglas firs. Signs are placed along the path to enlighten hikers on the forest's ecology. The trail also passes a great stretch of Willaby Creek running through a gorge.

The second loop is a larger undertaking of 4 miles. It ventures farther into the forest, crossing a swamp on well-built puncheons and passing Cascade Falls on Falls Creek. It returns to the trailhead via Lake Quinault Shoreline Trail. The final hike is into Willaby Creek. A steady forest of immense proportions follows hikers to a granddaddy of cedars. The trail crosses the creek, which can be tricky, and eventually peters out. All three trails offer typically large Olympic forests full of moss and ferns. These are trails for the whole family to relish, regardless of age or hiking ability.

User Groups: Hikers and leashed dogs. No horses or mountain bikes are allowed. No wheelchair access.

Open Seasons: This area is accessible year-round.

Permits: A federal Northwest Forest Pass is required to park here.

Maps: For a map of Olympic National Forest, contact the Outdoor Recreation Information Center at the downtown Seattle REI. For topographic maps, ask Green Trails for No. 197, Quinault Lake, or ask the USGS for Lake Quinault East.

Directions: From Forks, drive south on U.S. 101 to South Shore Road. Turn left (east) and drive 1.5 miles to the signed trailhead on the right side of the road.

Contact: Olympic National Forest, Quilcene Ranger Station, 295142 U.S. 101 South, Quilcene, WA 98376, 360/765-2200.

32 WYNOOCHEE PASS
7.2 mi/4.0 hrs

east of Quinault in Olympic National Park

Map 1.4, page 30

This is not a long trail, and that's the beauty of it. Smart hikers know that Wynoochee Pass provides easy access to Sundown Lake and the incredible high country of the area. These spots add many additional miles and feet of elevation when accessed via two other converging trails. The few hikers who visit this trail each year find superb forests of mountain hemlock and silver fir along the route. It's nearly the perfect trail; not too long, incredibly scenic, and rarely used.

Wynoochee Pass Trail begins along an old logging road within the national forest before quickly entering the pristine confines of the national park. The trail is set high above the Wynoochee River, which is nearly at the end of its journey. The trail makes a few switchbacks up to the small meadow at Wynoochee Pass, elevation 3,600 feet and just over two miles from the trailhead. From here, hikers should follow a lightly used footpath for one mile to Sundown Lake and meadowy Sundown Pass. Since it's so far out of the way, it's understandable that so few people visit this part of the Olympics. But others' loss is your gain on Wynoochee Pass Trail. In the best sense of the term, it really is a getaway.

User Groups: Hikers only. No dogs, horses, or mountain bikes are allowed. No wheelchair access.

Open Seasons: This trail is accessible May–November.

Permits: A federal Northwest Forest Pass is required to park here.

Maps: For a map of Olympic National Park,

contact the Outdoor Recreation Information Center at the downtown Seattle REI. For topographic maps, ask Green Trails for No. 166, Mount Christie, or ask the USGS for Mount Hoquim.

Directions: From Aberdeen, drive west 9 miles to Wynoochee River Road (just before Montesano). Turn left (north) and drive 33 miles to Forest Service Road 2270 (at a four-way intersection). Go straight on Forest Service Road 2270 and drive 12 miles to Forest Service Road 2270-400. Turn right and drive 2 miles to the signed trailhead.

Contact: Olympic National Park, Wilderness Information Center, 3002 Mount Angeles Road, Port Angeles, WA 98362, 360/565-3100.

33 GRAY WOLF RIVER
30.2 mi/3–4 days

south of Sequim in Olympic National Park

Map 1.4, page 30

When the rain gives you pause about your planned trip to the west side of the peninsula, the little-visited Gray Wolf may be one of your better options. It's conveniently situated in the rain shadow of the Olympics, where much less rain falls than in other parts of the peninsula. So when it's raining on the west side, you're likely to luck out and stay dry in the rain shadow. The trail is quite long with the best parts, of course, far up the trail. The lower section of Gray Wolf is lowland river hiking. It's only above Three Forks, where Cameron and Grand Creeks join Gray Wolf, that the trail develops real personality.

Skip the lower half of the river and access Gray Wolf via Three Forks Trail (5.5 miles). From here, Gray Wolf Trail passes through beautiful forests of hemlock, cedar, and Douglas fir. A shelter is at Falls Camp (10.7 miles). From here, one can hike a way trail three miles up to Cedar Lake, a very large subalpine lake set within a large meadow. This little-visited spot alone is well worth a trip of several days.

Gray Wolf Trail continues by crossing the river several times and then beginning its real ascent. The basin at the head of the Gray Wolf is rather large and expansive. Several high tarns are set amid groves of mountain hemlocks and bare slides of shale. The basin is surrounded by high peaks, including the Needles as they extend from Mount Deception. The trail continues by steeply descending to Dosewallips River Trail.

User Groups: Hikers only. No dogs, horses, or mountain bikes are allowed. No wheelchair access.

Open Seasons: This trail is usually accessible May–October.

Permits: A federal Northwest Forest Pass is required to park here. Overnight stays require backcountry camping permits, which are available at the Quilcene Ranger Station.

Maps: For a map of Olympic National Park, contact the Outdoor Recreation Information Center at the downtown Seattle REI. For topographic maps, ask Green Trails for No. 135, Mount Angeles, and No. 136, Tyler Peak, or ask the USGS for Tyler Peak, Maiden Peak, and Wellesley Peak.

Directions: From Sequim, drive 3 miles east on U.S. 101 to Palo Alto Road. Turn right (south) and drive 7.5 miles to Forest Service Road 2880. Turn right and drive 1 mile to Forest Service Road 2870. Turn right and drive .5 mile to the signed trailhead.

Contact: Olympic National Forest, Quilcene Ranger Station, 295142 U.S. 101 South, Quilcene, WA 98376, 360/765-2200.

34 MOUNT ZION
3.6 mi/2.0 hrs

west of Quilcene in Olympic National Forest

Map 1.4, page 30

This is one of the Olympics' easier, more accessible peaks. It's not one of the tallest peaks, yet it offers its fair share of views from the northeast corner of the peninsula. A forested trail deposits hikers at a fairly flat, open summit. In comparison to the rest of the Olympics, it is in close proximity to Seattle, making it a great day hike for those with an itch for the Olympics.

The trail's best attraction is the many rhododendrons that grace the forest blanketing the route. They are in full bloom during June and are likely to be one the lasting memories of the hike. The trail gains just 1,300 feet on its ascent, pretty light fare for summit hikes. The forest eventually gives way near the summit to grand views of Olympic ranges and peaks. Mount Baker and the Cascades are visible beyond Puget Sound on clear days. On days that aren't so clear, fear not. Mount Zion is in the Olympic rain shadow, a corner of the mountain range that receives much less rain than the other parts of the peninsula. So when it's raining elsewhere, Mount Zion will be much drier. In sum, Mount Zion is a wonderful trail for easy hiking and basking in the sun.

User Groups: Hikers, leashed dogs, horses, mountain bikes, and motorcycles. No wheelchair access.

Open Seasons: This trail is accessible mid-May–November (accessible nearly year-round with snowshoes).

Permits: A federal Northwest Forest Pass is required to park here.

Maps: For a map of Olympic National Forest, contact the Outdoor Recreation Information Center at the downtown Seattle REI. For topographic maps, ask Green Trails for No. 136, Tyler Peak, or ask the USGS for Mount Zion.

Directions: From Quilcene, drive north 1.5 miles on U.S. 101 to Lords Lake Road. Follow Lords Lake Road to the lake and turn left onto Forest Service Road 28. Drive to Bon Jon Pass and turn right onto Forest Service Road 2810. The trailhead is 2 miles ahead on the left.

Contact: Olympic National Forest, Quilcene Ranger Station, 295142 U.S. 101 South, Quilcene, WA 98376, 360/765-2200.

35 TUBAL CAIN
17.4 mi/2 days

west of Quilcene in the Buckhorn Wilderness of Olympic National Forest

Map 1.4, page 30

Tubal Cain Trail is more than a secluded forest or place of expansive mountain views. Unlike most wilderness settings, the route features a good deal of evidence of mankind. Along the route are a pair of easy-to-find old mines. Here, copper, manganese, and other minerals were extracted from the flanks of Iron and Buckhorn Mountains. But another unexpected find is made along a side trail, deep within a high basin. Tull Canyon is the final resting place for an old Air Force B-17. The plane crashed here more than 50 years ago and has been left intact.

The trail immediately crosses Silver Creek to climb the valley within thick growth of rhododendrons, in full bloom in June. At 3.2 miles is the junction with Tull Canyon Trail. Tubal Cain Mine (and campground) lies on the east side of the creek a short .5 mile later. The shaft of the mine ventures into the mountain nearly 3,000 feet. Although the mine shaft is unsafe for exploration, there are many old relics left outside the mine. From Tubal Cain Mine, the trail becomes more scenic as it climbs to Buckhorn Lake (5.5 miles). This is a good turnaround for day hikers. Buckhorn and Iron Mountains stand imposingly across the valley at this point, guarding their treasures. The trail ends at Marmot Pass among meadows awash in wildflowers during July.

User Groups: Hikers, leashed dogs, and horses. No mountain bikes are allowed. No wheelchair access.

Open Seasons: This trail is accessible June–October.

Permits: A federal Northwest Forest Pass is required to park here.

Maps: For a map of Olympic National Forest, contact the Outdoor Recreation Information Center at the downtown Seattle REI. For topographic maps, ask Green Trails for No. 136,

Tyler Peak, or ask the USGS for Mount Townsend and Mount Deception.

Directions: From Sequim, drive 3 miles east on U.S. 101 to Palo Alto Road. Turn right (south) and drive 7.5 miles to Forest Service Road 28. Stay left and drive 1 mile to Forest Service Road 2860. Turn right and drive a long 14.5 miles to the signed trailhead.

Contact: Olympic National Forest, Quilcene Ranger Station, 295142 U.S. 101 South, Quilcene, WA 98376, 360/765-2200.

36 ROYAL BASIN
16.2 mi/2 days

south of Sequim in Olympic National Park

Map 1.4, page 30

Unrivaled in beauty, Royal Basin Trail travels miles of old-growth forest before finding acres of parkland meadows beneath towering peaks. This is one trail that guidebook authors prefer to keep mum about.

Royal Basin Trail begins along Dungeness River Trail one mile from the trailhead, where Royal Creek enters the river. Stay to the right on Royal Basin Trail. Easy to follow and well maintained, the trail serves hikers of all abilities as it courses through forest and avalanche tracks. Progress up the trail is easy to gauge as the forest changes from Douglas firs and western hemlocks to silver firs, yellow cedars, and finally subalpine firs. Campsites are found at the first meadow, a good alternative to the traditional campground a mile farther at Royal Lake.

The trail clambers over a terrace to reach Royal Lake. The large basin reveals Mount Deception, the Olympics' second-highest peak, and the always impressive Needles, a long, jagged ridge. Explore to your heart's content, but stay on established trails, please. Parkland and meadows abound here, with wildflowers that catch fire in early summer. At the top of the basin is Royal Glacier, which you can walk on, while a trip to the shoulder below Mount Deception is also possible, revealing the Elwha River drainage. Royal Basin is sure to capture your heart. So hike Royal Basin and then lie about where you've been to anyone who asks.

User Groups: Hikers only. No dogs, horses, or mountain bikes are allowed. No wheelchair access.

Open Seasons: This trail is usually accessible mid-June–October.

Permits: A federal Northwest Forest Pass is required to park here. Overnight stays require backcountry camping permits, which are available at the Quilcene Ranger Station.

Maps: For a map of Olympic National Park, contact the Outdoor Recreation Information Center at the downtown Seattle REI. For topographic maps, ask Green Trails for No. 136, Tyler Peak, or ask the USGS for Mount Deception.

Directions: From Sequim, drive 3 miles east on U.S. 101 to Palo Alto Road. Turn right (south) and drive 7.5 miles to Forest Service Road 28. Stay left and drive 1 mile to Forest Service Road 2860. Turn right and drive 11 miles to signed Dungeness Trailhead.

Contact: Olympic National Park, Wilderness Information Center, 3002 Mount Angeles Road, Port Angeles, WA 98362, 360/565-3100; Quilcene Ranger District, 295142 U.S. 101 South, P.O. Box 280, Quilcene, WA 98376, 360/765-2200.

37 UPPER DUNGENESS
12.4 mi/6.0 hrs

west of Quilcene in the Buckhorn Wilderness of Olympic National Forest

Map 1.4, page 30

The Upper Dungeness River is one of the most picturesque of the Olympics' many rivers, and this trail captures much of its scenic beauty. The trail follows the Dungeness as it passes through outstanding forests and eventually reaches a major junction, high within a mountain basin. Along the way is Heather Creek Trail, a nonmaintained route heading directly into the Olympics' wild interior. Add the fact that the Dungeness receives less rain than most of the peninsula, and you have a popular off-season hike.

The trail makes its way along the valley bottom for the first mile to a junction with Royal

Basin Trail. Cross Royal Creek to stay on Dungeness Trail. The forest here is superb, with large Douglas firs, red cedars, and western hemlocks towering over an open understory. The trail eventually crosses the Dungeness to the east side and comes to Camp Handy, at 3.2 miles. Great camps are found within this slightly wooded meadow. From Camp Handy, Heather Creek Trail continues up the valley alongside the Dungeness for another four miles. This stretch is not maintained and is fairly undisturbed wilderness. Dungeness Trail leaves Camp Handy to begin climbing out of the valley and into parkland meadows. The trail ends at Boulder Camp, the junction with Constance Pass Trail and Big Quilcene Trail.

User Groups: Hikers, leashed dogs, and horses. No mountain bikes are allowed. No wheelchair access.

Open Seasons: This trail is accessible June–October.

Permits: A federal Northwest Forest Pass is required to park here.

Maps: For a map of Olympic National Forest, contact the Outdoor Recreation Information Center at the downtown Seattle REI. For topographic maps, ask Green Trails for No. 136, Tyler Peak, or ask the USGS for Mount Deception, Tyler Peak, and Mount Zion.

Directions: From Sequim, drive 3 miles east on U.S. 101 to Palo Alto Road. Turn right (south) and drive 7.5 miles to Forest Service Road 28. Stay left and drive 1 mile to Forest Service Road 2860. Turn right and drive 11 miles to signed Dungeness Trailhead.

Contact: Olympic National Forest, Quilcene Ranger Station, 295142 U.S. 101 South, Quilcene, WA 98376, 360/765-2200.

🔳 MOUNT TOWNSEND
7.8 mi/4.5 hrs

west of Quilcene in Buckhorn Wilderness of Olympic National Forest

Map 1.4, page 30

Upon reaching the top of Mount Townsend, hikers may be hard-pressed to decide if they're in the midst of mountains or perched above long stretches of Puget waterways. This lofty summit strategically puts you smack dab in the middle of the two settings. The grand, competing vistas are likely to vie for your attention for the length of your stay here. Be thankful. High mountain meadows scrubbed by forceful winds, complete with requisite berries, complement the experience. It's no wonder that Mount Townsend is one of the peninsula's more popular day hikes.

Mount Townsend Trail climbs steadily throughout its length. The couple of miles pass through forest punctuated by rhododendrons (catch them blooming in June). At 2.5 miles lies Camp Windy (not nearly as windy as Townsend's summit), and the trail soon reaches a junction with Silver Lakes Trail. Mount Townsend Trail harshly climbs through opening meadows, full of late summer's huckleberries. Snow and wind limit the growth of the subalpine trees, leaving vistas for hikers. The summit is long and flat with superb views. Nearly the full range of the Cascades lines the east, while Mount Deception and The Needles are highlights of the Olympic Range. The trail continues for another 1.4 miles down to Little Quilcene River Trail.

User Groups: Hikers, leashed dogs, and horses. No mountain bikes are allowed. No wheelchair access.

Open Seasons: This trail is accessible June–October.

Permits: A federal Northwest Forest Pass is required to park here.

Maps: For a map of Olympic National Forest, contact the Outdoor Recreation Information Center at the downtown Seattle REI. For topographic maps, ask Green Trails for No. 136, Tyler Peak, or ask the USGS for Mount Townsend.

Directions: From Quilcene, drive 1 mile south on U.S. 101 to Penny Creek Road. Turn right (west) and drive 1.5 miles to Big Quilcene Road. Stay to the left at this Y and drive 3 miles to the Forest Service boundary and paved Forest Service Road 27. Drive 9 miles to Forest

Service Road 2760. Drive 1 mile to the trailhead at road's end.

Contact: Olympic National Forest, Quilcene Ranger Station, 295142 U.S. 101 South, Quilcene, WA 98376, 360/765-2200.

39 SILVER LAKES
10.8 mi/6.0 hrs

west of Quilcene in the Buckhorn Wilderness of Olympic National Forest

Map 1.4, page 30

It takes a harsh rainstorm to ruin a trip to Silver Lakes. And that's a less-than-likely proposition since this trail is snugly tucked away in the peninsula's rain shadow. Silver Lakes nestle within a large basin rimmed with jagged peaks. Subalpine firs are amply spread around the lakes, mingling with meadows of heather. Alpine flowers add strokes of color unlikely to be forgotten for a long time after the trip. Throw in some good scrambles at the end to an extremely pleasant trail and you have yourself a thoroughly agreeable trip.

Silver Lakes Trail begins on Mount Townsend Trail, 2.9 miles from the trailhead (see listing in this chapter). The trail immediately drops into the forested valley, crosses Silver Creek, and makes a quick ascent to the larger Silver Lake. The smaller and less visited lake is just before the larger one, to the west off a visible side trail.

Parkland surrounds the lake, with large meadows of wildflowers mingling with small stands of subalpine fir. There are several campsites for overnight guests. The lake is favored by swimmers and fishermen alike. Be sure to scramble the slope rising to the south, between rocky peaks, for more wildflowers and the prime views.

User Groups: Hikers, leashed dogs, and horses. No mountain bikes are allowed. No wheelchair access.

Open Seasons: This trail is accessible July–October.

Permits: A federal Northwest Forest Pass is required to park here.

Maps: For a map of Olympic National Forest, contact the Outdoor Recreation Information Center at the downtown Seattle REI. For topographic maps, ask Green Trails for No. 136, Tyler Peak, or ask the USGS for Mount Townsend.

Directions: From Quilcene, drive 1 mile south on U.S. 101 to Penny Creek Road. Turn right (west) and drive 1.5 miles to Big Quilcene Road. Stay to the left at this Y and drive 3 miles to the Forest Service boundary and paved Forest Service Road 27. Drive 9 miles to Forest Service Road 2760. Drive 1 mile to the trailhead at road's end.

Contact: Olympic National Forest, Quilcene Ranger Station, 295142 U.S. 101 South, Quilcene, WA 98376, 360/765-2200.

40 UPPER BIG QUILCENE
10.6 mi/5.5 hrs

west of Quilcene in the Buckhorn Wilderness of Olympic National Forest

Map 1.4, page 30

Rarely can hikers get to such an outstanding viewpoint, with so much wild country spread before them, than with Upper Big Quilcene Trail. Passing through virgin timber and open, pristine meadows, the trail delivers hikers to Marmot Pass. This is an opportunity to view many of the Olympics' most impressive peaks, including Mount Mystery and Mount Deception. The trail is one of the best on the peninsula's east side and perfect for an outing with the dog.

The trail follows the river for several miles, where the forest consists of old-growth Douglas fir, western hemlock, and western red cedar. In June, rhododendrons light up the understory with fragrant blossoms. The trail then climbs gently but steadily out of the valley. Good camps are at Shelter Rock (2.6 mi) and Camp Mystery (4.6 mi), each next to water. The trail eventually broaches the confines of forest and finds itself at Marmot Pass, where one can finally see all that is to the north of the ridge. Grand views of near and far mountains are plentiful. The trail junctions here with

Tubal Cain Trail before dropping to Boulder Camp. Constance Pass and Upper Dungeness Trails meet at Boulder Camp.

User Groups: Hikers and leashed dogs. No horses or mountain bikes are allowed. No wheelchair access.

Open Seasons: This trail is accessible July–October.

Permits: A federal Northwest Forest Pass is required to park here.

Maps: For a map of Olympic National Forest, contact the Outdoor Recreation Information Center at the downtown Seattle REI. For topographic maps, ask Green Trails for No. 136, Tyler Peak, or ask the USGS for Mount Townsend and Mount Deception.

Directions: From Quilcene, drive 1 mile south on U.S. 101 to Penny Creek Road. Turn right (west) and drive 1.5 miles to Big Quilcene Road. Stay left at this Y and drive 3 miles to the Forest Service boundary and paved Forest Service Road 27. Drive 6 miles to Forest Service Road 2750. Stay to the left and drive 4.5 miles to the signed trailhead.

Contact: Olympic National Forest, Quilcene Ranger Station, 295142 U.S. 101 South, Quilcene, WA 98376, 360/765-2200.

41 TUNNEL CREEK
8.2 mi/4.5 hrs

west of Quilcene in the Buckhorn Wilderness of Olympic National Forest

Map 1.4, page 30

The trail up Tunnel Creek leads to a pair of subalpine lakes and a pass with far-reaching views. It's a popular day hike, whisking hikers from old-growth forests along the valley floor to open meadows and views up high. Never mind the steep final ascent to the lakes and 50-50 Pass, as you'll have plenty of time to rest while surveying the mountainous horizon.

The trail ventures easily through great forests of Douglas fir and western red cedar accompanied by numerous rhododendrons (blooming in June) for 2.7 miles. Here, the trail encounters Tunnel Creek Shelter, with a few campsites. Beyond this point, the route steeply climbs to the Twin Lakes (3.7 miles). The lakes are situated in a tiny basin and bounded by mountain hemlocks, an appealing setting. The trail climbs a bit more to 50-50 Pass, at elevation 5,050 feet. This is mostly just a rocky promontory, but the views are grand during clear weather. Nowhere is Mount Constance better seen, with pockets of snow often finding refuge among the many crags and faces. Views toward Puget Sound stand out as well. This is the ideal place to turn around; otherwise, a sharp descent awaits, into a valley other than where your car is parked.

User Groups: Hikers, leashed dogs, and horses. No mountain bikes are allowed. No wheelchair access.

Open Seasons: This trail is accessible mid-June–October.

Permits: A federal Northwest Forest Pass is required to park here.

Maps: For a map of Olympic National Forest, contact the Outdoor Recreation Information Center at the downtown Seattle REI. For topographic maps, ask Green Trails for No. 136, Tyler Peak, and No. 168, The Brothers, or ask the USGS for Mount Townsend.

Directions: From Quilcene, drive 1 mile south on U.S. 101 to Penny Creek Road. Turn right (west) and drive 1.5 miles to Big Quilcene Road. Stay left at this Y and drive 3 miles to the Forest Service boundary and Forest Service Road 2740. Stay to the left at this Y and drive 6.5 miles to the signed trailhead.

Contact: Olympic National Forest, Quilcene Ranger Station, 295142 U.S. 101 South, Quilcene, WA 98376, 360/765-2200.

42 WEST FORK DOSEWALLIPS
31.0 mi/3–4 days

south of Quilcene in Olympic National Park

Map 1.4, page 30

West Fork Dosewallips Trail is half of one of the premier routes for trekking across the Olympic Range. Making its way along the west fork of its namesake, the trail reaches Anderson Pass and connects to the legendary Enchanted Valley. This route has had its troubles in recent years. Several years ago, a new suspension bridge was blown out after only a year. Rebuilt, the bridge was again damaged in 2003. Be sure to call the Wilderness Information Center for current access status.

West Fork Dosewallips Trail begins 1.4 miles up Dosewallips River Trail (actually 6.5 miles because the road is permanently out five miles below the trailhead) at a signed junction. After a short distance lies the troubled bridge crossing over a beautiful canyon. Beyond, the trail weaves through grand old-growth forest. Big Timber Camp is at 4.2 miles (from the Dosewallips Ranger Station) and Diamond Meadows at 6.6 miles.

The trail climbs to Honeymoon Meadows, wide open meadows of grass and flowers, and eventually to Anderson Pass (access to the Enchanted Valley). This low pass is a real playground, with a trail leading to Anderson Glacier and its craggy home, the highlight of the trip. A final camp is just below the pass.

User Groups: Hikers and horses. No dogs or mountain bikes are allowed. No wheelchair access.

Open Seasons: This trail is accessible June–October.

Permits: A federal Northwest Forest Pass is required to park here. Overnight stays within the national park require backcountry camping permits, which are available at the Quilcene Ranger Station.

Maps: For a map of Olympic National Park, contact the Outdoor Recreation Information Center at the downtown Seattle REI. For topographic maps, ask Green Trails for No. 168, The Brothers, and No. 167, Mount Steel, or ask the USGS for The Brothers and Mount Steel.

Directions: From Quilcene, drive south 11.5 miles on U.S. 101 to Dosewallips River Road. Turn right (west) and drive about 10 miles to the road's end at a washout. The trail is on the right side of the road and climbs above the

washout before returning to the road, 5 miles from Dosewallips Ranger Station.

Contact: Olympic National Park, Wilderness Information Center, 3002 Mount Angeles Road, Port Angeles, WA 98362, 360/565-3100.

43 MAIN FORK DOSEWALLIPS RIVER
40.0 mi/4 days

south of Quilcene in Olympic National Park

Map 1.4, page 30

This exceptionally beautiful river valley has suddenly become much more remote. A few years back, the river wiped out the road to the trailhead, adding roughly five miles to the hike. This has weeded out a considerable number of visitors, and now this is a wilderness lover's dream come true. But don't worry about hiking an extra five miles, all of it on the old road. The hike is easily worth it.

After five miles along the old road, the abandoned car camp of Muscott Flats appears. The trail begins here at the ranger station. Dosewallips River Trail follows the river before splitting at 1.5 miles. Stay on the right fork to continue along the main Dosewallips Trail. Dosewallips Trail makes a long journey through typically grand forests of Douglas fir, hemlock, and cedar and passes three established camps on its way to Dose Meadows Camp, 12.5 miles from the end of the road.

The final 2.5 miles is the best part as it breaks out into spacious meadows. The trail begins a more steady ascent from here to Hayden Pass. Along the way is 1,000 Acre Meadow, a wildflower mecca off trail to the southeast for adventurous types. Those who make it to the pass will be rewarded. Countless peaks outline several valleys streaking away from this point. And, of course, Mount Olympus shines from the west.

User Groups: Hikers and horses. No dogs or mountain bikes are allowed. No wheelchair access.

Open Seasons: This trail is usually accessible mid-May–October.

Permits: A federal Northwest Forest Pass is required to park at the road washout. Overnight stays within the national park require back-country camping permits, which are available at the Quilcene Ranger Station.

Maps: For a map of Olympic National Park, contact the Outdoor Recreation Information Center at the downtown Seattle REI. For topographic maps, ask Green Trails for No. 135, Mount Angeles, No. 136, Tyler Peak, and No. 168, The Brothers, or ask the USGS for The Brothers, Mount Deception, and Wellesley Peak.

Directions: From Quilcene, drive south 11.5 miles on U.S. 101 to Dosewallips River Road. Turn right (west) and drive about 10 miles to the road's end at a washout. The trail is on the right side of the road and climbs above the washout before returning to the road, 5 miles from Dosewallips Ranger Station.

Contact: Olympic National Park, Wilderness Information Center, 3002 Mount Angeles Road, Port Angeles, WA 98362, 360/565-3100.

44 LAKE CONSTANCE
10.0 mi/6.0 hrs

south of Quilcene in Olympic National Park

Map 1.4, page 30

You're likely to hear two things about Lake Constance. First, folks always mention the incredible beauty of the lake. Craggy Mount Constance towers above mountain hemlocks and subalpine firs that border the deep blue lake. But there's a catch, which you're also likely to hear about Lake Constance. The trail is unbelievably steep—3,300 feet in just two miles. That's steep enough to be the toughest climb in the Olympics and steep enough that you can forget about switchbacks. The trail heads straight up the ridge. Your arms will get as much of a workout as your legs as you grab onto roots and branches, pulling yourself up what barely qualifies as a trail. It's a very difficult climb and should not be undertaken by those not ready for a strenuous ascent.

Camping is available at the lake, but because of heavy use, a permit and reservation are required for overnight stays. There are lots of opportunities to explore around the lake, but staying on established trails is important to prevent further ecosystem damage. Also, don't forget that the road up the Dosewallips is out and requires about three miles of hiking on the old road to get to the trail. Get in shape and make it up to Lake Constance, for it is well worth the effort.

User Groups: Hikers only. No dogs, horses, or mountain bikes are allowed. No wheelchair access.

Open Seasons: This trail is usually accessible June–October.

Permits: A federal Northwest Forest Pass is required to park here. Overnight stays at Lake Constance require reservations and backcountry camping permits.

Maps: For a map of Olympic National Park, contact the Outdoor Recreation Information Center at the downtown Seattle REI. For topographic maps, ask Green Trails for No. 168, The Brothers, or ask the USGS for The Brothers.

Directions: From Quilcene, drive south 11.5 miles on U.S. 101 to Dosewallips River Road. Turn right (west) and drive about 10 miles to the road's end at a washout. The trail is on the right side of the road and climbs above the washout before returning to the road, 3 miles from Lake Constance Trail.

Contact: Olympic National Park, Wilderness Information Center, 3002 Mount Angeles Road, Port Angeles, WA 98362, 360/565-3100.

45 DUCKABUSH RIVER
43.6 mi/3–4 days

south of Quilcene in the Brothers Wilderness of Olympic National Forest and Olympic National Park

Map 1.4, page 30

The Duckabush ranks as one of the longest river valley trails on the peninsula. It starts just six miles from Hood Canal and makes a long trek up to the river's headwaters. Much of the forest is big old-growth, and wildlife is regularly seen throughout the valley. Yet Duckabush Trail receives only moderate use, tapering off significantly farther up the lengthy valley. As wilderness lovers would say, "Other people's loss is our gain."

The main reasons few people venture far into the Duckabush are Little Hump and Big Hump. Elevation gains of 500 feet and 1,100 feet weed out many a noncommitted day hiker. Thank Big Hump, however, for preventing timber-cutting in the upper river valley. This obstacle kept much of the valley forested in old-growth, the main theme of the trail.

Good spots to throw down for the night are found at 5 Mile and 10 Mile Camps. The trail finally reaches the steep walls of Duckabush Basin after 20 miles. The trail makes a steep ascent to La Crosse Basin, a beautiful collection of high-country lakes, and O'Neil Pass. O'Neil Pass features scenery so spectacular that it's pretty much beyond compare to anything else in the Olympics. Magnificent mountains, valleys, and rivers sum it up best. It may be a lot of hard work to get very far on Duckabush Trail, but it will be well remembered.

User Groups: Hikers and horses. No dogs or mountain bikes are allowed. No wheelchair access.

Open Seasons: The lower part of this trail is accessible year-round (upper part is accessible July–October).

Permits: A federal Northwest Forest Pass is required to park here. Overnight stays require backcountry camping permits, which are available at Hoodsport Ranger Station.

Maps: For a map of Olympic National Park, contact the Outdoor Recreation Information Center at the downtown Seattle REI. For topographic maps, ask Green Trails for No. 167, Mount Steel, and No. 168, The Brothers, or ask the USGS for Mount Steel, The Brothers, and Mount Jupiter.

Directions: From Quilcene, drive 16 miles south on U.S. 101 to the Duckabush River Road (Forest Service Road 2510). Turn right (west) and drive 5.5 miles to Forest Service Road 2510-060. Turn right and drive .1 mile to a large parking lot and the signed trailhead.

Contact: Olympic National Park, Wilderness Information Center, 3002 Mount Angeles Road, Port Angeles, WA 98362, 360/565-3100; Olympic National Forest, Hoodsport Ranger District, 150 North Lake Cushman Road, Hoodsport, WA 98548, 360/877-5254.

46 LENA LAKES
6.0–12.0 mi/3.5 hrs–2 days

south of Quilcene in Olympic National Park

Map 1.4, page 30

Upper Lena Lake may possibly render hikers speechless with its beauty and open views. Meanwhile, the trail up to Lena Lake will certainly leave hikers breathless with its intense steep ascent and sections that require something more akin to scrambling than hiking. Lower Lena Lake is a much less strenuous excursion. Both lakes are great day hikes but also feature many campsites for overnight visits.

Lena Lake Trail climbs gently but steadily through three miles of shady forest to Lower Lena Lake. Dogs and mountain bikes are allowed up to this point, where numerous camps encircle the large lake. Upper Lena Lake Trail continues from the northeast corner of the lake and climbs strenuously for another three miles. This section features switchback after switchback as it ascends the steep valley. Be prepared for a rocky, narrow, and brushy trip.

The upper lake sits among some of the Olympics' best parkland meadows. Mount Bretherton stands to the south while Mount Lena fills the northern horizon. The National Park Service maintains numerous campsites around the eastern and southern shores of the lake. Footpaths create weblike patterns into the lakeside meadows. Be careful of treading

© SCOTT LEONARD

Upper Lena Lake, a strenuous but popular hike on Olympic westside

into revegetation plots, where the park is aiding regrowth of the very sensitive meadow ecosystem. Although Upper Lena Lake receives many visitors during the summer, it is worthy of all the attention it receives.

User Groups: Hikers only. No dogs, horses, or mountain bikes are allowed. No wheelchair access.

Open Seasons: This trail is accessible July–October.

Permits: A federal Northwest Forest Pass is required to park here. Overnight stays require backcountry camping permits, which are available at the park boundary.

Maps: For a map of Olympic National Park, contact the Outdoor Recreation Information Center at the downtown Seattle REI. For topographic maps, ask Green Trails for No. 168, The Brothers, or ask the USGS for Mount Washington and The Brothers.

Directions: From Quilcene, drive south 24 miles on U.S. 101 to Forest Service Road 25. Turn right and drive 8 miles to the Lena Lakes Trailhead.

Contact: Olympic National Park, Wilderness Information Center, 3002 Mount Angeles Road, Port Angeles, WA 98362, 360/565-3100.

47 THE BROTHERS
3.0 mi/2.0 hrs

south of Quilcene in the Brothers Wilderness of Olympic National Forest

Map 1.4, page 30

While The Brothers are the most easily recognized Olympic peaks from Seattle, visitors to the peninsula rarely hike this trail. That's because The Brothers Trail is primarily used by climbers to reach the base camp for a shot at the mountain's summit. The trail to the base camp is hikable for almost anyone, but since you won't see much, it's hardly worth it. To really appreciate The Brothers, you would have to go beyond the trail and ascend the mountain, which is not a job for amateurs. So unless you're ready for some real mountaineering, The Brothers Trail is best left as a through-way for climbers.

The trail begins near the northwest corner of Lena Lake, where Lena Creek empties into the lake. It is rocky and overcome with roots in places. It even requires some careful maneuvering over boulder fields. The trail enters the Valley of Silent Men, named for the climbers from Lena Lake passing through before the sun rises or the conversation heats up. The trail passes back and forth over East Lena Creek several times and after three miles crosses one last time, skirts a small pond, and ends at The Brothers base camp. Most hikers should turn around here.

Beyond the base camp, climbing The Brothers is recommended only with the proper gear and training. It's a pretty serious ascent, not a scramble for novices. Hikers intending to go up to the summit should consult climbing guides containing this peak or with the ranger station in Quilcene.

User Groups: Hikers, leashed dogs, and horses. No mountain bikes are allowed. No wheelchair access.

Open Seasons: This trail is accessible June–October.

Permits: A federal Northwest Forest Pass is required to park here.

Maps: For a map of Olympic National Forest, contact the Outdoor Recreation Information Center at the downtown Seattle REI. For topographic maps, ask Green Trails for No. 168, The Brothers, or ask the USGS for Mount Washington and The Brothers.

Directions: From Quilcene, drive south 24 miles on U.S. 101 to Forest Service Road 25. Turn right and drive 8 miles to the Lena Lakes Trailhead.

Contact: Olympic National Forest, Hoodsport Ranger Station, 150 North Lake Cushman Road, Hoodsport, WA 98548, 360/877-5254.

48 PUTVIN
8.0 mi/4.0 hrs

south of Quilcene in Mount Skokomish Wilderness of Olympic National Forest and in Olympic National Park

Map 1.4, page 30

Putvin Trail includes much of what is great about the Olympics. There are forests full of trees big enough to make your neck sore. There are prime subalpine meadows, full of heather and huckleberries, enough to make your mouth water. And, of course, there are outstanding views, enough to make you rub your eyes. It's

a steep trail, gaining 3,400 feet in just four miles. But as the pilgrims once said, there's redemption in suffering.

Putvin Trail starts off in the river bottom of the Hamma Hamma, climbing through an old logging tract. The trail eventually enters the Mount Skokomish Wilderness (1.5 miles) and a land of big trees. After briefly leveling out, Putvin resumes climbing, arriving at several small tarns. Keep going, as this is not Lake of the Angels. It is farther yet, set within a small glacier cirque called the Valley of Heaven. Heaven indeed. The lake is absolutely beautiful, surrounded by meadows and craggy peaks. Mount Skokomish and Mount Stone flank the valley's two ends. For outstanding views, hike the small footpath up to the long ridge separating the two peaks. From here, Putvin Trail's anonymity is hard to understand.

User Groups: Hikers and leashed dogs. No horses or mountain bikers are allowed. No wheelchair access.

Open Seasons: This trail is accessible mid-June–November.

Permits: A federal Northwest Forest Pass is required to park here. Overnight stays require backcountry camping permits, which are available at Hoodsport Ranger Station.

Maps: For a map of Olympic National Park and Olympic National Forest, contact the Outdoor Recreation Information Center at the downtown Seattle REI. For topographic maps, ask Green Trails for No. 167, Mount Steel, and No. 168, The Brothers, or ask the USGS for Mount Skokomish.

Directions: From Hoodsport, drive 14 miles north on U.S. 101 to Forest Service Road 25 (Hamma Hamma Recreation Area). Turn left (west) and drive 12 miles to the Putvin Historical Marker. The trail is on the right side of the road.

Contact: Olympic National Forest, Hoodsport Ranger Station, 150 North Lake Cushman Road, Hoodsport, WA 98548, 360/877-5254; Olympic National Park, Wilderness Information Center, 3002 Mount Angeles Road, Port Angeles, WA 98362, 360/565-3100.

49 MILDRED LAKES
9.8 mi/6.0 hrs

northwest of Hoodsport in Mount Skokomish Wilderness of Olympic National Forest

Map 1.4, page 30

Although Mildred Lakes is gaining in popularity, you're likely to experience fewer fellow hikers here than elsewhere in the Olympics. The Forest Service provides little maintenance on the trail to help keep this sensitive area in good condition, as an easy trail would likely lead to overuse. Nonetheless, Mildred Lakes are still out there and very much worth visiting.

The trail climbs through an old logging tract before entering virgin forest. The trail is relatively easy to follow through the pleasant forest of hemlock and fir. Before long, however, the trail becomes increasingly infested with rocks and roots. At about three miles, you must cross a ravine more than 20 feet deep. Now the trail becomes really rough. Head straight up the steep mountainside, pulling yourself up by rocks and roots. At 4.9 miles, crest the ridge to find the Mildred Lakes Basin.

The basin holds three lakes bordered by subalpine firs and meadows of heather. The Sawtooth Range runs along the north and western part of the basin, with Mount Cruiser and Mount Lincoln acting as bookends to the jagged ridge. There are a fair number of campsites up here, but Leave-No-Trace principles are to be emphasized, as heavy past use has been detrimental to the area.

User Groups: Hikers and leashed dogs. No horses or mountain bikes are allowed. No wheelchair access.

Open Seasons: This trail is accessible July–October.

Permits: A federal Northwest Forest Pass is required to park here.

Maps: For a map of Olympic National Forest, contact the Outdoor Recreation Information Center at the downtown Seattle REI. For topographic maps, ask Green Trails for No. 167, Mount Steel, or ask the USGS for Mount Skokomish.

Directions: From Hoodsport, drive north 14 miles on U.S. 101 to Forest Service Road 25 (Hamma Hamma Recreation Area). Turn left (west) and drive 14 miles to Mildred Lakes Trailhead at road's end.

Contact: Olympic National Forest, Hoodsport Ranger Station, 150 North Lake Cushman Road, Hoodsport, WA 98548, 360/877-5254.

50 STAIRCASE RAPIDS
2.0 mi/1.0 hr

northwest of Hoodsport in Olympic National Park

Map 1.4, page 30

Walks through the forest rarely get better than this. Set along the North Fork Skokomish River within an old-growth forest, Staircase Rapids Trail is perfect for families and older hikers. The flat, level trail encounters several sites where the river pours over bedrock or rumbles over rapids. And it all occurs within one of the eastern Olympics' most beautiful old-growth forests. The trail has a bit of history, as well, as it was part of the original route taken by the O'Neil Expedition in 1890. This is an excellent destination or just a side trip to a bigger excursion.

The trail starts at Staircase Ranger Station on the west side of the river. The exceptional old-growth forest is highlighted by Big Cedar (accessible by a side trail signed "Big Cedar"). Definitely check it out. Along the way to the rapids are Red Reef, an outcropping of red limestone that does its best to hold back the rushing river, and Dolly Varden Pool, where rocky cliffs loom over the river as it rumbles between large boulders. The climax of the walk is Staircase Rapids, a series of regularly spaced terraces over which the river spills. This is easily one of the Olympics' most scenic stretches of river and well worth a visit.

User Groups: Hikers only. No dogs, horses, or mountain bikes are allowed. No wheelchair access.

Open Seasons: This trail is accessible year-round.

Permits: A National Parks Pass is required to park here.

Maps: For a map of Olympic National Park, contact the Outdoor Recreation Information Center at the downtown Seattle REI. For topographic maps, ask Green Trails for No. 167, Mount Steel, or ask the USGS for Mount Skokomish.

Directions: From Hoodsport, drive west 9 miles on Lake Cushman Road (Highway 119) to Forest Service Road 24 (a T intersection). Turn left and drive 6.5 miles to Staircase Ranger Station for the trailhead and trailhead parking.

Contact: Olympic National Park, Wilderness Information Center, 3002 Mount Angeles Road, Port Angeles, WA 98362, 360/565-3100.

51 NORTH FORK SKOKOMISH
25.2 mi/2–3 days

northwest of Hoodsport in Olympic National Park

Map 1.4, page 30

The western rivers of the Olympic Mountains rightfully share reputations for forests of enormous proportions. While the North Fork Skokomish remains out of this limelight, it's no less impressive. The trail follows the North Fork Skokomish for 10 miles at relative ease, passing through a virgin forest full of massive trees. This route is historical, as well, having been blazed by Army Lieutenant Joseph P. O'Neil on the first east-west expedition of the Olympics in the winter of 1890.

The trail leaves Staircase Ranger Station along an old roadbed. It quickly encounters the Beaver Fire of 1985, where new firs are growing up among towering burned snags. At five miles, the trail crosses the Skokomish via a bridge where the slate-gray water passes through a beautiful box canyon bordered by colossal Douglas firs. The trail crosses several large streams, two of which lack a bridge and may be tricky in times of heavy runoff.

Camp Pleasant (6.4 miles) and Nine Stream Camp (9.3 miles) make for great places to spend the night and build a fire. After Nine

Stream, the trail begins its ascent to First Divide through large mountain hemlocks and Douglas firs. After 3.5 miles of climbing, the trail reaches First Divide and several small tarns. Views into the upper Duckabush reward the long trek. Just beyond the pass, Home Sweet Home (13.5 miles) offers another great site for camping in a meadow setting.

User Groups: Hikers and horses. No dogs or mountain bikes are allowed. No wheelchair access.

Open Seasons: The lower part of this trail is accessible year-round. The upper part is accessible June–October.

Permits: A National Parks Pass is required to park here. Overnight stays in the national park require backcountry camping permits, which are available at Hoodsport Ranger Station or at the trailhead.

Maps: For a map of Olympic National Park, contact the Outdoor Recreation Information Center at the downtown Seattle REI. For topographic maps, ask Green Trails for No. 167, Mount Steel, or ask the USGS for Mount Skokomish, Mount Olson, and Mount Steel.

Directions: From Hoodsport, drive west 9 miles on Lake Cushman Road (Highway 119) to Forest Service Road 24 (a T intersection). Turn left and drive 6.5 miles to Staircase Ranger Station for the trailhead and trailhead parking.

Contact: Olympic National Park, Wilderness Information Center, 3002 Mount Angeles Road, Port Angeles, WA 98362, 360/565-3100; Olympic National Forest, Hoodsport Ranger Station, 150 North Lake Cushman Road, Hoodsport, WA 98548, 360/877-5254.

52 WAGONWHEEL LAKE
5.8 mi/3.5 hrs

northwest of Hoodsport in Olympic National Park

Map 1.4, page 30

When people mention Wagonwheel Lake, they mostly condemn it to being nothing more than a conditioning hike. Consider that neither an insult nor compliment; it's mostly just the truth.

After all, the trail makes a brutal ascent of 3,200 feet in less than three miles. For most hikers, a pace of 1,000 feet per mile is considered "difficult." Throw in the fact that there are few views to be had along the way or at the lake and you get only the diehards or the foolhardy on the trail.

Nearly the entire length of the trail is a steep climb through the forest. The lower part of the trail climbs via switchback through second-growth forest tamed by fire before eventually reaching some old-growth hemlock. After nearly three miles of huffing and puffing, hikers are delivered to Wagonwheel Lake, set within a small basin on the north side of Copper Mountain and bounded by a dense forest offering relatively no views. With all the hard work, why come here? Because a day in the woods is always a good day.

User Groups: Hikers only. No dogs, horses, or mountain bikes are allowed. No wheelchair access.

Open Seasons: This trail is accessible July–November.

Permits: A National Parks Pass is required to park here. Overnight stays in the national park require backcountry camping permits, which are available at Hoodsport Ranger Station.

Maps: For a map of Olympic National Park, contact the Outdoor Recreation Information Center at the downtown Seattle REI. For topographic maps, ask Green Trails for No. 167, Mount Steel, or ask the USGS for Mount Skokomish.

Directions: From Hoodsport, drive west 9 miles on Lake Cushman Road (Highway 119) to Forest Service Road 24 (a T intersection). Turn left and drive 6.5 miles to Staircase Ranger Station for the trailhead and trailhead parking.

Contact: Olympic National Park, Wilderness Information Center, 3002 Mount Angeles Road, Port Angeles, WA 98362, 360/565-3100; Olympic National Forest, Hoodsport Ranger Station, 150 North Lake Cushman Road, Hoodsport, WA 98548, 360/877-5254.

53 FLAPJACK LAKES
16.0 mi/2 days

northwest of Hoodsport in Olympic National Park

Map 1.4, page 30

Flapjack Lakes is one of the most scenic and popular destinations in Olympic National Park. So popular, in fact, the Park Service instituted a permit system limiting the number of overnight campers here. Don't let that deter you, however, as it's a must hike on any to-do list of Olympic trails. Plus, Flapjack Lakes are easily accessible, especially for families on a weekend excursion.

The route follows North Fork Skokomish Trail for 3.5 miles, where Flapjack Lake Trail takes off to the east. The trail steadily ascends through a forest of impressively large trees while following Donahue Creek. At seven miles, the trail splits, with the left fork heading to Black and White Lakes. Stay to the right and find old mountain hemlocks, subalpine firs, and yellow cedars surrounding the two lakes. Mount Cruiser and the jagged ridge leading to Mount Lincoln enclose the eastern view; a way trail leading up to the Gladys Divide is a great side trip.

If the thought of crowds at Flapjacks is unappealing, an attractive alternative is Black and White Lakes. From the fork, a mile of walking brings hikers to an open ridge below Mount Gladys. The lakes are small and have fewer campsites, but they are much more open and offer outstanding views of the entire North Fork Skokomish drainage. With several options for exploration, Flapjack Lakes are definitely a destination for Olympic enthusiasts to undertake.

User Groups: Hikers only. No dogs, horses, or mountain bikes are allowed. No wheelchair access.

Open Seasons: This trail is accessible mid-May–October.

Permits: A National Parks Pass is required to park at North Fork Skokomish Trailhead. Overnight stays in the national park require backcountry camping permits, which are available at Staircase Ranger Station.

Maps: For a map of Olympic National Park, contact the Outdoor Recreation Information Center at the downtown Seattle REI. For topographic maps, ask Green Trails for No. 167, Mount Steel, or ask the USGS for Mount Skokomish and Mount Olson.

Directions: From Hoodsport, drive west 9 miles on Lake Cushman Road (Highway 119) to Forest Service Road 24 (a T intersection). Turn left and drive 6.5 miles to Staircase Ranger Station for the trailhead and trailhead parking.

Contact: Olympic National Park, Wilderness Information Center, 3002 Mount Angeles Road, Port Angeles, WA 98362, 360/565-3100.

54 SIX RIDGE
32.8 mi/3–4 days

northwest of Hoodsport in Olympic National Park

Map 1.4, page 30

If you are considering hiking Six Ridge, you are to be commended. You have a thirst for adventure and are undeterred by difficult ascents. You appreciate grand mountain views, love mountain meadows full of blooming wildflowers, and enjoy wilderness best when it's solitary. Six Ridge Trail is all that and more.

To access Six Ridge, one must first travel North Fork Skokomish Trail 5.6 miles, a flat and easy walk. Skokomish Trail crosses the river here and Six Ridge turns south. After crossing Seven Stream, the trail climbs gradually through forest to achieve the eastern end of Six Ridge. From here are eight miles of ridge walking. The trail passes through exceptional subalpine meadows for much of the route, although fields of scree, talus, and even snow are common. There are several camps on the ridge, most notably McGravey Lakes at 8.5 miles up the ridge. The trail technically ends at Six Ridge Pass, where it becomes Graves Creek Trail but continues to Lake Sundown in 1.2 miles.

User Groups: Hikers only. No dogs, horses, or mountain bikes are allowed. No wheelchair access.

Open Seasons: This trail is accessible mid-July–October.

Permits: A National Parks Pass is required to park here. Overnight stays in the national park require backcountry camping permits, which are available at the Staircase Ranger Station.

Maps: For a map of Olympic National Park, contact the Outdoor Recreation Information Center at the downtown Seattle REI. For topographic maps, ask Green Trails for No. 166, Mount Christie, and No. 167, Mount Steel, or ask the USGS for Mount Skokomish, Mount Olson, and Mount Hoquim.

Directions: From Hoodsport, drive west 9 miles on Lake Cushman Road (Highway 119) to Forest Service Road 24 (a T intersection). Turn left and drive 6.5 miles to Staircase Ranger Station for the trailhead and trailhead parking.

Contact: Olympic National Park, Wilderness Information Center, 3002 Mount Angeles Road, Port Angeles, WA 98362, 360/565-3100.

55 MOUNT ELLINOR
6.2 mi/3.0 hrs

northwest of Hoodsport in Mount Skokomish Wilderness of Olympic National Forest

Map 1.4, page 30

Tucked away in the southeastern corner of the Olympic Peninsula, Mount Ellinor is rarely high on peoples' radar when they are looking for a hike. It gets less attention than other nearby spots, such as Mount Rose or Flapjack Lakes. But the trip is no less beautiful and actually features some the area's best views.

The trail has two trailheads, the lower one adding about 1.5 miles and 800 feet elevation gain to the trip. Since it's not much farther, the lower trailhead is the better choice, as it follows a well-forested ridge that should not be missed. The trail is a steady climb, rarely leveling out for more than a few yards. The forest breaks into avalanche chutes and meadows about .5 mile from the summit. At the top, views of Hood Canal, Lake Cushman, and neighboring Olympic peaks can be found. Neither well known nor frequently visited, Mount Ellinor makes for a perfect day getaway.

User Groups: Hikers and leashed dogs. No horses or mountain bikes are allowed. No wheelchair access.

Open Seasons: This trail is accessible mid-June–November (accessible year-round with ice ax).

Permits: A federal Northwest Forest Pass is required to park here.

Maps: For a map of Olympic National Forest, contact the Outdoor Recreation Information Center at the downtown Seattle REI. For topographic maps, ask Green Trails for No. 167, Mount Steel, and No. 168, The Brothers, or ask the USGS for Mount Washington and Mount Skokomish.

Directions: From Hoodsport, drive east 9 miles on Hoodsport Road (County Road 44) to Forest Service Road 24. Turn right and drive 1.5 miles to Forest Service Road 2419 (Big Creek Road). Turn left and drive 6 miles to Forest Service Road 2419-014. Turn left and drive 1 mile to the signed trailhead at road's end.

Contact: Olympic National Forest, Hoodsport Ranger Station, 150 North Lake Cushman Road, Hoodsport, WA 98548, 360/877-5254.

56 MOUNT ROSE
6.4 mi/3.5 hr

northwest of Hoodsport in Mount Skokomish Wilderness of Olympic National Forest

Map 1.4, page 30

Mount Rose is one of the more popular summits in the southeastern Olympic Mountains. Which means it must be awfully scenic, as it is certainly not an easy route. The trail is unique for a summit route in that it is a loop. Laid out like a lasso, the trail ascends straight to the summit and then makes a circle along the ridge to the trail again. Overall elevation gain is 3,500 feet in just about three miles.

The trail navigates a mile of second-growth timber before entering the wilderness. The rise to the junction (1.8 miles) is rather steep despite the many switchbacks. Head to the right for the more gradual route along the ridge. The trail has peek-a-boo views of neighboring peaks and drainages. The summit is forested save for a small chuck of basalt that reaches up roughly 30 feet. From the top are grand, panoramic views of Hood Canal and numerous Olympic peaks. Good luck, and enjoy the workout.

User Groups: Hikers and leashed dogs. No horses or mountain bikes are allowed. No wheelchair access.

Open Seasons: This trail is accessible July–October.

Permits: Permits are not required. Parking and access are free.

Maps: For a map of Olympic National Forest, contact the Outdoor Recreation Information Center at the downtown Seattle REI. For topographic maps, ask Green Trails for No. 167, Mount Steel, or ask the USGS for Lightning Peak and Mount Skokomish.

Directions: From Hoodsport, drive west 9 miles on Lake Cushman Road (Highway 119) to Forest Service Road 24 (a T intersection). Turn left and drive 3 miles to the signed trailhead on the right side of the road.

Contact: Olympic National Forest, Hoodsport Ranger Station, 150 North Lake Cushman Road, Hoodsport, WA 98548, 360/877-5254.

57 UPPER SOUTH FORK SKOKOMISH
15.0 mi/1–2 days

west of Hoodsport in the Wonder Mountain Wilderness and Olympic National Park

Map 1.4, page 30

Upper South Fork Skokomish Trail is a great route through a typically great Olympic river valley. Unfortunately, it is much shorter than it once was. This trail has just what one could want out of Olympic river hike: a forest composed of large trees, a river carving through occasional canyons, and meadows at the river's headwaters along a high mountain ridge. And throw in an absence of people on the trail, which is all right with the folks who know of this place.

The trail leaves the road and sets off into a forest of large cedars, firs, and hemlocks, all old-growth and of good size. Streams and creeks regularly cross the trail, but few give any trouble. The trail crosses the river twice via bridges and makes a detour into the Startup Creek valley. Soon after the route enters the national park, it becomes little more than a beaten footpath. It's not exceptionally difficult to follow as long as snow isn't lingering on the ground (after mid-June). The trail climbs gradually through the headwaters of the South Fork of the Skokomish, eventually reaching Sundown Pass and Lake Sundown, a remote place of meadows and open subalpine forests. Backpackers will find overnight spots at Camp Riley (5.4 miles) and Sundown Pass.

User Groups: Hikers and horses. No dogs or mountain bikes are allowed. No wheelchair access.

Open Seasons: This trail is accessible mid-June–October.

Permits: A federal Northwest Forest Pass is required to park here.

Maps: For a map of Olympic National Park and Olympic National Forest, contact the Outdoor Recreation Information Center at the downtown Seattle REI. For topographic maps, ask Green Trails for No. 166, Mount Christie, No. 167, Mount Steel, and No. 199, Mount Tebo, or ask the USGS for Lightning Peak, Mount Tebo, Mount Olson, and Mount Hoquim.

Directions: From Hoodsport, drive south 7 miles to Skokomish Valley Road. Turn right (west) and drive 5.5 miles to Forest Service Road 23. Turn right and drive 13 miles to Forest Service Road 2361. Turn right and drive 5.5 miles to the signed trailhead at road's end.

Contact: Olympic National Forest, Hoodsport Ranger Station, 150 North Lake Cushman Road, Hoodsport, WA 98548, 360/877-5254.

58 RAINBOW CANYON
1.0 mi/0.5 hr

south of Quilcene in the Buckhorn Wilderness of Olympic National Forest

Map 1.5, page 31

This is a great leg-stretcher for those making a long trek along U.S. 101. Just outside Rainbow Campground (which is right off the highway), a short .5-mile hike accesses a nice waterfall on the way to Rainbow Canyon on the Big Quilcene River. The trail's drop is not much to speak of, making it easily accessible to hikers of all abilities.

Forests of Douglas fir tower over an understory that includes vine maple, a tangle of brilliant colors in September. An overlook peers into Elbo Creek, where the waterfall cascades into a small pool. The trail continues down to the Big Quilcene River, where it makes a gentle turn within the canyon walls. Moss and ferns line the sides. When the kids are getting antsy in the back seat, Rainbow Canyon is just the thing to burn off a little energy. Total distance for the round-trip excursion is just one mile.

User Groups: Hikers and leashed dogs. No horses or mountain bikes are allowed. No wheelchair access.

Open Seasons: This trail is accessible year-round.

Permits: Permits are not required. Parking and access are free.

Maps: For a map of Olympic National Forest, contact the Outdoor Recreation Information Center at the downtown Seattle REI. For topographic maps, ask the USGS for Mount Walker.

Directions: From Quilcene, drive 5 miles south on U.S. 101 to Rainbow Campground. While the trail begins from within the campground, it is a group site and the gate will be locked. Park across Highway 101 and walk into the site. The trailhead is at the back of the campground.

Contact: Olympic National Forest, Quilcene Ranger Station, 295142 U.S. 101 South, Quilcene, WA 98376, 360/765-2200.

59 LEADBETTER POINT

2.6–8.3 mi/1.5–4.5 hrs

northern tip of Long Beach in southwestern Washington

Map 1.6, page 32

It may not appear as though there is much going on at Leadbetter Point, but in fact the tip of Long Beach is extremely rich in wildlife. Comprising sand dunes and miles of grasses waving in the strong breeze, the area can look barren and a bit forbidding. On closer inspection, however, you'll see that hundreds of thousands of seabirds and shorebirds make this place home for a part of each year. Leadbetter Point is a bird-watcher's dream, home to snowy plovers, grouse, bald eagles, great herons, and woodpeckers. Although it's a good visit anytime of the year, winter is the peak of bird season. Just be ready for soggy trail in places.

A small network of trails courses around the ever-changing peninsula. Taken altogether, they make an 8.3-mile loop that includes sand dunes, coastal forest, Willapa Bay, and a stretch along the beach. Shorter hikes include Blue Trail, a 2.6-mile round-trip out to the Pacific Ocean. All of the trails are fairly level, climbing only over sand dunes and grassy knolls. The park is managed by State Parks but is also a National Wildlife Refuge because of its importance as a migratory stop for birds. Dogs are not allowed on any trails.

User Groups: Hikers only. No dogs, horses, or mountain bikes are allowed. No wheelchair access.

Open Seasons: This trail is accessible year-round.

Permits: A $5 day-use fee is required to park here and is payable at the trailhead, or you can get an annual State Parks Pass for $30; contact Washington State Parks and Recreation, 360/902-8500.

Maps: For topographic maps, ask the USGS for Oysterville and North Cove.

Directions: From Long Beach, drive north 18 miles on Highway 103 (Pacific Way) to Leadbetter Point State Park. The route passes through Oysterville and is well signed. The trailhead is at the end of the road within the Leadbetter Point State Park.

Contact: Willapa National Wildlife Refuge, 3888 U.S. 101, Ilwaco, WA 98624-9707, 360/484-3482.

60 LONG ISLAND

1.0–5.0 mi/2.0–5.0 hrs

in Willapa Bay in Southwestern Washington

Map 1.6, page 32

Talk about secluded. As the name implies, this is an island, and it's one with no bridges. One reaches Long Island by boat or kayak, with no other options. If that's not a problem (it actually makes the trip all the more special), then Long Island is a real gem.

Roughly five miles of trail and even more old road crisscross the island, two miles wide by seven miles long. Hiking along the shore is a real wildlife getaway, with a plethora of seabirds and shorebirds stopping by on their yearly migrations. Bald eagles, grouse, great herons, and snowy plovers are just a few of the many winged inhabitants. Inland, deer, bear, and elk are some of the bigger mammals to be found.

The highlight of the island is the ancient cedar grove in the center of the island. After crossing the bay to the island by boat (the crossing is about 200 feet and can be done only at high tide), hike north on the old logging road about 2.5 miles to the signed "Trail of the Ancient Cedars." Turn left and in .5 mile you will be among a large grove of massive cedars. Spared from logging because of its hard-to-reach locale, the stand is certain to instill a sense of awe for a forest that once covered the entire island. There are a number of primitive campgrounds around the lake, although there is no water during the summer.

User Groups: Hikers only. No dogs, horses, or mountain bikes are allowed. No wheelchair access.

Open Seasons: This trail is accessible year-round.

Permits: Permits are not required. Parking and access are free.

Maps: For topographic maps, ask the USGS for Long Island.

Directions: From Long Beach, drive north 13 miles on U.S. 101 to the signed Refuge Headquarters and trailhead.

Contact: Willapa National Wildlife Refuge, 3888 U.S. 101, Ilwaco, WA 98624-9707, 360/484-3482.

61 CAPE DISAPPOINTMENT STATE PARK
0.5–9.0 mi /0.5–4.5 hrs

southwest of Ilwaco in southwest Washington

Map 1.6, page 32

A network of trails through Cape Disappointment State Park makes for a great combination of forest and coastal hiking. All of the trails are extremely easy and highly scenic, providing parents a prime locale to take the kids on the weekend. Formerly known as Fort Canby, the state park covers the grounds where Lewis and Clark spent a wet winter. On Cape Disappointment, Washington's most southwestern point, the park overlooks both the Columbia River and Pacific Ocean.

The main route through the park is Washington Coast Trail, a long trek that gets its southern start here. Patched together from several trails, this 4.5-mile segment bisects the park through old-growth forest to link a pair of old lighthouses. Folks spending a full day here will want to hike the length of it, the best way to see the park.

Families looking for a shorter trip should hike to Beard's Hollow. The trail travels just .5 mile through coastal forest and sand dunes before finding the secluded cove, a gateway to more than 20 miles of beach to the north. Another beauty is Cape Disappointment Lighthouse Trail, 1.4 miles to the West Coast's oldest working lighthouse. Be sure to check out the Lewis and Clark Interpretive Center, atop a pair of enormous gun emplacements from World Wars I and II. The center features a cornucopia of artifacts from the Corps of Discovery's journey 200 years ago.

User Groups: Hikers, leashed dogs, and mountain bikes. No horses are allowed. Parts of the trails are wheelchair accessible.

Open Seasons: This area is accessible year-round.

Permits: A $5 day-use fee is required to park here and is payable at the trailhead, or you can get an annual State Parks Pass for $30; contact Washington State Parks and Recreation, 360/902-8500.

Maps: For topographic maps, ask the USGS for Cape Disappointment.

Directions: From Long Beach, drive south 3.5 miles on Pacific Way to Ilwaco. Turn right on North Head Road and drive 2.5 miles to North Head Lighthouse Road. Turn right and drive .5 miles to the well-signed park entrance. The main trailhead is located at the Lewis and Clark Interpretive Center, inside the park entrance.

Contact: Cape Disappointment State Park, P.O. Box 488, Ilwaco WA, 98624, 360/642-3078.

Chapter 2

© SCOTT LEONARD

Seattle and the San Juan Islands

Seattle and the San Juan Islands

Who says you have to go far from Seattle to enjoy the great outdoors? The Puget Sound area is undoubtedly one of the United State's most scenic locales for a major urban area, which is great for Seattleites. The North Cascades may be just an hour or two drive from Seattle, but the secluded parks and beaches of this region are even closer. Stretching from the San Juan Islands in Puget Sound (accessible only by ferry, one of the prettiest boat rides you'll ever embark upon) down to Seattle and Olympia, a strong network of state and city parks have preserved a bit of the wilderness for people to enjoy quickly and easily. Thanks to easy trails and loads of wildlife, these places are excellent trips for young hikers in training.

A number of great parks line the Sound, many located on the San Juans. Moran State Park is the best, not simply among these, but among all of Washington's state parks. Situated on horseshoe-shaped Orcas Island, the park boasts Mount Constitution as its highlight. From the lofty height of 2,409 feet, Mount Constitution lays Puget Sound and the Strait of Juan de Fuca below you. This makes a great hike, but the peak is accessible on four wheels as well. In Anacortes, Washington Park is a little-explored gem. It's convenient to access for people passing through Anacortes on their way to other places—be one of the few to stop and explore the trails and shoreline of this city park. On Whidbey Island are Deception Pass, Fort Ebey, and South Whidbey State Parks. These are great destinations any time of the year, with miles of trail along the water. Lucky visitors may spot sea lions or orcas swimming and playing in the sound.

Back on the mainland are several great wildlife refuges. The Puget Sound region sees millions of birds pass through the area each spring and fall on their way to warmer climes. Refuges like Tennant Lake near Bellingham, Padilla Bay near Mount Vernon, and Nisqually Wildlife Refuge near Olympia offer exceptional opportunities for quiet walks and wildlife sightings. Ducks and geese might be lounging in the marshlands while goshawks and falcons patrol the air in search of dinner.

And let's not forget the wealth of forests and trails within the city limits, either; Seattle's city park system rivals any in the nation. Carkeek Park overlooks Puget Sound from high bluffs and is home to one of Seattle's few remaining salmon streams (fall runs of salmon can still be seen in Piper Creek). Seward Park covers Bailey Peninsula in Lake Washington and still boasts some old-growth timber. At Discovery Park on the Sound, hikers can enjoy sunsets from on the hill or explore the tidal pools of Puget Sound during low tides. There's a lot to do in Seattle's own backyard.

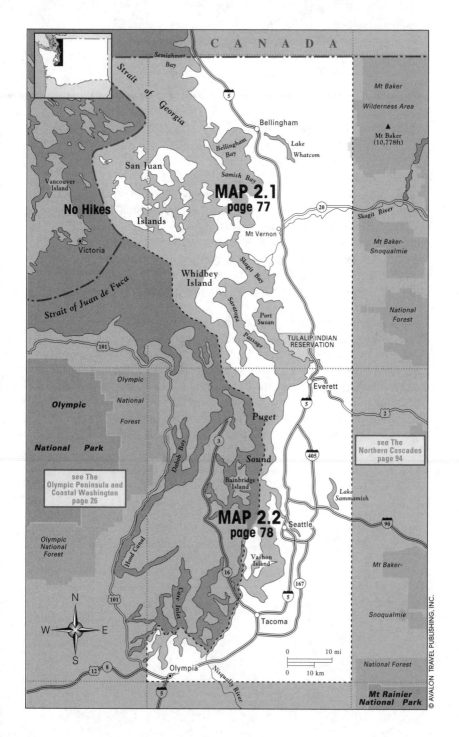

Map 2.1

Hikes 1–10
Pages 79–84

2.2

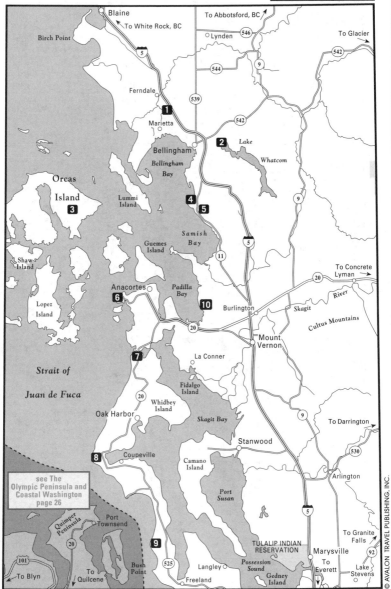

Map 2.2

Hikes 11–18
Pages 84–88

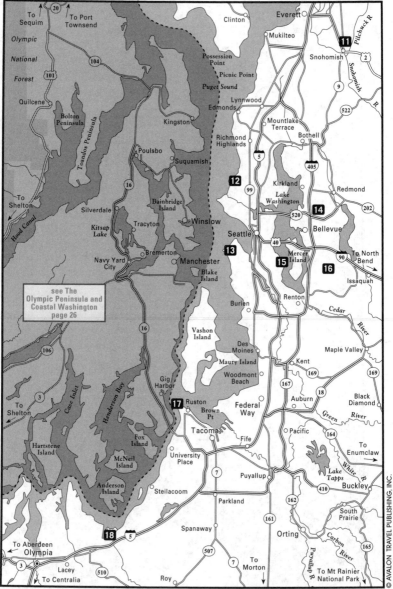

◼ TENNANT LAKE
0.8–4.4 mi/1.0–2.5 hrs

**south of Ferndale in Tennant Lake
County Park**

Map 2.1, page 77

Pristine wetlands are hard to come by within
the lower Nooksack River Valley, inundated by
suburban sprawl and the spreading fields of
agriculture, Fortunately, Tennant Lake Wildlife Area has preserved a chunk of these lands
that are so important to wildlife. Spread over
624 acres, Tennant Lake Wildlife Area is an
important spring and fall stopover for thousands of migratory birds, who make extensive
use of the shallow lake and surrounding wetlands, fields, and forest. Three flat, easy trails
meander through the park, a prime winter walk.

Tennant Lake Marsh Boardwalk is a 1.4-
mile loop that explores most of the park. A
well-built boardwalk helps to keep feet dry as
the trail explores the marshes and wetlands.
The route passes a 50-foot observation tower,
which provides an awesome panoramic view
of the area. A pair of binoculars comes in
handy from the top. A longer hike can be made
by following River Dike Trail (2.2 miles one-
way). The trail follows the meandering Nooksack River through forest, wetlands, and
neighboring farmlands. Finally, Hovander Park
Trail (.4 mile one-way) visits the historic Hovander Homestead along wooded boardwalk.
User Groups: Hikers and mountain bikes. No
dogs or horses are allowed. Two of the trails
are wheelchair accessible.
Open Seasons: This area is accessible year-
round.
Permits: Permits are not required. Parking and
access are free.
Maps: Maps of the trail system are posted at
trailheads. For a topographic map, ask the
USGS for Ferndale.
Directions: From Seattle, drive north on I-5 to
Ferndale (Exit 262). Turn left (west) on Main
Street and drive .5 mile to Hovander Road.
Turn left and drive to Nielsen Avenue. Turn
right and follow signs to Tennant Lake Inter-

pretive Center (end of Nielsen Avenue). The
trailhead is at the interpretive center.
Contact: Tennant Lake Interpretive Center,
5236 Nielsen Road, Ferndale, WA 98248,
360/384-3064.

◻ WHATCOM FALLS
0.5–2.0 mi/0.5–1.0 hr

in Bellingham

Map 2.1, page 77

Residents of Bellingham are lucky to have
Whatcom Falls in their own backyard. In one
of Washington's best municipal parks, several
miles of trail explore Whatcom Creek and its
large sets of falls. The park is ideal for rambling as the network of trails weaves along the
creek and through the forest. Pipeline Trail is
the main artery of the park, running for several miles along Whatcom Creek. This park
was once the scene of a tragic accident. In the
late 1990s, several people were killed when a
natural-gas pipeline exploded, igniting a fire
along half of the park. Burned trees and denuded slopes are a testament to this sad mis-
fortune, but the area is quickly revegetating.
A fish hatchery is in the center of the park and
is open to the public. Access to the hatchery
is via an old stone bridge constructed by the
Depression-era Works Progress Administra-
tion. The scenic bridge overlooks Whatcom
Falls, just one in a series of cascades. A short
distance downstream are another set of falls,
viewable from Pipeline Trail.
User Groups: Hikers, leashed dogs, and mountain bikes. No horses are allowed. Parts of the
trails are wheelchair accessible.
Open Seasons: This area is accessible year-
round.
Permits: Permits are not required. Parking and
access are free.
Maps: Maps of the trail system are posted at
trailheads. For a topographic map, ask the
USGS for Bellingham South.
Directions: From downtown Bellingham, drive
east on Lakeway Drive to Electric Avenue.

Turn right and drive .25 mile to Silver Beach Road. Turn left into the park entrance. The trailhead is on the west side of the parking lot. **Contact:** Bellingham City Parks, 3424 Meridian Street, Bellingham, WA 98225, 360/676-6985.

3 MORAN STATE PARK
0.5–7.4 mi/0.5–4.0 hrs

on Orcas Island in Moran State Park

Map 2.1, page 77

One of Washington's most beautiful and most popular state parks, Moran State Park rarely fails to impress. Situated on Orcas Island, the park is crowned by 2,409-foot Mount Constitution. It's the highest point in the San Juan Island chain, and the views from the summit are unbelievable. More than 30 miles of hiking trails lie within the park, exploring everything from forested lakes to the historic stone tower atop Mount Constitution. Whether you're visiting Orcas Island for a day or staying overnight at the campground, the trails of Moran State Park are well worth hiking.

The diversity of trails allows visitors to find a hike that is best for them. Many trails are short and flat. Among the best of the easy trails is Cascade Falls Trail, a quick .5-mile hike to the large waterfall on Cascade Creek. This is a real gusher during the springtime. Longer but just as flat is Mountain Lake Loop Trail, a 3.9-mile route around the park's largest body of water. Mountain Lake Trail starts at the large campground along the lake's shores.

The most popular destination for many visitors is the summit of Mount Constitution. Although one can drive to the top, Twin Lakes Trail is a survey of the park. Twin Lakes Trail skirts Mountain Lake before following a creek to Twin Lakes (1.5 miles), where loops circle both small lakes. The latter half of the trail switchbacks steeply to the summit (3.7 miles), where an old stone watchtower provides a panorama. The San Juans and Puget Sound are revealed in full glory, while Mount Baker rests behind the growing city of Bellingham.

User Groups: Hikers, leashed dogs, and mountain bikes (mountain bikes allowed September 15–May 15). No horses are allowed. No wheelchair access.
Open Seasons: This area is accessible year-round.
Permits: A $5 day-use fee is required to park here and is payable at the trailhead, or you can get an annual State Parks Pass for $30; contact Washington State Parks and Recreation, 360/902-8500.
Maps: Maps of the trail system are available at trailheads. For a topographic map, ask the USGS for Mount Constitution.
Directions: From the ferry terminal on Orcas Island, drive 13 miles on Horseshoe Highway (Orcas Road) to the park entrance. There are several trailheads within the park, all of them well signed.
Contact: Moran State Park, Star Route 22, Eastsound, WA, 98245, 360/376-2326.

4 LARRABEE STATE PARK
0.5–8.0 mi/1.0–4.0 hrs

south of Bellingham on Chuckanut Mountain

Map 2.1, page 77

Spanning an area from the shores of Puget Sound to the crest of Chuckanut Mountain, Larrabee State Park is a treasure for hikers. Larrabee was Washington's first state park and even today is one of its largest. A diverse mix of trails varies from a beach ramble to a hike to several high, forested lakes. Trails to Clayton Beach and Teddy Bear Cove (each about .5 mile round-trip, accessible from Highline Road) drop to the sandy shores of Chuckanut Bay and Puget Sound. The beaches are strewn with boulders and driftwood. Best of all, this area lies within the rain shadow of the Olympic Peninsula, meaning it receives about half the rain of the Seattle area.

Longer trails lead up the western slopes of Chuckanut Mountain to Fragrance (2 miles) and Lost Lakes (4 miles). Surrounded by lush forests, these large lakes are favorite haunts for both campers and anglers. Along the way to the lakes are numerous viewpoints of the San Juan Islands and Strait of Juan de Fuca.

User Groups: Hikers, leashed dogs, horses, and mountain bikes. No wheelchair access.

Open Seasons: This area is accessible year-round.

Permits: A $5 day-use fee is required to park here and is payable at the trailhead, or you can get an annual State Parks Pass for $30; contact Washington State Parks and Recreation, 360/902-8500.

Maps: For a topographic map, ask the USGS for Bellingham South.

Directions: From Seattle, drive north on I-5 to Chuckanut Drive (Exit 231). Turn left (west) and drive 14.5 miles to the park entrance. The trailhead is just inside the park entrance.

Contact: Larrabee State Park, 245 Chuckanut Drive, Bellingham, WA 98226, 360/676-2093.

5 PINE AND CEDAR LAKES
4.8 mi/3.0 hrs

south of Bellingham on Chuckanut Mountain

Map 2.1, page 77

Famous as a colorful drive during the fall, Chuckanut Mountain also has some great trails. Here, on the eastern end of the long mountain ridge, are Pine and Cedar Lakes. These are a pair of mountain lakes well regarded for their views and fishing. A single trail leads to both of them, just a few hundred yards apart. Pine and Cedar Lakes Trail climbs steeply for the first 1.5 miles through a terrific forest of broad-leafed trees. It's hikable year-round, but October is a grand time to visit, when the forest is ignited by autumn color. The trail reaches a junction—Cedar Lake to the left and Pine Lake to the right. Both lakes are forested and have a subalpine feel to them, odd given that the altitude here is 1,600 feet. Several campsites are also found at each lake. A loop trail encircles Cedar Lake, which also has a side trail leading to a high viewpoint.

User Groups: Hikers, leashed dogs, horses, and mountain bikes. No wheelchair access.

Open Seasons: This area is accessible year-round.

Permits: Permits are not required. Parking and access are free.

Maps: For a topographic map, ask the USGS for Bellingham South.

Directions: From Bellingham, drive south on I-5 to North Lake Samish Exit. Turn right (west) onto North Lake Samish Drive and drive to Old Samish Road. Turn left and drive 2.5 miles to the signed trailhead on the left.

Contact: Whatcom County Parks and Recreation, 3373 Mount Baker Highway, Bellingham, WA 98226, 360/733-2900.

6 WASHINGTON PARK
2.6 mi/1.5 hrs

in Anacortes on Puget Sound

Map 2.1, page 77

On the shores of Puget Sound and within the city limits of Anacortes, Washington Park gets far less attention than it deserves. Thousands of people pass right by the park on their way to the ferry to the San Juan Islands. But Washington Park is just as great, with more than 40,000 feet of shoreline and a 220-acre forest of cedar, fir, and madrona. Washington Park sits on a rocky point of Fidalgo Head, a large peninsula surrounded by saltwater and views. Although a road rounds the park, the best views are from Fidalgo Head Loop Trail, the main route through the park.

Fidalgo Head Loop Trail explores the perimeters of the park with frequent views of Puget Sound and the San Juan Islands. Numerous small side trails depart from this main artery, so it's a good idea to check out a trail map at the trailhead. Juniper Point and Burrows Trail are good, quick add-ons to Loop Trail. Elevation gains are modest, and the trail is easy enough for hikers of all abilities. Wildlife is plentiful, especially waterfowl. Brant, loons, murrelets, scoters, grebes, and hooded mergansers are frequently sighted, so a camera or binoculars are handy.

User Groups: Hikers, leashed dogs, and mountain bikes. No horses are allowed. No wheelchair access.

Open Seasons: This area is accessible year-round.

Permits: Permits are not required. Parking and access are free.

Maps: For a topographic map, ask the USGS for Anacortes North.

Directions: From Seattle, drive north on I-5 to Highway 20 (Exit 230). Head west on Highway 20 to Anacortes. Take Commercial Street to 12th Street. Turn left and drive 3 miles to Washington Park. The trailhead is located at the parking lot, just inside the park entrance.

Contact: Anacortes Parks and Recreation, P.O. Box 547, Anacortes, WA 98221, 360/293-1918.

◼7 DECEPTION PASS STATE PARK
1.0–12.0 mi/1.0–6.0 hrs

on northern Whidbey Island in Deception Pass State Park

Map 2.1, page 77

A wide network of trails winds throughout this park, one of Washington State's most beautiful. More than 35 miles of trails lead through great forests to loads of seashore exploring. Tides rush water through the pass between Skagit Bay and Rosario Strait as though it were a river. Beaches edged by contorted pines and madronas offer chances to see orcas and sea otters in the water. Numerous upland trails offer great opportunities for runs and more extended hiking.

The park is split between Fidalgo Island and Whidbey Island. A large bridge spans the pass to connect the two islands. The best beach hiking is along Rosario Beach, on Fidalgo Island, where the Samish legend of the Maiden of Deception Pass is recounted. Signed reader boards provide maps for a number of trails around Rosario Beach and Bowman Bay. Be sure to pick up a map, which shows trails and distances, to see the route and distance of the hike you wish to take.

On Whidbey Island, trails of interest include one running from West Point, on Rosario Strait, along the pass channel to Haypus Point and Goose Rock. The many upland trails on this side of the island are often visited by mountain bikers. In all, there are nine islands within the state park, some of which can be reached only by canoe. More than 250 campsites are here for those wishing to spend the night, but they go quickly, as nearly three million people a year visit the park. Finally, it pays to be cautious when hiking here. The park staff spends a considerable amount of time performing first aid and rescue for folks, especially kids, who wander too close to cliff edges.

User Groups: Hikers, leashed dogs, and mountain bikes. No horses are allowed. Some trails are wheelchair accessible.

Open Seasons: This area is accessible year-round.

Permits: A $5 day-use fee is required to park here and is payable at the trailhead, or you can get an annual State Parks Pass for $30; contact Washington State Parks and Recreation, 360/902-8500.

Maps: Maps of the trail system are available at trailheads. For a topographic map, ask the USGS for Deception Pass.

Directions: From Mount Vernon, drive west 18 miles on Highway 20 toward Oak Harbor. Entrances to the park, before and after crossing Deception Pass by way of a high bridge, are along Highway 20 and well signed. Trail maps at each entrance show the exact locations of each trailhead.

Contact: Deception Pass State Park, Highway 20, Oak Harbor, WA 98277, 360/675-2417.

◼8 FORT EBEY
6.0 mi/3.0 hrs

south of Oak Harbor on Whidbey Island

Map 2.1, page 77

Shake those wintertime blues and enjoy the drier climate of Whidbey Island. Situated in the rain shadow of the Olympic Mountains, America's longest island gets less than half the annual rainfall of Seattle. Fort Ebey is a great alternative to the crowds of people visiting the better-known Deception Pass State Park. A large trail network of more than 20 miles spreads out over the forested park, popular with mountain bikers. The highlight of Fort Ebey is Bluff Trail, six miles of wide, level trail extending along the high cliffs bordering the water. This is the most popular and scenic trail in the park, with outstanding views of the Olympic Mountains and Strait of Juan de Fuca. Lucky hikers may see a pod of orcas in the water below. Although rain is sparse here, wind isn't; remember an extra layer in all seasons. The park has several large cannon emplacements along the hillside overlooking the Strait of Juan de Fuca. Together with similar emplacements at Fort Worden and Fort Casey, these cannons formed a "Triangle of Fire," rendering the Puget Sound invulnerable to invasion during World War II. Fortunately, the invasion never arrived. There is a large car campground in the park, which is bordered by Kettles Park with even more trails to explore.

User Groups: Hikers, leashed dogs, and mountain bikes. No horses are allowed. No wheelchair access.

Open Seasons: This area is accessible year-round.

Permits: A $5 day-use fee is required to park here and is payable at the trailhead, or you can get an annual State Parks Pass for $30; contact Washington State Parks and Recreation, 360/902-8500.

Maps: Maps of the trail system are posted at trailheads. For a topographic map, ask the USGS for Port Townsend North.

Directions: From the ferry terminal in Clinton, on Whidbey Island, drive north 30 miles on Highway 525 to Libby Road. Turn left (west) and drive 1 mile to Valley Drive. Turn left and drive right into the park entrance. The trailhead is inside the park entrance and marked by a sign.

Contact: Fort Ebey State Park, 395 Fort Ebey Road, Coupeville, WA 98239, 360/678-4636.

9 SOUTH WHIDBEY STATE PARK
1.0–1.5 mi/1.0 hr

north of Clinton on Whidbey Island

Map 2.1, page 77

South Whidbey State Park remains far less known than its sister to the north, Deception Pass, but its scenery is just as great. On Admiralty Inlet, between Bush and Lagoon Points, the park offers great strolling along the peaceful beach or hiking within a stand of old-growth forest. From the day-use parking area, an unnamed path leads down to the water. The sandy beach stretches nearly a mile along Smugglers Cove. Wind-swept trees appear gnarly and stunted, growing out of the sides of the steep hillsides. Don't be surprised to spot sea otters playing and feeding offshore. A one-mile signed nature loop investigates the cliffs overlooking Admiralty Inlet, where lucky hikers can spot orcas in the water. For a quick and shady hike, Wilbert Trail winds 1.5 miles through an old, large forest of fir and cedar. All trails are family friendly. South Whidbey State Park is also home to a large car campground.

User Groups: Hikers and leashed dogs. No horses or mountain bikes are allowed. No wheelchair access.

Open Seasons: This area is accessible year-round.

Permits: A $5 day-use fee is required to park here and is payable at the trailhead, or you can get an annual State Parks Pass for $30; contact Washington State Parks and Recreation, 360/902-8500.

Maps: Maps of the trail system are posted at trailheads. For a topographic map, ask the USGS for Freeland.

Directions: From the ferry terminal in Clinton, drive north 10.5 miles on Highway 525 to Bush Point Road. Turn left and drive 5 miles (as the road becomes Smugglers Cove Road) to the park entrance on the left. The trailhead is inside the park entrance and marked by a sign.

Contact: South Whidbey State Park, 4128 Smugglers Cove Road, Freeland, WA 98249, 360/331-4559.

🔟 PADILLA BAY
0.8–4.6 mi/0.5–2.5 hrs

west of Mount Vernon on Puget Sound

Map 2.1, page 77

On the shores of large Padilla Bay, this wildlife refuge provides excellent walks through important wildlife habitat. Although the area was disturbed for agricultural use more than 100 years ago, the area is flourishing as bird habitat today. Thousands of migrating marsh and shore birds stop through the reserve during the spring and fall. The area is also important habitat for many marine animals. Open year-round, Padilla Bay makes a great place to stretch the legs during winter.

A pair of trails explores the federally protected reserve. Upland Trail, a short .8-mile loop, leaves from the Breazeale Center to explore open meadows and sparse forest. Interpretive guides are available from the Breazeale Center, explaining different sightings along the way. The beginning of the trail reaches a viewing platform and is accessible to wheelchairs.

A longer hike can be made along Shore Trail, a 2.3-mile graveled path along a dike bordering Padilla Bay. The route explores the tidal slough and open mud flats of the bay, a good place to see wildlife. Views of the Olympics and even Mount Baker can be had while enjoying the salty marine air of Puget Sound. The path ends at Bayview State Park, home to a large campground.

User Groups: Hikers, leashed dogs, and mountain bikes (dogs and mountain bikes allowed on Shore Trail). No horses are allowed. Parts of the trails are wheelchair accessible.

Open Seasons: This area is accessible year-round.

Permits: Permits are not required. Parking and access are free.

Maps: Maps of the trail system are posted at trailheads. For a topographic map, ask the USGS for Anacortes South and LaConner.

Directions: From Seattle, drive north on I-5 to Highway 20 (Exit 230). Turn left (west) and drive 5 miles to Farm to Market Road. Turn right (north) and drive 2 miles to Josh Wilson Road. Turn left and drive 1.5 miles to Bayview-Edison Road. Turn right and drive .5 miles to Breazeale Interpretive Center, where the trailhead is located.

Contact: Padilla Bay National Estuarine Research Reserve, 10441 Bayview-Edison Road, Mount Vernon, WA 98273, 360/428-1558.

🔟🔟 SNOHOMISH CENTENNIAL TRAIL
1.0–17.0 mi/1.0 hr–1 day

in Snohomish County

Map 2.2, page 78

One of Washington's many rails-to-trails projects, Snohomish Centennial Trail runs along 17 miles of old railroad line. The original segment of trail ran from Lake Stevens to Snohomish, but recent years have seen lengthy additions (an extra 10 miles between Lake Stevens and Arlington). Total length of the trail now runs 17 miles and is likely to continue growing. The trail rambles through the rural countryside of Snohomish County, through open fields into dense, shady forest. Views of the surrounding Cascade Mountains are nearly constant (except when in the woods, of course). This is a very popular mountain bike and equestrian trail. The 7 miles between Lake Stevens and Snohomish are paved. Hikers can take the trail for as long as they please; since the views are fairly consistent, they can turn around at any point.

User Groups: Hikers, leashed dogs, horses, and mountain bikes. The trail is wheelchair accessible (the trail is a mix of gravel and pavement).

Open Seasons: This area is accessible year-round.

Permits: Permits are not required. Parking and access are free.

Maps: For topographic maps, ask the USGS for Snohomish and Lake Stevens.

Directions: From Seattle, drive north on I-5 to Highway 2 (Exit 194). Drive east to the town of Snohomish. The trailhead is at the intersection of Maple Street and Pine Avenue.

Contact: Snohomish County Parks and Recreation, 9623 32nd Street Southeast, Everett, WA 98205, 425/388-6600.

12 CARKEEK PARK
0.5–3.0 mi/0.5–2.0 hrs

in Seattle on Puget Sound

Map 2.2, page 78

A flurry of recent work at Carkeek Park has turned it into one of Seattle's best in-city destinations for hiking. Trail work combined with revegetative plantings along several routes has shored up eroded areas and erased evidence of overuse and abuse. Stream restoration work has turned Piper Creek, which runs through the park, into one of Seattle's most promising salmon streams. Visit Carkeek in the spring or fall and you're likely to see salmon struggling up the short creek on their way to spawn. Wetland Trail is made of well-constructed boardwalk and explores Piper Creek for .5 mile. Other trails head up into the young forest covering the slopes of Carkeek Park. North Bluff Trail hits several great viewpoints overlooking Puget Sound and the wide beach below. Carkeek is a wonderful hideaway within the city limits.

User Groups: Hikers, leashed dogs, and mountain bikes. No horses are allowed. No wheelchair access.

Open Seasons: This area is accessible year-round.

Permits: Permits are not required. Parking and access are free.

Maps: Maps of the trail system are available at the trailhead kiosk.

Directions: From I-5 in Seattle, exit at Northgate Way (Exit 173). Head west on Northgate Way (it becomes 105th Street) to Greenwood Avenue. Turn right and drive to 110th Street. Turn left and drive about 1 mile as the street becomes Northwest Carkeek Park Road and curves down to the park entrance. The trail-

head is located at the main parking lot within the park, at the end of the road.

Contact: Seattle City Parks and Recreation, 100 Dexter Avenue North, Seattle, WA 98109, 206/684-4075.

13 DISCOVERY PARK
2.8 mi/1.5 hrs

in Seattle along Puget Sound

Map 2.2, page 78

Discovery Park is a perfect model of reclaiming an abandoned military base and releasing it to public use. Seattle City Parks took over the former Fort Lawton years ago and has turned it into one of the city's premier open spaces. The park sits on a high bluff overlooking Puget Sound. Watching the sun set over the Olympic Mountains from here makes for an evening to remember. Seven miles of trail explore the park, but the highlight is 2.8-mile Nature Loop Trail. The route enjoys a little bit of everything, passing old army barracks, weaving through old forest, and hitting a number of great viewpoints. Several steep side trails offer access to the sandy beach. The beach is well worth exploring during low tide, when tidal pools and their inhabitants (crabs, mussels, and tiny fish) are exposed. Although Discovery Park is in the midst of Washington's largest city, it's easy to feel as though you're miles away.

User Groups: Hikers, leashed dogs, and mountain bikes. No horses are allowed. No wheelchair access.

Open Seasons: This area is accessible year-round.

Permits: Permits are not required. Parking and access are free.

Maps: Maps of the trail system are posted at trailheads. For a topographic map, ask the USGS for Seattle North.

Directions: From Ballard (in Seattle), drive south on 15th Avenue Northwest to Emerson Street. Turn right and drive to West Gilman Street. Turn right and drive 2 miles to the park entrance. The main trailhead at the visitors center is .2 mile inside the entrance on the left. **Contact:** Seattle City Parks and Recreation, 100 Dexter Avenue North, Seattle, WA 98109, 206/684-4075.

14 BRIDLE TRAILS
1.0–4.8 mi/1.0–2.5 hrs

in Bellevue

Map 2.2, page 78

In the heart of Bellevue, Bridle Trails State Park is like stepping into a vortex. As busy shoppers crowd into the nearby shopping mall, a small oasis of lush forest crisscrossed by miles of trails offers a peaceful getaway. Hikers be forewarned, however, as this is a popular and heavily used equestrian park. The occasional piles of horse apples are a small price for such an accessible forest getaway. Nearly 30 miles of trail form a large network within the 500 acres of park. Few specific routes exist, as the best strategy is to just start rambling through the woods. A popular choice is to hike the perimeter of the park, a 4.8-mile loop. All trails within the park are relatively flat, wide, and easy to negotiate, and some are as short as 1 mile. Bridle Trails offers great springtime hiking, when the Cascades are full of snow but trillium and other flowers are blooming within the park.

User Groups: Hikers, leashed dogs, and horses. No mountain bikes are allowed. No wheelchair access.

Open Seasons: This area is accessible year-round.

Permits: A $5 day-use fee is required to park here and is payable at the trailhead, or you can get an annual State Parks Pass for $30; contact Washington State Parks and Recreation, 360/902-8500.

Maps: Maps of the trail system are posted at trailheads. For a topographic map, ask the USGS for Bellevue North.

Directions: From I-405 in Bellevue, take Exit 17. Turn right onto 116th Avenue and drive to Northeast 53rd Street. The park entrance is

on the left. The main trailhead is near the park entrance at the main parking area.

Contact: Washington State Parks and Recreation, P.O. Box 42650, Olympia, WA 98504-2669, 360/902-8844.

15 SEWARD PARK
1.8 mi/1.0 hr

in Seattle on Lake Washington

Map 2.2, page 78

One doesn't have to go far from Seattle to enjoy a stand of magnificent old-growth forest. In fact, one needn't even leave the city limits. On Bailey Peninsula, which juts into Lake Washington in South Seattle, Seward Park contains the largest stand of forest in the city. A wide, flat trail explores the forest and makes a loop along the waterfront. The forest has many large, towering Douglas firs and beautiful madronas with their peeling bark. A rich understory of salal, thimbleberry, and salmonberry creates a cool, peaceful interior. Although there is a network of small social trails, it's best to stick to the established path to avoid getting lost. The trail cuts through the park to the shore of Lake Washington. From here, hikers can walk the shore back to the parking area.

User Groups: Hikers, leashed dogs, and mountain bikes. No horses are allowed. The trails are wheelchair accessible.

Open Seasons: This area is accessible year-round.

Permits: Permits are not required. Parking and access are free.

Maps: Maps of the trail system are posted at trailheads. For a topographic map, ask the USGS for Seattle South.

Directions: From I-5 northbound, take Swift Avenue (exit 161) toward Albro Place. Turn right onto Swift Avenue and drive to Eddy Street. Turn left and drive to Beacon Avenue South. Turn left and drive to Orcas Street. Turn right and follow this street as it becomes Lake Washington Boulevard and hits the well-signed

Seward Park. The trailhead is at the main parking area at the end of the park entrance road.

Contact: Seattle City Parks and Recreation, 100 Dexter Avenue North, Seattle, WA 98109, 206/684-4075.

16 COUGAR MOUNTAIN
0.5–6.0 mi/0.5–3.0 hrs

south of Bellevue in Cougar Mountain Regional Park

Map 2.2, page 78

The most western of the Issaquah Alps, Cougar Mountain is sanctuary in Seattle's backyard. Now encroached upon by development on all sides, the county park has become a near island of forest. Despite the close proximity of the city, Cougar Mountain and its large network of trails can feel like a step into the wilderness. A pair of trailheads offers access to roughly 30 miles of trail crisscrossing the 3,000 acres of Cougar Mountain. Red Town lies near the bottom on the south side while a second trailhead exists atop the mountain at Anti-Aircraft Peak. This area is great for wintertime hiking, when snow covers much of the Cascades. Pick up a map, available at trailheads, to choose which hike you want to do.

From Red Town, a number of hikes can be custom-made. Coal Creek Trail runs through an open forest of big-leaf maple and red alder, encountering numerous mining artifacts. This area was heavily mined for coal until as recently as the 1960s. Be sure to carry a map, for many trails venture off the main artery. Good side trips include Bagley Seam Trail, Wildside Trail, and Rainbow Town Trail.

From Anti-Aircraft Peak, Anti-Aircraft Trail delves into the open forest that covers the mountain. Deer make common company along the way, as do coyotes and mountain beavers. Again, bring a map when hiking here. The trails are unmarked and it's easy to get turned around. The trails provide several opportunities for easy or challenging loops.

User Groups: Hikers, leashed dogs, horses, and mountain bikes. No wheelchair access.

Open Seasons: This area is accessible year-round.

Permits: Permits are not required. Parking and access are free.

Maps: Maps of the trail system are posted at trailheads. For a topographic map, ask the USGS for Bellevue South.

Directions: For Red Town, take Exit 13 off I-90 and turn south on Lakemount Boulevard. Drive 3 miles to the signed entrance on the left.

For Radar Park, which allows access to Anti-Aircraft Peak, take Exit 11 off I-90. Drive south on Southeast Newport Way to 164th Avenue. Turn right and drive to Cougar Mountain Drive. Turn right and drive 1 mile to the signed entrance.

Contact: Cougar Mountain Regional Wildland Park, King County Parks and Recreation, 201 South Jackson Street, Suite 700, Seattle, WA 98104, 206/296-8687.

17 POINT DEFIANCE
1.2–4.1 mi/2.0–4.0 hrs

in Tacoma on Puget Sound

Map 2.2, page 78

The feather in Tacoma's cap, Point Defiance is a rare respite from the noise of the city. Secluded on a large point jutting into Commencement Bay, Point Defiance lays claim to miles of waterfront and some of the Puget Sound's best views. While its exact ranking is left open to debate, Point Defiance is unquestionably one of the largest urban parks in North America. Large conifer forests grace nearly 20 miles of trail, a welcome change of scenery from Tacoma's industrial core. Point Defiance is also home to the city's zoo and aquarium; the roar of an elephant shouldn't be a surprise. Tacoma locals dearly love Point Defiance.

There are several options for exploring Point Defiance. Short walks can be made along Waterfront Promenade, stretching from Owen Beach to a small assortment of restaurants. This short trail (.6 mile) is paved and accessible to wheelchairs. Other trails take on more natural forms (dirt pathways) through the forest. Running along the cliffs that mark the edge of much of the park, Square Trail Outer Loop (4.1 miles) is by far the most scenic. It visits numerous overlooks of the sound, and scenes of the Tacoma Narrow Bridge are especially great. Triangle Trail Inner Loop (3.3 miles) makes a shorter trip with a couple of viewpoints of the sound, but it mostly stays within the forest. The most popular route is Spine Trail (2.1 miles), which runs straight through the park to a commanding viewpoint of Gig Harbor and the Narrows. Whatever your choice, enjoy the shady forest and rich ecosystem; even deer live within the park.

User Groups: Hikers, leashed dogs, and mountain bikes. No horses are allowed. The Waterfront Promenade is wheelchair accessible.

Open Seasons: This area is accessible year-round.

Permits: Permits are not required. Parking and access are free.

Maps: Maps of the trail system are posted at trailheads. For a topographic map, ask the USGS for Gig Harbor.

Directions: From I-5 in Tacoma, drive west on Highway 16 to Pearl Street exit. Turn right (north) and drive about 6 miles to the road's end at Point Defiance Park. Parking and trailheads are throughout the park.

Contact: Metro Parks Tacoma, 4702 South 19th Street, Tacoma, WA 98405, 253/305-1000.

18 NISQUALLY NATIONAL WILDLIFE REFUGE
1.0–5.0 mi/0.5–2.5 hrs

north of Olympia on Puget Sound

Map 2.2, page 78

One of Western Washington's largest undisturbed estuaries, Nisqually National Wildlife Refuge is an unnoticed treasure along I-5. Here, where freshwater meets saltwater, a rich habitat exists for animals of all sorts but especially birds. Thousands of migratory birds pass through the refuge each spring and fall on their

Nisqually National Wildlife Refuge, along boardwalk

way to warming climates or feeding grounds. Mallards, widgeons, teal, Canada geese, red-tailed hawks, and great blue heron are regular sightings. Fortunately for those of us stuck on the ground, two loop trails explore this area.

Much of the refuge is an expansive collection of marshes. The wide, slow-flowing Nisqually runs through the middle, but where the river ends and the sound begins is difficult to discern. Two loop trails run through the refuge. Both feature viewing platforms and blinds, where visitors can spy on wildlife without being noticed. It's a good idea to bring a pair of binoculars. A nice visitors center is open Wednesday–Sunday year-round.

Twin Barns Trail is a short one-mile loop with many interpretive signs explaining the history and ecology of the area. It's a great introduction to the refuge and the animals that live here. The trail is completely built of wooden boardwalk, making it accessible to all. A longer hike can be made by hiking Brown Farm Dike Trail, a five-mile loop around the perimeter of the refuge. This flat trail gets users close to the Nisqually River, Puget Sound, and McAllister Creek.

User Groups: Hikers only. No dogs, horses, or mountain bikes are allowed. The shorter of the two loops is wheelchair accessible.

Open Seasons: This area is accessible year-round.

Permits: A $3 day-use fee is required to park here and is payable at the trailhead.

Maps: Maps of the trail system are available at the visitor center. For a topographic map, ask the USGS for Nisqually.

Directions: From Seattle, drive south on I-5 to Nisqually (Exit 114). Turn right (west) onto Brown Farm Road and drive .3 mile to the well-signed trailhead.

Contact: Nisqually National Wildlife Refuge, 100 Brown Farm Road, Olympia, WA 98516, 360/753-9467.

Chapter 3

© SCOTT LEONARD

The Northern Cascades

The Northern Cascades

This region is home to a sizable chunk of Washington's greatest forests, mountains, and rivers. Hundreds of trails crisscross the enormous region, and nearly every one of them is great and exciting. It's truly hard to go wrong when setting out in the North Cascades. It's all a scenic playground, from ancient old-growth forests to alpine meadows, from wild and rushing rivers to enormous glaciers. (There are more glaciers here than in the rest of the lower 48 states combined!) The North Cascades are the playground of the Puget Sound region, with tons of trails less than two hours away.

Thanks to careful and diligent conservation, much of the North Cascades' natural beauty remains for us to enjoy. The region is home to one national park (North Cascades) and eight federally protected wildernesses (Alpine Lakes, Boulder River, Glacier Peak, Henry M. Jackson, Lake Chelan–Sawtooth, Mount Baker, Noisy-Diobsud, and Pasayten). Together, they make more than 2.5 million acres of protected land, possibly with more on the way. Another wilderness (the Big Sky, near Skykomish) has wide support from local communities and congresspeople and is very close to becoming official. (Unfortunately, a conservative congressman from California has repeatedly blocked this bill.)

The Alpine Lakes Wilderness offers the most easily accessed trails. Situated between Interstate 90 and Highway 2, many of these trailheads are less than a 90-minute drive from Seattle. Alpine Lakes is home to—you guessed it—hundreds of alpine lakes (technically subalpine). On the north side is the town of Leavenworth, up for debate as either cute or campy. Here, all buildings are required to incorporate Bavarian architecture, and it is certainly unlike any other town in the state (or outside of the Alps). It's interesting, to say the least. When you're itching to get outdoors for a quick hike, Alpine Lakes is a great place to start your search.

On the north side of Highway 2 are Henry M. Jackson and Glacier Peak Wildernesses. These two areas take up much of the North Cascades' central portion, about 670,000 acres. With glistening white glaciers covering its 10,541-foot summit, Glacier Peak is naturally the central focus of the area. Cady Ridge (both of them), Image Lake, and Buck Creek Pass are just a few of the excellent hikes in these wildernesses. These areas are also easily accessed by the Mountain Loop Highway. Cutting into the Cascades from Darrington, the route makes a large loop around the Boulder River Wilderness. This area is home to easy trails (Lake 22, Heather Lake, Goat Flats) and difficult trails alike (Mount Dickerson, Stujack Pass, Poodle Dog Pass).

Even with all these attractions, this isn't even half of what the North Cascades have to offer. The Mount Baker Wilderness, for one, contains alpine meadows that are absolutely amazing in July (when they're alive with wildflowers) and completely delicious in late August (when they're smothered in huckleberries). The insane beauty of Mount Baker and Mount Shuksan can almost go without saying. Head up Route 542 out of Bellingham for access to trails like Lake Ann, Hannegan Pass, and Chain Lakes.

Although North Cascades National Park and the Pasayten Wilderness are actually neighbors, they seem to be one entity. These two areas extend along a 70-mile stretch of the Canadian border, totaling 1,150,000 acres. Access is via Route 20, where glacier-capped mountains and old forests are regular sights from the road. Such a big area requires longer trips, and there are plenty to be found here. Day hikes to Driveway Butte and Desolation Peak are certainly possible, but such a short taste will definitely leave you wanting to spend at least four or five days on the trail. Copper Ridge, Whatcom Pass, Devil's Dome Loop, Boundary Trail, and Cathedral Basin are classics of the region. Folks on their way to the Pasayten will love the town of Winthrop, where the theme is Old West. A stop at Winthrop Brewing Company's local brewpub is a must, especially after your hike!

Finally, the east side of the Cascades is drier and often a great destination when the west side is rainy. (Like the Olympics, the Cascades act like a big squeegee, forcing moist air from the ocean to release most of its rain on the west side.) Many of the wilderness areas stretch across the Cascade Crest and have portions that benefit from this rain shadow effect. Highway 97 runs along the east side of the Cascades and provides access to many of these dry trails. The Lake Chelan–Sawtooth Wilderness is the heart and soul of the east side, with high, craggy peaks and mind-boggling views.

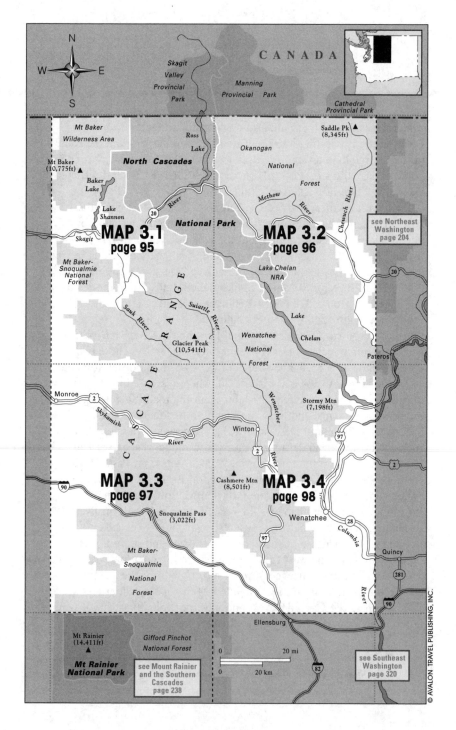

Map 3.1

Hikes 1–48
Pages 99–129

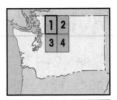

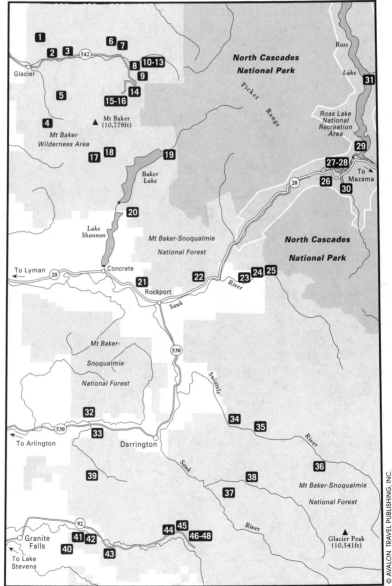

Map 3.2

Hikes 49–97
Pages 130–160

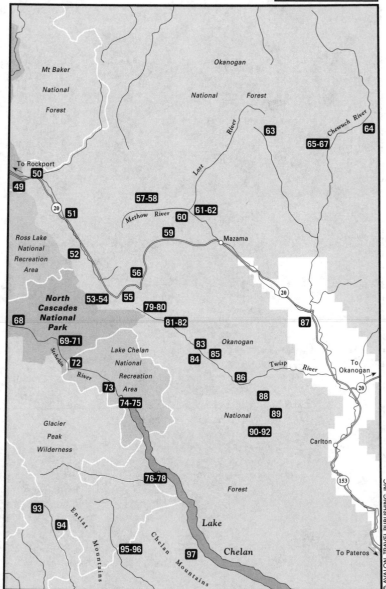

Map 3.3

Hikes 98-142
Pages 161-189

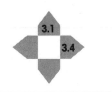

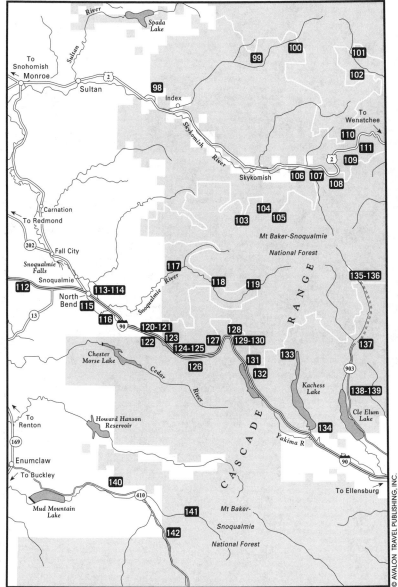

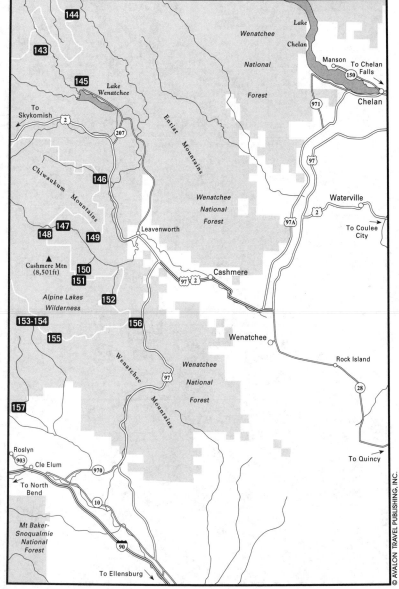

Map 3.4

Hikes 143–157
Pages 189-199

1 DAMFINO LAKES
1.4–19.6 mi/1.0–5.0 hrs

east of Bellingham in Mount Baker–Snoqualmie National Forest

Map 3.1, page 95

Damfino Lakes are merely a starting point for hiking and exploration, as Damfino Lakes serve as a junction to several beautiful hikes. Canyon Ridge, regarded highly by the few who know of it, is accessible only via this trail. Excelsior Ridge, normally a long, steep climb, is achieved much more easily via Damfino Lakes Trail. Damfino Lakes Trail is more about what lies beyond the lakes than the lakes themselves.

Damfino Lakes Trail climbs gently through forest to the pair of lakes (.7 mile). From here, turn north and encounter the high meadow run of Canyon Ridge Trail (up to 9.8 miles one-way). Turn north at the lakes to head to Cowap Peak (elevation 5,658 feet), a summit for great views. A map and compass are highly recommended for these two trails.

Turn south at the lakes to climb gradually to the vast meadows of Excelsior Ridge (3 miles). This is a quicker and much easier shortcut to the ridge (one-third of the elevation gain and half the distance than from the traditional trailhead). So don't head for Damfino Lakes and stop there; the two small lakes are just the beginning.

User Groups: Canyon Ridge Trail is open to hikers, leashed dogs, horses, llamas, bicycles, and motorcycles. South of Damfino Lakes is open to hikers and leashed dogs. Boundary Way Trail is open to hikers, leashed dogs, and llamas. No wheelchair access.

Open Seasons: This area is usually accessible August–September.

Permits: A federal Northwest Forest Pass is required to park here.

Maps: For a map of Mount Baker–Snoqualmie National Forest, contact the Outdoor Recreation Information Center at the downtown Seattle REI. For topographic maps, ask Green Trails for No. 13, Mount Baker, or ask the USGS for Bearpaw Mountain.

Directions: From Bellingham, drive 36 miles east on Highway 542 (Mount Baker Highway) to Canyon Creek Road (Forest Service Road 31). Turn left (north) and drive 14.5 miles to the trailhead, on the right side at a sharp turn in the road.

Contact: Mount Baker–Snoqualmie National Forest, Glacier Public Service Center, Glacier, WA 98244, 360/599-2714.

2 CHURCH MOUNTAIN
8.4 mi/6.0 hrs

east of Bellingham in Mount Baker–Snoqualmie National Forest

Map 3.1, page 95

One of the North Fork Nooksack River's finest hikes is fittingly one of its first. Church Mountain Trail rises through old-growth forest to an enormous basin and peak with views over the broad river valley to Mount Baker, Mount Shuksan, and much of Canada. It's not an easy height to achieve, as the 3,600-foot climb in just over four miles will attest. The trail offers enough wonder and inspiring views to more than make up for any weariness in the legs.

Church Mountain Trail starts off in a mean fashion, with a breath-stealing climb of switchbacks. These first two miles are mostly deep within virgin forest, with big trees providing welcome shade on warm, sunny days. The trail breaks out into the mountain's large glacial cirque, covered in subalpine meadows and streams. During July and early August, basin walls come afire with blooming wildflowers while heather and lupine thrive in the basin. This is a good turnaround for some, with Mount Baker directly across the basin, a real postcard view.

The final two miles are a steep ascent up basin walls, at times on tricky footing. This section is hot, dry, and exposed; plenty of water is a must. From atop Church Mountain, the views are panoramic and a topographic map is a necessity to identify the numerous mountains.

User Groups: Hikers and leashed dogs. No

horses or mountain bikes are allowed. No wheelchair access.

Open Seasons: This trail is usually accessible mid-July–early October.

Permits: A federal Northwest Forest Pass is required to park here.

Maps: For a map of Mount Baker–Snoqualmie National Forest, contact the Outdoor Recreation Information Center at the downtown Seattle REI. For topographic maps, ask Green Trails for No. 13, Mount Baker, or ask the USGS for Bearpaw Mountain.

Directions: From Bellingham, drive east 38 miles on Highway 542 (Mount Baker Highway) to Church Mountain Road (Forest Service Road 3040). Turn left (north) and drive 2.5 miles to the trailhead at road's end.

Contact: Mount Baker–Snoqualmie National Forest, Glacier Public Service Center, Glacier, WA 98244, 360/599-2714.

❸ EXCELSIOR RIDGE
11.2 mi/8.0 hrs

east of Bellingham in Mount Baker Wilderness of Mount Baker–Snoqualmie National Forest

Map 3.1, page 95

In a land where tough ascents and endless switchbacks are an accepted way of life on the trail, this hike makes others look tame. Excelsior Trail and Welcome Pass Trail climb from the valley floor to Excelsior Ridge, covered in meadows with views of mountains in every direction. Connecting them is High Divide Trail, 4.5 miles of ridgeline meadows. There's very little you won't see along this outstanding route.

To complete the whole loop, you must arrange a drop-off between the two trailheads. Better yet, drop off mountain bikes at the upper trailhead (Welcome Pass) and pick them up after hiking for an easy ride back to the car. For a one-way up-and-back trip, Welcome Pass is the best bet. Excelsior and Welcome Pass Trails both entail many switchbacks at an excruciating grade. The trails are mostly forested by old-growth, but they are nonetheless dry and hot.

The two trails are connected by High Divide Trail, which runs for 4.5 miles along the ridge. Views of Mount Baker and Mount Shuksan, just across the Nooksack River, are outstanding. The trail runs through seemingly endless meadows of wildflowers. Tomyhoi, Border Peaks, and a lot of Canada are visible from up here. Its south-facing orientation means that snow melts sooner here, making this one of the first trails to open in the valley.

User Groups: Hikers, leashed dogs, horses (horses allowed August 1–November 1), and llamas. No mountain bikes are allowed. No wheelchair access.

Open Seasons: This trail is usually accessible mid-June–early October.

Permits: A federal Northwest Forest Pass is required to park here.

Maps: For a map of Mount Baker–Snoqualmie National Forest, contact the Outdoor Recreation Information Center at the downtown Seattle REI. For topographic maps, ask Green Trails for No. 13, Mount Baker, and No. 14, Mount Shuksan, or ask the USGS for Bearpaw Mountain.

Directions: From Bellingham, drive east 41 miles on Highway 542 (Mount Baker Highway) to an unsigned trailhead on the left (north) side of the highway. This is Excelsior Pass Trailhead and is immediately past Nooksack Falls.

For Welcome Pass Trailhead, drive another 4.5 miles to Forest Service Road 3060. Turn left and drive 1 mile to the trailhead at road's end.

Contact: Mount Baker–Snoqualmie National Forest, Glacier Public Service Center, Glacier, WA 98244, 360/599-2714.

❹ HELIOTROPE RIDGE
5.0 mi/3.0 hrs

east of Bellingham in Mount Baker Wilderness of Mount Baker–Snoqualmie National Forest

Map 3.1, page 95

One of the best opportunities to see and hear a living glacier lies at the end of this popular trail. Heliotrope Ridge Trail ascends through beautiful forests to the terminus of the Coleman Glaciers. This is the most popular route for climbers who seek the summit of Mount Baker, which towers above the route. Huge glacial moraines shape the terrain above timberline, including the brightly layered Chromatic Moraine at the head of Glacier Creek. There's no shortage of hikers along the trail, but that should not detract from the great views and the ability to feel the mass of the slowly moving glaciers.

The trail leaves the trailhead and steadily ascends through beautiful forests of old-growth timber, crossing several ice-cold creeks. After two miles, the trail forks. The left fork crosses Heliotrope Creek and scrambles up to an overlook near an arm of the Coleman Glacier, where it terminates into a morass of mud and ice. Colorful Chromatic Moraine is just across the way.

The right fork at the junction climbs to a rocky terrain of wildflowers and whistling marmots. Mount Baker towers above a wide open area of scrambling opportunities. Climbers continue from here to the Coleman Glacier base camp. Be aware that the trickle of a stream you crossed in the morning may be a river by the afternoon. Plan carefully. Also, exploration on glaciers is not recommended without proper equipment and expertise—glacial crevasses prefer to swallow the foolish.

User Groups: Hikers and leashed dogs. No horses or mountain bikes are allowed. No wheelchair access.

Open Seasons: This trail is accessible August–early October.

Permits: A federal Northwest Forest Pass is required to park here.

Maps: For a map of Mount Baker-Snoqualmie National Forest, contact the Outdoor Recreation Information Center at the downtown Seattle REI. For topographic maps, ask Green Trails for No. 13, Mount Baker, or ask the USGS for Mount Baker and Goat Mountain.

Directions: From Bellingham, drive east 34 miles on Highway 542 (Mount Baker Highway) to Glacier Creek Road (Forest Service Road 39). Turn right (south) and drive 8.5 miles to the signed trailhead on the left.

Contact: Mount Baker-Snoqualmie National Forest, Glacier Public Service Center, Glacier, WA 98244, 360/599-2714.

5 SKYLINE DIVIDE
7.0 mi/4.0 hrs

east of Bellingham in Mount Baker Wilderness of Mount Baker-Snoqualmie National Forest

Map 3.1, page 95

Catch a sunset from Skyline Divide, and you'll never stop talking about it. This long ridge extending from Mount Baker is covered in meadows. Views stretch from the North Cascades to Puget Sound and from Mount Baker to British Columbia. The Skyline Trail truly lives in the sky.

The road to the trailhead was washed out at the time of publication; call the ranger station in Glacier for an update. Skyline Trail climbs two miles through grand forest of Pacific silver fir and western hemlock. The grade is constant and not difficult. Before long, the trail reaches the divide, and Mount Baker seems close enough to touch. The North Cascades unfold to the east for miles, and there is no end to the peaks one can identify. The ridge is dry and hot, so bring plenty of water.

Skyline Trail carries on south for another 1.5 miles, going up and down with the ridge and heading ever closer to Baker. To the west are the San Juan Islands in the sound, and Vancouver, British Columbia, is also discernible. Sunsets from here dazzle and are well worth the night hike down. Very little camping is found on the ridge; consider a hike by moonlight another part of a remarkable experience.

User Groups: Hikers, leashed dogs, and horses. No mountain bikes are allowed. No wheelchair access.

Open Seasons: This trail is accessible July–early October.

Permits: A federal Northwest Forest Pass is required to park here.

Maps: For a map of Mount Baker–Snoqualmie National Forest, contact the Outdoor Recreation Information Center at the downtown Seattle REI. For topographic maps, ask Green Trails for No. 13, Mount Baker, or ask the USGS for Mount Baker and Bearpaw Mountain.

Directions: From Bellingham, drive east 34 miles on Highway 542 (Mount Baker Highway) to Glacier Creek Road (Forest Service Road 39). Turn right (south) and quickly turn left onto Forest Service Road 37. Drive 15 miles to the trailhead at road's end.

Contact: Mount Baker–Snoqualmie National Forest, Glacier Public Service Center, Glacier, WA 98244, 360/599-2714.

6 YELLOW ASTER BUTTE
7.2 mi/3.5 hrs

east of Bellingham in Mount Baker Wilderness of Mount Baker–Snoqualmie National Forest

Map 3.1, page 95

This trail to the high country offers just about everything one could ask for in a trail. Wildflowers and huckleberries fill wide open meadows. A basin of subalpine lakes opens to reveal outstanding views of Baker and Shuksan, and a scramble yields Tomyhoi Peak. Best of all,

the trail starts high, saving energy for high-country rambling. Bring your swimsuit, as the lakes are too enticing to turn down. It's hard to imagine what's missing in this great subalpine parkland.

The route begins on Tomyhoi Lake Trail, which switchbacks through avalanche chutes and thick brush to a signed junction (1.4 miles). Take a left and climb through open meadows with non-stop views to the lake basin. Indian paintbrush, monkey flowers, and penstemon are just a few of the flowers you'll find blooming in late July. Facing south toward the sun, this trail can be very hot; bring extra water or a filter.

The basin is full of numerous small lakes, perfect for a dip. The meadows are delicate and deteriorating because of heavy use; camp only in designated sites and follow strict Leave-No-Trace principles. For the hardy, a well-used path leads to the top of Yellow Aster Butte and big views of Mount Larrabee, Border Peaks, and Mount Baker. Yellow Aster Butte is a must-do for dedicated North Cascades hikers.

User Groups: Hikers and leashed dogs. No horses or mountain bikes are allowed. No wheelchair access.

Open Seasons: This trail is accessible July–early October.

American (R) and Canadian (L) Border Peaks, from Yellow Aster Butte

© SCOTT LEONARD

Permits: A federal Northwest Forest Pass is required to park here.

Maps: For a map of Mount Baker–Snoqualmie National Forest, contact the Outdoor Recreation Information Center at the downtown Seattle REI. For topographic maps, ask Green Trails for No. 14, Mount Shuksan, or ask the USGS for Mount Larrabee.

Directions: From Bellingham, drive east 46 miles on Highway 542 (Mount Baker Highway) to Twin Lakes Road (Forest Service Road 3065), just beyond the Department of Transportation facility. Turn left (north) and drive 5 miles to the signed trailhead (where the road makes several switchbacks on an exposed slope).

Contact: Mount Baker–Snoqualmie National Forest, Glacier Public Service Center, Glacier, WA 98244, 360/599-2714.

7 WINCHESTER MOUNTAIN
3.8 mi/2.5 hrs

east of Bellingham in Mount Baker Wilderness of Mount Baker–Snoqualmie National Forest

Map 3.1, page 95

Winchester Mountain is home to a back-country favorite: an abandoned fire lookout. Built in 1935, the lookout is no longer used by the Forest Service but receives regular maintenance from a dedicated volunteer group. From up here, much of the North Cascades, in Washington and Canada, are revealed. Add to the spectacular views an enjoyable trail, flush with ripe huckleberries in September, and you have a great trail.

Winchester Mountain Trail is accessible at Twin Lakes (elevation 5,200 feet), an old base camp for miners and prospectors. The trail climbs steeply through meadows and patches of alpine trees. Be aware that the upper part of the trail is home to a hazardous snowfield that does not melt until late summer. Don't cross it without an ice ax. Otherwise it's best to drop below the snowfield and reconnect to the trail at the other side. The trail is a constant climb, but it's only 1,300 feet gain in about

two miles. Bring water and a tolerance for other hikers.

User Groups: Hikers and leashed dogs. No horses or mountain bikes are allowed. No wheelchair access.

Open Seasons: This trail is usually accessible late July–early October. (September is the ideal month to hike the trail, with the best chances of avoiding the snow field.)

Permits: A federal Northwest Forest Pass is required to park here.

Maps: For a map of Mount Baker–Snoqualmie National Forest, contact the Outdoor Recreation Information Center at the downtown Seattle REI. For topographic maps, ask Green Trails for No. 14, Mount Shuksan, or ask the USGS for Mount Larrabee.

Directions: From Bellingham, drive east 46 miles on Highway 542 (Mount Baker Highway) to Twin Lakes Road (Forest Service Road 3065), just beyond the Department of Transportation facility. Turn left (north) and drive 7 miles to the signed trailhead at road's end. The last two miles are not recommended for passenger cars. A four-wheel-drive vehicle with high clearance is highly recommended.

Contact: Mount Baker–Snoqualmie National Forest, Glacier Public Service Center, Glacier, WA 98244, 360/599-2714.

8 GOAT MOUNTAIN
6.4 mi/4.5 hrs

east of Bellingham in Mount Baker Wilderness of Mount Baker–Snoqualmie National Forest

Map 3.1, page 95

When June rolls around and the urge to explore the high country is strong, Goat Mountain is your sanctuary. The trail to this former lookout site lies on the south side of the mountain, making it one of the first to melt out in the summer. With views of Mount Shuksan and countless other peaks and ridges, this is a great first hike of the season. The climb is extremely strenuous, with more than 2,900 feet of elevation gain in just three miles, so it's a sure way to test your fitness for the coming summer of hiking.

Goat Mountain Trail is a steady climb up the side of the mountain. The first part passes through typically great forests of the Nooksack Valley. The trail enters Mount Baker Wilderness (2 miles) just as the forest gives way to open meadows. Huckleberries are as plentiful as the views of Shuksan and Baker. Be sure to bring water on this taxing ascent, as you won't find any on the way other than old patches of snow.

Below the summit sits an old lookout site, abandoned and torn down long ago. The views are excellent, and a long lunch break is well deserved after the hike. Those who are feeling adventurous and have the extra energy can continue scrambling up the ridge to the true summit, where the views only get better.

User Groups: Hikers, leashed dogs, and horses (horses allowed August 1–November 1). No mountain bikes are allowed. No wheelchair access.

Open Seasons: This trail is accessible late-June–October.

Permits: A federal Northwest Forest Pass is required to park here.

Maps: For a map of Mount Baker–Snoqualmie National Forest, contact the Outdoor Recreation Information Center at the downtown Seattle REI. For topographic maps, ask Green Trails for No. 14, Mount Shuksan, or ask the USGS for Mount Larrabee.

Directions: From Bellingham, drive east 46 miles on Highway 542 (Mount Baker Highway) to Hannegan Pass Road (Forest Service Road 32). Turn left and drive 2.5 miles to the trailhead on the left side. Parking is on the left immediately before the trailhead.

Contact: Mount Baker–Snoqualmie National Forest, Glacier Public Service Center, Glacier, WA 98244, 360/599-2714.

9 NOOKSACK CIRQUE
9.0 mi/5.0 hrs

east of Bellingham in Mount Baker Wilderness of Mount Baker–Snoqualmie National Forest

Map 3.1, page 95

Unlike any other trail in this valley, Nooksack Cirque Trail is an easy river hike with little elevation gain. This is a welcome respite from the area's straight-up, straight-down trails. Miles of forest rambling delivers hikers to Nooksack Cirque, one of the most easily accessible and largest glacial cirques you'll ever lay eyes upon.

Nooksack Cirque Trail starts by fording Ruth Creek (cross downed logs for a drier experience) and follows an old logging road. It's second-growth forest until the road ends at the wilderness boundary (3 miles), where old-growth forest starts. The two forests are hugely different. Enormous western hemlocks and Pacific silver firs give the feeling that one has been suddenly transported to the Olympic rainforests. Look for colonnades, straight lines of three or four ancient trees growing from a decomposed log.

The final mile is not maintained and becomes brushier as one goes along. Several times the trail breaks out onto the riverbed and route-finding is necessary (but not difficult—head upstream!). At the end sits the large, open cirque beneath the Nooksack Glacier. The ice-scraped cliffs covered in waterfalls are impressive if you're willing to endure the bushwhack. There are two large campsites about .5 mile inside the wilderness boundary.

User Groups: Hikers and leashed dogs. No horses or mountain bikes are allowed. No wheelchair access.

Open Seasons: This trail is usually accessible year-round.

Permits: A federal Northwest Forest Pass is required to park here.

Maps: For a map of Mount Baker–Snoqualmie National Forest, contact the Outdoor Recreation Information Center at the downtown Seattle REI. For topographic maps, ask Green

Trails for No. 14, Mount Shuksan, or ask the USGS for Mount Larrabee, Mount Sefrit, and Mount Shuksan.

Directions: From Bellingham, drive east 46 miles on Highway 542 (Mount Baker Highway) to Forest Service Road 32, just before you cross the Nooksack River. Turn left and drive 2 miles to Forest Service Road 34. Turn right and drive 1.5 miles to the trailhead at road's end.

Contact: Mount Baker–Snoqualmie National Forest, Glacier Public Service Center, Glacier, WA 98244, 360/599-2714.

10 HANNEGAN PASS
10.0 mi/5.0 hrs

east of Bellingham in Mount Baker Wilderness of Mount Baker–Snoqualmie National Forest

Map 3.1, page 95

More than a backcountry entrance to North Cascades National Park, Hannegan Trail is absolutely beautiful to boot. Passing beneath the looming Nooksack Ridge up to Hannegan Pass and down to Boundary Camp, the trail is one of the most scenic valley hikes anywhere. Leading to Copper Ridge, Chilliwack River, and Whatcom Pass, Hannegan Trail is a popular segment of longer treks. But the trail reaches Hannegan Peak, one of the best vistas in all of the North Cascades.

Hannegan Trail follows Ruth Creek back to its headwaters beneath Ruth Mountain. Much of the route is open avalanche chutes, revealing the enormous, vertical ridges on either side. Soon, the 7,100-foot Ruth Mountain appears with its enormous glacier and glacially polished walls. Beneath Ruth is Hannegan Camp (3.5 miles), a large and picturesque campground.

Hannegan Trail climbs to the meadows of Hannegan Pass (4 miles) and down to Boundary Camp (5 miles). At the pass is Hannegan Peak Trail, a steep pitch through meadows to the 6,186-foot peak. The views are grand, including Ruth, Mount Shuksan, Mount Baker, the Picketts, and countless other Cascade peaks. Just about every footstep along this hike is un-

believably beautiful. To hike this trail and not visit Hannegan Peak is a missed opportunity.

User Groups: Hikers, leashed dogs, and horses. No mountain bikes are allowed. No wheelchair access.

Open Seasons: This trail is usually accessible July–early October.

Permits: A federal Northwest Forest Pass is required to park here. Overnight stays within the national park (Boundary Camp or beyond) require backcountry camping permits, which are available at Glacier Public Service Center. No permit is required for staying at Hannegan Camp.

Maps: For a map of Mount Baker–Snoqualmie National Forest, contact the Outdoor Recreation Information Center at the downtown Seattle REI. For topographic maps, ask Green Trails for No. 14, Mount Shuksan, or ask the USGS for Mount Sefrit.

Directions: From Bellingham, drive east 46 miles on Highway 542 (Mount Baker Highway) to Hannegan Pass Road (Forest Service Road 32). Turn left and drive 5 miles to the signed trailhead at road's end.

Contact: Mount Baker–Snoqualmie National Forest, Glacier Public Service Center, Glacier, WA 98244, 360/599-2714.

11 COPPER RIDGE LOOP
34.5 mi/4–5 days

east of Bellingham in North Cascades National Park

Map 3.1, page 95

Strike up a conversation with a North Cascades hiking veteran and you'll invariably be asked, "Have you done Copper Ridge yet?" This backcountry trek maintains cultlike popularity, thanks to being one of the most scenic and beloved routes in the state. Views and meadows abound along this high-country route. Several lakes highlight the ridge run, which also leads to an old lookout. The wild ridge is isolated in the upper national park and makes an excellent loop with Chilliwack Trail.

Copper Ridge is accessible via Hannegan

Pass (see previous listing). At Boundary Camp (5 miles) the trail splits—up to Copper Ridge and down to Chilliwack River (see listing in this chapter). Your direction will depend upon available camp reservations (the National Park Service requires permits to camp within the park). Much of the trail enjoys open meadows. Great views, but it's hot and dry, too; prepare to pack water.

Copper Ridge Trail leaves Boundary Camp and climbs around Hells Gorge to the ridge. Silesia Camp and Egg Lake Camp (8.2 miles) offer great camps and a refreshing dip in Egg Lake. An old lookout offers the route's highest point at 6,260 feet (10.7 miles). Below the long arm of Copper Mountain lies Copper Lake Camp (11.9 miles). The trail continues four additional miles on the ridge before dropping to Chilliwack River (19.4 miles). Become a North Cascades veteran and make plans for Copper Ridge.

User Groups: Hikers and horses. No dogs or mountain bikes are allowed. No wheelchair access.

Open Seasons: This trail is usually accessible August–September.

Permits: A federal Northwest Forest Pass is required to park here. Overnight stays within the national park require backcountry camping permits, which are are available at Glacier Public Service Center.

Maps: For a map of North Cascades National Park, contact the Outdoor Recreation Information Center at the downtown Seattle REI. For a topographic map, ask Green Trails for No. 14, Mount Shuksan, and No. 15, Mount Challenger, or ask the USGS for Mount Sefrit and Copper Mountain.

Directions: From Bellingham, drive east 46 miles on Highway 542 (Mount Baker Highway) to Hannegan Pass Road (Forest Service Road 32). Turn left and drive 5 miles to the signed trailhead at road's end.

Contact: North Cascades National Park, Wilderness Information Center, 7280 Ranger Station Road, Marblemount, WA 98267, 360/873-4500;

Mount Baker–Snoqualmie National Forest, Glacier Public Service Center, Glacier, WA 98244, 360/599-2714.

12 WHATCOM PASS
34.0 mi/4 days
east of Bellingham in North Cascades National Park

Map 3.1, page 95

The legend of Whatcom Pass frequently and quickly makes its way around hiking circles. It's not a legend of Sasquatch or a miner's ghost, but instead true accounts of the beauty found at Whatcom Pass. Nestled at the base of the Picket Range, Whatcom Pass enjoys the North Cascades' most impressive range. Some old-timers even proclaim Whatcom Pass the king of all backcountry destinations. That sounds about right.

The route follows the beautiful Hannegan Pass and Chilliwack River Trails (see listings in this chapter) to Brush Creek (12.3 miles). By this point, the scenery should have knocked your boots off. Brush Creek Trail splits from the Chilliwack and climbs five miles to the subalpine splendor of Whatcom Pass. Graybeal Camp sits at 12.3 miles, but pass it up for a camp near the pass. Take care in this delicate ecosystem by staying on established trails and avoiding campfires. Appreciate the view of Mount Challenger and its enormous glacier. Make great side trips by scrambling north to Tapto Lakes or south along the Whatcom Arm.

User Groups: Hikers only. No dogs, horses, or mountain bikes are allowed. No wheelchair access.

Open Seasons: This trail is accessible August–September.

Permits: A federal Northwest Forest Pass is required to park here. Overnight stays within the national park require reservations and backcountry camping permits, which are available at Glacier Public Service Center.

Maps: For a map of North Cascades National Park, contact the Outdoor Recreation Information Center at the downtown Seattle REI.

For topographic maps, ask Green Trails for No. 14, Mount Shuksan, and No. 15, Mount Challenger, or ask the USGS for Mount Sefrit, Copper Mountain, Mount Redoubt, Mount Challenger, and Mount Blum.

Directions: From Bellingham, drive east 46 miles on Highway 542 (Mount Baker Highway) to Hannegan Pass Road (Forest Service Road 32). Turn left and drive 5 miles to the signed trailhead at road's end.

Contact: North Cascades National Park, Wilderness Information Center, 7280 Ranger Station Road, Marblemount, WA 98267, 360/873-4500; Mount Baker-Snoqualmie National Forest, Glacier Public Service Center, Glacier, WA 98244, 360/599-2714.

13 CHILLIWACK RIVER
40.0 mi/4 days

east of Bellingham in North Cascades National Park

Map 3.1, page 95

As the miles pass underfoot on Chilliwack River Trail, the solitude of the wilderness grows ever more lonely. Most often hiked to reach Copper Ridge or Whatcom Pass, Chilliwack River Trail is grand by itself, too. Miles of large old-growth forest tower over the trail, pleasantly following the rambling river. This is real wilderness, where bears and elk are regular hiking partners. Regardless of one's destination, Chilliwack River Trail is an enjoyable journey.

Chilliwack Trail is accessible via Boundary Camp on Hannegan Pass Trail (5 miles). Chilliwack Trail drops through ever-thickening forest to Copper Creek Camp (8.5 miles) and U.S. Cabin Camp (11.1 miles). The trail crosses the river at one of the state's unique river crossings: A cable car whisks hikers above the river to the opposite shore.

Brush Creek Trail (12.9 miles) ventures south up to Whatcom Pass (12.9 miles) while Copper Ridge Trail climbs to the west (16.5 miles). Beyond this point, the trail rambles through beautiful lowland river forests, where green dominates the scenery. Bear Creek Camp (18.3 miles) and

Little Chilliwack Camp (20.7 miles) offer campsites before entering Canada (24 miles one-way). Few ever make it so deep into this wild place. **User Groups:** Hikers and horses. No dogs or mountain bikes are allowed. No wheelchair access.

Open Seasons: This trail is accessible from Hannegan Pass July–September and from Canada nearly year-round.

Permits: A federal Northwest Forest Pass is required to park at the Hannegan Pass trailhead. Overnight stays within the national park require backcountry camping permits.

Maps: For a map of North Cascades National Park, contact the Outdoor Recreation Information Center at the downtown Seattle REI. For topographic maps, ask Green Trails for No. 14, Mount Shuksan, and No. 15, Mount Challenger, or ask the USGS for Mount Sefrit and Copper Mountain.

Directions: From Bellingham, drive east 46 miles on Highway 542 (Mount Baker Highway) to Hannegan Pass Road (Forest Service Road 32). Turn left and drive 5 miles to the signed trailhead at road's end.

Contact: North Cascades National Park, Wilderness Information Center, 7280 Ranger Station Road, Marblemount, WA 98267, 360/873-4500.

14 LAKE ANN
8.6 mi/6.0 hrs

east of Bellingham in Mount Baker Wilderness of Mount Baker-Snoqualmie National Forest

Map 3.1, page 95

When you finally crest the meadowy pass and spot Lake Ann lying beneath Mount Shuksan, you will know that you have arrived someplace special. Rocky alpine meadows surround this high-country lake, while the towering cliffs and glaciers of Mount Shuksan stand above. The journey is through four miles of old-growth forest and berry-filled meadows. This is one of the best hikes in an area full of beautiful country.

Lake Ann Trail quickly drops through forest

Mount Baker, from along Lake Ann Trail, a great hike

into Swift Creek Basin (1.5 miles). Despite an average of 700 inches of snow each winter, mountain hemlocks swell massively. In the basin, acres of meadows brim with huckleberries, making this a sweet hike in August. The trail crosses Swift Creek (look downstream to Mount Baker) and climbs two miles through more meadows to a pass above Lake Ann.

Surrounded by alpine meadows and mountain views, Lake Ann presents a nice place to rest awhile. Take a dip in the cool water while watching marmots play in the meadows. On Mount Shuksan, the Curtis Glaciers can be heard breaking and settling in the summer heat. There is plenty of camping space, but it can go quickly. This trail is a perfect midweek or late-season trip.

User Groups: Hikers and leashed dogs. No horses or mountain bikes are allowed. No wheelchair access.

Open Seasons: This area is usually accessible July–early October.

Permits: A federal Northwest Forest Pass is required to park here.

Maps: For a map of Mount Baker–Snoqualmie National Forest, contact the Outdoor Recreation Information Center at the downtown Seattle REI. For topographic maps, ask Green Trails for No. 14, Mount Shuksan, or ask the USGS for Shuksan Arm.

Directions: From Bellingham, drive east 56 miles on Highway 542 (Mount Baker Highway) to the signed trailhead on the left, past Heather Meadows Visitor Center.

Contact: Mount Baker–Snoqualmie National Forest, Glacier Public Service Center, Glacier, WA 98244, 360/599-2714.

15 GALENA CHAIN LAKES
6.5 mi/4.0 hrs

east of Bellingham in Mount Baker Wilderness of Mount Baker–Snoqualmie National Forest

Map 3.1, page 95

Galena Chain Lakes have been a backcountry destination for hikers and backpackers for generations. Nestled among towering mountains, these four lakes are picturesque examples of the subalpine. Chain Lakes are immersed in meadows and huckleberries and offer lots of great camping. They can be fished for dinner as well. This trail is great for families and is accessible for both day hikers visiting Heather Meadows as well as overnight backpackers.

The route is best done as a loop, starting at Artist Point. Chain Lakes Trail heads toward Ptarmigan Ridge before turning right at a signed junction (1 mile). Before you know it, you've reached Mazama Lake (2 miles). There are four choice camps here, set on the small ridge between the lake and Mount Baker. The trail makes its way to large Iceberg Lake, which sits below the vertical walls of Table Mountain. Reportedly, the fish are biggest here. A side trail leads to four camps along Hayes Lake, which requires a bit of up and down.

To exit the basin, the trail climbs to a saddle between Table and Mazama Dome, the best vista of the trail, and drops two steep miles to the visitors center. Wild Goose Trail returns hikers to Artist Point, but drivers passing through here are always happy to pick up a few riders for the two-mile drive. This is a popular trail in season.

User Groups: Hikers and leashed dogs. No horses or mountain bikes are allowed. No wheelchair access.

Open Seasons: This trail is usually accessible July–September.

Permits: A federal Northwest Forest Pass is required to park here.

Maps: For a map of Mount Baker–Snoqualmie National Forest, contact the Outdoor Recreation Information Center at the downtown Seattle REI. For topographic maps, ask Green Trails for No. 14, Mount Shuksan, or ask the USGS for Shuksan Arm.

Directions: From Bellingham, drive east 58 miles on Highway 542 (Mount Baker Highway) to Artist's Point at the end of the highway. The trailhead is on the northwest side of the parking lot.

Contact: Mount Baker-Snoqualmie National Forest, Glacier Public Service Center, Glacier, WA 98244, 360/599-2714.

16 PTARMIGAN RIDGE
8.0 mi/4.0 hrs

east of Bellingham in Mount Baker Wilderness of Mount Baker–Snoqualmie National Forest

Map 3.1, page 95

Just as one might expect from an arm of Mount Baker, Ptarmigan Ridge Trail revels in an excess of natural beauty. Wildflowers paint miles

of meadows while even more miles of views extend in all directions. Mount Shuksan looms from the east, and Mount Baker towers directly above. Marmots and picas are local residents, living it up with location, location, location. It's not possible to ask too much of Ptarmigan Ridge on a sunny, summer day.

Before leaving, be aware of several safety issues. Snowfields linger along the route well into summer, sometimes all year long. They are steep and should be crossed only by experienced hikers. Along this precipitous ridge, a misstep can have grave consequences. Mount Baker's weather changes rapidly, so be ready to use map and compass should a storm blow in and create a whiteout. That said, Ptarmigan Ridge Trail presents an exciting trip for those prepared for it.

The route uses Chain Lakes Trail before cutting left at a signed junction (1 mile). Ptarmigan Ridge Trail follows the cusp of the ridge as it ascends to Coleman Pinnacle (4.5 miles). Along the way are miles of wildflower meadows and fields of rock. Summer days are blistering hot in the sun, so extra water is a must. A scramble to the top of Coleman Pinnacle rewards with close views of Rainbow Glacier and Mount Baker. Climbers use this route to approach Mount Baker from Camp Kiser.

User Groups: Hikers and leashed dogs. No horses or mountain bikes are allowed. No wheelchair access.

Open Seasons: This trail is accessible August–September.

Permits: A federal Northwest Forest Pass is required to park here.

Maps: For a map of Mount Baker–Snoqualmie National Forest, contact the Outdoor Recreation Information Center at the downtown Seattle REI. For topographic maps, ask Green Trails for No. 14, Mount Shuksan (No. 13, Mount Baker, is helpful in identifying ridges and peaks on the mountain), or ask the USGS for Shuksan Arm.

Directions: From Bellingham, drive east 58 miles on Highway 542 (Mount Baker Highway)

to Artist's Point at the end of the highway. The trailhead is on the northwest side of the parking lot.

Contact: Mount Baker–Snoqualmie National Forest, Glacier Public Service Center, Glacier, WA 98244, 360/599-2714.

BELL PASS/CATHEDRAL PASS/MAZAMA PARK
17.0 mi/1–2 days

east of Bellingham in Mount Baker Wilderness of Mount Baker–Snoqualmie National Forest

Map 3.1, page 95

On the southwestern slopes of Washington's youngest volcano, Bell Pass Trail offers a more reclusive entry into the wonders of the Mount Baker high country. The trail presents a longer route into a parkland of expansive meadows, crackling glaciers, and wide vistas. That means fewer people travel along it than on the Park Butte and Scott Paul Trails, an enticing consideration.

Bell Pass Trail begins along Elbow Lake Trail, cutting switchbacks through the forest on its way to a junction (3.5 miles); Bell Pass Trail heads to the right. Elk sightings are an ordinary occurrence here. The trail departs the forest to find itself at Bell Pass (5.5 miles), where views of the Twin Sister Range are great. The trail levels out while it traverses above Ridley Creek. The meadows of Mazama Park (8.5 miles) are exceptional anytime in summer, but especially so in July during full bloom. Campsites are here. The trail continues up through Cathedral Pass to meet Park Butte Trail. A great lookout sits atop Park Butte, well worth the extra effort.

User Groups: Hikers, leashed dogs, and horses. No mountain bikes are allowed. No wheelchair access.

Open Seasons: This area is accessible July–October.

Permits: A federal Northwest Forest Pass is required to park here.

Maps: For a map of Mount Baker–Snoqualmie

National Forest, contact the Outdoor Recreation Information Center at the downtown Seattle REI. For topographic maps, ask Green Trails for No. 45, Hamilton, or ask the USGS for Twin Sisters Mountain and Mount Baker.

Directions: From Sedro-Woolley, drive east 16 miles on Highway 20 to Mile Marker 82. Turn left (north) on Baker Lake Highway (Forest Service Road 11) and drive 12 miles to Forest Service Road 12. Turn left and drive 14 miles to a signed spur road on the left. Turn left on this road and drive .25 mile to Elbow Lake Trailhead.

Contact: Mount Baker–Snoqualmie National Forest, Mount Baker Ranger District Office, 810 Highway 20, Sedro-Woolley, WA 98284, 360/856-5700.

18 PARK BUTTE/RAILROAD GRADE/SCOTT PAUL TRAIL
7.0–8.0 mi/4.0 hrs

east of Bellingham in Mount Baker Wilderness of Mount Baker–Snoqualmie National Forest

Map 3.1, page 95

This is arguably the finest terrain in all of the North Cascades. Three trails lead to high subalpine meadows set at the foot of Mount Baker, where glaciers crumble off the mountain and the sky opens up around you. Spend days roaming the high country here, spotting wildflowers and wildlife. The three trails form a network offering wide exploration, so it's best to have a map when picking your route through this area. Campsites spread throughout the area for magical overnight stays. This place attracts lots of visitors, so come for the scenery, not the solitude.

Park Butte Trail (7 miles round-trip, up and back) climbs through forest to open meadows and Park Butte lookout. The trail crosses Sulphur and Rocky Creeks (clear in the morning but milky white with glacial flour by afternoon). Marmots whistle from meadows while picas peep from atop boulders. The trail splits in Morovitz Meadow (2 miles); the left fork climbs a ridge to the lookout, with views of the mountain and Twin Sisters.

Scott Paul Trail (8 miles round-trip loop) leaves the Park Butte Trail in Morovitz Meadow to climb up Metcalf Moraine and meet the interesting terminus of Easton Glacier. The moraine exposes barren rock and mud, detailing an infant landscape before mountain meadows encroach. The trail continues east through meadows to climb a high crest with views of Mount Shuksan and the North Cascades before dropping through forest to the trailhead. Railroad Grade (6 miles round-trip, up and back) is a side trail shooting up to the mountain out of Morovitz Meadow. The trail is on a moraine created by the Easton Glacier and brings you close to the living glacier.

User Groups: Hikers, leashed dogs, and horses. No mountain bikes are allowed. No wheelchair access.

Open Seasons: This area is accessible July–October.

Permits: A federal Northwest Forest Pass is required to park here.

Maps: For a map of Mount Baker–Snoqualmie National Forest, contact the Outdoor Recreation Information Center at the downtown Seattle REI. For topographic maps, ask Green Trails for No. 45, Hamilton, or ask the USGS for Baker Pass.

Directions: From Sedro-Woolley, drive east 16 miles on Highway 20 to Mile Marker 82. Turn left (north) on Baker Lake Highway (Forest Service Road 11) and drive 12 miles to Forest Service Road 12. Turn left and drive 3.5 miles to Forest Service Road 13. Turn right and drive 5.5 miles to the trailhead at road's end.

Contact: Mount Baker-Snoqualmie National Forest, Mount Baker Ranger District Office, 810 Highway 20, Sedro-Woolley, WA 98284, 360/856-5700.

19 BAKER LAKE AND BAKER RIVER

3.6–28.6 mi/2.0 hr–2 days

east of Sedro-Woolley in Mount Baker–Snoqualmie National Forest

Map 3.1, page 95

For year-round forest wandering, Mount Baker presents hikers these two trails. Baker Lake Trail meanders 14.3 miles along the eastern shore of the large, dogleg-shaped lake. Baker River Trail continues from the north part of the lake and ventures eight miles up the river into North Cascades Park. Exceptional old-growth forests line the lengths of both trails, and water is always at hand. These are great trails for both day hikes and more extended adventures.

Short hikes along Baker Lake Trail are best begun from the south end. The trail contours along the eastern shores of the lake through stands of large trees. Anderson Point, a good turnaround, juts into the lake with campsites (1.8 miles); there are also three other campgrounds. The grade is level and easy, perfect for families with small children.

At the north end of the lake is Baker River Trail. Baker River Trail passes through terrific stands of virgin timber and even a beaver pond as it follows the river. In contrast to wildlife, people are relatively scarce here. The maintained trail ends when it crosses Sulphide Creek, impassable during times of high water. If you ford the river, a social trail continues beside the milky river five miles before truly petering out. For the adventurous, solitude and an enjoyable time are highly likely.

User Groups: Hikers, leashed dogs, and horses. No mountain bikes are allowed. No wheelchair access.

Open Seasons: This trail is accessible year-round.

Permits: A federal Northwest Forest Pass is required to park here.

Maps: For a map of Mount Baker–Snoqualmie National Forest, contact the Outdoor Recreation Information Center at the downtown Seattle REI. For topographic maps, ask Green

Trails for No. 46, Lake Shannon, or ask the USGS for Welker Peak, Bacon Peak, and Mount Shuksan.

Directions: From Sedro-Woolley, drive east 16 miles on Highway 20 to Mile Marker 82. Turn left (north) on Baker Lake Highway (Forest Service Road 11). For Baker Lake Trailhead, drive 14 miles to Baker Dam Road. Turn right and drive across Upper Baker Dam to Forest Service Road 1107. Turn left and drive 1 mile to the trailhead on the left side. For Baker River Trailhead, drive 25.5 miles on Forest Service Road 11 to the trailhead at road's end.

Contact: Mount Baker–Snoqualmie National Forest, Mount Baker Ranger District Office, 810 Highway 20, Sedro-Woolley, WA 98284, 360/856-5700.

20 ANDERSON AND WATSON LAKES
2.5 mi/2.0 hrs

east of Bellingham in Noisy-Diobsud Wilderness of Mount Baker–Snoqualmie National Forest

Map 3.1, page 95

High in the Noisy-Diobsud Wilderness is a trail with several options. Watson Lakes Trail passes by Anderson Butte, a former lookout site full of views, on its way to two sets of picturesque subalpine lakes. Accessible by hikers of all abilities, these lakes serve grand views of distant peaks and offer superb fishing for those with dinner in mind. Throw in old-growth forest and subalpine meadows, and this is a day hike or overnight trip that has it all.

Watson Lakes Trail leaves the lofty trailhead (elevation 4,200 feet) and proceeds through virgin timber and meadows to Anderson Butte junction (.9 mile). A .5-mile climb achieves the summit, a great place to see Mount Baker and North Cascade peaks. Include this side trip in a hike to the lakes.

Watson Lakes Trail soon arrives at another junction (1.5 miles). To the right are Anderson Lakes (2 miles), three small subalpine lakes surrounded by meadows and trees. The left

fork in the trail leads over a shoulder and down to Watson Lakes (2.5 miles), a larger pair of lakes with more mountain views. Both lakes are ringed by big trees and meadows. Camping at both lakes is in designated sites only. Also, both lake basins are notoriously buggy. Access to both sets of lakes is easy and hikers of all abilities will enjoy visiting them.

User Groups: Hikers and leashed dogs. No horses or mountain bikes are allowed. No wheelchair access.

Open Seasons: This area is accessible mid-June–October.

Permits: A federal Northwest Forest Pass is required to park here.

Maps: For a map of Mount Baker–Snoqualmie National Forest, contact the Outdoor Recreation Information Center at the downtown Seattle REI. For topographic maps, ask Green Trails for No. 46, Lake Shannon, or ask the USGS for Bacon Peak.

Directions: From Sedro-Woolley, drive east 16 miles on Highway 20 to Mile Marker 82. Turn left (north) on Baker Lake Highway (Forest Service Road 11). Drive 14 miles to Baker Dam Road. Turn right and drive across Upper Baker Dam to Forest Service Road 1107. Turn left and drive 10 miles to Forest Service Road 022. Turn left and drive to the trailhead at road's end.

Contact: Mount Baker–Snoqualmie National Forest, Mount Baker Ranger District Office, 810 Highway 20, Sedro-Woolley, WA 98284, 360/856-5700.

21 SAUK MOUNTAIN
4.2 mi/4.0 hrs

west of Marblemount in Mount Baker–Snoqualmie National Forest

Map 3.1, page 95

This is a great short day hike that offers outstanding vistas the entire way. Sauk Mountain Trail starts and ends in meadows smothered with alpine flowers. Most would say that it's difficult to find anything better than that. Of course, the terrific nature of the trail attracts loads of folks, but solitude is always difficult to find so close to Highway 20.

The trail is well laid out, with many switchbacks cutting the 1,300 feet of elevation gain to a much easier grade. This is exclusive meadow country, and in midsummer, flower enthusiasts will find themselves in heaven. Expect to find paintbrush, phlox, tiger lilies, aster, columbine, and lupine on display. Sauk Mountain Trail splits (1.5 miles), with the left fork heading to the summit and the right fork leading down to Sauk Lake, which is set between the rocky slopes of Sauk and Bald Mountains. The summit is a former fire lookout site with panoramic views. Gaze from the San Juans to the rugged North Cascades, from Mount Baker and Mount Shuksan all the way south to Mount Rainier. This trail gets a lot of use, so please stick to the path and don't cut switchbacks.

User Groups: Hikers and leashed dogs. No horses or mountain bikes are allowed. No wheelchair access.

Open Seasons: This trail is accessible mid-June–October.

Permits: A federal Northwest Forest Pass is required to park here.

Maps: For a map of Mount Baker–Snoqualmie National Forest, contact the Outdoor Recreation Information Center at the downtown Seattle REI. For topographic maps, ask Green Trails for No. 46, Lake Shannon, or ask the USGS for Sauk Mountain.

Directions: From Sedro-Woolley, drive east on Highway 20 for 32 miles. At Mile Marker 96, turn left on Sauk Mountain Road (Forest Service Road 1030). Follow Forest Service Road 1030 for 7 miles to the junction of Forest Service Road 1036. Turn right on Road 1036 and follow to the road's end, where the trailhead is located.

Contact: Mount Baker–Snoqualmie National Forest, Mount Baker Ranger District Office, 810 Highway 20, Sedro-Woolley, WA 98284, 360/856-5700.

22 THORNTON LAKES
9.5 mi/5.0 hrs

west of Newhalem in North Cascades National Park

Map 3.1, page 95

The three Thornton Lakes are high in an outstretched arm of Mount Triumph along the western side of North Cascades National Park. The trail does not offer much until near the very end, where Mount Triumph and Thornton Lakes come into view along a ridge crest. Here, Mount Triumph towers over the lakes while Eldorado Peak stands to the south. The best views are not at the lake but rather atop Trappers Peak to the north.

Thornton Lakes Trail was never actually built by a trail crew but instead was fashioned over time simply by boots. The first half of the trail follows an old logging road, brushy with alders, before finding the makeshift trail. It climbs steeply through second-growth forest before breaking out into open meadows.

The trail reaches a ridge (4.5 miles) above Lower Thornton Lake, where hikers have three options. For access to the lower lake, the biggest of the three, drop down the ridge along the obvious trail. The upper lakes, often covered with snow and ice well into summer, are reached by traversing the west slopes of the lower lake along small footpaths. And finally, view seekers should follow the ridge crest to the north to scramble Trappers Peak. From up here, the close Pickett Range comes into full view along with much of the surrounding North Cascades. There are not many sites for camping here, so the trip is definitely recommended as a day hike.

User Groups: Hikers only. No dogs, horses, or mountain bikes are allowed. No wheelchair access.

Open Seasons: This trail is accessible July–October.

Permits: A federal Northwest Forest Pass is required to park here.

Maps: For a map of North Cascades National Park, contact the Outdoor Recreation Information Center at the downtown Seattle REI.

For topographic maps, ask Green Trails for No. 47, Marblemount, or ask the USGS for Mount Triumph.

Directions: Drive east on Highway 20 from Marblemount. Look for the Thornton Lakes Trail sign near Mile Marker 117. Turn north on the gravel road and drive 5 miles to the road's end, where the trailhead is located.

Contact: North Cascades National Park, Wilderness Information Center, 7280 Ranger Station Road, Marblemount, WA 98267, 360/873-4500.

23 MONOGRAM LAKE/ LOOKOUT MOUNTAIN
9.4 mi/5.0 hrs

east of Marblemount in Mount Baker–Snoqualmie National Forest and North Cascades National Park

Map 3.1, page 95

At the western edge of North Cascades National Park are two exceptional destinations accessible from one trail. Monogram Lake sits in a small cirque on a high alpine ridge, framed by meadows and high mountain views. On the other hand, the lookout atop creatively named Lookout Mountain offers scores of extraordinary vistas of North Cascade peaks. The catch is well over 4,000 feet of elevation gain from the trailhead to either point. Don't worry about reaching only one. It will still be a memorable trip, and there's something left for next weekend.

Both routes begin on Lookout Mountain Trail, a treacherously steep series of switchbacks through shady old-growth forest. The trail splits (2.8 miles), with Lookout Mountain to the left and Monogram Lake to the right. Lookout Mountain Trail continues climbing harshly but now through open meadows teeming with blooming wildflowers in July and early August. At the summit (4.7 miles, 5,719 feet) rests a functional lookout at the edge of a mighty drop-off. As expected, the views are spectacular from this height.

Monogram Lake Trail soon enters wildflower meadows and traverses open slopes to the lake

(4.9 miles). This is national park territory, a place where dogs are strictly not allowed. A multitude of exploring exists around the lake, perfect for those with an itch for scrambling. Backpackers can stay at Monogram Lake Camp, but don't forget reservations with the Park Service.

User Groups: Monogram Lake Trail is open to hikers. Lookout Mountain Trail is open to hikers and leashed dogs. No horses or mountain bikes are allowed. No wheelchair access.

Open Seasons: This trail is accessible mid-July–October.

Permits: A federal Northwest Forest Pass is required to park here.

Maps: For a map of Mount Baker-Snoqualmie National Forest and North Cascades National Park, contact the Outdoor Recreation Information Center at the downtown Seattle REI. For topographic maps, ask Green Trails for No. 47, Marblemount, or ask the USGS for Big Devil Peak.

Directions: From Sedro-Woolley, drive east on Highway 20 for 39 miles to the community of Marblemount. On the east end of town, turn right on the Cascade River Road, which immediately crosses the Skagit River. Drive 6.5 miles on Cascade River Road to the signed trailhead on the north side of the road, just inside the national forest boundary.

Contact: North Cascades National Park, Wilderness Information Center, 7280 Ranger Station Road, Marblemount, WA 98267, 360/873-4500.

24 HIDDEN LAKE PEAKS
9.0 mi/5.0 hrs

east of Marblemount in Mount Baker–Snoqualmie National Forest and North Cascades National Park

Map 3.1, page 95

An aura surrounds trails that are open for short periods each year. Thanks to heavy winter snowfall, some routes are accessible just a few fleeting months each summer. Thus trips to these destinations are rare and special. That's the case with Hidden Lake, often locked away from hikers by snow until late summer. But if you bide your time, you won't be disappointed. Hidden Lake and its accompanying lookout are high in the sky but surrounded by even higher Cascade peaks.

Hidden Lake Peaks Trail is classic North Cascades: lots of elevation gain. As usual, the 3,500 feet of climbing is well worth it. The trail climbs through a forest of Pacific silver fir before giving way to the meadows and views of Sibley Creek Basin. Sunbathing marmots on the granite boulders are as common as lingering patches of snow.

Hidden Lake Peaks Trail climbs to a saddle from which Hidden Lake is finally revealed. Hikers can either drop to the lake or climb to Hidden Lake Lookout for views. If snow lingers along either route, it's best to simply enjoy the great views from the saddle.

User Groups: Hikers and leashed dogs (up to the park boundary at the saddle). No horses or mountain bikes are allowed. No wheelchair access.

Open Seasons: This trail is accessible August–October.

Permits: A federal Northwest Forest Pass is required to park here.

Maps: For a map of Mount Baker–Snoqualmie National Forest and North Cascades National Park, contact the Outdoor Recreation Information Center at the downtown Seattle REI. For topographic maps, ask Green Trails for No. 48, Diablo Dam, and No. 80, Cascade Pass, or ask the USGS for Eldorado Peak and Sonny Boy Lake.

Directions: From Sedro-Woolley, drive east on Highway 20 for 39 miles to the community of Marblemount. On the east end of town, turn right on Cascade River Road, which immediately crosses the Skagit River. At about 10 miles, turn left onto Sibley Creek Road (Forest Service Road 1540, also signed "Hidden Lake Trail") and drive to the end, about 5 miles.

Contact: North Cascades National Park, Wilderness Information Center, 7280 Ranger Station Road, Marblemount, WA 98267, 360/873-4500.

25 CASCADE PASS
7.4 mi/3.5 hrs

east of Marblemount in North Cascades National Park

Map 3.1, page 95

From the parking lot at the trailhead, there is little doubt that Cascade Pass Trail is one magnificent hike. With the mighty Johannesburg Mountain to the south, Cascade Pass Trail carries hikers to the Cascade Crest at the foot of several tall, massive peaks. Wildflowers and glacial views are the norm along the entire route, an entrance to the Stehekin Valley and much of North Cascades National Park.

Cascade Pass Trail climbs steadily but gently throughout its length. A grand forest of mountain hemlock and Pacific silver fir offers welcome shade before breaking into expansive meadows. At Cascade Pass (3.7 miles), acres of wildflowers compete for attention with the neighboring glacier-capped ridges and peaks. This is a dry trail, so bring plenty of water. Also, this area sees plenty of traffic, so stay on designated trails and make this a day hike only.

Cascade Pass is a fine turnaround, but options for further exploration do exist. Sahale Arm Trail heads north from the pass, gaining big elevation and bigger views. A less difficult path heads in the opposite direction to scale Mix-up Peak and find a small tarn. Trekkers will be glad to know that Cascade Pass Trail continues east and drops to the Stehekin River. This route to Lake Chelan has been used for thousands of years by Native American traders.

User Groups: Hikers only. No dogs, horses, or mountain bikes are allowed. No wheelchair access.

Open Seasons: This trail is accessible July–October.

Permits: A federal Northwest Forest Pass is required to park here.

Maps: For a map of North Cascades National Park, contact the Outdoor Recreation Information Center at the downtown Seattle REI. For topographic maps, ask Green Trails for

No. 80, Cascade Pass, or ask the USGS for Cascade Pass.

Directions: From the town of Marblemount on Highway 20, drive 23 miles on Cascade River Road to the trailhead at road's end.

Contact: North Cascades National Park, Wilderness Information Center, 7280 Ranger Station Road, Marblemount, WA 98267, 360/873-4500.

26 PYRAMID LAKE
4.2 mi/2.0 hrs

south of Diablo in Ross Lake National Recreation Area

Map 3.1, page 95

Pyramid Lake Trail provides easy access to a deep lake set far below the towering summit of Pyramid Peak. The trail follows the gentle Pyramid Creek through a forest of large and small trees, where a recent burn killed some trees but spared others. The trail is a popular one since it's one of the easier hikes within the park. It's a great destination for folks passing through the park along the highway and looking for a short hike to stretch the legs.

Pyramid Lake Trail gains 1,500 feet in two miles. Closely spaced lodgepole pine and Douglas fir compete to revegetate the forest after a slope-clearing fire. Farther on, larger trees begin appearing, particularly some western red cedars. The trail crosses the creek at the one-mile mark, which may result in some wet feet during times of heavy flow. The trail climbs at a steady rate to the lake, bound by vertical cliffs on two sides. Pyramid Peak stands tall to the southwest, seemingly barren and without a tree to speak of. The lake lies within a National Research Area because of the high levels of biodiversity here. Camping is strictly prohibited, and exploration around the lake should be confined to clearly established trails. Please keep dogs on leashes at all times!

User Groups: Hikers and leashed dogs. No horses or mountain bikes are allowed. No wheelchair access.

Open Seasons: This trail is accessible May–October.

Permits: A federal Northwest Forest Pass is required to park here.

Maps: For a map of North Cascades National Park, contact the Outdoor Recreation Information Center at the downtown Seattle REI. For topographic maps, ask Green Trails for No. 48, Diablo Dam, or ask the USGS for Diablo Dam and Ross Dam.

Directions: From Newhalem, drive east on Highway 20 to the trailhead on the north side of the road, just beyond Mile Marker 126.

Contact: North Cascades National Park, Wilderness Information Center, 7280 Ranger Station Road, Marblemount, WA 98267, 360/873-4500.

27 SOURDOUGH MOUNTAIN
11.5 mi/6.0 hrs

north of Diablo in Ross Lake National Recreation Area and North Cascades National Park

Map 3.1, page 95

Sourdough Mountain Trail is all about two very simple things: unrivaled views of the North Cascades and steepness. Views extend in every direction, up, down, east and west, and north and south. Countless peaks are within sight, including Colonial and Snowfield Peaks and the celebrated Pickett Range, often called simply "the Picketts." This vista comes with a dear cost, however, as the trail is one of the steepest you'll come across. From trailhead to summit is a grueling 5,100-foot ascent in just 5.7 miles. It's a real hoofer, but those who complete it will not soon forget it.

Sourdough Mountain Trail gets to work immediately, climbing 3,000 feet in the first three miles. Great forests of Douglas fir and western hemlock provide shade along the exhausting climb. The trail eventually reaches grand subalpine meadows and the sky-high summit. Sourdough Lookout sits atop the 5,985-foot summit. The panoramic views are top-notch and difficult to duplicate within the park. A pair of camps are on either side of the lookout for those wishing to recover tired legs with a night's rest.

User Groups: Hikers only. No dogs, horses,

or mountain bikes are allowed. No wheelchair access.

Open Seasons: This trail is accessible July–October.

Permits: A federal Northwest Forest Pass is required to park here.

Maps: For a map of North Cascades National Park, contact the Outdoor Recreation Information Center at the downtown Seattle REI. For topographic maps, ask Green Trails for No. 48, Diablo Dam, and No. 16, Ross Lake, or ask the USGS for Diablo Dam and Ross Dam.

Directions: From Marblemount, drive east on Highway 20. Turn left at the town of Diablo, near Mile Marker 126. Sourdough Mountain Trailhead is behind the domed swimming pool near the back of the town.

Contact: North Cascades National Park, Wilderness Information Center, 7280 Ranger Station Road, Marblemount, WA 98267, 360/873-4500.

28 DIABLO LAKE
7.6 mi/4.0 hrs

near Diablo in Ross Lake National Recreation Area

Map 3.1, page 95

By itself, Diablo Lake Trail is an excellent way to pass an afternoon, with views of emerald Diablo Lake and pristine old-growth forests. There are a multitude of activities, however, that can be enjoyed in conjunction with the trail to make the day that much more memorable. For instance, during the summer, hike the trail to Ross Dam and then take a Seattle City Light ferry on the lake back down to the trailhead. Tours of the dams are also available, allowing folks to see why their lights turn on at the flip of a switch. Several campgrounds and picnic sites are also nearby for those using their cars as a base.

Diablo Lake Trail actually never nears the lakeshore, and instead takes a higher route that provides more views. Numerous peaks and ridges of the North Cascades are visible along the trail, especially from the viewpoint halfway down the

trail. The trail is a great place to bird-watch, as scores of species make the forests here their home. While there is some elevation gain along the route, few hikers will have any difficulty with it. That makes it great for families (but keep an eye on little ones near the viewpoints). The trail eventually connects to Ross Dam, the end of one lake but the beginning of another.

User Groups: Hikers and leashed dogs. No horses or mountain bikes are allowed. No wheelchair access.

Open Seasons: This trail is accessible when Highway 20 is open. Highway 20 closure depends on seasonal snow, and it is usually closed November–April.

Permits: A federal Northwest Forest Pass is required to park here.

Maps: For a map of North Cascades National Park, contact the Outdoor Recreation Information Center at the downtown Seattle REI. For topographic maps, ask Green Trails for No. 48, Diablo Dam, or ask the USGS for Diablo Dam and Ross Dam.

Directions: From Marblemount, drive east on Highway 20. Turn left at Diablo Dam. The parking area is before crossing the dam, which is closed to car traffic. The trailhead is a .5-mile walk down the old road.

Contact: North Cascades National Park, Wilderness Information Center, 7280 Ranger Station Road, Marblemount, WA 98267, 360/873-4500.

29 BEAVER LOOP
32.5 mi/4 days

west of Ross Lake in North Cascades National Park

Map 3.1, page 95

Not so long ago, glaciers a mile thick slid down the Big Beaver and Little Beaver Valleys, carving them into wide U-shaped troughs. If you need proof, the Beaver Loop through the two valleys will surely provide it. This well-known backpacking route gains little elevation but enjoys some of Washington's largest stands of old-growth forest. Beaver Pass offers grand views of enormous valleys framed by even larger peaks.

The route follows Little Beaver Creek before crossing into Big Beaver Creek Valley. It's necessary to arrange a water taxi with Ross Lake Resort to deposit yourself at the mouth of Little Beaver Creek. Little Beaver Trail threads up the valley through 11 miles of remarkable forest. Camps are situated at the boat landing, at Perry Creek at 4.6 miles, and Stillwell Camp at 11.2 miles.

At Stillwell Camp, Big Beaver Trail cuts off and climbs to the pass. This requires a ford of Little Beaver Creek, difficult if not impossible in early summer when the snows are in full melt, so be prepared. At Big Beaver Pass (13.7 miles and home to Beaver Pass Camp), exploration will yield amazing views into the Luna Valley and its basin, while the Picketts tower over the valley. Big Beaver Trail drops into the wide, U-shaped valley and travels 13.5 miles to Ross Lake through stands of western red cedar more than 1,000 years old. The cedars alone are worth the 26.5 miles. Luna Camp is 2.7 miles from Beaver Pass, 39 Mile Camp is seven miles from the pass, and Pumpkin Mountain Camp is at Ross Lake. To get back to the car, hike the Ross Lake Trail six miles or make arrangements with the water taxi for a pickup at Big Beaver.

User Groups: Hikers only. No dogs, horses, or mountain bikes are allowed. No wheelchair access.

Open Seasons: This trail is accessible July–September.

Permits: A federal Northwest Forest Pass is required to park here. Overnight stays within the national park require reservations and backcountry camping permits, which are available at the Wilderness Information Center.

Maps: For a map of North Cascades National Park, contact the Outdoor Recreation Information Center at the downtown Seattle REI. For topographic maps, ask Green Trails for No. 15, Mount Challenger, and No. 16, Ross Lake, or ask the USGS for Pumpkin Mountain, Mount Prophet, Mount Redoubt, Mount Spickard, and Hozomeen Mountain.

Directions: From Marblemount, drive east 20 miles on Highway 20 to signed Diablo Dam. Turn left and cross the dam and turn immediately right for the parking area for Ross Lake Resort. Here, a ferry carries passengers to the Ross Lake Water Taxi for transportation to the trailheads.

Contact: North Cascades National Park, Wilderness Information Center, 7280 Ranger Station Road, Marblemount, WA 98267, 360/873-4500; Ross Lake Resort Water Taxi, 206/386-4437.

30 THUNDER CREEK
38.8 mi/4 days

south of Diablo Lake in North Cascades National Park

Map 3.1, page 95

This is one of the North Cascades' classic routes, leading deep into the park and out to Lake Chelan. The trail is also great for short day hikes up the creek, as there is plenty to see and do within the first several miles. Immense, icy peaks line the valley ridges while massive cedars and firs fill the forest along the trail. Thunder Creek is deservedly considered one of the park's classic hikes.

Thunder Creek Trail sets off within a large forest of western red cedar and Douglas fir. Hikers looking for a short day hike will enjoy Thunder Creek Nature Loop (.5 mile up Thunder Creek Trail), a one-mile loop that ventures off into old-growth forest. Thunder Creek Trail stays relatively flat for 7.5 miles to McAllister Camp, a good turnaround for long day hikes. Here, a bridge spans the creek as it rushes through a small canyon of granite, a wonderful place for lunch.

Farther along Thunder Creek Trail, the wilderness grows deeper, with views of rugged, glacial peaks to the west. Enormous glaciers cover these mountains and provide the creek with much of its rock flour. The trail continues through the forested valley to Park Creek Pass, a one-way total of 19.4 miles. Stehekin lies eight miles beyond. Numerous campsites are situated throughout the valley. Thunder

Creek makes a wonderful segment of a long trek through the North Cascades.

User Groups: Hikers, leashed dogs (dogs allowed on the first 6.5 miles but not within the national park), and horses. No mountain bikes are allowed. No wheelchair access.

Open Seasons: This trail is accessible April–November.

Permits: A federal Northwest Forest Pass is required to park here. Overnight stays within the national park require backcountry camping permits, which are available at the Wilderness Information Center.

Maps: For a map of North Cascades National Park, contact the Outdoor Recreation Information Center at the downtown Seattle REI. For topographic maps, ask Green Trails for No. 48, Diablo Dam, No. 49, Mount Logan, and No. 81, McGregor Mountain, or ask the USGS for Ross Dam, Forbidden Peak, and Mount Logan.

Directions: From Newhalem, drive east on Highway 20 to Mile Marker 130 and Colonial Creek Campground. Turn right and park in the lot above the boat ramp. The signed trailhead is located at the end of the parking lot.

Contact: North Cascades National Park, Wilderness Information Center, 7280 Ranger Station Road, Marblemount, WA 98267, 360/873-4500.

31 DESOLATION PEAK
13.6 mi/8.0 hrs

east of Ross Lake in North Cascades National Park

Map 3.1, page 95

Jack Kerouac made Desolation Peak world-famous when he included the mountain in his book *Desolation Angels*. The book is based on his time with the Forest Service, when he was stationed at the still-functional lookout atop the lofty peak. Kerouac has helped to keep the peak a well-visited locale despite its truly desolate location.

Ross Lake Resort offers boat transportation to Desolation Landing near Lightning Creek. After disembarking from the boat, hike Desolation Peak Trail north along Ross Lake for two miles before making a very steep ascent to Des-

olation Peak. Although there is some shade along the way, much of the hillside was burned in a fire 75 years ago and gets a lot of sun. The views improve as the elevation increases, creating the opportunity for regular breaks. Bringing extra water is a must, as snow is the only source this high. From the open slopes of Desolation Peak, numerous peaks and ridges are visible. Ross Lake appears particularly agreeable after such a long hike. Overnight hikers will enjoy Desolation Camp, just below tree line.

User Groups: Hikers only. No dogs, horses, or mountain bikes are allowed. No wheelchair access.

Open Seasons: This trail is accessible mid-June–September.

Permits: A federal Northwest Forest Pass is required to park here. Overnight stays within the national park require reservations and backcountry camping permits, which are available at the Wilderness Information Center.

Maps: For a map of North Cascades National Park, contact the Outdoor Recreation Information Center at the downtown Seattle REI. For topographic maps, ask Green Trails for No. 16, Ross Lake, or ask the USGS for Hozomeen Mountain.

Directions: From Marblemount, drive east 20 miles on Highway 20 to signed Diablo Dam. Turn left and cross the dam and turn immediately right for the parking area for Ross Lake Resort. Here, a ferry carries passengers to the Ross Lake Water Taxi for transportation to the trailheads.

Contact: North Cascades National Park, Wilderness Information Center, 7280 Ranger Station Road, Marblemount, WA 98267, 360/873-4500; Ross Lake Resort Water Taxi, 206/386-4437.

32 MOUNT HIGGINS
9.0 mi/5.0 hrs

west of Darrington in Mount Baker-Snoqualmie National Forest

Map 3.1, page 95

Mount Higgins is best known by Mountain Loop Highway drivers as the first big mountain they pass under. Highly visible from the road is the long band of rock capping the ridge and leading into the tilted slats of Mount Higgins. The hike up is every bit as rewarding and as strenuous as it would seem from the car.

Mount Higgins Trail endures 3,300 feet of harsh elevation gain on the way. That's a lot of climbing, and only boggy and buggy Myrtle Lake offers a little respite along the way. Weary hikers who turn back early will still have a good time, but they miss the climax that makes all the hard work worth it. After passing a clear-cut, the trail enters virgin national forest. The grade eventually levels out, and the Myrtle Lake Trail soon breaks to the left, at 3.3 miles. Myrtle Lake is a short .5 mile away. Mount Higgins Trail continues climbing to an abandoned lookout post, just below the summits of Mount Higgins. These peaks are best left to true rock climbers. The view from the old lookout encompasses miles of mountains, including the Olympics across Puget Sound.

User Groups: Hikers and leashed dogs. No horses or mountain bikes are allowed. No wheelchair access.

Open Seasons: This trail is accessible July–October.

Permits: A federal Northwest Forest Pass is required to park here.

Maps: For a map of Mount Baker–Snoqualmie National Forest, contact the Outdoor Recreation Information Center at the downtown Seattle REI. For topographic maps, ask Green Trails for No. 77, Oso, or ask the USGS for Oso.

Directions: From Arlington, drive east 16 miles on the Mountain Loop Highway (Highway 530) to C-Post Road (just before Mile Marker 38). Turn right (north) onto C-Post Road. Continue on the road for 2.8 miles after crossing over the North Fork Stillaguamish River. The road dead-ends at the signed trailhead, and the trail is on the right side (east) of the road. Some parking is available along the road.

Contact: Mount Baker–Snoqualmie National Forest, Darrington Ranger Station, 1405 Emmens Street, Darrington, WA 98241, 360/436-1155.

33 BOULDER RIVER
8.6 mi/4.5 hrs

within the Boulder River Wilderness southwest of the town of Darrington

Map 3.1, page 95

When the snow still lingers in the alpine regions during the springtime, Boulder River Trail offers an excellent chance to stretch the legs and get ready for summer. The trail wanders four miles into the river valley to a picturesque setting of camps. Along the way are several outstanding waterfalls dropping into the river, which makes much of its way through narrow gorges. With little elevation gain, the trail is a favorite for hikers of all ages and abilities.

Boulder River Trail follows an old logging road to the wilderness boundary, where great old-growth forest begins (1 mile). The first of Boulder's two high waterfalls soon comes into view. While this is a nice turnaround spot for the less serious, it's advisable to trek the next three miles.

Boulder River Trail continues through exceptional old-growth forests, often high above the noisy river. Early-season hikers will en-

Boulder River Trail, a good year-round hike

counter numerous trilliums and other understory flowers in full bloom. The trail empties out onto the river's banks (4.3 miles), where Three Fingers Peak can be seen up the valley. Expect to linger here a while. Boulder River is a great overnight trip as well, with several campsites clustered around the end of the trail.

User Groups: Hikers and leashed dogs. No horses or mountain bikes are allowed. No wheelchair access.

Open Seasons: This trail is accessible year-round.

Permits: A federal Northwest Forest Pass is required to park here.

Maps: For a map of Mount Baker–Snoqualmie National Forest, contact the Outdoor Recreation Information Center at the downtown Seattle REI. For topographic maps, ask Green Trails for No. 77, Oso, and No. 109, Granite Falls, or ask the USGS for Granite Falls.

Directions: From Arlington, drive east on Mountain Loop Highway (Highway 530) to French Creek Road. Turn right and drive 4 miles to the trailhead at road's end.

Contact: Mount Baker–Snoqualmie National Forest, Darrington Ranger Station, 1405 Emmens Street, Darrington, WA 98241, 360/436-1155.

34 HUCKLEBERRY MOUNTAIN
14.0 mi/9.0 hrs

east of Darrington in Glacier Peak Wilderness of Mount Baker–Snoqualmie National Forest

Map 3.1, page 95

Huckleberry Mountain is a hike for the serious North Cascade hiker. Few trails in the state are as strenuous as Huckleberry Mountain—5,000 feet of vertical ascent in seven miles is evidence of that. But don't be scared off too easily. If you are looking for a rough, challenging hike, there is no better trail than this. The route climbs steeply through layers of forest zones before emerging among mountaintop meadows and expansive views.

Huckleberry Mountain Trail heads in one direction, which is up. Take relief in the cascading streams running nearby and the shade provided by the old-growth forest. The trail finally levels out after five miles, where it finds the crest of large, wide Huckleberry Mountain. The trail now heads north along the ridge before ending at the site of an old lookout. The expansive views soothe weary legs.

There are camps along the trail for those wishing to make a night of it. Be sure to carry extra water; once the snow is gone, so is your water. An early start is recommended for day hikers and backpackers alike. A group of lakes several miles north are accessible only by cross-country travel.

Note: Suiattle River Road was severely washed out in 2003, and a timeline for repair was not set at time of publication. Call ahead to see if the trail is accessible.

User Groups: Hikers, leashed dogs, and horses. No mountain bikes are allowed. No wheelchair access.

Open Seasons: This trail is accessible July–October.

Permits: A federal Northwest Forest Pass is required to park here.

Maps: For a map of Mount Baker–Snoqualmie National Forest, contact the Outdoor Recreation Information Center at the downtown Seattle REI. For topographic maps, ask Green Trails for No. 79, Snowking Mountain, or ask the USGS for Huckleberry Mountain.

Directions: From Darrington, drive north 7 miles on Highway 530 toward Rockport to Suiattle River Road (Forest Service Road 26). Turn right and drive 15 miles to the trailhead on the left.

Contact: Mount Baker–Snoqualmie National Forest, Darrington Ranger Station, 1405 Emmens Street, Darrington, WA 98241, 360/436-1155.

35 GREEN MOUNTAIN
8.0 mi/5.0 hrs

west of Darrington in Glacier Peak Wilderness of Mount Baker–Snoqualmie National Forest

Map 3.1, page 95

Green Mountain has it all. Enjoy lush old-growth forest before breaking out into wide open meadows that give the mountain its name. Wildflowers cover the slopes in bright colors during July, while August brings a feast of huckleberries. Several small tarns tucked into a small basin present the perfect place for a rest and meal before the final ascent to the climax of the route. At the top of Green Mountain, at a lofty 6,500 feet, stands an old lookout soaking up panoramic views of the Cascades. There's not much one can ask of a trail that Green Mountain doesn't deliver.

Green Mountain trail starts high, at 3,500 feet, making it easier to stomach than most trails in the area. The forest breaks after one mile to revel in unbroken views. Several small tarns (2.5 miles) offer a rest stop (or turnaround) before the final climb to the summit. Built in 1933, the historic lookout perseveres atop Green Mountain. Glacier Peak rises spectacularly to the east while countless ridges and peaks fill the horizon. If we had just one day to spend hiking in the Mountain Loop Highway region, this would be it.

Note: Suiattle River Road was severely washed out in 2003, and a timeline for repair was not set at time of publication. Call ahead to see if the trail is accessible.

User Groups: Hikers, leashed dogs, and horses. No mountain bikes are allowed. No wheelchair access.

Open Seasons: This trail is accessible July–October.

Permits: A federal Northwest Forest Pass is required to park here.

Maps: For a map of Mount Baker–Snoqualmie National Forest, contact the Outdoor Recreation Information Center at the downtown Seattle REI. For topographic maps, ask Green Trails for No. 80, Cascade Pass, or ask the USGS for Downey Mountain.

Directions: From Darrington, drive north 7 miles on Highway 530 toward Rockport to Suiattle River Road (Forest Service Road 26). Turn right and drive 20.5 miles to Forest Service Road 2680. Turn left (north) and drive 6 miles to the trailhead at road's end.

Contact: Mount Baker–Snoqualmie National Forest, Darrington Ranger Station, 1405 Emmens Street, Darrington, WA 98241, 360/436-1155.

36 IMAGE LAKE
33.0 mi/3–4 days

in Glacier Peak Wilderness of Mount Baker–Snoqualmie National Forest

Map 3.1, page 95

When you finally reach Image Lake, you'll likely recognize the spectacular scene from numerous book covers and friends' pictures. Understandably, it's one of Washington's best-known scenes. Within a small high-country cirque, Image Lake reflects perfectly the majestic Glacier Peak, just seven miles distant.

The route follows Suiattle River Trail before breaking away and climbing to the upper ridge. The river valley is one of Washington's finest, filled with a lush forest of ancient timber. At 10.8 miles, veer left on Miners Ridge Trail and climb 5.5 miles to the subalpine splendor of Miners Ridge and Image Lake.

The trip can be done in three days, if you're quick, but it's best to take at least four days. It's possible to stay at a different camp each night. First- and last-night campsites can be found at Canyon Creek Camp (6.5 miles) and before Miners Ridge Trail junction (9.5 miles). Numerous campsites are at Image Lake and on Miners Ridge, but they manage to go quickly on summer weekends. One mile beyond Image Lake is Lady Camp with equally great views. Activities other than gazing at Glacier Peak include rambling along Miners Ridge, covered in wildflowers during July. Near the western end sits a lookout still maintained by the Forest Service.

Note: Suiattle River Road was severely washed out in 2003, and a timeline for repair was not set at time of publication. Call ahead to see if the trail is accessible.

User Groups: Hikers and leashed dogs. No horses or mountain bikes are allowed. No wheelchair access.

Open Seasons: This trail is accessible July–September.

Permits: A federal Northwest Forest Pass is required to park here.

Maps: For a map of Mount Baker–Snoqualmie National Forest, contact the Outdoor Recreation Information Center at the downtown Seattle REI. For topographic maps, ask Green Trails for No. 112, Glacier Peak, or ask the USGS for Lime Mountain and Gamma Peak.

Directions: From Darrington, drive north 7 miles on Highway 530 toward Rockport to Suiattle River Road (Forest Service Road 26). Drive 24 miles on Suiattle River Road to the trailhead at road's end.

Contact: Mount Baker–Snoqualmie National Forest, Darrington Ranger Station, 1405 Emmens Street, Darrington, WA 98241, 360/436-1155.

37 MOUNT PUGH (STUJACK PASS)
7.0 mi/5.0 hrs

in Mount Baker–Snoqualmie National Forest

Map 3.1, page 95

In true North Cascades form, Mount Pugh Trail makes a challenging climb (nearly 4,000 feet) to expansive views that encompass a multitude of peaks. Stujack Pass is a small saddle on the ridge below mighty Pugh Mountain. The terrain is inspiring, where patches of small, weather-beaten trees grow in gardens of rock and heather. If this isn't enough, there is a footpath that leads to the summit of Mount Pugh. The question won't be if you want to summit Mount Pugh. The question will be if you have the energy to summit.

Mount Pugh Trail is in good shape to the pass, but beyond it is not much more than a rocky path. The trail moves through old-growth forest and encounters small Lake Meten (1.5 miles). Get used to switchbacks, for they are the story of the day. The forest eventually breaks and the route provides loads of views as it scales the rocky slope. Stujack Pass is a welcome sight. It's a great reward when you hit the pass and so much is finally revealed to the east. Hearty hikers can climb another 1,500 feet (in

just 1.5 miles) to the summit via a tricky foot path along the ridge. From the summit, views from Rainier to Baker embrace too much of the Cascades to absorb in just one afternoon.

User Groups: Hikers and leashed dogs. No horses or mountain bikes are allowed. No wheelchair access.

Open Seasons: This trail is accessible August–October.

Permits: A federal Northwest Forest Pass is required to park here.

Maps: For a map of Mount Baker–Snoqualmie National Forest, contact the Outdoor Recreation Information Center at the downtown Seattle REI. For topographic maps, ask Green Trails for No. 111, Sloan Peak, or ask the USGS for Pugh Mountain and White Chuck Mountain.

Directions: From Darrington, drive east 14 miles on Mountain Loop Highway to Forest Service Road 2095. Turn left and drive 1.5 miles to the trailhead on the right.

Contact: Mount Baker–Snoqualmie National Forest, Darrington Ranger Station, 1405 Emmens Street, Darrington, WA 98241, 360/436-1155.

38 MEADOW MOUNTAIN
21.0 mi/2–3 days

in Glacier Peak Wilderness of Mount Baker–Snoqualmie National Forest

Map 3.1, page 95

A long approach to Meadow Mountain has made it much wilder than many of its counterparts. Closure of the access road added 5.5 miles to the hike, weeding out the day-hiker crowd. That's good news for those seeking an easy but satisfying weekend trip to sublime meadows and mountain views. Huckleberries, wildflowers, and marmots are all over, indulging hikers in paradise. The trail gets only better the farther one travels, tracing an open ridge to Fire Mountain.

The first 5.5 miles are along Forest Service Road 2710, whose closure is a mixed blessing. It's never much fun to hike a road, but say goodbye to the crowds. Meadow Mountain Trail climbs steeply and quickly to a pass, where

the trail forks (7.5 miles). The left route drops slightly to Meadow Lake (8.2 miles), encircled by rocky cliffs and meadows. The main trail follows the ridge east, passing through subalpine parkland. Big Glacier Peak stands almost alarmingly close. Emerald and Diamond Lakes (10.5 miles) lie to the north of the trail, requiring some easy cross-country travel. Few spots are as peaceful Meadow Mountain. Campsites are scattered along the route but good, established sites are found at each of the lakes.
User Groups: Hikers, leashed dogs, and horses. No mountain bikes are allowed. No wheelchair access.

Open Seasons: This trail is accessible July–October.

Permits: A federal Northwest Forest Pass is required to park here.

Maps: For a map of Mount Baker–Snoqualmie National Forest, contact the Outdoor Recreation Information Center at the downtown Seattle REI. For topographic maps, ask Green Trails for No. 111, Sloan Peak, and No. 112, Glacier Peak, or ask the USGS for Pugh Mountain and Glacier Peak.

Directions: From Darrington, drive east 9 miles on Mountain Loop Highway to White Chuck Road (Forest Service Road 23). Turn left (east) and drive 6 miles to Forest Service Road 27 (signed "Meadow Mountain Trail"). Turn left (north) and drive 2.4 miles to Forest Service Road 2710, which is gated, and the new trailhead.

Contact: Mount Baker–Snoqualmie National Forest, Darrington Ranger Station, 1405 Emmens Street, Darrington, WA 98241, 360/436-1155.

39 GOAT FLATS
10.0 mi/5.0 hrs

in the Boulder River Wilderness, within Mount Baker–Snoqualmie National Forest

Map 3.1, page 95

It's hard to believe that such great hiking is so close to the Seattle area. Proximity to the city brings out the crowds, but the high-country beauty of Goat Flats deserves to be experienced by all. Three Fingers Trail travels five miles to the paradise of Goat Flats. Ancient forests surrender to views of old, craggy mountains. This is undoubtedly the best stretch of trail in Boulder River Wilderness.

Three Fingers Trail climbs through old-growth forest before encountering Saddle Lake (2.5 miles), modest in size but inviting nonetheless. Overnight guests need to make camp at least 200 feet from the lake. Three Fingers Trail continues its ascent through alpine meadows and increasingly rewarding views. Goat Flats sit in a particularly wide saddle along the ridge (5.5 miles), offering a grand perspective on the Cascades. Enjoy the meadows overflowing with flowers in midsummer and the huckleberries in the late summer. The trail continues one mile to Tin Can Gap and another mile to an old lookout atop Three Fingers. Tin Can Gap is too strenuous of an effort to be worthwhile and the lookout is usually reserved for climbers. Bring your lunch, stick to Goat Flats, and you'll be talking about it for months.

User Groups: Hikers and leashed dogs. No horses or mountain bikes are allowed. No wheelchair access.

Open Seasons: This trail is accessible July–October.

Permits: A federal Northwest Forest Pass is required to park here.

Maps: For a map of Mount Baker–Snoqualmie National Forest, contact the Outdoor Recreation Information Center at the downtown Seattle REI. For topographic maps, ask Green Trails for No. 109, Granite Falls, and No. 110, Silverton, or ask the USGS for Granite Falls and Silverton.

Directions: From Granite Falls, drive 7 miles east to Tupso Pass Road (Forest Service Road 41). Turn right and drive this long, gravel road to its end, 18 miles later. Watch for road markers, as many small roads branch off the main road, Forest Service Road 41.

Contact: Mount Baker–Snoqualmie National Forest, Verlot Public Service Center, 33515 Mountain Loop Highway, Granite Falls, WA 98252, 360/691-7791.

40 MOUNT PILCHUCK
6.0 mi/3.5 hrs

east of Verlot in Mount Baker–Snoqualmie National Forest and Mount Pilchuck State Park

Map 3.1, page 95

An outstanding hike, the greatest attraction along Mount Pilchuck Trail is undoubtedly the restored fire lookout at the summit. Built in 1920, the lookout was restored by the Everett Chapter of the Mountaineers to a condition equaling the outstanding views from within. The lookout peers out to the entire Puget Sound Basin, with Seattle's buildings distant specks, up to Mount Baker and over many North Cascade peaks to Glacier Peak. The lookout contains a full history of the site as well as a great map of visible peaks. This is all on top of a hike through a beautiful old-growth forest and parkland meadows among the granite slabs of the mountain.

Mount Pilchuck Trail begins within a forest teeming with giant mountain hemlocks. The trail climbs steadily the entire way but never at an excruciating grade. The trail turns north and works its way around Little Pilchuck to enter the north basin. Hemlocks and Alaskan yellow cedar find ground amid enormous slabs of granite. Snow lingers late into summer along this north-facing basin, although it rarely poses a problem. The ascent to the summit is the steepest part of the trail but well worth it. On a sunny day, there is no grander view of the Puget Sound Basin. Check the weather, as Pilchuck has a nasty legend for fast-arriving fog, a definite view spoiler.

User Groups: Hikers and leashed dogs. No horses or mountain bikes are allowed. No wheelchair access.

Open Seasons: This trail is accessible June–November.

Permits: A federal Northwest Forest Pass is required to park here.

Maps: For a map of Mount Baker–Snoqualmie National Forest, contact the Outdoor Recreation Information Center at the downtown Seattle REI. For topographic maps, ask Green Trails for No. 109, Granite Falls, or ask the USGS for Granite Falls.

Directions: From Granite Falls, drive east 12 miles on Mountain Loop Highway (Highway 530) to Pilchuck Road (Forest Service Road 42). Turn right and drive 7 miles to the trailhead at road's end.

Contact: Mount Baker–Snoqualmie National Forest, Verlot Public Service Center, 33515 Mountain Loop Highway, Granite Falls, WA 98252, 360/691-7791.

41 HEATHER LAKE
3.8 mi/3.0 hrs

east of Granite Falls in Mount Baker–Snoqualmie National Forest

Map 3.1, page 95

Below the north face of Mount Pilchuck, Heather Lake is one of the Mountain Loop Highway's most beautiful day hikes. A stretch among giant timber brings Heather Lake, inviting hikers to stick around for a while with a loop around the lake. In the latter part of summer, tasty huckleberries stain your hands while lofty peaks strain your neck. For proximity to the Seattle area and overall grandeur, there are few better destinations.

Heather Lake Trail climbs steadily but at an easy grade. While the path may have been overcome by roots or rocks at times, it is wide enough to easily accommodate the crowds that hike it. The first mile winds through long-ago-logged land, with enormous cedar stumps testament to the old forests. Notice several 80-foot western hemlocks growing atop cedar stumps, with roots snaking to the ground. Soon, the trail enters virgin forest set upon steep slopes, and one can begin to see the challenges the old lumberjacks faced. The trail drops into Heather Lake Basin, with views of Mount Pilchuck's steep walls and a trail with numerous structures to take you around the lake. Time your hike right (in August) and feast on berries.

User Groups: Hikers and leashed dogs. No

horses or mountain bikes are allowed. No wheelchair access.

Open Seasons: This trail is accessible mid-May–November.

Permits: A federal Northwest Forest Pass is required to park here.

Maps: For a map of Mount Baker–Snoqualmie National Forest, contact the Outdoor Recreation Information Center at the downtown Seattle REI. For topographic maps, ask Green Trails for No. 109, Granite Falls, or ask the USGS for Verlot.

Directions: From Granite Falls, drive east 12 miles on the Mountain Loop Highway (Highway 530) to Pilchuck Road (Forest Service Road 42). Turn right and drive 1.5 miles to the signed trailhead.

Contact: Mount Baker–Snoqualmie National Forest, Verlot Public Service Center, 33515 Mountain Loop Highway, Granite Falls, WA 98252, 360/691-7791.

42 LAKE 22
5.4 mi/4.0 hrs

east of Granite Falls in Mount Baker–Snoqualmie National Forest

Map 3.1, page 95

The designation of Lake 22 Research Natural Area preserved the landscape around this trail, making it the jewel of the southern Mountain Loop Highway. Climbing entirely through old-growth forest, the journey is as beautiful as the destination, which is a tall order in Lake 22's case. Along the trail, cascading waterfalls work to draw your attention from enormous Douglas firs and western red cedars. At the lake, steep walls leading to a rugged ridge of granite compete for attention with bushes of huckleberries.

Lake 22 Trail climbs steadily along 22 Creek, rumbling with several large cascades. The tread is well maintained, and the number of log structures is impressive. Just in time, the grade flattens and Lake 22 stands before you, guarded by the towering north face of Mount Pilchuck. The lake is stocked, so a fishing pole is put to

good use here. This is a great day hike from Seattle and is very popular. But no size of crowd should keep hikers from experiencing Lake 22.

User Groups: Hikers only. No dogs, horses, or mountain bikes are allowed. No wheelchair access.

Open Seasons: This trail is accessible mid-May–November.

Permits: A federal Northwest Forest Pass is required to park here.

Maps: For a map of Mount Baker–Snoqualmie National Forest, contact the Outdoor Recreation Information Center at the downtown Seattle REI. For topographic maps, ask Green Trails for No. 109, Granite Falls, or ask the USGS for Verlot.

Directions: From Granite Falls, drive east 13 miles on the Mountain Loop Highway (Highway 530) to the signed trailhead on the right.

Contact: Mount Baker–Snoqualmie National Forest, Verlot Public Service Center, 33515 Mountain Loop Highway, Granite Falls, WA 98252, 360/691-7791.

43 ASHLAND LAKES/ BALD MOUNTAIN
4.0–9.8 mi/2.0–10.0 hrs

south of Verlot on Washington Department of Natural Resources land

Map 3.1, page 95

This is one of the Seattle area's lesser-known hikes. On Washington Department of Natural Resources land, which is usually less than scenic, the Ashland Lakes and Bald Mountain area actually retains its old-growth forests and meadows. Perhaps the nickname Department of Nothing Left is not entirely appropriate after all. A small network of trails visits several sets of lakes and rides the crest of a long ridge. Much of it is easily accessible to hikers of all ages. For just an hour out of Seattle, it doesn't get much better than this.

Hikers can access Bald Mountain from the west or east end. Bald Mountain Trail runs along the crest of Bald Mountain, more like a ridge than a mountain. On the eastern side are Cutthroat Lakes (9.8 miles), a large grouping of tarns and small lakes set in subalpine meadows. On the western end of the trail are Ashland Lakes (4 miles). This pair of lakes, along with Beaver Plant Lake, are immersed in grand old-growth forest. DNR constructed nice, large campsites at each of the lakes. A little farther down the trail from these lakes are Twin Falls, where Wilson Creek makes an enormous cascade off a cliff into a small lake.

User Groups: Hikers and leashed dogs. No horses or mountain bikes are allowed. No wheelchair access.

Open Seasons: This trail is accessible May–November.

Permits: A federal Northwest Forest Pass is required to park here.

Maps: For a map of this area, contact the Outdoor Recreation Information Center at the downtown Seattle REI. For topographic maps, ask Green Trails for No. 110, Silverton, and No. 142, Index, or ask the USGS for Silverton and Index.

Directions: For Ashland Lakes, drive 4.5 miles east of Verlot to Forest Serice Road 4020. Turn right (south) and drive 2.3 miles to Forest Service Road 4021. Turn right and drive 1.5 miles to Forest Service Road 4021-016. Turn left onto Forest Service Road 4021-016 and drive to the Ashland trailhead at road's end.

For Cutthroat Lakes, drive east 7 miles from Verlot to Forest Service Road 4030. Turn right (south) and drive 1 mile to Forest Service Road 4032. Turn right and drive 8 miles to the trailhead at road's end.

Contact: Mount Baker-Snoqualmie National Forest, Verlot Public Service Center, 33515 Mountain Loop Highway, Granite Falls, WA 98252, 360/691-7791.

44 MOUNT FORGOTTEN MEADOWS

8.0 mi/5.0 hrs

east of Granite Falls in Mount Baker-Snoqualmie National Forest

Map 3.1, page 95

When Perry Creek Trail breaks out of the forest onto the open ridge and Mount Forgotten stares down on you, the previous four miles of steep ascent become worth every step. Great mountain views are finally at hand. But the best is yet to come. Continuing to the meadows of Mount Forgotten delivers expansive and panoramic views of numerous North Cascades peaks.

At first, Perry Creek Trail climbs slowly through several open avalanche fields. As the trail enters the forest, Perry Creek Falls greets hikers as it rushes through a small gorge. From here, the trail gets mean. The route switchbacks up through old-growth forest of Alaskan yellow cedars and Pacific silver firs, whose shade and understory of huckleberries compensate for the climb.

Soon, the trail breaks out onto the ridge, with Mount Baker visible from afar and Mount Forgotten finally apparent. Just before the ridge, follow a small footpath to the right. Mount Forgotten Meadows await a few hundred yards away, with spectacular views of Glacier Peak and other surrounding mountains. There are few better picnic spots in the Mountain Loop Highway area.

User Groups: Hikers and leashed dogs. No horses or mountain bikes are allowed. No wheelchair access.

Open Seasons: This trail is accessible June–October.

Permits: A federal Northwest Forest Pass is required to park here.

Maps: For a map of Mount Baker-Snoqualmie National Forest, contact the Outdoor Recreation Information Center at the downtown Seattle REI. For topographic maps, ask Green Trails for No. 111, Sloan Peak, or ask the USGS for Bedal.

Directions: From Granite Falls, drive east 26 miles on Mountain Loop Highway (Highway 530) to Perry Creek Road (Forest Service Road 4063). Turn left and drive 1.5 miles (stay left at the fork) to the trailhead at road's end.

Contact: Mount Baker-Snoqualmie National Forest, Verlot Public Service Center, 33515 Mountain Loop Highway, Granite Falls, WA 98252, 360/691-7791.

45 MOUNT DICKERMAN
8.6 mi/5.0 hrs

east of Granite Falls in Mount Baker–Snoqualmie National Forest

Map 3.1, page 95

Mount Dickerman persists as a Mountain Loop Highway favorite in spite of its punishing nature. After all, prolific berry bushes and expansive mountain views have the tendency to cancel out killer ascents. During the burly hike up countless switchbacks, keep your mind focused on the August berries that will surely revive your step. And during the final rise, keep your attention on the opening and expanding scenes, culminated by a near orgy of views at the summit.

Mount Dickerman Trail starts off as serious as a heart attack, making a full-on assault on the hillside. The valley floor disappears while you zigzag up through a cool forest with a few creeks for splashdowns. The trail levels off a bit to enter open meadows chock-full of huckleberry bushes. The trail keeps on climbing to make the final ascent to the summit. Glacier Peak is an imposing neighbor while all of the Monte Cristo peaks make their own appearance. It can be a busy trail in the summer, but as always with North Cascade summits, it's well worth it.

User Groups: Hikers and leashed dogs. No horses or mountain bikes are allowed. No wheelchair access.

Open Seasons: This trail is accessible July–October.

Permits: A federal Northwest Forest Pass is required to park here.

Maps: For a map of Mount Baker–Snoqualmie National Forest, contact the Outdoor Recreation Information Center at the downtown Seattle REI. For topographic maps, ask Green Trails for No. 111, Sloan Peak, or ask the USGS for Bedal.

Directions: From Granite Falls, drive east on the Mountain Loop Highway (Highway 530) for 28 miles. The signed trailhead is on the left (north) side of the highway.

Contact: Mount Baker–Snoqualmie National Forest, Verlot Public Service Center, 33515 Mountain Loop Highway, Granite Falls, WA 98252, 360/691-7791.

46 GOTHIC BASIN
9.0 mi/5.0 hrs

east of Granite Falls in Henry M. Jackson Wilderness of Mount Baker–Snoqualmie National Forest

Map 3.1, page 95

While little remains of the once-bustling mining town of Monte Cristo, the miners' trails live on. The trail up to Gothic Basin, one of many mines in the area, reveals the job's greatest perk: unbelievable views of mountains and valleys. Indeed, Gothic Basin Trail is a testament to the hardiness of the old miners. In a successful effort to get to the worksite quickly, it makes a very steep ascent to the basin, a barren moonscape save for large Foggy Lake.

Hike or bike Monte Cristo Road 1.1 miles to Gothic Basin Trail, just before the road crosses the Sauk River. It's a quick and dirty climb to the basin using steep switchbacks, but several impressive waterfalls alleviate the tough ascent. Snow lingers late within several creek gorges, making the route strongly not recommended when significant snowpack remains on the hillside. The trail eventually reaches the Gothic Basin (4.6 miles), an expansive bowl of heather meadows. Del Campo and Gothic Peaks tower above Foggy Lake on either side. For the rockhounds out there, this is a great place to explore. Numerous types of rocks are found up here, including conglomerates, granite, limestone, and sandstone. It's amazing to think that this place used to be, for miners, just another day at the office.

User Groups: Hikers, leashed dogs, and mountain bikes (mountain bikes on Monte Cristo Road). No horses are allowed. No wheelchair access.

Open Seasons: This trail is accessible late July–October.

Permits: A federal Northwest Forest Pass is required to park here.

Maps: For a map of Mount Baker–Snoqualmie National Forest, contact the Outdoor Recreation Information Center at the downtown Seattle REI. For topographic maps, ask Green Trails for No. 111, Sloan Peak, and No. 143, Monte Cristo, or ask the USGS for Monte Cristo.

Directions: From Granite Falls, drive east 30 miles on the Mountain Loop Highway (Highway 530) to the trailhead at Barlow Pass.

Contact: Mount Baker–Snoqualmie National Forest, Verlot Public Service Center, 33515 Mountain Loop Highway, Granite Falls, WA 98252, 360/691-7791.

47 POODLE DOG PASS/ TWIN LAKES

17.4 mi/1–2 days

east of Granite Falls in Henry M. Jackson Wilderness of Mount Baker–Snoqualmie National Forest

> Map 3.1, page 95

Poodle Dog Pass is one of the Mountain Loop Highway's premier hikes, set about as deep as one can get within the Cascades. This is high country, where meadows of heather cover the hillsides and mountain peaks dominate the skyline. The closure of Monte Cristo Road has made this a much longer trek, subsequently helping the path ditch most of its crowds. Rugged peaks and mountains are the theme to this hike, some of the best of the Monte Cristo region.

Accessing Poodle Dog Pass requires an easy four-mile hike or bike down Monte Cristo Road. While the road is closed to vehicles, it's not closed to mountain bikes, a popular way of cutting eight miles off the round-trip. From Monte Cristo, Poodle Dog Pass Trail steadily climbs out of the forest and into meadows, climbing over 1,600 feet in just 1.7 miles. From Poodle Dog Pass (1.7 miles), a side trail leads to large Silver Lake, set beneath the cliffs of Silvertip Peak. Beyond the pass, Twin Lakes Trail continues through superb terrain of mead-

ows and rock fields, shooting right between Twin Peaks before dropping to Twin Lakes. The long ridge of Columbia Peak stands more than 2,400 feet above the lakes, creating a large, ringed basin. Established campsites are found at each of the three lakes, and camping should be restricted to these sites only.

User Groups: Hikers, leashed dogs, and mountain bikes (mountain bikes on Monte Cristo Road). No horses are allowed. No wheelchair access.

Open Seasons: This trail is accessible July–October.

Permits: A federal Northwest Forest Pass is required to park here.

Maps: For a map of Mount Baker–Snoqualmie National Forest, contact the Outdoor Recreation Information Center at the downtown Seattle REI. For topographic maps, ask Green Trails for No. 111, Sloan Peak, and No. 143, Monte Cristo, or ask the USGS for Monte Cristo.

Directions: From Granite Falls, drive east 30 miles on the Mountain Loop Highway (Highway 530) to Monte Cristo Trail at Barlow Pass.

Contact: Mount Baker–Snoqualmie National Forest, Verlot Public Service Center, 33515 Mountain Loop Highway, Granite Falls, WA 98252, 360/691-7791.

48 GLACIER BASIN

12.2 mi/8.0 hrs

east of Granite Falls in Henry M. Jackson Wilderness of Mount Baker–Snoqualmie National Forest

> Map 3.1, page 95

Glacier Basin has the ability to make a person feel about as big as an ant. With massive mountains towering several thousand feet above the basin on every side, any understanding of "perspective" slips off into the thin mountain air. The imposing cliffs and peaks of Cadet and Monte Cristo seem to redefine scale. Glacier Basin is the perfect locale to reset the human ego.

Glacier Basin Trail departs from the old town of Monte Cristo, an easy four-mile walk down the closed-to-vehicles Monte Cristo Road. A popular means for arriving here is via mountain bike, riding along the road and then hiking the trail. The trail sets off at a decent pace before sharply quickening in its ascent. Rising up the valley, the trail passes a dramatic waterfall on Glacier Creek before taking a turn up over Mystery Hill (6 miles), the place for overnight camps.

By now the forest has faded away and meadows fill in between talus slopes. Picas and marmots are heard frequently, just before they scuttle off beneath the rocks. The trail gradually levels out and enters the basin, which is filled with meadows and interlocked braids of creeks. This is beautiful alpine territory, not so long ago buried beneath massive glaciers.

User Groups: Hikers, leashed dogs, and mountain bikes (mountain bikes on Monte Cristo Road). No horses are allowed. No wheelchair access.

Open Seasons: This trail is accessible July–October.

Permits: A federal Northwest Forest Pass is required to park here.

Maps: For a map of Mount Baker–Snoqualmie National Forest, contact the Outdoor Recreation Information Center at the downtown Seattle REI. For topographic maps, ask Green Trails for No. 111, Sloan Peak, and No. 143, Monte Cristo, or ask the USGS for Monte Cristo and Blanca Lake.

Directions: From Granite Falls, drive east 30 miles on the Mountain Loop Highway (Highway 530) to the trailhead at Barlow Pass.

Contact: Mount Baker–Snoqualmie National Forest, Verlot Public Service Center, 33515 Mountain Loop Highway, Granite Falls, WA 98252, 360/691-7791.

49 FOURTH OF JULY PASS
12.2 mi/5.0 hrs

east of Newhalem in Ross Lake National Recreation Area and North Cascades National Park

Map 3.2, page 96

This is one of the few passes in the North Cascades that does not inspire a cold sweat in hikers. Unlike many of its kin, this is not a steep, near-vertical trail leading to the pass. On the contrary, the route along Panther Creek is extremely beautiful and easy to hike. Numerous cascades and waterfalls are the result of the creek's course over ever-present boulders. The total elevation gain of 1,800 feet is spread out over six miles, so Fourth of July Pass can be achieved by the whole family. Wide views of glacially capped mountains await at the top. And for those with the means for transportation, the trail continues to Thunder Creek for a great through-hike.

The best route up to the pass is definitely via Panther Creek. Panther Creek Trail stays near the gushing creek as it passes through a luxuriant forest of large western red cedars. At 3.1 miles is Panther Camp, with several sites. The trail begins to climb up the hillside when the creek makes a hard turn to the southeast to venture deep into the wilderness. Glaciers carved the pass long ago to avoid Ruby Mountain, leaving it wide and flat. Panther Potholes offer a cool respite on hot days. The best views are from Fourth of July Camp. From here are expansive views of the Neve Glacier sliding down off Snowfield Peak and Colonial Peak. The trail continues 2.5 miles to Thunder Creek Trail (2.1 miles from the trailhead).

User Groups: Hikers only. No dogs, horses, or mountain bikes are allowed. No wheelchair access.

Open Seasons: This trail is accessible July–October.

Permits: A federal Northwest Forest Pass is required to park here.

Maps: For a map of North Cascades National Park, contact the Outdoor Recreation Information Center at the downtown Seattle REI. For topographic maps, ask Green Trails for No. 48, Diablo Dam, and No. 49, Mount Logan, or ask the USGS for Crater Mountain and Ross Dam.

Directions: From Marblemount, drive east on Highway 20 to East Bank Trailhead, 8 miles beyond Colonial Creek Campground. Park at

East Bank Trailhead, cross the highway, and walk .3 mile east to the trailhead on the south side of the highway.

Contact: North Cascades National Park, Wilderness Information Center, 7280 Ranger Station Road, Marblemount, WA 98267, 360/873-4500.

50 DEVIL'S DOME LOOP
41.7 mi/4–5 days

east of Ross Lake in North Cascades National Park and Pasayten Wilderness

Map 3.2, page 96

The North Cascades National Park is well known for its large selection of extended backpacking trips. Devil's Dome Loop is one of its best, even trekking across part of the Pasayten Wilderness. Set along the high ridges east of Ross Lake, the loop encircles mammoth Jack Mountain while enjoying miles of far-flung vistas, acres of old-growth forests, and privacy in the deep wilderness. The route is a tough one and should be undertaken only by those ready for four or more days in the backcountry.

Heading counterclockwise, Jackita Ridge Trail climbs steeply from Canyon Creek onto the barren, rocky slopes of Crater Mountain. From here, 11 miles of trail traverses Jackita Ridge before encountering Devil's Ridge Trail at Devil's Pass. Devil's Ridge Trail heads east for another five miles of high-country hiking. From this point, the trail drops to Ross Lake. The East Bank Trail follows the shore 15 miles before returning to Canyon Creek Trailhead. While a four-day trip is possible, five or six days is much better.

Water is an important consideration, as the ridge is extremely dry once the snowpack has melted. Along the way are many established camps. Most notable are (from Canyon Creek Trailhead): Devil's Park (7 miles), Devil's Pass Shelter (16 miles), Skyline Camp (18 miles), Devil's Dome (20 miles), and Bear Skull (22 miles). The East Bank Trail has many camps spread along its shores. The Devil's Dome Loop is highly respected for its ability to challenge even veteran hikers.

User Groups: Hikers only. No dogs, horses, or mountain bikes are allowed. No wheelchair access.

Open Seasons: This area is accessible mid-July–October.

Permits: A federal Northwest Forest Pass is required to park here. Overnights stays within the national park require backcountry camping permits, which are available at the Wilderness Information Center.

Maps: For a map of North Cascades National Park, contact the Outdoor Recreation Information Center at the downtown Seattle REI. For topographic maps, ask Green Trails for No. 16, Ross Lake, No. 17, Jack Mountain, No. 48, Diablo Dam, and No. 49, Mount Logan, or ask the USGS for Crater Mountain, Azurite Peak, Shull Mountain, Jack Mountain, and Pumpkin Mountain.

Directions: From Marblemount, drive east on Highway 20 to the Canyon Creek Trailhead, near Mile Marker 142.

Contact: North Cascades National Park, Wilderness Information Center, 7280 Ranger Station Road, Marblemount, WA 98267, 360/873-4500.

51 EAST CREEK
16.0 mi/2 days

west of Winthrop in North Cascades Scenic Highway and Okanogan National Forest

Map 3.2, page 96

Despite an easily accessible trailhead on Highway 20, few people bother to visit East Creek. Perhaps the trail is overshadowed by the reputations of bigger, better-known trails. Other folks' loss is your gain should you undertake East Creek. Eight miles of trail travel through terrific old-growth forest and open meadow to Mebee Pass, where views are finally afforded. From the pass, scramble to surrounding peaks, peer into the long Methow River valley, bask in the sun, and most of all, enjoy the solitude.

East Creek Trail crosses Granite Creek via footbridge before making a quick ascent along East Creek. A ford of East Creek is required (2.5 miles), a difficult endeavor when the winter's snows are still melting. Late July is best, as runoff has lowered but wildflowers are still in bloom. The trail continues up the valley, crossing numerous creeks. The last 1.5 miles is a steep climb up the side of the valley, breaking out of the forest into meadows. At the pass stands an old fire lookout, built in 1933 and recently renovated. Camps are situated at several places along the trail, but the best are just below Mebee Pass in the meadows.

User Groups: Hikers, leashed dogs, and horses. No mountain bikes are allowed. No wheelchair access.

Open Seasons: This trail is accessible July–October.

Permits: A federal Northwest Forest Pass is required to park here.

Maps: For a map of Okanogan National Forest, contact the Outdoor Recreation Information Center at the downtown Seattle REI. For topographic maps, ask Green Trails for No. 49, Mount Logan, or ask the USGS for Azurita Peak.

Directions: From Marblemount, drive east on Highway 20 to the East Creek Trailhead, near Mile Marker 146.

Contact: Okanogan National Forest, Methow Valley Ranger District, 24 West Chewuch Road, Winthrop, WA 98862, 509/996-4003.

52 EASY PASS/FISHER CREEK
7.0 mi/5.0 hrs

east of Newhalem in Okanogan National Forest and North Cascades National Park

Map 3.2, page 96

Easy Pass is easily one of the biggest misnomers within the North Cascades, as there is nothing easy about it. After all, a rugged, rocky climb of 2,800 feet is rarely easy. It certainly isn't here. The scenery, however, is easy on the eyes. The colossal Mount Logan, cloaked in ice, stares from across the valley while Fisher Peak stands at the head of the basin. Wildflowers and wildlife roam freely below in the

wild and undisturbed valley. The trail continues by dropping into the basin and wandering out Fisher Creek Valley to Thunder Creek, an exceptional trek.

Easy Pass Trail immediately crosses boulder-strewn Granite Creek and starts a long, arduous climb to the pass. After two miles, the trail breaks out of forest and enters an avalanche chute between the steep walls of Ragged Ridge. The name Easy Pass stems from the fact that this was the easiest (and only) place for a trail over Ragged Ridge. The trail finally reaches the pass after 3.5 miles. Here, subalpine larches claim whatever soil they can for a home, turning a brilliant gold in the fall. There is no camping at the pass.

For overnight trips, Easy Pass Trail continues down to Fisher Creek (within the national park). This is black-bear country, and the animals are frequently spotted roaming the hillsides munching on huckleberries. Fisher Camp is at the lower part of the flower-filled basin and makes a great overnight resting spot. The trail proceeds down through the forested valley to Thunder Creek, 11 miles from Easy Pass.

User Groups: Hikers and leashed dogs (dogs to Easy Pass only). No horses or mountain bikes are allowed. No wheelchair access.

Open Seasons: This trail is accessible mid-July–mid-October.

Permits: A federal Northwest Forest Pass is required to park here. Overnights stays within the national park require backcountry camping permits.

Maps: For a map of Okanogan National Forest and North Cascades National Park, contact the Outdoor Recreation Information Center at the downtown Seattle REI. For topographic maps, ask Green Trails for No. 49, Mount Logan, or ask the USGS for Mount Arriva and Mount Logan.

Directions: From Winthrop, drive about 40 miles west on Highway 20 (or 46 miles east from Marblemount) to Easy Pass Trailhead. The trailhead is on the south side of the highway.

Contact: North Cascades National Park, Wilderness Information Center, 7280 Ranger Station Road, Marblemount, WA 98267, 360/873-4500.

53 RAINY LAKE NATURE TRAIL
1.8 mi/1.0 hr
west of Winthrop in Okanogan National Forest
Map 3.2, page 96

The achievement of motoring up a pass is usually a call for celebration and a little leg stretching. Rainy Lake Nature Trail provides the perfect excuse to pull over and work out the cramps. Only a mile to the lake, with no elevation change, Rainy Lake Trail is easily accomplished by folks of all ages and abilities. The paved path has educational signs pointing out plant species or ecological processes. Some of the trees on the trail are downright imposing. At the end lies Rainy Lake, sitting within a glacial cirque. The Lyall Glacier sits above with its meltwater cascading into the lake. This is a great stop!

User Groups: Hikers and leashed dogs. No horses or mountain bikes are allowed. The trail is wheelchair accessible.

Open Seasons: This trail is accessible mid-June–October.

Permits: A federal Northwest Forest Pass is required to park here.

Maps: For a map of Okanogan National Forest, contact the Outdoor Recreation Information Center at the downtown Seattle REI. For topographic maps, ask Green Trails for No. 50, Washington Pass, or ask the USGS for Washington Pass.

Directions: From Newhalem, drive Highway 20 to Mile Marker 157. Turn right into the south trailhead. The north trailhead is only for Cutthroat Pass and the Pacific Crest Trail.

Contact: Okanogan National Forest, Methow Valley Ranger District, 24 West Chewuch Road, Winthrop, WA 98862, 509/996-4003.

54 LAKE ANN/MAPLE PASS
3.8–7.6 mi/2.0–4.5 hrs
west of Winthrop in Okanogan National Forest
Map 3.2, page 96

With good reason, Lake Ann is one of Highway 20's most-often-recommended day hikes. Just two miles of hiking delivers a beautiful lake surrounded by towering ridges. It's a great place for bird-watching, offers the chance to do a little fishing, and makes for a nice picnic. Plus, it can be added as a side trip to Maple Pass.

Lake Ann Trail heads up through a great old-growth forest filled with Pacific silver fir and mountain hemlock. The path is well maintained and the grade climbs gently. Marmots are likely to greet you with a shrill whistle while you pass through the meadows. The trail divides (1.5 miles), with the Maple Pass Trail heading to the right. Stay to the left and soon you'll be at Lake Ann. (If you don't go back to do Maple Pass, your trip will be 3.8 miles round-trip.) Unfortunately there is no camping at Lake Ann because of previous overuse and abuse. The lake basin is a result of glacial carving nearly a million years ago. As the glacier retreated, the rocks and dirt it deposited formed a natural dam, creating Lake Ann. Meadows abound here, even on a small island in the south part of the lake. And there is always a chance of seeing a black bear here. So keep that picnic nearby at all times.

In local hiking circles, Maple Pass is considered one of the best day hikes in the region. And rightfully so, as this trail takes hikers above two shimmering blue lakes to a level with glaciers. It takes you through mountain meadows teeming with marmots and visited by mountain goats and black bears. Most impressively, it takes you on even terms with so many major peaks that you need six topo maps to name them all. This really is a trail to remember and visit again and again.

The loop is best started counterclockwise. This makes the ascent a little easier to handle. In the other direction, a sign forewarns,

"Trail beyond steeper but more scenic." Maple Pass Trail follows Lake Ann trail for 1.5 miles before climbing the basin wall to Heather Pass. Lake Ann glitters below and mountain heather lights up the meadows in August. Black Peak, 8,970 feet, emerges and rarely leaves your sight. The trail moves up the western ridge through high meadows. Alpine larches grace any fertile spot possible, and the northern peaks stand out. Maple Pass is a good climb, and from it an understanding of several major creek drainages can be had. On clear days, even Glacier Peak is visible. The trail, now even with the Lyall Glacier, continues down, moving between views of Rainy Lake and Lake Ann. A steep drop through a wonderful forest brings you to the car again. The experience will likely keep you coming back to Maple Pass.

User Groups: Hikers and leashed dogs (dogs allowed on the loop but may not complete it, as Maple Pass is in the national park). No horses or mountain bikes are allowed. No wheelchair access.

Open Seasons: This trail is usually accessible mid-July–early October.

Permits: A federal Northwest Forest Pass is required to park here.

Maps: For a map of Okanogan National Forest, contact the Outdoor Recreation Information Center at the downtown Seattle REI. For topographic maps for the Lake Ann Trail, ask Green Trails for No. 50, Washington Pass, or ask the USGS for Washington Pass. For topographic maps for Maple Pass, ask Green Trails for No. 49, Mount Logan, and No. 50, Washington Pass, or ask the USGS for Washington Pass and Mount Arriva.

Directions: From Newhalem, drive Highway 20 to Mile Marker 157. Turn right into the south trailhead. The north trailhead is only for Cutthroat Pass and the Pacific Crest Trail.

Contact: Okanogan National Forest, Methow Valley Ranger District, 24 West Chewuch Road, Winthrop, WA 98862, 509/996-4003.

55 BLUE LAKE
4.4 mi/2.5 hrs

west of Winthrop in Okanogan National Forest

Map 3.2, page 96

Blue Lake is a natural masterpiece. To begin, Blue Lake Trail climbs through shady old-growth forests. The destination is a short two miles, a lake sparkling deep turquoise, making Blue Lake a most appropriate name. Enormous craggy peaks and ridges skirted in rock and talus stand to three sides. The 7,800-foot Early Winters Spires rise to the northeast trying to steal the show. And the high mountain subalpine forests bring it all to life.

Blue Lake is a truly fantastic hike, considering its easy accessibility and attractiveness in all seasons. The first mile of trail climbs gradually through virgin forest. Before long, it breaks into meadows, and Cutthroat Peak is visible across the valley. The trail was built well and receives good maintenance, as it seems much shorter than its stated distance. The path finds the lake before you know it. Mountain hemlock, alpine larch, and subalpine fir find home in the smallest crevasses and complete the scene. The alpine larch make a late-season hike here highly appealing. During autumn, the larch seem to catch on fire, their needles turning orange and then yellow before falling off. There is no camping allowed at Blue Lake, so please keep it to a day hike.

User Groups: Hikers and leashed dogs. No horses or mountain bikes are allowed. No wheelchair access.

Open Seasons: This trail is accessible mid-June–mid-October.

Permits: A federal Northwest Forest Pass is required to park here.

Maps: For a map of Okanogan National Forest, contact the Outdoor Recreation Information Center at the downtown Seattle REI. For topographic maps, ask Green Trails for No. 50, Washington Pass, or ask the USGS for Washington Pass.

Directions: From Winthrop, drive west on Highway 20 to Blue Lake Trailhead. The signed trailhead is on the left, about .5 mile west of Washington Pass.

Contact: Okanogan National Forest, Methow Valley Ranger District, 24 West Chewuch Road, Winthrop, WA 98862, 509/996-4003.

56 CUTTHROAT PASS
11.0 mi/6.0 hrs

near Washington Pass in Okanogan National Forest

Map 3.2, page 96

Cutthroat Pass is perfect for all kinds of hikers, from beginners to the experienced, which has made it a popular destination over the years. The pass isn't a difficult journey, making it a great trip for first-timers in the North Cascades. Cutthroat Lake offers a good turnaround point for those uninterested in climbing to the pass and simply wanting a great, short day hike. Conversely, the views from the pass will inspire even the most trail hardened of hikers, who may think they have seen it all.

Cutthroat Pass Trail leisurely climbs through the valley's forest to a junction (1.7 miles). Here, Cutthroat Lake Trail breaks to the left. The lake is a short .25 mile down the trail, lined by boulders, forests, and steep basin walls. Those wanting an easy overnighter will find campsites here. Make sure it's an established site, though, and at least 200 feet from the lakeshore.

Continuing on Cutthroat Pass Trail takes hikers abruptly up to the pass. Expect a lot of wildflowers in the expansive meadows during the month of July. The views are exceptional, distant, and rewarding. Visitors often return home with stories of seeing or encountering mountains goats, who regularly frequent the area. Camps are situated around the pass, although water is nonexistent once the snowpack is gone. The pass sees its fair share of traffic because the Pacific Crest Trail runs right through it.

User Groups: Hikers, leashed dogs, and horses. No mountain bikes are allowed. No wheelchair access.

Open Seasons: This trail is accessible July–September.

Permits: A federal Northwest Forest Pass is required to park here.

Maps: For a map of Okanogan National Forest, contact the Outdoor Recreation Information Center at the downtown Seattle REI. For topographic maps, ask Green Trails for No. 50, Washington Pass, or ask the USGS for Washington Pass.

Directions: From Winthrop, drive west 26 miles on Highway 20 to Forest Service Road 400. Turn right (north) and drive 1 mile to the trailhead at road's end.

Contact: Okanogan National Forest, Methow Valley Ranger District, 24 West Chewuch Road, Winthrop, WA 98862, 509/996-4003.

57 WEST FORK METHOW RIVER
16.0 mi/2–6 days

northwest of Mazama in Okanogan National Forest

Map 3.2, page 96

The West Fork of the Methow River serves as an access point to one of the Pacific Crest Trail's most scenic sections. The trail follows the river eight miles up the valley to the PCT. The trail along the river is well known by anglers, who come here to catch and release cutthroat and other trout. Campsites appear regularly along the way, usually directly on the river. The trail eventually leaves the riverside to reach the PCT.

From here, hikers have several options. They can join the PCT as it heads north through Brush Creek and along a high ridge to Hart's Pass (20.7 miles). Expect lots of meadows, views, and probably mountain goats. Or one can travel south on the PCT. The famous trail continues south through the river valley, up to meadowy ridges and on to Rainy Pass Trailhead via three major passes (26.4 miles). And the East Creek Trail ventures out of the Methow Valley to Mebee Pass, an old fire lookout, and eventually to East Creek Trailhead (17.9 miles). These three options require two cars, however, which is sometimes a difficult undertaking. If you have only one car, there's no shame in hiking out the same way you came in.

User Groups: Hikers, leashed dogs, horses, and mountain bikes. No wheelchair access.

Open Seasons: This trail is accessible July–mid-October.

Permits: A federal Northwest Forest Pass is required to park here.

Maps: For a map of Okanogan National Forest, contact the Outdoor Recreation Information Center at the downtown Seattle REI. For topographic maps, ask Green Trails for No. 49, Mount Logan, and No. 50, Washington Pass, or ask the USGS for Robinson Mountain and Slate Peak.

Directions: From Winthrop, drive west 17 miles on Highway 20 to Mazama. Turn right (north) onto Mazama Road and drive .2 mile to Hart's Pass Road (County Road 9140/Forest Service Road 5400). Turn left and drive to Rattlesnake Trailhead, .3 mile beyond River Bend Campground.

Contact: Okanogan National Forest, Methow Valley Ranger District, 24 West Chewuch Road, Winthrop, WA 98862, 509/996-4003.

58 BUCKSKIN RIDGE
22.2 mi/2 days

northwest of Mazama in Pasayten Wilderness of Okanogan National Forest

Map 3.2, page 96

Thanks to Slate Pass, a trailhead conveniently situated at 6,200 feet of elevation, access to Buckskin Ridge is a piece of cake. Well, maybe a little more difficult than cake, but still, very little of the North Cascades is as accessible. Buckskin Ridge Trail runs the long, jagged ridge at a steady elevation. Major peaks of the Pasayten Wilderness are close enough to touch at times (or even climb). Buckskin Trail passes a pair of lakes before dropping to the Pasayten River, which offers a pair of excellent river hike loop options.

From Hart's Pass, hike the road up to Slate Pass (1.4 miles) and where Buckskin Ridge

Trail begins. The trail enjoys open meadows for much of its length. The trail winds around the east side of the ridge to good camping at Silver Lake (6 miles) and on to Silver Pass (8 miles). The trail now runs the west side of the ridge, with all new peaks to admire. This segment has several steep and challenging sections, so be prepared for a slow time. Buckskin Lake (11.1 miles) marks the northern end of the ridge and also makes for a good campsite. The obvious return route is back along the ridge. But those seeking a loop can continue on Buckskin Trail to the Pasayten River. Here, trails up the West and Middle Forks return to Slate Peak. Each is about 35 miles in total length.

User Groups: Hikers, leashed dogs, and horses (horses permitted but highly not recommended). No mountain bikes are allowed. No wheelchair access.

Open Seasons: This trail is accessible July–October.

Permits: A federal Northwest Forest Pass is required to park here.

Maps: For a map of Okanogan National Forest, contact the Outdoor Recreation Information Center at the downtown Seattle REI. For topographic maps, ask Green Trails for No. 18, Pasayten Peak, and No. 50, Washington Pass, or ask the USGS for Slate Peak, Pasayten Peak, and Frosty Creek.

Directions: From Winthrop, drive west 17 miles on Highway 20 to Mazama. Turn right (north) onto Mazama Road and drive .2 mile to Hart's Pass Road (County Road 9140/Forest Service Road 5400). Turn left and drive 18.5 miles to Hart's Pass. Turn right on Forest Service Road 5400-600 and drive 5 miles to Slate Pass at road's end. Hart's Pass Road is prone to frequent washouts; call the ranger station for current status.

Contact: Okanogan National Forest, Methow Valley Ranger District, 24 West Chewuch Road, Winthrop, WA 98862, 509/996-4003.

59 DRIVEWAY BUTTE

8.0 mi/5.0 hrs

north of Highway 20 in Okanogan National Forest

Map 3.2, page 96

This is a steep ascent to a former lookout site atop Driveway Butte. If the Forest Service once used a peak to scan for fires, you can be certain that it has an expansive view. Indeed it does, looking out over many surrounding valleys, ridges, and peaks, all the way into the Pasayten Wilderness. Driveway Butte Trail gains about 3,000 feet, which is no easy feat. Complicating the task is a trail that can be rocky and rough at times. For those prepared for a strenuous hike, however, the vista is a wonderful reward.

Driveway Butte Trail leaves Early Winters Creek very near Highway 20. The first two miles are brutal, climbing steeply up Indian Creek through forest. At a small pass, the trail heads around the headwaters of McGee Creek. Subalpine meadows finally appear before the top of the Butte, with grand views of Silver Star Mountain and many other Cascade peaks. Once the snow is gone, very little water is to be found along the trail, so carrying extra water is important, especially on hot summer days. The panoramic views will be well appreciated by those who accomplish the summit.

User Groups: Hikers, leashed dogs, and horses. No mountain bikes are allowed. No wheelchair access.

Open Seasons: This trail is accessible mid-May–October.

Permits: A federal Northwest Forest Pass is required to park here.

Maps: For a map of Okanogan National Forest, contact the Outdoor Recreation Information Center at the downtown Seattle REI. For topographic maps, ask Green Trails for No. 50, Washington Pass, or ask the USGS for Silverstar Mountain and Robinson Mountain.

Directions: From Winthrop, drive west on Highway 20 for 18.5 miles to Klipchuck Campground. Near the self-service fee station is a gated service road. The trail begins about 100 yards down this road.

Contact: Okanogan National Forest, Methow Valley Ranger Station, 24 West Chewuch Road, Winthrop, WA 98862, 509/996-4003.

60 WEST FORK PASAYTEN

31.0 mi/3–4 days

northwest of Mazama in Pasayten Wilderness of Okanogan National Forest

Map 3.2, page 96

The West Fork of the Pasayten is easily accessible via Slate Peak, a trailhead conveniently situated at an elevation of 6,800 feet. Start high and drop into the large, wide valley of the Pasayten's West Fork. The trail sticks to the river valley, passing through ancient forests of pine and fir with frequent views to the towering peaks lining the valley ridges. This trail experiences some of the Pasayten's wildest regions, where sightings of bear and other wildlife are frequent. Best of all, the trail makes two excellent loops when combined with trails that run along the top of the valley's ridges.

West Fork Pasayten Trail drops from the high vantage of Slate Peak into the river valley below. Snow lingers a little late on the north side of Slate Peak and you must ford the river (4 miles). That means late July or early August are prime times to hit this trail. Campsites are littered along the route, frequently right on the river. At 8.5 miles is a junction for Holman Creek and up to Pacific Crest Trail, the first of the two great loop possibilities. Hike up to Holman Pass and head south on PCT back to Slate Peak for a total of 21 miles. Many call this the best of PCT. Anywhere.

The main trail continues another seven miles to a major junction. Head south on the Buckskin Ridge Trail, a 16.6-mile trip back to Slate Peak. This section of trail can be obscure and difficult to find at times, but experienced routefinders will love it.

User Groups: Hikers, leashed dogs, and horses. No mountain bikes are allowed. No wheelchair access.

Open Seasons: This trail is accessible mid-July–mid-October.

Permits: A federal Northwest Forest Pass is required to park here. A free wilderness permit is also required to hike here and is available at the trailhead.

Maps: For a map of Okanogan National Forest, contact the Outdoor Recreation Information Center at the downtown Seattle REI. For topographic maps, ask Green Trails for No. 18, Pasayten Peak, and No. 50, Washington Pass, or ask the USGS for Slate Peak, Pasayten Peak, and Frosty Creek.

Directions: From Winthrop, drive west 17 miles on Highway 20 to Mazama. Turn right (north) onto Mazama Road and drive .2 mile to Hart's Pass Road (County Road 9140/Forest Service Road 5400). Turn left and drive 18.5 miles to Hart's Pass. Turn right on Forest Service Road 5400-600 and drive 5 miles to Slate Pass at road's end. Hart's Pass Road is prone to frequent washouts; call the ranger station for current status.

Contact: Okanogan National Forest, Methow Valley Ranger District, 24 West Chewuch Road, Winthrop, WA 98862, 509/996-4003.

61 ROBINSON PASS
55.0 mi/5–10 days

north of Mazama in Pasayten Wilderness of Okanogan National Forest

Map 3.2, page 96

By no means must you hike this trail 27.5 miles in only to come out the same 27.5 miles. Instead, Robinson Creek Trail can be drastically shortened or dramatically lengthened. Heading over Robinson Pass into the Middle Fork Pasayten River valley, the trail ventures into the most secluded section of the already remote wilderness. Numerous trails intersect the trail along the Pasayten River, making hikes easily customizable. Even a straight trip up and back isn't all that bad.

Robinson Creek Trail follows the creek to Robinson Pass (8.8 miles). Campsites are scattered along the creek and are usually forested;

the better ones are near the pass. The trail now drops elevation for the next 19 miles down through the Pasayten River Valley. The wide, U-shaped valley is regularly broken up by enormous avalanche chutes, revealing the tall, rounded peaks lining the valley. Campsites are abundant in this valley and are often along the river.

Trails frequently break off to head over the ridge or up another major creek drainage. Trails lead up the West Fork of Pasayten (20.5 miles), Rock Creek (21.6 miles), and Frosty Creek (22.8 miles), each more desolate than the one before it. High-country treks can be made up to Freds Lake and Doris Lake (15.7 miles) or Tatoosh Buttes (20.7 miles). The Pasayten Wilderness is a place where grizzly bears and gray wolves still roam the countryside, and Robinson Creek Trail is the gateway to all of it.

User Groups: Hikers, leashed dogs, and horses. No mountain bikes are allowed. No wheelchair access.

Open Seasons: This trail is accessible mid-June–mid-October.

Permits: A federal Northwest Forest Pass is required to park here. A free wilderness permit is also required to hike here and is available at the trailhead.

Maps: For a map of Okanogan National Forest, contact the Outdoor Recreation Information Center at the downtown Seattle REI. For topographic maps, ask Green Trails for No. 18, Pasayten Peak, and No. 50, Washington Pass, or ask the USGS for Robinson Mountain, Slate Peak, Pasayten Peak, and Mount Lago.

Directions: From Winthrop, drive west 17 miles on Highway 20 to Mazama. Turn right (north) onto Mazama Road and drive .2 mile to Hart's Pass Road (County Road 9140/Forest Service Road 5400). Turn left and drive 9.5 miles to Robinson Creek Trailhead. Hart's Pass Road is prone to frequent washouts; call the ranger station for current status.

Contact: Okanogan National Forest, Methow Valley Ranger District, 24 West Chewuch Road, Winthrop, WA 98862, 509/996-4003.

62 LOST RIVER
8.5 mi/5.0 hrs

northwest of Mazama in Pasayten Wilderness of Okanogan National Forest

Map 3.2, page 96

While the Pasayten Wilderness is best known for its long treks into the backcountry, it does have its share of great day hikes. This easy stroll through the woods leads to the convergence of two large gorges, the Lost River and Eureka Creek. Along the way, the Lost River makes for noisy company, cascading over boulders and small rapids. With very little elevation gain along the route, the trail is perfect for hikers of all abilities and families. As an additional bonus, the low-lying trail opens earlier than other high routes, making the Lost River a good springtime outing.

Monument Creek Trail follows Lost River through forests of pine and fir, regularly breaking out for views of the valley ridges. Four miles in, the trail comes to Eureka Creek. Spilling out of a deep gorge, the creek passes over impressive falls before joining the Lost River. Cross a bridge over Eureka to streamside campsites, a very pleasant place to have lunch or spend the night. The narrow Lost River Gorge is viewable from the end of the trail, although it gets even more rugged and remote up the valley—so much so that trail construction isn't possible up the gorge. Folks who are ready for serious cross-country navigation can leave the two streams' confluence and hike up to Pistol Pass and on to Monument Creek (15.4 miles), a strenuous, even hellish, up and down.

User Groups: Hikers, leashed dogs, and horses. No mountain bikes are allowed. No wheelchair access.

Open Seasons: This trail is accessible April–October.

Permits: A federal Northwest Forest Pass is required to park here.

Maps: For a map of Okanogan National Forest, contact the Outdoor Recreation Information Center at the downtown Seattle REI. For topographic maps, ask Green Trails for No.

50, Washington Pass, and No. 51, Mazama, or ask the USGS for Robinson Mountain and McLeod Mountain.

Directions: From Winthrop, drive west 17 miles on Highway 20 to Mazama. Turn right (north) onto Mazama Road and drive .2 mile to Hart's Pass Road (County Road 9140/Forest Service Road 5400). Turn left and drive 9.5 miles to Monument Creek Trailhead. Hart's Pass Road is prone to frequent washouts; call the ranger station for current status.

Contact: Okanogan National Forest, Methow Valley Ranger District, 24 West Chewuch Road, Winthrop, WA 98862, 509/996-4003.

63 BURCH MOUNTAIN
9.8 mi/5.5 hrs

north of Winthrop in Okanogan National Forest

Map 3.2, page 96

From atop Burch Mountain, feel awash in a sea of rocky peaks, with waves of mountain ridges extending in every direction. The vastness of the Pasayten Wilderness is easily felt from this high point of 7,782 feet. Catch the trail during the early summer and the journey is as grand as the summit, with open forests providing cool shade and wildflowers taking over open meadows. Venture here later in the season and you're sure to experience hot, dry weather. If you come in August, bring plenty of water.

The route starts on Billy Goat Pass Trail, which gains a hefty 1,800 feet of elevation in three miles. At the pass, double back to the south on Burch Mountain Trail. This path scales the side of Eightmile Ridge at a less harsh pitch. Meadows and vistas are the norm along the way. After 1.5 miles, the trail has reached the base of Burch Mountain and a side trail scrambles to the summit. Big Craggy Peak lives up to its name across Eightmile Creek, while numerous other peaks and ridges shine in the not-so-far distance. Bring a map, for many of the peaks deserve to be identified.

User Groups: Hikers, leashed dogs, and horses.

No mountain bikes are allowed. No wheelchair access.

Open Seasons: This trail is accessible July–September.

Permits: A federal Northwest Forest Pass is required to park here.

Maps: For a map of Okanogan National Forest, contact the Outdoor Recreation Information Center at the downtown Seattle REI. For topographic maps, ask Green Trails for No. 19, Billy Goat Mountain, or ask the USGS for Billy Goat Mountain and Sweetgrass Butte.

Directions: From Winthrop, drive north on Chewuch River Road (across Highway 20 from the visitors center) 10 miles to Forest Service Road 5140. Turn left and drive 11 miles to the trailhead at road's end.

Contact: Okanogan National Forest, Methow Valley Ranger District, 24 West Chewuch Road, Winthrop, WA 98862, 509/996-4003.

64 CHEWUCH RIVER
36.0 mi/4 days

north of Winthrop in Pasayten Wilderness of Okanogan National Forest

Map 3.2, page 96

This long, river valley trail makes connections to several trails branching off into the Pasayten Wilderness before arriving at some of the area's most beautiful country. But it also makes for a good day hike, with Chewuch Falls a short three miles up the trail. Those looking for an extended trip will enjoy Remmel Lake at the head of the Chewuch. Trips up Tungsten Creek, Topaz Mountain, and Coleman Peak are also begun from the Chewuch River.

Chewuch River Trail is popular with those riding horses or driving stock, meaning that it can be wide and dusty. Overall, the hike gains little elevation as it passes through forests of lodgepole pine, some of it burned in 2003. Campsites are scattered along the length of the trail, and water is never far away. Keep plodding and the trail eventually rises into Remmel Basin to find Remmel Lake (18 miles), surrounded by meadows and larches. The high,

flat terrain makes the surrounding 8,000-plus-feet peaks seem like rolling hills. At the lake, make camp at established campsites more than 200 feet from the lakeshore.

User Groups: Hikers, leashed dogs, and horses. No mountain bikes are allowed. No wheelchair access.

Open Seasons: This trail is accessible July–September.

Permits: A federal Northwest Forest Pass is required to park here. A free wilderness permit is also required to hike here and is available at the trailhead.

Maps: For a map of Okanogan National Forest, contact the Outdoor Recreation Information Center at the downtown Seattle REI. For topographic maps, ask Green Trails for No. 20, Coleman Peak, or ask the USGS for Coleman Peak, Bauerman Ridge, and Remmel Mountain.

Directions: From Winthrop, drive north on Chewuch River Road (across Highway 20 from the visitors center) 30 miles to Thirtymile Trailhead at road's end.

Contact: Okanogan National Forest, Methow Valley Ranger District, 24 West Chewuch Road, Winthrop, WA 98862, 509/996-4003.

65 COLEMAN RIDGE
31.7 mi/3–4 days

north of Winthrop in Pasayten Wilderness of Okanogan National Forest

Map 3.2, page 96

While Coleman Ridge Trail runs more than 20 miles along the high alpine ridge, the best part of the trip is contained in the upper part of ridge, near Four Point Lake. Here, scattered among glacially scraped boulders, are meadows full of early summer wildflowers and far-reaching vistas. Four Point Lake makes for a wonderful camp, where captivating stars illuminate the night sky.

The route follows the Chewuch River before making a lazy loop up to Coleman and back down. Hike the Chewuch River, passing Chewuch Falls along the way, until you reach Fire Creek Trail (6 miles), heading off to the left. You must ford the Chewuch, a difficult crossing when the snowpack runoff is high. The trail climbs up Fire Creek, eventually becoming Coleman Ridge Trail (10.7 miles), and finds a high mountain pass complete with views. Campsites are scattered along the route, with nice spots on the creek and a couple atop the ridge.

Coleman Ridge Trail heads north on the ridge and passes below Remmel Mountain, a worthy peak for an easy side trip. Four Point Lake is off a short side trail (16.5 miles). Be sure to use the established sites at the lake. The route then drops down Four Point Creek to the Chewuch River, 12.9 miles from the trailhead. Good times for a trip here are July, when wildflowers are blooming, and late September, when larches seem to have caught fire.

User Groups: Hikers, leashed dogs, and horses. No mountain bikes are allowed. No wheelchair access.

Open Seasons: This trail is accessible July–September.

Permits: A federal Northwest Forest Pass is required to park here. A free wilderness permit is also required to hike here and is available at the trailhead.

Maps: For a map of Okanogan National Forest, contact the Outdoor Recreation Information Center at the downtown Seattle REI. For topographic maps, ask Green Trails for No. 20, Coleman Peak, or ask the USGS for Coleman Peak, Mount Barney, and Bauerman Ridge.

Directions: From Winthrop, drive north on Chewuch River Road (across Highway 20 from the visitors center) 30 miles to Thirtymile Trailhead at road's end.

Contact: Okanogan National Forest, Methow Valley Ranger District, 24 West Chewuch Road, Winthrop, WA 98862, 509/996-4003.

66 CATHEDRAL BASIN
39.0 mi/5–6 days

north of Winthrop in Pasayten Wilderness of Okanogan National Forest

Map 3.2, page 96

For folks seeking to experience the best of what the Pasayten Wilderness has to offer, this is the trail. More than 20 miles from the nearest car lies resplendent Cathedral Basin. Lakes are set inside basins, illuminated by wildflowers in the summer, larches in the fall, and multitudes of stars every night. The Cathedral Pass journey is one of the prizes of the Pasayten.

The best access is via Andrews Creek, an excellent, although long, valley hike. It's 12.5 miles along the forested creek to Andrews Pass. Some of the route was burned in 2003. Throughout

Cathedral Basin—hard to get to but one of Washington's most beautiful places.

the valley are tremendous views of surrounding peaks and ridges. Camps are scattered regularly along the trail here. It's another three miles from the pass to a junction with Boundary Trail. Head east to encounter Lower Cathedral Lake (18.6 miles) and Upper Cathedral (20.5 miles). Campsites are scarce around the lakes, so be ready to set up camp near the Boundary Trail junction or other available sites.

Above the lakes, Cathedral Peak and Amphitheater Mountain form worthy sentinels, standing on either side of the pass. Marmots rumble across the tundralike meadows while bears forage for berries. Scrambles are possible up many of the neighboring peaks, where the views extend across the wilderness to the Cascades and Canada.

User Groups: Hikers, leashed dogs, and horses. No mountain bikes are allowed. No wheelchair access.

Open Seasons: This trail is accessible July–September.

Permits: A federal Northwest Forest Pass is required to park here. A free wilderness permit is also required to hike here and is available at the trailhead.

Maps: For a map of Okanogan National Forest, contact the Outdoor Recreation Information Center at the downtown Seattle REI. For topographic maps, ask Green Trails for No. 20, Coleman Peak, or ask the USGS for Coleman Peak, Mount Barney, and Remmel Mountain.

Directions: From Winthrop, drive north on Chewuch River Road (across Highway 20 from the visitors center) 24 miles to signed Andrew's Creek Trailhead.

Contact: Okanogan National Forest, Methow Valley Ranger District, 24 West Chewuch Road, Winthrop, WA 98862, 509/996-4003.

67 PEEPSIGHT
28.0 mi/3–4 days

north of Winthrop in Pasayten Wilderness of Okanogan National Forest

Map 3.2, page 96

Off Andrews Creek and normally a route to other places, the trail to Peepsight Mountain and Peepsight Lake is a worthy journey in itself. The eight-mile trail leaves Andrews Creek to scale the side of Peepsight Mountain. This is high country, full of meadows and views. A trip to Peepsight Mountain, elevation 8,146 feet, is a window on the Pasayten, laying much of the vast wilderness at your tired feet. And Peepsight Lake lies on the other side of the pass, but it usually opens later in the season because of snow melting slowly on the pass. The trail winds back down to Andrews Creek to form a loop.

The route follows Andrews Creek Trail to Peepsight Trail (8.5 miles). A ford of Andrews Creek is necessary, not an easy task in the early summer. Peepsight Trail climbs to a junction (12.6 miles); to the west lies Peepsight Lake, a welcome sight when fall larches are burning with color. Peepsight Mountain is an easy scramble from this trail. The right fork in the trail skirts Peepsight Mountain and makes for Crazy Man Pass and Rock Lake before dropping back to Andrews Pass, 12.5 miles from the trailhead. Campsites are found at many places along the route; when possible, stick to established sites.

User Groups: Hikers, leashed dogs, and horses. No mountain bikes are allowed. No wheelchair access.

Open Seasons: This trail is accessible August–September.

Permits: A federal Northwest Forest Pass is required to park here. A free wilderness permit is also required to hike here and is available at the trailhead.

Maps: For a map of Okanogan National Forest, contact the Outdoor Recreation Information Center at the downtown Seattle REI. For topographic maps, ask Green Trails for No. 20, Coleman Peak, or ask the USGS for Coleman Peak and Remmel Mountain.

Directions: From Winthrop, drive north on Chewuch River Road (across Highway 20 from the visitors center) 24 miles to signed Andrew's Creek Trailhead.

Contact: Okanogan National Forest, Methow Valley Ranger District, 24 West Chewuch Road, Winthrop, WA 98862, 509/996-4003.

68 HORSESHOE BASIN (STEHEKIN)
7.8–16.4 mi/2 days

north of Stehekin in North Cascades National Park

Map 3.2, page 96

Fortunately, one of the North Cascades' most beautiful basins is a convenient trip for folks on both the west side and east side of the Cascades. Hikers living on the rainy side of the state can reach Horseshoe Basin via Cascade Pass in 8.2 up-down-and-up-again miles. Eastsiders can take a shorter route via Stehekin, which involves a beautiful ferry ride on Lake Chelan. On either route, the enormous cliffs and waterfalls ringing Horseshoe Basin make for an awesome trip.

Folks seeking access to Horseshoe Basin from the west need to hike to Cascade Pass (3.7 miles; see listing in this chapter) and drop to the Stehekin River and Horseshoe Basin Trail junction (6.7 miles). From Chelan, ride the ferry to Stehekin and catch the shuttle to Cottonwood Campground, at the end of Stehekin Valley. From here, Horseshoe Basin junction is a quick hike (2.4 miles).

Horseshoe Basin Trail wanders up Basin Creek 1.5 miles to the head of the basin. Covered in meadows, the basin offers impressive views of the enormous mountains and glaciers towering 4,000 feet above. Campers, please stick to established campsites, scattered throughout the basin. This area is dotted by numerous mines, operated decades ago, and their remains are worth checking out. Horseshoe Basin is a North Cascades classic.

User Groups: Hikers only. No dogs, horses, or mountain bikes are allowed. No wheelchair access.

Open Seasons: This trail is accessible July–mid-October

Permits: A federal Northwest Forest Pass is required to park at Cascade Pass, for hikers entering from the west. Overnight stays within the national park require reservations and backcountry camping permits, which are available at the Wilderness Information Center in Marblemount or the visitors center in Stehekin.

Maps: For a map of North Cascades National Park, contact the Outdoor Recreation Information Center at the downtown Seattle REI. For topographic maps, ask Green Trails for No. 80, Cascade Pass, or ask the USGS for McGregor Mountain, Goode Mountain, and Mount Logan.

Directions: For the eastern entrance, from Wenatchee, drive north 33 miles on U.S. 97 to Chelan. Lady of the Lake Ferry Terminal is on U.S. 97 Alternate just before entering downtown. Catch the passenger ferry to Stehekin and ride the shuttle to Cottonwood Camp Trailhead.

For the western entrance, from the town of Marblemount on Highway 20, drive 23 miles on Cascade River Road to the Cascade Pass Trailhead at road's end.

Contact: North Cascades National Park, Golden West Visitor Center, Stehekin, WA, 360/856-5700, ext. 340; Lady of the Lake Ferry Service, 1418 West Woodin Avenue, Chelan, WA 98816, 509/682-4584.

69 NORTH FORK BRIDGE CREEK
19.4 mi/3 days

north of Stehekin in North Cascades National Park

Map 3.2, page 96

A high, rugged ridge dotted by glaciers surrounds the large basin at the head of North Fork Bridge Creek. The high peaks of Goode Mountain, Storm King, and Mount Logan stand impressively over the open, rocky expanse of North Fork Meadows. The splendor of it all is easily accessible via a gentle trail along valley floors and a trio of great camps, easy stuff for beginner backpackers.

North Fork Bridge Creek Trail is accessible through Stehekin, which requires a ride on the

Lake Chelan passenger ferry. Catch the shuttle from Stehekin to Bridge Creek Trailhead. The first three miles are along Bridge Creek Trail. Shortly after crossing the creek, via bridge, North Fork Trail takes off to the left (north). At 5.2 miles is Walker Park Camp, for hikers and horses, while at 6.2 miles are Grizzly Creek Camps, one each for horses and hikers. Camping beyond is now forbidden because of excessive abuse in the meadows.

North Fork Bridge Creek Trail alternates between old forests and avalanche chutes. The views from the openings get successively better. From Grizzly Camps, it's a quick hike to North Fork Meadows (8.5 miles). The bulky valley walls shoot skyward to enormous peaks. Glaciers struggle to cling to the steep slopes. Enjoy.

User Groups: Hikers and horses. No dogs or mountain bikes are allowed. No wheelchair access.

Open Seasons: This trail is accessible July–mid-October

Permits: Overnight stays within the national park require reservations and backcountry camping permits, which are available at the visitors center in Stehekin.

Maps: For a map of North Cascades National Park, contact the Outdoor Recreation Information Center at the downtown Seattle REI. For topographic maps, ask Green Trails for No. 49, Mount Logan, and No. 81, Mc-Gregor Mountain, or ask the USGS for Mc-Gregor Mountain, Goode Mountain, and Mount Logan.

Directions: From Wenatchee, drive north 33 miles on U.S. 97 to Chelan. Lady of the Lake Ferry Terminal is on U.S. 97 Alternate just before entering downtown. Catch the passenger ferry to Stehekin and ride the shuttle to Bridge Creek Trailhead.

Contact: North Cascades National Park, Golden West Visitor Center, Stehekin, WA, 360/856-5700, ext. 340; Lady of the Lake Ferry Service, 1418 West Woodin Avenue, Chelan, WA 98816, 509/682-4584.

70 GOODE RIDGE
10.0 mi/6.0 hrs

north of Stehekin in North Cascades National Park

Map 3.2, page 96

Doing things the old-fashioned way, Goode Ridge Trail starts low in the valley before climbing to a high valley ridge. Make no mistake; Goode Ridge Trail is a steep one, gaining 4,400 feet of elevation in just five miles. Its challenging but not overwhelming ascent is perfect for those who are craving some mean vistas but who aren't crazy enough to challenge Mc-Gregor Mountain to a fight.

Goode Ridge Trail is in the northern part of the Stehekin Valley. For that, one must hop the passenger ferry from Chelan and then a shuttle from Stehekin. All that is not possible for one day, so plan on camping in the valley somewhere at least one night. The trail makes a steady climb away from the river, passing through forests for the first half before breaking out into open meadows. Expect hot, dry weather during the summer and bring extra water. The trail eventually reaches the southern end of Goode Ridge. The views of the surrounding peaks, lakes, and valleys are impressive. McGregor, Goode, Storm King, and Glacier Peak are the most memorable from a long list of visible peaks.

User Groups: Hikers only. No dogs, horses, or mountain bikes are allowed. No wheelchair access.

Open Seasons: This trail is accessible July–September.

Permits: Overnight stays within the national park require reservations and backcountry camping permits, which are available at the visitors center in Stehekin.

Maps: For a map of North Cascades National Park, contact the Outdoor Recreation Information Center at the downtown Seattle REI. For topographic maps, ask Green Trails for No. 81, McGregor Mountain, or ask the USGS for Goode Mountain.

Directions: From Wenatchee, drive north 33

miles on U.S. 97 to Chelan. Lady of the Lake Ferry Terminal is on U.S. 97 Alternate just before entering downtown. Catch the passenger ferry to Stehekin and ride the shuttle to Goode Ridge Trailhead.

Contact: North Cascades National Park, Golden West Visitor Center, Stehekin, WA, 360/856-5700, ext. 340; Lady of the Lake Ferry Service, 1418 West Woodin Avenue, Chelan, WA 98816, 509/682-4584.

71 RAINBOW LAKE
23.8 mi/3 days

north of Stehekin in North Cascades National Park and Lake Chelan National Recreation Area

Map 3.2, page 96

Since there are no car-carrying ferries to Stehekin, there are no cars in the small town. A shuttle bus is your only option for access to the valley's nine trailheads. But the lack of a car makes through-hikes extremely easy. Rainbow Lake Trail is a perfect example. Have the shuttle drop you off upriver and hike your way back to Stehekin. This route is a grand one, via four creek valleys and a stop at a high alpine lake.

The route is best done from north to south, since the north trailhead is 1,000 feet higher. Disembark from the Stehekin shuttle at Bridge Creek Trailhead and hike the famed Pacific Crest Trail to South Fork Bridge Creek junction (6.8 miles). Good first-night camps are found at Sixmile Camp (6 miles) and South Fork Camp (6.8 miles). South Fork Bridge Creek Trail climbs to Bowan Pass (13.1 miles), passing Dans Camp (9.8 miles). The pass lies directly below the rocky and sheer face of Bowan Mountain.

Rainbow Lake rests just on the other side of the pass, set within open meadows dotted by larches, colorful in the early fall. An established camp is found here at 14 miles, near Rainbow Lake, and two more are at 15.4 miles and 16 miles, down in the North Fork Rainbow Creek Valley. Follow the trail through

forests of pine and fir, out the valley, and down Rainbow Creek Trail to Stehekin. Enjoy a meal and a beer in Stehekin and then ride Lady of the Lake to Chelan and your unmissed auto.

User Groups: Hikers and horses. No dogs or mountain bikes are allowed. No wheelchair access.

Open Seasons: This trail is accessible July–September.

Permits: Overnight stays within the national park require reservations and backcountry camping permits, which are available at the visitors center in Stehekin.

Maps: For a map of North Cascades National Park, contact the Outdoor Recreation Information Center at the downtown Seattle REI. For topographic maps, ask Green Trails for No. 81, McGregor Mountain, and No. 82, Stehekin, or ask the USGS for McGregor Mountain, McAlester Mountain, and Stehekin.

Directions: From Wenatchee, drive north 33 miles on U.S. 97 to Chelan. Lady of the Lake Ferry Terminal is on U.S. 97 Alternate just before entering downtown. Catch the passenger ferry to Stehekin and ride the shuttle to to Bridge Creek Trailhead.

Contact: North Cascades National Park, Golden West Visitor Center, Stehekin, WA, 360/856-5700, ext. 340; Lady of the Lake Ferry Service, 1418 West Woodin Avenue, Chelan, WA 98816, 509/682-4584.

72 McGREGOR MOUNTAIN
15.4 mi/2–3 days

north of Stehekin in Lake Chelan National Recreation Area

Map 3.2, page 96

It's difficult to verify, but it's my opinion that McGregor Mountain is the steepest trail in the state. And with all the steep trails in the North Cascades, Olympics, and Mount Rainier, that's a fine distinction. From trailhead to summit, McGregor Mountain Trail climbs 6,300 feet. Few care to continue counting past 50 the number of switchbacks to the top of an 8,122-foot peak. Keep in mind that pain on the trail always pays off at top.

High Bridge Trailhead is in the Stehekin River Valley, meaning you'll need to catch the passenger ferry from Chelan to Stehekin and subsequently ride the shuttle bus to High Bridge Camp. Start on Pacific Crest Trail before turning right (east) onto McGregor Mountain Trail (1.3 miles). The ascent starts immediately and doesn't end until Heaton Camp at 7,000 feet. Much of the trail lies in open, rocky meadows. The trail is dry, so bring enough water for hiking and for meals at camp. Heaton Camp offers exceptional views. A short scramble reaches the ridge below McGregor's summit, revealing far-flung views to the east. Finally, before you hit the trail, ask yourself, "Are you sure you want to do this when there's a nice bakery in Stehekin instead?"

User Groups: Hikers only. No dogs, horses, or mountain bikes are allowed. No wheelchair access.

Open Seasons: This trail is accessible July–September.

Permits: Permits are not required. Parking and access are free.

Maps: For a map of North Cascades National Park, contact the Outdoor Recreation Information Center at the downtown Seattle REI. For topographic maps, ask Green Trails for No. 81, McGregor Mountain, or ask the USGS for McGregor Mountain.

Directions: From Wenatchee, drive north 33 miles on U.S. 97 to Chelan. Lady of the Lake Ferry Terminal is on U.S. 97 Alternate just before entering downtown. Catch the passenger ferry to Stehekin and ride the shuttle to High Bridge Trailhead.

Contact: North Cascades National Park, Golden West Visitor Center, Stehekin, WA, 360/856-5700, ext. 340; Lady of the Lake Ferry Service, 1418 West Woodin Avenue, Chelan, WA 98816, 509/682-4584.

73 COMPANY/DEVORE CREEKS LOOP

27.5 mi/3 days

west of Stehekin in Glacier Peak Wilderness of Wenatchee National Forest

Map 3.2, page 96

This is another excellent through-hike within Stehekin Valley. The route heads up long, wide Company Creek Valley and circles around a sharp ridge of craggy peaks before dropping through Fourth of July Basin on the way to Stehekin. The crowds are rather thin along the trail, having been drawn to other, better known trails farther up the valley. That's good news for those who venture here, a wild place full of things to see.

The route begins on Company Creek Trail with a long but scenic climb to Hilgard Pass (11.3 miles). Avalanche chutes expose Tupshin and Devore Peaks for long distances. You must ford Company Creek five miles in, difficult during times of heavy runoff. Well-established campsites are found at 3.5 miles, 10 miles, and 11.5 miles. At 6,600 feet, Hilgard Pass offers some scenic views.

The route now drops 1,900 feet before gaining 1,800 back on the way to Tenmile Pass (15.8 miles). If it sounds like a lot of work, it is. But enormous Fourth of July Basin awaits on the other side. This is premier high country, with sweeping views of the Devore Creek drainage. Bears and coyotes are frequent visitors, but they rarely approach close enough for mug shots. Excellent second-night camps are found at Tenmile Pass and within Fourth of July Basin. The trail drops to Bird Creek Camp (20 miles) and Weaver Point Camp (25 miles) before arriving at Devore Creek Trailhead.

User Groups: Hikers, leashed dogs, and horses. No mountain bikes are allowed. No wheelchair access.

Open Seasons: This trail is accessible July–September.

Permits: Permits are not required. Parking and access are free.

Maps: For a map of Wenatchee National For-

est, contact the Outdoor Recreation Information Center at the downtown Seattle REI. For topographic maps, ask Green Trails for No. 81, McGregor Mountain, No. 82, Stehekin, No. 113, Holden, and No. 114, Lucerne, or ask the USGS for Stehekin, Mount Lyall, and Holden.
Directions: From Wenatchee, drive north 33 miles on U.S. 97 to Chelan. Lady of the Lake Ferry Terminal is on U.S. 97 Alternate just before entering downtown. Catch the passenger ferry to Stehekin and ride the shuttle to Company Creek Trailhead.
Contact: North Cascades National Park, Golden West Visitor Center, Stehekin, WA, 360/856-5700, ext. 340; Lady of the Lake Ferry Service, 1418 West Woodin Avenue, Chelan, WA 98816, 509/682-4584.

7.4 STEHEKIN TRAILS
0.5–9.0 mi/0.5–5.0 hrs

around Stehekin north of Lake Chelan

Map 3.2, page 96

Accessible only by passenger ferry or plane, Stehekin is as remote as it gets. The small village consists of resorts and cabins, several small restaurants and bakeries, and no fewer than 12 campgrounds. Scattered around town and valley are 18 different trails, many of which are full-scale adventures (covered elsewhere in this chapter). Some are perfect day hikes for families, including Agnes Gorge, Bullion Loop (a section of PCT), and Rainbow Loop Trail.

Agnes Gorge Trail, on the north side of Agnes Creek (different trail), travels 2.5 easy miles up the creek as it runs through a tight chasm. At the end, the trail finds the creek as it passes over a small waterfall. Rainbow Loop Trail goes 5 miles along the eastern ridge above Stehekin. The trail gains little elevation and gets in a couple of views of Lake Chelan. Pacific Crest Trail also runs through the upper valley. Using the shuttle, make a 6.5-mile through-hike from Bullion Camp past Coon Lake up to Bridge Creek Camp. The Stehekin Valley is beautiful, and now you can say you've hiked PCT.

User Groups: Hikers, leashed dogs, and horses. No mountain bikes are allowed. No wheelchair access.
Open Seasons: This area is accessible March–November.
Permits: Permits are not required. Parking and access are free.
Maps: For a map of North Cascades National Park, contact the Outdoor Recreation Information Center at the downtown Seattle REI. For topographic maps, ask Green Trails for No. 82, Stehekin, and No. 81, McGregor Mountain, or ask the USGS for Stehekin.
Directions: From Wenatchee, drive north 33 miles on U.S. 97 to Chelan. Lady of the Lake Ferry Terminal is on U.S. 97 Alternate just before entering downtown. Catch the passenger ferry to Stehekin and ride the shuttle to the various trailheads.
Contact: North Cascades National Park, Golden West Visitor Center, Stehekin, WA, 360/856-5700, ext. 340; Lady of the Lake Ferry Service, 1418 West Woodin Avenue, Chelan, WA 98816, 509/682-4584.

7.5 CHELAN LAKESHORE
16.9 mi one-way/2–4 days

south of Stehekin in Lake Chelan–Sawtooth Wilderness of Okanogan National Forest

Map 3.2, page 96

April and May are great times to hike Lake Chelan Lakeshore Trail, before the summer's heat makes it unbearable. Besides, summers should be reserved for the alpine. Lakeshore Trail travels 17 miles along the eastern bank to the hamlet of Stehekin, soaking up much of the lake's scenery.

Park in the town of Chelan and ride the passenger ferry to the landing of Prince Creek, on the eastern shore. After your hike, catch lunch in Stehekin and a returning ferry to Chelan. The trail follows the lakeshore, often climbing a few hundred yards above the waterline. Open forests of enormous ponderosa pine and Douglas fir line the hillside, and snowy peaks appear across the lake.

A number of established camps lie along the trail, including Prince Creek, Cascade Creek (5.5 miles), Meadow Creek (7.6 miles), Moore Point (10.6 miles), Flick Creek (13.5 miles) and Purple Point, in Stehekin. The trail can be done in two days, but three or four days is best, allowing for great side trips. Spend a day hiking up Fish Creek to Boulder Lake or Prince Creek to the Sawtooth Range. It may be only a lakeshore trail, but those who hike it know there is much more to it than that.

User Groups: Hikers only. No dogs, horses, or mountain bikes are allowed. No wheelchair access.

Open Seasons: This trail is accessible year-round.

Permits: Permits are not required. Parking and access are free.

Maps: For a map of Okanogan National Forest, contact the Outdoor Recreation Information Center at the downtown Seattle REI. For topographic maps, ask Green Trails for No. 82, Stehekin, No. 114, Lucerne, and No. 115, Prince Creek, or ask the USGS for Prince Creek, Lucerne, and Stehekin.

Directions: From Wenatchee, drive north 33 miles on U.S. 97 to Chelan. Lady of the Lake Ferry Terminal is on U.S. 97 Alternate just before entering downtown. Catch the passenger ferry to Stehekin and ride the shuttle to Prince Creek Landing.

Contact: North Cascades National Park, Golden West Visitor Center, Stehekin, WA, 360/856-5700, ext. 340; Lady of the Lake Ferry Service, 1418 West Woodin Avenue, Chelan, WA 98816, 509/682-4584.

76 LYMAN LAKES
18.2 mi/3–4 days

west of Lake Chelan in Glacier Peak Wilderness of Wenatchee National Forest

Map 3.2, page 96

For years, this has been one of the state's most frequented glaciers. Dropping off into the upper lake, Lyman Glacier displays the workings of the Ice Age, albeit on a smaller scale.

The hike is a great trip up Railroad Creek Valley to large Lyman Lake, an outstanding place to spend the night. Further adventures and wide open meadows await up the trail in this high-country parkland. The lakes are often visited as a stop along a larger loop, but they make for a great trip in themselves.

The trailhead is accessible via passenger ferry from Chelan. Disembark at Lucerne and catch a ride on a privately operated bus to the village of Holden. Railroad Creek Trail ascends the forested valley to Hart Lake (3.5 miles) and Lyman Lake (8.1 miles). Camps are scattered along the way and at Lyman Lake. Lyman Spur Trail (8.1) climbs to Spider Gap, a steep but scenic ascent.

Deep within Glacier Peak Wilderness, wildlife is found everywhere. Mountain goats roam the high ridges while deer and bear roam the valleys. Be sure to hang bear sacks when camping. The trail continues south another mile to the upper lake and meadow bliss. Lyman Glacier is safe for careful exploration. For those on an extended stay, a trip up to Cloudy Pass (12.1 miles) and Suiattle Pass (13.1 miles) delivers grand views of the Cascades.

User Groups: Hikers, leashed dogs, and horses. No mountain bikes are allowed. No wheelchair access.

Open Seasons: This trail is accessible July–October.

Permits: Permits are not required. Parking and access are free.

Maps: For a map of Wenatchee National Forest, contact the Outdoor Recreation Information Center at the downtown Seattle REI. For topographic maps, ask Green Trails for No. 113, Holden, or ask the USGS for Holden.

Directions: From Wenatchee, drive north 33 miles on U.S. 97 to Chelan. Lady of the Lake Ferry Terminal is on U.S. 97 Alternate just before entering downtown. Catch the passenger ferry to Lucerne, the drop-off for Holden. Take the bus to the town of Holden. The trailhead is located at Holden Campground.

Contact: North Cascades National Park, Golden West Visitor Center, Stehekin, WA, 360/856-5700, ext. 340; Lady of the Lake Ferry Service, 1418 West Woodin Avenue, Chelan, WA 98816, 509/682-4584.

77 DOMKE LAKE
7.0 mi/4.0 hrs–2-plus days

west of Lake Chelan in Wenatchee National Forest

Map 3.2, page 96

This large lake sits within a small valley above and away from Lake Chelan. More than a mile long, the lake is a favorite stop for hikers, anglers, and families looking to do some camping. While the lake is accessible only by passenger ferry, it still receives a fair amount of traffic. While Domke Lake isn't as large as Lake Chelan, its water is warmer and thus more inviting for extended swims.

Domke Lake is just 3.5 miles from Lucerne, the boat drop-off point. The trail ascends just 1,000 feet to the forested lake. Camps are at the northeast and southeast corners while yet another camp is reached by boat on the western shore. Make the lake a base camp to explore the area on Domke Mountain Trail. Its junction is just below the lake on the main trail. Three miles of trail gain nearly 3,000 feet to a grand viewpoint of the lakes and imposing mountains.

User Groups: Hikers, leashed dogs, horses, and mountain bikes. No wheelchair access.

Open Seasons: This trail is accessible June–October.

Permits: Permits are not required. Parking and access are free.

Maps: For a map of Wenatchee National Forest, contact the Outdoor Recreation Information Center at the downtown Seattle REI. For topographic maps, ask Green Trails for No. 114, Lucerne, or ask the USGS for Lucerne.

Directions: From Wenatchee, drive north 33 miles on U.S. 97 to Chelan. Lady of the Lake Ferry Terminal is on U.S. 97 Alternate just before entering downtown. Catch the passenger ferry to Lucerne. The trailhead is located at the ferry stop.

Contact: North Cascades National Park, Golden West Visitor Center, Stehekin, WA, 360/856-5700, ext. 340; Lady of the Lake Ferry Service, 1418 West Woodin Avenue, Chelan, WA 98816, 509/682-4584.

78 EMERALD PARK
14.2 mi/1–3 days

within Glacier Peak Wilderness west of Lake Chelan

Map 3.2, page 96

Set below the high summits of the Chelan Mountains, Emerald Park is a lush escape from the surrounding dry climate. Green meadows sit within a deep, rocky basin, where Emerald Peak and Pinnacle Peak tower 3,000 feet above Emerald Park. The trail can be accomplished as a full day of hiking, but two or three days is best. The basin deserves exploration and a trip up to Millham Pass is well recommended. The area is remote and belongs mostly to coyotes and the stars.

A passenger ferry is the only option to the trailhead at Lucerne, three-quarters of the way up Lake Chelan on the western shore. The route spends 1.6 miles on Domke Lake Trail before heading off on Emerald Park Trail. A short .5 mile later the trail splits again; head to the left, saving Railroad Creek for another day. Five miles of trail slowly makes its way up the valley, gaining 3,000 feet. The trail is often far above the creek, making water scarce. At Emerald Park, the forest gives way to green, open meadows and astounding views of the basin. Emerald Park Camp is 7.1 miles from Lucerne.

User Groups: Hikers, leashed dogs, and horses. No mountain bikes are allowed. No wheelchair access.

Open Seasons: This trail is accessible May–October.

Permits: Permits are not required. Parking and access are free.

Maps: For a map of Wenatchee National Forest, contact the Outdoor Recreation Information Center at the downtown Seattle REI. For topographic maps, ask Green Trails for No.

114, Lucerne, or ask the USGS for Holden, Pinnacle Mountain, and Lucerne.

Directions: From Wenatchee, drive north 33 miles on U.S. 97 to Chelan. Lady of the Lake Ferry Terminal is on U.S. 97 Alternate just before entering downtown. Catch the passenger ferry to Lucerne. The trailhead is located at the ferry stop.

Contact: North Cascades National Park, Golden West Visitor Center, Stehekin, WA, 360/856-5700, ext. 340; Lady of the Lake Ferry Service, 1418 West Woodin Avenue, Chelan, WA 98816, 509/682-4584.

79 TWISP PASS
4.2 mi/3.0 hrs

northwest of Twisp in Lake Chelan–Sawtooth Wilderness of Okanogan National Forest

Map 3.2, page 96

The upper Sawtooth Mountain Range is full of natural beauty; wildflowers envelop mountain meadows in color in the early summer while subalpine larches burn up the hillsides during the fall. The trail to Twisp Pass encounters both, as well as impressive views of crowded mountain peaks in all directions. It's one of the best day hikes in the Twisp Valley, but it also serves hikers looking for longer trips. The trail is a major route into the North Cascades National Park, on the western side of the pass. An additional 4.3 miles delivers hikers to Bridge Creek and a junction of four major trails. Day hikers will be content with the pass and Dagger Lake, just inside the park.

The trail is a steep one, gaining 2,400 feet on the way to the pass. The first two miles are well forested and come to a trail junction. The right fork heads up to Copper Pass, an equally impressive gap within the mighty Sawtooths. A great loop can be made via Copper Pass and Bridge Creek for 20.5 miles. Stay to the left for Twisp Pass, climbing steeply through rocky meadows to Twisp Pass. Water is scarce after the junction, so bring plenty. Lincoln Butte and Twisp Mountain stand tall on either side of the pass, while Dagger Lake sparkles

from below. A quick mile's descent into the park arrives at an established camp at Dagger Lake. A backcountry permit from the national park is required for overnight stays here.

User Groups: Hikers, leashed dogs (up to Twisp Pass, but not beyond), and horses. No mountain bikes are allowed. No wheelchair access.

Open Seasons: This trail is accessible July–September.

Permits: A federal Northwest Forest Pass is required to park here.

Maps: For a map of Okanogan National Forest, contact the Outdoor Recreation Information Center at the downtown Seattle REI. For topographic maps, ask Green Trails for No. 82, Stehekin, or ask the USGS for Gilbert.

Directions: From Twisp, drive east 26 miles on Twisp River Road (Forest Service Road 44 becomes Forest Service Road 4440) to the trailhead at road's end.

Contact: Okanogan National Forest, Methow Valley Ranger Station, 24 West Chewuch Road, Winthrop, WA 98862, 509/996-4003.

80 NORTH CREEK
9.2 mi/4.5 hrs

northwest of Twisp in Lake Chelan–Sawtooth Wilderness of Okanogan National Forest

Map 3.2, page 96

North Creek presents one of the Twisp Valley's more gentle and accessible lake hikes. The trail climbs just 2,200 feet over 4.6 miles, a relative cakewalk compared to the routes for some other lakes in the valley. The valley nearly encircles Gilbert Mountain, offering a chance to view the rugged peak from nearly every side. To add color to the scenery, wildflowers light up the open meadows around the lake during July.

After passing through an old timber harvest, the trail climbs through a forest of Douglas fir and ponderosa pine. The trail occasionally passes through avalanche chutes where snow can stick around into July some years. When it does, passage is difficult. Despite the arid conditions of Eastern Cascades, this valley received a fair amount of carving by Ice Age glaciers, leaving it flat and wide. The trail follows the creek for the most part, following the natural loop of the valley, eventually turning south before encountering the lake. Gilbert Mountain looms high above from the south, more than 2,000 feet overhead. Exploration above the lake is best avoided; vertical shafts and loose rock remain from previous mining activity, as well as fragile meadows that don't endure hiking boots well.

User Groups: Hikers, leashed dogs, and horses. No mountain bikes are allowed. No wheelchair access.

Open Seasons: This trail is accessible June–October.

Permits: A federal Northwest Forest Pass is required to park here.

Maps: For a map of Okanogan National Forest, contact the Outdoor Recreation Information Center at the downtown Seattle REI. For topographic maps, ask Green Trails for No. 82, Stehekin, or ask the USGS for Gilbert.

Directions: From Twisp, drive east 26 miles on Twisp River Road (Forest Service Road 44 becomes Forest Service Road 4440) to the trailhead at road's end.

Contact: Okanogan National Forest, Methow Valley Ranger Station, 24 West Chewuch Road, Winthrop, WA 98862, 509/996-4003.

81 LOUIS LAKE
11.4 mi/6.0 hrs

northwest of Twisp in Lake Chelan–Sawtooth Wilderness of Okanogan National Forest

Map 3.2, page 96

Louis Lake is one of the best deals in the Twisp Valley. Less grueling than other routes in the valley, Louis Lake Trail visits the most scenic lakes in the Sawtooth Range. Grand examples of Englemann spruce, Douglas fir, and whitebark pine battle with mountain views for your attention. It's an epic bout, although the great ridges dominating the skyline win out. To top it all off, Louis Lake sits within a narrow, rugged valley surrounded by some of the range's most jagged ridges. Visitors from afar are well

advised to give Louis Lake serious consideration as a recipient for their effort.

The route begins along South Creek Trail before Louis Lake Trail cuts to the south (2.1 miles). The trail heads straight toward the ridge before the valley turns 90 degrees, revealing a narrow slot. The forest breaks into meadows often, revealing South Creek Butte and Crescent Mountain. Louis Lake (5.3 miles) is a pictorial setting, surrounded by meadows of heather and harboring a small, tree-covered island. Steep valley walls lead to a sharp ridge around the basin, highlighted by a tall peak of 81,42 feet. Despite its popularity during the summer, Louis Lake is an outstanding Twisp Valley destination.

User Groups: Hikers, leashed dogs, and horses. No mountain bikes are allowed. No wheelchair access.

Open Seasons: This trail is accessible mid-June–October.

Permits: A federal Northwest Forest Pass is required to park here.

Maps: For a map of Okanogan National Forest, contact the Outdoor Recreation Information Center at the downtown Seattle REI. For topographic maps, ask Green Trails for No. 82, Stehekin, or ask the USGS for Gilbert.

Directions: From Twisp, drive east 22 miles on Twisp River Road (Forest Service Road 44 becomes Forest Service Road 4440) to South Creek Trailhead on the right.

Contact: Okanogan National Forest, Methow Valley Ranger Station, 24 West Chewuch Road, Winthrop, WA 98862, 509/996-4003.

82 SCATTER CREEK
8.6 mi/6.0 hrs

northwest of Twisp in Lake Chelan–Sawtooth Wilderness of Okanogan National Forest

Map 3.2, page 96

The prime time to visit Scatter Lake is fall, when wildly colorful larches mark the perimeter of this deep blue pool. To add to the array of colors, afternoon sunlight brings out the deep red of high Abernathy Peak. Scatter Lake offers lots of color to make up for the punishing hike. In fact, punishing may be a light word for 3,800 feet of elevation gain contained within four short miles. But that's the way of the Twisp Valley. The scenery around Scatter Lake easily makes up for it.

The route begins along Twisp River Trail but quickly turns onto Scatter Creek Trail (.2 mile). The trail begins a short series of switchbacks before abandoning them altogether for the alternative of a straight ascent up the valley. Scatter Creek is always at hand offering a cool refreshment. Scatter Creek Trail crosses the creek before climbing the final mile to the lake. Wildflowers are prolific in the open meadows during July. Abernathy Peak, 8,321 feet, looks down from the talus-strewn ridge around the lake basin.

User Groups: Hikers, leashed dogs, and horses. No mountain bikes are allowed. No wheelchair access.

Open Seasons: This trail is accessible June–October.

Permits: A federal Northwest Forest Pass is required to park here.

Maps: For a map of Okanogan National Forest, contact the Outdoor Recreation Information Center at the downtown Seattle REI. For topographic maps, ask Green Trails for No. 82, Stehekin, or ask the USGS for Gilbert and Midnight Mountain.

Directions: From Twisp, drive east 22 miles on Twisp River Road (Forest Service Road 44 becomes Forest Service Road 4440) to South Creek Trailhead on the right.

Contact: Okanogan National Forest, Methow Valley Ranger Station, 24 West Chewuch Road, Winthrop, WA 98862, 509/996-4003.

83 SLATE CREEK
10.2 mi/6.0 hrs

northwest of Twisp in Lake Chelan–Sawtooth Wilderness of Okanogan National Forest

Map 3.2, page 96

Slate Lake is the most brutal of the Twisp Valley lake hikes. Other appropriate synonyms include terrorizing, demanding, and exceptionally beautiful. Such words go along with 3,800-foot elevation gains laid out over just three miles. The lake is set back within a recess along the Abernathy Ridge, nearly becoming a part of the Wolf Creek drainage. Instead, the lake drains into Little Slate Creek and down to Twisp River. The terrain is fairly open, as the forest struggles to thicken for lack of much precipitation. This makes for good views and excellent scrambling.

Slate Creek Trail gets all the work out of the way in the first three miles. In this stretch, the trail climbs straight up to a knob on the west side of the creek. This ascent is dry and extremely demanding on hot summer days. From this point, however, the views are outstanding. The rugged Sawtooth Range stretches out across from the entire length of the Twisp River. Midnight and 3 A.M. Mountains are directly across Little Slate Creek. From here, the trail follows at a nearly even grade along the ridge enclosing Slate Lake. Those with energy left can take advantage of the great scrambling opportunities around the lake. Despite the treacherous ascent up, Slate Lake is the best lake in the valley for those with an adventurous spirit.

User Groups: Hikers, leashed dogs, and horses. No mountain bikes are allowed. No wheelchair access.

Open Seasons: This trail is accessible June–October.

Permits: A federal Northwest Forest Pass is required to park here.

Maps: For a map of Okanogan National Forest, contact the Outdoor Recreation Information Center at the downtown Seattle REI. For topographic maps, ask Green Trails for No. 83, Buttermilk Butte, or ask the USGS for Midnight Mountain.

Directions: From Twisp, drive east 18 miles on Twisp River Road (Forest Service Road 44 becomes Forest Service Road 4440) to Slate Creek Trailhead on the right.

Contact: Okanogan National Forest, Methow Valley Ranger Station, 24 West Chewuch Road, Winthrop, WA 98862, 509/996-4003.

84 WILLIAMS CREEK

13.6 mi/8.0 hrs

northwest of Twisp in Lake Chelan–Sawtooth Wilderness of Okanogan National Forest

Map 3.2, page 96

Williams Creek Trail starts low and ends high. Make no mistake about that. If you're into difficult 3,700-foot elevation gains, then perhaps this is the perfect trail for you. The most distinctive facet of the route is its passage through an old forest burn. Although the fire occurred decades ago, the forest remains open. Significant regenerative growth has taken place, staging an interesting example of forest dynamics.

Williams Lake is set within a great bowl, where Williams Butte and War Creek Ridge rim the basin. Meadows are prolific around the lake, with July flowers as bright as the sky. The trail to the lake follows the creek the entire way, staying to the north side. The trail is popular with equestrians, as there is a horse camp just before the lake. While the lake is stocked, fishing reviews are mixed. If you're going to hike almost seven miles, though, you might as well bring your pole and try to catch some lunch.

User Groups: Hikers, leashed dogs, and horses. No mountain bikes are allowed. No wheelchair access.

Open Seasons: This trail is accessible June–October.

Permits: A federal Northwest Forest Pass is required to park here.

Maps: For a map of Okanogan National Forest, contact the Outdoor Recreation Information Center at the downtown Seattle REI. For topographic maps, ask Green Trails for No. 82, Stehekin, and No. 83, Buttermilk Butte, or ask the USGS for Gilbert, Midnight Mountain, and Sun Mountain.

Directions: From Twisp, drive east 19 miles on Twisp River Road (Forest Service Road 44) to Mystery Campground. Turn left on Forest Service Road 4430, cross the river, and stay left for .5 mile to Williams Creek Trailhead on the right.

Contact: Okanogan National Forest, Methow Valley Ranger Station, 24 West Chewuch Road, Winthrop, WA 98862, 509/996-4003.

85 NORTH WAR CREEK

19.0 mi/2 days

west of Twisp in Lake Chelan–Sawtooth Wilderness of Okanogan National Forest

Map 3.2, page 96

North War Creek Trail is the most northern and scenic route to Chelan Summit Trail. The trail makes a long gradual ascent to War Creek Pass, where the high-country Lake Juanita awaits. A side trail leads to the summit of Boulder Butte, where the views of much of the North Cascades are superb. Most hikers on this trail are completing the longer Chelan Summit Loop and wish to exit via the Twisp River. Nonetheless, War Creek is a great excursion for those wanting to see what the Sawtooth Ridge has to offer.

North War Creek Trail parallels the stream for nearly its entire length. The grade is gentle until the end, where the last mile rises to the pass. Forests of old-growth pine and spruce blanket the valley, adding shade on hot days, although parts of the forest are scarred from a 1994 fire. The trail crests at War Creek Pass in a subalpine setting, where meadows cover the crest and views extend in many directions. Lake Juanita is below with a hiker and horse camp. The trail up to Boulder Butte is highly recommended and not to be missed by any who have ventured this far. From War Creek Pass, trails lead down Purple Creek to Stehekin, up Boulder Creek, and down the crest of the Sawtooth Mountains.

User Groups: Hikers, leashed dogs, and horses. No mountain bikes are allowed. No wheelchair access.

Open Seasons: This trail is accessible July–October.

Permits: A federal Northwest Forest Pass is required to park here.

Maps: For a map of Okanogan National Forest, contact the Outdoor Recreation Information

Center at the downtown Seattle REI. For topographic maps, ask Green Trails for No. 82, Stehekin, and No. 83, Buttermilk Butte, or ask the USGS for Sun Mountain and Oval Peak.

Directions: From Twisp, drive east 15 miles on Twisp River Road (Forest Service Road 44) to Forest Service Road 4430. Turn left on Forest Service Road 4430, cross the river, and stay right for 1 mile to Forest Service Road 100. Turn left and drive 1.5 miles to the trailhead at road's end.

Contact: Okanogan National Forest, Methow Valley Ranger Station, 24 West Chewuch Road, Winthrop, WA 98862, 509/996-4003.

86 OVAL LAKES
15.0–22.6 mi/2–3 days

west of Twisp in Lake Chelan–Sawtooth Wilderness of Okanogan National Forest

Map 3.2, page 96

The Sawtooth Range east of Lake Chelan is full of great adventures and destinations. Situated along the high mountainous crest, Oval Lakes are one of the range's most beautiful locales. These three lakes lie within small, rocky basins at the head of Oval Creek. Subalpine larches eke out a living here, at nearly 7,000 feet. The lakes have great camping and offer great exploration, with loads of views from Oval Pass.

The route begins on Eagle Creek Trail but soon cuts off on Oval Creek Trail (1.9 miles). The old forest provides welcome shade for a while but begins to break into meadows and views. West Oval Lake is achieved via a short side trail (at 7.2 miles) but is not open to camping. Check it out, get a taste of what's ahead, and continue to Middle Oval Lake (8.9 miles) or East Oval Lake (9.4 miles). The fishing's good but the camping's even better. One look at the rocky ridges ringing the lakes, and you'll know why this is called the Sawtooths.

Between West Oval and Middle Oval Lakes, be sure to hike a quick .25 mile to Oval Pass and views of Tuckaway Basin. Adventurous hikers with a map can initially follow Eagle

Creek Trail to Eagle Pass and around Tuckaway Lake to Oval Pass, a lasso-shaped loop of 22.6 miles

User Groups: Hikers, leashed dogs, and horses. No mountain bikes are allowed. No wheelchair access.

Open Seasons: This trail is accessible July–October.

Permits: A federal Northwest Forest Pass is required to park here.

Maps: For a map of Okanogan National Forest, contact the Outdoor Recreation Information Center at the downtown Seattle REI. For topographic maps, ask Green Trails for No. 83, Buttermilk Butte, or ask the USGS for Sun Mountain and Oval Peak.

Directions: From Twisp, drive east 15 miles on Twisp River Road (Forest Service Road 44) to Forest Service Road 4430. Turn left on Forest Service Road 4430, cross the river, and stay to the left for 1 mile to Forest Service Road 080. Turn right and drive 1.5 miles to the trailhead at road's end.

Contact: Okanogan National Forest, Methow Valley Ranger Station, 24 West Chewuch Road, Winthrop, WA 98862, 509/996-4003.

87 WOLF CREEK
19.8 mi/2 days

west of Winthrop in Lake Chelan–Sawtooth Wilderness of Okanogan National Forest

Map 3.2, page 96

Gardner Meadows caps one of the region's most beautiful valley treks. Wolf Creek Trail ventures 10 miles into Wolf Creek valley, ending where Abernathy Ridge and Gardner Mountain loom high above the open parkland. Although the trail is popular with equestrians and hunters during fall, an abundance of wildlife awaits to be seen. Lupine and glacier lilies paint the meadows in color during early summer while deer and coyotes roam the open expanse. And there's no end to exploring off the main trail, as several nonmaintained trails lead into side valleys.

Wolf Creek Trail ascends gently over 10

miles to Gardner Meadows. The trail never strays far from the creek, which is locally known for booming bull trout populations. Most of the route passes through forests of huge Douglas fir and ponderosa pines. Side trails include one up the North Fork Wolf Creek at 2.7 miles, the South Fork Wolf Creek at 6.5 miles, and another up Hubbard Creek at 7.2 miles, none of which is maintained. Less maintenance, however, usually means more adventure.

Gardner Meadows is set upon wide open rolling hills. Patches of trees litter the terrain, which runs up to steep, scree-covered slopes. Scrambles farther up to Abernathy Lake or to the top of Abernathy Ridge are well advised for those looking for off-trail travel. Rumors continue to persist regarding gray wolves within the appropriately named valley. Reported sightings have not been confirmed and are more likely coyotes, which are abundant here. Sightings of gray wolves in the North Cascades have been confirmed only north of Highway 20.

User Groups: Hikers, leashed dogs, and horses. No mountain bikes are allowed. No wheelchair access.

Open Seasons: This trail is accessible June–October.

Permits: A federal Northwest Forest Pass is required to park here.

Maps: For a map of Okanogan National Forest, contact the Outdoor Recreation Information Center at the downtown Seattle REI. For topographic maps, ask Green Trails for No. 83, Buttermilk Butte, or ask the USGS for Thompson Ridge, Gilbert, and Midnight Mountain.

Directions: From Winthrop, drive east on Highway 20 to Twin Lakes Road (County Road 9120). Turn right (west) and drive 1.5 miles to Wolf Creek Road (County Road 1145). Turn right and drive 5 miles to the trailhead at road's end.

Contact: Okanogan National Forest, Methow Valley Ranger Station, 24 West Chewuch Road, Winthrop, WA 98862, 509/996-4003.

88 EAST FORK BUTTERMILK CREEK

15.0 mi/1–2 days

west of Twisp in Lake Chelan–Sawtooth Wilderness of Okanogan National Forest

Map 3.2, page 96

East Fork Buttermilk Creek is much like the West Fork. It's a hike through a forest that really isn't worth the time it takes to hike it. It's always nice to get out and enjoy nature, but there are many other trails within the area that are far more deserving of your time. That said, there are still some good things about this trail. Those good things are mainly limited to large forests near the creek and some great views at Hoodoo Pass. Unless you've hiked many other trails in the area and are looking for a new experience, East Fork Buttermilk Creek just isn't all that special.

The trail is laid out on an old mining road for the first four miles. Forests of Englemann spruce and lodgepole pine cover the valley and occasionally provide glimpses of surrounding ridges. The trail is not steep until it reaches the headwaters of the creek in Hoodoo Basin. Here, it abruptly ascends to Hoodoo Pass (7.5 miles). Views to the north and south are well worth a long stop here. The trail drops to Chelan Summit Trail (8.8 miles). Backpackers should plan on camping at Hoodoo Pass or at the junction of Chelan Summit Trail.

User Groups: Hikers, leashed dogs, and horses. No mountain bikes are allowed. No wheelchair access.

Open Seasons: This trail is accessible mid-June–October.

Permits: A federal Northwest Forest Pass is required to park here.

Maps: For a map of Okanogan National Forest, contact the Outdoor Recreation Information Center at the downtown Seattle REI. For topographic maps, ask Green Trails for No. 83, Buttermilk Butte, and No. 115, Prince Creek, or ask the USGS for Hoodoo Peak and Martin Peak.

Directions: From Twisp, drive east 11 miles on

Twisp River Road to Forest Service Road 43. Turn left and drive 6 miles to Forest Service Road 400. Turn right and drive 3.5 miles to the trailhead on the left.

Contact: Okanogan National Forest, Methow Valley Ranger Station, 24 West Chewuch Road, Winthrop, WA 98862, 509/996-4003.

89 LIBBY CREEK
10.4 mi/6.0 hrs

southwest of Twisp in Lake Chelan–Sawtooth Wilderness of Okanogan National Forest

Map 3.2, page 96

Libby Lake sits within its own amphitheater. Large, towering walls of granite ringing the high lake give way to large slopes of boulders and talus. But the lake is not easy to reach. Several elevation drops along the way are relentlessly followed by difficult climbs. But Libby Lake is well regarded and always enjoyable.

Libby Creek Trail begins on an old logging road and climbs steadily before becoming a real trail. The path eventually drops to cross the North Fork of Libby Creek, a great time to dip one's head in the cold water and cool off. The trail remains within the wide, forested valley bottom, crossing another pair of small creeks, sometimes dry. Tall Hoodoo Peak is to the north. The trail makes a final charge upward just before the lake. Remnants of a very old cabin can be seen to the side of the trail, beaten up by heavy winter snowfalls. There are several campsites below the lake, a quiet and inviting overnight stay. The lake itself is ringed by broken talus and subalpine larches, subsisting in this harsh, almost barren, mountain hideaway.

User Groups: Hikers, leashed dogs, and horses. No mountain bikes are allowed. No wheelchair access.

Open Seasons: This trail is accessible July–September.

Permits: A federal Northwest Forest Pass is required to park here.

Maps: For a map of Okanogan National Forest, contact the Outdoor Recreation Information Center at the downtown Seattle REI. For topographic maps, ask Green Trails for No. 83, Buttermilk Butte, and No. 115, Prince Creek, or ask the USGS for Hoodoo Peak.

Directions: From Twisp, drive east 3 miles on Highway 20 to Highway 153. Turn right onto Okanogan County Road 1045 and drive to Forest Service Road 43. Turn left and drive 5.5 miles to Forest Service Road 4340. Turn left and drive 1.5 miles to Forest Service Road 4340-700. Turn right and drive 1.5 miles to Forest Service Road 4340-750. Turn left and drive to the signed trailhead.

Contact: Okanogan National Forest, Methow Valley Ranger Station, 24 West Chewuch Road, Winthrop, WA 98862, 509/996-4003.

90 MARTIN LAKES
14.2 mi/2 days

southwest of Twisp in Lake Chelan–Sawtooth Wilderness of Okanogan National Forest

Map 3.2, page 96

Martin Lakes are a great first experience of the Sawtooths, a place of high lakes and higher peaks. Surrounded on three sides by woods and on another by the larch-dotted base of Martin Peak, the lakes offer a lot of peace, quiet, and most likely, solitude. Dinner's never more than a few casts away, either, as the lakes sport a good deal of healthy trout. It's enough to make hungry hikers curse forgotten poles.

The trail is in good condition and makes a steady, modest incline. The route begins on Eagle Lakes Trail but splits onto Martin Creek Trail (2.3 miles). The trail regularly opens to provide views of the opposing ridge and beyond, preventing feelings of forest claustrophobia. The two Martin Lakes are down a short and signed side trail at 6.3 miles. Several good campsites are found at the lower lake. High peaks and ridges surround the large basin. Clark's nutcrackers swoop about the whitebark pines, and hawks give the numerous chipmunks chase.

User Groups: Hikers, leashed dogs, horses, mountain bikes, and motorcycles (motorcycles most of the way). No wheelchair access.

Open Seasons: This trail is accessible July–mid-October.

Permits: A federal Northwest Forest Pass is required to park here.

Maps: For a map of Okanogan National Forest, contact the Outdoor Recreation Information Center at the downtown Seattle REI. For topographic maps, ask Green Trails for No. 115, Prince Creek, or ask the USGS for Martin Peak.

Directions: From Pateros, drive north on Highway 153. Turn left onto Gold Creek Loop Road, south of the town of Carlton. Turn left (west) onto Forest Service Road 4340. Drive about 6 miles to Forest Service Road 4340-300. Turn left and drive for about 5 miles to the trailhead at road's end.

Contact: Okanogan National Forest, Methow Valley Ranger Station, 24 West Chewuch Road, Winthrop, WA 98862, 509/996-4003.

91 CRATER LAKE
7.4 mi/4.0 hrs

southwest of Twisp in Lake Chelan–Sawtooth Wilderness of Okanogan National Forest

Map 3.2, page 96

Crater Lake is not the result of a large meteor hitting the Sawtooths. Nor was it created by a long-ago volcanic eruption. So erase the image of a crater from your mind, and replace it with tall, jagged ridges, craggy peaks, colorful larches, and blue mountain water. Voilà, you have a picture of the real Crater Lake. It's a good day hike and shows what the Sawtooths have to offer.

The route begins on Eagle Lake Trail, cutting to the right just after crossing Crater Creek (.5 mile). It moves quickly up the valley at a moderate grade. Crossing the creek again, it climbs more steeply. Before long, you'll be swearing the trail feels like more than the posted three miles from the junction. After a large granite outcrop, which reveals most of Eastern Washington, the trail levels off and hits the lake. There are several spots for camping at the outlet of the lake. This is a favorite spot for high-country anglers.

User Groups: Hikers, leashed dogs, horses, and mountain bikes. No wheelchair access.

Open Seasons: This trail is accessible July–mid-October.

Permits: A federal Northwest Forest Pass is required to park here.

Maps: For a map of Okanogan National Forest, contact the Outdoor Recreation Information Center at the downtown Seattle REI. For topographic maps, ask Green Trails for No. 115, Prince Creek, or ask the USGS for Martin Peak.

Directions: From Pateros, drive north on Highway 153. Turn left onto Gold Creek Loop Road, south of the town of Carlton. Turn left (west) onto Forest Service Road 4340. Drive about 6 miles to Forest Service Road 4340-300. Turn left and drive for about 5 miles to the trailhead at road's end.

Contact: Okanogan National Forest, Methow Valley Ranger Station, 24 West Chewuch Road, Winthrop, WA 98862, 509/996-4003.

92 EAGLE LAKES
12.3 mi/1–2 days

southwest of Twisp in Lake Chelan–Sawtooth Wilderness of Okanogan National Forest

Map 3.2, page 96

Take a trip to Eagle Lakes and you are likely to run into folks who have been coming here for 35 years or more. They enthusiastically call it home, and it's easy to understand why. Set below the towering granite walls of Mount Bigelow, Upper Eagle Lake enjoys a grand forest of subalpine larch and fir. A beautiful trail to the lakes and pretty decent fishing make this a popular choice in the South Sawtooth Range.

Eagle Lakes Trail climbs for much of its length but never too steeply. After Martin Lakes junction (2.5 miles), the forest begins to open up along Eagle Lakes Trail, providing a welcome view and appreciation of how far one has come. The trail passes granite outcroppings and very large Douglas firs and ponderosa pines. The junction for Upper Eagle Lake arrives first (5.8 miles) and climbs a short .5 mile to the lake.

Campsites ring the eastern shore, opposite the rocky slopes of the western shore. Upper Lake is definitely the better choice. Lower Eagle Lake Trail drops to the left (6.1 miles) to the more forested and larger lake, home to a horse camp.

User Groups: Hikers, leashed dogs, horses, mountain bikes, and motorcycles. No wheelchair access.

Open Seasons: This trail is accessible July–mid-October.

Permits: A federal Northwest Forest Pass is required to park here.

Maps: For a map of Okanogan National Forest, contact the Outdoor Recreation Information Center at the downtown Seattle REI. For topographic maps, ask Green Trails for No. 115, Prince Creek, or ask the USGS for Martin Peak.

Directions: From Pateros, drive north on Highway 153. Turn left onto Gold Creek Loop Road, south of the town of Carlton. Turn left (west) onto Forest Service Road 4340. Drive about 6 miles to Forest Service Road 4340-300. Turn left and drive for about 5 miles to the trailhead at road's end.

Contact: Okanogan National Forest, Methow Valley Ranger Station, 24 West Chewuch Road, Winthrop, WA 98862, 509/996-4003.

93 BUCK CREEK PASS
20.5 mi/2 days

north of Trinity in Glacier Peak Wilderness of Wenatchee National Forest

Map 3.2, page 96

Great by itself, Buck Creek Pass is also the means to grander ends. The pass is between three high peaks, each of them offering exceptional views of surrounding peaks and mountain ranges. The views are first-rate, but the wildflower meadows are what draw crowds of folks up the trail each year. In fact, Flower Dome could not be better named, for a blanket of flowers covers its entirety during July. Glacier Peak is a regular fixture, its mighty glaciers well revealed.

Buck Creek Trail leaves the town of Trinity along the road but quickly enters Glacier Peak Wilderness. The trail splits (2 miles), so stick to

the left, cross the Chiwawa River via bridge, and head up Buck Creek Valley through large forests of Douglas fir, Englemann spruce, and hemlock.

Buck Creek Pass is achieved after a tiring 10 miles. Numerous campsites line the trail and are widespread at the pass. Once camp is set up, the exploration can begin. Absolutely necessary is a one-mile trip up Flower Dome, awash in wildflower color. Another trail climbs to the top of Liberty Cap. For the hearty, a difficult trail heads toward High Pass and barren Triad Lake. Much of the area is delicate and receives heavy traffic, so be sure to take care where you step.

User Groups: Hikers, leashed dogs, and horses. No mountain bikes are allowed. No wheelchair access.

Open Seasons: This trail is accessible July–September.

Permits: A federal Northwest Forest Pass is required to park here.

Maps: For a map of Wenatchee National Forest, contact the Outdoor Recreation Information Center at the downtown Seattle REI. For topographic maps, ask Green Trails for No. 113, Holden, or ask the USGS for Trinity, Clark Mountain, and Suiattle Pass.

Directions: From Leavenworth, drive west on Highway 2 to Highway 207, at Coles Corner. Veer Left to Fish Lake and drive 1 mile to Chiwawa Valley Road (Forest Service Road 62). Turn left and drive to Trinity. The trailhead is at road's end, just beyond Phelps Creek Campground.

Contact: Wenatchee National Forest, Lake Wenatchee Ranger District, 22976 Highway 207, Leavenworth, WA 98826, 509/763-3103.

94 PHELPS CREEK (SPIDER MEADOW)
17.0 mi/2 days

north of Lake Wenatchee in Glacier Peak Wilderness of Wenatchee National Forest

Map 3.2, page 96

Officially, the route is named Phelps Creek Trail. But within Washington hiking circles, it is better known as Spider Meadow, after the enormous meadows within the elongated valley. At the head of the valley slides Spider Glacier, Washington's easiest glacier to explore. Nearly a mile long but not more than 150 feet across, Spider Glacier ends at scenic Spider Gap, with views of the North Cascades. Few trails this scenic are this easy.

Phelps Creek Trail follows an old logging road but soon enters Glacier Peak Wilderness (1 mile). The forest grows older and larger, and edible mushrooms are regularly spotted. Chicken-of-the-woods and bear's head tooth fungus are easily identifiable by beginners, but be sure to leave trailside specimens alone for others to enjoy. The trail breaks into Spider Meadow (4 miles). The obvious U shape to the valley is the work of the valley's previous tenant, a glacier. Camping must be at established campsites, of which there are about 30 throughout the lower valley.

After climbing out of the meadow (5 miles), the trail climbs to Spider Glacier, to the east. This glacier is completely nontechnical and can be traversed easily by all. At the top is Spider Gap, with views to the north of the larger Lyman Glacier and various North Cascade peaks. There are an additional 10 campsites within this upper basin. Expect a lot of people here on summer weekends.

User Groups: Hikers, leashed dogs, and horses (horses allowed up to Spider Meadow only). No mountain bikes are allowed. No wheelchair access.

Open Seasons: This trail is accessible mid-June–September.

Permits: A federal Northwest Forest Pass is required to park here.

Maps: For a map of Wenatchee National Forest, contact the Outdoor Recreation Information Center at the downtown Seattle REI. For topographic maps, ask Green Trails for No. 113, Holden, or ask the USGS for Trinity, Holden, and Suiattle Pass.

Directions: From Leavenworth, drive west on Highway 2 to Highway 207, at Coles Corner. Turn left and drive to Fish Lake and drive 1 mile to Chiwawa Valley Road (Forest Service Road 62). Turn left and drive toward Trinity. Just before Trinity, turn right on Forest Service Road 6211 and drive to the trailhead at road's end.

Contact: Wenatchee National Forest, Lake Wenatchee Ranger District, 22976 Highway 207, Leavenworth, WA 98826, 509/763-3103.

95 ENTIAT MEADOWS
29.6 mi/3–4 days

northwest of Entiat in Glacier Peak Wilderness of Wenatchee National Forest

Map 3.2, page 96

After 15 miles, a trail needs to offer something special. I'm talking large peaks or glaciers, wide open meadows with wildflowers, or lots of wildlife. Actually, that's what Entiat River Trail delivers, making its easy but long route well worth the trip.

Entiat River Trail quietly follows the Entiat River to its headwaters, making little substantial change in elevation. The first 10 miles are forested by large Englemann spruce, silver fir, and Douglas fir. Soon, the valley opens into meadows, and Tin Pan Mountain welcomes you to true backcountry. The trail turns west with the valley and Seven Fingered Jack beckons from the end of the valley, encouraging hikers to keep moving. There are good camps throughout this section of the trail for resting tired feet. Many hours from the car, Entiat River Trail arrives at its terminus among meadows and enormous piles of glacier moraine.

Entiat Glacier covers the backside of Maude Mountain, breaking and crackling during warm summer days. Mountain goats regularly patrol the steep valley walls in pursuit of dinner. Their bright white coats are easy to spot. There are many deer in the valley and always a good chance of seeing a bear or cat. This spot is far from any civilization, a very welcome bargain indeed.

User Groups: Hikers, leashed dogs, and horses. No mountain bikes are allowed. No wheelchair access.

Open Seasons: This trail is accessible June–October.

Permits: A federal Northwest Forest Pass is required to park here.

Maps: For a map of Wenatchee National Forest, contact the Outdoor Recreation Information Center at the downtown Seattle REI. For topographic maps, ask Green Trails for No. 113, Holden, and No. 114, Lucerne, or ask the USGS for Holden and Saska Peak.

Directions: From Wenatchee, drive north along U.S. 97 Alternate to Entiat. Turn left on Entiat River Road and drive 38 miles to the road's end, where the trailhead is located.

Contact: Wenatchee National Forest, Entiat Ranger Station, 2108 Entiat Way, P.O. Box 476, Entiat, WA 98822, 509/784-1511.

96 ICE LAKES
25.6 mi/2–3 days

northwest of Entiat in Glacier Peak Wilderness of Wenatchee National Forest

Map 3.2, page 96

Ice Lakes are true high country. Other than subalpine larches and big mountains, there is little else here. No worries, because Ice Lakes is phenomenally beautiful. Think of the Enchantments, but without the crowds or discouraging permit process. The upper Entiat Mountains rise above Ice Valley and surround the lakes. Hike up here in late September and the larches will add radiant yellows and oranges to the landscape. Best of all, this trail is not exceptionally well known.

The journey to Ice Lakes is no piece of cake. First, hike eight miles up Entiat River Trail. Cross the Entiat (troublesome in the spring) and wind up Ice Creek Valley through a forest filled with large Englemann spruce. First-night spots can be found on either side of the Entiat River crossing (8 miles), where Pomas Creek runs into Ice Creek (8.8 miles), and at Ice Camp (12.7 miles).

At Ice Camp, the trail turns downright nasty, scaling the valley wall (a 1,300-foot climb in one mile). This section often requires 90 minutes or more, so don't be discouraged. At the

top is Lower Ice Lake, and a short mile farther is Upper Ice Lake. There is lots of camping to be had at the lakes, particularly the lower one. Plan for time to kick back and relax here, as it's time well spent. There are lots of scrambles to be had from here, including an ascent of 9,082-foot Mount Maude.

User Groups: Hikers, leashed dogs, and horses (horses up to Ice Camp; they won't be able to make it farther). No mountain bikes are allowed. No wheelchair access.

Open Seasons: This trail is usually accessible mid-July–October.

Permits: A federal Northwest Forest Pass is required to park here.

Maps: For a map of Wenatchee National Forest, contact the Outdoor Recreation Information Center at the downtown Seattle REI. For topographic maps, ask Green Trails for No. 113, Holden, and No. 114, Lucerne, or ask the USGS for Holden, Saska Peak, and Pinnacle Mountain.

Directions: From Wenatchee, drive north along U.S. 97 Alternate to Entiat. Turn left on Entiat River Road and drive 38 miles to the road's end, where the well-signed trailhead is located.

Contact: Wenatchee National Forest, Entiat Ranger Station, 2108 Entiat Way, P.O. Box 476, Entiat, WA 98822, 509/784-1511.

97 PYRAMID MOUNTAIN
18.4 mi/1–2 days

west of Lake Chelan in Wenatchee National Forest

Map 3.2, page 96

Pyramid Mountain is for hikers looking to seemingly stand atop the state. From the lofty elevation of 8,243 feet, Pyramid Mountain provides a panorama rarely matched in the region. From the high ridge and even higher peak, one can see much of Lake Chelan, surrounding mountain ranges, and much of the Cascades. To attain such a high vantage is relatively easy thanks to a trailhead at 6,500 feet. Vistas this grand don't come this cheaply very often.

Pyramid Mountain Trail spends the length of its time along the Chelan Mountains ridgeline among sparse meadows and subalpine trees. Passing Crow Hill, the trail hits a junction (2.7 miles); stay right to skirt below Graham Mountain. Endure a pair of elevation losses before climbing Pyramid Mountain, where an old fire lookout once stood. Camping can be done in accordance with Leave-No-Trace principles, but fires are never a good idea in this dry climate. Carrying extra water is important here, where the summer sun is scorching.

User Groups: Hikers, leashed dogs, horses, and mountain bikes. No wheelchair access.

Open Seasons: This trail is accessible mid-July–September.

Permits: A federal Northwest Forest Pass is required to park here.

Maps: For a map of Wenatchee National Forest, contact the Outdoor Recreation Information Center at the downtown Seattle REI. For topographic maps, ask Green Trails for No. 114, Lucerne, or ask the USGS for Pyramid Mountain and Saksa Peak.

Directions: From Entiat, drive east on Entiat River Road to Forest Service Road 5900, just beyond Lake Creek Campground. Turn right and drive 8.5 miles to Forest Service Road 113 at Shady Pass. Turn left and drive 2 miles to the trailhead at road's end. This is a rough road and a high-clearance vehicle is recommended.

Contact: Wenatchee National Forest, Entiat Ranger Station, 2108 Entiat Way, P.O. Box 476, Entiat, WA 98822, 509/784-1511.

98 WALLACE FALLS
5.6 mi/3.0 hrs

north of Gold Bar in Wallace Falls State Park

Map 3.3, page 97

There are few better trails within such easy reach of Seattle. Wallace Falls are some of the Cascades' best known waterfalls, with more than nine drops of at least 50 feet. The tallest cascade, with a drop of 265 feet, is visible from Highway 2. Why see something from the highway when you can check it out up close?

There are two options for reaching the falls,

thanks to the hard work of volunteers. A direct route to the falls is achieved in 2.8 miles while a longer, gentler loop adds a mile. Either way, Wallace Falls is certainly made for the whole family and for all hikers. The trail leaves the trailhead before splitting into Woody Trail and Railroad Grade (the longer of the two). Traveling through forests of alder and fir, the trails meet near the bridge over the North Wallace River. Another mile up the trail reveals the numerous falls. It's wonderful during the spring, when snowmelt turns Wallace River into a torrent and adds spectacular drama to the falls. Also during the spring, many forest plants and flowers are in bloom, adding much color to the setting. The trail gets its fair share of visitors during the summer, but it's understandable why.

User Groups: Hikers and leashed dogs. No horses or mountain bikes are allowed. No wheelchair access.

Open Seasons: This trail is accessible year-round.

Permits: A $5 day-use fee is required to park here and is payable at the trailhead, or you can get an annual State Parks Pass for $30; contact Washington State Parks and Recreation, 360/902-8500.

Maps: For topographic maps, ask Green Trails for No. 142, Index, or ask the USGS for Gold Bar and Wallace Lake.

Directions: From Everett, drive east on U.S. 2 to the town of Gold Bar. Turn left (north) on 1st Street and follow the signs to the park entrance. The well-signed trailhead is near the main parking area in the park.

Contact: Wallace Falls State Park, P.O. Box 230, Gold Bar, WA 98251, 360/793-0420.

99 BLANCA LAKE
7.0 mi/4.0 hrs

northeast of Index in Henry M. Jackson Wilderness of Mount Baker–Snoqualmie National Forest

Map 3.3, page 97

Below a trio of towering peaks, Blanca Lake makes a scenic trip. With the large Columbia Glacier feeding the lake a steady stream of silt-filled runoff, the lake turns an intense turquoise and makes for fine photographs. The beauty of the lake and its surroundings are not without grinding effort. The trail makes a steep ascent to a pass at Virgin Lake before steeply dropping to the lake. From amid parkland meadows, however, views of Glacier Peak help to ease the leg-numbing switching.

Blanca Lake Trail dances the switchback shuffle, ascending 2,700 feet in just three miles. Forests of red cedar, Douglas fir, and western hemlock shade the way. Near the crest (2.7 miles), enjoy views of the inner peaks and ridges of the Cascades. Pass Virgin Lake and drop to Blanca Lake. Columbia Peak, Monte Cristo Peak, and Kyes Peak ring the large basin. Trails for exploration wander around the lake, but Columbia Glacier should be treated as off-limits. A number of good campsites ring the lake, but they see a lot of use, especially on summer weekends. Blanca Lake is well worth writing home about.

User Groups: Hikers and leashed dogs. No horses or mountain bikes are allowed. No wheelchair access.

Open Seasons: This trail is accessible July–October.

Permits: A federal Northwest Forest Pass is required to park here.

Maps: For a map of Mount Baker–Snoqualmie National Forest, contact the Outdoor Recreation Information Center at the downtown Seattle REI. For topographic maps, ask Green Trails for No. 143, Monte Cristo, or ask the USGS for Blanca Lake.

Directions: From Everett, drive east on U.S. 2 to Index. At the Index turnoff, turn left (north) onto the North Fork Skykomish River Road (Forest Road 63). Drive 18.1 miles to the trailhead.

Contact: Mount Baker–Snoqualmie National Forest, Skykomish Ranger Station, 74920 Northeast Stevens Pass Highway, Skykomish, WA 98288, 360/677-2414.

100 WEST CADY RIDGE
7.0–17.0 mi/1–2 days

north of Skykomish in Henry M. Jackson Wilderness of Mount Baker–Snoqualmie National Forest

Map 3.3, page 97

West Cady Ridge is blessed with miles of wide open big-sky meadows. The views are supreme from nearly every inch of the trail, which rides the crest of the ridge straight to PCT. Meadows of heather and wildflower aplenty cover the ridge, making July the time to hit this trail. Splendor this grand rarely comes at so easy a price. And topping it all off is the panoramic vista from atop Benchmark Mountain.

West Cady Ridge Trail reaches meadows in a quick but steep hike through great Cascade old-growth forest. The trees shrink before your eyes as you steadily climb higher. The trail finds the crest (3.5 miles, a good turnaround point for a shorter hike) and follows it to PCT (8.5 miles). There are some ups and downs, but at all times the trail is easy to follow. Huckleberries line the route, an encouragement to take things slowly. A side trail (at 7 miles) shoots up Benchmark Mountain to the summit. Backpackers are encouraged to explore this trail. At 5,816 feet, the summit reveals much of the Cascades. Hiking north on PCT brings hikers to Pass Creek Trail, which can be used to make a loop out of West Cady Ridge.

User Groups: Hikers, leashed dogs, and horses. No mountain bikes are allowed. No wheelchair access.

Open Seasons: This trail is accessible July–October.

Permits: A federal Northwest Forest Pass is required to park here.

Maps: For a map of Mount Baker–Snoqualmie National Forest, contact the Outdoor Recreation Information Center at the downtown Seattle REI. For topographic maps, ask Green Trails for No. 143, Monte Cristo, and No. 144, Benchmark Mountain, or ask the USGS for Blanca Lake and Benchmark Mountain.

Directions: From Everett, drive east on U.S.

2 to Index. At the Index turnoff, turn left (north) onto North Fork Skykomish River Road (Forest Service Road 63). Drive 20 miles to the trailhead on the right.

Contact: Mount Baker–Snoqualmie National Forest, Skykomish Ranger Station, 74920 Northeast Stevens Pass Highway, Skykomish, WA 98288, 360/677-2414.

101 CADY CREEK/ LITTLE WENATCHEE LOOP
19.0 mi/2–3 days

north of Lake Wenatchee in Henry M. Jackson Wilderness of Wenatchee National Forest

Map 3.3, page 97

This is an excellent trip along Pacific Crest Trail. Using Cady Creek and Little Wenatchee River Trails, the route offers access to a pair of superb high country destinations. Meadows of wildflowers and sweeping vistas are the name of the game here, one of PCT's most beautiful stretches. While the loop can be made in two days, three is far better. A more relaxed pace allows for side trips and more time in this exceptional place.

The route begins along Cady Creek, a gradual climb through old-growth forests to Cady Pass (5.2 miles). Cady Creek must be forded, but the cool water is refreshing on hot summer days. Hike north on PCT through terrific meadows to Lake Sally Ann (10 miles) below Skykomish Peak. Lake Sally Ann has several great campsites.

PCT continues north to Meander Meadow (12.3 miles), a large, flat basin overflowing with wildflowers. Several great camps are near the outlet of the meadow. Kodak Peak stands over the basin, offering panoramic views from the summit. Much of Glacier Peak and Henry M. Jackson Wildernesses are within sight. The route returns to the trailhead via Little Wenatchee River Trail, which is full of great forests and waterfalls. Much of PCT is along north-facing slopes, where snow lingers late into summer, a consideration. All in all, this is an outstanding three-day weekend.

User Groups: Hikers, leashed dogs, and horses. No mountain bikes are allowed. No wheelchair access.

Open Seasons: This trail is accessible mid-July–October.

Permits: A federal Northwest Forest Pass is required to park here.

Maps: For a map of Wenatchee National Forest, contact the Outdoor Recreation Information Center at the downtown Seattle REI. For topographic maps, ask Green Trails for No. 144, Benchmark Mountain, or ask the USGS for Poe Mountain and Benchmark Mountain.

Directions: From Leavenworth, drive west on U.S. 2 to Highway 207, at Coles Corner. Turn left and drive to Little Wenatchee Road (Forest Service Road 65). Veer left and drive to the signed trailhead at road's end.

Contact: Wenatchee National Forest, Lake Wenatchee Ranger Station, 22976 Highway 207, Leavenworth, WA 98826, 509/763-3103.

102 FORTUNE PONDS
17.0 mi/1–2 days

north of Skykomish in Henry M. Jackson Wilderness of Mount Baker–Snoqualmie National Forest

Map 3.3, page 97

Don't be fooled by the name of the hike. Tradition dictates that the hike be called Fortune Ponds, even though they are but a small feature of this wonderful route. The bigger features are Pear and Peach Lakes, two large high-country lakes enclosed by parkland meadows and outstanding views. And for those seeking even more adventure, a climb to the top of Fortune Mountain is easy and well recommended.

Meadow Creek Trail immediately climbs a steep valley wall through a burned-out forest. The trail levels out and gradually climbs along Meadow Creek. The creek must be crossed twice, a wet ordeal during the early summer. By the time the forest thins and eventually breaks, you reach Fortune Ponds. Benchmark Mountain stands to the north, framed nicely behind the lakes. The trail continues another mile to Pear Lake and an intersection with Pacific Crest Trail. Peach Lake is to the south and over a small ridge. Subalpine fir and mountain hemlocks line the lakes, where established camps can be found. This is the high country, where huckleberries madly grow before bears can madly eat them. A side trail leads up Fortune Mountain, which at 5,903 feet presents much of the surrounding wilderness.

User Groups: Hikers, leashed dogs, and horses. No mountain bikes are allowed. No wheelchair access.

Open Seasons: This trail is accessible July–October.

Permits: A federal Northwest Forest Pass is required to park here.

Maps: For a map of Wenatchee National Forest, contact the Outdoor Recreation Information Center at the downtown Seattle REI. For topographic maps, ask Green Trails for No. 144, Benchmark Mountain, or ask the USGS for Captain Point and Benchmark Mountain.

Directions: From Everett, drive east on U.S. 2 until .5 mile east of the town of Skykomish. Turn left (north) onto the Beckler River Road (Forest Service Road 65) and drive for 6 miles to the junction with Rapid River Road (Forest Service Road 6530). Turn right and continue for 4.5 miles to trailhead.

Contact: Mount Baker–Snoqualmie National Forest, Skykomish Ranger Station, 74920 Northeast Stevens Pass Highway, Skykomish, WA 98288, 360/677-2414.

103 SNOQUALMIE AND DOROTHY LAKES

4.0–15.0 mi/2.5 hr–2 days

south of Skykomish in Alpine Lakes Wilderness of Mount Baker–Snoqualmie National Forest

Map 3.3, page 97

This great route offers two ways to experience it. Snoqualmie and Dorothy Lake Trails make a long, east-west journey through the Alpine Lakes Wilderness, progressing from the Taylor River in the Snoqualmie drainage over to

the Miller River in the Skykomish drainage. Along the way are a number of great waterfalls and no fewer than five large lakes. There's lots to explore here with a chance for hikers of all abilities to experience it.

Snoqualmie, Dear, Bear, and Dorothy Lakes lie within 2.5 miles of each other. These big lakes feature grand forests reaching to the shores, with big peaks visible over the basin's gentle ridges. Quick and easy access is gained from Miller River Trailhead, just two miles from enormous Lake Dorothy. This access point is preferred by families and those seeking the lakes but not a long trek. From the west trailhead, the route makes a longer (15 miles round-trip), more scenic trek to the lakes. Also, a steep side trail (6.3 miles) shoots up to isolated Nordrum Lake. Campsites are located at each of the lakes.

User Groups: Hikers, leashed dogs, horses, and mountain bikes (horses and mountain bikes allowed on the first six miles of Taylor River Road). No wheelchair access.

Open Seasons: This trail is accessible mid-May–November.

Permits: A federal Northwest Forest Pass is required to park here.

Maps: For a map of Mount Baker–Snoqualmie National Forest, contact the Outdoor Recreation Information Center at the downtown Seattle REI. For topographic maps, ask Green Trails for No. 175, Skykomish, or ask the USGS for Snoqualmie Lake and Big Snow Mountain.

Directions: Taylor River Trailhead: From Seattle, drive east on I-90 to Exit 34. Turn left onto 468th Avenue North. At .6 mile, turn right onto Middle Fork Road (Forest Service Road 56). Stay on Forest Service Road 56 for 12.5 miles to the Taylor River Trailhead. Forest Service Road 56 splits just after it crosses the Taylor River; stay to the left. The trailhead is .5 mile farther at a gate.

East Miller River Trailhead: From Everett, drive east on U.S. 2 to Money Creek Campground, 2.8 miles before the town of Skykomish. Turn south onto the Old Cascade Highway.

The road is just west of the highway tunnel. Drive the Old Cascade Highway for 1 mile, then turn right (south) onto the Miller River Road (Forest Service Road 6410). Continue on Forest Service Road 6410 for 9.5 miles to the road's end at the trailhead.

Contact: Mount Baker–Snoqualmie National Forest, North Bend Ranger Station, 42404 Southeast North Bend Way, North Bend, WA 98045, 425/888-1421.

104 FOSS LAKES
13.6 mi/2 days

east of Skykomish in Alpine Lakes Wilderness of Mount Baker–Snoqualmie National Forest

Map 3.3, page 97

This classic Alpine Lakes Wilderness trail takes in no fewer than five lakes, offering a day hike or overnighter that never gets boring. The upper lakes are set among a rugged landscape once dominated by glaciers. Even today, it sees a lot of winter snow. But be forewarned: Within two hours of Seattle and with easy accessibility up to even the farthest lake, this trail sees a lot of use, even bordering on abuse. If you're willing to forgo solitude, then Foss Lakes is a must visit.

The trail begins very easily, with little elevation gain along the first 1.5 miles to Trout Lake. Along the way, the trail passes one of the biggest Douglas firs you'll ever see. Only the largest of families will be able to wrap their arms around this one. Surrounded by forest, Trout Lake whets the appetite for the alpine lakes to come. This is a good turnaround for less serious hikers.

From Trout Lake, West Fork Foss Trail climbs steeply to Lake Malachite, cruising in and out of forest alongside a beautiful cascading stream that offers needed refreshment on hot days. This is the trail's big climb, gaining 1,800 feet in two miles. From Lake Malachite, another three lakes (Copper, Little Heart, and Big Heart) lie within three miles' distance. The lakes seem to get better as you progress,

with the blues of the lakes getting deeper and the rocky ridges getting steeper and higher. From Big Heart Lake, trails lead to Lake Angeline and the many ridges and lakes beyond. There is camping at each of the lakes, although it goes quickly during the summer season. These are true alpine lakes, sure to stick in your hiking memory.

User Groups: Hikers and leashed dogs. No horses or mountain bikes are allowed. No wheelchair access.

Open Seasons: This trail is usually accessible June–October.

Permits: A federal Northwest Forest Pass is required to park here.

Maps: For a map of Mount Baker–Snoqualmie National Forest, contact the Outdoor Recreation Information Center at the downtown Seattle REI. For topographic maps, ask Green Trails for No. 175, Skykomish, or ask the USGS for Big Snow Mountain and Skykomish.

Directions: From Everett, drive east on U.S. 2 to 1.7 miles east of the town of Skykomish. Turn right (south) onto Foss River Road (Forest Service Road 68). Stay on this main road, avoiding any turnoffs, to the trailhead at road's end.

Contact: Mount Baker–Snoqualmie National Forest, Skykomish Ranger Station, 74920 Northeast Stevens Pass Highway, Skykomish, WA 98288, 360/677-2414.

105 NECKLACE VALLEY
16.0 mi/1–2 days

west of Stevens Pass in Alpine Lakes Wilderness of Mount Baker–Snoqualmie National Forest

Map 3.3, page 97

It's a long, hard hike into Necklace Valley. After five miles of river valley, the trail climbs 2,500 feet in a little more than two miles. Not exactly the stuff for beginners. For those who endure the challenge of reaching the Necklace Valley, however, ample compensation awaits. The Necklace Valley hosts a string of handsome lakes dotting a narrow, high valley. On nearly all sides are rocky slopes and ridges, where patches of snow linger late into summer. The upper valley is wide and very open, leaving lots of room to explore.

Necklace Valley Trail quickly enters the wilderness (1.5 miles) and enjoys four miles of old-growth forest along the East Fork Foss River. From here, the trail shoots up through the forest quickly and mercilessly into Necklace Valley (7 miles). A map is a necessity up here, as there are a number of lakes and lots of room to get lost. The best plan of action is to just start wandering, as there is no such thing as a bad section of the Necklace Valley. The lower lakes are forested and provide good shelter, while the upper lakes are open with meadows. All of the lakes here have established campsites. The scenery only gets better as the trail follows the valley up past La Bohn Lakes to La Bohn Gap. From here, Mount Hinman and Bears Breast Mountain stand tall to the south and north.

User Groups: Hikers and leashed dogs. No horses or mountain bikes are allowed. No wheelchair access.

Open Seasons: This trail is accessible July–October.

Permits: A federal Northwest Forest Pass is required to park here.

Maps: For a map of Mount Baker–Snoqualmie National Forest, contact the Outdoor Recreation Information Center at the downtown Seattle REI. For topographic maps, ask Green Trails for No. 175, Skykomish, and No. 176, Stevens Pass, or ask the USGS for Skykomish, Big Snow Mountain, and Mount Daniel.

Directions: From Everett, drive east on U.S. 2 to 1.7 miles east of the town of Skykomish. Turn right (south) onto Foss River Road (Forest Service Road 68) and drive 4.1 miles to the trailhead.

Contact: Mount Baker–Snoqualmie National Forest, Skykomish Ranger Station, 74920 Northeast Stevens Pass Highway, Skykomish, WA 98288, 360/677-2414.

106 TONGA RIDGE

9.2 mi/5.0 hrs

west of Stevens Pass in Alpine Lakes Wilderness of Mount Baker–Snoqualmie National Forest

Map 3.3, page 97

This is a great opportunity for the whole family to experience the high country. Starting out at a lofty 4,300 feet elevation, the trail rides out Tonga Ridge for more than four miles, offering Mount Sawyer and Fisher Lake for excellent side trips. The route stays below 5,000 feet the entire length, making for very little climbing yet excellent mountain views. The trail is popular with hikers because of its extensive meadows overflowing with huckleberries. Never mind the late August crowds; stay focused on the terrific views of nearby peaks.

Tonga Ridge Trail travels 4.6 miles along Tonga Ridge, connecting at each end to a part of Forest Service Road 6830-310. The first and closest trailhead is recommended, save for those looking for a shorter hike to Fisher Lake. Subalpine meadows dominate the route, as do great views of Mounts Hinman and Daniel. During August, hikers quickly take note of the plentiful huckleberry bushes. A side trail leads to the summit of Mount Sawyer for a 360-degree view of the surrounding peaks and much of the Cascades. A side trail also leads to Fisher Lake. The rough trail heads up and over a small crest to the large and impressive lake, set beneath towering cliffs.

User Groups: Hikers and leashed dogs. No horses or mountain bikes are allowed. No wheelchair access.

Open Seasons: This trail is accessible July–October.

Permits: A federal Northwest Forest Pass is required to park here.

Maps: For a map of Mount Baker–Snoqualmie National Forest, contact the Outdoor Recreation Information Center at the downtown Seattle REI. For topographic maps, ask Green Trails for No. 175, Skykomish, and No. 176,

Stevens Pass, or ask the USGS for Skykomish and Scenic.

Directions: From Everett, drive east on U.S. 2 to 1.7 miles east of the town of Skykomish. Turn right (south) onto Foss River Road (Forest Service Road 68). Drive on Forest Service Road 68 for 3.5 miles to Forest Service Road 6830. Turn left onto Forest Service Road 6830 and drive for 6 miles to Forest Service Road 6830-310. Turn right onto Forest Service Road 6830-310 and drive 1 mile to the end of the road.

Contact: Mount Baker–Snoqualmie National Forest, Skykomish Ranger Station, 74920 Northeast Stevens Pass Highway, Skykomish, WA 98288, 360/677-2414.

107 DECEPTION CREEK
20.6 mi/2 days

west of Stevens Pass in Alpine Lakes Wilderness of Mount Baker–Snoqualmie National Forest

Map 3.3, page 97

Some trips into the wilderness need not culminate at a vista or high alpine lake. Sometimes, simple travel within giant forests and along a cool, murmuring creek is the end in itself. That is certainly the case with Deception Creek, a great stroll through shady cool Cascade forest with access to high-country lakes. But the real point of Deception Creek is simply an excursion into wilderness.

Deception Creek Trail parallels the stream for six miles. It crosses the swirling creek below a nice waterfall (.5 mile). The route features a bit of up and down as it slowly climbs up the valley. This is Cascadia at its best, with the forest full of large Douglas firs, western red cedars, and western hemlocks. Moss grows on most everything while the forest floor becomes a carpet of ferns at times.

Deception Creek Trail eventually leaves the valley floor to ascend the valley wall. A connector trail (7.3 miles) leads up to Deception Lakes, a good option as a destination. Deception Pass (10.3 miles) is a junction for Pacific Crest Trail and Marmot and Hyas

Lakes. Campsites are scattered liberally along the trail.

User Groups: Hikers and leashed dogs. No horses or mountain bikes are allowed. No wheelchair access.

Open Seasons: This trail is accessible April–November.

Permits: A federal Northwest Forest Pass is required to park here.

Maps: For a map of Mount Baker–Snoqualmie National Forest, contact the Outdoor Recreation Information Center at the downtown Seattle REI. For topographic maps, ask Green Trails for No. 176, Stevens Pass, or ask the USGS for Scenic and Mount Daniel.

Directions: From Everett, drive east on U.S. 2 to Forest Service Road 6088, immediately beyond Deception Falls picnic area. Turn right and drive .3 mile to the trailhead at road's end.

Contact: Mount Baker–Snoqualmie National Forest, Skykomish Ranger Station, 74920 Northeast Stevens Pass Highway, Skykomish, WA 98288, 360/677-2414.

108 SURPRISE LAKE
8.0 mi/4.0 hrs

near Stevens Pass in Alpine Lakes Wilderness of Mount Baker–Snoqualmie National Forest

Map 3.3, page 97

By the time one has hiked a mile up Surprise Creek, the surprise should be over. Within the first half hour, it is readily evident that this is a beautiful hike. It gets only better as it progresses. But perhaps a surprise does exist, because the view from Pieper Pass seems almost too good to be true. This is a great part of the Alpine Lakes Wilderness, with many lakes and lots of stunning scenery.

Surprise Creek Trail quickly says good-bye to civilization and enters old-growth forest. Surprise Creek makes a number of small falls and cascades. The grade is gentle until the trail makes a quick rise to a narrow gap between two ridges. Reach the notch and Surprise Lake (4 miles); Glacier Lake is a bit farther up the long, narrow basin (5 miles). Forest and meadow fringe the lakes, and the tall cliffs of Surprise Mountain drop to Glacier Lake. Numerous campsites are found around each lake.

For additional exploration, hike PCT up to 6,000-foot Pieper Pass to view the large glaciers on Mount Hinman and Mount Daniel. Spark Plug and Thunder Mountains are good scrambles as well. There is a lot of high country to explore around here, and likely more than a few extra surprises.

User Groups: Hikers and leashed dogs. No horses or mountain bikes are allowed. No wheelchair access.

Open Seasons: This trail is accessible July–October.

Permits: A federal Northwest Forest Pass is required to park here.

Maps: For a map of Mount Baker–Snoqualmie National Forest, contact the Outdoor Recreation Information Center at the downtown Seattle REI. For topographic maps, ask Green Trails for No. 176, Stevens Pass, or ask the USGS for Scenic.

Directions: From Everett, drive east on U.S. 2 to Mile Marker 58. Turn right (south) onto an unmarked road to the service center for Burlington-Northern Railroad. Cross the railroad tracks and turn onto the spur road on the far right. Continue for .2 mile to the trailhead.

Contact: Mount Baker–Snoqualmie National Forest, Skykomish Ranger Station, 74920 Northeast Stevens Pass Highway, Skykomish, WA 98288, 360/677-2414.

109 CHAIN LAKES
22.0 mi/2 days

near Stevens Pass in Alpine Lakes Wilderness of Wenatchee National Forest

Map 3.3, page 97

Chain Lakes are tucked way, way back in the Alpine Lakes Wilderness. Eleven miles from the nearest trailhead, there are few people back in these parts. Great old-growth forest lines much of the route before it breaks into subalpine meadows and views, with several spec-

tacular lakes. Chain Lakes are an excellent destination for a long weekend. They definitely deserve three days for exploration rather than two cramped days spent mostly hiking.

Chain Lakes are accessible by either Stevens Pass or Icicle Creek out of Leavenworth. These are two different approaches to the shared segment of Chain Lakes Trail. From near Stevens Pass, PCT climbs above Josephine Lake and Lake Susan Jane before dropping into the Icicle Creek drainage and Chain Lakes Trail (5 miles). Traveling from Icicle Creek (6.5 miles) takes you through a more typical east-side forest, drier with more pines.

The two routes converge at Chain Lakes Trail, which climbs quickly to the lakes. Chain Lakes lie within a narrow basin, filled with parkland and meadows along the upper lakes, where jagged crags line the rim of the basin. There are several established campsites near the lower two lakes. The trail heads over the jagged ridge through a gap and drops to Doelle Lakes, two more great high lakes with camping.

User Groups: Hikers, leashed dogs, and horses (horses allowed day use of Chain Lakes). No mountain bikes are allowed. No wheelchair access.

Open Seasons: This trail is accessible July–October.

Permits: A federal Northwest Forest Pass is required to park here.

Maps: For a map of Mount Baker–Snoqualmie National Forest, contact the Outdoor Recreation Information Center at the downtown Seattle REI. For topographic maps, ask Green Trails for No. 176, Stevens Pass, and No. 177, Chiwaukum Mountains, or ask the USGS for Stevens Pass.

Directions: From Everett, drive east on U.S. 2 to Forest Service Road 6960 (about 4 miles east of Stevens Pass). Turn right and drive 4 miles to the parking lot at the road's gated end. Turn right (south) onto an unmarked road to the service center for Burlington-Northern Railroad. Cross the railroad tracks and turn onto the spur road on the far right. Continue for .2 mile to the trailhead.

Contact: Mount Baker–Snoqualmie National Forest, Skykomish Ranger Station, 74920 Northeast Stevens Pass Highway, Skykomish, WA 98288, 360/677-2414.

110 NASON RIDGE
6.0–22.1 mi/3.5 hr–2 days
east of Stevens Pass in Wenatchee National Forest

Map 3.3, page 97

This subalpine ridge provides hikers with a lot of trail and several excellent destinations. Running the length of Nason Ridge, Nason Ridge Trail passes three lakes and an alpine lookout, summits several peaks more than 6,000 feet elevation, and features five different access points. It is not, however, an easy ascent to any part of Nason Ridge. Every trailhead has at least 2,000 feet of climbing to the ridge. The splendor of Nason Ridge is well worth it.

The main attractions along the ridge are Rock Mountain and Lake (9.2 miles round-trip), Merritt Lake (6 miles round-trip), and Alpine Lookout. Rock Mountain (6,852 feet) stands on the western end of Nason Ridge. Rock Lake sits below, in a small cirque and surrounded by subalpine forest. Farther east are Crescent and Merritt Lakes. Merritt is accessible by its own trail right off Highway 2. The lakes on the ridge have established campsites that should be used at all times. Alpine Lookout is a staffed Forest Service fire watchtower, about five miles from Butcher Creek Trailhead. Spread out on the ridge between these points are 20 miles of trail threading through high meadow, the perfect place for mountain goats. The two ends of the trail also have trailheads, on Butcher Creek and Snowy Creek. These are accessible from Highway 2 and Lake Wenatchee. There is much to do and see on Nason Ridge, and it gets better later in the season.

User Groups: Hikers, leashed dogs, and mountain bikes. No horses are allowed. No wheelchair access.

Open Seasons: This trail is open mid-July–October.

Permits: A federal Northwest Forest Pass is required to park here.

Maps: For a map of Wenatchee National Forest, contact the Outdoor Recreation Information Center at the downtown Seattle REI. For topographic maps, ask Green Trails for No. 145, Lake Wenatchee, or ask the USGS for Labyrinth Mountain, Mount Howard, and Lake Wenatchee.

Directions: From Leavenworth, drive west on U.S. 2 to Forest Service Road 6910 for Alpine Lookout, Forest Service Road 657 for Merritt Lake or Rock Mountain Trailhead (on U.S. 2).

Contact: Wenatchee National Forest, Lake Wenatchee Ranger Station, 22976 Highway 207, Leavenworth, WA 98826, 509/763-3103.

111 IRON GOAT
12.0 mi one-way/6.0 hrs

west of Stevens Pass along Highway 2

Map 3.3, page 97

Iron Goat Trail is the result of a lot of volunteer labor. Volunteers for Outdoor Washington have led the effort to remake an old railway into one of Washington's best rails-to-trails projects. The route follows the old path of the Great Northern Railway, the first rail service to cross Stevens Pass back in the late 1800s. Volunteers have done an excellent job of cleaning up debris, refurbishing the trail, and adding many interesting interpretive signs along the way. The route is great for families and hikers of all abilities—you can turn around at any point for a satisfying hike. Along the way are many old artifacts from the railway. Several tunnels lead off into the hillside, appearing as deep, dark caverns. As a railway, the route was plagued by trouble from the uncooperative Cascades. Snowslides and avalanches were frequent problems, as were fires. The trail is accessible at its two ends, each of which is on the west side of Stevens Pass. This is an excellent trip not only for families and young children, but for anyone crossing the pass and needing a break.

User Groups: Hikers and leashed dogs. No horses or mountain bikes are allowed. Part of the trail is wheelchair accessible (near Martin Creek).

Open Seasons: This trail is usually accessible April–November.

Permits: A federal Northwest Forest Pass is required to park at the trailheads.

Maps: Maps of this trail are best obtained at the trailheads. Current Green Trails and USGS maps do not show the Iron Goat.

Directions: From Everett, drive east on U.S. 2 beyond the town of Skykomish. At Mile Marker 55 (6 miles east of the town of Skykomish), turn left (north) onto the Old Cascade Highway (Forest Service Road 67). Drive 2.3 miles to Forest Service Road 6710 and turn left onto Forest Service Road 6710. Drive 1.4 miles to the Martin Creek Trailhead.

To get to Wellington Trailhead, drive to Mile Marker 64.3, just west of Stevens Pass, and turn left (north) onto the Old Cascade Highway. Drive 2.8 miles to Road 050. Turn right onto Road 050. Turn right and drive to the trailhead.

Contact: Mount Baker–Snoqualmie National Forest, Skykomish Ranger Station, 74920 Northeast Stevens Pass Highway, Skykomish, WA 98288, 360/677-2414.

112 TIGER MOUNTAIN
1.0–5.2 mi/1.0–5.0 hrs

within Tiger Mountain State Forest

Map 3.3, page 97

Tiger Mountain State Forest is a shining example of what a great place Seattle is to live. More than 80 miles of trail lie within 13,000 acres of this wooded park less than a half hour from the city. That makes it the state's busiest trailhead, with cars often parked along the entrance all the way to the freeway. But don't be dismayed by the parking, as the many miles of wandering trails offer many chances for casual forest strolling or intensive hiking. The park's easy accessibility makes it extremely popular among hikers of all abilities and especially for families.

There are many trails to explore here. The best strategy is to peruse the signboard at the trailhead and pick one that suits your mood. Your own map will also be handy in navigating the vast network of trails. The most popular is West Tiger 3, which leads to the western summit. With an elevation gain of more than 2,000 feet in just 2.6 miles, it satisfies even serious hikers. It offers grand views of the Seattle and Puget Sound region, the adjacent Issaquah Alps, and even Mount Rainier. Other favorites with less climbing include Poo Poo Point Trail and Seattle View Trail. Easier, more level hikes include Around the Lake Trail, leading to Tradition Lake, and Bus Road Trail. Children will love Swamp Monster Trail, a level interpretive trail with signboards telling the story of a lovable raccoon.

User Groups: Hikers, leashed dogs, horses, and mountain bikers. No wheelchair access.

Open Seasons: This area is usually accessible year-round.

Permits: Permits are not required. Parking and access are free.

Maps: For topographic maps, ask Green Trails for No. 204S, Tiger Mountain, or ask the USGS for Fall City and Hobart.

Directions: From Seattle, drive east on I-90 to Exit 20, High Point Road. Take a right, and then another quick right, following the sign for Tradition Lake Trailhead. The gate is open seven days a week dawn–8 P.M.

Contact: Washington Department of Natural Resources, P.O. Box 47001, Olympia, WA 98504-7001, 360/902-1375.

113 MOUNT SI
8.0 mi/4.0 hrs

north of North Bend in Mount Si Natural Resources Conservation Area

Map 3.3, page 97

Mount Si is like the Disneyland of Seattle hiking: more crowds than you can shake a stick at. Busloads of folks from the metropolitan area descend upon this mountain, the closest high peak to Seattle. It's literally the most heavily used trail in the state. Experienced and novice hikers alike come here for the views of the Cascades, Seattle, and Puget Sound Basin. The trail is steep and at times rocky, often used by folks as a late-spring training hike for the upcoming summer. It's certainly not an ideal trail for those seeking wilderness exploration, but it scratches the itch for wooded hikes and commanding views.

Mount Si Trail is a continuous climb through the forest. Views into the Snoqualmie River Valley are few until the top. A good stop is at Snag Flats (2 miles), where giant Douglas fir offer a great rest. This is the only level section of the trail, where extensive puncheon and turnpike has been installed by EarthCorps crews. A few interpretive signs discuss a fire that hit the area almost a century ago.

From Snag Flats is yet more incline, eventually turning into serious switchbacks. The summit, best left for those with rock-climbing experience, is marked by a haystack. The views from up here are wide, from Puget Sound to deep into the Cascades. Mount Rainier is often visible to the south. It's a great hike if you don't mind hiking with half of Seattle.

User Groups: Hikers and leashed dogs. No horses or mountain bikes are allowed. No wheelchair access.

Open Seasons: This trail is usually accessible May–November.

Permits: Permits are not required. Parking and access are free.

Maps: For topographic maps, ask Green Trails for No. 206S, Mount Si, or ask the USGS for Mount Si.

Directions: From Seattle, drive east on I-90 to Exit 32. Turn left on 468th Avenue and drive to North Bend Way. Turn left and drive to Mount Si Road. Turn right and drive 4 miles to the trailhead on the left.

Contact: Washington Department of Natural Resources, P.O. Box 47001, Olympia, WA 98504-7001, 360/902-1375.

114 LITTLE SI

5.0 mi/2.5 hrs

north of North Bend in Mount Si Natural Resources Conservation Area

Map 3.3, page 97

Appropriately named, Little Si is Mount Si in a nutshell. A shorter hike, less of an incline, and fewer people all make this a nice early- or late-season hike when other, more intriguing trails are out of reach because of snow. The trail offers a pretty good workout nonetheless, making an ascent most of its length. There are a number of side trails, so it's best to have a map and good memory of which direction you came. The views from the top extend across the Snoqualmie Valley to Rattlesnake Mountain and up to Mount Si and Mount Washington.

Little Si Trail immediately climbs an outcropping of exposed rock. The main trail goes straight ahead while spur trails stray to the sides. These side trails can be good extracurricular journeys, and some great new ones have been built by EarthCorps crews. Most side trails lead to exposed rock heavily used by local climbers. Mostly second-growth forest covers the trail, although some granddaddy trees can be seen in places. The summit of the Little Si is exposed to reveal the surrounding countryside, quickly becoming "North Bend: The Strip Mall." A fun and manageable hike for the whole family.

User Groups: Hikers and leashed dogs. No horses or mountain bikes are allowed. No wheelchair access.

Open Seasons: This area is usually accessible March–December.

Permits: Permits are not required. Parking and access are free.

Maps: For topographic maps, ask Green Trails for No. 206S, Mount Si, or ask the USGS for North Bend.

Directions: From Seattle, drive east on I-90 to Exit 32. Turn left on 468th Avenue and drive to North Bend Way. Turn left and drive to Mount Si Road. Turn right and drive 1 mile to the trailhead on the left.

Contact: Washington Department of Natural Resources, P.O. Box 47001, Olympia, WA 98504-7001, 360/902-1375.

115 RATTLESNAKE MOUNTAIN
3.0–11.3 mi/1.5 hrs

within the Cedar River Municipal Watershed and on Washington Department of Natural Resources Land

Map 3.3, page 97

Unbeknownst to most hikers, Rattlesnake Mountain Trail is actually an 11.3-mile trail that spans nearly the entire east-to-west length of the mountain. Most folks hike only the northern part of the trail to Rattlesnake Ledge, an immense outcropping of rock that offers great views of the surrounding area. The trail is new, built by Washington Trails Association and EarthCorps crews in conjunction with Mountains to Sound Greenway Trust and the City of Seattle. The new trail is a vast improvement over the old, which was essentially a straight-up assault on the hill. Now a consistent, manageable, and wide grade whisks hundreds of hikers to the ledge each day.

The route to Rattlesnake Ledge starts in the Cedar River watershed. The trail passes through second-growth forest rich in undergrowth flowers and ferns before arriving at the ledge (1.5 miles). The ledge literally drops straight down, so take care with dogs and children. Views extends across the Snoqualmie Valley to Mount Si and eastward into the watershed, the source of Seattle's drinking water.

The trail actually continues over the mountain. The view into the watershed grows bigger, and on clear days Mount Rainier looms surreally large to the south. The trail is a makeshift collection of trails and old logging roads, although a more continuous replacement is being built. The trail ends at Snoqualmie Point 11.3 miles later, making for a long and enjoyable hike with a car shuttle.

User Groups: Hikers and leashed dogs. No horses or mountain bikes are allowed. No wheelchair access.

Open Seasons: This trail is usually accessible year-round.

Permits: Permits are not required. Parking and access are free.

Maps: For topographic maps, ask Green Trails for No. 205S, Rattlesnake Mountain, or ask the USGS for North Bend.

Directions: From Seattle, drive east on I-90 to Exit 32. Turn right on 468th Avenue (becomes Southeast Edgewick Road) and drive 5 miles to the signed trailhead at Rattlesnake Lake.

Contact: Cedar River Watershed Education Center, 425/831-6780.

116 TWIN FALLS
2.6 mi/1.5 hrs

east of North Bend in Twin Falls State Park

Map 3.3, page 97

Twin Falls Trail makes an excellent winter hike, when high-country trails are covered with the excessive white of winter's work and the rivers are flowing with Washington's most ordinary commodity, rain. Twin Falls are much more than just a pair; rather, the South Fork of the Snoqualmie River makes a series of cascades that concludes with an impressive plummet of more than 150 feet. The trail is easy going for hikers of all abilities. The journey is nothing to shake your head at, either, as it passes through old-growth forest and one particular grand-daddy of a tree.

A well-maintained trail ambles alongside the Snoqualmie River to the falls. Several enormous cedars line the trail, spared the long, cutting arm of the timber industry. A number of boardwalks and bridges are strategically placed to keep feet dry in even the wettest of weather. At the falls (1.3 miles), a platform offers misty views of the falls. Above, a bridge spans the river in the midst of the cascades. The optimum time to visit is the winter and spring, when more than 75,000 gallons of water flow over the falls each minute. During dry summers, this torrent vanishes to just 200 gallons. The trail continues to connect to John Wayne

Pioneer Trail, which provides access to a trailhead at Exit 38.

User Groups: Hikers and leashed dogs. No horses or mountain bikes are allowed. No wheelchair access.

Open Seasons: This trail is accessible year-round.

Permits: A $5 day-use fee is required to park here and is payable at the trailhead, or you can get an annual State Parks Pass for $30; contact Washington State Parks and Recreation, 360/902-8500.

Maps: For topographic maps, ask Green Trails for No. 206, Bandera, or ask the USGS for Chester Morse Lake.

Directions: From Seattle, drive east on I-90 to Exit 34. Turn right off the freeway on 468th Avenue Southeast and drive south .5 mile to Southeast 159th Street. Drive .5 mile to the trailhead at road's end.

Contact: Washington State Parks and Recreation, P.O. Box 42650, Olympia, WA 98504-2669, 360/902-8844.

117 MIDDLE FORK SNOQUALMIE RIVER
1.0–10.0 mi/0.5–5.0 hrs

northeast of North Bend in Mount Baker–Snoqualmie National Forest

Map 3.3, page 97

The Middle Fork of the Snoqualmie River is a fantastic trail close to the Seattle area and accessible year-round. Much of the trail passes through old-growth forests that survived the saw or ax. Along the upper reaches of trail are the privately operated Goldmeyer Hot Springs, one of the best in Washington. The trail has been undergoing an intense amount of reconstruction by the Forest Service in the past few years, opening up many more miles of trail along the river.

Middle Fork Trail works its way through the river valley for roughly 12 miles along the south shore. It is accessible at two trailheads, one near the Taylor River and another near Dingford Creek. Customize your hike by turning

around when the mood strikes—even a stroll of just 1 mile out and back will feel satisfying. Near the Taylor River, at Middle Fork Trailhead, Middle Fork Trail crosses the river on a new, extraordinary wooden bridge and meanders up the river valley, swooping near and away from the river. Above Dingford Trailhead, the trail encounters routes up to Snow, Gem, and Wildcat Lakes. Goldmeyer Hot Springs are roughly five miles from the trailhead and require reservations. The Middle Fork rarely gets snow, making it an excellent escape during the winter.

User Groups: Hikers, leashed dogs, horses, and mountain bikes. No wheelchair access.

Open Seasons: This trail is accessible year-round.

Permits: A federal Northwest Forest Pass is required to park at the trailheads.

Maps: For a map of Mount Baker–Snoqualmie National Forest, contact the Outdoor Recreation Information Center at the downtown Seattle REI. For topographic maps, ask Green Trails for No. 174, Mount Si, No. 175, Skykomish, and No. 207, Snoqualmie Pass, or ask the USGS for Lake Phillipa and Snoqualmie Lake.

Directions: From Seattle, drive east on I-90 to Exit 34. Turn left onto 468th Avenue North and drive .6 mile to Middle Fork Road. Turn right and drive 3 miles to Forest Service Road 56. Turn left and drive 11 miles to Middle Fork Snoqualmie Trailhead.

To reach the upper trailhead at Dingford, continue on Forest Service Road 56 for 6 miles.

Contact: Mount Baker–Snoqualmie National Forest, North Bend Ranger Station, 42404 Southeast North Bend Way, North Bend, WA 98045, 425/888-1421.

118 DINGFORD CREEK
11.0 mi/6.0 hrs

northeast of North Bend in Alpine Lake Wilderness of Mount Baker–Snoqualmie National Forest

Map 3.3, page 97

Hester and Myrtle Lakes are just two of many

wonderful high-country lakes off Dingford Creek Trail. Hester and Myrtle are the largest and best known, attracting a majority of Dingford Trail's visitors. The hikes to the lakes are exceptional and offer miles of further exploration in the high-country meadows. Old-growth forest of hemlock, cedar, and fir make the journey along rumbling Dingford Creek an excellent day hike.

Dingford Creek Trail makes a quick ascent through second-growth forest before leveling out and strolling through ancient forests. At three miles the trail splits; head right for Hester Lake (5.5 miles). Hester Lake is large and encircled by forests of subalpine fir and mountain hemlock. Anglers love the lake for its stocked trout. From here, adventurous folks can reach Little Hester Lake and explore Mount Price.

Dingford Creek Trail continues following the stream up to Myrtle Lake (5.5 miles), fringed with forest and talus shores. Folks with off-trail experience can get to three small lakes to the west or climb up to Big Snow Lake, which sits directly under Big Snow Mountain. The trail grows faint from Myrtle Lake but does head up to Little Myrtle Lake and two other, smaller lakes. Regardless of destination, any route up Dingford Creek Trail is outstanding.

User Groups: Hikers and leashed dogs. No horses or mountain bikes are allowed. No wheelchair access.

Open Seasons: This trail is accessible July–early November.

Permits: A federal Northwest Forest Pass is required to park here.

Maps: For a map of Mount Baker–Snoqualmie National Forest, contact the Outdoor Recreation Information Center at the downtown Seattle REI. For topographic maps, ask Green Trails for No. 175, Skykomish, or ask the USGS for Snoqualmie Lake and Big Snow Mountain.

Directions: From Seattle, drive east on I-90 to Exit 34. Turn left onto 468th Avenue North and drive .5 mile to Middle Fork Road. Turn right and drive 3 miles (via the left fork in the road). Turn left on Forest Service Road 56 and drive 14 miles to Dingford Trailhead. Park in

the wide turnout on the right; the trailhead is on the left.

Contact: Mount Baker–Snoqualmie National Forest, North Bend Ranger Station, 42404 Southeast North Bend Way, North Bend, WA 98045, 425/888-1421.

119 DUTCH MILLER GAP
15.0 mi/8.0 hrs

northeast of North Bend in Alpine Lakes Wilderness of Mount Baker–Snoqualmie National Forest

Map 3.3, page 97

A trip to Dutch Miller Gap is a trip to the headwaters of the mighty Middle Fork Snoqualmie River. Here, deep within the river's valley, wilderness reigns supreme in the old-growth forests and meadows. Tall, rocky peaks dominate the wild landscape. As a bonus, there are several options for exploration in the high country, including Williams Lake and beautiful La Bohn Gap and La Bohn Lakes.

Middle Fork Snoqualmie Trail gradually climbs four miles up the valley alongside the river. The river makes a number of cascades and creates lots of pools for dipping. A short but noticeable rise, where the trail climbs a glacial step, delivers hikers into subalpine meadows with frequent rock slides. Camp Pedro is at six miles and has several great campsites.

After Camp Pedro, the trail splits, with the right fork climbing to Dutch Miller Gap through meadows and talus. The surrounding peaks tower over hikers at the pass. Expect lots of ripe huckleberries in August. The other fork leads up to Williams Lake, set within meadows in a glacial cirque. Footpaths lead up to La Bohn Gap, which features views as great as those of Dutch Miller, and down to the Necklace Valley. With so many excellent places up here, hikers can't go wrong.

User Groups: Hikers, leashed dogs, and horses. No mountain bikes are allowed. No wheelchair access.

Open Seasons: This trail is accessible July–October.

Permits: A federal Northwest Forest Pass is required to park here.

Maps: For a map of Mount Baker–Snoqualmie National Forest, contact the Outdoor Recreation Information Center at the downtown Seattle REI. For topographic maps, ask Green Trails for No. 175, Skykomish, and No. 176, Stevens Pass, or ask the USGS for Big Snow Mountain and Mount Daniel.

Directions: From Seattle, drive east on I-90 to Exit 34. Turn left onto 468th Avenue North and drive .5 mile to Middle Fork Road. Turn right and drive 3 miles (via the left fork in the road). Turn left on Forest Service Road 56 and drive 20 miles to the trailhead at road's end. Forest Service Road 56 is often very rough and may require a high-clearance vehicle.

Contact: Mount Baker–Snoqualmie National Forest, North Bend Ranger Station, 42404 Southeast North Bend Way, North Bend, WA 98045, 425/888-1421.

120 MOUNT DEFIANCE/ MASON LAKES

16.6 mi/8.0 hrs

east of North Bend in Alpine Lakes Wilderness of Mount Baker–Snoqualmie National Forest

Map 3.3, page 97

New Ira Spring Trail couples great high lakes with a high peak chock-full of views. Recently rebuilt, the trail to Mount Defiance and Mason Lakes commemorates one of Washington's strongest wilderness advocates, trail guide guru Ira Spring. Fields of heather and huckleberries are prolific along this route, as are the blackflies and mosquitoes in early summer. This trail encounters numerous lakes stocked with trout and is complemented with a scramble atop Mount Defiance.

Ira Spring Trail travels two miles on an old road before the newly built trail begins with spectacular results. Lazy switchbacks climb through open meadows before it tops a crest and descends to a wide, forested basin and Mason Lake. The main trail continues east to Rainbow Lake, filled to the brim with what else, rainbow trout. A side trail leads to Island Lake, the prime swimming hole (deep, cool, and sunny). All of the lakes have several campsites, although they go quickly.

Just beyond Mason Lake lies the Mount Defiance Trail junction. Turn left and climb through huckleberry meadows to the great views atop the summit. Cascade peaks line the horizons to the north, east, and south, while Puget Sound Basin and the Olympics stand out to the west. It's a great viewpoint.

User Groups: Hikers and leashed dogs. No horses or mountain bikes are allowed. No wheelchair access.

Open Seasons: This trail is accessible July–October.

Permits: A federal Northwest Forest Pass is required to park here. A free wilderness permit is also required to hike here and is available at the trailhead.

Maps: For a map of Mount Baker–Snoqualmie National Forest, contact the Outdoor Recreation Information Center at the downtown Seattle REI. For topographic maps, ask Green Trails for No. 206, Bandera, or ask the USGS for Bandera.

Directions: From Seattle, drive east on I-90 to Exit 45. Turn left (north, over the freeway) to Forest Service Road 9030. Turn left and drive left .5 mile to Forest Service Road 9031. Veer left on Forest Service Road 9031 and drive 4 miles to the trailhead at road's end.

Contact: Mount Baker–Snoqualmie National Forest, North Bend Ranger Station, 42404 Southeast North Bend Way, North Bend, WA 98045, 425/888-1421.

121 BANDERA MOUNTAIN

7.0 mi/4.0 hrs

east of North Bend in Alpine Lakes Wilderness of Mount Baker–Snoqualmie National Forest

Map 3.3, page 97

Bandera has a reputation for two things: a steep, difficult ascent and breathtaking panoramic views. The second feature far outweighs the first. A new trail built by the Forest Service makes access to Bandera Trail much easier and should encourage even more folks to visit this great place. That's good for everyone, since Bandera is less than an hour from Seattle. The trail is awash in mountain views in every direction, offering one of Washington's best sunsets.

The route to Bandera follows Mason Lakes Trail for 2.5 miles before splitting off to the right at a signed junction. By this point, hikers are out of woods and immersed in wide open mountain meadows, kept in check by heavy snowpacks and regular (every 100 years or so) fires. The views are grand along the way and only get better as the trail reaches the summit of Bandera. Mount Rainier is enormous to the south, behind McClellan Butte. Miles and miles of forest and mountain ridges give way to Glacier Peak to the east and Mount Baker to the north. Total elevation gain is about 3,000 feet, a rough day's work, but the memories of the great views will outlast any soreness.

User Groups: Hikers and leashed dogs. No horses or mountain bikes are allowed. No wheelchair access.

Open Seasons: This trail is accessible June–mid-November.

Permits: A federal Northwest Forest Pass is required to park here. A free wilderness permit is also required to hike here and is available at the trailhead.

Maps: For a map of Mount Baker–Snoqualmie National Forest, contact the Outdoor Recreation Information Center at the downtown Seattle REI. For topographic maps, ask Green Trails for No. 206, Bandera, or ask the USGS for Bandera.

Directions: From Seattle, drive east on I-90 to Exit 45. Turn left (north, over the freeway) to Forest Service Road 9030. Turn left and drive left .5 mile to Forest Service Road 9031. Veer left on Forest Service Road 9031 and drive 4 miles to the trailhead at road's end.

Contact: Mount Baker–Snoqualmie National Forest, North Bend Ranger Station, 42404 Southeast North Bend Way, North Bend, WA 98045, 425/888-1421.

122 McCLELLAN BUTTE
9.2 mi/5.0 hrs

east of North Bend in Mount Baker–Snoqualmie National Forest

Map 3.3, page 97

A tough, steep, rocky path leads to the top of McClellan Butte. Few hikers will have kind words for a trail that asks so much. That is, until hikers reach the top with miles of forests and peaks revealed at their feet. Adversity is often just an exercise in building character (thanks, Dad). McClellan Butte may be a difficult climb, but it's an excellent alternative to other trails that are busier and just as difficult (Mount Si, for instance).

McClellan Butte Trail climbs through forest for nearly its entire length. After .6 mile it intersects the Iron Horse Trail; follow it west .4 mile, then turn south on McClellan Butte Trail. A great number of steep switchbacks scale the hillside, crossing several avalanche chutes that can remain filled with snow until July. Be aware that when filled with snow, they are dangerous because of avalanches. Overuse has exposed many frustrating rocks and roots.

The trail eventually finds the southern edge of the butte at the border of the Cedar River watershed. The trail ends below the true summit, a rocky point with vertical walls, best left for rock climbers. Nevertheless, there are great views just below the summit, with Mount Rainier in the distance and Chester Morse Lake directly below. Think of all the character you just built after that treacherous climb. Cheers!

User Groups: Hikers and leashed dogs. No horses or mountain bikes are allowed. No wheelchair access.

Open Seasons: This trail is accessible July–October.

Permits: A federal Northwest Forest Pass is required to park here.

Maps: For a map of Mount Baker–Snoqualmie National Forest, contact the Outdoor Recreation

Information Center at the downtown Seattle REI. For topographic maps, ask Green Trails for No. 206, Bandera, or ask the USGS for Bandera.

Directions: From Seattle, drive east on I-90 to Exit 42. Turn right (south) and then turn left onto Forest Service Road 55. Drive .3 mile to a signed gravel road. Turn right and drive .2 mile to the trailhead at road's end.

Contact: Mount Baker–Snoqualmie National Forest, North Bend Ranger Station, 42404 Southeast North Bend Way, North Bend, WA 98045, 425/888-1421.

123 TALAPUS AND OLALLIE LAKES
4.0–6.0 mi/2.0–3.0 hrs

east of North Bend in Alpine Lakes Wilderness of Mount Baker–Snoqualmie National Forest

Map 3.3, page 97

Although they're not showy or flashy, this pair of forested lakes can be the perfect respite from the city. Talapus and Olallie Lakes are greatly accessible, situated within an hour's drive of Seattle. The easy trail gains less than 1,000 feet, perfect for hikers young and old. The result during the summer is swarms of families to match the swarms of bugs. Regardless, the lakes make great overnight destinations with many nice campsites. And forests of virgin Douglas fir and western hemlock surround the lakes to offer shade for those not inclined to jump in the water.

Talapus Lake Trail begins on an old cat track but soon becomes a true trail. The trail dances a laid-back switchback shuffle through a cool, shady forest. Alpine Lakes Wilderness is entered just before a marshy area, below Talapus Lake. Many paths diverge from here, leading to good camping spots around Talapus. This trail is very busy, so the camping spots go early during the summer.

For Olallie Lake, continue .5 mile along the main trail to a junction; veer left for .5 mile to the forested shores of Olallie. Again, there are many camps along the lake for the many visitors. Keep in mind that both lakes harbor a lot of mosquitoes. Olallie visitors should follow Pratt Lake Trail above the lake for a picturesque view of Mount Rainier.

User Groups: Hikers and leashed dogs. No horses or mountain bikes are allowed. No wheelchair access.

Open Seasons: This trail is accessible June–October.

Permits: A federal Northwest Forest Pass is required to park here. A free wilderness permit is also required to hike here and is available at the trailhead.

Maps: For a map of Mount Baker–Snoqualmie National Forest, contact the Outdoor Recreation Information Center at the downtown Seattle REI. For topographic maps, ask Green Trails for No. 206, Bandera, or ask the USGS for Bandera.

Directions: From Seattle, drive east on I-90 to Exit 45. From the off-ramp, turn north (left) onto Forest Service Road 9031 for about .5 mile. Turn right onto Forest Service Road 9030 and drive 2 miles to road's end, where the trailhead is located.

Contact: Mount Baker–Snoqualmie National Forest, North Bend Ranger Station, 42404 Southeast North Bend Way, North Bend, WA 98045, 425/888-1421.

124 GRANITE MOUNTAIN
8.6 mi/5.0 hrs

east of North Bend in Alpine Lakes Wilderness of Mount Baker–Snoqualmie National Forest

Map 3.3, page 97

Let's not mince words; Granite Mountain Trail is a hell of a climb to one of the best summit views in the region. The trail ascends nearly 4,000 feet in just over four miles but rewards with broad meadows of huckleberries and copious views of surrounding peaks. The summit is home to the last functioning fire lookout operated by the Forest Service in the area. If the Forest Service is here, you know it has views.

Granite Mountain Trail begins 1.3 miles up Pratt Lake Trail. As the hum of the freeway fades away, Granite Mountain Trail takes off to the right. The ascent is certainly steep, making numerous switchbacks up through the forest. Be thankful for the shade, as there is unlikely to be any water on the route. The trail eventually emerges into open meadows with Mount Rainier off in the distance.

This south-facing slope melts out early in the year, but the trail soon levels out and jumps to the north slope of the hill. Here, snow lingers late and avalanche danger persists even into June. Head-turning views will likely slow your ascent and help to keep your heart rate reasonable. All of the Snoqualmie-area peaks are on parade as are Mount Baker and Glacier Peak on clear days.
User Groups: Hikers, leashed dogs, llamas, and goats. No horses or mountain bikes are allowed. No wheelchair access.
Open Seasons: This trail is accessible July–October.
Permits: A federal Northwest Forest Pass is required to park here.
Maps: For a map of Mount Baker–Snoqualmie National Forest, contact the Outdoor Recreation Information Center at the downtown Seattle REI. For topographic maps, ask Green Trails for No. 207, Snoqualmie Pass, or ask the USGS for Snoqualmie Pass.
Directions: From Seattle, drive east on I-90 to Exit 47. Turn left (north) from the off-ramp and turn left at the T in the road. Drive .5 mile to the signed trailhead.
Contact: Mount Baker–Snoqualmie National Forest, North Bend Ranger Station, 42404 Southeast North Bend Way, North Bend, WA 98045, 425/888-1421.

125 PRATT LAKE
11.4 mi/6.0 hrs

east of North Bend in Alpine Lakes Wilderness of Mount Baker–Snoqualmie National Forest

Map 3.3, page 97

Pratt Lake is one of the nicest but least-visited destinations in Alpine Lakes Wilderness. The journey to the lake is just as great as the destination. Great forests, views of Mount Rainier, berries for everyone, and lots of lakeshore to explore are yours for the enjoying. What's more is that there are often few people along this route. That's amazing, since it is easily one of the best loops anywhere near I-90 and Seattle.

Pratt Lake Trail begins in the shade of forest, much needed during summer days. The trail climbs gently, crossing several small creeks on its way to Olallie Lake. It passes signed junctions for Granite Mountain and Talapus Lake. As the trail contours above Olallie Lake, the forest breaks for an amazing view of Mount Rainier.

The trail splits along a ridge; the left fork leads to Mount Defiance, so head right, down to Pratt Lake through fields of granite boulders. The chirping you hear is picas saying hello. Mount Roosevelt stands out across from the basin, above Pratt Lake. Numerous campsites are at the north end of the lake, where it drains into the Pratt River. Remnants of abandoned Pratt River Trail are on the western shore, ripe for exploration. At night, with the moon and stars at play in the sky, this place seems very far away from everything, yet it is less than an hour from Seattle.
User Groups: Hikers, leashed dogs, and llamas. No horses or mountain bikes are allowed. No wheelchair access.
Open Seasons: This trail is accessible mid-June–October.
Permits: A federal Northwest Forest Pass is required to park here. A free wilderness permit is also required to hike here and is available at the trailhead.
Maps: For a map of Mount Baker–Snoqualmie National Forest, contact the Outdoor Recreation Information Center at the downtown Seattle REI. For topographic maps, ask Green Trails for No. 206, Bandera, and No. 207, Snoqualmie Pass, or ask the USGS for Bandera and Snoqualmie Pass.
Directions: From Seattle, drive east on I-90 to Exit 47. Turn left (north) from the off-ramp and turn left at the T in the road. Drive .5 mile to the signed trailhead.

Contact: Mount Baker–Snoqualmie National Forest, North Bend Ranger Station, 42404 Southeast North Bend Way, North Bend, WA 98045, 425/888-1421.

126 ANNETTE LAKE

7.0 mi/4.0 hrs

in the Mount Baker–Snoqualmie National Forest, south of Snoqualmie Pass

Map 3.3, page 97

Nothing is especially unique about Annette Lake. Then again, Annette is another beautiful alpine lake, set between large peaks, with waterfalls and beautiful forest. Add it all up, and it's definitely a great place to spend the day. The trail up to Annette Lake is fairly easy to hike, and that's never a bad thing.

Annette Lake Trail proceeds through dense forest on its way to the lake. In the beginning, the trail follows an old service road and soon crosses an old railway line (now Iron Horse Trail). Switchbacks rise steeply on the side of Silver Peak, high above Humpback Creek. Avalanche chutes open the canopy in places, providing some views of Humpback Mountain. The trail continues smoothly for the last mile, arriving at Annette Lake.

Annette Lake sits directly between Silver Peak and Abiel Peak. Steep cliffs drop into the woods and lingering snowfields that surround the lake. It's not your typically deep blue alpine lake, but it does make for some decent fishing. There is some camping around the lake for those seeking an overnighter.

User Groups: Hikers and leashed dogs. No horses or mountain bikes are allowed. No wheelchair access.

Open Seasons: This trail is accessible June–mid-November.

Permits: A federal Northwest Forest Pass is required to park here. A free wilderness permit is also required to hike here and is available at the trailhead.

Maps: For a map of Mount Baker–Snoqualmie National Forest, contact the Outdoor Recreation Information Center at the downtown

Seattle REI. For topographic maps, ask Green Trails for No. 207, Snoqualmie Pass, or ask the USGS for Snoqualmie Lake and Lost Pass.

Directions: From Seattle, drive east on I-90 to Exit 47. Turn right (south) and then left on Forest Service Road 55. Drive .5 mile to the signed trailhead at road's end.

Contact: Mount Baker–Snoqualmie National Forest, North Bend Ranger Station, 42404 Southeast North Bend Way, North Bend, WA 98045, 425/888-1421.

127 DENNY CREEK AND LAKE MELAKWA

9.0 mi/4.5 hrs

east of North Bend in Alpine Lakes Wilderness of Mount Baker–Snoqualmie National Forest

Map 3.3, page 97

This may well be the most beautiful hike in the I-90 corridor. Two series of incredible waterfalls parallel the trail. After crossing Hemlock Pass, Lake Melakwa sits within a beautiful, large basin, rimmed by jagged peaks giving way to forests of subalpine trees. This is a perfect introduction to all that the Alpine Lakes Wilderness has to offer; accordingly, it attracts flocks of people during the summer. Don't be dismayed, as there is plenty to see for all.

Denny Creek Trail begins along Denny Creek as cars and trucks pass overhead on I-90. The highway overpass preserves important corridors, allowing wildlife to move uninhibited through the forests. The trail encounters Keekwulee Falls at 1.5 miles; at two miles are Snowshoe Falls. These cascades form large pools on slabs of granite with lots of nooks and crannies.

The trail switchbacks up through avalanche chutes and fields of huckleberries to Hemlock Pass; Lake Melakwa lies another .3 mile beyond. There are many campsites at the lake, on both the eastern and western shores. Be sure to stay on footpaths, as the meadows here have taken a beating. Sharp-toothed Chair Peak is the tallest peak of the jagged rim around the basin. More great lakes lie beyond Lake Melakwa for the adventurous. The trail drops with Melakwa Creek to Lower Tuscohatchie Lake, a favorite backcountry swimming hole.

User Groups: Hikers and leashed dogs. No horses or mountain bikes are allowed. No wheelchair access.

Open Seasons: This trail is accessible July–October.

Permits: A federal Northwest Forest Pass is required to park here. A free wilderness permit is also required to hike here and is available at the trailhead.

Maps: For a map of Mount Baker–Snoqualmie National Forest, contact the Outdoor Recreation Information Center at the downtown Seattle REI. For topographic maps, ask Green Trails for No. 207, Snoqualmie Pass, or ask the USGS for Snoqualmie Pass.

Directions: From Seattle, drive east on I-90 to Exit 47. Turn left (north) from the off-ramp and turn right at the T in the road. Drive .4 mile to Forest Service Road 58. Turn left and drive about 4 miles to the signed trailhead.

Contact: Mount Baker–Snoqualmie National Forest, North Bend Ranger Station, 42404 Southeast North Bend Way, North Bend, WA 98045, 425/888-1421.

128 SNOW LAKE
6.0 mi/3.0 hrs

north of Snoqualmie Pass in Alpine Lakes Wilderness of Mount Baker–Snoqualmie National Forest

Map 3.3, page 97

Everything about this place seems supersized. Snow Lake is remarkably large, especially for an alpine lake. The basin itself is enormous, easily absorbing the large crowds that trek to the area. Big meadows satisfy appetites with large numbers of prime huckleberries. And of course the surrounding peaks and ridges are large, looming over the lake and making for some striking vistas. It's all large and all exceptionally grand.

Snow Lake Trail gently works its way to-

ward tiny Source Lake. This section is mostly open, providing great views of the jagged valley ridges. Switchbacks climb steeply to a ridge looking down on Snow Lake. The trail is occasionally rocky, mostly because of the high use. The ridge is a turnaround point for many, as the trail then drops about 500 feet in .5 mile to Snow Lake. Unless you're on a strict time schedule (you shouldn't be), it's worth the effort to continue.

Snow Lake is cloaked in typical Alpine Lakes Wilderness beauty. The cliffs of Chair Peak tower over meadows and groves of mountain hemlock surrounding the lake. Camping at Snow Lake is discouraged because of the heavy use of the trail; alpine meadows have delicate makeups. If you're not satisfied with stopping here, then you're in for a treat. A climb over a steep ridge ends up at Gem and Wildcat Lakes.

User Groups: Hikers and leashed dogs. No horses or mountain bikes are allowed. No wheelchair access.

Open Seasons: This trail is accessible June–October.

Permits: A federal Northwest Forest Pass is required to park here. A free wilderness permit is also required to hike here and is available at the trailhead.

Maps: For a map of Mount Baker–Snoqualmie National Forest, contact the Outdoor Recreation Information Center at the downtown Seattle REI. For topographic maps, ask Green Trails for No. 207, Snoqualmie Pass, or ask the USGS for Bandera and Snoqualmie Pass.

Directions: From Seattle, drive east on I-90 to Exit 52 (West Summit). Turn left (under the freeway) and left again on Alpental Road. Drive .2 mile and turn right on Forest Service Road 9040. Drive 1.5 miles to a large gravel parking lot on the left. The trailhead is on the right.

Contact: Mount Baker–Snoqualmie National Forest, North Bend Ranger Station, 42404 Southeast North Bend Way, North Bend, WA 98045, 425/888-1421.

129 COMMONWEALTH BASIN/RED PASS

10.0 mi/5.0 hrs

near Snoqualmie Pass in Alpine Lakes
Wilderness of Mount Baker–Snoqualmie
National Forest

Map 3.3, page 97

This is one of the better trails out of the Snoqualmie Pass area. The trailhead literally starts at Snoqualmie Pass and climbs 5 miles to a spectacular viewpoint atop Red Pass. Along the way are old-growth forests of enormous mountain hemlocks that give way to wide open meadows and fields of blueberry bushes. The trail needn't be hiked its entire length to be fully enjoyed. That makes this trail a great family hike, in case little ones get tuckered out early.

The first half of the route follows Pacific Crest Trail. Along this stretch, the trail gently and gradually climbs through shady forest to reach a junction (2.5 miles). Stick to the left on Commonwealth Basin Trail as the basin opens into parkland, meadows mixed with pockets of forest. You must make a crossing of Commonwealth Creek (4 miles), but it is unlikely to be much trouble by mid-July. The last mile is a descent climb of about 1,200 feet. Halfway up is Red Pond and a nice campsite. Finally, after more switchbacks, Red Pass is achieved. Views extend in nearly all directions, taking in countless peaks of the Alpine Lakes Wilderness.

User Groups: Hikers and leashed dogs. No horses or mountain bikes are allowed. No wheelchair access.

Open Seasons: This trail is accessible July–October.

Permits: A federal Northwest Forest Pass is required to park here.

Maps: For a map of Mount Baker–Snoqualmie National Forest, contact the Outdoor Recreation Information Center at the downtown Seattle REI. For topographic maps, ask Green Trails for No. 207, Snoqualmie Pass, or ask the USGS for Snoqualmie Pass.

Directions: From Seattle, drive east on I-90 to Exit 52. Turn north at the exit ramp and take the first right into the PCT-North parking area. The lot to the left is intended for stock; hikers can continue straight to the main parking lot. The trail starts at the east end of the parking lot.

Contact: Mount Baker–Snoqualmie National Forest, North Bend Ranger Station, 42404 Southeast North Bend Way, North Bend, WA 98045, 425/888-1421.

130 KENDALL KATWALK

11.0 mi/6.0 hrs

north of Snoqualmie Pass in Alpine Lakes
Wilderness of Mount Baker–Snoqualmie
National Forest

Map 3.3, page 97

Without a doubt, Kendall Katwalk is one of the most unforgettable and exciting stretches of Pacific Crest Trail. Heading north from Snoqualmie Pass, PCT encounters a long granite wall on the side of Kendall Peak, with a slope of roughly 75 degrees. That's pretty close to vertical. With a little ingenuity and even more dynamite, trail engineers blasted a 100-yard stretch of trail into the slope. Named Kendall Katwalk, it's now famous across the country.

PCT leaves Snoqualmie Pass and wastes little time before beginning the ascent to the high country. Shady and well graded, the trail passes underfoot quickly. Stay right at Commonwealth Basin junction (2.5 miles) and continue climbing with PCT. The forest soon breaks, and numerous neighboring peaks and ridges come into view. In August, ripe huckleberries fuel the climb to Katwalk (5.5 miles). This is a crowded segment of PCT, but take the time to walk Katwalk a couple of times anyway. Although the trail is plenty wide, watch your step; Silver Creek Valley is a good 1,200-foot drop. Campers will need to hike an extra two miles to Gravel and Ridge Lakes.

User Groups: Hikers, leashed dogs, and horses. No mountain bikes are allowed. No wheelchair access.

Open Seasons: This trail is accessible mid-June–September.

Permits: A federal Northwest Forest Pass is required to park here.

Maps: For a map of Mount Baker–Snoqualmie National Forest, contact the Outdoor Recreation Information Center at the downtown Seattle REI. For topographic maps, ask Green Trails for No. 207, Snoqualmie Pass, or ask the USGS for Snoqualmie Pass.

Directions: From Seattle, drive east on I-90 to Exit 52. Turn north at the exit ramp and take the first right into the PCT-North parking area. The lot to the left is intended for stock; hikers can continue straight to the main parking lot. The trail starts at the east end of the parking lot.

Contact: Mount Baker–Snoqualmie National Forest, North Bend Ranger Station, 42404 Southeast North Bend Way, North Bend, WA 98045, 425/888-1421.

131 GOLD CREEK VALLEY
8.0 mi/4.0 hrs

north of Snoqualmie Pass in Alpine Lakes Wilderness of Mount Baker–Snoqualmie National Forest

Map 3.3, page 97

Gold Creek Trail is an easy venture through old-growth forest on the east side of the crest. The trail gains just 400 feet of elevation in four miles of maintained trail, making it accessible by hikers of all abilities. Meadows and avalanche chutes are numerous, providing ample views of the surrounding peaks and ridges. Although it is along the Cascade Crest, the trail sits low in the valley. It is often one of the first trails in the area to be snow free. That makes it a great selection in June. Hikers looking for a challenge can continue on nonmaintained trails to Alaska or Joe Lakes, each situated high on the valley's ridges.

Gold Creek Trail travels for a mile before crossing into Alpine Lakes Wilderness. An old-growth forest of fir and hemlock provides needed shade as Gold Creek gushes with the winter's snowmelt. The trail crosses several streams along the way, including Gold Creek,

and may be difficult or even impassable when stream flow is high. The route eventually crosses Silver Creek, where maintenance of the trail ends. From here, audacious hikers can bushwhack it to steep footpaths to Alaska and Joe Lakes. These high lakes in small cirques are set within subalpine parkland. A specific destination is not required on Gold Creek Trail, as the entire length of the trail is excellent hiking.

User Groups: Hikers and leashed dogs. No horses or mountain bikes are allowed. No wheelchair access.

Open Seasons: This trail is accessible mid-May–November.

Permits: A federal Northwest Forest Pass is required to park here.

Maps: For a map of Mount Baker–Snoqualmie National Forest, contact the Outdoor Recreation Information Center at the downtown Seattle REI. For topographic maps, ask Green Trails for No. 207, Snoqualmie Pass, or ask the USGS for Chikamin Peak.

Directions: From Seattle, drive east on I-90 to Exit 54. Turn left and drive .2 mile to Forest Service Road 4832. Turn right and drive 1 mile to Forest Service Road 144. Turn left and drive 2 miles to the signed trailhead.

Contact: Mount Baker–Snoqualmie National Forest, North Bend Ranger Station, 42404 Southeast North Bend Way, North Bend, WA 98045, 425/888-1421.

132 MARGARET AND LILLIAN LAKES
9.2–10.6 mi/5.0–6.0 hrs

northeast of Snoqualmie Pass in Alpine Lakes Wilderness of Wenatchee National Forest

Map 3.3, page 97

Margaret and Lillian Lakes are just two in a series of high-country lakes within the south end of Rampart Ridge. These subalpine lakes enjoy knockout views of the inner Cascade Crest. You'd never guess from the jumble of cars at the trailhead that this trail is a steep one or that it endures a stretch of road hiking for the first two miles. Never mind, for this is a great hike just 90 minutes from Seattle.

The signed trailhead is just uphill from the parking lot on Forest Service Road 4934. Passing through the gates, hike the old road for nearly two miles before finding true trail. Subalpine fir and mountain hemlock provide welcome shade on this hot, dry trail. Extra water will be appreciated during the summer heat. The trail soon splits at a saddle (3.5 miles), with the right fork dropping to Margaret Lake (4.6 miles). Rocky meadows surround the cool lake below Mount Margaret.

For a slightly longer hike, stay left at the junction, continuing to follow Rampart Ridge Trail down to Twin Lakes (4.5 miles) and on to Lake Lillian (5.3 miles). Both lakes revel in wildflower blooms in July, and views across Gold Creek to Kendall Peak are awesome. Campers need to stay away from lakeshores and find established sites. Adhere to the trails at all times, for these are fragile environs.

User Groups: Hikers and leashed dogs. No horses or mountain bikes are allowed. No wheelchair access.

Open Seasons: This trail is accessible mid-June–mid-October.

Permits: A federal Northwest Forest Pass is required to park here.

Maps: For a map of Wenatchee National Forest, contact the Outdoor Recreation Information Center at the downtown Seattle REI. For topographic maps, ask Green Trails for No. 207, Snoqualmie Pass, or ask the USGS for Chikamin Peak and Stampede Pass.

Directions: From Seattle, drive east on I-90 to Exit 54 (Hyak). Turn left and drive .3 mile to Forest Service Road 4832. Turn right and drive 5 miles to Forest Service Road 4934. Turn left and drive .5 mile to the parking area. The signed trailhead is a short walk up Forest Service Road 4934 behind a gated road.

Contact: Wenatchee National Forest, Cle Elum Ranger Station, 803 West 2nd Street, Cle Elum, WA 98922, 509/852-1100.

133 RACHEL LAKE
7.6 mi/4.0 hrs

northeast of Snoqualmie Pass in Alpine Lakes Wilderness of Wentachee National Forest

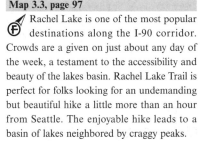
Map 3.3, page 97

Rachel Lake is one of the most popular destinations along the I-90 corridor. Crowds are a given on just about any day of the week, a testament to the accessibility and beauty of the lakes basin. Rachel Lake Trail is perfect for folks looking for an undemanding but beautiful hike a little more than an hour from Seattle. The enjoyable hike leads to a basin of lakes neighbored by craggy peaks.

The first three miles of Rachel Lake Trail are relatively flat and pass quickly. This section passes through forest and occasional avalanche chutes, where colorful fireweed dominates the openings. The last mile gets interesting and much tougher, climbing steeply through a classic box canyon. The views begin to appear as you enter the high country. Rachel Lake is the largest of three lakes and many small tarns beneath Rampart Ridge, each tempting with their cool water.

Rampart Ridge and the lakes have seen a lot of use, with denuded areas abounding. This is unfortunate, as beautiful alpine meadows used to be prolific here. Alta Mountain stands tall to the north and offers a good scramble to the top. There is a lot of country to explore from Rachel Lake, and much of it already has been. Yet Rachel Lake is a beautiful destination and will always be a solidly popular day hike.

User Groups: Hikers and leashed dogs. No horses or mountain bikes are allowed. No wheelchair access.

Open Seasons: This trail is accessible June–October.

Permits: A federal Northwest Forest Pass is required to park here. A free wilderness permit is also required to hike here and is available at the trailhead.

Maps: For a map of Wenatchee National

Forest, contact the Outdoor Recreation Information Center at the downtown Seattle REI. For topographic maps, ask Green Trails for No. 207, Snoqualmie Pass, or ask the USGS for Snoqualmie Pass.

Directions: From Seattle, drive east on I-90 to Exit 62. Turn left on Kachess Lake Road and drive 5.5 miles to Forest Service Road 4930. Turn right and drive 3.5 miles to the trailhead at road's end.

Contact: Wenatchee National Forest, Cle Elum Ranger District, 803 West 2nd Street, Cle Elum, WA 98922, 509/852-1100.

134 KACHESS RIDGE
13.1 mi one-way/7.0 hrs

north of Easton in Wenatchee National Forest

Map 3.3, page 97

High above two large reservoirs, Kachess Ridge Trail traverses more than 13 miles along a high, meadowy ridge. Along the way are several worthy side trips to high vistas or alpine lakes. The trail works well as a through-hike, but if two cars are out of the question, no worries. Four other access points make getting to a particular spot quite easy.

For a through-hike, it's best to travel north to south, conveniently losing 2,500 feet of net elevation along the way. The route follows the crest of No Name Ridge. At 2.3 miles is a junction for Red Mountain Trail, a seldom-used trail passing Little Joe Lake (nice) on the way to an alternate trailhead (not recommended). At 3.8 miles is the junction dropping to inviting Thorp Lake and another trailhead. A short .25 mile later a side trail heads steeply to the summit of Thorp Mountain, the high point of the trip, in both altitude and experience. At 5,854 feet, see much of the surrounding Cascades, most spectacularly Mount Rainier.

The trail follows the ridge three miles through meadows and continuous views, passing Know Creek Trail (another trailhead) and French Cabin Creek Trail (a fourth trailhead). The trail now begins its drop into Silver Creek Basin

and down to the trailhead. Kachess Beacon Trail, 1.9 miles from the southern trailhead, leads up to a nice viewpoint at 4,615 feet.

User Groups: Hikers, leashed dogs, horses, and mountain bikes. No wheelchair access.

Open Seasons: This trail is accessible mid-June–October.

Permits: A federal Northwest Forest Pass is required to park here.

Maps: For a map of Wenatchee National Forest, contact the Outdoor Recreation Information Center at the downtown Seattle REI. For topographic maps, ask Green Trails for No. 208, Kachess Lake, or ask the USGS for Kachess Lake.

Directions: From Seattle, drive east on I-90 to Exit 70 (Easton). Drive north over the freeway and turn left on West Sparks Road. Drive one mile to Forest Service Road 4818. Turn right and drive one mile to Forest Service Road 203. Turn right and drive 2 miles to the signed trailhead at road's end.

Contact: Wenatchee National Forest, Cle Elum Ranger District, 803 West 2nd Street, Cle Elum, WA 98922, 509/852-1100.

135 DECEPTION PASS LOOP
14.7 mi/1–3 days

north of Cle Elum in Alpine Lakes Wilderness of Wenatchee National Forest

Map 3.3, page 97

The climax of the trip is not at Deception Pass but instead beneath the amazing Cathedral Rock and the parkland surrounding its base. Cathedral Rock looms high above Pacific Crest Trail, with towering rock cliffs that somehow sing and make cathedral the only word fit to describe the peak. Throw in great views of the Wenatchee Mountains and Mount Stuart, and you have the makings for a great weekend of hiking.

The hike works either clockwise or counterclockwise, but the latter makes for less strenuous climbing and is described here. Start at Tucquala Lake and head north through Cle Elum Valley to the pass, which is wooded and offers few views. Here, Marmot Lake and Lake Clarice are four miles to the north along a down-and-up trail, each with campsites.

From Deception Pass, the route follows PCT south past impressive mountain hemlocks before arriving at the base of Cathedral Rock. A pair of stream crossings may be difficult in times of heavy runoff. At Cathedral Rock, the trail climbs to beautiful parkland meadows of huckleberries, heather, and small trees. Peggy's Pond lies a short .5 mile around the base of Cathedral Rock and is worth visiting. The route drops steeply to the trailhead via Cathedral Rock Trail, passing Squaw Lake along the way.

User Groups: Hikers, leashed dogs, and horses (horses will be unable to cross a blown-out ford on a stream along the PCT). No mountain bikes are allowed. No wheelchair access.

Open Seasons: This trail is accessible June–October.

Permits: A federal Northwest Forest Pass is required to park here.

Maps: For a map of Wenatchee National Forest, contact the Outdoor Recreation Information Center at the downtown Seattle REI. For topographic maps, ask Green Trails for No. 176, Stevens Pass, or ask the USGS for Mount Daniel and The Cradle.

Directions: From Seattle, drive east on I-90 to Exit 80 (Roslyn). Turn left on Bullfrog Cutoff Road and drive to Highway 903. Turn left and drive to Salmon La Sac and Forest Service Road 4330. Continue straight on Forest Service Road 4330 to Tucquala Meadows Trailhead at road's end.

Contact: Wenatchee National Forest, Cle Elum Ranger District, 803 West 2nd Street, Cle Elum, WA 98922, 509/852-1100.

136 TUCK AND ROBIN LAKES
12.8 mi/1–2 days

north of Cle Elum in Alpine Lakes
Wilderness of Wentachee National Forest

Map 3.3, page 97

These two picturesque lakes are classics among folks who regularly hike this area. Set high

on the west side of the Wenatchee Ridge, Robin Lake reveals typical but never-tiring beauty of mountain hemlocks, heather, and huckleberries. This is a great destination, but with a little more effort, Tuck Lake delivers an outstanding high-mountain landscape uncommon in the Northwest. At an elevation of 6,100 feet, vegetation becomes scarce, large bare slabs of Granite Mountain beg for exploration, and a feeling of high alpine is always in the air.

The trail begins on Deception Pass Trail. The first three miles are flat and easy as the trail moves up the upper reaches of the Cle Elum River Valley. From here, the trail climbs well up through lazy switchbacks and at 4.5 miles is the cutoff for Tuck and Robin Lakes. Turning right, the trail ascends steeply, 1,100 feet in two miles, on sometimes rocky and difficult trail. After two miles, you've arrived at Robin Lake in subalpine forest. Bare slabs of granite mix with patches of mountain hemlocks and heather. Tuck Lake is about 1.5 miles farther on a way path that can provide some difficulty, as it climbs another 900 feet. At Tuck, the landscape is barren, with large slabs of granite exposed for lack of any decent soil at such an altitude. Blue sky and massive peaks fill the horizon.

While camping is available at both lakes, don't count on getting a spot if you show up late. This is a popular trail, and disappearing vegetation is a concern with established campsites going early. During the summer and early fall, it is best as a day hike.

User Groups: Hikers and leashed dogs. No horses or mountain bikes are allowed. No wheelchair access.

Open Seasons: This trail is accessible late June–early October.

Permits: A federal Northwest Forest Pass is required to park here.

Maps: For a map of Wenatchee National Forest, contact the Outdoor Recreation Information Center at the downtown Seattle REI. For topographic maps, ask Green Trails for No.

176, Stevens Pass, or ask the USGS for Mount Daniel and The Cradle.

Directions: From Seattle, drive east on I-90 to Exit 80 (Roslyn). Turn left on Bullfrog Cutoff Road and drive to Highway 903. Turn left and drive to Salmon La Sac and Forest Service Road 4330. Continue straight on Forest Service Road 4330 to Tucquala Meadows Trailhead at road's end.

Contact: Wenatchee National Forest, Cle Elum Ranger District, 803 West 2nd Street, Cle Elum, WA 98922, 509/852-1100.

137 PADDY-GO-EASY PASS
6.0 mi/3.5 hrs

north of Roslyn in Alpine Lakes Wilderness of Wenatchee National Forest

Map 3.3, page 97

Trailblazers must be sarcastic folk, especially when it comes to naming their new trails. Experienced hikers know as a general rule of thumb that when the word "easy" is used in a trail name, that trail is usually anything but easy. Regardless of the effort, hikers are often pleased with the outstanding views of many nearby peaks and ridges. The route travels outstanding high-country terrain, full of meadows covered in wildflowers. To top off the trip is Sprite Lake, an all-star lake set before The Cradle.

French Creek Trail makes a steady and steep ascent to the pass. Forest lines most of the way up before thinning to great meadows. This is a very colorful place in early July, when wildflowers are in full bloom. The trail gains roughly 2,700 feet in three miles. The pass is superb, with views of numerous peaks. Mounts Daniel, Stuart, and Rainier are particularly memorable. The pass lies at the crest of the Wenatchee Mountains, a beautiful ridge in its own right.

For further exploration, Sprite Lake lies a short distance over the pass within a small glacial cirque, with rocky slopes and scrubby subalpine trees. Across the valley below stands The Cradle, a tall, rocky, and barren peak.

No, Paddy, it's not an easy hike, but it certainly is spectacular.

User Groups: Hikers, leashed dogs, and horses. No mountain bikes are allowed. No wheelchair access.

Open Seasons: This trail is accessible July–mid-October.

Permits: A federal Northwest Forest Pass is required to park here.

Maps: For a map of Wenatchee National Forest, contact the Outdoor Recreation Information Center at the downtown Seattle REI. For topographic maps, ask Green Trails for No. 176, Stevens Pass, or ask the USGS for The Cradle.

Directions: From Seattle, drive east on I-90 to Exit 80 (Roslyn). Turn left on Bullfrog Cutoff Road and drive to Highway 903. Turn left and drive to Salmon La Sac and Forest Service Road 4330. Continue straight on Forest Service Road 4330 to Paddy-Go-Easy Pass, 1 mile before road's end.

Contact: Wenatchee National Forest, Cle Elum Ranger Station, 803 West 2nd Street, Cle Elum, WA 98922, 509/852-1100.

138 WAPTUS RIVER VALLEY
29.6 mi/4 days

north of Salmon La Sac in Alpine Lakes Wilderness of Wenatchee National Forest

Map 3.3, page 97

Waptus River Valley is not an end in itself. The trail leads to a number of high-country destinations, including Spade Lake and Dutch Miller Gap, two highlights of the Alpine Lakes Wilderness. It's a bit like those old books in which you can choose your own adventure. Take a number of trips up the river, each with different destinations and results. Of course, Waptus River and Waptus Lake are not to be overlooked. The route up the valley is beautiful, while Waptus Lake is the Alpine Lakes' largest lake, with excellent camping.

Waptus River Trail follows the river closely within surrounding forests. Waptus Lake (8.5 miles) has campsites and views of massive Summit Chief and Bears Breast Mountains. The main trail skirts the lake and continues to the head of the valley, where it makes for Dutch Miller Gap. Near the top of the tough ascent to the pass lies Lake Ivanhoe, a high lake set within shores of granite. Dutch Miller Gap leads down into the Middle Fork Snoqualmie.

One of the most popular side trips is Spade Lake. From Waptus Lake, Spade Lake Trail climbs steeply to Spade Lake. The views are good until the lake, where they become excellent. Other adventures along Waptus River Trail include trails up gentle Trail Creek, Waptus Pass over to Escondido Creek, and Pacific Crest Trail, which crosses the valley just above Waptus Lake.

User Groups: Hikers, leashed dogs, and horses. No mountain bikes are allowed. No wheelchair access.

Open Seasons: This trail is accessible July–October.

Permits: A federal Northwest Forest Pass is required to park here.

Maps: For a map of Wenatchee National Forest, contact the Outdoor Recreation Information Center at the downtown Seattle REI. For topographic maps, ask Green Trails for No. 176, Stevens Pass, and No. 208, Kachess Lake, or ask the USGS for Mount Daniel and Polallie Ridge.

Directions: From Seattle, drive east on I-90 to Exit 80 (Roslyn). Turn left on Bullfrog Cutoff Road and drive to Highway 903. Turn left and drive to Salmon La Sac Campground. Waptus Trailhead is on the right, just after you cross Cle Elum River.

Contact: Wenatchee National Forest, Cle Elum Ranger Station, 803 West 2nd Street, Cle Elum, WA 98922, 509/852-1100.

139 JOLLY MOUNTAIN
12.4 mi/8.0 hrs

north of Cle Elum in Wenatchee National Forest

Map 3.3, page 97

At 6,443 feet elevation, Jolly Mountain is well capable of delivering excellent views of surrounding ridges and mountains. On clear days, which are easier to come by here on the east side of the Cascades, the tall peak delivers. The route climbs up along Salmon La Sac Creek to a ridge, before making the final ascent to Jolly Mountain. The way is extremely steep, gaining more than 4,000 feet in just six miles of trail. This trail is definitely for the well conditioned, except for those traveling by mountain bike or motorcycle, which are allowed on the trail.

Jolly Mountain Trail makes a steady and steep climb up the creek valley, crossing it at 2.6 miles (difficult ford when the snows are still melting, until mid-July). The views are plentiful, as are the wildflowers blooming in early summer. The trail makes a final steep rise to the summit of Jolly Mountain. The peak provides wide views in all directions, and the vast size of Mount Stuart is readily apparent. The trail is very dry, so be sure to carry lots of water.

User Groups: Hikers, leashed dogs, horses, mountain bikes, and motorcycles. No wheelchair access.

Open Seasons: This trail is accessible June–November.

Permits: A federal Northwest Forest Pass is required to park here.

Maps: For a map of Wenatchee National Forest, contact the Outdoor Recreation Information Center at the downtown Seattle REI. For topographic maps, ask Green Trail for No. 208, Kachess Lake, or ask the USGS for Davis Peak.

Directions: From Seattle, drive east on I-90 to Exit 80 (Roslyn). Turn left on Bullfrog Cutoff Road and drive to Highway 903. Turn left and drive to Salmon La Sac. Jolly Mountain Trailhead is on the right, just beyond Cayuse Horse Camp.

Contact: Wenatchee National Forest, Cle Elum Ranger Station, 803 West 2nd Street, Cle Elum, WA 98922, 509/852-1100.

140 SUMMIT LAKE/ BEARHEAD MOUNTAIN
5.0–6.0 mi/3.0 hrs

south of Enumclaw in Clearwater Wilderness of Mount Baker–Snoqualmie National Forest

Map 3.3, page 97

One trailhead provides access to these two destinations, one a high, subalpine lake and the other an even higher mountain summit. Most folks pick one and take it easy, rather than cram both hikes into one long, strenuous day. A trip to Summit Lake, an ideal midsummer swimming hole, is 2.5 miles one-way and a 1,000-foot elevation gain. A trip to the panoramic viewpoint of Bearhead Mountain is three miles one-way, climbing 1,700 feet.

The routes follow Summit Lake Trail into Clearwater Wilderness, climbing to Twin Lake (.8 mile). The trail splits here; Summit Lake Trail turns left while Carbon Trail heads right to Bearhead Mountain. The climb to Bearhead traverses the base of the mountain before turning to climb straight up the shoulder on Bearhead Mountain Trail (2.2 miles). From 6,089 feet, the views are stupendous. Mountains to the north, mountains to the east, and mountains to the south.

A slight majority of hikers turn toward Summit Lake and its meadowy shores. Wildflowers arrive in July while huckleberries wait until late August. Mount Rainier is easily seen from the shore, an incredible dream. Those with an itch for views will enjoy knowing that an easy scramble leaves from the lake to a peak rising west of the lake with great views.

User Groups: Hikers, leashed dogs, and horses. No mountain bikes are allowed. No wheelchair access.

Open Seasons: This trail is accessible mid-June–September.

Permits: A federal Northwest Forest Pass is required to park here.

Maps: For a map of Mount Baker–Snoqualmie National Forest, contact the Outdoor Recreation Information Center at the downtown Seattle REI. For topographic maps, ask Green Trails for No. 237, Enumclaw, or ask the USGS for Bearhead Mountain.

Directions: From Enumclaw, drive west 5 miles to Highway 165 (on the west side of Buckley). Turn left (south) and drive 10.5 miles to Carbon River Highway. Turn left and drive 7.7 miles to Cayada Creek Road (Forest Service Road 7810). Turn left and drive 7 miles to the trailhead at road's end.

Contact: Mount Baker–Snoqualmie National Forest, Enumclaw Ranger Station, 450 Roosevelt Avenue East, Enumclaw, WA 98022, 360/825-6585.

141 GREENWATER RIVER
15.2 mi/1–2 days

south of Enumclaw in Norse Peak Wilderness of Mount Baker–Snoqualmie National Forest

Map 3.3, page 97

In one of the few virgin river valleys left in the southern Mount Baker–Snoqualmie National Forest, Greenwater River Trail explores it all. Coursing more than 10 miles to Corral Pass, its highlights are several lakes gracing the route. Being rather flat and certainly easy, this is a great full day hike or overnight trip for young or beginner backpackers, especially early or late in the year, when snow still blankets the high country.

Greenwater River Trail never ventures far from the beautiful, lively river. Endure a quick spell of old logging before immersing yourself in an ancient forest of Douglas fir, western hemlock, and western red cedar. A pair of small lakes (Meeker and Upper Greenwater) appear at two and 2.4 miles. These lakes are good turnarounds for a short day hike. Continuing up, the trail passes a pair of signed junctions to Echo Lake (6.9 miles). A number of campgrounds are found at the south end of the lake (7.4 miles). Don't forget the fly rod, because the trout in this lake make a sizable dinner.

User Groups: Hikers, leashed dogs, and horses. No mountain bikes are allowed. No wheelchair access.

Open Seasons: This trail is accessible April–November.

Permits: A federal Northwest Forest Pass is required to park here.

Maps: For a map of Mount Baker–Snoqualmie National Forest, contact the Outdoor Recreation Information Center at the downtown Seattle REI. For topographic maps, ask Green Trails for No. 239, Lester, or ask the USGS for Lester SW.

Directions: From Enumclaw, drive east on Highway 410 20.5 miles to Greenwater Road (Forest Service Road 70). Turn left (north) and drive 10 miles to Forest Service Road 7033. Turn right and drive .5 mile to the signed trailhead on the right.

Contact: Mount Baker–Snoqualmie National Forest, Enumclaw Ranger Station, 450 Roosevelt Avenue East, Enumclaw, WA 98022, 360/825-6585.

142 NOBLE KNOB
7.4 mi/4.0 hrs

south of Enumclaw in Norse Peak Wilderness of Mount Baker–Snoqualmie National Forest

Map 3.3, page 97

Tally it all up: $10 national park fee? No. Pure meadow bliss, complete with wildflowers in July? Yes. Long, taxing climb? No. Miles and miles of brilliant views? Yes. If you're not sold already, keep reading. The trail to Noble Knob is one of ease and excitement, a glorious ramble through the high country to a magnificent viewpoint. Noble Knob Trail starts high, at 5,700 feet elevation, an altitude that changes little throughout the hike. Skirting the base of Mutton Mountain and the slopes of Dalles Ridge, the trail arrives at the base of Noble Knob, a small rounded peak. A short side trail leads to the summit, the former site of a fire lookout. Mountain views appear from every direction (Olympics to the northwest), but of course Mount Rainier steals the show. Expect

to see a lot of company on Noble Knob Trail, especially on summer weekends.

User Groups: Hikers, leashed dogs, horses, and mountain bikes. No wheelchair access.

Open Seasons: This trail is accessible June–September.

Permits: A federal Northwest Forest Pass is required to park here.

Maps: For a map of Mount Baker–Snoqualmie National Forest, contact the Outdoor Recreation Information Center at the downtown Seattle REI. For topographic maps, ask Green Trails for No. 239, Lester, or ask the USGS for Suntop and Lester SW.

Directions: From Enumclaw, drive east 32 miles on Highway 410 to Corral Pass Road (Forest Service Road 7174). Turn left (east) and drive 6.7 miles to the trailhead just before Corral Pass Campground.

Contact: Mount Baker–Snoqualmie National Forest, Enumclaw Ranger Station, 450 Roosevelt Avenue East, Enumclaw, WA 98022, 360/825-6585.

143 MOUNT DAVID
14.0 mi/8.0 hrs

north of Lake Wenatchee in Glacier Peak Wilderness of Wenatchee National Forest

Map 3.4, page 98

This is about as high as one can get in the Glacier Peak Wilderness, other than Glacier Peak itself. It certainly feels that way. Tucked up north of Lake Wenatchee, Mount David towers over surrounding peaks for miles and miles. That leaves unmatched panoramic views for those who summit the challenging peak. Neighboring ridges and peaks fall away from beneath, melting into scores of other ridges as far as the eye can see. Challenging is an understatement for this trail. Make no mistake, this is a long, taxing ascent to the top. Alpine ridges and never-ending views make all the hard work worthwhile.

The route begins on Panther Creek Trail but Mount David Trail takes off to the right (west) after one mile. Here, the climbing begins. It's a steady assault on the mountain, but thanks to the excellent layout of the trail, it's never too much. The total elevation gain is 5,100 feet, or what is known as a "full day." No water is to be found along the trail, so be sure to bring several liters per person. From the ridge, the views open up as the trail contours on or just below the sharp ridge. The mountain falls away precipitously at your feet, down to the valley bottom far below. The trail seems to become steeper nearer the end, but that is likely because of complaints from weary legs. A small scramble conquers the summit. There's no end to the visible peaks, certainly too many to list here. At 7,431 feet tall, Mount David feels like the top of the world.

User Groups: Hikers and leashed dogs. No horses or mountain bikes are allowed. No wheelchair access.

Open Seasons: This trail is accessible August–October.

Permits: A federal Northwest Forest Pass is required to park here.

Maps: For a map of Wenatchee National Forest, contact the Outdoor Recreation Information Center at the downtown Seattle REI. For topographic maps, ask Green Trails for No. 145, Wenatchee Lake, or ask the USGS for Wenatchee Lake.

Directions: From Leavenworth, drive west on U.S. 2 to Highway 207 (at Coles Corner). Turn right and drive to White River Road, north of Lake Wenatchee (Forest Service Road 6400). Turn right and drive to the trailhead at road's end.

Contact: Wenatchee National Forest, Lake Wenatchee Ranger Station, 22976 Highway 207, Leavenworth, WA 98826, 509/763-3103.

144 LITTLE GIANT PASS
10.0 mi/7.0 hrs

north of Lake Wenatchee in Glacier Peak Wilderness of Wenatchee National Forest

Map 3.4, page 98

From Little Giant Pass, the views are nearly indescribable. From the pass, enjoy expansive views stretching miles to dozens of mountains

and ridges. Don't forget to look down, as well, for the perspective of not one but two immense, glacially carved valleys at your feet. This is one knee-knocking, lung-busting, hell-raiser of a hike—3,800 vertical feet in a brisk five miles. In addition to views are vast wildflower meadows within beautiful basins.

Little Giant Trail begins with a ford of Chiwawa River, a wet ordeal in the summer and fall but an impassable obstacle any other time. The trail wastes no time and immediately begins a long series of switchbacks out of the valley. Old-growth forest covers the trail and keeps hikers cool with shade. The trail crosses Little Giant Creek (other than remnant snowpack, the route's only water source) and begins entering exposed meadows. The climbing isn't done until you reach the pass. The wide, U-shaped valleys of the Chiwawa and Napeequa Rivers reveal their glacial origins. Snowcapped peaks and ridges line the horizon in every direction. Remember extra water or a water filter on this trip; you'll definitely need it.

User Groups: Hikers, leashed dogs, and horses (horses not recommended). No mountain bikes are allowed. No wheelchair access.

Open Seasons: This trail is accessible June–October.

Permits: A federal Northwest Forest Pass is required to park here.

Maps: For a map of Wenatchee National Forest, contact the Outdoor Recreation Information Center at the downtown Seattle REI. For topographic maps, ask Green Trails for No. 113, Holden, or ask the USGS for Trinity and Clark Mountain.

Directions: From Leavenworth, drive west on U.S. 2 to Highway 207, at Coles Corner. Turn left, drive to Fish Lake, and drive 1 mile to Chiwawa Valley Road (Forest Service Road 62). Turn left and drive toward Trinity to Little Giant Trailhead on the left, 1.5 miles beyond Nineteenmile Campground.

Contact: Wenatchee National Forest, Lake Wenatchee Ranger Station, 22976 Highway 207, Leavenworth, WA 98826, 509/763-3103.

145 DIRTY FACE
9.0 mi/5.0 hrs

north of Lake Wenatchee in Wenatchee National Forest

Map 3.4, page 98

We won't throw around terms such as cruel or nasty, but Dirty Face is not a stroll in the park. This trail is a straight-up assault on the mountain. Fair enough, for hikers are armed with endless switchbacks and Nalgenes of water to help achieve the top. A successful hiker is rewarded with views of Lake Wenatchee and numerous peaks of the Glacier Peak Wilderness. The site formerly hosted a Forest Service lookout to take advantage of the wide vista. Don't be discouraged if the hike sounds difficult. It is challenging, but it is beautiful as well.

Dirty Face Trail changes little over its length, composed entirely of switchbacks—reports vary between 70 and 90. After about 25 or so, the simple act of counting becomes easier said than done. The trail runs into an abandoned logging road (1.5 miles), which must be followed to its end, where the trail begins again. Ponderosa pine provides poor shade along the trail before patches of subalpine trees offer even less. The trail reaches a ridge, then switchbacks up even more to the former lookout site. The views are grand to the east and west, encompassing much of the Glacier Peak Wilderness. Lake Wenatchee glimmers in the sunshine below.

User Groups: Hikers, leashed dogs, horses, and mountain bikes. No wheelchair access.

Open Seasons: This trail is accessible mid-June–October.

Permits: A federal Northwest Forest Pass is required to park here.

Maps: For a map of Wenatchee National Forest, contact the Outdoor Recreation Information Center at the downtown Seattle REI. For topographic maps, ask Green Trails for No. 145, Wenatchee Lake, or ask the USGS for Wenatchee Lake.

Directions: From Leavenworth, drive west on U.S. 2 to Highway 207 (at Coles Corner). Turn right and drive to the trailhead at Lake Wenatchee Ranger Station.

Contact: Wenatchee National Forest, Lake Wenatchee Ranger Station, 22976 Highway 207, Leavenworth, WA 98826, 509/763-3103.

146 CHIWAUKUM CREEK
24.4 mi/2–3 days

near Leavenworth in Alpine Lakes Wilderness of Wenatchee National Forest

Map 3.4, page 98

Little-known Chiwaukum Creek is a trail corridor with all sorts of options. Several decades ago the road to the trailhead closed, adding a couple of miles to the hike in. Apparently an old road is grounds for dismissal of a trail, perhaps because there are so many other great hikes in the area. Fewer people sounds good. The options exist because the trail heads up the valley before splitting into North and South Forks. Each of these trails then splits again. It quickly becomes a full summer of weekends trying to hike it all. The crown jewel of the valley is Larch Lake, attained via 12 miles on North Fork Trail.

Chiwaukum Trail heads up the valley for six miles before splitting, staying close to the cool water of the creek among great forests of pine and fir. The beautiful and rarely traveled South Fork heads left, eventually splitting to reach Icicle Ridge Trail at Ladies Pass or Index Creek. The route via Ladies Pass travels between Lake Brigham and Lake Flora, outstanding high-country lakes. Also on the South Fork is a trail up Palmer Creek, to the Badlands and Icicle Ridge again.

North Fork Trail crosses Glacier Creek (8 miles) before climbing to reach the forested shores of Chiwaukum Lake (10 miles). Rocky mountain ridges surround the cool, blue water of the lake, as do numerous campsites. The trail continues to Larch Lake (12.2 miles), an area of meadows and jagged ridges. Larches and subalpine firs cover the landscape.

User Groups: Hikers, leashed dogs, and horses (horses allowed only to Glacier Creek).

No mountain bikes are allowed. No wheelchair access.

Open Seasons: This trail is accessible late July–October.

Permits: A federal Northwest Forest Pass is required to park here.

Maps: For a map of Wenatchee National Forest, contact the Outdoor Recreation Information Center at the downtown Seattle REI. For topographic maps, ask Green Trails for No. 177, Chiwaukum Mountains, or ask the USGS for Winton, Big Jim Mountain, and Chiwaukum Mountain.

Directions: From Stevens Pass, drive 25 miles east on U.S. 2 to Mile Marker 89. Turn right onto Chiwaukum Creek Road (Forest Service Road 7908) just beyond the marker. Drive to a junction and stay to the right. Drive to the road's end and the trailhead.

Contact: Wenatchee National Forest, Leavenworth Ranger Station, 600 Sherbourne, Leavenworth, WA 98826, 509/548-6977.

147 CHATTER CREEK/ LAKE EDNA
11.5 mi/8.0 hrs

near Leavenworth in Alpine Lakes Wilderness of Wenatchee National Forest

Map 3.4, page 98

Some folks hike the Alpine Lakes for a relaxing time away from home. Others come here looking for a relentless workout that offers killer views. Chatter Creek Trail up to Lake Edna is definitely for the latter type of hiker. It gains nearly 4,000 feet in just over five miles. That is undoubtedly considered a workout. As steep as the trail may be, however, it pays off with a terrific lake set in parkland and panoramic views of the Cascades. Lake Edna is situated along Icicle Ridge Trail, making Chatter Creek a quick but grueling access to the high ridge trail.

Chatter Creek Trail quickly begins climbing, where old forests provide welcome shade on hot days. The trail crosses the creek (tricky before June) and continues its relentless ascent

to the ridgeline (5 miles). At least it spends its last half among wide open meadows. The views begin to really emerge at this point.

Chatter Creek Trail contours a basin before making a final climb to the lake at 6,735 feet. The lake lies within a northside basin, so snow may linger well into August. The shores are fairly barren of trees; only scrubs and meadow endure this high up. The best vistas are found atop Cape Horn, a steep scramble to the west. At over 7,000 feet, much of the Cascades is exposed. Those planning to camp at the lake or along the ridge must use established campsites and refrain from camping on the fragile meadows.

User Groups: Hikers, leashed dogs, and horses. No mountain bikes are allowed. No wheelchair access.

Open Seasons: This trail is accessible July–October.

Permits: A federal Northwest Forest Pass is required to park here.

Maps: For a map of Wenatchee National Forest, contact the Outdoor Recreation Information Center at the downtown Seattle REI. For topographic maps, ask Green Trails for No. 177, Chiwaukum Mountains, or ask the USGS for Jack Ridge and Chiwaukum Mountain.

Directions: From Leavenworth, drive south on Icicle Creek Road (Forest Service Road 7600) 16 miles to Chatter Creek Campground and Trailhead, on the right.

Contact: Wenatchee National Forest, Leavenworth Ranger Station, 600 Sherbourne, Leavenworth, WA 98826, 509/548-6977.

148 JACK CREEK
23.2 mi/1–3 days

near Leavenworth in Alpine Lakes Wilderness of Wenatchee National Forest

Map 3.4, page 98

A lot awaits off Jack Creek Trail. Several trails lead off from Jack Creek, connecting to other major drainages of Icicle Creek and thereby creating spectacular loops for backpacking. Alone, the trail travels more than 11 miles to

Stuart Pass and exceptional subalpine parkland. Most of the route is forested, the trail surrounded by old-growth forests of Douglas fir, Englemann spruce, and pines. The full length of the trail is rarely traveled, making Jack Creek a preferred backcountry route.

Jack Creek Trail follows the stream closely for most of its length. The trail to Trout Lake cuts off just over a mile in. This is a great loop when connected to Eightmile Lake (see listing in this chapter). A couple of miles later another trail leads to Trout Lake, much more steeply. Meadow Creek heads off to the west, providing a pair of loops; one climbs to Blackjack Ridge and Cradle Lake, an excellent highcountry route, while the other crosses Meadow Creek Pass and drops into French Creek. Any of these routes are well chosen.

Jack Creek Trail slowly but surely gains in elevation to Stuart Pass (11.6 miles, 6,400 feet). Mount Stuart looms large to the east, and the Esmerelda Peaks are in view. The trail is a great valley hike, with plenty of camping along the way. It's an excellent trail to simply see where you end up.

User Groups: Hikers, leashed dogs, and horses. No mountain bikes are allowed. No wheelchair access.

Open Seasons: This trail is accessible mid-June–November.

Permits: A federal Northwest Forest Pass is required to park here.

Maps: For a map of Wenatchee National Forest, contact the Outdoor Recreation Information Center at the downtown Seattle REI. For topographic maps, ask Green Trails for No. 177, Chiwaukum Mountains, and No. 210, Liberty, or ask the USGS for Jack Ridge and Mount Stuart.

Directions: From Leavenworth, drive south on Icicle Creek Road (Forest Service Road 7600) 16 miles to Trout/Jack Creek Trailhead on the left, just beyond Rock Island Campground.

Contact: Wenatchee National Forest, Leavenworth Ranger Station, 600 Sherbourne, Leavenworth, WA 98826, 509/548-6977.

149 ICICLE RIDGE
10.0–25.0 mi/3.5 hrs–4 days

near Leavenworth in Alpine Lakes Wilderness of Wenatchee National Forest

Map 3.4, page 98

This long ridge trail is a favorite among Leavenworth locals. Extending for 25 miles and more, the trail takes in a wide variety of high country. Alpine meadows full of early summer flowers dominate nearly the entire route, while a number of high lakes occupy the western end. The route has a number of access points, both from Icicle Creek Road and the backcountry. Views are as prolific as the wildflowers, extending over much of the Alpine Lakes Wilderness and south to Mount Stuart and Mount Daniel. This high country is outstanding and thankfully preserved by the Alpine Lakes Wilderness.

At the eastern trailhead, Icicle Ridge Trail seemingly starts right in the town of Leavenworth. Little time is wasted in reaching the ridge, as the trail climbs quickly and steeply and then runs the crest. A steep trail from Icicle Creek Road via Fourth of July Creek reaches the ridge in this section. It's extremely dry in the summer, and the snow melts here before the rest of the trail, providing early access.

Icicle Ridge Trail drops off the ridge to cross Cabin Creek and reach large Lake Augusta, at 6,854 feet. Set beneath Big Jim Mountain, this is a great place for camping. The stars at night are surreal. The trail meanders along the north side of the ridge for a while, making junctions with Palmer Creek Trail and Index Creek Trail. Another ascent delivers Lakes Edna and craggy Cape Horn. Chatter Creek Trail accesses the ridge here in a 10-mile trip. The trail stays at or above 7,000 feet for several miles before dropping to Mary and Margaret Lakes. Hikers have access to Frosty or Whitehorse Creek Trails, both backcountry exits.

User Groups: Hikers, leashed dogs, and horses. No mountain bikes are allowed. No wheelchair access.

Open Seasons: This trail is accessible July–October (the eastern end opens in late May).

Permits: A federal Northwest Forest Pass is required to park here.

Maps: For a map of Wenatchee National Forest, contact the Outdoor Recreation Information Center at the downtown Seattle REI. For topographic maps, ask Green Trails for No. 177, Chiwaukum Mountains, and No. 178, Leavenworth, or ask the USGS for Big Jim Mountain, Cashmere Mountain, and Leavenworth.

Directions: From Leavenworth, drive south on Icicle Creek Road (Forest Service Road 7600) 16 miles to Chatter Creek Campground and Trailhead, on the right.

Contact: Wenatchee National Forest, Leavenworth Ranger Station, 600 Sherbourne, Leavenworth, WA 98826, 509/548-6977.

150 EIGHTMILE AND TROUT LAKE LOOP

18.0 mi/–2 days

near Leavenworth in Alpine Lakes Wilderness of Wenatchee National Forest

Map 3.4, page 98

This is an outstanding loop through tall, rocky ridges and mountains in the Alpine Lakes Wilderness. Windy Pass connects Trout Lake to Eightmile Lake via miles of excellent high-country hiking, achieving lakes and views that will not soon be forgotten. Windy Pass stands at 7,300 feet, revealing much of the surrounding wilderness. Cashmere Mountain stands to the east, Mount Stuart to the south, and countless other peaks and ridges line the horizon. Trout and Eightmile Lakes are excellent destinations by themselves for day hikes or overnighters.

The loop requires a car drop or hitchhike from a friendly passerby. Starting from Eightmile Creek, the trail climbs moderately to Little Eightmile Lake and Eightmile Lake (3.3 miles), each dwarfed by the surrounding mountains. Camping along this route requires hikers to obtain a permit at the Leavenworth Ranger Station. The trail next reaches open parkland meadows and Lake Caroline (6.8 miles).

The prime moment of the hike comes at Windy Pass (7,200 feet), one of the best panoramic views on any trail in the region. Flowers and larches add color to the scene, each at their own times of the year. The trail descends three miles from Windy Pass to Trout Lake (12.3 miles), surrounded by trees and even more high ridges and peaks. From Trout Lake, the trail drops to Icicle Creek (18 miles).

User Groups: Hikers, leashed dogs, and horses (horses day use only). No mountain bikes are allowed. No wheelchair access.

Open Seasons: This trail is accessible July–early November.

Permits: A federal Northwest Forest Pass is required to park here. Overnight stays require backcountry camping permits ($3 per person per day), which are available at Leavenworth Ranger Station.

Maps: For a map of Wenatchee National Forest, contact the Outdoor Recreation Information Center at the downtown Seattle REI. For topographic maps, ask Green Trails for No. 177, Chiwaukum Mountains, or ask the USGS for Cashmere Mountain and Jack Ridge.

Directions: From Leavenworth, drive south on Icicle Creek Road (Forest Service Road 7600) 10 miles to Forest Service Road 7601 (Bridge Creek Campground). Turn left and drive 3 miles to the signed trailhead on the right.

Contact: Wenatchee National Forest, Leavenworth Ranger Station, 600 Sherbourne, Leavenworth, WA 98826, 509/548-6977.

151 COLCHUCK AND STUART LAKES

9.0 mi/6.0 hrs

near Leavenworth in Alpine Lakes Wilderness of Wenatchee National Forest

Map 3.4, page 98

These are two favorite destinations for many Alpine Lakes hikers. Each lake is a beautiful turquoise and is surrounded by great subalpine forests. Massive, rocky mountains enclose the lakes, and typically awesome mountain views are encountered along the trails. The lakes are great to hike no matter what your timeframe for the trip, as they are challenging day hikes as well as excellent overnighters. The trails can be fairly busy during the summer with day hikers, but an overnight permitting system keeps campers to a reasonable number. Colchuck and Stuart Lakes are wonderful and wild mountain lakes.

The route to the two lakes follows cool and refreshing Mountaineer Creek before splitting (2.5 miles). The left fork climbs to Colchuck Lake, a steep grade of switchbacks. A cool waterfall eases the pain. Colchuck Lake sits within patches of forest, directly beneath the enormous walls of Dragontail and Colchuck Peaks. Their rocky cliffs drop straight to the water.

From the junction, Stuart Lake Trail makes an easy and gentle climb through meadows to Stuart Lake. The way is full of views of the surrounding ridges and peaks, with Mount Stuart towering 4,000 feet above the lake. Impressive stuff, indeed. At both lakes, camping is grand. Regardless of which lake you choose, it's difficult to go wrong once you've stepped foot onto this trail.

User Groups: Hikers only. No dogs, horses, or mountain bikes are allowed. No wheelchair access.

Open Seasons: This area is accessible July–October.

Permits: A federal Northwest Forest Pass is required to park here. Overnight stays require backcountry camping permits ($3 per person per day), which are available at Leavenworth Ranger Station.

Maps: For a map of Wenatchee National Forest, contact the Outdoor Recreation Information Center at the downtown Seattle REI. For topographic maps, ask Green Trails for No. 177, Chiwaukum Mountains, and No. 209, Mount Stuart, or ask the USGS for Cashmere and Enchantment Lakes.

Directions: From Leavenworth, drive south on Icicle Creek Road (Forest Service Road 7600) 5 miles to Snow Creek Trailhead on the left.

Contact: Wenatchee National Forest, Leavenworth Ranger Station, 600 Sherbourne, Leavenworth, WA 98826, 509/548-6977.

152 THE ENCHANTMENTS
16.8 mi/2–4 days

south of Leavenworth in Alpine Lakes Wilderness of Wenatchee National Forest

Map 3.4, page 98

Ahh, the Enchantments. Just the thought of this spectacular playground of high country makes the heart warm. Nowhere is quite like the Enchantments; this is the Shangri-la of Washington hiking. This series of high basins is filled with lakes of unsurpassed quality, with acres of subalpine parkland. Larches are everywhere, making late September a time not to miss. These high ridges have the craggiest rock you've seen. No trail description can ever do justice to the true beauty of the Enchantments.

The Enchantments are best reached via Snow Lakes. An excellent loop can be made by hiking down Aasgard Pass to Colchuck Lake. This requires a car-drop, however. So this description will stick to the Snow Lakes access. Because of large crowds of people visiting the area, folks planning on staying overnight, which is recommended, must obtain a permit from the Leavenworth Ranger Station.

Snow Lakes Trail crosses Icicle Creek and immediately climbs to Snow Lakes (6.5 miles). Fortunately, much of the route is in old-growth forest. Snow Lakes are a common first-night camp for those unable to make it all the way to the Lower Enchantments. Between Snow Lakes and the first basin, the trail makes a very steep, rugged climb. The trees gradually give way, and hikers finally find themselves within the Enchantments (8 miles).

The Enchantments are a series of basins filled with lakes. A good map is necessary, as a network of trails laces the area. Marmots frolic in the meadows and sun themselves on the boulders while wind rustles the needles of subalpine firs and larches. The basins are rimmed by a number of ridges jutting into the sky with their sharp, craggy peaks. The main trail passes lake after lake on its way farther up and deeper into the basin. Glaciers overhang many of the upper lakes and are often heard cracking and breaking. The trail reaches Aasgard Pass (10.7 miles) before dropping steeply to Colchuck Lake, far below. Backpackers looking to spend a night or two in the Enchantments have numerous campsite options. Dozens of sights are located at nearly every lake. Just remember to pitch it on a hard, durable, and established spot.

User Groups: Hikers only. No dogs, horses, or mountain bikes are allowed. No wheelchair access.

Open Seasons: This trail is accessible mid-July–October.

Permits: A federal Northwest Forest Pass is required to park here. Overnight stays within the Enchantments require backcountry camping permits, which are awarded by lottery at the Leavenworth Ranger Station.

Maps: For a map of Wenatchee National Forest, contact the Outdoor Recreation Information Center at the downtown Seattle REI. For topographic maps, ask Green Trails for No. 209S, The Enchantments, or ask the USGS for Cashmere, Enchantment Lakes, and Blewett.

Directions: From Leavenworth, drive south on Icicle Creek Road (Forest Service Road 7600) 5 miles to Snow Creek Trailhead on the left.

Contact: Wenatchee National Forest, Leavenworth Ranger Station, 600 Sherbourne, Leavenworth, WA 98826, 509/548-6977.

153 ESMERELDA BASIN
4.5 mi/3.0 hrs

northwest of Cle Elum in Wenatchee National Forest

Map 3.4, page 98

The lazy trail to Esmerelda Basin is perfectly suited for those seeking subalpine meadows and rocky peaks without the difficulty of a major climb. Esmerelda Basin is filled with meadows of wildflowers set among rock. Total elevation gain is 1,700 feet, making it easy to understand the popularity of the trail. From the basin, several attractive options await. Fortune Creek Pass offers distant views of mountains. Alternatively, the trail meanders on the ridgeline to find small Lake Ann, set on the barren slopes of Ingalls Peak, an outstanding destination.

Esmerelda Basin Trail begins at a lofty elevation of 4,300 feet, providing an easy journey to a grand landscape. The route pleases immediately and consistently, passing back and forth between subalpine forests and open meadows. The rocky Esmerelda Peaks line the route to the south. Esmerelda Basin is about two miles from the trailhead. At this junction, head left to climb to Fortune Creek Pass, where the views become sublime. Turn right at the junction for another adventure, a trail riding the crest toward Fortune Peak and Lake Ann. These are highly recommended as extended day hikes.

User Groups: Hikers, leashed dogs, and horses. No mountain bikes are allowed. No wheelchair access.

Open Seasons: This trail is accessible July–October.

Permits: A federal Northwest Forest Pass is required to park here.

Maps: For a map of Wenatchee National Forest, contact the Outdoor Recreation Information Center at the downtown Seattle REI. For topographic maps, ask Green Trails for No. 209, Mount Stuart, or ask the USGS for Mount Stuart.

Directions: From Seattle, drive east on I-90 to Exit 86. Turn left on Highway 970 and drive 7 miles to Teanaway River Road. Turn left and drive 13 miles to Forest Service Road 9737. Drive 10 miles to the trailhead at road's end.

Contact: Wenatchee National Forest, Cle Elum Ranger Station, 803 West 2nd Street, Cle Elum, WA 98922, 509/852-1100.

154 LONGS PASS AND LAKE INGALLS
6.0–10.8 mi/3.5–6.0 hrs

northwest of Cle Elum in Wenatchee National Forest

Map 3.4, page 98

Longs Pass and Lake Ingalls are two of the

Cle Elum area's best destinations. Larches are ablaze in the fall while amazing views of Mount Stuart linger year-round. The high elevation trailhead makes it easy to achieve the best of the eastern Cascades. Open subalpine forests provide constant views of surrounding peaks, valleys, and forests on a steady climb to Longs Pass and Lake Ingalls. From Longs Pass, the view of Mount Stuart is unbeatable, with the massive mountain staring directly at hikers from across Ingalls Creek. Lake Ingalls is bound by glacially scraped granite and patches of meadows. Day hikes as good as this are hard to come by so easily.

The route starts high, at 4,400 feet, on Esmerelda Basin Trail. At the first junction (.4 mile), veer right for Ingalls Way Trail. Two miles of switchbacks end at another junction; left for Lake Ingalls, right for Longs Pass. Both trails are moderately steep and exposed, so bring plenty of water. Open meadows are scattered with larches brightening the slopes in the fall. Longs Pass (3 miles) has the Cascades' best view of Stuart, set among superb meadows with larches to boot. Ingalls Lake (5.4 miles) rests directly beneath its own craggy mountain, Ingalls Peak. While they get quite dry and scorching hot in the dead of summer, both of these trails are wonderful early summer and fall trips.

User Groups: Hikers, leashed dogs, and horses. No mountain bikes are allowed. No wheelchair access.

Open Seasons: This trail is accessible July–October.

Permits: A federal Northwest Forest Pass is required to park here.

Maps: For a map of Wenatchee National Forest, contact the Outdoor Recreation Information Center at the downtown Seattle REI. For topographic maps, ask Green Trails for No. 209, Mount Stuart, or ask the USGS for Mount Stuart.

Directions: From Seattle, drive east on I-90 to Exit 86. Turn left on Highway 970 and drive 7 miles to Teanaway River Road. Turn left and drive 13 miles to Forest Service Road 9737. Drive 10 miles to the trailhead at road's end.

Contact: Wenatchee National Forest, Cle Elum Ranger Station, 803 West 2nd Street, Cle Elum, WA 98922, 509/852-1100.

155 BEVERLY TURNPIKE

6.4 mi/3.5 hrs

northeast of Cle Elum in Wenatchee National Forest

Map 3.4, page 98

Connecting the Teanaway River to Ingalls Creek, Beverly and Turnpike Trails meet in the most beautiful of circumstances. At 5,800 feet, Beverly-Turnpike Pass is endowed with excellent views of mountain ridges and peaks, particularly the nearby and impressive Mount Stuart. Like most high-country routes, this trail passes through miles of subalpine meadows and revels in swaths of wildflowers. The route drops to the Ingalls Creek Trail, making for a good loop if a car-drop can be arranged.

Beverly Turnpike Trail climbs steadily from Teanaway River Valley up along Beverly Creek. It's not very impressive at first, as it travels an old road and passes through a clear-cut. As the trail progresses, however, unspoiled forests and meadows enter the scene. Rocky ridges line the way, their slopes covered in meadows. A trail cuts off to the right to Fourth Creek, also an access to Ingalls Creek. Stay left and follow the main trail to the pass. The best views are achieved here, where Mount Stuart appears to the north. A steep side trip up to Iron Peak, just before the pass, is well recommended for panoramic views. The route then follows Turnpike Creek through old-growth forest to Ingalls Creek and a necessary ford to reach that trail.

User Groups: Hikers, leashed dogs, and horses. No mountain bikes are allowed. No wheelchair access.

Open Seasons: This trail is accessible July–October.

Permits: A federal Northwest Forest Pass is required to park here.

The Enchantments, Washington's best and most revered destination

Maps: For a map of Wenatchee National Forest, contact the Outdoor Recreation Information Center at the downtown Seattle REI. For topographic maps, ask Green Trails for No. 209, Mount Stuart, or ask the USGS for Red Top Mountain, Enchantment Lakes, and Mount Stuart.

Directions: From Seattle, drive east on I-90 to Exit 86. Turn left on Highway 970 and drive 7 miles to Teanaway River Road. Turn left and drive 13 miles to Forest Service Road 9737. Drive 3 miles to Forest Service Road 112. Turn right and drive 1.5 miles to the trailhead at road's end.

Contact: Wenatchee National Forest, Cle Elum Ranger Station, 803 West 2nd Street, Cle Elum, WA 98922, 509/852-1100.

156 INGALLS CREEK
32.0 mi/3–4 days 3 ⛰ 10

southeast of Leavenworth in Alpine Lakes Wilderness of Wenatchee National Forest

Map 3.4, page 98

The longest river hike in the Alpine Lakes Wilderness, this valley route leads to unbelievably beautiful country. Set below massive Mount Stuart and numerous other craggy peaks and mountains, Ingalls Creek makes an impressive trek through eastside forest to superb subalpine meadows. An early summer hike reveals untold treasures in melting snowfields and natural bouquets of wildflowers. Few treks left in the Alpine Lakes area can boast of such remoteness and wildness. That makes this a very special place to those who visit it.

Ingalls Creek Trail rarely strays far from the banks of Ingalls Creek. The route is mostly old-growth ponderosa pines and Douglas firs. Campsites are numerous along the trail, which keeps an easy grade for most of its path.

At Porcupine Creek (10 miles), the trail begins climbing, emerging from the forest into excellent subalpine parkland. Surrounding ridges and peaks break out into view. The Wenatchee Mountains, while quite big, pale in comparison to Mount Stuart directly to the north. Ingalls Lake is a favorite site, set among larches on granite slabs. While camping is not allowed at the lake, plentiful campsites are to be found nearby. The trail ends by climbing to Stuart Pass at 6,400 feet.

User Groups: Hikers, leashed dogs, and horses. No mountain bikes are allowed. No wheelchair access.

Open Seasons: This trail is accessible June–November.

Permits: A federal Northwest Forest Pass is required to park here.

Maps: For a map of Wenatchee National Forest, contact the Outdoor Recreation Information Center at the downtown Seattle REI. For topographic maps, ask Green Trails for No. 209, Mount Stuart, and No. 210, Liberty, or ask the USGS for Mount Stuart, Enchantment Lakes, and Blewett.

Directions: From Seattle, drive east on I-90 to Highway 970 (Exit 86). Drive north to U.S. 97. Drive north to Ingalls Creek Road, 12 miles north of Blewett Pass. Turn left and drive 1 mile to the trailhead at road's end.

Contact: Wenatchee National Forest, Leavenworth Ranger Station, 600 Sherbourne, Leavenworth, WA 98826, 509/548-6977.

157 YELLOW HILL AND ELBOW PEAK

6.0–10.0 mi/4.0–6.0 hrs

northeast of Cle Elum in Wenatchee National Forest

Map 3.4, page 98

Yellow Hill and Elbow Peak are all about views. Situated in the Teanaway drainage, these two mountaintops offer wide vistas of the surrounding Cascades. The route itself is not anything special, being mainly composed of roads and dirt tracks fit for bikes. Nothing keeps hikers from enjoying these trails other than the steep climbs, but that's what trails offering breathtaking views are all about.

Yellow Hill Trail follows a logging road high above the Teanaway Valleys. Second-growth forests offer shade on this dry trail as it switchbacks up a ridge. The trees gradually thin out

along the path, giving hikers great views of neighboring ridges and peaks. The trail makes it to Yellow Hill at three miles and 5,527 feet elevation. Mount Stuart appears surprisingly close while Mount Rainier stands to the south. Elbow Peak is another two miles of hiking along a high ridge, definitely a pleasant way to spend a few hours. The views are not much different from those at Yellow Hill, but people are much more scarce. From their lofty perches, both peaks provide a proper outlook on the numerous ridges and valleys of the Teanaway Valleys.

User Groups: Hikers, leashed dogs, horses, mountain bikes, and motorcycles. No wheelchair access.

Open Seasons: This trail is accessible mid-June–October.

Permits: A federal Northwest Forest Pass is required to park here.

Maps: For a map of Wenatchee National Forest, contact the Outdoor Recreation Information Center at the downtown Seattle REI. For topographic maps, ask Green Trails for No. 208, Kachess Lake, and No. 209, Mount Stuart, or ask the USGS for Cle Elum Lake, Teanaway Butte, and Davis Peak.

Directions: From Seattle, drive east on I-90 to Exit 86. Turn left on Highway 970 and drive 7 miles to Teanaway River Road. Turn left and drive 7 miles to West Fork Teanaway Road. Turn left and drive 1 mile to Middle Fork Teanaway Road. Turn right and drive 6 miles to the signed trailhead on the right.

Contact: Wenatchee National Forest, Cle Elum Ranger Station, 803 West 2nd Street, Cle Elum, WA 98922, 509/852-1100.

© SCOTT LEONARD

Northeast Washington

t's easy to find folks who are experts on hiking in the Alpine Lakes or Glacier Peak Wildernesses. The same goes for finding authoritative voices on North Cascades National Park or even the desolate Pasayten Wilderness. But hikers with an intricate knowledge of northeastern Washington are few and far between. Sure, westsiders have plenty to keep them occupied with the Cascades and Olympic Mountains. But never visiting or exploring Colville National Forest is a missed opportunity.

Locals from places like Republic, Colville, or Metaline Falls don't mind this lack of attention because that means they have nearly two million acres of national forest practically to themselves. The likelihood of running into a crowd out here is pretty much zilch. In fact, except for hunting season, you're unlikely to see other folks in the backcountry.

The wild Kettle and Selkirk Ranges are two major subregions of northeast Washington, and they are crisscrossed by great trails. Hit the trail in the Kettle Range and don't be surprised by elk, deer, or even moose. When hiking in the Selkirks, be on the lookout for caribou, gray wolves, or even grizzlies. Transecting northeast Washington, Highway 20 from Anacortes to Newport is easily the state's most scenic highway. Expect to come across places like Republic, Kettle Falls, Colville, and Metaline Falls. Never heard of them? Most folks haven't.

The Kettle Mountains are located east of the Cascades proper but west of the mighty Columbia River rise. The range runs south to north, and most peaks top 7,000 feet of elevation. Many of the trails networking the mountains start low and work their way up to the main travelway, the Kettle Crest Trail, which runs along the length of the ridge. The Columbia Mountain Trail offers a great and quick experience of the Kettles. With a trailhead at Sherman Pass right on Highway 20, the trail climbs quickly to the peak of Columbia Mountain, giving up views for miles. The southwest side of the range was burned severely in 1988, but the Edds Mountain and Barnaby Butte Trails are still great trails despite the charred forest lining their routes.

Great trails are found in the low country, as well. Outside of Republic (another great small town, complete with a co-op grocery) are Fish and Swan Lakes. In addition to great fishing and a good car campground, trails loop each lake. On the east side of the Kettle Range is Hoodoo Canyon, a short hike through a narrow gorge, complemented by a lake and good campground.

Farther east (much farther east) lie the Selkirk Mountains. Many of the peaks in the Selkirks, like Grassy Top, Thunder Mountain, and Shedroof Mountain, fall in the 6,000- to 7,000-foot range. The most popular adventures in this area occur at Sullivan Lake, a large, glacially cut lake bordered by old forests. A pair of great campgrounds makes this a regular summer destination for families and boaters.

Tucked away into Washington's borders with Canada and Idaho, the Salmo-Priest Wilderness protects 40,000 acres of the Colville National Forest. The wilderness is shaped like a horseshoe and protects the high ridges framing Sullivan Creek. Several great trails explore the peaks and meadows of the Salmo-Priest. Crowell Ridge, Grassy Top, and Shedroof Divide are all fine trails.

In short, if you don't know the Selkirks or the Kettles, you should. It's well worth the trip from west of the Cascades to see how the other half plays.

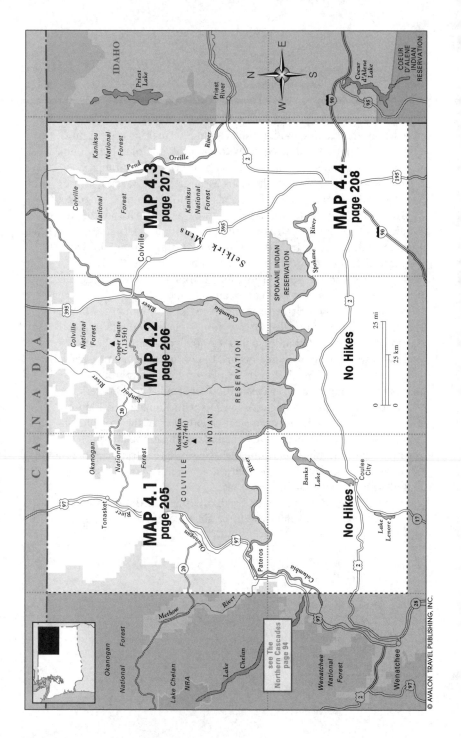

Map 4.1

Hikes 1–10
Pages 209–214

4.2

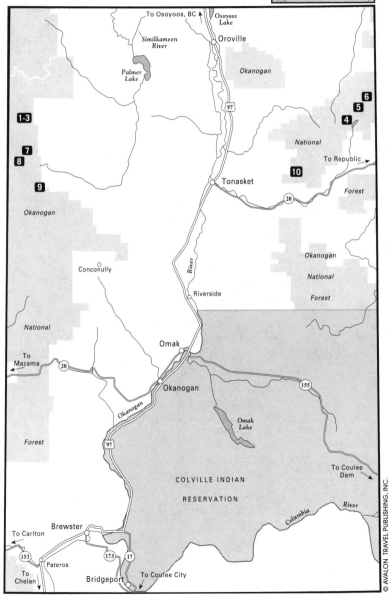

To Osoyoos, BC

Osoyoos Lake

Oroville

Similkameen River

Palmer Lake

Okanogan

97

1-3

7

8

9

Okanogan

Conconully

National

To Mazama

20

National

Forest

6

5

4

To Republic

10

Forest

20

Tonasket

Okanogan

National

Forest

River

Riverside

Omak

Okanogan

155

Omak Lake

Okanogan

97

To Coulee Dam

COLVILLE INDIAN

RESERVATION

River

Columbia

Brewster

To Carlton

153

Pateros

To Chelan

173

17

Bridgeport

To Coulee City

© AVALON TRAVEL PUBLISHING, INC.

Map 4.2

Hikes 11–29
Pages 215–225

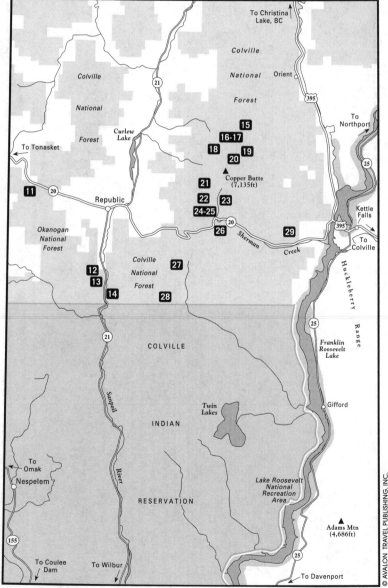

To Christina Lake, BC

Colville

National

Orient

Forest

395

To Northport

Colville

National

Forest

Curlew Lake

To Tonasket

15

16-17

18   **19**

20

Copper Butte (7,135ft)

21

11   20   Republic

22   **23**

24-25

20

26   Sherman   Creek   **29**

Kettle Falls

395

To Colville

Okanogan National Forest

Colville National Forest

27

12

13

14   **28**

Huckleberry Range

21   Sanpoil

COLVILLE

25

Franklin Roosevelt Lake

INDIAN

Twin Lakes

Gifford

To Omak

Nespelem

River

RESERVATION

Lake Roosevelt National Recreation Area

155

To Coulee Dam   To Wilbur

Adams Mtn (4,686ft)

25

To Davenport

© AVALON TRAVEL PUBLISHING, INC.

Map 4.3

Hikes 30–43
Pages 225–233

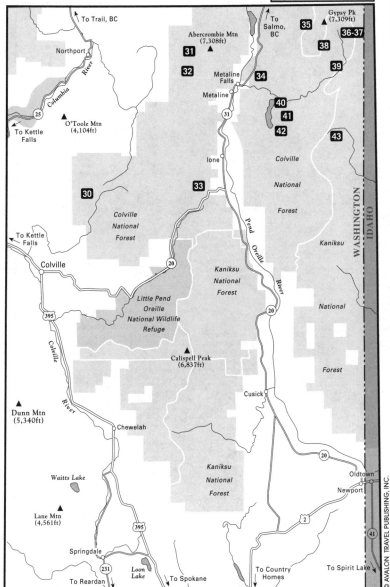

Map 4.4

Hike 44
Page 233

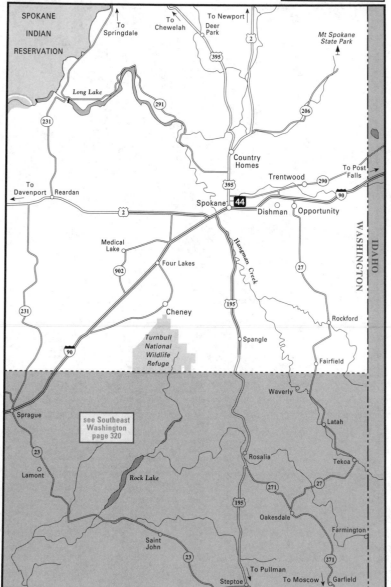

SPOKANE INDIAN RESERVATION

To Springdale

To Chewelah

To Newport

Deer Park

Mt Spokane State Park

Long Lake

291

231

395

206

Country Homes

Trentwood

To Post Falls

To Davenport

Reardan

2

Spokane

44

Dishman

Opportunity

290

90

WASHINGTON

IDAHO

Medical Lake

Four Lakes

Hangman Creek

902

231

Cheney

195

27

Rockford

90

Turnbull National Wildlife Refuge

Spangle

Fairfield

Waverly

Sprague

see Southeast Washington page 320

Latah

23

Lamont

Rock Lake

Rosalia

Tekoa

271

27

195

Oakesdale

Farmington

Saint John

23

To Pullman

Steptoe

To Moscow

Garfield

271

© AVALON TRAVEL PUBLISHING, INC.

1 BOUNDARY TRAIL
98.0 mi/9–10 days

near the Canadian border in Pasayten Wilderness of Okanogan National Forest

Map 4.1, page 205

One of Washington's granddaddy trails, Boundary Trail runs across the entirety of America's largest wilderness, the Pasayten. The route follows the Canadian border, hence the name. It is an extremely high route, much of it occurring at 6,000 feet or more. The area is completely wild and one of the few places in the lower 48 where grizzly bears and gray wolves still roam. The route needn't be hiked end to end; there are many great trips accessing just a part of the trail. At least eight major trails provide access for small loops.

The Boundary Trail begins at Castle Pass on Pacific Crest Trail. Start at Hart's Pass and hike north 18 miles to Castle Pass and "Ol' 533," the trail's number. From here, it heads east 73 miles to Iron Gate Trailhead, in the middle of nowhere. Along the way it climbs dozens of high passes and ridges, crosses the Pasayten River, and basks in endless views of mountains. The summer is a prime time to visit, when wildflowers are in bloom, as is the fall, when larches do their thing. Established camps are littered along the route, and off-trail camping is OK as long as it's low impact. Also, if you hike this route without the maps, you likely won't come back. Good luck.

User Groups: Hikers, leashed dogs, and horses. No mountain bikes are allowed. No wheelchair access.

Open Seasons: This trail is accessible July–September.

Permits: A federal Northwest Forest Pass is required to park here. A free wilderness permit is also required to hike here and is available at the trailhead.

Maps: For a map of Okanogan National Forest, contact the Outdoor Recreation Information Center at the downtown Seattle REI. For topographic maps, ask Green Trails for

No. 17, Jack Mountain, No. 18, Pasayten Peak, No. 19, Billy Goat Mountain, No. 20, Coleman Peak, and No. 21, Horseshoe Basin, or ask the USGS for Horseshoe Basin, Bauerman Ridge, Remmel Mountain, and Ashnola Pass.

Directions: Harts Pass: From Winthrop, drive west 17 miles on Highway 20 to Mazama. Turn right (north) onto Mazama Road and drive .2 mile to Hart's Pass Road (County Road 9140/Forest Service Road 5400). Turn left and drive to Rattlesnake Trailhead, .3 mile beyond River Bend Campground.

Iron Gate: From Tonasket, drive north on Tonasket–Oroville Westside Road to Loomis-Oroville Road. Turn left and drive through Enterprise and Loomis to Sinlahekin Valley Road (County Road 9425). Turn right and drive 2 miles to Touts Coulee Road (Forest Service Road 39). Turn left and drive 14 miles to Iron Gate Road. Turn right and drive 5 miles to the trailhead at road's end.

Contact: Okanogan National Forest, Methow Valley Ranger District, 24 West Chewuch Road, Winthrop, WA 98862, 509/996-4003.

2 HORSESHOE BASIN (PASAYTEN)
13.0 mi/2–4 days

north of Winthrop in Pasayten Wilderness of Okanogan National Forest

Map 4.1, page 205

This is not the well-known Horseshoe Basin trail at the head of the Stehekin River. Instead, this is a much more remote and hence lesser-known Horseshoe Basin deep within the Pasayten Wilderness. The terrain, high rolling hills covered in tundralike meadows, is unlike that anywhere else in Washington. Many of the peaks top out over 8,000 feet, an impressive height. One of the best trails the Pasayten has to offer, Horseshoe Basin is appropriate for backpackers with moderate experience.

Starting at Iron Gate Trailhead, follow Boundary Trail as it climbs through scenic forest and meadow to Sunny Pass (5.2 miles). Boundary

Trail turns north and finds expansive Horseshoe Pass and Basin (6.7 miles). Incredible camps are found at Sunny Pass, Horseshoe Pass, Louden Lake, and Smith Lake. The ecosystem is delicate at this elevation and necessitates strict Leave-No-Trace camping.

The basin is ripe for exploration. Each of the many peaks is an easy walk, little more than 1,000 feet above the high pass. Armstrong Mountain lines the Canadian border while Arnold Peak and Horseshoe Mountain are worthy American peaks. Any side trip is highly recommended. Although the snowpack is gone by Memorial Day, be prepared for adverse weather, even a snowstorm, well into summer.

User Groups: Hikers, leashed dogs, and horses. No mountain bikes are allowed. No wheelchair access.

Open Seasons: This trail is accessible mid-May–October.

Permits: A federal Northwest Forest Pass is required to park here. A free wilderness permit is also required to hike here and is available at the trailhead.

Maps: For a map of Okanogan National Forest, contact the Outdoor Recreation Information Center at the downtown Seattle REI. For topographic maps, ask Green Trails for No. 21, Horseshoe Basin, or ask the USGS for Horseshoe Basin.

Directions: From Tonasket, drive north on Tonasket–Oroville Westside Road to Loomis-Oroville Road. Turn left and drive through Enterprise and Loomis to Sinlahekin Valley Road (County Road 9425). Turn right and drive 2 miles to Touts Coulee Road (Forest Service Road 39). Turn left and drive 14 miles to Iron Gate Road. Turn right and drive 5 miles to the trailhead at road's end.

Contact: Okanogan National Forest, Methow Valley Ranger District, 24 West Chewuch Road, Winthrop, WA 98862, 509/996-4003.

3 WINDY PEAK
12.8 mi/6.5 hrs

north of Winthrop in Pasayten Wilderness of Okanogan National Forest

Map 4.1, page 205

The tallest point in the area, Windy Peak makes an attractive summit on clear days. There are no fewer than four different routes to the peak, but this wilderness trail up Windy Creek is the shortest and best. Passing through old-growth forests, it climbs to the vast open meadows along the flanks of Windy Peak. Wildflowers, views, and indeed a little wind is about all you'll find at 8,334 feet. This is one of Washington's most expansive views.

From Iron Gate Trailhead, begin on Boundary Trail but turn left on Clutch Creek Trail (.7 mile). Climbing the ridge through forests of fir and pine, the route turns right on Windy Peak Trail (4.4 miles). The trail climbs straight up, but it's a meadow walk from here on to the top. At the summit (6.4 miles), much of the Pasayten is laid bare at your feet, spread out in front of the Cascades Mountains. Don't forget extra water and food on this dry, strenuous trip.

User Groups: Hikers, leashed dogs, and horses. No mountain bikes are allowed. No wheelchair access.

Open Seasons: This trail is accessible July–October.

Permits: A federal Northwest Forest Pass is required to park here. A free wilderness permit is also required to hike here and is available at the trailhead.

Maps: For a map of Okanogan National Forest, contact the Outdoor Recreation Information Center at the downtown Seattle REI. For topographic maps, ask Green Trails for No. 21, Horseshoe Basin, or ask the USGS for Horseshoe Basin.

Directions: From Tonasket, drive north on Tonasket–Oroville Westside Road to Loomis-Oroville Road. Turn left and drive through Enterprise and Loomis to Sinlahekin Valley Road (County Road 9425). Turn right and drive 2 miles to Touts Coulee Road (Forest Service Road 39). Turn left and drive 20 miles to the trailhead at Long Swamp Campground.

Contact: Okanogan National Forest, Methow Valley Ranger District, 24 West Chewuch Road, Winthrop, WA 98862, 509/996-4003.

4 SOUTH SIDE BONAPARTE
11.2 mi/6.0 hrs

northwest of Tonasket in Okanogan National Forest

Map 4.1, page 205

Mount Bonaparte registers as one of eastern Washington's tallest summits, standing tall at 7,257 feet. Being that the peak is in the north-central part of the state, you're assured of spectacular views of distant mountains in every direction. South Side Trail is the shortest and easiest way to reach the summit out of four possible options. While much of the route is forested, the upper parts of the trail are fairly open, cloaked in meadows and steep slopes. The summit of Mount Bonaparte is rounded like a large dome, meaning trees obscure most views until one climbs the 90-year-old fire lookout stationed atop the mountain. That the lookout still stands is a testament to its hardy construction in 1914. The snow-capped North Cascades are readily visible to the west while the Kettle River Range stands to the east. Rarely seen mountains of Canada stand to the north.

User Groups: Hikers, leashed dogs, and horses. No mountain bikes are allowed. No wheelchair access.

Open Seasons: This trail is accessible May–November.

Permits: Permits are not required. Parking and access are free.

Maps: For a map of Okanogan National Forest, contact the Outdoor Recreation Information Center at the downtown Seattle REI. For a topographic map, ask the USGS for Mount Bonaparte.

Directions: From Tonasket, drive east 20 miles on Highway 20 to County Road 4953. Turn left (north) and drive 9 miles to Forest Service

Road 33. Turn left and drive 7 miles to Forest Service Road 33-100. Turn left and drive 3.5 miles to the trailhead.

Contact: Okanogan National Forest, Tonasket Ranger Station, 1 West Winesap, Tonasket, WA 98855, 509/486-2186.

5 STRAWBERRY MOUNTAIN
3.0 mi/1.5 hrs

northwest of Tonasket in Okanogan National Forest

Map 4.1, page 205

While the summit of big brother Mount Bonaparte towers over little brother Strawberry Mountain, the latter boasts the easier and more enjoyable hike. Strawberry Trail climbs from a great campground on Lost Lake up through some magnificent old-growth forest. Enormous ponderosa pines, Douglas firs, and western larches highlight the trip to Strawberry Mountain's summit. These trees have survived through the centuries thanks to strong natural defenses against fire (thick bark, wide spacing). The trail climbs the north side of the mountain steadily but gently all the way to the top. Although the summit is more than 2,500 feet below the peak of Mount Bonaparte, the forest breaks open to reveal great views of Lost and Bonaparte Lakes below. Strawberry Trail is a definite must-hike trail for anyone camping at Lost Lake or in the general area. And proving that life is truly sweet, you can expect to find strawberries (small ones) along the route.

User Groups: Hikers, leashed dogs, and horses. No mountain bikes are allowed. No wheelchair access.

Open Seasons: This trail is accessible May–November.

Permits: Permits are not required. Parking and access are free.

Maps: For a map of Okanogan National Forest, contact the Outdoor Recreation Information Center at the downtown Seattle REI. For a topographic map, ask the USGS for Mount Bonaparte.

Directions: From Tonasket, drive east 20 miles

on Highway 20 to Bonaparte Lake Road (County Road 4953). Turn left (north) and drive 9 miles to Forest Service Road 33. Turn left and drive 5.5 miles to Lost Lake Campground. The trailhead is 50 yards down the small side road (Forest Service Road 33-050) immediately before the campground (but park in the campground's day-use area).

Contact: Okanogan National Forest, Tonasket Ranger Station, 1 West Winesap, Tonasket, WA 98855, 509/486-2186.

6 BIG TREE BOTANICAL LOOP
0.7 mi/0.5 hr

northwest of Tonasket in Okanogan National Forest

Map 4.1, page 205

Big trees indeed. This easy-to-navigate trail shows that the east side of the Cascades can grow enormous evergreens much like the west side does. The short loop trail, with a wide, flat, and graveled path for wheelchair access, walks through an old-growth forest of ponderosa pine, Douglas fir, Englemann spruce, and western larch. Many of the trees are upward of 300 years old. Although the forest underwent selective logging about 40 years ago (to remove trees doomed to die by bark beetles), the forest is a great example of eastern climax forests. The trees are widely spaced with a sparse undergrowth of grasses and small shrubs. These understory plants are meant to burn regularly, at low intensities. The fire burns quickly with little chance to ignite the large trees. At the end of the loop is the highlight of the hike, where two gigantic western larches grow in a small depression. These two granddaddy tamaracks are more than 900 years old, on par with some of the biggest trees in the Olympics. Here's to another 900 years!

User Groups: Hikers and leashed dogs. No horses or mountain bikes are allowed. This trail is wheelchair accessible.

Open Seasons: This trail is accessible year-round.

Permits: Permits are not required. Parking and access are free.

Maps: For a map of Okanogan National Forest, contact the Outdoor Recreation Information Center at the downtown Seattle REI. For a topographic map, ask the USGS for Mount Bonaparte.

Directions: From Tonasket, drive east on Highway 20 to Bonaparte Lake Road (County Road 4953). Turn left (north) and drive 9 miles to Forest Service Road 33. Turn left and drive 3.5 miles to the well-signed trailhead and parking area on the right side of the road.

Contact: Okanogan National Forest, Tonasket Ranger Station, 1 West Winesap, Tonasket, WA 98855, 509/486-2186.

7 TIFFANY MOUNTAIN
8.2 mi/4.5 hrs

east of Winthrop in Okanogan National Forest

Map 4.1, page 205

The roadless area surrounding Tiffany Mountain is distinct from the rest of the North Cascades. High, rolling hills dominate the horizons, while wetlands and meadows populate many of the valleys. Open forests of fir and pine create beautiful parkland on the slopes of mountains, while their summits are covered in wildflowers, grasses, and mosses. It's a more subtle beauty than the jagged peaks of the North Cascades. If you're here in July, expect a lot of green for such an easterly locale.

Tiffany Mountain is reachable via four routes, making a loop trip easy and promising. Pick or choose, but Tiffany Lake Trail is the best choice. This route passes timbered Tiffany Lake (an excellent base camp) before climbing to Whistler Pass. The four trails converge here and may be confusing, so bring a map and compass. A scramble to the top of Tiffany Mountain yields vistas extending for miles. Peer into the vast Pasayten Wilderness, then turn and survey much of the Cascade Range. A walk along flowered Freezeout Ridge is an easier but equally great side trip. The area is protected as a botanical reserve, so if camping here, stick to established camps and observe strict Leave-No-Trace principles.

User Groups: Hikers, leashed dogs, horses, and mountain bikes. No wheelchair access.

Open Seasons: This trail is accessible mid-June–September.

Permits: A federal Northwest Forest Pass is required to park here.

Maps: For a map of Okanogan National Forest, contact the Outdoor Recreation Information Center at the downtown Seattle REI. For topographic maps, ask Green Trails for No. 53, Tiffany Mountain, or ask the USGS for Tiffany Mountain.

Directions: From the town of Conconully, drive Okanogan County Road 2017 around the reservoir for three miles. Turn right onto Forest Service Road 37 and continue for 21 miles. After crossing Bernhardt Creek, turn right onto Forest Service Road 39 and drive 8 miles north to Tiffany Springs Campground and the trailhead.

Contact: Okanogan National Forest, Methow Valley Ranger District, 24 West Chewuch Road, Winthrop, WA 98862, 509/996-4003.

8 BERNHARDT MINE
5.0 mi/3.0 hrs

northeast of Winthrop in Okanogan National Forest

Map 4.1, page 205

Mention the word "mine" to a hiker, and you're likely to get a nasty scowl in return. After all, who wants to toil along a trail just to check out a big hole? Well, Bernhardt Mine Trail is really much more than a field trip to an old mine. The trail passes several old, barely standing cabins along the way, testaments to the hardy living of the old settlers. And there's the mine itself, a tame model of extraction compared to modern practices, when bulldozers rip up entire hillsides and chemical solutions strip streams into lifelessness. Enjoy the mine, but keep hiking to Clark Peak, where you'll forget all about industry thanks

to sweeping meadows of wildflowers that reveal distant mountain ranges.

The route to the mine is steep but only two miles. Pass through soggy wetlands and climb almost straight up to the miner's cabin and an accompanying mine. Hike a little higher to intersect North Summit Trail. This trail runs north to Tiffany Mountain and makes possible an 11-mile loop (hike Freezeout Ridge Trail to Forest Service Road 39 and walk the road two miles to your car). If you're looking for something shorter, just scramble to the top of Clark Peak. Expansive views and grassy meadows will be your reward.

User Groups: Hikers, leashed dogs, horses, and mountain bikes. No wheelchair access.

Open Seasons: This trail is accessible July–mid-October.

Permits: A federal Northwest Forest Pass is required to park here.

Maps: For a map of Okanogan National Forest, contact the Outdoor Recreation Information Center at the downtown Seattle REI. For topographic maps, ask Green Trails for No. 53, Tiffany Mountain, or ask the USGS for Tiffany Mountain.

Directions: From the town of Conconully, drive Okanogan County Road 2017 around the reservoir three miles. Turn right onto Forest Service Road 37 and continue for 21 miles. After crossing Bernhardt Creek, turn right onto Forest Service Road 39 and drive 1 mile north to the trailhead on the right.

Contact: Okanogan National Forest, Methow Valley Ranger District, 24 West Chewuch Road, Winthrop, WA 98862, 509/996-4003.

9 GRANITE MOUNTAIN
11.0 mi/6.0 hrs

northeast of Winthrop in Okanogan National Forest

Map 4.1, page 205

In the early 1990s, more than 700 local residents sent letters to the U.S. Forest Service, objecting to plans to build more than 30 miles of road through the Granite Mountain Roadless

Area. The roads were to help log thousands of acres of forest, spoiling one of the Okanogan's best forests. Fortunately for hikers today, their efforts were successful. Granite Mountain Trail climbs steeply to Granite's 7,366-foot summit, surveying the protected forests as well as many distant peaks and ranges. If you're not into a full hike, you can still obtain views from Little Granite Mountain, a six-mile round-trip.

Granite Mountain Trail climbs steeply through forests of lodgepole pine and fir to a small ridge. A side trail leads north to the top of Little Granite (2 miles). The main trail continues toward much larger Granite Mountain through a gap between ridges. A stiff scramble almost straight up leads to the summit and the requisite views. Although it passes near Little Granite Creek, the trail is usually very dry once the snowpack has disappeared, so extra water is a must.

User Groups: Hikers, leashed dogs, horses, and mountain bikes. No wheelchair access.

Open Seasons: This trail is accessible July–mid-October.

Permits: A federal Northwest Forest Pass is required to park here.

Maps: For a map of Okanogan National Forest, contact the Outdoor Recreation Information Center at the downtown Seattle REI. For topographic maps, ask Green Trails for No. 53, Tiffany Mountain, and No. 85, Loup Loup, or ask the USGS for West Conconully and Loup Loup Summit.

Directions: From Conconully, drive southwest 2 miles on Okanogan County Road 2017. The road branches to Forest Service Road 42 and Forest Service Road 37; turn right onto Road 37. Drive 1 mile and turn left onto Forest Service Road 37-100. Drive 4 miles and turn right onto Forest Service Road 37-120. The trailhead is .5 mile ahead, on the right.

Contact: Okanogan National Forest, Methow Valley Ranger District, 24 West Chewuch Road, Winthrop, WA 98862, 509/996-4003.

🔟 FOURTH OF JULY RIDGE
9.0 mi/5.0 hrs

northwest of Tonasket in Okanogan National Forest

Map 4.1, page 205

Fourth of July Ridge is less about big views than it is a trip back into time. Along the trail are several old cabins built more than 100 years ago by some of the region's first settlers. In the 19th century, folks slowly moved into the upper Okanogan for the deceptively rich natural resources of the area. Although the forests and prairies appear dry during much of the summer, this area is really an ideal place to raise cattle. Geologically, the land of the Okanogan is very old and composed of metamorphic rocks, a type of rock that is often home to vast mineral deposits. That attracted miners to these parts. The cabins along the ridge have long ago been abandoned, yet old artifacts can still found among their remains. After passing the cabins (1.5 miles), Fourth of July Trail slowly traverses Mount Bonaparte by climbing the southeast slope. At 3.5 miles is Lightning Spring, usually dry by June, and at 4.5 miles the trail intersects Southside Trail, access to Mount Bonaparte's summit (see listing for South Side Bonaparte in this chapter).

User Groups: Hikers, leashed dogs, and horses. No mountain bikes are allowed. No wheelchair access.

Open Seasons: This trail is accessible May–November.

Permits: Permits are not required. Parking and access are free.

Maps: For a map of Okanogan National Forest, contact the Outdoor Recreation Information Center at the downtown Seattle REI. For topographic maps, ask the USGS for Havillah and Mount Bonaparte

Directions: From Tonasket, drive north 15 miles on County Road 9467 (Tonasket-Havillah Road) to Forest Service Road 3230. Turn right and drive 4 miles to the signed trailhead.

Contact: Okanogan National Forest, Tonasket Ranger Station, 1 West Winesap, Tonasket, WA 98855, 509/486-2186.

⓫ FIR MOUNTAIN
4.0 mi/2.5 hrs

east of Tonasket in Okanogan National Forest

Map 4.2, page 206

Although the route up Fir Mountain is nothing to write home about, much of your sweat is paid off with a great summit view. Fir Mountain Trail shows no qualms about its intention of climbing straight up the hillside to the summit, a long craggy mass of exposed rock. The trail is mostly forested until it reaches the summit, meaning you'll have to wait until you're well invested in the hike to achieve any views. This is a good place to see deer or elk browsing in the forest, or to hear the whoomp-whoomp-whoomp of grouse. The summit has good vistas of the Kettle River Range and the white-capped North Cascades to the east. Expect the trail to be hot and dry with no water to be found along the way. The trailhead is across Highway 20 from Sweat Creek Campground, a nice place to call home for the night.

User Groups: Hikers and leashed dogs. No horses or mountain bikes are allowed. No wheelchair access.

Open Seasons: This trail is accessible May–October.

Permits: Permits are not required. Parking and access are free.

Maps: For a map of Okanogan National Forest, contact the Outdoor Recreation Information Center at the downtown Seattle REI. For a topographic map, ask the USGS for Wauconda Summit.

Directions: From Republic, drive west 9 miles on Highway 20 to Forest Service Road 31. Turn left (south) and drive 1.5 miles to the signed trailhead.

Contact: Okanogan National Forest, Tonasket Ranger Station, 1 West Winesap, Tonasket, WA 98855, 509/486-2186.

⓬ SWAN AND LONG LAKE LOOPS
1.3–1.8 mi/1.0 hr

south of Republic in Colville National Forest

Map 4.2, page 206

These are a pair of outstanding lakeshore loops leaving from a pair of great campgrounds. The two trails encircle Swan Lake (1.8 miles) and Long Lake (1.3 miles), passing through old-growth ponderosa pine forest with steady views of the lakes. Swan Lake is large and open atop a high plateau. Long

Long Lake, a short and easy lake loop near a car campground

Lake lies in a narrow valley between two rocky cliffs. The trails are flat and easy, perfect for hikers of all ages and abilities. Moose and elk are often heard calling out from around the lake during late evening, while loons, geese, and ducks fill the woods with sound during the morning. The two campgrounds are great for casual campers, as they feature full car-camping amenities. Anglers in pursuit of the well-stocked trout in the lakes will most appreciate the trails since they pass countless secluded fishing holes.

User Groups: Hikers, leashed dogs, and mountain bikes. No horses are allowed. No wheelchair access.

Open Seasons: This trail is accessible March–November.

Permits: Permits are not required. Parking and access are free.

Maps: For a map of Colville National Forest, contact the Outdoor Recreation Information Center at the downtown Seattle REI. For a topographic map, ask the USGS for Swan Lake.

Directions: From Republic, drive south 7.5 miles on Highway 21 to Scatter Creek Road. Turn right (west) and drive 7 miles to Swan Lake Campground. The trailhead is in the day-use area.

Contact: Colville National Forest, Republic Ranger Station, 180 North Jefferson, Republic, WA 99166, 509/775-7400.

⓭ TENMILE
5.0 mi/2.5 hrs

south of Republic in Colville National Forest

Map 4.2, page 206

Unlike many of the summit hikes in the area, Tenmile Trail hikes through a small, rugged canyon up into nice parkland forests of fir and pine. The route leaves San Poil Campground (conveniently situated alongside Highway 21) and climbs through the lightly forested canyon. Ponderosa pines line the steep walls while cottonwoods inhabit the wet canyon bottom. This

is a great place to see deer, hear elk, and maybe even stumble across a moose. Don't forget about bears or the possibility of a rattlesnake. Tenmile Trail climbs 1.5 miles in the canyon before reaching the plateau above, a good turn-around point. The last mile works its way up through a draw to Tenmile Road, a good access point for those staying at Swan or Long Lake Campgrounds.

User Groups: Hikers and leashed dogs. No horses or mountain bikes are allowed. No wheelchair access.

Open Seasons: This trail is accessible June–October.

Permits: Permits are not required. Parking and access are free.

Maps: For a map of Colville National Forest, contact the Outdoor Recreation Information Center at the downtown Seattle REI. For topographic maps, ask the USGS for Bear Mountain and Swan Lake.

Directions: From Republic, drive 10 miles south on Highway 21 to San Poil Campground. Turn right (west) into the campground. The trailhead is near the day-use parking area.

For the upper trailhead, turn right onto Scatter Creek Road (7.5 miles from Republic) and drive 4 miles to Tenmile Road. Turn left and drive 2.5 miles to the signed trailhead.

Contact: Colville National Forest, Republic Ranger Station, 180 North Jefferson, Republic, WA 99166, 509/775-7400.

⓮ 13 MILE
16.5 mi one-way/8.0 hrs

southeast of Republic in Colville National Forest

Map 4.2, page 206

A trail with options is 13 Mile, making for a great trek through the southern reach of the Kettle River Range. The route has three trailheads, making the entire stretch of trail (more than 16 miles) easily accessible. The views are unbeatable from the high ridge, whether they be looking out to other Kettle peaks or out over San Poil Valley.

All three trailheads offer something different and worthwhile. From 13 Mile Campground, the trail climbs quickly to views of the beautiful San Poil River canyon. Hawks and eagles looking for dinner are commonly seen high above the valley. The trail intersects Forest Service Road 2054 and the middle trailhead at about four miles. Thirteen Mile Trail continues east to grassy meadows along the south slopes of 13 Mile Mountain before dropping into a creek valley. Deer and elk are frequently encountered on this lightly used section of the route. The high point (in elevation) is achieved when the trail reaches the saddle between Fire and 17 Mile Mountains, just 2.5 miles from the east trailhead. The great thing about 13 Mile Trail is that with three trailheads, it's like three trails in one and each is equally fun. Water sources are undependable (especially in late summer) along this high route, so be sure to carry an adequate supply. A few camps are dispersed throughout, but best bets are to find a flat spot 50 yards from the trail and to call it home for the night.

User Groups: Hikers, leashed dogs, horses, and mountain bikes. No wheelchair access.

Open Seasons: This trail is accessible June–October.

Permits: Permits are not required. Parking and access are free.

Maps: For a map of Colville National Forest, contact the Outdoor Recreation Information Center at the downtown Seattle REI. For topographic maps, ask the USGS for Thirteenmile Creek, Bear Mountain, and Edds Mountain.

Directions: West access: From Republic, drive 13 miles south on Highway 21 to 13 Mile Campground on the left (east) side of the road. The 13 Mile Trailhead is within the campground.

East access: From Republic, drive east 7 miles to Hall Creek Road (County Road 99, which turns into Forest Service Road 2054). Turn right (south) and drive 5.5 miles to Forest Service Road 600. Turn left onto Forest Service Road 600 and drive 5 miles to the signed trailhead on the right (west) side of the road.

Middle Access: From Republic, drive east 7 miles to Hall Creek Road (County Road 99). Turn right (south) and drive 1.5 miles to County Road 233. Turn right and drive 1.5 miles to Forest Service Road 2053. Veer left and drive 1 mile to Forest Service Road 2054. Turn right and drive 5.5 miles to Cougar Trailhead.

Contact: Colville National Forest, Republic Ranger Station, 180 North Jefferson, Republic, WA 99166, 509/775-7400.

15 TAYLOR RIDGE
8.0 mi/4.0 hrs

northwest of Kettle Falls in Colville National Forest

Map 4.2, page 206

Taylor Ridge Trail has just about everything you could ask for from a trail. The route traverses the high ridge, frequently leaving the timber to take in good views of the surrounding peaks and valleys. Water is frequently available along the route and there are several good campsites, making overnight ventures a good bet. The trail is also split in half by a Forest Service road, making upper sections of the ridge easily accessible. From the bisecting road, the two segments are each about four miles in length. Head east on Taylor Ridge Trail to follow the ridge for a short while before dropping sharply to Boulder Creek. The trail to the west gently climbs higher, passing through meadows and vistas as the ridge works its way toward the Kettle Crest. Find camps near the road and up higher on the trail. Water can be found from several streams and springs along the route.

User Groups: Hikers, leashed dogs, horses, mountain bikes, and motorcycles. No wheelchair access.

Open Seasons: This trail is accessible May–October.

Permits: Permits are not required. Parking and access are free.

Maps: For a map of Colville National Forest, contact the Outdoor Recreation Information Center at the downtown Seattle REI. For topographic maps, ask the USGS for Mount Leona and Bulldog Mountain.

Directions: From Kettle Falls, drive north 22 miles to Boulder–Deer Creek Road (Forest Service Road 6100). Turn left (west) and drive 8 miles to Forest Service Road 6113. Turn left (south) and drive 7 miles to the signed trailhead.

Contact: Colville National Forest, Kettle Falls Ranger Station, 255 West 11th Avenue, Kettle Falls, WA 99141, 509/738-7700.

16 PROFANITY
6.0 mi/3.5 hrs

northeast of Republic in Colville National Forest

Map 4.2, page 206

Rarely used by anyone other than hunters, Profanity Peak Trail offers a firsthand glimpse at the impact of forest fires on dry, east-side forests. The Leona Fire roared through this area in 2001, destroying much of the forest. Already, the area has begun to regenerate. Ground covers revealed by the now-gone canopy are doing extremely well in the sunlight. Seedlings have already taken root in many places and are working on creating a forest of their own. It's a welcome sight to see nature taking care of itself, especially after the doomsday coverage forest fires often receive.

The first half of Profanity Trail climbs through parts of the fire on its way up to Kettle Crest Trail. At this point, the views are grand to the east and west. Those with a cursing streak can exercise it by heading south on Kettle Crest Trail and scaling the summit of Profanity Peak. Grand vistas await those who do.

User Groups: Hikers, leashed dogs, horses, and mountain bikes. No wheelchair access.

Open Seasons: This trail is accessible May–October.

Permits: Permits are not required. Parking and access are free.

Maps: For a map of Colville National Forest, contact the Outdoor Recreation Information Center at the downtown Seattle REI. For a topographic map, ask the USGS for Mount Leona.

Directions: From Republic, drive east 2.5 miles on Highway 20 to Highway 21. Turn left (north) and drive 13 miles to Aeneas Creek Road (County Road 566). Turn right and drive 8 miles (the road becomes Forest Service Road 2160) to the trailhead at road's end.

Contact: Colville National Forest, Republic Ranger Station, 180 North Jefferson, Republic, WA 99166, 509/775-7400.

17 STICK PIN
2.6 mi/2.0 hrs

northwest of Kettle Falls in Colville National Forest

Map 4.2, page 206

Stick Pin, one of the many trails offering access to Kettle Crest Trail, is unique in that water is readily available nearly the length of the trail. Thanks go out to the trail engineer who laid out Stick Pin, as it follows the South Fork of Boulder Creek up to its headwaters in the Kettle River Range. The cool water is refreshing on hot summer days. Most of Stick Pin Trail is covered by thick forests of Douglas fir, western larch, and lodgepole pine. Deer and elk are plentiful in this area, as are easy-to-startle grouse. The trail threads between Ryan Hill and Stickpin Hill to make a steep climb up to Kettle Crest Trail and the requisite meadow views.

User Groups: Hikers, leashed dogs, horses, and mountain bikes. No wheelchair access.

Open Seasons: This trail is accessible May–October.

Permits: Permits are not required. Parking and access are free.

Maps: For a map of Colville National Forest, contact the Outdoor Recreation Information Center at the downtown Seattle REI. For a topographic map, ask the USGS for Mount Leona.

Directions: From Kettle Falls, drive west approximately 22 miles on Highway 20 to Albian Hill Road. Turn right (north) and drive 12.1 miles to Forest Service Road 2030-921, a small side road. Follow this road .5 mile to its end and the signed trailhead. A primitive camp is at the trailhead.

Contact: Colville National Forest, Kettle Falls Ranger Station, 255 West 11th Avenue, Kettle Falls, WA 99141, 509/738-7700.

18 LEONA
3.2 mi/1.5 hrs

northeast of Republic in Colville National Forest

Map 4.2, page 206

It may be hard to distinguish between the many trails leading up to Kettle Crest Trail, but Leona is one of the best. Much of the trail features glorious views of Curlew Valley and out to the North Cascades. And when you reach Kettle Crest Trail, you can gaze out over the Columbia River Valley and up and down the Kettle River Range. Leona Trail climbs steadily, but the grade is easily managed, especially since this is such a short trail. At the halfway point is Leona Spring, a rare source of water at this elevation. At the crest, hike north along signed Leona Loop Trail, which combines with Kettle Crest Trail to a make a six-mile loop (total). Cutting off from the loop is a trail to the summit of Leona, a well-recommended vista.

User Groups: Hikers, leashed dogs, horses, and mountain bikes. No wheelchair access.

Open Seasons: This trail is accessible May–October.

Permits: Permits are not required. Parking and access are free.

Maps: For a map of Colville National Forest, contact the Outdoor Recreation Information Center at the downtown Seattle REI. For a topographic map, ask the USGS for Mount Leona.

Directions: From Republic, drive east 2.5 miles on Highway 20 to Highway 21. Turn left (north) and drive 11.5 miles to St. Peter's Creek Road (County Road 584). Turn right (east) and drive 7 miles (it will turn into Forest Service Road 2157) to a roadblock and road's end. The trailhead is to the right of the roadblock.

Contact: Colville National Forest, Republic

Ranger Station, 180 North Jefferson, Republic, WA 99166, 509/775-7400.

19 US MOUNTAIN
5.2 mi/3.0 hrs

northeast of Kettle Falls in Colville National Forest

Map 4.2, page 206

One of the few trails in this region not connecting to Kettle Crest Trail, US Mountain Trail instead undertakes a summit of the 6,200-foot peak. As can be expected, the summit opens to reveal meadows and spectacular views. Most notable is that from this vantage it is possible to see much of the Kettle River Range. US Mountain is set off to the east side of the divide, thus making the northern half of the mountains well discernable. US Mountain Trail makes a steady ascent on the mountain but is not terribly steep. The forest can be pretty thick in places, but parts of the trail are covered in swaths of meadows (and flowers during the early summer). Although the trail continues down into the South Fork Boulder Creek Valley, hikers are well advised to turn back after reaching the top of US Mountain. This is a hot and dry trail, so extra water is an important consideration.

User Groups: Hikers, leashed dogs, horses, mountain bikes, and motorcycles. No wheelchair access.

Open Seasons: This trail is accessible May–October.

Permits: Permits are not required. Parking and access are free.

Maps: For a map of Colville National Forest, contact the Outdoor Recreation Information Center at the downtown Seattle REI. For a topographic map, ask the USGS for Copper Butte.

Directions: From Kettle Falls, drive west approximately 22 miles on Highway 20 to Albian Hill Road. Turn right (north) and drive 7.3 miles to a difficult-to-find trailhead on the right (east) side of the road.

Contact: Colville National Forest, Kettle Falls Ranger Station, 255 West 11th Avenue, Kettle Falls, WA 99141, 509/738-7700.

20 OLD STAGE ROAD
3.2–10.6 mi/1.5–6.0 hrs

northeast of Republic in Colville National Forest

Map 4.2, page 206

As far as unique histories go, Old Stage Road Trail takes the cake. This is the last remaining section of the first Washington State Highway. Well, highway is hardly the proper word. How about calling it a bumpy, dusty, rocky route over the mountains? Today it's not so bad, thanks to lots of volunteer work from Inland Empire Chapter of Backcountry Horsemen of Washington. The trail is popular with folk on horseback but is perfectly suited for families on foot.

In 1892, the Washington Legislature commissioned a road to be built from Marblemount, west of the Cascades, to Marcus on the Columbia River. The old road came up from the west to the Kettle River Range and crossed it via this route. It lasted only about six years before a better route over Sherman Pass was recognized and built. Much of the hike is forested as the trail gently climbs to Kettle Crest Trail. The trail stretches up to the crest (1.6 miles), a good turnaround point for shorter excursions, before dropping down through forest. Hikers today will find a trail much more suited for boots than wagon wheels, but it is amazing to see what folks once went through just to get across the state.

User Groups: Hikers, leashed dogs, horses, and mountain bikes. No wheelchair access.

Open Seasons: This trail is accessible mid-May–October.

Permits: Permits are not required. Parking and access are free.

Maps: For a map of Colville National Forest, contact the Outdoor Recreation Information Center at the downtown Seattle REI. For a topographic map, ask the USGS for Copper Butte.

Directions: From Kettle Falls, drive 25 miles west on Highway 20 to Albian Hill Road (Forest Service Road 2030). Turn right (north) and drive 7.1 miles to Forest Service Road 2030-

380. The signed trailhead lies a few hundred yards up Forest Service Road 2030-380.

Contact: Colville National Forest, Republic Ranger Station, 180 North Jefferson, Republic, WA 99166, 509/775-7400.

21 MARCUS
7.0 mi/3.5 hrs

northeast of Republic in Colville National Forest

Map 4.2, page 206

To say the least, Marcus Trail provides an easy and extremely beautiful access to Kettle Crest Trail. What should really be known about the trail is that leads to the foot of Copper Butte, the tallest point in the Kettle River Range. Parts of Copper Butte were burned by a 1996 fire. Marcus makes a steady ascent to Kettle Crest Trail. After two miles of old, open forest, the trail breaks out into open meadows, aflame in wildflower color during the early summer. The trail traverses a south-facing slope, making it accessible a little earlier than others in the area, but hot and dry, without water. Once you reach Kettle Crest Trail, don't miss the highlight of the trip, a summit of Copper Butte. At 7,135 feet, the peak soaks up the views of numerous distant mountain ranges within two countries and two states, with Glacier Peak to the west.

User Groups: Hikers, leashed dogs, horses, and mountain bikes. No wheelchair access.

Open Seasons: This trail is accessible May–October.

Permits: Permits are not required. Parking and access are free.

Maps: For a map of Colville National Forest, contact the Outdoor Recreation Information Center at the downtown Seattle REI. For topographic maps, ask the USGS for Cooke Mountain and Copper Butte.

Directions: From Republic, drive east on Highway 20 about 3 miles to Highway 21. Turn left (north) and drive 2.5 miles to County Road 284. Turn right and drive 2.5 miles until it turns into Forest Service Road 2152. Continue on Forest Service Road 2152 for 2.7 miles to Forest Service Road 2040. Turn left and drive 5.2 miles to Forest Service Road 250. Turn right and drive 1.5 miles to the signed trailhead. A primitive campsite is at the trailhead.

Contact: Colville National Forest, Republic Ranger Station, 180 North Jefferson, Republic, WA 99166, 509/775-7400.

22 SHERMAN
2.6 mi/1.5 hrs

east of Republic along SR20 in Colville National Forest

Map 4.2, page 206

Sherman Trail provides quick but difficult access to the northern section of Kettle Crest Trail. By itself, the trail is rather miserable. But Kettle Crest Trail is prime country for exploration, and it lends itself well to making longer trips possible. Sherman gains nearly 1,600 feet of elevation in a short 1.3 miles. Much of the route is within a thick, young forest. Although the views are eaten up by the surrounding thicket of trees, at least they provide shade on this normally hot and dry route. Not until you reach the end of the trail, along the crest of the range, does the forest break and the views come out. For hikers looking to continue along Kettle Crest Trail, Jungle Hill lies to the south (2 total miles) and Wapaloosie to the north (3.5 total miles).

User Groups: Hikers, leashed dogs, horses, and mountain bikes. No wheelchair access.

Open Seasons: This trail is accessible June–October.

Permits: Permits are not required. Parking and access are free.

Maps: For a map of Colville National Forest, contact the Outdoor Recreation Information Center at the downtown Seattle REI. For topographic maps, ask the USGS for Cooke Mountain and Copper Butte.

Directions: From Republic, drive east approximately 12 miles to Forest Service Road 2040. Turn left (north) and drive 2.5 miles to Forest Service Road 065. Turn right (east) and drive 2 miles to the signed trailhead.

Contact: Colville National Forest, Republic Ranger Station, 180 North Jefferson, Republic, WA 99166, 509/775-7400.

23 WAPALOOSIE
5.5 mi/3.0 hrs

northwest of Kettle Falls in Colville National Forest

Map 4.2, page 206

More than a worthy candidate for a tongue-twister contest, Wapaloosie is an excellent scenic route to North Kettle Crest Trail. The summit of Wapaloosie itself is a grand adventure, challenging for some hikers and just right for others. Wapaloosie Trail takes advantage of numerous switchbacks to make a slow but steady ascent on the mountain. The trail gains roughly 2,000 feet of elevation in a short 2.75 miles, not an effort to snicker at. After 1.5 miles, the trail breaks out into open slopes covered in grasses and wildflowers. Deer and elk are likely to be seen in the early mornings or late evenings. Hawks are regularly soaring above, keeping an eye on all below. Wapaloosie Trail reaches Kettle Crest Trail just below Wapaloosie Mountain. A short side trail leads to the summit, offering panoramic views of the surrounding countryside. This is a great way to get in some views and exercise at the same time.

User Groups: Hikers, leashed dogs, horses, and mountain bikes. No wheelchair access.

Open Seasons: This trail is accessible June–October.

Permits: Permits are not required. Parking and access are free.

Maps: For a map of Colville National Forest, contact the Outdoor Recreation Information Center at the downtown Seattle REI. For a topographic map, ask the USGS for Copper Butte.

Directions: From Kettle Falls, drive west approximately 22 miles on Highway 20 to Albian Hill Road. Turn right (north) and drive 3.2 miles to the signed trailhead.

Contact: Colville National Forest, Kettle Falls Ranger Station, 255 West 11th Avenue, Kettle Falls, WA 99141, 509/738-7700.

24 COLUMBIA MOUNTAIN
7.1 mi/3.5 hrs

east of Republic along SR20 in Colville National Forest

Map 4.2, page 206

Columbia Mountain offers the most easily accessible and most encompassing viewpoint within the Kettle River Range. Directly off Highway 20, Columbia Mountain Trail cuts off from Kettle Crest Trail to create a loop encircling the 6,700-foot butte. Within the loop is a side trail leading to an abandoned lookout and the summit of Columbia Mountain. This is one of the best vantages in the Kettle River Range, with long views of the divide to the north and south. The devastation of the 1988 White Mountain fire is readily apparent, with much of the southern mountain range nothing but miles of dead snags.

The route follows Kettle Crest Trail two miles through forest and eventually open meadows. On clear days, the North Cascades are well visible to the west. At Columbia Spring, a sea-

View from Columbia Mountain (in Kettle Range), looking north

sonal source of water, Columbia Mountain Trail cuts right and backtracks up the slopes. The trail diverges after .5 mile to create a loop around the mountain, much like a lasso. On the north side of the loop you'll find the trail up to the peak. Mountains appear across the distant horizons, with snow-capped peaks in Canada and Idaho joining in. Outside of the North Cascades, nowhere else along Highway 20 will you find a better hike.

User Groups: Hikers, leashed dogs, horses, and mountain bikes. No wheelchair access.

Open Seasons: This trail is accessible June–October.

Permits: Permits are not required. Parking and access are free.

Maps: For a map of Colville National Forest, contact the Outdoor Recreation Information Center at the downtown Seattle REI. For a topographic map, ask the USGS for Sherman Peak.

Directions: From Republic, drive 17 miles east on Highway 20 to Sherman Pass. On the east side of the pass, turn left (north) into the signed trailhead.

Contact: Colville National Forest, Republic Ranger Station, 180 North Jefferson, Republic, WA 99166, 509/775-7400.

25 KETTLE CREST NORTH
30.3 mi one-way/3 days

northeast of Republic in Colville National Forest

Map 4.2, page 206

This is a long, rugged, and popular route through the high country of the Kettle River Range. Stretching 30 miles from Sherman Pass all the way to Deer Creek Summit, North Kettle Crest Trail starts high and stays that way. The trail climbs or skirts the base of numerous mountains and buttes, including Columbia (2 miles from Sherman Pass), Wapaloosie (7 miles), Copper (13 miles), Ryan Hill (20 miles), Profanity (22 miles), and Sentinel (28 miles). Each peak along the way can be scrambled to the top to reveal expansive views in all directions. Much of the route is swathed in open meadows of grass and wildflowers. June is usually a great month to get some color on the trail.

Although parts of Kettle Crest North Trail are relatively well traveled, much of the trail has few visitors most of the year (hunting season in the fall brings increased use). That means animals are aplenty in these parts, with deer, elk, and moose spotted along the trail regularly. Signs of bear and cougar are frequently seen along the trail; these big predators scratch trees to mark their territory, leaving behind stripped bark and exposed trunk. Campsites are scattered throughout the length of the trail. Water is a less dependable commodity. There are some springs and streams along the route, but by late summer they are not reliable; rationing of water is smart planning. The best bet is to set up a through-hike with a car at each end. Many access trails lead to the Kettle Crest, so many options exist for a customized hike. For a decent backpacking experience, there's no better trail in this area.

User Groups: Hikers, leashed dogs, horses, and mountain bikes. No wheelchair access.

Open Seasons: This trail is accessible June–October.

Permits: Permits are not required. Parking and access are free.

Maps: For a map of Colville National Forest, contact the Outdoor Recreation Information Center at the downtown Seattle REI. For topographic maps, ask the USGS for Sherman Peak, Copper Butte, and Mount Leona.

Directions: South access: From Republic, drive 17 miles east on Highway 20 to Sherman Pass. On the east side of the pass, turn left (north) into the signed trailhead.

North access: From Republic, drive north approximately 20 miles to the town of Curlew. Turn east on County Road 602 and drive 12 miles to Deer Creek Summit Trailhead.

Contact: Colville National Forest, Republic Ranger Station, 180 North Jefferson, Republic, WA 99166, 509/775-7400.

26 KETTLE CREST SOUTH
13.3 mi one-way/8.0 hrs

east of Republic along Highway 20 in Colville National Forest

Map 4.2, page 206

The southern leg of Kettle Crest Trail is highly memorable for two reasons. Most of this high route is along the crest of the Kettle River Range and thus offers expansive views of the surrounding country, from the North Cascade Mountains in the west to the Columbia River Valley to the east. Even more remarkable is the charred forest that covers much of the route. In 1988, eight lightning strikes created six fires. Because of extremely dry conditions, the fires merged to create the White Mountain Complex. The fire eventually burned more than 20,000 acres of forest, leaving behind miles of dead trees, known as snags. The fire burned along much of Kettle Crest Trail but did leave pockets of older forest. Where the fire burned, it burned hot and left little. As nature tends to do, the area is quickly recovering. Small pines and lush ground cover are filling in the area, well on the way to creating a forest of their own.

Kettle Crest South Trail truly follows the crest of this large range for much of its length. From Sherman Pass, it climbs around Sherman Peak and Snow Peak, each of which is tall and reached via side trails. Bald Mountain, Barnaby Buttes, and White Mountain are other peaks easily bagged along the way. It's best done as a through-hike, with a second car positioned at White Mountain Trailhead. Water can be obtained via several springs and streams scattered along the route. Campsites are strewn frequently along the route.

User Groups: Hikers, leashed dogs, horses, and mountain bikes. No wheelchair access.

Open Seasons: This trail is accessible June–October.

Permits: Permits are not required. Parking and access are free.

Maps: For a map of Colville National Forest, contact the Outdoor Recreation Information Center at the downtown Seattle REI.

For a topographic map, ask the USGS for Sherman Peak.

Directions: North access: From Republic, drive 17 miles east on Highway 20 to Sherman Pass. On the east side of the pass, turn left (north) into the signed trailhead.

South access: From Republic, drive 20 miles east on Highway 20 to Forest Service Road 2020 (about three miles beyond Sherman Pass). Turn right (south) and drive 5 miles to Forest Service Road 2014. Turn right and drive 4 miles to Forest Service Road 2020-250. Turn right and drive 3.5 miles to White Mountain Trailhead.

Contact: Colville National Forest, Kettle Falls Ranger Station, 255 West 11th Avenue, Kettle Falls, WA 99141, 509/738-7700.

27 EDDS MOUNTAIN
8.4 mi/4.0 hrs
southeast of Republic in Colville National Forest

Map 4.2, page 206

Edds Mountain Trail offers the most scenic route to South Kettle Crest Trail. The route passes below Edds Mountain and Bald Mountain, a pair of 6,800-foot peaks, each of which is an easy scramble to broad views. The North Cascades line the western horizon over Sanpoil Valley, while the Kettle River Range fills the east. Parts of the route are in forest, other parts are in open meadows. June is a great time to see wildflowers covering these south-facing slopes. The trail offers a great firsthand look at the White Mountain Complex fire of 1988, passing through several sections of charred forest that is once again teeming with plant life. Although the trail gains just 1,000 feet over four miles, parts of the path are steep and rocky. Extra water is a must on this hot and dry trail.

User Groups: Hikers, leashed dogs, horses, and mountain bikes. No wheelchair access.

Open Seasons: This trail is accessible June–October.

Permits: Permits are not required. Parking and access are free.

Maps: For a map of Colville National Forest, contact the Outdoor Recreation Information Center at the downtown Seattle REI. For a topographic map, ask the USGS for Edds Mountain.

Directions: From Republic, drive east 7 miles on Highway 20 to Hall Creek Road (County Road 99, which turns into Forest Service Road 2054). Turn right (south) and drive 4 miles to Forest Service Road 300. Turn left and drive 1.5 miles to road's end and the trailhead.

Contact: Colville National Forest, Republic Ranger Station, 180 North Jefferson, Republic, WA 99166, 509/775-7400.

28 BARNABY BUTTE
14.0 mi/8.0 hrs
southeast of Republic in Colville National Forest

Map 4.2, page 206

Barnaby Butte Trail offers a lot more than just a summit of the two rounded peaks. For starters, it offers a good workout. The trail climbs more than 3,000 feet over the course of seven miles, a decent day's work for anyone. Barnaby Butte Trail passes through a wide variety of ecosystems, most notably recently burned areas of forests. These patches were engulfed by the White Mountain Fire of 1988 and are now home to stands of small young pines. Animals are never far from this seldom-used route. These open areas make for great wildlife habitat, providing open space for deer to graze and countless snags from which hawks conduct their hunt. And, of course, the trail makes a grand summit of Barnaby Buttes, the site of a former lookout. The view of the southern Kettle River Range is great, and the bird's-eye view of the fire's impact is incredible. It's important to carry extra water and sunscreen on this trail because of its long and exposed (hot) nature. Water will likely not be available along the way.

User Groups: Hikers, leashed dogs, horses, and mountain bikes. No wheelchair access.

Open Seasons: This trail is accessible June–October.

Permits: Permits are not required. Parking and access are free.

Maps: For a map of Colville National Forest, contact the Outdoor Recreation Information Center at the downtown Seattle REI. For a topographic map, ask the USGS for Sherman Peak.

Directions: From Republic, drive east 7 miles on Highway 20 to Hall Creek Road (County Road 99, which turns into Forest Service Road 2054). Turn right (south) and drive 5.5 miles to Forest Service Road 600. Turn left onto Forest Service Road 600 and drive 7 miles to the signed trailhead on the left (east) side of the road. The first two miles of trail is old Road 680.

Contact: Colville National Forest, Republic Ranger Station, 180 North Jefferson, Republic, WA 99166, 509/775-7400.

29 HOODOO CANYON
4.5 mi/2.5 hrs

west of Kettle Falls in Colville
National Forest

Map 4.2, page 206

Hoodoo Canyon provides one of the best day hikes in northeastern Washington. Departing from a great campground on a well-stocked fishing lake, Hoodoo Canyon Trail climbs the wall of a narrow canyon to a viewpoint. The way is steep and rough at times, but always well worth the effort. And it can all be done in a morning or afternoon hike, with enough time to make s'mores at Trout Lake under the stars.

Hoodoo Canyon Trail departs Trout Lake Campground and quickly switchbacks up the canyon wall. It then traverses the length of the canyon with Trout and Emerald Lakes reflecting from far below. The forest mingles with open slopes along the way, making the hike especially scenic. The trail can be rocky and narrow at points; be careful. The trail climbs to a bluff overlooking the glacially carved canyon. To the north are the eastern peaks of the Kettle River Range. The trail continues two miles down to Deadman Creek and a northern trail-

head. The much better option is to return to Trout Lake and catch yourself some dinner.

User Groups: Hikers and leashed dogs. No horses or mountain bikes are allowed. No wheelchair access.

Open Seasons: This trail is accessible April–November.

Permits: Permits are not required. Parking and access are free.

Maps: For a map of Colville National Forest, contact the Outdoor Recreation Information Center at the downtown Seattle REI. For topographic maps, ask the USGS for Bangs Mountain, Boyds, and Jackknife Mountain.

Directions: From Kettle Falls, drive west 8 miles on Highway 20 to Trout Lake Road (Forest Service Road 020). Turn right (north) and drive 5 miles to Trout Lake Campground. The trailhead is within the campground.

Contact: Colville National Forest, Kettle Falls Ranger Station, 255 West 11th Avenue, Kettle Falls, WA 99141, 509/738-7700.

30 GILLETTE RIDGE
12.5 mi/6.0 hrs

north of Colville in Colville National Forest

Map 4.3, page 207

Gillette Ridge provides something of a rarity in the state: an easy-to-access and easy-to-complete ridge run. Starting at 4,700 feet, Gillette Ridge Trail traverses the crest of the ridge and tops out on the north section at 5,775 feet. Although there are a few saddles in which to lose hard-earned elevation, don't fret and instead munch on some huckleberries. The trail makes a good tour of the ridge, with plenty of views along the way. Various mountains appear from near and far on the horizons, but far more scenic is the valley below. It's hard to miss the distinctive U shape of the valley, sculpted roughly 12,000 years ago by glaciers. Even more impressive is that the glaciers that ground out Deep Creek Valley also smoothed out the ridge you're on. Back in 10,000 B.C., you'd be under hundreds of feet of ice. That's a refreshing thought on hot summer days, which is most of them up here. Water isn't to be found along the route, so bring plenty to drink with the huckleberries you'll harvest.

User Groups: Hikers, leashed dogs, horses, and mountain bikes. No wheelchair access.

Open Seasons: This trail is accessible mid-May–October.

Permits: Permits are not required. Parking and access are free.

Maps: For a map of Colville National Forest, contact the Outdoor Recreation Information Center at the downtown Seattle REI. For topographic maps, ask the USGS for Aladdin and Gillette Mountain.

Directions: From Colville, drive north approximately 14.5 miles on Alladin Road (County Road 9435) to Forest Service Road 500. Turn left (west) and drive 6 miles to the trailhead on the left side of the road.

Contact: Colville National Forest, Colville Ranger Station, 755 South Main, Colville, WA 99114, 509/684-7000.

31 ABERCROMBIE MOUNTAIN
6.5 mi/3.5 hrs

north of Colville in Colville National Forest

Map 4.3, page 207

From the high vantage point afforded by Abercrombie Mountain, one can seemingly peer into forever. At 7,308 feet, the peak is one of the tallest in eastern Washington. On clear days, visitors can literally look out over hundreds of square miles, well into Canada and Idaho. Just five miles from the Canadian border, the peak towers above the surrounding country. Trails scale Abercrombie from the east and west, but the road to the west trailhead is more accessible. Abercrombie Trail cuts steep switchbacks up the hillside, passing through a variety of environments, from forests of lodgepole pine to clear-cuts to forests long ago ravaged by fire. The remains of an old fire lookout lie strewn about the summit, remnants of a once-awesome place to wake up and go to work. Bring plen-

ty of water, as this is hot and dry country with no refreshment along the way.

User Groups: Hikers, leashed dogs, and horses. No mountain bikes are allowed. No wheelchair access.

Open Seasons: This trail is accessible June–October.

Permits: Permits are not required. Parking and access are free.

Maps: For a map of Colville National Forest, contact the Outdoor Recreation Information Center at the downtown Seattle REI. For topographic maps, ask the USGS for Leadpoint and Abercrombie Mountain.

Directions: From Colville, drive north 25 miles on Alladin Road (County Road 9435) to Deep Creek Road (County Road 9445). Turn right and drive 7 miles to County Road 4720. Turn right and drive 2 miles to Forest Service Road 070. Drive 3.5 miles to road's end and the signed trailhead.

Contact: Colville National Forest, Colville Ranger Station, 755 South Main, Colville, WA 99114, 509/684-7000.

32 SHERLOCK PEAK
2.5 mi/2.0 hrs

north of Colville in Colville National Forest

Map 4.3, page 207

Abercrombie's little brother to the south, Sherlock Peak, is on par when it comes to bragging rights. While not as tall as Abercrombie Mountain, Sherlock Peak delivers a better journey to the final destination. The route starts high, resulting in a less strenuous hike. A seasonal cold-water spring is found along the route, providing a refresher early in the summer. And best of all, much of the route is in open forest and meadows. That may make the hike hotter, but it makes it more scenic, too. Just munch on some of the huckleberries found along the trail to make up for any sunburn. From the top of Sherlock, gaze east to the Selkirk Range running into Idaho and Canada or west to the Columbia River Valley.

User Groups: Hikers, leashed dogs, and horses. No mountain bikes are allowed. No wheelchair access.

Open Seasons: This trail is accessible June–October.

Permits: Permits are not required. Parking and access are free.

Maps: For a map of Colville National Forest, contact the Outdoor Recreation Information Center at the downtown Seattle REI. For topographic maps, ask the USGS for Leadpoint and Deep Lake.

Directions: From Colville, drive north 25 miles on Alladin Road (County Road 9435) to Deep Creek Road (County Road 9445). Turn right and drive 7 miles to County Road 4720. Turn right and drive 2 miles to Forest Service Road 070. Turn right and drive .5 mile to Forest Service Road 075, a rough dirt road. Drive 4 miles to road's end and the trailhead.

Contact: Colville National Forest, Colville Ranger Station, 755 South Main, Colville, WA 99114, 509/684-7000.

33 TIGER/COYOTE ROCK LOOPS
1.8–4.8 mi/1.0–2.5 hrs

west of Ione in Colville National Forest

Map 4.3, page 207

This pair of nice and easy loops makes for an excellent break from a long drive across Highway 20. With little elevation gain, Tiger and Coyote Rock Loops can be tackled by hikers of all abilities, particularly little ones. The two loops are situated in a small basin filled with wildlife. Beavers swim in Frater Lake while deer, elk, and moose often feed in the open meadows. Tiger Loop is the smaller of the two (1.8 miles) and takes only an hour to complete. It follows the shore of Frater Lake before journeying over to the waving grasses of Tiger Meadows. The trail junctions with Coyote Loop; turn left to return to the trailhead. Coyote Loop is just under five miles long, a more moderate distance for a full morning or afternoon. The

trail passes through stands of Douglas fir and lodgepole pine to reach several viewpoints of the surrounding valley, at Coyote Rock and Shelter Rock. Be sure to bring water with you, as it won't be found along the way.

User Groups: Hikers, leashed dogs, mountain bikes, and motorcycles. No horses are allowed. No wheelchair access.

Open Seasons: This area is accessible April–November.

Permits: Permits are not required. Parking and access are free.

Maps: For a map of Colville National Forest, contact the Outdoor Recreation Information Center at the downtown Seattle REI. For a topographic map, ask the USGS for Ione.

Directions: From Ione, drive south on Highway 31 to the junction with Highway 20. Turn right (west) and drive approximately 15 miles to the well-signed trailhead on the right (north) side of the highway.

Contact: Colville National Forest, Colville Ranger Station, 755 South Main, Colville, WA 99114, 509/684-7000.

34 HALLIDAY/NORTH FORK
19.0 mi/2 days

east of Metaline Falls in the Salmo-Priest Wilderness of Colville National Forest

Map 4.3, page 207

This pair of trails combines to make a well-used route up to Crowell Ridge, in the northern arm of the Salmo-Priest Wilderness. Unfortunately, this promising route into the high country is actually a bit of a disappointment. For such a long trip, little water is to be found along the way. Much of the route is in the deep forest, revealing little of the surrounding mountains or valleys. And there's a big drop in the middle, resulting in a dreaded loss of hard-earned elevation. However, the trail offers an excellent opportunity to come across a large sampling of wildlife. Most folks have seen deer or grouse when out hiking. But how about moose or caribou? Or the symbol of wilderness, grizzly bears? You're likely to find them here.

The first trail is Halliday, which starts from Slate Creek and soon passes a marsh and ponds, a likely place to find moose feeding. Halliday then climbs the shoulder of Crowell Mountain before dropping sharply to North Fork Sullivan Trail. This trail doesn't get near the refreshing creek, which is rather annoying on hot days. Desperate hikers will have to bushwhack through underbrush for a cooldown. North Fork Trail climbs steeply in its last two miles to reach Crowell Ridge and spectacular payoff views. Inconveniently, the only campsite is a few miles below Crowell Ridge, a long and tiring day. With so much working against it, one might question why this backcountry route gets any use. Hunters love it.

User Groups: Hikers, leashed dogs, and horses. No mountain bikes are allowed. No wheelchair access.

Open Seasons: This trail is accessible May–October.

Permits: Permits are not required. Parking and access are free.

Maps: For a map of Colville National Forest, contact the Outdoor Recreation Information Center at the downtown Seattle REI. For topographic maps, ask the USGS for Boundary Dam and Gypsy Peak.

Directions: From Metaline Falls, drive north 6.5 miles on Highway 31 to Forest Service Road 180. Turn right and the trailhead is 200 yards down a dirt road, on the left of the large clearing.

Contact: Colville National Forest, Sullivan Lake Ranger Station, 12641 Sullivan Lake Road, Metaline Falls, WA 99153, 509/446-7500.

35 SLATE CREEK
8.6 mi/4.5 hrs

east of Metaline Falls in Colville National Forest

Map 4.3, page 207

Slate Creek is one of the more difficult trails in the Sullivan Lake area. After crossing its namesake, Slate Creek Trail climbs steeply through the forest to a small depression with-

in a small ridge. From there, lace your boots tightly for a quick descent into Uncas Gulch, only to climb right out of it again. It's a significant up and down of about 500 feet and is likely to leave you a bit spent for the extra effort. Plenty of good things will more than make up for your effort. Hikers who wallk quietly are likely to encounter wildlife, whether it be as small as a rabbit or grouse, or as large as an elk, caribou, or grizzly bear. The trail is mostly used only during the fall hunting seasons, so the animals are unlikely to be expecting you. A campsite and the trail's only water are at Uncas Gulch Creek. The trail ends after 4.3 miles at a junction with North Fork Sullivan Trail, where the forest finally opens to reveal the surrounding mountains.

User Groups: Hikers, leashed dogs, and horses. No mountain bikes are allowed. No wheelchair access.

Open Seasons: This trail is accessible June–October.

Permits: Permits are not required. Parking and access are free.

Maps: For a map of Colville National Forest, contact the Outdoor Recreation Information Center at the downtown Seattle REI. For a topographic map, ask the USGS for Gypsy Peak.

Directions: From Metaline Falls, drive north on Highway 31 for 9 miles to Forest Service Road 3155. Turn right and drive 5.5 miles to the trailhead on the right side of the road.

Contact: Colville National Forest, Sullivan Lake Ranger Station, 12641 Sullivan Lake Road, Metaline Falls, WA 99153, 509/446-7500.

36 SALMO LOOP
17.8 mi/2–3 days

east of Metaline Falls in the Salmo-Priest Wilderness of Colville National Forest

Map 4.3, page 207

Backcountry trekkers, this is the hike for you. Salmo Loop explores the old-growth forests of Salmo River while also climbing to the peak of Snowy Top, a 7,500-foot peak that's actually in Idaho. The route feels as if it's some of the deepest wilderness in the country for a reason: It is. The symbol of wilderness in North America, the grizzly bear, still lives here. Not to mention herds of deer, elk, caribou, and moose. The trail encounters old-growth western hemlock and western red cedar within the Salmo Basin but passes through sublime alpine meadows near the peak of Little Snowy Top. This is one trail that certainly makes the long drive out to this little-known corner of the state worthwhile.

Salmo Basin Trail drops from Salmo Divide Trailhead steeply to South Salmo River (3.1 miles). The bridge may or may not be passable when you get there, so be sure to consider carefully before fording this river during times of high snow runoff. The trail then follows the South Salmo River up to the ridgeline between Snowy Top and Little Snowy Top (8.8 miles). It may be out of the way to hike the side trail up to Snowy Top, but it's the perfect spot for a long break. Possession of a camera is recommended here. The route then follows Shedroof Divide Trail back down to Salmo Divide Trail (14.8 miles), three miles from the car.

Campsites are scattered liberally throughout the trip, most notably along the South Salmo River. A pair are also up on the Shedroof Divide. Water is plentiful in the Salmo Basin, but may be tricky if not impossible to secure once you're on the ridge. Be sure to top off your water before leaving the river. Other than that, be prepared for an amazing trip.
User Groups: Hikers, leashed dogs, and horses. No mountain bikes are allowed. No wheelchair access.
Open Seasons: This trail is accessible mid-June–October.
Permits: Permits are not required. Parking and access are free.
Maps: For a map of Colville National Forest, contact the Outdoor Recreation Information Center at the downtown Seattle REI. For topographic maps, ask the USGS for Salmo Mountain and Continental Mountain (Idaho).
Directions: From Metaline Falls, drive north

2 miles on Highway 31. Turn right onto County Road 9345 and drive 5 miles to Forest Service Road 22. Turn left and drive 20 miles (the road becomes Forest Service Road 2220 at 6.5 miles) to the road's end and the trailhead.
Contact: Colville National Forest, Sullivan Lake Ranger Station, 12641 Sullivan Lake Road, Metaline Falls, WA 99153, 509/446-7500.

37 SHEDROOF DIVIDE
18.7 mi one-way/2 days
east of Metaline Falls in the Salmo-Priest Wilderness of Colville National Forest
Map 4.3, page 207

Cutting through the heart of Salmo-Priest Wilderness, Shedroof Divide Trail revels in open meadows and expansive views of the surrounding Selkirk Mountains. This high route along the crest of a long ridge is hard to equal in its beauty, making for a backpacker's dream. Big game abounds in this high country, with scores of deer, elk, and even caribou roaming the hillsides. Hikers may encounter a bear (both black bears and grizzly bears live here) or a more elusive cougar. Don't worry, these big predators prefer to mind their own business; just remember to look big if you come across one.

Shedroof Divide Trail is accessible via several trails and trailheads, including Shedroof Mountain (the northern trailhead), Pass Creek Pass (southern trailhead), Thunder Creek Trail, and Shedroof Cutoff Trail. A through-hike is recommended to take in all of the route, but bringing two cars to this remote part of Washington can prove problematic. Single-car hikers are best advised to start at the northern trailhead and hike in from there as time allows. Shedroof Divide Trail follows the crest, passing below a number of peaks, including Shedroof, Thunder, and Round Top Mountains. Side trails to their peaks are a must-do diversion. Much of the route is awash in open meadows and grand views deep into Idaho and Canada. Water may be difficult to find along the trail, but there are a couple of seasonal cold-water springs for help. Camps are dispersed along the route, with good, established sites just north of Round Top and just south of Thunder Mountain. Shedroof Divide Trail is the way best way to experience the vastness of the Selkirk Mountains.

User Groups: Hikers, leashed dogs, and horses. No mountain bikes are allowed. No wheelchair access.

Open Seasons: This trail is accessible mid-June–October.

Permits: Permits are not required. Parking and access are free.

Maps: For a map of Colville National Forest, contact the Outdoor Recreation Information Center at the downtown Seattle REI. For topographic maps, ask the USGS for Salmo Mountain, Helmer Mountain, and Pass Creek.

Directions: North access: From Metaline Falls, drive north 2 miles on Highway 31. Turn right onto County Road 9345 and drive 5 miles to Forest Service Road 22. Turn left and drive 20.5 miles to the end of the road and the signed trailhead.

South access: From Metaline Falls, drive north 2 miles on Highway 31. Turn right onto County Road 9345 and drive 5 miles to Forest Service Road 22. Turn left and drive 6.5 miles to a signed junction. Stay to the right on Forest Service Road 22 and drive 7.5 miles to Pass Creek Pass and the signed trailhead.

Contact: Colville National Forest, Sullivan Lake Ranger Station, 12641 Sullivan Lake Road, Metaline Falls, WA 99153, 509/446-7500.

38 CROWELL RIDGE
12.0 mi/8.0 hrs

east of Metaline Falls in the Salmo-Priest Wilderness of Colville National Forest

Map 4.3, page 207

Visitors to Crowell Ridge will think they have accidentally hiked into the North Cascades. Glacial basins and snowy peaks greet hikers as they traverse this high ridge in the northern arm of Salmo-Priest Wilderness. Undisturbed forests of subalpine fir and Englemann spruce give way to big meadows and bigger vistas. Ex-

pect to see a large assortment of wildlife, from bald eagles patrolling the skies for a meal to deer, elk, and bighorn sheep grazing along the steep hillsides.

Crowell Ridge Trail leaves Bear Pasture Trailhead and immediately climbs to Crowell Ridge. The trees quickly disappear from the rocky ridge and open meadows. At more than 7,300 feet, Gypsy Peak stands as a beacon from the north with a large glacial basin and lakes at the bottom of steep slopes. If you're interested in seeing wildflowers, try late June and early July, when the winter's snowpack has finally melted out. The trail heads south and makes a junction with North Fork Sullivan Trail at 3.7 miles. Here is the trail's only campsite, a grand place to set up camp. Crowell Ridge Trail continues 4.1 miles through open meadow over to Sullivan Mountain Trailhead, the trail's end. If you had only one day to spend in the Sullivan Lake area, this would be the trail to hike.

User Groups: Hikers, leashed dogs, and horses. No mountain bikes are allowed. No wheelchair access.

Open Seasons: This trail is accessible mid-June–October.

Permits: Permits are not required. Parking and access are free.

Maps: For a map of Colville National Forest, contact the Outdoor Recreation Information Center at the downtown Seattle REI. For a topographic map, ask the USGS for Gypsy Peak.

Directions: From Metaline Falls, drive north 2 miles on Highway 31. Turn right onto County Road 9345 and drive 5 miles to Forest Service Road 22. Turn left and drive 8 miles (the road becomes Forest Service Road 2220 at 6.5 miles) to Forest Service Road 2212. Turn left and drive 3 miles to Forest Service Road 200. Turn right and drive 6 miles to the road's end and Bear Pasture Trailhead.

Contact: Colville National Forest, Sullivan Lake Ranger Station, 12641 Sullivan Lake Road, Metaline Falls, WA 99153, 509/446-7500.

39 THUNDER CREEK
10.2 mi/5.0 hrs

east of Metaline Falls in the Salmo-Priest Wilderness of Colville National Forest

Map 4.3, page 207

Less traveled than many other trails in the region, Thunder Creek Trail serves as an excellent way to step into the heart of Shedroof Divide. The first half of the trail follows an old road through the forest, passing many small streams and wet spots. After 2.2 miles, the road ends and the trail becomes a true footpath as it crosses into Salmo-Priest Wilderness. Old-growth western hemlock and western red cedar fill the forests, making prime habitat for a variety of big game animals. Deer, elk, bear, and even caribou are found in these forests. Thunder Creek Trail finds Shedroof Divide Trail after 5.1 miles, complete with open meadows and encouraging views. From here, hikers can head north or south along the backbone of Salmo-Priest Wilderness. Although the trail can often be wet, suitable drinking water may be difficult to find. Folks looking to make a night out of it will want to pitch their tents up on the divide in previously used spots.

User Groups: Hikers, leashed dogs, and horses. No mountain bikes are allowed. No wheelchair access.

Open Seasons: This trail is accessible mid-June–October.

Permits: Permits are not required. Parking and access are free.

Maps: For a map of Colville National Forest, contact the Outdoor Recreation Information Center at the downtown Seattle REI. For topographic maps, ask the USGS for Salmo Mountain and Helmer Mountain.

Directions: From Metaline Falls, drive north 2 miles on Highway 31. Turn right onto County Road 9345 and drive 5 miles to Forest Service Road 22. Turn left and drive 13 miles (the road becomes Forest Service Road 2220 at 6.5 miles) to Gypsy Meadows. The signed trailhead is on the right side of Forest Service Road 2220.

Contact: Colville National Forest, Sullivan Lake Ranger Station, 12641 Sullivan Lake Road, Metaline Falls, WA 99153, 509/446-7500.

40 SULLIVAN LAKESHORE
8.4 mi/4.0 hrs

east of Metaline Falls in Colville National Forest

Map 4.3, page 207

Situated between two national forest campgrounds, Sullivan Lakeshore Trail is a great hike for families. Four miles of level hiking along Sullivan Lake is highlighted by a great self-guided nature trail at one end. The trail runs between East Sullivan and Noisy Creek Campgrounds along the eastern shore of Sullivan Lake, making for two easily accessible trailheads. The better bet is to start from East Sullivan, where a short .5-mile nature loop cuts off the main trail into the heart of the forest. Hikers can pick up a brochure to follow as they hike, learning about different processes of the forest ecosystem. This short trail is ideal for little ones.

Sullivan Lakeshore Trail runs along the edge of Sullivan Lake, passing in and out of a mixed forest of hardwoods and conifers. The trail frequently breaks out to views of the lake and Sand Creek Mountain to the west. Often, hikers will turn around and peer up from the foot of Hall Mountain to see mountain goats scaling the rocky cliffs. Hikers young and old will appreciate this lakeside trail.

User Groups: Hikers and leashed dogs. No horses or mountain bikes are allowed. The nature trail is wheelchair accessible.

Open Seasons: This trail is accessible year-round.

Permits: Permits are not required. Parking and access are free.

Maps: For a map of Colville National Forest, contact the Outdoor Recreation Information Center at the downtown Seattle REI. For a topographic map, ask the USGS for Metaline Falls.

Directions: From Metaline Falls, drive north

2 miles on Highway 31. Turn right onto County Road 9345 and drive 5 miles to Forest Service Road 22. Turn left and drive .5 mile to East Sullivan Campground. Turn right and drive .3 mile to the well-signed trailhead on the left.

Contact: Colville National Forest, Sullivan Lake Ranger Station, 12641 Sullivan Lake Road, Metaline Falls, WA 99153, 509/446-7500.

41 HALL MOUNTAIN
5.0 mi/2.5 hrs

east of Metaline Falls in Colville National Forest

Map 4.3, page 207

Hall Mountain Trail is one of the best day hikes in the Sullivan Lake area. The trail up Hall Mountain is relatively short, never too steep for even younger hikers, and ends at an old lookout site, an obvious spot for views of the surrounding mountains. Hall Mountain Trail starts along an old road before arriving at a junction with Noisy Creek Trail (.7 mile). Take a right and keep climbing through the forest of subalpine fir and Englemann spruce. Big-game encounters are possible, with scores of deer, elk, and even caribou filling the woods during different seasons. More likely, you'll be startled by the sudden noise of a grouse taking off from under your feet. Hall Mountain Trail breaks out of the forest to find old remains of the Hall Mountain fire lookout. Sand Creek Mountain stands opposite the deep, blue water of Sullivan Lake, a tempting refresher for the end the day. Lucky hikers will peer down the steep slopes of Hall Mountain to find bighorn sheep scaling the hillside.

User Groups: Hikers, leashed dogs, horses, and mountain bikes. No wheelchair access.

Open Seasons: This trail is accessible June–October.

Permits: Permits are not required. Parking and access are free.

Maps: For a map of Colville National Forest, contact the Outdoor Recreation Information Center at the downtown Seattle REI. For topographic maps, ask the USGS for Metaline Falls and Pass Creek.

Directions: From Metaline Falls, drive north 2 miles on Highway 31. Turn right onto County Road 9345 and drive 5 miles to Forest Service Road 22. Turn left and drive 3.5 miles to Forest Service Road 500. Turn right and drive 7 miles to the road's end and the trailhead. This road is open only July 1–August 14, to minimize disturbances to wildlife habitat. Hall Mountain is accessible via Grassy Top or Noisy Creek during other times of the year.

Contact: Colville National Forest, Sullivan Lake Ranger Station, 12641 Sullivan Lake Road, Metaline Falls, WA 99153, 509/446-7500.

42 NOISY CREEK
10.6 mi/4.0 hrs

east of Metaline Falls in Colville National Forest

Map 4.3, page 207

In a region of high mountains, Noisy Creek Trail offers an easier hike perfectly suited for more laid-back hikers. The trail follows Noisy Creek, an appropriate name for the gushing stream during the spring snowmelt, for five miles through forests new and old. The first 1.3 miles climbs gently through the valley up to a vista of Sullivan Lake. This is a great turnaround for those seeking a shorter day hike, as it's about the only view you're going to find. More serious hikers will want to follow the trail farther up the creek valley as it makes its way through a forest of western hemlock, western red cedar, grand fir, and western larch, a hard-to-find species in Washington. Watch for camp robbers (not bandits, just gray jays) following you from the trailhead, hoping for a trail-mix handout. Woodpeckers pound away on dead snags while deer and elk frequently cross hikers' paths. Noisy Creek Trail crosses its namesake once (1.8 miles), a wet and even troublesome ford when the stream is running strongly. The trail makes a steep, mile-long climb out of the valley before ending at a junction with Hall Mountain Trail, at 5.3 miles.

User Groups: Hikers, leashed dogs, horses, and mountain bikes. No wheelchair access.

Open Seasons: This trail is accessible year-round.

Permits: Permits are not required. Parking and access are free.

Maps: For a map of Colville National Forest, contact the Outdoor Recreation Information Center at the downtown Seattle REI. For topographic maps, ask the USGS for Metaline Falls and Pass Creek.

Directions: From Metaline Falls, drive north 2 miles on Highway 31. Turn right onto County Road 9345 and drive 9.8 miles to Noisy Creek Campground. The well-signed trailhead is between the group and individual camp sections.

Contact: Colville National Forest, Sullivan Lake Ranger Station, 12641 Sullivan Lake Road, Metaline Falls, WA 99153, 509/446-7500.

43 PASS CREEK/GRASSY TOP
7.6 mi/4.0 hrs

east of Metaline Falls in Colville National Forest

Map 4.3, page 207

A mountain summit covered in grass means few trees. Few trees means expansive views of the surrounding mountains. One of the easier and more beautiful peaks to bag in the Sullivan Lake area is Grassy Top, a challenging but not overwhelming trail to the mountain's summit. All of this lies just outside of Salmo-Priest Wilderness but that is no harm to the appeal of this hike.

Grassy Top Trail begins at lofty Pass Creek Pass, a low point in the Shedroof Divide. The trail heads south along the ridge and steadily climbs toward Grassy Top. The forest of subalpine fir, Englemann spruce, and whitebark pine breaks open into expansive meadows of wildflowers (during the early summer) and waves of grass. These meadows are great places to catch deer grazing or bears scavenging. The trail passes just below Grassy Top, but a side trail leads to the summit. The surrounding Selkirk Range is in full splendor from this van-

tage, a delight on clear days. Remember to pack enough water, as it's nonexistent along the trail. Overnight hikers will need to find a place to camp off trail as there are no developed sites. We recommend atop Grassy Top.

User Groups: Hikers, leashed dogs, horses, and mountain bikes. No wheelchair access.

Open Seasons: This trail is accessible mid-June–October.

Permits: Permits are not required. Parking and access are free.

Maps: For a map of Colville National Forest, contact the Outdoor Recreation Information Center at the downtown Seattle REI. For a topographic map, ask the USGS for Pass Creek.

Directions: From Metaline Falls, drive north 2 miles on Highway 31. Turn right onto County Road 9345 and drive 5 miles to Forest Service Road 22. Turn left and drive 6.5 miles to a signed junction. Stay to the right on Forest Service Road 22 and drive 7.5 miles to Pass Creek Pass and the signed trailhead.

Contact: Colville National Forest, Sullivan Lake Ranger Station, 12641 Sullivan Lake Road, Metaline Falls, WA 99153, 509/446-7500.

44 LITTLE SPOKANE RIVER NATURAL AREA
7.5 mi/4.0 hrs

east of Spokane in Little Spokane River Natural Area

Map 4.4, page 208

Little Spokane River Natural Area provides a great escape from the city into an undisturbed wilderness. Contrasting greatly with the dry pine forests common to the Spokane area, the lowland bordering the river is rich in life. It's a prime spot to see animals normally viewed only on wildlife shows. The river ecosystem is fertile habitat for wildlife, including beaver, muskrat, porcupines, raccoons, coyotes, white-tailed deer, and even the occasional moose. The river also serves as important habitat for birds, including woodpeckers, bald eagles, red-tailed hawks, mergansers, and wood ducks. During the spring, this area serves as a rookery (nesting site) for great blue herons. The Little Spokane River is also a great place to cast a fishing line, and the trail offers access to many secluded fishing holes where rainbow and cutthroat trout lurk below the surface.

From the central Painted Rocks Trailhead, the main trail runs to the east and west along the river. An informative brochure is available at the trailhead, providing a natural-history lesson as one wanders the trails. There is no true destination along the trail; a hike of any length is certain to be great trip. Be sure to investigate rock outcroppings for ancient Indian pictographs; these paintings are found all along the trail. Hikers who lead a double life as river rats will be happy to know that the Little Spokane River is a favorite haunt for canoeists and kayakers.

User Groups: Hikers only. No dogs, horses, or mountain bikes are allowed. No wheelchair access.

Open Seasons: This trail is accessible year-round.

Permits: Permits are not required. Parking and access are free.

Maps: For topographic maps, ask the USGS for Dartford and Ninemile Falls.

Directions: From Spokane, drive north on Highway 291 to Rutter Parkway. Turn right (east) and drive to the trailhead, on the left just after you cross the river.

Contact: Riverside State Park, 9711 West Charles Street, Nine Mile Falls, WA 99026, 509/465-5537.

Chapter 5

© SCOTT LEONARD

Mount Rainier and
the Southern Cascades

Mount Rainier and the Southern Cascades

asily the Northwest's tallest point (by more than 2,000 feet),
Mount Rainier never seems to be far from view. At 14,411 feet,
the towering mass of The Mountain looms over life in Puget
Sound, southern Washington, and a good chunk of the east side as
well. Perhaps because Mount Rainier is such familiar sight, many of
the forests and mountains to her south go unnoticed. That's a shame,
for the South Cascades of Washington are home to some excellent adventures in waiting. This area not only contains the living outdoor laboratory that is Mount St. Helens, it also has the glaciers and meadows
of Mount Adams and Goat Rocks.

First and foremost on the agendas of most visitors to the region is
Mount Rainier, since it is, to say the least, the embodiment of hiking
in the Evergreen State. From old-growth forest to alpine meadows,
from icy glaciers to milky white rivers, Mount Rainier has it all. A
total of 26 glaciers grace the slopes of Takhoma (which, in Puyallup,
means "breast of the milk-white waters"). These glistening masses of
ice give birth to opalescent rivers flowing in every direction.

There are several points of access to one of the nation's most famous
and heavily visited national parks: Route 410 and 123 transect the eastern side of the park, accessing Sunrise (6,400 feet), where great day
hikes and longer trips exploring the north and east sides of Mount
Rainier begin. Along the south side of the park, Nisqually and Stevens
Canyon Roads meet at the high country of glory of Paradise. Again,
numerous trails branch out from the visitor center and historic Park
Lodge, exploring the meadows and glaciers of the area. Skyline Trail is
a mecca for wildflowers. Although the west side of the park is inaccessible by car, Mowich Lake and Carbon River in the northwest corner
can still be reached by road, the easiest park access from Seattle.

To the south is the Cascades' most restless sister, Mount St. Helens.
Once one of the nation's most majestic mountains, it erupted in a
mighty explosion in 1980, drastically altering its figure. Cubic miles of
rock and mud slid off the mountain, and many square miles of forest
were completely leveled. Today, life around the mountain is making a
comeback. Shrubs and wildflowers are taking hold, and trees are even
popping up here and there. But the devastation of the eruption is still
readily evident. Coldwater Ridge and Johnston Ridge Visitor Centers

are great stops, with trails leading from each into the blast zone. Folks can actually drive right into the blast zone at Windy Ridge Viewpoint, on the east side. A hike along Plains of Abraham or Meta Lake are great day trips.

Not to be outdone, the Gifford Pinchot National Forest boasts two beautiful wildernesses. Near White Pass are the snowcapped and rocky peaks of Goat Rocks. Numerous trails access this complex of obsolete volcanoes. Snowgrass Flats and Goat Ridge are the most scenic—and popular—routes into the area. And yes, there are goats here: A bet that you'll see a few is definitely worth a wager. Farther south in Indian Heaven, another group of high peaks and ridges were left over from old volcanoes. Thomas Lake and Indian Heaven Trails are great routes to explore the meadows and get good views of Mounts Hood, Adams, St. Helens, and even Rainier.

The rest of the Gifford Pinchot National Forest is crisscrossed by a large network of paved and unpaved roads. Numerous campgrounds and trails are easy to access, and even Sunday drivers will enjoy a trip into the Gipo. Mount Adams stands as Washington's second tallest peak and enjoys a wealth of trails and campgrounds. Although Round-the-Mountain doesn't actually make it all the way around, it's a great through-hike amongst meadows and waterfalls. Mount Adams is also one of Washington's easiest summits. Well, easy as in no ropes or climbing, but there is still the small matter of 8,000 feet elevation gain via South Climb. Much of the Gifford Pinchot remains unprotected as federal wilderness. Before hikers rise up in protest, mountain bikers should remind them that there are other users out there. In fact, many ridge trails are perfect for those on wheels (check out Langille Ridge, Boundary Trail, or Badger Ridge). Thanks to all the volcanic soil of the South Cascades, huckleberries are a plentiful backcountry harvest, and Juniper Ridge, Dark Meadows, and Hidden Lakes are great berry-picking trails. Rounding out the hiking selection is every kid's favorite school field trip: Ape Cave, a long underground lava tube. For water lovers, there's the White Salmon River, a very popular white-water rafting river, and while driving along the Columbia River Gorge, perhaps on your way to hike Beacon Rock, you're sure to notice hundreds of windsurfers on the river near Hood River.

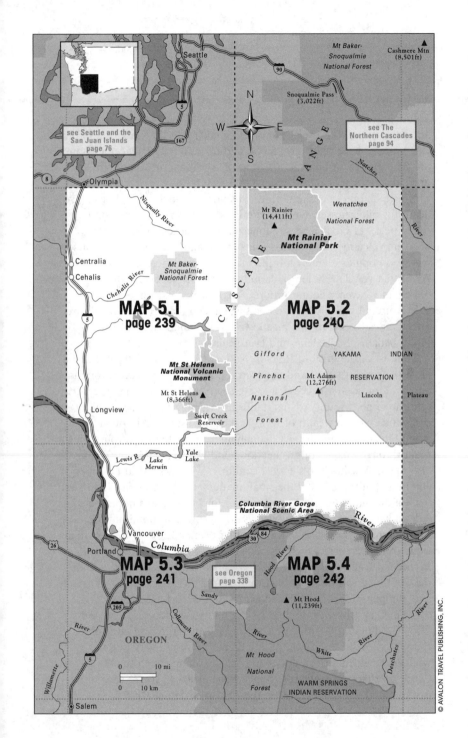

Map 5.1

Hikes 1–17
Pages 243–252

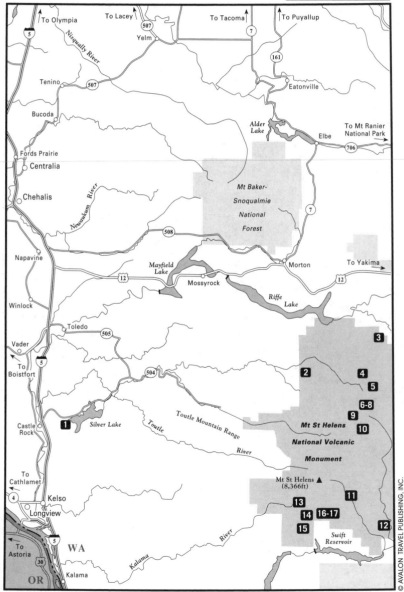

Map 5.2

Hikes 18–110
Pages 253–309

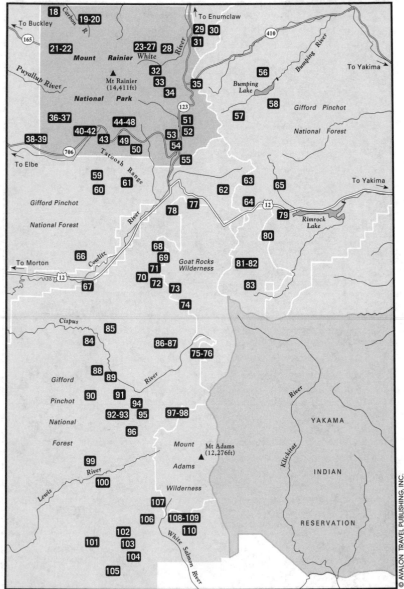

Map 5.3

Hikes 111–112
Pages 310–311

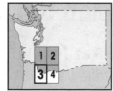

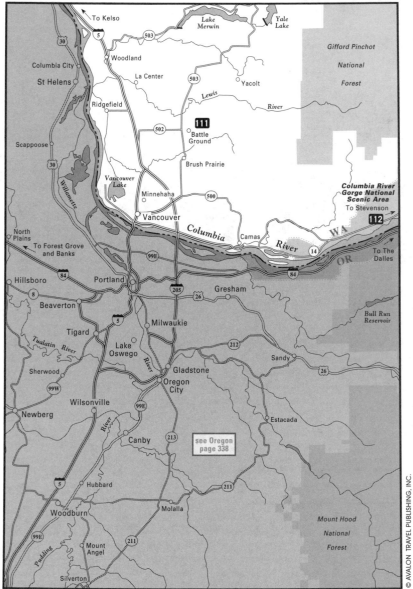

© AVALON TRAVEL PUBLISHING, INC.

Map 5.4

Hikes 113–119
Pages 311–314

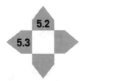

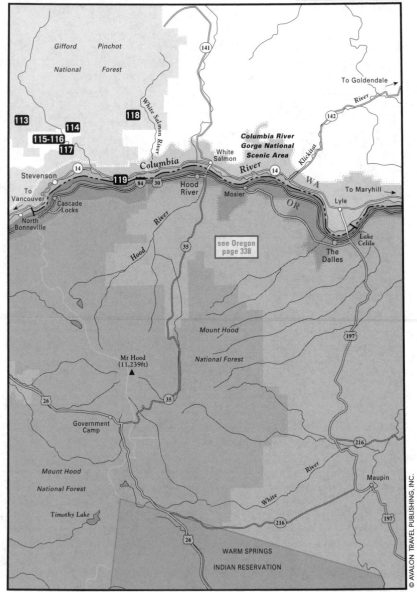

◼ SILVER LAKE
1.0 mi/0.5 hr

east of Castle Rock in Silver Lake State Park

Map 5.1, page 239

The quick, one-mile loop of Silver Lake Trail is a great leg stretcher for folks hitting up the Silver Lake Visitor Center. The trail delves into the growing wetlands that in turn are slowly shrinking Silver Lake. The lake itself was formed by lava flows more than 2,000 years ago and is now on its last legs. Although the outlook may not be good for the lake, wildlife still finds it a happy home and is abundant around the lake. This is a favorite winter haunt for deer and elk, while spring and fall bring loads of migrating waterfowl. On clear days, Mount St. Helens is visible across Silver Lake. The trail is barrier free and accessible to wheelchairs.

User Groups: Hikers and leashed dogs. No horses or mountain bikes are allowed. The trail is wheelchair accessible.

Open Seasons: This trail is accessible year-round.

Permits: A federal Northwest Forest Pass is required to park here.

Maps: For a topographic map, ask the USGS for Silver Lake.

Directions: From Castle Rock, drive east 5 miles on Highway 504 to Silver Lake Mount St. Helens Visitor Center. The trailhead is on the south side of the visitors center.

Contact: Gifford Pinchot National Forest, Mount St. Helens National Volcanic Monument, 42218 Northeast Yale Bridge Road, Amboy, WA 98601, 360/449-7871.

◻ COLDWATER LAKE
5.5 mi/3.0 hrs

east of Castle Rock in Mount St. Helens National Volcanic Monument of Gifford Pinchot National Forest

Map 5.1, page 239

Hikers along the shores of Coldwater Lake can thank the 1980 eruption of Mount St. Helens for the trail they're enjoying. That's because before the blast, there was no Coldwater Lake. Massive amounts of mud and debris rushed down from the erupting volcano and created a large natural dam on Coldwater Creek, slowly filling up to become Coldwater Lake.

Coldwater Lake Trail follows the shores of this lake before climbing abruptly to the ridge above. The trail is easy to reach, beginning at the Coldwater Ridge Visitor Center. The trail follows the shores, now regenerating with small shrubs and plants. Although the gray, ashen hillsides look unfit for survival, many species of wildlife are spotted here, including deer, elk, squirrels, and frogs, and trout have been stocked in the lake. The trail hugs the shoreline for nearly three miles before climbing steeply. It's best to turn around and enjoy the walk back before the steep ascent.

User Groups: Hikers only. No dogs, horses, or mountain bikes are allowed. No wheelchair access.

Open Seasons: This trail is accessible April–November.

Permits: A federal Northwest Forest Pass is required to park here.

Maps: For a map of Gifford Pinchot National Forest, contact the Outdoor Recreation Information Center at the downtown Seattle REI. For a topographic map, ask Green Trails for No. 364, Mount St. Helens, or ask the USGS for Elk Rock and Spirit Lake West.

Directions: From Castle Rock, drive east 35 miles to the Coldwater Visitor Center in Mount St. Helens National Monument. The signed trailhead is immediately following the visitors center on the left.

Contact: Gifford Pinchot National Forest, Mount St. Helens National Volcanic Monument, 42218 Northeast Yale Bridge Road, Amboy, WA 98601, 360/449-7871.

❸ STRAWBERRY MOUNTAIN
12.0 mi/6.0 hrs

south of Randle in Mount St. Helens National Volcanic Monument of Gifford Pinchot National Forest

Map 5.1, page 239

Running south to north along the edge of Mount St. Helens' blast zone, Strawberry Mountain tells a great story of the effects of the 1980 eruption. Strawberry Mountain Trail rides the crest of the long mountain (which is more a ridge than a mountain). Along the western side, entire forests were leveled by a wave of searing gas and ash. The blast leveled the trees like blades of grass, leaving them arranged in neat rows. On the eastern side, it's business as usual. Subalpine meadows filled with wildflowers now dominate the southern part of the route, which climbs to a pair of open peaks.

Strawberry Mountain Trail runs the length of the ridge, 11 miles in all. The southern trailhead saves a lot of elevation gain and is more open and scenic. Thus it's the preferred route. Start at Bear Meadows and hike Boundary Trail to Strawberry Mountain Trail (.4 mile). Turn left and follow Strawberry Mountain Trail north. Old-growth forest is mixed with open meadows. A short side trail (2.7 miles) cuts off to the west and quickly finds an expansive viewpoint. Views of the alpine Mount Margaret backcountry and the crater within Mount St. Helens are terrific. The trail continues into open meadows of heather and lupine (5 miles). It's a good time to turn around and retrace your steps to the car when you've had your fill of views. Don't expect to find any water along this high route.

User Groups: Hikers, leashed dogs, horses, and mountain bikes. No wheelchair access.

Open Seasons: This trail is accessible June–October.

Permits: A federal Northwest Forest Pass is required to park here.

Maps: For a map of Gifford Pinchot National Forest, contact the Outdoor Recreation Information Center at the downtown Seattle REI.

For a topographic map, ask Green Trails for No. 332, Spirit Lake, or ask the USGS for Cowlitz Falls and Vanson Peak.

Directions: From Randle, drive south 1 mile on Highway 131 to Forest Service Road 25. Stay to the right and drive 19 miles to Forest Service Road 99. Turn right and drive 6 miles to Bear Meadow Trailhead. The trail starts on the north side of Road 99.

Contact: Gifford Pinchot National Forest, Mount St. Helens National Volcanic Monument, 42218 Northeast Yale Bridge Road, Amboy, WA 98601, 360/449-7871.

❹ QUARTZ CREEK BIG TREES
0.5 mi/0.5 hr

southwest of Randle in Gifford Pinchot National Forest

Map 5.1, page 239

So close to such devastated landscape, it's amazing to see what much of the forest near Mount St. Helens previously looked like. Not far from the blast zone, Quartz Creek Big Trees Trail is a short loop into an ancient forest of Douglas fir, western hemlock, and western red cedar. Mosses and ferns blanket every branch and inch of ground, a moist contrast to the barren landscapes just a few miles away over the ridge. Quartz Creek Big Trees Trail is flat, level, and barrier free, perfect for hikers of all ages and abilities. The trail makes a short .5-mile loop within this old-growth forest.

User Groups: Hikers and leashed dogs. No horses or mountain bikes are allowed. The trail is wheelchair accessible.

Open Seasons: This trail is accessible year-round.

Permits: A federal Northwest Forest Pass is required to park here.

Maps: For a map of Gifford Pinchot National Forest, contact the Outdoor Recreation Information Center at the downtown Seattle REI. For a topographic map, ask Green Trails for No. 332, Spirit Lake, or ask the USGS for Cowlitz Falls.

Directions: From Randle, drive south 1 mile on Highway 131 to Forest Service Road 25. Stay to the right and drive 8 miles to Forest Service Road 26. Turn right and drive 8 miles to Forest Service Road 2608. Turn left and drive 1.5 miles to the signed trailhead on the right.

Contact: Gifford Pinchot National Forest, Cowlitz Valley Ranger Station, 10024 U.S. 12, Randle, WA 98377, 360/497-1100.

5 GOAT MOUNTAIN
8.0 mi/5.0 hrs

north of Mount St. Helens in Gifford Pinchot National Forest

Map 5.1, page 239

Situated 12 miles north of Mount St. Helens (as the crow flies), Goat Mountain managed to escape much of the eruption's devastating impact. Thank goodness, for Goat Mountain is a subalpine wonderland. Covered in open meadows, this rocky ridge provides great views of the eruption's impact to the south. Goat Mountain is an excellent way to see the altered landscape yet still enjoy a hike among lush meadows.

Goat Mountain Trail climbs from Ryan Lake, zigzaging in and out of affected forest, now a graveyard of standing dead trees. The trail reaches the ridge (1.5 miles) and navigates a mix of meadows and rocky bluffs, each awash in wildflowers (bear grass, lupine, siprea, and stonecrop, to name a few). The towering slopes of Mount Margaret loom from the south.

Goat Mountain Trail traverses the ridge for three spectacular miles, eventually dropping to Deadman Lake (4.8 miles) and on to Vanson Lake (8.1 miles). Unless you're looking for a long hike or tough climb back, the best turnaround is before the trail drops to Deadman Lake. You'll see that Goat Mountain is an appropriate name. Fluffy white goats are a common sight, scrambling along the rocky cliffs.

User Groups: Hikers, leashed dogs, horses, and mountain bikes. No wheelchair access.

Open Seasons: This trail is accessible June–September.

Permits: A federal Northwest Forest Pass is required to park here.

Maps: For a map of Gifford Pinchot Nation-

al Forest, contact the Outdoor Recreation Information Center at the downtown Seattle REI. For a topographic map, ask Green Trails for No. 332, Spirit Lake, or ask the USGS for Cowlitz Falls and Vanson Peak.

Directions: From Randle, drive south 1 mile on Highway 131 to Forest Service Road 25. Stay to the right and drive 8 miles to Forest Service Road 26. Turn right and drive 14 miles to Forest Service Road 2612. Turn right and drive .5 mile to the trailhead on the right.

Contact: Gifford Pinchot National Forest, Mount St. Helens National Volcanic Monument, 42218 Northeast Yale Bridge Road, Amboy, WA 98601, 360/449-7871.

6 BOUNDARY, WEST END
12.0 mi/5.0–6.0 hrs

in Mount St. Helens National Monument

Map 5.1, page 239

This western end of Boundary Trail is the most glorious stretch of trail in Mount St. Helens National Monument. This section of Boundary Trail runs 13.8 miles (one-way) between Johnston Ridge Observatory and Norway Pass, near Winder Ridge Viewpoint. A car-drop between these two points involves hundreds of miles of driving and is hardly worthwhile. No worries, because each trailhead offers access to a great peak in about 12 miles.

Visitors to Johnston Ridge Observatory can hike to Coldwater Peak (12.2 miles round-trip), an up-close look at the crater. From the observatory, hike east on Boundary Trail above sprawling plains of ash and mud. The trail heads north and climbs above St. Helens Lake, a site of total devastation. A side trail leads to the summit (elevation 5,727 feet).

From Forest Service Road 99, a hike to Mount Margaret (11.6 miles round-trip) makes for an incredible trip through alpine meadows and views of sparkling lakes. From Norway Pass Trailhead, hike west on Boundary Trail to Norway Pass (2.2 miles). The trail travels through the heart of the blast zone, but lush meadows survived to the north. A side trail leads to Margaret's summit.

At the time of publication, this trail was closed due to the 2004 eruption of Mount St. Helens. Look on the park website or call the USDA Forest Service to check current trail conditions.

User Groups: Hikers only. No dogs, horses, or mountain bikes are allowed. No wheelchair access.

Open Seasons: This trail is accessible June–mid-October.

Permits: A federal Northwest Forest Pass is required to park here.

Maps: For a map of Gifford Pinchot National Forest, contact the Outdoor Recreation Information Center at the downtown Seattle REI. For a topographic map, ask Green Trails for No. 332, Spirit Lake, or ask the USGS for Spirit Lake West and Spirit Lake East.

Directions: From Randle, drive south 1 mile on Highway 131 to Forest Service Road 25. Stay to the right and drive 19 miles to Forest Service Road 99. Turn right and drive 11 miles to Forest Service Road 26. Turn right and drive 1.5 miles to Norway Pass Trailhead.

Contact: Gifford Pinchot National Forest, Mount St. Helens National Volcanic Monument, 42218 Northeast Yale Bridge Road, Amboy, WA 98601, 360/449-7871, 360/891-5202, www.fs.fed.us/gpnf .mshnvm.

7 BOUNDARY TRAIL
27.8 mi one-way/3.0 days

across Gifford Pinchot National Forest

Map 5.1, page 239

Boundary Trail is a long through-hike traversing Gifford Pinchot National Forest west to east. The trail previously began near the Mount Margaret backcountry, but the 1980 eruption destroyed the western trailhead and made the western six miles an adventuresome and entirely new out-and-back hike (see previous listing). The eastern contiguous section of Boundary Trail gets in miles of meadow rambling and even some old-growth shade.

The best place to start is Elk Pass, an easy access on Forest Service Road 25. From here, Boundary Trail travels alternating patches of old-growth and clear-cuts for about seven miles. The trail gets interesting as it skirts Badger and Craggy Peaks, where meadows and views reign supreme. The trail leads to the southern ends of Langille and Juniper Ridges, an exposed and beautiful 11-mile segment. The remainder of the trail (9 miles) sticks mostly to forest, ending at Council Lake.

Many so-called feeder trails offer access to Boundary Trail, making numerous segments of the route accessible for day hikes. Water is often scarce along the route, so plan well and bring plenty of capacity. Campsites are rarely designated; low-impact cross-country camping is necessary. At the time of publication, this trail was closed due to the 2004 eruption of Mount St. Helens. Look on the park website or call the USDA Forest Service to check current trail conditions.

User Groups: Hikers, leashed dogs, horses, mountain bikes, and motorcycles. No wheelchair access.

Open Seasons: This trail is accessible July–mid-October.

Permits: A federal Northwest Forest Pass is required to park at the trailheads.

Maps: For a map of Gifford Pinchot National Forest, contact the Outdoor Recreation Information Center at the downtown Seattle REI. For a topographic map, ask Green Trails for No. 332, Spirit Lake, No. 333, McCoy Peak, and No. 334, Blue Lake, or ask the USGS for French Butte, McCoy, Spirit Lake East, and Spirit Lake West.

Directions: From Randle, drive south 1 mile on Highway 131 to Forest Service Road 25. Stay to the right and drive 23 miles to the well-signed trailhead.

Contact: Gifford Pinchot National Forest, Cowlitz Valley Ranger Station, 10024 U.S. 12, Randle, WA 98377, 360/497-1100, 360/891-5202, www .fs.fed.us/gpnf/mshnvm.

8 META LAKE
0.5 mi/0.5 hr

northeast of Mount St. Helens in Mount St. Helens National Volcanic Monument in Gifford Pinchot National Forest

Map 5.1, page 239

Lying behind a small ridge, Meta Lake received less than a death blow from Mount St. Helens' eruption despite being squarely in the blast zone. It helped that a snowpack lingered around the still-frozen lake, providing plants and trees a modest insulation from the searing heat and gas. With such protection in place, Meta Lake survived the blast and today provides a great example of the regeneration of life after the 1980 eruption.

Meta Lake Trail makes a quick trip to the lake (just .25 mile one-way). Several interpretive signs line the route, filling visitors in on the ability of life to survive and thrive here. Firs and hemlocks are once again creating a forest among blown-down logs, with lots of huckleberry bushes filling in the holes. Brook trout are still found in the lake, as are salamanders and frogs. The path is paved and is one of the best in the area with access for wheelchairs.

User Groups: Hikers only. No dogs, horses, or mountain bikes are allowed. The trail is wheelchair accessible.

Open Seasons: This trail is accessible June–September.

Permits: A federal Northwest Forest Pass is required to park here.

Maps: For a map of Gifford Pinchot National Forest, contact the Outdoor Recreation Information Center at the downtown Seattle REI. For a topographic map, ask Green Trails for No. 332, Spirit Lake, or ask the USGS for Spirit Lake East.

Directions: From Randle, drive south 1 mile on Highway 131 to Forest Service Road 25. Stay to the right and drive 19 miles to Forest Service Road 99. Turn right and drive 11.5 miles to the signed trailhead on the right.

Contact: Gifford Pinchot National Forest, Mount St. Helens National Volcanic Monument, 42218

Northeast Yale Bridge Road, Amboy, WA 98601, 360/449-7871.

9 HARMONY FALLS
2.0 mi/1.5 hrs

northeast of Mount St. Helens in Mount St. Helens National Volcanic Monument in Gifford Pinchot National Forest

Map 5.1, page 239

Before the 1980 eruption of Mount St. Helens, Spirit Lake was home to houses and lodges, campgrounds, and an old, lush forest. All of that was quickly destroyed by the eruption, which left behind a surreal landscape. Harmony Trail passes right through this devastated area down to Spirit Lake, surveying the enormously changed scene.

Harmony Trail provides the only access to Spirit Lake, reaching the lakeshore where Harmony Falls drops in. The trail drops 600 feet to the lake, a considerable climb out. Bare trees lie scattered on the hillsides in neat rows, leveled by the searing gases of the eruption. Part of Spirit Lake is covered by dead trees, neatly arranged in the northern arm. On the hillsides, small plants and shrubs work hard to revegetate the land. With a significant chunk of the mountain lying at the bottom of the lake, the shores of Spirit Lake were raised 200 feet. This significantly enlarged the lake and cut off much of the height of Harmony Falls. At the time of publication, this trail was closed due to the 2004 eruption of Mount St. Helens. Look on the park website or call the USDA Forest Service to check current trail conditions.

User Groups: Hikers only. No dogs, horses, or mountain bikes are allowed. No wheelchair access.

Open Seasons: This trail is accessible June–September.

Permits: A federal Northwest Forest Pass is required to park here.

Maps: For a map of Gifford Pinchot National Forest, contact the Outdoor Recreation Information Center at the downtown Seattle REI. For a topographic map, ask Green Trails for

No. 332, Spirit Lake, or ask the USGS for Spirit Lake West and Spirit Lake East.

Directions: From Randle, drive south 1 mile on Highway 131 to Forest Service Road 25. Stay to the right and drive 19 miles to Forest Service Road 99. Turn right and drive 16 miles to the signed trailhead on the right.

Contact: Gifford Pinchot National Forest, Mount St. Helens National Volcanic Monument, 42218 Northeast Yale Bridge Road, Amboy, WA 98601, 360/449-7871, 360/891-5202, www.fs.fed.us/gpnf/mshnvm.

10 PLAINS OF ABRAHAM
9.0 mi/5.0 hrs

south of Randle in Mount St. Helens National Volcanic Monument in Gifford Pinchot National Forest

Map 5.1, page 239

Other than Loowit Trail, a round-the-mountain trek, no route gets closer to Mount St. Helens than Abraham Trail. The route, shaped like a lasso, spends its entirety within the blast zone, a barren landscape leveled by the 1980 eruption.

The route begins at popular Windy Ridge Viewpoint and follows the ridge on Truman Trail. Turn left on Abraham Trail (1.7 miles) as the path rounds five narrow draws (3 miles) to Loowit Trail (4 miles), within the Plains of Abraham. The plains are a wide, barren landscape repeatedly pounded by mud and landslides. Other than the smallest of plants and mosses, life is absent. It's an eerie but impressive scene.

Turn right on Loowit Trail to climb to Windy Pass (5 miles), an appropriate name on most days. The loop returns to the car via Truman Trail (6 miles) and Windy Ridge. July and August are great months to hike Abraham Trail, when wildflowers are at their peak. Water and shade are not found at any time along the trail, so consider extra water and sunscreen.

At the time of publication, this trail was closed due to the 2004 eruption of Mount St. Helens. Look on the park website or call the USDA Forest Service to check current trail conditions.

User Groups: Hikers only. No dogs, horses, or mountain bikes are allowed. No wheelchair access.

Open Seasons: This trail is accessible June–October.

Permits: A federal Northwest Forest Pass is required to park here.

Maps: For a map of Gifford Pinchot National Forest, contact the Outdoor Recreation Information Center at the downtown Seattle REI. For a topographic map, ask Green Trails for No. 364S, Mount St. Helens NW, or ask the USGS for Spirit Lake East.

Directions: From Randle, drive south 1 mile on Highway 131 to Forest Service Road 25. Stay to the right and drive 19 miles to Forest Service Road 99. Turn right and drive to Windy Ridge Trailhead at road's end.

Contact: Gifford Pinchot National Forest, Mount St. Helens National Volcanic Monument, 42218 Northeast Yale Bridge Road, Amboy, WA 98601, 360/449-7871, 360/891-5202, www.fs.fed.us/gpnf/mshvm.

11 LAVA CANYON
2.0 mi/1.5 hrs

northeast of Cougar in Mount St. Helens National Volcanic Monument in Gifford Pinchot National Forest

Map 5.1, page 239

The 1980 eruption created a raging torrent of mud and debris that gushed through the narrow gorge. The violent flow scoured the canyon bottom clean, leaving only barren bedrock for the Muddy River. That was a good thing, as it created a colorful river canyon with numerous pools and cascades.

The first section of Lava Canyon Trail descends a steep series of switchbacks to several views of the canyon (.5 mile). This section is paved and accessible to wheelchairs, although it's very steep and assistance is usually needed. From here, a signed loop crosses the river via a bridge and follows the river down. This section of river has many pools and channels carved into the bedrock. The loop crosses back over the river via a high suspension bridge (1 mile). Although Lava Canyon Trail continues to a lower trailhead (2.5 miles), the lower suspension bridge marks a good time to head back.

At the time of publication, this trail was closed due to the 2004 eruption of Mount St. Helens. Look on the park website or call the USDA Forest Service to check current trail conditions. **User Groups:** Hikers and leashed dogs. No horses or mountain bikes are allowed. Part of the trail is wheelchair accessible (for the first half mile, down to a viewpoint of the canyon, although very steep).

Open Seasons: This trail is accessible May–November.

Permits: A federal Northwest Forest Pass is required to park here.

Maps: For a map of Gifford Pinchot National Forest, contact the Outdoor Recreation Information Center at the downtown Seattle REI. For a topographic map, ask Green Trails for No. 364, Mount St. Helens, or ask the USGS for Smith Creek Butte.

Directions: From Vancouver, drive north on I-5 to Highway 503 (Woodland, exit 21). Drive east 35 miles to Forest Service Road 83. Turn left and drive 10 miles to the signed trailhead at road's end.

Contact: Gifford Pinchot National Forest, Mount St. Helens National Volcanic Monument, 42218 Northeast Yale Bridge Road, Amboy, WA 98601, 360/449-7871, 360/891-5202, www.fs.fed.us/gpnf/mshnvm.

12 CEDAR FLATS
1.0 mi/0.5 hr

north of Cougar in Gifford Pinchot National Forest

Map 5.1, page 239

Quick and easy, Cedar Flats Trail ventures through Southern Washington's most impressive old-growth forest. It's easy to imagine you've been transported to the Olympic Peninsula when wandering among these giants. Douglas fir, western hemlock, and western red cedar create a forest of immense proportions. The

area is preserved as part of Cedar Flats Natural Area, which was set aside in the 1940s. This area serves as important, undisturbed habitat for a variety of animals. Herds of elk winter in this area and deer are year-round inhabitants. Cedar Flats Trail makes a short and flat loop, arranged like a lasso, making this a great walk for families and hikers who prefer to avoid difficult hikes. Part of the trail nears the steep cliffs overlooking the Muddy River (inaccessible from the trail). The trail can be easily walked in a half hour, but it's well worth spending an afternoon in this peaceful setting. **User Groups:** Hikers and leashed dogs. No horses or mountain bikes are allowed. No wheelchair access.

Open Seasons: This trail is accessible year-round.

Permits: A federal Northwest Forest Pass is required to park here.

Maps: For a map of Gifford Pinchot National Forest, contact the Outdoor Recreation Information Center at the downtown Seattle REI. For a topographic map, ask Green Trails for No. 364, Mount St. Helens, or ask the USGS for Cedar Flat.

Directions: From Cougar, drive east on Highway 503 (Forest Service Road 90) to Forest Service Road 25, at Pine Creek Information Station. Turn left and drive 6 miles to the trailhead on the right.

Contact: Gifford Pinchot National Forest, Mount St. Helens National Volcanic Monument, 42218 Northeast Yale Bridge Road, Amboy, WA 98601, 360/449-7871.

13 SHEEP CANYON
4.4 mi/3.0 hrs

north of Cougar in Mount St. Helens National Volcanic Monument of Gifford Pinchot National Forest

Map 5.1, page 239

Not all of Mount St. Helens' destruction in May 1980 was the result of searing gas and ash. Areas not directly in the line of fire were instead affected by torrents of mud, water, and debris. That's what happened along Sheep Creek, a muddy, ashen stream running through a steep canyon. The trail provides access to Loowit Trail, the route running around the mountain, home to impressive views of the flattened volcano.

Sheep Canyon Trail quickly leaves a patch of clear-cut land to enter an old-growth forest of noble fir. The route climbs much of its length, gaining more than 1,400 feet, rendering the shady, old forest a welcome friend. The highlight of the trail is Sheep Canyon, where Sheep Creek flows between vertical rock walls. Finally, the trail climbs harshly to Loowit Trail, where hikers can add extra miles by exploring to the north or south.

At the time of publication, this trail was closed due to the 2004 eruption of Mount St. Helens. Look on the park website or call the USDA Forest Service to check current trail conditions.
User Groups: Hikers and leashed dogs. No horses or mountain bikes are allowed. No wheelchair access.
Open Seasons: This trail is accessible June–October.
Permits: A federal Northwest Forest Pass is required to park here.
Maps: For a map of Gifford Pinchot National Forest, contact the Outdoor Recreation Information Center at the downtown Seattle REI. For a topographic map, ask the USGS for Mount St. Helens and Goat Mountain.
Directions: From Vancouver, drive north on I-5 to Highway 503 (Woodland, exit 21). Drive east 35 miles to Forest Service Road 83. Turn left and drive 3.5 miles to Forest Service Road 81. Turn left and drive to Forest Service Road 8123. Turn right and drive to the signed trailhead at road's end.
Contact: Gifford Pinchot National Forest, Mount St. Helens National Volcanic Monument, 42218 Northeast Yale Bridge Road, Amboy, WA 98601, 360/449-7871, 360/891-5202, www.fs.fed.us/gpnf/mshnvm.

🔟 APE CAVE
2.5 mi/3.0 hrs

north of Cougar in Mount St. Helens National Volcanic Monument in Gifford Pinchot National Forest

Map 5.1, page 239

The name Ape Cave conjures images of Sasquatch huddled in a narrow underground passage. Sorry to disappoint. The caves were first explored by members of a local outdoors club, "The Apes," hence the name. Ape Cave is a long, large cave (known as a lava tube) naturally carved into the basalt by lava and water through thousands of years. These deep, pitch-black tunnels are an eerie and memorable experience.

From the main entrance, the cave heads in two directions. The Lower Passage is easier and shorter. It delves about .7 mile past a number of formations, including a Lava Ball and mudflow floor. The Upper Passage is 1.3 miles long underground with a 1.3-mile trail aboveground that returns to the trailhead. The Upper Passage is more challenging, with segments that climb over rock piles and a small lava ledge.

Be prepared for a chilly hike. Year-round temperature is a steady 42°F. Two sources of light are recommended, and headlamps don't count. The deep darkness of the caves requires very strong flashlights or, preferably, large gas lanterns. Parts of the upper passage are rocky, so sturdy shoes and pants are also recommended.

At the time of publication, this trail was closed due to the 2004 eruption of Mount St. Helens. Look on the park website or call the USDA Forest Service to check current trail conditions.
User Groups: Hikers only. No dogs, horses, or mountain bikes are allowed. No wheelchair access.
Open Seasons: This trail is accessible year-round.
Permits: A federal Northwest Forest Pass is required to park here.
Maps: For a map of Gifford Pinchot National Forest, contact the Outdoor Recreation

Information Center at the downtown Seattle REI. For a topographic map, ask Green Trails for No. 364, Mount St. Helens, or ask the USGS for Mount Mitchell.

Directions: From Vancouver, drive north on I-5 to Highway 503 (Woodland, exit 21). Drive east 35 miles to Forest Service Road 83. Turn left and drive 2 miles to Forest Service Road 8303. Turn left and drive 1.5 miles to the signed trailhead on the right.

Contact: Gifford Pinchot National Forest, Mount St. Helens National Volcanic Monument, 42218 Northeast Yale Bridge Road, Amboy, WA 98601, 360/449-7871, 360/891-5202. www.fs.fed.us/gpnf/mshnvm.

15 TRAIL OF TWO FORESTS
0.3 mi/0.5 hr

northeast of Cougar in Mount St. Helens National Volcanic Monument in Gifford Pinchot National Forest

Map 5.1, page 239

Trail of Two Forests is a quick nature loop into one of the most unlikely natural phenomena in the Northwest. Nearly two millennia ago, Mount St. Helens sent a wave of molten lava down her south flank. Trail of Two Forests is perfectly situated near the bottom of the flow, where the lava still moved but was not hot enough to immediately destroy trees. Here, lava cooled around the trees, which eventually decomposed and left small tunnels, caves, and pits as a testament to the old forest. Boardwalk lines the entire route, making Trail of Two Forests accessible to wheelchairs. The boardwalk also protects the fragile forest ground, so please stay on the trail. The one chance visitors have to get off-trail is a chance to crawl through a tunnel, or lava tube, nearly 30 feet long. It's a trip!

At the time of publication, this trail was closed due to the 2004 eruption of Mount St. Helens. Look on the park website or call the USDA Forest Service to check current trail conditions.
User Groups: Hikers and leashed dogs. No horses or mountain bikes are allowed. No wheelchair access.

Open Seasons: This trail is accessible March–November.
Permits: A federal Northwest Forest Pass is required to park here.
Maps: For a map of Gifford Pinchot National Forest, contact the Outdoor Recreation Information Center at the downtown Seattle REI. For a topographic map, ask Green Trails for No. 364, Mount St. Helens, or ask the USGS for Mount Mitchell.
Directions: From Vancouver, drive north on I-5 to Highway 503 (Woodland, exit 21). Drive east 35 miles to Forest Service Road 83. Turn left and drive 2 miles to Forest Service Road 8303. Turn left and drive .1 mile to the signed trailhead on the left.
Contact: Gifford Pinchot National Forest, Mount St. Helens National Volcanic Monument, 42218 Northeast Yale Bridge Road, Amboy, WA 98601, 360/449-7871, 360/891-5202, www.fs.fed.us/gpnf/mshnvm.

16 JUNE LAKE
2.8 mi/2.0 hrs

northeast of Cougar in Mount St. Helens National Volcanic Monument in Gifford Pinchot National Forest

Map 5.1, page 239

June Lake achieves recognition by being the only subalpine lake on the slopes of Mount St. Helens, complete with waterfall. Subalpine forest and meadow ring the lake, which has a sandy beach perfect for summer afternoon lounging.

June Lake Trail gains just 500 feet in 1.4 miles and is ideal for families. It courses its way through young forest with views of a gorge before emerging upon a large field of basalt boulders (1 mile). The trail sticks to the forest and soon finds June Lake. For a view of Mount St. Helens, hike past the lake a few hundred yards on Loowit Trail. Several campsites are scattered around the lake, and campers are expected to follow strict Leave-No-Trace principles.

At the time of publication, this trail was closed

due to the 2004 eruption of Mount St. Helens. Look on the park website or call the USDA Forest Service to check current trail conditions.
User Groups: Hikers and leashed dogs. No horses or mountain bikes are allowed. No wheelchair access.
Open Seasons: This trail is accessible May–November.
Permits: A federal Northwest Forest Pass is required to park here.
Maps: For a map of Gifford Pinchot National Forest, contact the Outdoor Recreation Information Center at the downtown Seattle REI. For a topographic map, ask Green Trails for No. 364S, Mount St. Helens NW, or ask the USGS for Mount St. Helens.
Directions: From Vancouver, drive north on I-5 to Highway 503 (Woodland, exit 21). Drive east 35 miles to Forest Service Road 83. Turn left and drive 6 miles to the signed trailhead on the left.
Contact: Gifford Pinchot National Forest, Mount St. Helens National Volcanic Monument, 42218 Northeast Yale Bridge Road, Amboy, WA 98601, 360/449-7871, 360/891-5202, www.fs.fed.us/gpnf/mshvm.com

🔲 LOOWIT TRAIL
30.5 mi/3–4 days

around the mountain in Mount St. Helens National Volcanic Monument in Gifford Pinchot National Forest

Map 5.1, page 239

Loowit Trail is the grand loop encircling Mount St. Helens. It was an interesting trip before 1980, and the eruption of the mountain turned this trek into an unforgettable outing. Loowit experiences everything imaginable—old-growth forest, alpine meadows, and barren, ravaged landscapes. Compared to Wonderland Trail, elevation changes along the route are modest. Still, many sections of the trail are difficult and rocky.

Loowit Trail has no definite trailhead. Instead, several feeder trails lead to the 27.7-mile loop. Among these trails are June Lake in the south (1.7 miles one-way), Truman Trail at

Windy Ridge (3 miles), and Sheep Canyon on the west side (2.2 miles). Diligent planning is a must before setting out on Loowit Trail. Water sources and campsites are limited throughout the route and often change year to year. The Forest Service suggests that you call ahead to get the current scoop. Finally, be ready for ash, lots and lots of ash. The fine, gray particles will invade everything you own. Bring a coffee filter to tie around your water filter and protect it. Also, take special care with cameras, binoculars, or eyeglasses, all easily damaged by ash.

Loowit Trail is often hiked counterclockwise. From June Lake, the trail climbs beneath the rocky toe of the Worm Flows to Shoestring Glacier, from the barren Plains of Abraham to Loowit Falls and impressive views of the crater.

At the time of publication, this trail was closed due to the 2004 eruption of Mount St. Helens. Look on the park website or call the USDA Forest Service to check current trail conditions.
User Groups: Hikers only. No dogs, horses, or mountain bikes are allowed. No wheelchair access.
Open Seasons: This trail is accessible June–October.
Permits: A federal Northwest Forest Pass is required to park here.
Maps: For a map of Gifford Pinchot National Forest, contact the Outdoor Recreation Information Center at the downtown Seattle REI. For a topographic map, ask Green Trails for No. 364S, Mount St. Helens NW, or ask the USGS for Mount St. Helens, Smith Creek Butte, and Goat Mountain.
Directions: From Vancouver, drive north on I-5 to Highway 503 (Woodland, exit 21). Drive east 35 miles to Forest Service Road 83. Turn left and drive 6 miles to the signed trailhead on the left for June Lake (the shortest access on the south side).
Contact: Gifford Pinchot National Forest, Mount St. Helens National Volcanic Monument, 42218 Northeast Yale Bridge Road, Amboy, WA 98601, 360/449-7871, 360/891-5202, www.fs.fed.us/gpnf/mshnvm

18 GREEN LAKE
3.6 mi/2.0 hrs

in northwest Mount Rainier National Park

Map 5.2, page 240

You don't need amnesia to forget about Mount Rainier when hiking the trail to Green Lake. Grabbing your attention from the start are grand-daddy Douglas firs and western hemlocks. These giants tower over the trail in the Carbon River Valley and are estimated to be more than 800 years of age. The trail then climbs alongside Ranger Creek, within earshot but mostly out of sight. A must-see stop is a small side trail to Ranger Falls (1 mile). During the spring snow-melt, this large series of cascades creates a thunderous roar heard throughout the forest. The trail switchbacks .5 mile before leveling and crossing the creek. Green Lake sits among pristine forest and a little meadow. Anglers can try their luck here for trout. South of the lake and peeking through a large valley stands Tolmie Peak. Green Lake is a great day hike during the summer but also makes a good snowshoe trek during the winter. Old-growth forest, big waterfalls, and a serene mountain lake—now what was the name of that mountain everyone keeps talking about?

User Groups: Hikers only. No dogs, horses, or mountain bikes are allowed. No wheelchair access.

Open Seasons: This area is usually accessible April–November.

Permits: A National Parks Pass is required to enter the park.

Maps: For a map of Mount Rainier National Park, contact the Outdoor Recreation Information Center at the downtown Seattle REI. For a topographic map, ask Green Trails for No. 269, Mount Rainier West, or ask the USGS for Mowich Lake.

Directions: From Tacoma, drive east on Highway 410 to Buckley. Turn south on Highway 165 and drive 14 miles to Carbon River Road. Turn left and drive 8 miles to Carbon River Entrance Station. Continue 3 miles to the trailhead on the right.

Contact: Mount Rainier National Park, Wilkeson Wilderness Information Center, P.O. Box 423, Wilkeson, WA 98396, 360/569-6020.

19 WINDY GAP
13.0–17.0 mi/8.0 hr–2 days

in northern Mount Rainier National Park

Map 5.2, page 240

Mount Rainier grabs the most attention (it stands more than 14,000 feet tall, after all). But the park holds miles of amazing terrain, tucked away from the mountain's view. Windy Gap is a perfect example. The enjoyable trail climbs into a high-country playground of meadows and rocky peaks, with plenty to see and do. Hikes to Lake James and the Natural Bridge (a large rock arch) start here. A full day of hiking, Windy Gap features two backcountry camps for overnight visits.

The route starts from Ipsut Creek Campground and joins Wonderland Trail (.5 mile), eventually leaving to cross the Carbon River (2.4 miles). Turn left and do the switchback shuffle up Northern Loop Trail to Windy Gap. The sighting of colorful Yellowstone Cliffs (5.1 miles) signals the arrival of parkland meadows, reflective tarns, and craggy horizons. Boulder-strewn Windy Gap (6.4 miles), a good place to turn around, is truly a blustery experience, and mountain goats roam the surrounding ridges.

Beyond Windy Gap, Northern Loop Trail drops 1.5 miles to lightly visited Lake James, clad in subalpine meadows. Beyond Windy Gap .25 mile, a signed trail leads to Natural Bridge. Rising out of the forest, the large rock formation seems lost from the sea. After crossing the Carbon, the trail is dry; bring plenty of water. Beautiful backcountry camps are situated at Yellowstone Cliffs and Lake James and require camping permits.

User Groups: Hikers only. No dogs, horses, or mountain bikes are allowed. No wheelchair access.

Open Seasons: This area is usually accessible mid-July–September.

Permits: A National Parks Pass is required to enter the park. Overnight stays within the national park require backcountry camping permits, which are available at Wilkeson Wilderness Information Center.

Maps: For a map of Mount Rainier National Park, contact the Outdoor Recreation Information Center at the downtown Seattle REI. For a topographic map, ask Green Trails for No. 269, Mount Rainier West, and No. 270, Mount Rainier East, or ask the USGS for Mowich Lake and Sunrise.

Directions: From Tacoma, drive east on Highway 410 to Buckley. Turn south on Highway 165 and drive 14 miles to Carbon River Road. Turn left and drive 8 miles to Carbon River Entrance Station. Continue 5 miles to Ipsut Creek Campground at road's end. The trailhead is well marked.

Contact: Mount Rainier National Park, Wilkeson Wilderness Information Center, P.O. Box 423, Wilkeson, WA 98396, 360/569-6020.

20 CARBON GLACIER/ MYSTIC LAKE

15.5 mi/8.0 hr–2 days

north of The Mountain in Mount Rainier National Park

Map 5.2, page 240

Situated on the famed Wonderland Trail, there isn't a lake closer to Mount Rainier than Mystic Lake. This seven-mile stretch of Washington's most esteemed trail is incredibly diverse. It travels through old-growth forest on the Carbon River, past Rainier's lowest and longest glacier, and upward to rocky alpine meadows and a majestic lake. This is one of the park's premier hikes.

The length of the route follows Wonderland Trail. The trail starts mildly, cruising through ancient forests. After crossing Carbon River (3 miles), however, the trail climbs unrelentingly to Mystic Lake. Somehow, the trail finds a path between Carbon Glacier and the valley wall. Those cracking noises you hear are the glacier giving way to the hot summer sun; walking on the glacier is ill advised without an ice ax and proper training.

Wonderland Trail parts ways with the glacier as it enters Moraine Park (5.5 miles), acres of wildflower meadows. A welcome sight on hot days, Mystic Lake lies just below Mineral Mountain. Although it stands 800 feet above the lake, Mineral Mountain can do little to block Mount Rainier and its ragged Willis Wall. Backcountry camps are situated at Dick Creek (4 miles) and Mystic Lake (7.7 miles); they require permits and are usually occupied by Wonderland trekkers.

User Groups: Hikers only. No dogs, horses, or mountain bikes are allowed. No wheelchair access.

Open Seasons: This area is usually accessible mid-July–September.

Permits: A National Parks Pass is required to enter the park. Overnight stays within the national park require backcountry camping permits, which are available at Wilkeson Wilderness Information Center.

Maps: For a map of Mount Rainier National Park, contact the Outdoor Recreation Information Center at the downtown Seattle REI. For a topographic map, ask Green Trails for No. 269, Mount Rainier West, or ask the USGS for Mowich Lake.

Directions: From Tacoma, drive east on Highway 410 to Buckley. Turn south on Highway 165 and drive 14 miles to Carbon River Road. Turn left and drive 8 miles to Carbon River Entrance Station. Continue 5 miles to Ipsut Creek Campground at road's end. The trailhead is well marked.

Contact: Mount Rainier National Park, Wilkeson Wilderness Information Center, P.O. Box 423, Wilkeson, WA 98396, 360/569-6020.

21 TOLMIE PEAK LOOKOUT

6.5 mi/3.5 hrs

northwest of Tahoma in Mount Rainier National Park

Map 5.2, page 240

The best job in the United States is a summer spent staffing the Tolmie Peak Lookout. The job description includes: a three-mile commute through pristine subalpine forest, picturesque

Eunice Lake surrounded in parkland meadows, and panoramic views from the office, encompassing The Mountain and miles of national forest. Ready to sign up?

Tolmie Peak Trail begins at Mowich Lake, a spectacular setting itself. The trail leaves the large, forested lake and rises gently to Ipsut Pass (1.5 miles), a junction with Carbon River Trail. Stay to the left and continue climbing to Eunice Lake (2.3 miles), where meadows reach to the lake's edges. The trail then climbs steeply one more mile to Tolmie Lookout (elevation 5,939 feet) atop the windswept peak. Mount Rainier is the obvious attraction, but Mount St. Helens and the North Cascades make appearances as well. Talk about your prime picnic spots. If the final steep climb to the lookout sounds unappealing, stopping short at Eunice Lake is a good hike as well. In late July, wildflowers fill the meadows bordering Eunice, and views of Mount Rainier are still to be had.

User Groups: Hikers only. No dogs, horses, or mountain bikes are allowed. No wheelchair access.

Open Seasons: This area is accessible June–October.

Permits: A National Parks Pass is required to enter the park.

Maps: For a map of Mount Rainier National Park, contact the Outdoor Recreation Information Center at the downtown Seattle REI. For a topographic map, ask Green Trails for No. 269, Mount Rainier West, or ask the USGS for Mowich Lake and Golden Lakes.

Directions: From Tacoma, drive east on Highway 410 to Buckley. Turn south on Highway 165 and drive 14 miles to Carbon River Road junction. Stay to the right on Mowich Lake Road and drive 17 miles to Mowich Lake Campground at road's end. The trailhead is well marked.

Contact: Mount Rainier National Park, Wilkeson Wilderness Information Center, P.O. Box 423, Wilkeson, WA 98396, 360/569-6020.

22 SPRAY PARK
8.8 mi/4.5 hrs

northwest of The Mountain in Mount Rainier National Park

Map 5.2, page 240

Spray Park is without a doubt one of the most beautiful places on Mount Rainier. Meadows measured by the square mile cover the upper reaches of this trail, dominated by the imposing stature of The Mountain. Wildflowers erupt and blanket the high country in late July, while black bears in search of huckleberries roam in late August. The trail is one of the greats in the national park and receives heavy use.

Spray Park Trail leaves from Mowich Lake, an inviting dip after a hot summer day on the trail. The trail meanders through the forest to Eagle Cliff (1.5 miles), where the trail follows the precipitous slope. A side trail wanders over to Spray Falls (1.9 miles) before making a steep ascent on switchbacks. The reward for the effort is a breakout from forest into open meadow. Spray Park Trail wanders through this open country, past tarns and rock fields to a saddle (elevation 6,400 feet) with views of even more meadows. The saddle is a good turnaround point, as the trail drops beyond it to Carbon River. Be sure to bring ample water, a rarity beyond Spray Falls. And remember, the meadows here are very fragile; please stay on established trails.

User Groups: Hikers only. No dogs, horses, or mountain bikes are allowed. No wheelchair access.

Open Seasons: This area is usually accessible July–September.

Permits: A National Parks Pass is required to enter the park.

Maps: For a map of Mount Rainier National Park, contact the Outdoor Recreation Information Center at the downtown Seattle REI. For a topographic map, ask Green Trails for No. 269, Mount Rainier West, or ask the USGS for Mowich Lake.

Directions: From Tacoma, drive east on Highway 410 to Buckley. Turn south on Highway

165 and drive 14 miles to Carbon River Road junction. Stay to the right on Mowich Lake Road and drive 17 miles to Mowich Lake Campground at road's end. The trailhead is well marked.

Contact: Mount Rainier National Park, Wilkeson Wilderness Information Center, P.O. Box 423, Wilkeson, WA 98396, 360/569-6020.

23 SUNRISE NATURE TRAILS
1.5–3.2 mi/0.5–1.5 hrs
near Sunrise in Mount Rainier National Park

Map 5.2, page 240

The beauty of Sunrise's high placement means that hikers don't have to venture far for an incredible hike. Although the views start at the parking lot, pavement is usually something we're trying to avoid. Several great options are well suited to hikers of all abilities. Options vary from trips to Shadow Lake or Frozen Lake to a nature trail and a walk through a silver forest. These are perfect trails for families with little ones or for folks conducting an auto tour around the park.

Although the network of trails surrounding Sunrise seems like a jumbled cobweb, every junction is well signed and easy to navigate. Trails to the two lakes are easy walks. Shadow Lake is a level three-mile round-trip, with meadows and views of Rainier all the way. Frozen Lake gains a little more elevation and peers out over the colorful meadows of Berkeley Park (3.2 miles round-trip).

The west end of Sourdough Ridge Trail features a self-guided nature trail, a 1.5-mile loop with some elevation gain. Lupine and bistort are on full display in July. On the south side of the visitors center is Silver Forest Trail (2.4 miles), a unique path through a forest of bare snags, long ago killed but not toppled by fire.

User Groups: Hikers only. No dogs, horses, or mountain bikes are allowed. No wheelchair access.

Open Seasons: This area is usually accessible July–September.

Permits: A National Parks Pass is required to enter the park.

Maps: For a map of Mount Rainier National Park, contact the Outdoor Recreation Information Center at the downtown Seattle REI. For a topographic map, ask Green Trails for No. 270, Mount Rainier East, or ask the USGS for Sunrise.

Directions: From Puyallup, drive east 52 miles on Highway 410 to Sunrise Road in Mount Rainier National Park. Turn right and drive 15 miles to the trailhead at Sunrise Visitor Center.

Contact: Mount Rainier National Park, White River Wilderness Information Center, 70004 Highway 410 East, Enumclaw, WA 98022, 360/569-6030.

24 BERKELEY AND GRAND PARKS
7.6–15.2 mi/4.0–8.0 hrs
out of Sunrise in Mount Rainier National Park

Map 5.2, page 240

A grand destination indeed, wide, flat Grand Park stretches for more than a mile with incredible views of Mount Rainier. On the way, Berkeley Park dazzles with its own wildflower displays and beautiful stream. In a land of many high-country meadows, this is a dandy of a choice.

The route leaves the high country of Sunrise and gently wanders through meadows to Frozen Lake (1.5 miles), tucked beneath Mount Fremont and Burroughs Mountain. Follow the Wonderland Trail for one mile to Northern Loop Trail and drop into Berkeley Park (2.5 miles), where streams crisscross the lush meadows. This is a good turnaround for hikers uninterested in making the longer trip to Grand Park.

Northern Loop Trail leaves Berkeley Park and travels through open subalpine forest to Grand Park (7.6 miles). Grand Park and its meadows stretch more than a mile to the north. Deer and elk are frequent visitors to the meadows, where they find an abundance

Mount Rainier from Grand Park

of summer grazing. Although Grand Park is preferably accomplished in a day, hikers hoping to spend the night can pitch camp at Berkeley Camp (3.8 miles) or hike 3.3 miles beyond Grand Park to Lake Eleanor (11.4 miles one-way). Access to Lake Eleanor via an unofficial trail from national forest land is frowned upon by the Park Service; besides, it misses out on the best sections of the route.

User Groups: Hikers only. No dogs, horses, or mountain bikes are allowed. No wheelchair access.

Open Seasons: This area is usually accessible mid-July–September.

Permits: A National Parks Pass is required to enter the park.

Maps: For a map of Mount Rainier National Park, contact the Outdoor Recreation Information Center at the downtown Seattle REI. For a topographic map, ask Green Trails for No. 270, Mount Rainier East, or ask the USGS for Sunrise.

Directions: From Puyallup, drive east 52 miles on Highway 410 to Sunrise Road in Mount Rainier National Park. Turn right and drive 15 miles to the trailhead at Sunrise Visitor Center.

Contact: Mount Rainier National Park, White River Wilderness Information Center, 70004 Highway 410 East, Enumclaw, WA 98022, 360/569-6030.

25 MOUNT FREMONT LOOKOUT

6.0 mi/3.0 hrs

out of Sunrise in Mount Rainier National Park

Map 5.2, page 240

Where there's a lookout, there are views. And there's no lookout closer to Mount Rainier than the one atop Mount Fremont. Never mind that the lookout doesn't sit on Fremont's summit. There are still plenty of views along this great trail. Hiking in Rainier high country is all about meadows, and this trail is no different. It travels exclusively through open meadows, and as long as the weather is clear (never a guarantee around The Mountain), you can expect knock-your-boots-off views. Best of all, Mount Fremont is an easy trail to navigate for hikers, gaining just 1,200 feet in about three miles.

Mount Fremont Trail leaves the popular Sunrise Visitor Center and quickly climbs to Sourdough Ridge. Mount Rainier is almost too close, crowding much of the southern horizon. Pass picturesque Frozen Lake at 1.5 miles as the trail encounters a large but well-signed junction. Mount Fremont Trail heads north along the rocky ridge, tops out in elevation, and drops to the lookout, built in the 1930s. Although it's hard to take your eyes off Tahoma and its glaciers, the Cascades and Olympics will call from distant horizons. The vast meadows of Grand Park below the lookout are a painter's palette of color in July. Be sure to carry enough water for the trip; there's none to be found along the way.

User Groups: Hikers only. No dogs, horses, or mountain bikes are allowed. No wheelchair access.

Open Seasons: This trail is accessible mid-July–September.

Permits: A National Parks Pass is required to enter the park.

Maps: For a map of Mount Rainier National Park, contact the Outdoor Recreation Information Center at the downtown Seattle REI. For a topographic map, ask Green Trails for No. 270, Mount Rainier East, or ask the USGS for Sunrise.

Directions: From Puyallup, drive east 52 miles on Highway 410 to Sunrise Road in Mount Rainier National Park. Turn right and drive 15 miles to the trailhead at Sunrise Visitor Center.

Contact: Mount Rainier National Park, White River Wilderness Information Center, 70004 Highway 410 East, Enumclaw, WA 98022, 360/569-6030.

26 SOURDOUGH RIDGE/ DEGE PEAK

2.5 mi/1.5 hrs

near Sunrise in Mount Rainier National Park

Map 5.2, page 240

Sourdough Ridge Trail covers more than four miles of immaculate subalpine meadows immersed in grand views of Mount Rainier and much more. The trail follows Sourdough Ridge from Sunrise Visitor Center out to Dege Peak and Sunrise Point on the east end. A visit here in July will yield acre upon acre of blooming wildflowers, with swaths of paintbrush, lupine, and daisies on the mountainside. This is a popular and heavily used trail near the Sunrise Visitor Center, and rightfully so. There may be no easier or quicker way to get a view of Tahoma.

Sourdough Ridge Trail quickly climbs away

from Sunrise Visitor Center into meadows. Every step leads to a better view. Of course The Mountain is impressively big, but the Cowlitz Chimneys and Sarvent Glaciers are seen best from this route. Those who survive the ascent of the first mile have seen the worst. The trail follows the ridge beneath Antler Peak and Dege Peak, the trail's highlight (a side trail leads to its summit). Look north over meadowy ridges to the Palisades and all the way up to Glacier Peak. This is a great hike for families visiting Sunrise; the trail gains less than 600 feet.

User Groups: Hikers only. No dogs, horses, or mountain bikes are allowed. No wheelchair access.

Open Seasons: This area is usually accessible mid-June–September.

Permits: A National Parks Pass is required to enter the park.

Maps: For a map of Mount Rainier National Park, contact the Outdoor Recreation Information Center at the downtown Seattle REI. For a topographic map, ask Green Trails for No. 270, Mount Rainier East, or ask the USGS for Sunrise.

Directions: From Puyallup, drive east 52 miles on Highway 410 to Sunrise Road in Mount Rainier National Park. Turn right and drive 15 miles to the trailhead at Sunrise Visitor Center.

Contact: Mount Rainier National Park, White River Wilderness Information Center, 70004 Highway 410 East, Enumclaw, WA 98022, 360/569-6030.

27 BURROUGHS MOUNTAIN LOOP

5.5 mi/3.0 hrs

near Sunrise in Mount Rainier National Park

Map 5.2, page 240

One of Mount Rainier's best day hikes, Burroughs Mountain is also one of its most challenging. Many hikers set out on this hike only to be turned back by snowfields that linger well into August. It's best to check in with the ranger at Sunrise and get a trail report. Snow or not, there's definitely lots to see along the way. Along the way you'll find meadows of flowers and marmots before reaching the tundralike expanses atop Burroughs Mountain. Add to it a lake for lunch and views of glaciers, and Burroughs Loop seems to have it all.

Burroughs Mountain Trail makes a five-mile loop up to the high, rocky plateau of Burroughs Mountain. A clockwise direction is best, especially if the north side is still snowy. From the visitors center, the trail crosses over crystal streams and colorful meadows to Shadow Lake and an overlook of Emmons Glacier and the White River (1.4 miles). Hikers start dropping off as the trail climbs 900 feet to First Burroughs Mountain (2.8 miles). Guaranteed: Mount Rainier has never looked so big in your life.

Burroughs Mountain Trail wanders the wide, flat plateau and drops to Frozen Lake (3.6 miles). Snowfields like to linger along this northern half of the loop. These steep slopes can be crossed when snowy, but an ice ax is highly, highly recommended. The well-signed trail heads back to the visitors center.

User Groups: Hikers only. No dogs, horses, or mountain bikes are allowed. No wheelchair access.

Open Seasons: This area is usually accessible July–September.

Permits: A National Parks Pass is required to enter the park.

Maps: For a map of Mount Rainier National Park, contact the Outdoor Recreation Information Center at the downtown Seattle REI. For a topographic map, ask Green Trails for No. 270, Mount Rainier East, or ask the USGS for Sunrise.

Directions: From Puyallup, drive east 52 miles on Highway 410 to Sunrise Road in Mount Rainier National Park. Turn right and drive 15 miles to the trailhead at Sunrise Visitor Center.

Contact: Mount Rainier National Park, White River Wilderness Information Center, 70004 Highway 410 East, Enumclaw, WA 98022, 360/569-6030.

28 PALISADES LAKES
6.6 mi/3.5 hrs–2 days

near Sunrise in Mount Rainier National Park

Map 5.2, page 240

There is no easier lake hike in Mount Rainier National Park than Palisades Lakes Trail. It has no big views of Tahoma; those are blocked by the rugged Sourdough Mountains. But Palisades Lakes Trail offers seven subalpine lakes and many smaller tarns, each among acres of meadows and rocky ridges. The trail is up and down but never significantly, making this a perfect hike for younger hikers. The short length of the trail means it's easily hiked in an afternoon, but a pair of backcountry camps are enticing enough to warrant an overnight visit.

Palisades Lakes Trail leaves Sunrise Road and quickly climbs to Sunrise Lake (.4 mile), where a short side trail leads to the small, forested lake. Palisades Trail continues past Clover Lake (1.4 miles) and Hidden Lake (2.5 miles), each surrounded by subalpine groves and meadows. Another mile of trail through acres of meadows, brimming with wildflowers in early August, arrives at Upper Palisades Lake. The lake gets its name from the rocky ridge, known as the Palisades, framing the basin. Marmots and picas are sure to be heard whistling from the talus slopes, and mountain goats are residents of the area too. For an overnight stay, you must make camp at either Dicks Lake or Upper Palisades.

User Groups: Hikers only. No dogs, horses, or mountain bikes are allowed. No wheelchair access.

Open Seasons: This area is usually accessible mid-June–September.

Permits: A National Parks Pass is required to enter the park. Overnight stays within the national park require backcountry camping permits, which are available at Sunrise Visitor Center.

Maps: For a map of Mount Rainier National Park, contact the Outdoor Recreation Information Center at the downtown Seattle REI.

For a topographic map, ask Green Trails for No. 270, Mount Rainier East, or ask the USGS for White River Park.

Directions: From Puyallup, drive east 52 miles on Highway 410 to Sunrise Road in Mount Rainier National Park. Turn right and drive 13 miles to Sunrise Point and the trailhead.

Contact: Mount Rainier National Park, White River Wilderness Information Center, 70004 Highway 410 East, Enumclaw, WA 98022, 360/569-6030.

29 CRYSTAL MOUNTAIN
9.0 mi/4.5 hrs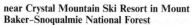

near Crystal Mountain Ski Resort in Mount Baker–Snoqualmie National Forest
Map 5.2, page 240

Better known for ski runs, Crystal Mountain features a good hiking trail. Getting there isn't quite as easy as using a ski lift, however, unless you actually ride the resort's chair lift, which is possible. Crystal Mountain Trail spends a fair amount of time in unimpressive woods before breaking out into miles of more-than-wonderful ridge hiking. This is a great place to view Mount Rainier and munch on huckleberries.

Crystal Mountain Trail begins with little flair, enduring clear-cuts and second-growth forest for three miles as it ascends 1,600 feet. That's the requirement to achieve Crystal Ridge and any notable rewards. At the ridge, Mount Rainier appears above the White River Valley. The trail climbs another three miles along the ridge through wide, rounded meadows mixed with steep, rocky slopes. Wildflowers are in full gear during early June while huckleberries make the trip twice as sweet in early August. Anywhere along the ridge is a good turnaround. Water is nonexistent, so carry plenty of extra water.

Crystal Mountain Trail can be completed several other ways, but they aren't as enjoyable. The trail forms a loop back to the ski resort, passing several small mountain lakes (a total of 13.8 miles, 2.5 on the road). An all-downhill version can be had by riding a ski lift up to the ridge and hiking back down.

User Groups: Hikers, leashed dogs, horses, and mountain bikes. No wheelchair access.

Open Seasons: This trail is accessible June–September.

Permits: A federal Northwest Forest Pass is required to park here.

Maps: For a map of Mount Baker–Snoqualmie National Forest, contact the Outdoor Recreation Information Center at the downtown Seattle REI. For topographic maps, ask Green Trails for No. 270, Mount Rainier East, and No. 271, Bumping Lake, or ask the USGS for Bumping Lake and White River.

Directions: From Puyallup, drive east 47 miles on State Highway 410 to Crystal Mountain Road (Forest Service Road 7190). Turn left (east) and drive 4.4 miles to Forest Service Road 7190-510. Turn right and drive .4 mile to Sand Flats camping area and the trailhead.

Contact: Mount Baker–Snoqualmie National Forest, Enumclaw Ranger Station, 450 Roosevelt Avenue East, Enumclaw, WA 98022, 360/825-6585.

30 NORSE PEAK
11.2–13.8 mi/6.0–7.5 hrs

near Crystal Mountain Ski Resort in Mount Baker–Snoqualmie National Forest
Map 5.2, page 240

Ignored by the masses at Mount Rainier, Norse Peak and Cascade Crest are equally deserving of attention. Although steep, Norse Peak Trail travels miles of meadows to a former lookout site west of Rainier. Conveniently, the trail offers a detour of even more meadowy hiking on the way. When in this region, it's often hard to justify not visiting the national park. Not here. Norse Peak is worth it.

Norse Peak Trail spends all of its time climbing, gaining 2,900 feet to the lookout. It's well laid out and never too steep, but it's certainly tiring under a hot summer sun. Most of the trail is exposed in high-country meadows, so bringing plenty of water and sunscreen are good ideas. Norse Peak Trail spends less than two miles in the forest before emerging into the open. As the trail climbs, Tahoma rises from behind Crystal Mountain. At 3.6 miles lies Goat Lake junction and at 4.9 miles is Norse Peak Lookout junction; stay to the right both times for the lookout, 6,856 feet of views. Tahoma is its usual magnificent self, but numerous other peaks are noteworthy too.

You can make a loop to visit beautiful Big Crow Basin. Descend from the lookout to the upper junction. Turn right and pass through the large basin of meadows to Pacific Crest Trail and back again via Goat Lake Trail. Even with a trip to the lookout, the loop is less than 14 miles.

User Groups: Hikers, leashed dogs, horses, and mountain bikes (no mountain bikes in Big Crow Basin). No wheelchair access.

Open Seasons: This trail is accessible mid-June–September.

Permits: A federal Northwest Forest Pass is required to park here.

Maps: For a map of Mount Baker–Snoqualmie National Forest, contact the Outdoor Recreation Information Center at the downtown Seattle REI. For a topographic map, ask Green Trails for No. 271, Bumping Lake, or ask the USGS for Norse Peak.

Directions: From Puyallup, drive east 47 miles on State Highway 410 to Crystal Mountain Road (Forest Service Road 7190). Turn left (east) and drive 4 miles to Forest Service Road 7190-410. Parking is on the right side of Crystal Mountain Road (Forest Service Road 7190); the signed trailhead is several hundred yards up Forest Service Road 7190-410.

Contact: Mount Baker–Snoqualmie National Forest, Enumclaw Ranger Station, 450 Roosevelt Avenue East, Enumclaw, WA 98022, 360/825-6585.

31 CRYSTAL LAKES
6.0 mi/3.5 hrs

near Sunrise in Mount Rainier National Park

Map 5.2, page 240

Crystal Lakes Trail presents hikers a choice between two inspiring destinations. One route heads to Crystal Lakes, a pair of sublime subalpine lakes cloaked in wildflower meadows. As the lakes are in a large basin beneath Sourdough Gap and Crystal Peak, the distant views are limited (but hardly missed). The second option bypasses the two lakes and climbs to Crystal Peak Lookout. Naturally, the views of The Mountain are great. Either way, a great trip is assured.

Crystal Lakes Trail leaves Highway 410 and hastily climbs the valley wall within forest. At 1.3 miles lies the decisive junction. Left for the lakes, right for the lookout. Crystal Lakes Trail keeps climbing, soon entering the open subalpine and Lower Crystal Lake (2.3 miles). Upper Crystal Lake is just a short climb away (3 miles). Acres of wildflowers light up the basins in early August. Backcountry camps are at each lake and require a camping permit. For those itching to get to a high viewpoint, the Crystal Peak Trail climbs 2.5 miles from the junction along a dry, open slope to the lookout (elevation 6,615 feet). On a clear day, five Cascades volcanoes are within view, not to mention much of the national park and surrounding national forest.

User Groups: Hikers only. No dogs, horses, or mountain bikes are allowed. No wheelchair access.

Open Seasons: This trail is usually accessible mid-July–September.

Permits: A National Parks Pass is required to enter the park. Overnight stays within the national park require backcountry camping permits, which are available at Sunrise Visitor Center.

Maps: For a map of Mount Rainier National Park, contact the Outdoor Recreation Information Center at the downtown Seattle REI. For a topographic map, ask Green Trails for No. 270, Mount Rainier East, or ask the USGS for White River Park.

Directions: From Puyallup, drive east 51 miles on Highway 410 to Crystal Lakes Trailhead, just before the White River Wilderness Information Center.

Contact: Mount Rainier National Park, White River Wilderness Information Center, 70004 Highway 410 East, Enumclaw, WA 98022, 360/569-6030.

32 GLACIER BASIN

3.8–7.0 mi/2.0–3.5 hrs

near Sunrise in Mount Rainier National Park

Map 5.2, page 240

Mount Rainier may be known best for the immense glaciers covering its slopes. More than two dozen massive ice sheets radiate from the mountain's summit, sculpting entire valleys and ridges. Glacier Basin Trail provides a close look at two of Mount Rainier's glaciers, Emmons Glacier and Inter Glacier, hard at work. If you find glaciers boring, then shift your attention to the hillsides and look for mountain goats among the meadows.

Here's a little geology lesson first. Glaciers are massive sheets of ice produced through thousands of years. Snowfall slowly accumulates through the years and becomes compacted into a sheet of ice. Enter gravity, which slowly pulls the glacier down the valley, scraping and sculpting the terrain as it moves. It may take a while (millennia), but glaciers are heavy-duty landscapers. When glaciers retreat (melt faster than they form, as they are now), they leave a denuded valley filled with moraine (piles of rock and dirt), which you'll see here. Got it? You're ready for Glacier Basin Trail.

The trail has two forks: Glacier Basin Trail (7 miles round-trip) and Emmons Glacier Trail (3.8 miles). The trail departs White River Campground and gently climbs to the junction (.9 mile): Head left for Emmons Glacier (the largest in the lower 48 states), right for Inter Glacier. Both trails provide great views of the glaciers. Being a glacier is dirty work, apparent from the enormous piles of rock and mud covering the ice. Glacier Basin is most popular with mountaineers seeking a summit of The Mountain.

User Groups: Hikers only. No dogs, horses, or mountain bikes are allowed. No wheelchair access.

Open Seasons: This trail is usually accessible mid-July–September.

Permits: A National Parks Pass is required to enter the park.

Maps: For a map of Mount Rainier National Park, contact the Outdoor Recreation Information Center at the downtown Seattle REI. For a topographic map, ask Green Trails for No. 270, Mount Rainier East, or ask the USGS for White River Park.

Directions: From Puyallup, drive east 52 miles on Highway 410 to Sunrise Road in Mount Rainier National Park. Turn right and drive 5.5 miles to White River Road. Turn left and drive 2 miles to White River Campground and signed trailhead.

Contact: Mount Rainier National Park, White River Wilderness Information Center, 70004 Highway 410 East, Enumclaw, WA 98022, 360/569-6030.

33 SUMMERLAND/ PANHANDLE GAP

8.6–11.4 mi/4.5–6.0 hrs

near Sunrise in Mount Rainier National Park

Map 5.2, page 240

Many hikers who have completed Wonderland Trail, a 93-mile trek around The Mountain, claim the country surrounding Panhandle Gap as their favorite. The meadows of Summerland and Ohanapecosh Park lie on either side of Panhandle Gap. Above, the ancient volcano of Little Tahoma stands before its big sister, Mount Rainier. Traveling this high country via Wonderland Trail at White River is a diverse and scenic trip.

The route leaves White River Campground and follows Wonderland through old-growth forest of large western hemlock, western red cedar, and Douglas fir. Little Tahoma, with Fryingpan Glacier hanging off its side, signals your arrival in the meadows and wildflowers of Summerland (4.3 miles). Large herds of mountain goats are frequently seen on the rocky slopes surrounding Summerland.

The curious and energetic can follow Wonderland Trail another 1.4 miles as it ascends steeply to the wind-swept terrain of Panhandle Gap. From this high point, the meadows of Ohanapecosh Park unfold beneath several high waterfalls. A word of caution: This high country is rocky and fairly barren. In many places, the trail is designated by rock cairns. No matter the season, be prepared for adverse weather. Tahoma has a system of its own, one that changes rapidly and unexpectedly, so bring warm clothes and know how to use your compass.

User Groups: Hikers only. No dogs, horses, or mountain bikes are allowed. No wheelchair access.

Open Seasons: This area is usually accessible August–September.

Permits: A National Parks Pass is required to enter the park.

Maps: For a map of Mount Rainier National Park, contact the Outdoor Recreation Information Center at the downtown Seattle REI. For a topographic map, ask Green Trails for No. 270, Mount Rainier East, or ask the USGS for Sunrise and White River Park.

Directions: From Puyallup, drive east 52 miles on Highway 410 to Sunrise Road in Mount Rainier National Park. Turn right and drive 4.5 miles to Fryingpan Trailhead on the left.

Contact: Mount Rainier National Park, White River Wilderness Information Center, 70004 Highway 410 East, Enumclaw, WA 98022, 360/569-6030.

34 OWYHIGH LAKES
7.6 mi/4.0 hrs

east of Tahoma in Mount Rainier National Park

Map 5.2, page 240

With such a dominating presence, Mount Rainier makes it easy to miss some of the other outstanding scenery in the park. Plenty of great hiking is to be had that doesn't include

bulky views of the massive volcano. Owyhigh Lakes Trail is one such hike, traveling up through old but dense forest to parkland lakes. Meadows of wildflowers surround the several lakes and light up the scenery during early August. If you're worried about missing out on seeing rocky peaks and ridges, don't fret. The lakes are situated between craggy Governors Ridge and stately Tamanos Mountain, home of four prominent pinnacles known as the Cowlitz Chimneys.

Adding to Owyhigh Trail's allure is its lack of people. When the crowds at the park visitors centers make you begin to think it's holiday shopping season at the mall, Owyhigh Lakes is likely to be vacant. Folks hoping to spend the night can pitch their shelters at Tamanos Creek Camp, .5 mile before the lakes; just remember to pick up your permit. The trail continues beyond the lakes, crests a pass, and drops five miles to Deer Creek Trailhead, requiring a car-drop. Day hikers should turn around at Owyhigh Lakes.

User Groups: Hikers only. No dogs, horses, or mountain bikes are allowed. No wheelchair access.

Open Seasons: This trail is accessible mid-July–September.

Permits: A National Parks Pass is required to enter the park.

Maps: For a map of Mount Rainier National Park, contact the Outdoor Recreation Information Center at the downtown Seattle REI. For a topographic map, ask Green Trails for No. 270, Mount Rainier East, or ask the USGS for White River Park and Chinook Pass.

Directions: From Puyallup, drive east 52 miles on Highway 410 to Sunrise Road in Mount Rainier National Park. Turn right and drive 3 miles to the signed trailhead on the left.

Contact: Mount Rainier National Park, White River Wilderness Information Center, 70004 Highway 410 East, Enumclaw, WA 98022, 360/569-6030.

35 CHINOOK PASS HIKES
1.0–13.0 mi/0.5–6.0 hrs
at Chinook Pass in Mount Baker–Snoqualmie National Forest

Map 5.2, page 240

Chinook Pass is one of the most beautiful of Washington's Cascade passes. So it comes as no surprise that it is a starting point for some amazing hiking. Three great hikes originate here, two of them routes along famed Pacific Crest Trail. Tipsoo Lake Trail is extremely easy, perfect for families with little ones. Naches Loop is longer but also easy, full of big-time views. Sourdough Gap and Pickhandle Point offer views and meadows along PCT.

Tipsoo Lake is a short one-mile walk around the high mountain lake. Wildflowers light up the meadows in July, with views of Mount Rainier. The trail around Tipsoo Lake is flat with many picnic sites.

Making a four-mile loop around Naches Peak, PCT connects to Naches Trail among acres of wildflower-filled meadows. The preferred route is clockwise, so as to keep Mount Rainier in front of you. The trail gains just 400 feet but is exposed and dry, becoming hot on summer afternoons.

A longer trip from Chinook Pass heads along PCT to Sourdough Gap and Pickhandle Point. This is one of PCT's most beautiful segments, traveling through open meadows to Sourdough Gap (3 miles one-way) and Pickhandle Point (6.5 miles). Pickhandle Point lies south and above the lifts of the local ski resort; skiers accustomed to a snowy landscape will be just as pleased with the summertime look.

User Groups: Hikers, leashed dogs, and horses. No mountain bikes are allowed. Tipsoo Lake Trail is wheelchair accessible.

Open Seasons: This area is accessible June–mid-October.

Permits: A federal Northwest Forest Pass is required to park here.

Maps: For a map of Mount Baker–Snoqualmie National Forest, contact the Outdoor Recreation Information Center at the downtown Seattle REI.

For a topographic map, ask Green Trails for No. 270, Mount Rainier East, and No. 271, Bumping Lake, or ask the USGS for Chinook Pass.

Directions: From Puyallup, drive east 60 miles on Highway 410 to Tipsoo Lake Trailhead, on the west side of Chinook Pass.

Contact: Wenatchee National Forest, Naches Ranger Station, 10237 Highway 12, Naches, WA 98937, 509/653-2205.

36 KLAPATCHE PARK
21.0 mi/2 days
near Longmire in Mount Rainier National Park

Map 5.2, page 240

The one sure way to instantly turn a popular backcountry destination into a remote and lonely journey is to close the access road. That's exactly what happened to Klapatche Park, now mostly enjoyed by trekkers on Wonderland Trail. A washout on Westside Road extended a trip into Klapatche from five miles round-trip into 21 miles. That's 16 miles of road—but don't miss out on the miles of meadows and high country lakes of Klapatche Park. Instead, hop on a mountain bike and turn this into Washington's best ride and hike.

The best access to Klapatche Park is via Klapatche Ridge Trail, eight miles up Westside Road. The trail climbs through old-growth forest to the high meadows of Klapatche Park and Aurora Lake (2.5 miles). Mount Rainier towers above fields of lupine, aster, and penstemon. The giant meadows of St. Andrew's Park are a must side trip, just a mile south on Wonderland Trail. This certainly qualifies as some of the park's best high country. Return back via Klapatche Ridge Trail or make a loop of it via South Puyallup Trail. Camping is allowed only at Klapatche Park Camp or South Puyallup Camp and requires reservations. Road or not, this is a gorgeous hike.

User Groups: Hikers and mountain bikes (mountain bikes on Westside Road). No dogs or horses are allowed. No wheelchair access.

Open Seasons: This trail is accessible July–mid-October.

Permits: A National Parks Pass is required to enter the park.

Maps: For a map of Mount Rainier National Park, contact the Outdoor Recreation Information Center at the downtown Seattle REI. For a topographic map, ask Green Trails for No. 269, Mount Rainier West, or ask the USGS for Mount Wow and Mount Rainier West.

Directions: From Tacoma, drive south 40 miles on Highway 7 to Elbe. Turn east on Highway 706 and drive 10 miles to the Nisqually Entrance Station. Continue 1 mile to Westside Road. Turn left and drive to the trailhead at the washout. Hike or bike 8 miles on the closed road to the trailhead on the right.

Contact: Mount Rainier National Park, Longmire Wilderness Information Center, Tahoma Woods, Star Route, Ashford, WA 98304, 360/569-4453.

37 EMERALD RIDGE LOOP
16.2 mi/1–2 days

near Longmire in Mount Rainier National Park

Map 5.2, page 240

More remote and less accessible than other faces, Mount Rainier's western side features few trails outside of Mowich. And the trails that do explore The Mountain's western slopes are fading into obscurity thanks to the closure of Westside Road. That's a shame, as Emerald Ridge is a beauty of a trail. With old-growth forest, alpine meadows, and an almost-close-enough-to-touch encounter with Tahoma Glacier, there's little left to desire.

Westside Road once provided easy access to the trailheads. But after a washout, the Park Service decided not to reopen it. That has kept the crowds out and the animals wild. It also means some road walking, about 8.3 miles of road out of a 16.2-mile total loop. The park does allow mountain bikes on the road; the smart hiker bikes to the upper trailhead, hikes the loop, and coasts back to the car.

On the trail, the loop follows Round Pass Trail and South Emerald Ridge Trail up to Wonder-

land Trail (2.1 miles). An interesting outcrop of columnar basalt (hexagonal columns formed as erupted lava cooled) is found just before the junction. Wonderland Trail climbs to emerald meadows and Tahoma Glacier (4.3 miles). Glacier Island, encircled by glaciers as recently as the 1930s, stands before the towering bulk of Mount Rainier. The loop drops to Tahoma Creek Trail (5.8 miles) and to the lower trailhead (7.9 miles). Backpackers need to plan on setting up for the night at South Puyallup Camp (the only site along the trail), located at the junction of South Emerald Ridge and Wonderland Trails.

User Groups: Hikers and mountain bikes (mountain bikes on Westside Road). No dogs or horses are allowed. No wheelchair access.

Open Seasons: This trail is accessible July–mid-October.

Permits: A National Parks Pass is required to enter the park.

Maps: For a map of Mount Rainier National Park, contact the Outdoor Recreation Information Center at the downtown Seattle REI. For a topographic map, ask Green Trails for No. 269, Mount Rainier West, or ask the USGS for Mount Wow and Mount Rainier West.

Directions: From Tacoma, drive south 40 miles on Highway 7 to Elbe. Turn east on Highway 706 and drive 10 miles to the Nisqually Entrance Station. Continue 1 mile to Westside Road. Turn left and drive to the trailhead at the washout. Hike or bike 5 miles on the closed road to the trailhead on the right.

Contact: Mount Rainier National Park, Longmire Wilderness Information Center, Tahoma Woods, Star Route, Ashford, WA 98304, 360/569-4453.

38 GLACIER VIEW WILDERNESS
1.5–7.0 mi/1.0–3.5 hrs

west of Mount Rainier in Glacier View Wilderness of Gifford Pinchot National Forest

Map 5.2, page 240

Excluded from the national park but protected by wilderness designation, Glacier View

Wilderness is a gem hidden from the masses. This small enclave on the west side of Mount Rainier National Park features several pristine mountain lakes and a pair of gorgeous viewpoints. When you want to see The Mountain in all its glory but don't want to bump elbows with the crowds at Sunrise or Paradise, head to Glacier View Wilderness.

The wilderness is bisected by Glacier View Trail, which runs north to south and has two trailheads. The southern trailhead provides easy access to Lake Christine. The trail climbs gently to the mountain lake (.75 mile), cloaked by mountain hemlock and subalpine fir. There are several great campsites, and the fishing is supposedly not half bad either. From the lake, a side trail leads one mile to the summit of Mount Beljica, awash in big views of Rainier.

The northern trailhead provides access to Glacier View Lookout. Glacier View Trail runs north along a forested ridge to Glacier View Lookout (2 miles; elevation 5,450). This high forest is chock-full of ancient trees and bear grass with its huge blooms. The lookout provides great views of Rainier and surrounding countryside. Beyond the lookout are Lake West (2.3 miles) and Lake Helen (3.5 miles). Both lakes have several campsites. You'll likely be able to count on one hand the people you run across.

User Groups: Hikers and leashed dogs. No horses or mountain bikes are allowed. No wheelchair access.

Open Seasons: This area is accessible mid-June–October.

Permits: A federal Northwest Forest Pass is required to park here.

Maps: For a map of Gifford Pinchot National Forest, contact the Outdoor Recreation Information Center at the downtown Seattle REI. For a topographic map, ask Green Trails for No. 269, Mount Rainier West, or ask the USGS for Mount Wow.

Directions: From Tacoma, drive south 40 miles on Highway 7 to Elbe. Turn east on Highway 706 and drive to Copper Creek Road (Forest Service Road 59). Turn left and drive 4.5 miles to Forest Service Road 5920. Turn right and drive to the unsigned trailhead at road's end.

Contact: Gifford Pinchot National Forest, Cowlitz Valley Ranger Station, 10024 U.S. 12, Randle, WA 98377, 360/497-1100.

39 GOBBLER'S KNOB/ LAKE GEORGE

6.4–8.8 mi/3.5–4.5 hrs

west of Mount Rainier in Glacier View Wilderness and Mount Rainier National Park

Map 5.2, page 240

Gobbler's Knob is the best deal in the Mount Rainier area. Pristine old-growth forest blankets this grand route as it passes a beautiful mountain lake on its way to the national park, a viewpoint, and another impressive lake. From atop Gobbler's Knob, Mount Rainier looms large with its impressive stature. Lake George lies beneath Mount Wow. Wow means "goat" in the Salish, the language of local American Indians in the Puget Sound region, and it's likely what you'll be mouthing as you watch mountain goats rambling along the steep slopes.

The preferred route to Gobbler's Knob and Lake George crosses Glacier View Wilderness. A washout on Westside Road increased access via the national park by three miles (all on old road). Avoid park fees and an unsightly road walk by hiking through the wilderness. Puyallup Trail meanders through Beljica Meadows to the junction with Lake Christine Trail (.9 mile). Head left as the trail drops through old-growth mountain hemlock and subalpine fir to Goat Lake (2.3 miles). Campsites are scattered around the lake and require no backcountry permits.

Puyallup Trail then climbs to a saddle between Gobbler's Knob and rocky Mount Wow (3.2 miles). A side trail leads to Gobbler's Knob Lookout and its drop-dead views of Mount Rainier and its glaciers. What a place to watch a sunset! Lake George lies 1,200 feet below, surrounded by forest and rocky slopes. Lake George Camp requires backcountry permits from the National Park Service. The trail continues .8 mile to the abandoned Westside Road.

User Groups: Hikers only. No dogs, horses, or mountain bikes are allowed. No wheelchair access.

Open Seasons: This area is accessible mid-June–October.

Permits: A federal Northwest Forest Pass is required to park here.

Maps: For a map of Mount Rainier National Park and Gifford Pinchot National Forest, contact the Outdoor Recreation Information Center at the downtown Seattle REI. For a topographic map, ask Green Trails for No. 269, Mount Rainier West, or ask the USGS for Mount Wow.

Directions: From Tacoma, drive south 40 miles on Highway 7 to Elbe. Turn east on Highway 706 and drive to Copper Creek Road (Forest Service Road 59). Turn left and drive 4.5 miles to Forest Service Road 5920. Turn right and drive to the unsigned trailhead at road's end. (For access via the national park, follow directions for the Emerald Ridge listing in this chapter.)

Contact: Mount Rainier National Park, Longmire Wilderness Information Center, Tahoma Woods, Star Route, Ashford, WA 98304, 360/569-4453.

40 INDIAN HENRY'S HUNTING GROUND

11.4 mi/7.0 hrs

near Longmire in Mount Rainier National Park

Map 5.2, page 240

Home to some of Mount Rainier's most beautiful scenery, Kautz Creek Trail to Indian Henry's Hunting Ground has it all. The trail passes through old-growth forest, where Douglas firs, western hemlocks, and western red cedars have been standing together for centuries. Upper sections of the route are enveloped in subalpine meadows, where bear, deer, and marmots roam the parkland. And of course, The Mountain makes a grand appearance, towering above the high country with rocky arms and glistening glaciers. It's a full day of hiking, but enjoyable every step of the way.

There are three ways into Indian Henry's Hunting Ground, the best being via Kautz Creek, described below. Other options include Wonderland Trail out of Longmire (an up and down 13.8 miles) and Tahoma Creek Trail (a steeper, less scenic 10 miles). Kautz Creek Trail quickly crosses its namesake on an old floodplain. The trail then climbs through stands of old-growth forest on its way to high-country meadows (3.5 miles). The grade becomes more gentle in its final two miles, providing plenty of time to snack on huckleberries in the fall. A great side trip is Mirror Lakes (an extra 1.2 miles round-trip), where Tahoma reflects in the small subalpine tarns. At Indian Henry's Hunting Ground stands a historic patrol cabin still staffed by the Park Service. The only campground within the area is Devils Dream Camp (reservations required), usually full with Wonderland Trail trekkers.

User Groups: Hikers only. No dogs, horses, or mountain bikes are allowed. No wheelchair access.

Open Seasons: This area is usually accessible year-round.

Permits: A National Parks Pass is required to enter the park. Overnight stays within the national park require backcountry camping permits, which are available at Longmire Wilderness Information Center in Ashford.

Maps: For a map of Mount Rainier National Park, contact the Outdoor Recreation Information Center at the downtown Seattle REI. For a topographic map, ask Green Trails for No. 269, Mount Rainier West, and No. 301, Randle, or ask the USGS for Mount Rainier West.

Directions: From Tacoma, drive south 40 miles on Highway 7 to Elbe. Turn east on Highway 706 and drive 10 miles to the Nisqually Entrance Station. Continue 7 miles to Longmire Wilderness Information Center. The trailhead is across the street in Kautz Creek Picnic Area.

Contact: Mount Rainier National Park, Longmire Wilderness Information Center, Tahoma Woods, Star Route, Ashford, WA 98304, 360/569-4453.

41 RAMPART RIDGE LOOP
4.5 mi/2.5 hrs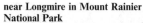

near Longmire in Mount Rainier National Park

Map 5.2, page 240

Climbing atop one of Rainier's ancient lava flows, Rampart Ridge Trail delivers the requisite views and meadows needed in any hike. The trail offers some of the best views of Tahoma (Mount Rainier) from the Longmire Visitor Center. Included in the deal are old-growth forests and some likely encounters with wildlife. Deer, grouse, squirrels, and woodpeckers are regular residents of the area. Gaining little more than 1,100 feet, it's a great trail for all hikers.

The loop is best done clockwise, hiking along the ridge toward the mountain. Rampart Ridge Trail begins on Trail of the Shadows, just 300 yards from the parking lot. From there, it switchbacks at a moderate but steady grade around the steep cliffs of Rampart Ridge. The forest here is great old-growth mountain hemlocks and subalpine firs, decked out in gowns of moss and lichens. The trail finds the top of the ridge (1.5 miles) and follows the level plateau for more than a mile. Forest is regularly broken up by meadows of wildflowers (try the month of July) and huckleberries (usually ripe in August). Although The Mountain dominates the skyline, Rampart Ridge offers a great view of the large, U-shaped Nisqually River Valley (thank you, glaciers). The trail circles back to Longmire via Wonderland Trail.

User Groups: Hikers only. No dogs, horses, or mountain bikes are allowed. No wheelchair access.

Open Seasons: This trail is usually accessible July–mid-October.

Permits: A National Parks Pass is required to enter the park.

Maps: For a map of Mount Rainier National Park, contact the Outdoor Recreation Information Center at the downtown Seattle REI. For a topographic map, ask Green Trails for No. 269, Mount Rainier West, or ask the USGS for Mount Rainier West.

Directions: From Tacoma, drive south 40 miles on Highway 7 to Elbe. Turn east on Highway 706 and drive 10 miles to the Nisqually Entrance Station. Continue 18 miles to the National Park Inn at Paradise. The trailhead is behind the inn.

Contact: Mount Rainier National Park, Longmire Wilderness Information Center, Tahoma Woods, Star Route, Ashford, WA 98304, 360/569-4453.

42 COMET FALLS/ VAN TRUMP PARK
6.2 mi/3.5 hrs

near Longmire in Mount Rainier National Park

Map 5.2, page 240

Two of the most scenic spots in Mount Rainier National Park are conveniently on the same trail. One of Rainier's highest waterfalls, Comet Falls, plunges off a rocky cliff more than 320 feet. It's the largest of several cascades along the route. As great as Comet Falls may be, Van Trump Park is arguably even better. Acre upon acre of meadow unfolds beneath behemoth Tahoma, with wildflowers coloring the entire scene during the summer. That rumbling is just Kautz and Van Trump Glaciers doing their thing, cracking and breaking in the summer heat.

You can bet that with so much to see, the trail will be busy. In fact, this is one of the park's most popular hikes. Unfortunately, it has a small trailhead with no alternate parking; be ready to choose another hike if the parking lot is full. Van Trump Park Trail leaves the trailhead and briskly climbs alongside the constantly cascading Van Trump Creek. Christine Falls is a short 10-minute walk from the trailhead. Old-growth forest provides shade all the way to Comet Falls. Shutterbugs rejoice, but save some film for later. From the falls, Van Trump Park Trail switchbacks up to open meadows and prime views. Clear days reveal the Tatoosh Range, Mount Adams, and Mount St. Helens to the south. Be sure to stick to established trails; in such a heavily used area, meadows are quickly destroyed by wayward feet.

User Groups: Hikers only. No dogs, horses, or mountain bikes are allowed. No wheelchair access.

Open Seasons: This trail is usually accessible July–mid-October.

Permits: A National Parks Pass is required to enter the park.

Maps: For a map of Mount Rainier National Park, contact the Outdoor Recreation Information Center at the downtown Seattle REI. For a topographic map, ask Green Trails for No. 269, Mount Rainier West, or ask the USGS for Mount Rainier West.

Directions: From Tacoma, drive south 40 miles on Highway 7 to Elbe. Turn east on Highway 706 and drive 10 miles to the Nisqually Entrance Station. Continue 12 miles to the signed trailhead on the left.

Contact: Mount Rainier National Park, Longmire Wilderness Information Center, Tahoma Woods, Star Route, Ashford, WA 98304, 360/569-4453.

43 EAGLE PEAK
7.2 mi/4.0 hrs

near Longmire in Mount Rainier National Park

Map 5.2, page 240

Directly out of Longmire, Eagle Peak Trail climbs skyward through old-growth forest and meadows to Eagle Peak Saddle on the north side of Tatoosh Range. At an elevation of 5,700 feet, Mount Rainier looms large while several other Cascade volcanoes are well within sight. The trail is fairly steep, gaining 2,700 feet in just 3.6 miles. Despite its close proximity to Longmire, the ascent keeps the trail less traveled than those near Sunrise or Paradise Visitor Centers.

Eagle Peak Trail climbs quickly and steeply through the mature forest. Douglas fir and mountain hemlock quickly give way to their relatives, mountain hemlock and subalpine fir. The forest covers the trail for three miles, keeping it relatively cool; the only water is found when the trail crosses a small stream (2 miles). The final .5 mile is a steep ascent in flower-clad meadows, with Eagle Peak towering above. The trail ends in a large saddle between Eagle and Chutla Peaks. Scrambles to either peak are recommended only for experienced and outfitted climbers. From this outpost of the Tatoosh Range, miles and miles of surrounding countryside (some forested, some denuded) are revealed. Hikers who neglect to bring a camera never fail to regret it.

User Groups: Hikers only. No dogs, horses, or mountain bikes are allowed. No wheelchair access.

Open Seasons: This area is usually accessible mid-July–September.

Permits: A National Parks Pass is required to enter the park.

Maps: For a map of Mount Rainier National Park, contact the Outdoor Recreation Information Center at the downtown Seattle REI. For a topographic map, ask Green Trails for No. 269, Mount Rainier West, and No. 301, Randle, or ask the USGS for Mount Rainier West and Wahpenayo.

Directions: From Tacoma, drive south 40 miles on Highway 7 to Elbe. Turn east on Highway 706 and drive 10 miles to the Nisqually Entrance Station. Continue 7 miles to Longmire Museum for parking. The signed trailhead is on the opposite side of the suspension bridge crossing the Nisqually River, on the left.

Contact: Mount Rainier National Park, Longmire Wilderness Information Center, Tahoma Woods, Star Route, Ashford, WA 98304, 360/569-4453.

44 PARADISE NATURE TRAILS
1.5–2.8 mi/0.7–1.5 hrs

near Paradise in Mount Rainier
National Park

Map 5.2, page 240

World-famous and Mount Rainier's most visited setting, Paradise fails to disappoint even the highest expectations. Directly below The Mountain among acres of subalpine meadows, Paradise sports a striking visitors center as well as the historic Paradise Inn. Folks have been coming here to experience Mount Rainier for well over 100 years. And Paradise is a great place to become acquainted with Washington's tallest peak on a number of easy and highly scenic trails. From glacier viewpoints to wildflower rambles, the trails of Paradise easily put visitors into seventh heaven.

The large network of trails near Paradise may appear confusing on a map, but all junctions are well signed. The meadows of this high country are extremely fragile and wither away quickly under the stomp of a boot. Be sure to stick to designated trails at all times. For a view of enormous Nisqually Glacier and its expansive moraine, hike from the visitors center to Nisqually Vista (1.6 miles). This level and wide trail makes a loop (shaped like a lasso) and is perfect for hikers of any ability. Also accessible from the visitors center is Alta Vista Trail (1.5 miles), a gentle climb to a viewpoint. From this small knob, Rainier's bulk astounds even the most veteran of hikers. Look south to take in views of southern Washington's other volcanic peaks, Mount St. Helens and Mount Adams.

Paradise Inn also offers an array of trails, easily customized to any length desired. A good hike is to Golden Gate (2.8 miles) and the vast meadows of Edith Creek Basin. Also beginning in Paradise but long enough to warrant their own listings in this chapter are Skyline Loop, Mazama Ridge, and Paradise Glacier Trails (see next listings).

User Groups: Hikers only. No dogs, horses, or mountain bikes are allowed. No wheelchair access.

Open Seasons: This area is accessible mid-June–October.

Permits: A National Parks Pass is required to enter the park.

Maps: For a map of Mount Rainier National Park, contact the Outdoor Recreation Information Center at the downtown Seattle REI. For a topographic map, ask Green Trails for No. 270S, Paradise, or ask the USGS for Mount Rainier East.

Directions: From Tacoma, drive south 40 miles on Highway 7 to Elbe. Turn east on Highway 706 and drive 10 miles to the Nisqually Entrance Station. Continue 17.5 miles to the Henry M. Jackson Visitor Center or 18 miles to the Paradise National Park Inn. The trails emanate from the visitors center and the lodge. Consult a map to see which trailhead to access.

Contact: Mount Rainier National Park, Longmire Wilderness Information Center, Tahoma Woods, Star Route, Ashford, WA 98304, 360/569-4453.

45 PARADISE GLACIER
6.0 mi/3.0 hrs

near Paradise in Mount Rainier
National Park

Map 5.2, page 240

To discover what millions of tons of ice look and sound like, take scenic Paradise Glacier Trail, which gently climbs through wide open meadows, rock fields, and snowfields to the living Paradise Glacier. Centuries of snowfall built up this massive block of ice slowly sliding down Mount Rainier. The upper reaches of the trail reveal the barren landscapes that are trademarks of retreating glaciers. Paradise Glacier Trail is the park's best chance to view up close the mountain's most famous features.

The route to Paradise Glacier follows Skyline Trail (counterclockwise from Paradise Inn) 1.9 miles to Paradise Glacier Trail junction, just above Sluiskin Falls. Also here is Stevens–Van Trump Historical Memorial, commemorating their 1870 ascent of Mount

Rainier, one of the first by white men. Paradise Glacier Trail begins here and heads directly for the glacier (3 miles), cracking, creaking, and breaking apart before your very eyes and ears. Although the terrain appears barren, it is very fragile; be sure to stick to designated trails. The high country here is pretty close to true tundra, with tiny plants doing their best to survive on the barren slopes. Streams cascade all around. Paradise Glacier used to sport several large ice caves that could be explored, but warm weather through the last few decades has left them destroyed or unsafe. Walking on the glacier is also unsafe and prohibited.

User Groups: Hikers only. No dogs, horses, or mountain bikes are allowed. No wheelchair access.

Open Seasons: This trail is accessible mid-June–October.

Permits: A National Parks Pass is required to enter the park.

Maps: For a map of Mount Rainier National Park, contact the Outdoor Recreation Information Center at the downtown Seattle REI. For a topographic map, ask Green Trails for No. 270S, Paradise, or ask the USGS for Mount Rainier East.

Directions: From Tacoma, drive south 40 miles on Highway 7 to Elbe. Turn east on Highway 706 and drive 10 miles to the Nisqually Entrance Station. Continue 18 miles to the National Park Inn at Paradise. The trailhead is behind the inn.

Contact: Mount Rainier National Park, Longmire Wilderness Information Center, Tahoma Woods, Star Route, Ashford, WA 98304, 360/569-4453.

46 MAZAMA RIDGE
5.4 mi/2.5 hrs

near Paradise in Mount Rainier National Park

Map 5.2, page 240

Walking away from The Mountain, Mazama Ridge avoids the mall-like crush of visitors along other Paradise trails. Such a beautiful hike still gets plenty of use, however, and for good reason. The easy trail spends its entirety wandering amid subalpine meadows with big views of the big mountain. To the south stands the jagged Tatoosh Range. And to cap it all off is a series of small tarns, idyllic spots for lunch.

The theme of Mazama Ridge Trail is meadows, meadows, meadows. The route leaves Paradise Inn and follows Skyline Trail 1.5 miles to a signed junction; to the right is Mazama Ridge Trail. The trail follows the wide, flat ridgeline south. During July, lupine, daisies, and countless other wildflowers add shrouds of color to green meadows.

The trail reaches a number of small lakes and tarns (2.5 miles) along the flat top of Faraway Rock. Below its steep slopes lie Louise and Reflection Lakes and Wonderland Trail. With little elevation change, this is a great trail for families with little ones.

User Groups: Hikers only. No dogs, horses, or mountain bikes are allowed. No wheelchair access.

Open Seasons: This trail is accessible mid-June–October.

Permits: A National Parks Pass is required to enter the park.

Maps: For a map of Mount Rainier National Park, contact the Outdoor Recreation Information Center at the downtown Seattle REI. For a topographic map, ask Green Trails for No. 270S, Paradise, or ask the USGS for Mount Rainier East.

Directions: From Tacoma, drive south 40 miles on Highway 7 to Elbe. Turn east on Highway 706 and drive 10 miles to the Nisqually Entrance Station. Continue 18 miles to the National Park Inn at Paradise. The trailhead is behind the inn.

Contact: Mount Rainier National Park, Longmire Wilderness Information Center, Tahoma Woods, Star Route, Ashford, WA 98304, 360/569-4453.

47 SKYLINE LOOP
5.0 mi/3.0 hrs

out of Paradise in Mount Rainier National Park

Map 5.2, page 240

Skyline Trail may well be the premier hike in Mount Rainier National Park. The trail delivers miles of alpine meadows, peers over the enormous Nisqually Glacier, and summits Panorama Point. This high vista is as close to The Mountain as you can get without ropes and a harness. Acres of blooming wildflowers line the trail in late July, and if big-time views bore you, several streams and waterfalls are thrown in for good measure. This is a popular trip for folks visiting the Paradise Visitor Center. The overall elevation gain is 1,400 feet, a respectable but not strenuous workout.

The best route is a clockwise one. Although numerous trails crisscross this area, Skyline Trail is well signed at every junction. Starting at Paradise, the trail skirts Alta Vista Peak and climbs through meadows to the ridge above Nisqually Glacier (1.3 miles). On hot summer days, the silence of the high country is broken only by whistling marmots and the cracking glacier.

Panorama Point (2.5 miles; elevation 6,800 feet) is an appropriate name for this high vista. Mount Rainier towers above the viewpoint, and the rocky and jagged Tatoosh Range stands to the south. On clear days, Mount Adams, Goat Rocks, Mount St. Helens, and even Mount Hood in Oregon make appearances. Panorama indeed! Because you definitely packed your camera, save some film for the last half of the trail. Descending to Paradise, Skyline Trail passes Stevens–Van Trump Memorial (commemorating an ascent of Mount Rainier), Sluiskin Falls, and Myrtle Falls. Camping is not permitted in the Paradise area.

User Groups: Hikers only. No dogs, horses, or mountain bikes are allowed. Part of the trail is wheelchair accessible (but somewhat steep).

Open Seasons: This trail is accessible mid-July–September.

Permits: A National Parks Pass is required to enter the park.

Maps: For a map of Mount Rainier National Park, contact the Outdoor Recreation Information Center at the downtown Seattle REI. For a topographic map, ask Green Trails for No. 270S, Paradise, or ask the USGS for Mount Rainier East.

Directions: From Tacoma, drive south 40 miles on Highway 7 to Elbe. Turn east on Highway 706 and drive 10 miles to the Nisqually Entrance Station. Continue 18 miles to the National Park Inn at Paradise. The trailhead is behind the inn.

Contact: Mount Rainier National Park, Longmire Wilderness Information Center, Tahoma Woods, Star Route, Ashford, WA 98304, 360/569-4453.

48 WONDERLAND TRAIL
93.0 mi/10 days

around Tahoma in Mount Rainier National Park

Map 5.2, page 240

Wonderland Trail is considered by many to be the be-all and end-all of Washington hiking. The long, demanding trek makes a full circle around the behemoth mountain, exploring old-growth forest, high alpine meadows, and everything in between. Tahoma (Mount Rainier's Native American name) is the center of attention at almost every turn, towering above the trail with massive glaciers and windswept snowfields. The Wonderland passes through the park's most beautiful terrain. Acres and acres of wildflower meadows dominate Spray Park, Indian Henry's Hunting Ground, and Summerland. Outstanding lakes and streams are repeat encounters, with Mowich Lake, Carbon River, and Martha Falls a sampling of many highlights.

Wonderland Trail is certainly one of the most demanding hikes in the state. The route repeatedly climbs out of low river valleys to high ridges radiating from Tahoma. Although some folks complete the hike in as few as seven or eight days, plan for at least 10 full days. This makes for a leisurely pace of about 10 miles per day. Besides, there's far too much to see to rush through it. The best starting points include Longmire, Sunrise, or Paradise Visitor Centers. Smart hikers plan carefully and leave a food cache at a visitors center halfway through the route. Because of the trail's popularity, the Park Service requires reservations for all backcountry camps (cross-country camping—that is, selecting a temporary site somewhere off-trail, is not allowed). Spots are limited and regularly fill up in April (reservations can be made after April 1). And finally, be prepared for adverse weather in any season. Tahoma creates its own weather systems, sometimes in just minutes. Set out upon this epic trail and you will not be disappointed, guaranteed!

User Groups: Hikers only. No dogs, horses, or mountain bikes are allowed. No wheelchair access.

Open Seasons: This trail is accessible mid-July–September.

Permits: A National Parks Pass is required to enter the park.

Maps: For a map of Mount Rainier National Park, contact the Outdoor Recreation Information Center at the downtown Seattle REI. For a topographic map, ask Green Trails for No. 269, Mount Rainier West, and No. 270, Mount Rainier East, or ask the USGS for Mount Rainier West, Mount Rainier East, Mowich Lake, Sunrise, Golden Lakes, Mount Wow, White River Park, and Chinook Pass.

Directions: From Tacoma, drive south 40 miles on Highway 7 to Elbe. Turn east on Highway 706 and drive 10 miles to the Nisqually Entrance Station. Continue 18 miles to the National Park Inn at Paradise. The well-signed trailhead is beside the inn. Other access points include Sunrise Visitor Center or Mowich Lake.

Contact: Mount Rainier National Park, Longmire Wilderness Information Center, Tahoma Woods, Star Route, Ashford, WA 98304, 360/569-4453.

49 PINNACLE SADDLE
2.6 mi/2.5 hrs

near Paradise in Mount Rainier National Park

Map 5.2, page 240

Pinnacle Peak Trail is one of the park's steepest trails. An elevation gain of 1,050 feet passes underfoot in a short 1.3 miles, delivering hikers to a wonderful viewpoint. The steep, rocky path keeps the crowds at bay, leaving the route for only the most determined hikers and view junkies. Although it starts gently, much of the trail does little but climb skyward. Mount Rainier remains visible the entire way. Because the trail is situated on the north-facing slopes of the Tatoosh Range, snow lingers here late, sometimes into August. Marmots and picas whistle and scurry about the rocky meadows while mountain goats frequently patrol the jagged ridge. The trail eventually reaches Pinnacle Saddle, between Pinnacle and Denham Peaks, in the heart of the Tatoosh Range. To the north stands The Mountain, above Paradise meadows; to the south, snowy Goat Rocks and Mount Adams are visible. The truly adventurous can undertake a rocky scramble to the summit of Pinnacle Peak. It's a gain of 600 feet, but few views are to be gained for the extra effort. Other than snowmelt, little water is to be found along the way; be sure to pack your own.

User Groups: Hikers only. No dogs, horses, or mountain bikes are allowed. No wheelchair access.

Open Seasons: This area is accessible August–September.

Permits: A National Parks Pass is required to enter the park.

Maps: For a map of Mount Rainier National Park, contact the Outdoor Recreation Information Center at the downtown Seattle REI. For a topographic map, ask Green Trails for No. 270, Mount Rainier East, or ask the USGS for Mount Rainier East.

Directions: From Tacoma, drive south 40 miles on Highway 7 to Elbe. Turn east on Highway

706 and drive 10 miles to the Nisqually Entrance Station. Continue 16 miles to Stevens Canyon Road. Turn right and drive 2.5 miles to the signed trailhead on the right.

Contact: Mount Rainier National Park, Longmire Wilderness Information Center, Tahoma Woods, Star Route, Ashford, WA 98304, 360/569-4453.

50 SNOW AND BENCH LAKES
2.6 mi/1.5 hrs

near Paradise in Mount Rainier National Park

Map 5.2, page 240

Short, flat, and beautiful best describe Snow Lake Trail. The perfect hike for folks young and old, Snow Lake Trail features a pair of subalpine lakes enclosed by meadows and rocky peaks. The total elevation gain is about 200 feet, practically unnoticeable. Away from the bustle of the Paradise area, Snow Lake offers visitors prime hiking without the crowds.

Snow Lake Trail leaves Stevens Canyon Road and quickly reaches The Bench, a wide, flat meadow with perfect views of Mount Rainier. Bear grass occupies the large meadows, sending its large blooms skyward during August. Bench Lake occupies part of the large meadow. The trail continues another .5 mile to Snow Lake, tucked away within a large basin. The lake got its name from the heavy snowpack that lingers around the lake (and on the trail) until late July. Craggy Unicorn Peak rises above the lake and talus slopes from the south. Visitors interested in spending the night will appreciate Snow Lake Camp, the park's most accessible backcountry campground (permits required).

User Groups: Hikers only. No dogs, horses, or mountain bikes are allowed. No wheelchair access.

Open Seasons: This trail is usually accessible August–September.

Permits: A National Parks Pass is required to enter the park. Overnight stays within the national park require backcountry camping permits, which are available at Sunrise Visitor Center.

Maps: For a map of Mount Rainier National Park, contact the Outdoor Recreation Information Center at the downtown Seattle REI. For a topographic map, ask Green Trails for No. 270, Mount Rainier East, or ask the USGS for Mount Rainier East.

Directions: From Tacoma, drive south 40 miles on Highway 7 to Elbe. Turn east on Highway 706 and drive 10 miles to the Nisqually Entrance Station. Continue 16 miles to Stevens Canyon Road. Turn right and drive 4 miles to the signed trailhead on the right.

Contact: Mount Rainier National Park, Longmire Wilderness Information Center, Tahoma Woods, Star Route, Ashford, WA 98304, 360/569-4453.

51 SHRINER PEAK LOOKOUT
8.4 mi/5.0 hrs –2 days

near Stevens Canyon entrance in Mount Rainier National Park

Map 5.2, page 240

Probably nothing is more beautiful than waking to Mount Rainier basking in the glow of the rising sun. And probably there is no better place to behold such a sight than Shriner Peak. But this extraordinary place requires extraordinary effort. Shriner Peak Trail gains extensive elevation in open terrain, made hot by the afternoon sun. Easily done in a day, Shriner Camp invites hikers to spend the night and enjoy the daybreak view.

Shriner Peak Trail is not for the faint of heart. The trail gains more than 3,400 feet in just 4.2 miles, a steep ascent by any standard. Plus, much of the route lies on an exposed, south-facing slope (the hottest of them all). As you sweat and trudge uphill, keep in mind that nature rewards those who work the hardest. The trail winds its way through shady forest before entering an old burn area and eventually open meadows (2.5 miles). The upper half of the route is awash in views of Mount Rainier and surrounding valleys. Shriner Camp is just below the summit off a short side trail; unfortunately it's a dry camp. Shriner Peak is best undertaken early in the day, before the sun is high. Finally, be sure to carry extra water; even if it's cloudy and cool, you'll need it.

User Groups: Hikers only. No dogs, horses, or mountain bikes are allowed. No wheelchair access.

Open Seasons: This area is accessible August–September.

Permits: A National Parks Pass is required to enter the park. Overnight stays within the national park require backcountry camping permits, which are available at the Longmire and White River Wilderness Information Centers.

Maps: For a map of Mount Rainier National Park, contact the Outdoor Recreation Information Center at the downtown Seattle REI. For a topographic map, ask Green Trails for No. 270, Mount Rainier East, or ask the USGS for Chinook Pass.

Directions: From Puyallup, drive east 56 miles on Highway 410 to Highway 123. Turn right (south) and drive 7.5 miles to the trailhead on the left side of the road.

Contact: Mount Rainier National Park, White River Wilderness Information Center, 70004 Highway 410 East, Enumclaw, WA 98022, 360/569-6030.

52 LAUGHINGWATER CREEK
11.4 mi/6.0 hrs–2 days

near Stevens Canyon entrance in Mount Rainier National Park

Map 5.2, page 240

A rarity in this national park, Laughingwater Creek Trail forsakes mountain meadows and views of Mount Rainier. Instead, this lightly used trail makes a grand trip through old-growth forest to Three Lakes, set among open subalpine forest. The trail provides a quiet reintroduction to the Cascade Mountains after the crowds of Mount Rainier's visitors centers. The only sounds around these parts are the noisy rumbling of Laughingwater Creek and the bellows of elk.

Laughingwater Creek Trail gains more than

2,500 feet between the trailhead and Three Lakes. Most of the climb is spread moderately along the route, easy enough for hikers young and old. The trail sticks close to the creek and passes within view of a waterfall at 2.5 miles. Western hemlocks gives way to mountain hemlocks and subalpine fir replaces Douglas fir as the trail nears the crest of the hike.

Three Lakes lie in a small basin atop the ridge. A wonderful backcountry camp is situated here with an aged shelter. This is an out-of-the-way section of the national park (if any remain these days), with few visitors spending the night at Three Lakes Camp. If you have an itch to see The Mountain, continue on the trail past Three Lakes toward Pacific Crest Trail and meadow vistas.

User Groups: Hikers and horses. No dogs or mountain bikes are allowed. No wheelchair access.

Open Seasons: This area is usually accessible July–September.

Permits: A National Parks Pass is required to enter the park.

Maps: For a map of Mount Rainier National Park, contact the Outdoor Recreation Information Center at the downtown Seattle REI. For a topographic map, ask Green Trails for No. 270, Mount Rainier East, and No. 271, Bumping Lake, or ask the USGS for Chinook Pass.

Directions: From Puyallup, drive east 56 miles on Highway 410 to Highway 123. Turn right (south) and drive 10.5 miles to the trailhead on the left side of the road, just south of Stevens Canyon entrance.

Contact: Mount Rainier National Park, White River Wilderness Information Center, 70004 Highway 410 East, Enumclaw, WA 98022, 360/569-6030.

53 SILVER FALLS LOOP
3.0 mi/1.5 hrs

out of Ohanapecosh in Mount Rainier National Park

Map 5.2, page 240

Silver Falls Loop is one of Mount Rainier's

best river trails, perfect for families and hikers of all abilities. The route is a gentle grade along the bustling river to one of the park's most impressive cascades. Silver Falls Trail follows Ohanapecosh River a gentle 1.5 miles to Silver Falls. Old-growth trees dominate the forest found along the route, making the trail a cool and shady respite from hot and sunny meadows. Squirrels and woodpeckers are often found scurrying among the timber while deer and elk browse the forest floor. Anglers are frequent visitors to the trail, thanks to its easy access to the trout-laden river.

Silver Falls is a thunderous waterfall, where the glacial-fed Ohanapecosh makes a series of cascades. The climax is a 70-foot drop into a large punch bowl. The trail crosses a deep gorge via a bridge immediately below the falls, showering hikers in mist when the river is roaring. Although beautiful, the falls are dangerous if explored off-trail. Keep a short leash on little ones and stick to the established trail. The loop heads directly back to Ohanapecosh Campground along the opposite bank of the river, a quick and easy outing.

User Groups: Hikers only. No dogs, horses, or mountain bikes are allowed. No wheelchair access.

Open Seasons: This trail is accessible year-round.

Permits: A National Parks Pass is required to enter the park.

Maps: For a map of Mount Rainier National Park, contact the Outdoor Recreation Information Center at the downtown Seattle REI. For a topographic map, ask Green Trails for No. 270, Mount Rainier East, or ask the USGS for Ohanapecosh Hot Springs and Chinook Pass.

Directions: From Puyallup, drive east 56 miles on Highway 410 to Highway 123. Turn right (south) and drive 13 miles to Ohanapecosh Campground. Turn left into the campground; the trailhead is near the visitor center.

Contact: Mount Rainier National Park, White River Wilderness Information Center, 70004 Highway 410 East, Enumclaw, WA 98022, 360/569-6030.

54 GROVE OF THE PATRIARCHS
1.5 mi/1.0 hr

near Stevens Canyon entrance in Mount Rainier National Park

Map 5.2, page 240

Competing with Olympic rainforests, here, in the low valley of the Ohanapecosh River, is one of Washington's most impressive stands of old-growth timber. On a small island in the middle of the river, this grove of Douglas fir, western hemlock, and western red cedar has been growing undisturbed for nearly 1,000 years. That's right, a full millennium. Isolated by the river from the surrounding forest, Grove of the Patriarchs has been able to avoid fire and other natural disturbances, living up to its full potential. This is a true climax forest. The trail to Grove of the Patriarchs is flat and easily navigated. The trail heads upstream for .5 mile through an impressive (yet comparatively small) forest. The trail crosses the river via bridge and loops around the island. Many of the trees measure more than 25 feet around the trunk, with one granddaddy fir rounding out at 35 feet in circumference. In this ancient place, the only hazard is a strained neck.

User Groups: Hikers only. No dogs, horses, or mountain bikes are allowed. No wheelchair access.

Open Seasons: This area is accessible mid-May–October.

Permits: A National Parks Pass is required to enter the park.

Maps: For a map of Mount Rainier National Park, contact the Outdoor Recreation Information Center at the downtown Seattle REI. For a topographic map, ask Green Trails for No. 270, Mount Rainier East, or ask the USGS for Ohanapecosh Hot Springs.

Directions: From Puyallup, drive east 56 miles on Highway 410 to Highway 123. Turn right (south) and drive 11 miles to Stevens Canyon

Road/entrance. Turn right and the trailhead is just beyond the guard station on the right.

Contact: Mount Rainier National Park, White River Wilderness Information Center, 70004 Highway 410 East, Enumclaw, WA 98022, 360/569-6030.

55 EAST SIDE TRAIL
3.0–5.0 mi/1.5–3.5 hrs

near Stevens Canyon entrance in Mount Rainier National Park

Map 5.2, page 240

East Side Trail follows Chinook Creek and Ohanopecosh River as they wind their ways through exceptional old-growth forests. The trail has three trailheads, including near Cayuse Pass and Ohanapecosh Campgrounds. The distance between these two endpoints is 12 miles. The best access, however, is via Deer Creek in the middle of the route. This .5-mile access trail joins East Side Trail within a mile of spectacular waterfalls to the north and south. Deer Creek Trail drops to East Side Trail at the backcountry camp of Deer Creek. The best option is to turn left (south) and follow the level trail one mile to where it crosses Chinook Creek. Here, the stream cascades through a narrow gorge directly below the footbridge. Bigger Stafford Falls is another mile down the trail. From Deer Creek Camp, the trail climbs kindly toward Cayuse Pass, passing more falls and cascades. This is a great trail for families with little ones; just keep a short leash on them near all stream crossings.

User Groups: Hikers only. No dogs, horses, or mountain bikes are allowed. No wheelchair access.

Open Seasons: This area is usually accessible April–October.

Permits: Permits are not required. Parking and access are free.

Maps: For a map of Mount Rainier National Park, contact the Outdoor Recreation Information Center at the downtown Seattle REI. For a topographic map, ask Green Trails

for No. 270, Mount Rainier East, or ask the USGS for Ohanapecosh Hot Springs and Chinook Pass.

Directions: From Puyallup, drive east 56 miles on Highway 410 to Highway 123. Turn right (south) and drive 4 miles to the signed trailhead on the right side of the road.

Contact: Mount Rainier National Park, White River Wilderness Information Center, 70004 Highway 410 East, Enumclaw, WA 98022, 360/569-6030.

56 AMERICAN RIDGE
10.2–26.2 mi/5.0 hrs–3 days

in William O. Douglas Wilderness of Wenatchee National Forest

Map 5.2, page 240

A major route bisecting the northern William O. Douglas Wilderness, American Ridge Trail offers hikers many options to customize a hike. From the Bumping River all the way up to Pacific Crest Trail, American Ridge stretches more than 26 miles. Eight different access trails, including PCT, create a whole slew of opportunities. The eastern end is primarily high forests; the middle third reaches into high, ridgeline meadows with lots of views; the western end offers access to a number of high-country lakes and meadows (see next listing).

Four trails reach American Ridge from Highway 410, with Mesatchee Creek Trail a favorite. Mesatchee Trail climbs 5.3 miles and 2,200 feet through forest and intermittent meadows to the ridge. East of this junction delivers more than five miles of meadows. Also from Highway 410, Goat Peak Trail climbs 3,000 feet in four miles to a lookout.

Three trails reach the ridge from Bumping River, Goose Prairie Trail being the preferred route. This is a 5.1-mile ascent to the ridge. Hike west for tiny Kettle Lake and miles of meadows. All of these trails are very hot in the late summer and always lack any water, an important consideration. They're also lonely routes into a beautiful backcountry.

User Groups: Hikers, leashed dogs, and horses.

No mountain bikes are allowed. No wheelchair access.

Open Seasons: This trail is accessible April–October.

Permits: A federal Northwest Forest Pass is required to park here.

Maps: For a map of Wenatchee National Forest, contact the Outdoor Recreation Information Center at the downtown Seattle REI. For a topographic map, ask Green Trails for No. 271, Bumping Lake, and No. 272, Old Scab Mountain, or ask the USGS for Norse Peak, Cougar Peak, Bumping Lake, Goose Prairie, and Old Scab Mountain.

Directions: From Yakima, drive west on Highway 410 to Forest Service Road 460, just west of Lodgepole Campground. Turn left and drive .3 mile to the trailhead at road's end.

Contact: Wenatchee National Forest, Naches Ranger Station, 10237 Highway 12, Naches, WA 98937, 509/653-2205.

57 COUGAR LAKES
12.0–20.0 mi/6.0 hrs –2 days
in William O. Douglas Wilderness of Wenatchee National Forest

Map 5.2, page 240

Cougar Lakes lie at the western end of American Ridge, directly below the Cascade Crest. They make a great day hike or easy overnighter. Also in the area is Pacific Crest Trail, which lends itself to an excellent loop hike connecting to Cougar Lakes. This is a great weekend hike, encompassing one of the best sections of PCT in southern Washington. Meadows and mountain lakes are prominent themes on both routes. Each route is great for hikers of all abilities, gaining moderate elevation gently.

To reach Cougar Lakes, the route begins with Swamp Lake Trail, a gradual, forested ascent to Swamp Lake (4 miles) and American Ridge Trail (4.6 miles). Hike west toward PCT; Cougar Lakes junction (5.2 miles) cuts south to the two lakes (6 miles). Around the lakes, subalpine meadows unfold beneath tall, rocky

cliffs. Numerous campsites are around the basin. Whether on a day hike or overnighter, be sure to scramble the crest for a view of Mount Rainier.

To hike the longer loop on PCT, continue west on American Ridge Trail toward PCT (6.7 miles). The loop route goes south on PCT, passing Two Lakes, Crag Lake, and Buck Lake. This is meadow country with prime viewing of Mount Rainier and many other mountains. The route intersects Bumping River Trail (13.1 miles) and turns east to return to the trailhead (20 miles). All lakes along the way offer camping and are the sole sources of water.

User Groups: Hikers, leashed dogs, and horses. No mountain bikes are allowed. No wheelchair access.

Open Seasons: This trail is accessible June–mid-October.

Permits: A federal Northwest Forest Pass is required to park here.

Maps: For a map of Wenatchee National Forest, contact the Outdoor Recreation Information Center at the downtown Seattle REI. For a topographic map, ask Green Trails for No. 271, Bumping Lake, or ask the USGS for Cougar Lake.

Directions: From Yakima, drive west on Highway 410 to Bumping Lake Road (Forest Service Road 1800). Turn left and drive 17 miles to the trailhead at road's end.

Contact: Wenatchee National Forest, Naches Ranger Station, 10237 Highway 12, Naches, WA 98937, 509/653-2205.

58 MOUNT AIX
11.0 mi/6.0 hrs
in William O. Douglas Wilderness of Wenatchee National Forest

Map 5.2, page 240

Steep, rocky, and downright treacherous at times, Mount Aix does its best to discourage visitors. It stands at 7,766 feet, and hikers must scale 4,000 feet in just 5.5 miles to reach the summit. And the mountain offers no water to aid the trek, a harsh slight on the hot, exposed slopes. Demanding as it may be, Mount Aix rewards with much more than it asks. Miles of meadows chock-full of wildflowers highlight the upper half as do exceptional views of Mount Rainier and surrounding mountains. Mount Aix is definitely best for seasoned hikers who are looking for a good workout.

Mount Aix Trail rests on the east side of the Cascade Crest, meaning the route receives less snow than trails just a few miles west. This is one of the earliest high-country routes to open in the state. Switchbacks are the name of the game, rising out of the forest into the open meadows. At 3.7 miles is a junction with Nelson Ridge Trail. This is a nice option, offering several miles of ridgeline meadows before dozens of miles in the William O. Douglas Wilderness. Head right and climb another two miles to the summit. This last effort to the trail's climax is rocky and sometimes a scramble.

User Groups: Hikers, leashed dogs, and horses. No mountain bikes are allowed. No wheelchair access.

Open Seasons: This trail is accessible mid-May–mid-October.

Permits: A federal Northwest Forest Pass is required to park here.

Maps: For a map of Wenatchee National Forest, contact the Outdoor Recreation Information Center at the downtown Seattle REI. For a topographic map, ask Green Trails for No. 271, Bumping Lake, or ask the USGS for Timberwolf Mountain and Bumping Lake.

Directions: From Yakima, drive west on Highway 410 to Bumping Lake Road (Forest Service Road 1800). Turn left and drive 14 miles to Forest Service Road 1808. Turn left and drive 1.5 miles to the signed trailhead on the left side.

Contact: Wenatchee National Forest, Naches Ranger Station, 10237 Highway 12, Naches, WA 98937, 509/653-2205.

59 SAWTOOTH LAKES
7.0 mi/4.0 hrs

south of Mount Rainier in Gifford Pinchot National Forest

Map 5.2, page 240

Along the north side of Sawtooth Ridge lie four high lakes among forest and meadows. Just outside the national park boundary, these lakes are highly ignored by the masses headed for Mount Rainier. That's good news for peace and quiet, at least until July 1. After that date motorcycles are allowed on the trail. Visit here in late May or June, and you'll have these great swimming holes all to yourself. Old forest and peek-a-boo views of The Mountain vie for attention along the way. And to cap off the hike is a neck-straining view of High Rock's 600-foot vertical cliff.

The best route to Sawtooth Lakes is via Teeley Creek Trail. After a quick climb past Pothole Lake, the trail levels out completely. At Osborne Mountain Trail junction (.7 mile), stay left on Teeley Creek Trail and soon reach the two largest and best lakes, Bertha May (1.2 miles) and Granite (1.8 miles). The trail continues along the north side of Sawtooth Ridge to meadows directly beneath the cliffs of High Rock (3.1 miles). Although the trail continues two miles to Cora Lake and additional trailheads, the meadows below High Rock are a great turnaround. On hot summer days, a dip in the lakes will be calling your name.

User Groups: Hikers, leashed dogs, horses, mountain bikes, and motorcycles (motorcycles allowed after June 30). No wheelchair access.

Open Seasons: This trail is accessible mid-June–October.

Permits: A federal Northwest Forest Pass is required to park here.

Maps: For a map of Gifford Pinchot National Forest, contact the Outdoor Recreation Information Center at the downtown Seattle REI. For a topographic map, ask Green Trails for No. 301, Randle, or ask the USGS for Sawtooth Ridge.

Directions: From Tacoma, drive south 40 miles

on Highway 7 to Elbe. Turn east on Highway 706 and drive 7 miles to Forest Service Road 52. Turn right and drive 4.5 miles to Forest Service Road 84. Turn right and drive 1.5 miles to Forest Service Road 8410. Turn right and drive 4.5 miles to the trailhead on the left.

Contact: Gifford Pinchot National Forest, Cowlitz Valley Ranger Station, 10024 U.S. 12, Randle, WA 98377, 360/497-1100.

60 HIGH ROCK LOOKOUT
3.2 mi/2.0 hrs

south of Mount Rainier in Gifford Pinchot National Forest

Map 5.2, page 240

Towering over the adjacent Sawtooth Ridge at 5,685 feet, this peak is certainly high. And with a sheer 600-foot drop on its north face, it definitely qualifies as a rock. And yet the name is an understatement. High Rock might be an imposing sight from below, but the Forest Service Lookout stationed on the summit boasts some of the best views in the Gifford Pinchot. The mountain is separated from Mount Rainier National Park only by Nisqually Valley. Thus, broad views but sparse crowds.

Atop the tallest peak in Sawtooth Range, High Rock Lookout Trail endures a short but sharp climb: 1,600 feet in just 1.5 miles. It wastes little time reaching high meadows and glorious views along High Rock's southern arm. Southern-oriented meadows means sunny, exposed, and dry. Bring water. The lookout stands at 5,685 feet and revels in views of Goat Rocks, Mount Adams, and Mount St. Helens. That enormous mountain just a stone's throw away is Mount Rainier. The northern edge is a sharp drop, so watch your step. Over the edge lie three high lakes along Sawtooth Ridge (see previous listing).

User Groups: Hikers and leashed dogs. No horses or mountain bikes are allowed. No wheelchair access.

Open Seasons: This trail is accessible mid-June–October.

Permits: A federal Northwest Forest Pass is required to park here.

Maps: For a map of Gifford Pinchot National Forest, contact the Outdoor Recreation Information Center at the downtown Seattle REI. For a topographic map, ask Green Trails for No. 301, Randle, or ask the USGS for Sawtooth Ridge.

Directions: From Tacoma, drive south 40 miles on Highway 7 to Elbe. Turn east on Highway 706 and drive 7 miles to Forest Service Road 52. Turn right and drive 1 mile to Forest Service Road 85. Continue straight and drive 5 miles to Forest Service Road 8440. Stay to the left and drive 4.5 miles to the trailhead on the left at Towhead Gap.

Contact: Gifford Pinchot National Forest, Cowlitz Valley Ranger Station, 10024 U.S. 12, Randle, WA 98377, 360/497-1100.

61 TATOOSH RIDGE
5.0 mi/3.5 hrs

south of Mount Rainier in Tatoosh Wilderness of Gifford Pinchot National Forest

Map 5.2, page 240

Tatoosh Range stands less than 10 miles from Mount Rainier (as the crow flies), practically a smaller sister to the dominating mountain. And Tatoosh Ridge Trail boasts incredible views of The Mountain, yet it seems so far away— far away from the crowds in the national park, that is. Just south of the park boundary but protected by its own wilderness, Tatoosh Range receives just a fraction of the visitors that trails inside the park do. It's good habitat for lonely views, high lakes, and mountain meadows.

Tatoosh Ridge Trail runs along the southern spine of Tatoosh Ridge, with trailheads at either end. Both ends are steep switchback shuffles, but the northern trailhead offers access to much more scenic terrain. Tackle 2,600 feet of elevation in just two miles before reaching Tatoosh Lakes junction. This side trail (1 mile round-trip) leads up to a saddle of epic views and down to Tatoosh Lakes, lying among rocky slopes and meadows. Several great camps are found along the lakeshore.

From the first junction, Tatoosh Ridge Trail

continues over rocky and exposed terrain to another junction (3.9 miles), this time leading up to Tatoosh Lookout. At 6,310 feet, here are your epic views. The trail drops from the second junction, below Butter Peak and to the southern trailhead (9 miles one-way). Pack sunscreen and extra water, as the trail is hot, often exposed, and without water, save for the lakes.

User Groups: Hikers, leashed dogs, and horses. No mountain bikes are allowed. No wheelchair access.

Open Seasons: This trail is accessible July–September.

Permits: A federal Northwest Forest Pass is required to park here.

Maps: For a map of Gifford Pinchot National Forest, contact the Outdoor Recreation Information Center at the downtown Seattle REI. For a topographic map, ask Green Trails for No. 302, Packwood, or ask the USGS for Tatoosh Lakes.

Directions: To the northern trailhead: From Packwood, drive north 4 miles on Skate Creek Road (Forest Service Road 52) to Forest Service Road 5270. Turn right and drive 6 miles to the signed trailhead on the right.

To the southern trailhead: From Packwood, drive north on Skate Creek Road and turn right on Forest Service Road 5290. Drive 5 miles, staying on the main gravel road, then veer left, remaining on Forest Service Road 5290 for 3.5 miles to the trailhead at road's end.

Contact: Gifford Pinchot National Forest, Cowlitz Valley Ranger Station, 10024 U.S. 12, Randle, WA 98377, 360/497-1100.

62 DUMBBELL LAKE LOOP
15.8 mi/2 days

southeast of Mount Rainier in William O. Douglas Wilderness of Gifford Pinchot National Forest

Map 5.2, page 240

Dumbbell Lake knows how to treat a hiker well. It offers not only beautiful scenery but the opportunity for lots of exploring. It's situated on a high plateau, where the firs are plentiful and form a nice surrounding forest. On the north side, a connected chain of small islands extends into the lake and encourages lots of investigation.

The hike to Dumbbell begins along Pacific Crest Trail out of White Pass. Follow PCT for 6.5 miles as it climbs gently onto the plateau. The trail passes small Sand Lake before dropping to Buesch Lake, where good camping is to be had. Abandon PCT and join Trail 56, where Dumbbell lies just .5 mile away. The best camping is found near the middle of the lake on the north side, beyond the burned section at the west end. The trail continues past Cramer Lake while gradually dropping elevation back to the trailhead.

On these high flatlands, dense groves of subalpine firs and mountain hemlocks frequently give way to open meadows. The many small lakes and large open meadows on this high plateau make for great day excursions. If you try this hike in the summer, expect people and bugs. Both can be pesky, but don't miss this hike.

User Groups: Hikers, leashed dogs, and horses. No mountain bikes are allowed. No wheelchair access.

Open Seasons: This trail is usually accessible July–mid-October.

Permits: A federal Northwest Forest Pass is required to park here.

Maps: For a map of Gifford Pinchot National Forest, contact the Outdoor Recreation Information Center at the downtown Seattle REI. For topographic maps, ask Green Trails for No. 303, White Pass, or ask the USGS for White Pass and Spiral Lake.

Directions: From Randle, drive east on Highway 12 to White Pass Campground, on the north side of the highway just east of the pass. The trailhead is located just before the campground entrance and is signed as the Pacific Crest Trail.

Contact: Gifford Pinchot National Forest, Cowlitz Valley Ranger Station, 10024 U.S. 12, Randle, WA 98377, 360/497-1100.

63 TWIN SISTERS
2.4 mi/1.5 hrs

southeast of Mount Rainier in William O. Douglas Wilderness of Gifford Pinchot National Forest

Map 5.2, page 240

It's almost too easy to get to Twin Sisters. A place so beautiful usually loses out when access is so easy, and that's nearly the case here. A pair of large, stunning high lakes are the Twin Sisters, surrounded by a wilderness of firs and hemlocks. The lakes are popular destinations for folks of all types because of their easy accessibility, great camping, and extensive opportunities for side trips, including the great Tumac Mountain.

This hike serves well both as a day hike or as an extended backpacking trip. The grade up Deep Creek is short and never taxing. The lakes are surrounded by forests of subalpine fir and mountain hemlock. To the north, almost between the lakes, lies a small butte. Most of the terrain in this area is gentle, rolling hills. At the lakes, excessive use through the years created numerous campsites. Camping must now be at least 200 feet from the lakeshore to keep damage to a minimum. If the crowds feel too thick at Twin Sisters, many other small lakes are worth seeking out.

A necessary side trip is Tumac Mountain, a relatively small and young High Cascades volcano. Just two miles from the east lake, the 6,340-foot summit of Tumac includes a crater and stunning views of Mount Rainier. Other easy expeditions are to Fryingpan Lake, Snow Lake, or Blakenship Lakes, and Pacific Crest Trail is not far.

User Groups: Hikers, leashed dogs, and horses. No mountain bikes are allowed. No wheelchair access.

Open Seasons: This area is usually accessible July–early October.

Permits: A federal Northwest Forest Pass is required to park here.

Maps: For a map of Gifford Pinchot National Forest, contact the Outdoor Recreation Information Center at the downtown Seattle REI. For a topographic map, ask Green Trails for No. 303, White Pass, or ask the USGS for Spiral Lake, Bumping Lake, and White Pass.

Directions: From Yakima, drive west on Highway 410 to Bumping Lake Road (Forest Service Road 1800). Turn left and drive 13 miles to Forest Service Road 1808. Turn left and drive 6.5 miles to Deer Creek Campground and the trailhead at road's end.

Contact: Gifford Pinchot National Forest, Cowlitz Valley Ranger Station, 10024 U.S. 12, Randle, WA 98377, 360/497-1100.

64 SPIRAL BUTTE
12.0 mi/6.0 hrs

southeast of Mount Rainier in William O. Douglas Wilderness of Gifford Pinchot National Forest

Map 5.2, page 240

Forget all the gear, time, and trouble it takes to summit Mount Rainier or Mount Adams. Getting atop a High Cascades volcano can be done in a day with nothing more than a sturdy pair of hiking boots. That's the allure of Spiral Butte, a small peak just north of Highway 12 near White Pass. The scene from the top is panoramic, offering views of Mount Rainier, Goat Rocks, and other surrounding peaks and ridges.

The trail is a steady climb nearly all the way, gaining 2,500 feet. Sand Ridge Trail climbs through a typical east-side forest. Take a left onto Shellrock Lake Trail (3 miles) and another left on Spiral Butte Trail (4 miles). Here, western larches begin to appear and add some needed color on autumn days. Spiral Butte is so named because of a long, twisting arm of the mountain that swings out from the north. It is on this arm that the trail climbs, providing a great alternative to switchbacks but nevertheless gaining 1,100 feet in the final two miles.

Spiral Butte is relatively young, about one million years old, and consists of andesite, a volcanic rock that breaks into large and beautiful gray chunks. Large slopes of talus are visible, revealing the difficulty vegetation can encounter when trying to pioneer such tough terrain.

User Groups: Hikers, leashed dogs, mountain bikes, and horses. No wheelchair access.

Open Seasons: This trail is usually accessible mid-June–early October.

Permits: A federal Northwest Forest Pass is required to park here.

Maps: For a map of Gifford Pinchot National Forest, contact the Outdoor Recreation Information Center at the downtown Seattle REI. For topographic maps, ask Green Trails for No. 303, White Pass, or ask the USGS for Spiral Butte.

Directions: From Randle, drive east on Highway 12 to White Pass. Continue east on Highway 12 for 6 miles to the trailhead (signed "Sand Ridge") on the north side of the highway.

Contact: Gifford Pinchot National Forest, Cowlitz Valley Ranger Station, 10024 U.S. 12, Randle, WA 98377, 360/497-1100.

65 IRONSTONE MOUNTAIN
11.0 mi/6.0 hrs

north of White Pass in William O. Douglas Wilderness of Wenatchee National Forest

Map 5.2, page 240

Aided by a high trailhead (elevation 6,300 feet), Ironstone Mountain presents the easiest ridge hike in the area. Sparse, open forest regularly gives way to open meadows and great views. Ironstone Mountain Trail leaves Forest Service Road 199 and follows the ups and downs of the ridge to Ironstone Mountain. Along the way are several trail junctions, including Burnt Mountain Trail (2.5 miles) and Shellrock Peak (4.5 miles). These two side trails can be combined to form a loop option down (way down) to Rattlesnake Creek and back. A full trip out to Ironstone Mountain is nearly 20 miles round-trip. The best option is to hike the ridge to Shellrock Peak Trail and head north on this trail. Within a mile is easy access to Shellrock Peak, a panoramic vista at 6,835 feet. This is a great viewpoint to see Mount Rainier, the Cascade Crest, and Goat Rocks. Remember to carry plenty of water. This trail is on the east side of the Cascades and can be extremely hot and dry.

User Groups: Hikers, leashed dogs, and horses. No mountain bikes are allowed. No wheelchair access.

Open Seasons: This trail is accessible June–October.

Permits: A federal Northwest Forest Pass is required to park here.

Maps: For a map of Wenatchee National Forest, contact the Outdoor Recreation Information Center at the downtown Seattle REI. For a topographic map, ask Green Trails for No. 304, Rimrock, or ask the USGS for Spiral Butte and Rimrock Lake.

Directions: From White Pass, drive east 18 miles to Bethel Ridge Road (Forest Service Road 1500) at Bethel Ridge Sno-Park. Turn left and drive 9.5 miles to Forest Service Road 199. Turn left and drive 2.5 miles to the trailhead at road's end.

Contact: Wenatchee National Forest, Naches Ranger Station, 10237 Highway 12, Naches, WA 98937, 509/653-2205.

66 PURCELL MOUNTAIN
7.4–15.4 mi/4.0–8.0 hrs

north of Randle in Gifford Pinchot National Forest

Map 5.2, page 240

Conveniently situated along Highway 12 near Randle, Purcell Mountain reaches into the high country and snags meadows and views. It's not an easy trip, however, despite two separate access trails. Expect some significant climbing along either end, with switchbacks the name of the game. The reward for such efforts? Expansive meadows of flowers spread before vast mountain vistas.

Purcell Mountain Trail runs the ridge of the long mountain, almost eight miles from end to end with a total elevation gain of 4,500 feet. From Highway 12, the trail wastes no time and quickly climbs among old timber. The forest provides welcome shade but breaks occasionally for valley views. Meadows appear before Prairie

Mountain (5 miles) and dominate the eastern slopes at Little Paradise (6 miles). The trail ends atop Purcell Mountain (7.7 miles).

A shorter but more strenuous option is Purcell Lookout Trail to the upper ridge. The trail climbs from a logging road to the top of Purcell Mountain (elevation 5,442 feet), gaining 2,400 feet in 3.7 miles. The lookout is long gone, but the views stuck around. Across miles of logged national forest land, Mount Rainier, Mount St. Helens, and Goat Rocks make inspiring neighbors.

On either route, water is a scarce commodity; be sure to carry adequate supplies. Campsites are also scarce, but a couple may be found below Little Paradise Meadows and at the two trails' junction.

User Groups: Hikers, leashed dogs, horses, and mountain bikes. No wheelchair access.

Open Seasons: This trail is accessible mid-June–October.

Permits: A federal Northwest Forest Pass is required to park here.

Maps: For a map of Gifford Pinchot National Forest, contact the Outdoor Recreation Information Center at the downtown Seattle REI. For a topographic map, ask Green Trails for No. 301, Randle, or ask the USGS for Randle.

Directions: Lower trailhead: From Randle, drive east 6 miles on Highway 12 to the signed trailhead, on the left (north) side.

Upper trailhead: From Randle, drive east 6 miles to Davis Creek Road. Turn left and drive 1 mile to Forest Service Road 63. Turn left and drive 4.5 miles to Forest Service Road 6310. Turn left and drive 1 mile to the trailhead on the right.

Contact: Gifford Pinchot National Forest, Cowlitz Valley Ranger Station, 10024 U.S. 12, Randle, WA 98377, 360/497-1100.

steep trip to a high viewpoint overlooking the Cowlitz River Valley. The trailhead actually bisects the trail, eliminating 2,500 feet of knee-knocking elevation gain along Kilborn Creek. That sounds good. From Kilborn Springs at the trailhead, Pompey Peak Trail climbs quickly and steadily through shady old-growth forest. Douglas fir and western hemlock give way to silver fir as the trail climbs. A social trail breaks off from the main trail (1.5 miles) and makes a short scramble to the summit (elevation 5,180 feet). Mount Rainier towers above the Tatoosh Range, while the peaks of Goat Rocks peek out from the east. Those with a hankering to put more trail underfoot can wander along Pompey Peak Trail another 2.8 miles along the ridge to Klickitat Trail, near Twin Sisters Mountain. And for a bit of history: Pompey Peak was named for a pack mule belonging to an old settler. The mule fell to its death on the upper part of the trail in the 1890s.

User Groups: Hikers, leashed dogs, horses, and mountain bikes. No wheelchair access.

Open Seasons: This trail is accessible June–October.

Permits: A federal Northwest Forest Pass is required to park here.

Maps: For a map of Gifford Pinchot National Forest, contact the Outdoor Recreation Information Center at the downtown Seattle REI. For a topographic map, ask Green Trails for No. 301, Randle, or ask the USGS for Purcell Mountain.

Directions: From Randle, drive south 1. mile on Highway 131 to Forest Service Road 23. Turn left and drive 3.5 miles to Forest Service Road 2404. Turn left and drive to the trailhead at road's end.

Contact: Gifford Pinchot National Forest, Cowlitz Valley Ranger Station, 10024 U.S. 12, Randle, WA 98377, 360/497-1100.

67 POMPEY PEAK
3.2 mi/2.0 hrs

southwest of Packwood in Gifford Pinchot National Forest

Map 5.2, page 240

Pompey Peak Trail offers a quick, beautiful, but

68 PACKWOOD LAKE
9.2 mi/5.0 hrs

east of Packwood in Goat Rocks Wilderness of Gifford Pinchot National Forest

Map 5.2, page 240

Here's a hike the whole family can enjoy. Packwood Lake Trail skirts the base of Snyder Mountain through a forest of big trees to the large, scenic lake. Peaks of the Goat Rocks are visible to the south and Mount Rainier's summit to the north. The lake's crystal-blue water is inviting to swimmers and anglers alike; it holds a healthy population of trout. Elk are a frequent visitor during the winter. The idyllic setting is punctuated by a small forested island in the middle.

Although Packwood Lake Trail is forested and shady, little water is to be found along the way. The elevation gain of 900 feet is barely noticeable, well spread over the 4.6 miles of trail. Clear-cuts and second-growth forests are quickly passed by before you enter stands of old timber. The lake is a favorite overnight destination for families, with campsites found around the shores of the lake. A trail winds around the east shore, with trails leading to Mosquito (6.8 miles) and Lost Lakes (8.8 miles).
User Groups: Hikers, leashed dogs, and horses. No mountain bikes are allowed. No wheelchair access.

Open Seasons: This trail is accessible year-round.

Permits: A federal Northwest Forest Pass is required to park here.

Maps: For a map of Gifford Pinchot National Forest, contact the Outdoor Recreation Information Center at the downtown Seattle REI. For a topographic map, ask Green Trails for No. 302, Packwood, or ask the USGS for Packwood.

Directions: From Randle, drive east 16 miles to Packwood. Turn right on Forest Service Road 1260 (near the ranger station) and drive south 5 miles to the trailhead at road's end.

Contact: Gifford Pinchot National Forest, Cowlitz Valley Ranger Station, 10024 U.S. 12, Randle, WA 98377, 360/497-1100.

69 LILY BASIN
12.0 mi/6.0 hrs

south of Mount Rainier in Goat Rocks Wilderness of Gifford Pinchot National Forest

Map 5.2, page 240

Lily Basin Trail is full of great views of the South Cascade volcanoes and blooming wildflowers. Contouring around the head of Glacier Creek, the trail gives a bird's-eye view of Lily Basin, where bugling elk and howling coyotes are frequently heard. Johnson Peak towers above the trail before Heart Lake, set within subalpine meadows, comes into view below the trail. Many hikers leave with a camera full of great pictures.

The trail begins quite high, at 4,200 feet, and quickly enters Goat Rocks Wilderness. The trees along the ridge fight the heavy winter snowpack to attain large girths. The trail follows the ridge for four miles before arriving high above Lily Basin. Large populations of elk often graze in Lily Basin. The trail becomes tricky as it contours around the basin through avalanche chutes and talus. The slope falls away quickly, and hikers should take care when tackling this section. Wildflowers are abundant in these high open slopes.

At six miles is the junction with Angry Mountain Trail. From here, one can gaze down onto either side of the ridge, and no fewer than three of the major volcanoes are within view. A couple of possible camps lie along the trail, with the best camping a quick descent to Heart Lake.
User Groups: Hikers, leashed dogs, and horses (horses may have difficulty navigating the last couple of miles around the basin). No mountain bikes are allowed. No wheelchair access.

Open Seasons: This area is accessible July–October.

Permits: A federal Northwest Forest Pass is required to park here.

Maps: For a map of Gifford Pinchot National Forest, contact the Outdoor Recreation Information Center at the downtown Seattle REI. For a topographic map, ask Green Trails for No. 302, Packwood, or ask the USGS for Packwood.

Directions: From Randle, drive east 14 miles on Highway 12 to Forest Service Road 48. Turn right (south) and drive 9.5 miles to the trailhead on the right. This is shortly after a sharp left-hand turn in a creek bottom.

Contact: Gifford Pinchot National Forest, Cowlitz Valley Ranger Station, 10024 U.S. 12, Randle, WA 98377, 360/497-1100.

70 SOUTH POINT LOOKOUT
7.0 mi/4.0 hrs
south of Randle in Gifford Pinchot National Forest

Map 5.2, page 240

The lookout may be long gone, but the far-reaching views remain. South Point Lookout Trail makes a rugged assault on South Point Mountain, gaining 3,200 feet in just 3.5 miles. That's steep by anyone's standards. The payoff is grand, though, with views of Mount Rainier, Mount St. Helens, and Goat Rocks, not to mention many surrounding ridges and peaks. Much of the trail climbs within an open forest burned long ago. The resulting forest of snags provides increasingly better vistas along the ascent but also makes the hike a hot one (and dry, so bring extra water). The trail ends at the summit, where the lookout once stood. Adventurous folk will enjoy scrambling south along the rocky, meadowy ridge.

User Groups: Hikers, leashed dogs, horses, and mountain bikes. No wheelchair access.

Open Seasons: This trail is accessible June–October.

Permits: A federal Northwest Forest Pass is required to park here.

Maps: For a map of Gifford Pinchot National Forest, contact the Outdoor Recreation Information Center at the downtown Seattle REI. For a topographic map, ask Green Trails for No. 302, Packwood, or ask the USGS for Packwood.

Directions: From Randle, drive east 11 miles on Highway 12 to Forest Service Road 20. Turn right (south) and drive 4 miles (crossing Smith Creek) to the signed trailhead on the left.

Contact: Gifford Pinchot National Forest, Cowlitz Valley Ranger Station, 10024 U.S. 12, Randle, WA 98377, 360/497-1100.

71 GLACIER LAKE
4.0 mi/2.0 hrs

south of Mount Rainier in Goat Rocks Wilderness of Gifford Pinchot National Forest

Map 5.2, page 240

The trail to Glacier Lake is short, has just 800 feet of gain, and leads to a great lake full of trout. The name is misleading, as there are no glaciers near the lake. Instead, beautiful forests of old-growth fir and hemlock encase the lake with a small meadow at the west end making for a great picnicking spot. Elk roam Lily Basin farther up the creek and often make it down to the lake.

Glacier Lake Trail starts off from the trailhead in a young forest logged several decades ago. Within a mile the trail enters the wilderness and virgin forests. The trail is well maintained and never very steep, making easy access for all. A footpath skirts the large lake for exploration by anglers and families alike.

User Groups: Hikers, leashed dogs, and horses. No mountain bikes are allowed. No wheelchair access.

Open Seasons: This trail is accessible May–November.

Permits: A federal Northwest Forest Pass is required to park here.

Maps: For a map of Gifford Pinchot National Forest, contact the Outdoor Recreation Information Center at the downtown Seattle REI. For a topographic map, ask Green Trails for No. 302, Packwood, or ask the USGS for Packwood.

Directions: From Randle, drive east 12 miles on Highway 12 to Forest Service Road 21. Turn right (south) and drive 5 miles to Forest Service Road 2110. Turn left and drive .5 mile to the trailhead on the right.

Contact: Gifford Pinchot National Forest, Cowlitz Valley Ranger Station, 10024 U.S. 12, Randle, WA 98377, 360/497-1100.

72 ANGRY MOUNTAIN
16.8 mi/8.0 hrs

**south of Mount Rainier in Goat
Rocks Wilderness of Gifford Pinchot
National Forest**

Map 5.2, page 240

Despite the name of the mountain, few people leave Angry Mountain in a foul mood. Out of breath and quite tired, but angry, not likely. The trail climbs 3,400 feet along the long ridge of the mountain with the help of plenty of switchbacks. Mount Rainier seems never to be far off, constantly in view to the north. The route ventures deep into the Goat Rocks Wilderness, ending at Heart Lake, a beautiful high lake sure to calm flared tempers and sore feet.

Angry Mountain Trail is difficult from the get-go. It quickly switchbacks up the west end of the mountain through nice forests of Douglas fir and hemlock. The forest soon opens, with large trees spaced farther apart because of heavy winter snowpacks. The trail follows the ridge, which drops steeply to the south. The severe cliffs along the south side of the mountain are a likely source of the name Angry Mountain. Or maybe it's the steep ascent.

Angry Mountain Trail continues by making another series of steep switchbacks, nearing the high point of the mountain and a viewpoint. The trail enters its prime from here, meandering along the ridge. Wildflowers go crazy during June and July. The trail eventually connects to Lily Basin Trail, near the head of Jordan Basin. A great overnight stay is found at Heart Lake (9 miles).

User Groups: Hikers, leashed dogs, and horses. No mountain bikes are allowed. No wheelchair access.

Open Seasons: This area is usually accessible mid-June–October.

Permits: A federal Northwest Forest Pass is required to park here.

Maps: For a map of Gifford Pinchot National Forest, contact the Outdoor Recreation Information Center at the downtown Seattle REI. For topographic maps, ask Green Trails for

No. 302, Packwood, or ask the USGS for Packwood Lake.

Directions: From Randle, drive east 12 miles on Highway 12 to Forest Service Road 21. Turn right (south) and drive 7.5 miles to Forest Service Road 2120. Turn left and drive .5 mile to the trailhead on the right.

Contact: Gifford Pinchot National Forest, Cowlitz Valley Ranger Station, 10024 U.S. 12, Randle, WA 98377, 360/497-1100.

73 GOAT RIDGE
11.0 mi/6.0 hrs

**south of Mount Rainier in Goat
Rocks Wilderness of Gifford Pinchot
National Forest**

Map 5.2, page 240

This is one of the most popular trails in Goat Rocks and for good reason. After climbing into the subalpine with miles of views, the trail finds beautiful but cold Goat Lake. Guarantees are rare, but it's likely that you'll see mountain goats on the high ridges surrounding the lake in the evening. So if you're after goats, wildflowers, or views, Goat Ridge is your hike.

The trail begins from Berry Patch Trailhead and climbs quickly through the forest. A loop option is available (1.2 miles) and is highly recommended. It climbs to the site of a former lookout, where three Cascade volcanoes sit close by. The loop returns to the main Goat Ridge Trail and adds little distance to the hike.

Scaling the slopes of Jordan Basin, the trail passes through wide open meadows that ignite with wildflower blooms in the summer. The trail intercepts Jordan Basin Trail (5.1 miles), a great side trip. Goat Lake lies another .5 mile on Goat Ridge Trail, set deep among high alpine ridges, home to white fuzzy goats.

Goat Ridge makes a great loop. Beyond Goat Lake, hike to Snowgrass Flats (7.8 miles), where hikers can drop back to the trailhead (13.3 miles) via Snowgrass Trail. This is an outstanding overnight trip.

User Groups: Hikers, leashed dogs, and horses.

No mountain bikes are allowed. No wheelchair access.

Open Seasons: This trail is usually accessible July–September.

Permits: A federal Northwest Forest Pass is required to park here.

Maps: For a map of Gifford Pinchot National Forest, contact the Outdoor Recreation Information Center at the downtown Seattle REI. For topographic maps, ask Green Trails for No. 334, Blue Lake, and No. 303, White Pass, or ask the USGS for Hamilton Butte and Old Snowy Mountain.

Directions: From Randle, drive east 12 miles on Highway 12 to Forest Service Road 21. Turn right (south) and drive 14 miles to Forest Service Road 2150. Turn left and drive 3.5 miles. Stay right at the Chambers Lake turnoff and then left to the north Berry Patch Trailhead. (There are two trailheads named Berry Patch—check signboards to verify you're at the one you want.)

Contact: Gifford Pinchot National Forest, Cowlitz Valley Ranger Station, 10024 U.S. 12, Randle, WA 98377, 360/497-1100.

74 SNOWGRASS FLATS
8.4 mi/5.0 hrs

south of Mount Rainier in Goat Rocks Wilderness of Gifford Pinchot National Forest

Map 5.2, page 240

Some trails feature smile-inducing views or open vistas. Others showcase beautiful vegetation or wildlife. When a trail delivers both, it enters a realm reserved for few hikes. Snowgrass Flats is one of those hikes. The trail starts with a diverse forest featuring trees of inspiring size. Next are a pair of beautiful streams. And at the top lies Snowgrass Flats, a wide open parkland featuring more than acres of meadow. And last, the towering peaks of the Goat Rocks.

Snowgrass Trail leaves Berry Patch Trailhead and climbs over the end of Goat Ridge. It crosses Goat Creek on a nice bridge, where the stream cascades and courses over bedrock. Giant yellow cedars, Douglas firs, silver firs, and mountain hemlocks grow here. The trail passes another cascading stream, and the scenery only gets better. Numerous trees cost hikers time on the trail to ponder their ages.

After fairly steady climbing, the trail reaches Snowgrass Flats. This is open parkland for the most part, with meadows spreading far and wide. Here the trail runs into Pacific Crest Trail. Hiking about two miles south on PCT is well worth the effort, as the trail climbs to the base of Old Snowy and the views north become wide open. Old Snowy, at almost 8,000 feet, beckons you to climb farther with a very steep but trouble-free way trail to the summit. This is a hike to remember. Unfortunately, camping is prohibited within Snowgrass Flats.

User Groups: Hikers, leashed dogs, and horses. No mountain bikes are allowed. No wheelchair access.

Open Seasons: This trail is usually accessible July–September.

Permits: A federal Northwest Forest Pass is required to park here.

Maps: For a map of Gifford Pinchot National Forest, contact the Outdoor Recreation Information Center at the downtown Seattle REI. For topographic maps, ask Green Trails for No. 334, Blue Lake, No. 335, Walupt Lake, and No. 303, White Pass, or ask the USGS for Hamilton Butte and Walupt Lake.

Directions: From Randle, drive east 12 miles on Highway 12 to Forest Service Road 21. Turn right (south) and drive 14 miles to Forest Service Road 2150. Turn left and drive 3.5 miles. Stay right at Chambers Lake turnoff and then right on Forest Service Road 2150-405, toward the south Berry Patch Trailhead. (There are two trailheads named Berry Patch—check signboards to verify you're at the one you want.)

Contact: Gifford Pinchot National Forest, Cowlitz Valley Ranger Station, 10024 U.S. 12, Randle, WA 98377, 360/497-1100.

Goat Lake, seen here from the PCT near Snowgrass Flats, is a popular destination.

75 NANNIE RIDGE
9.0 mi/5.5 hrs

south of White Pass in Goat Rocks Wilderness of Gifford Pinchot National Forest

Map 5.2, page 240

Nannie Ridge Trail, in the southern Goat Rocks Wilderness, makes a scenic trip along the high crest. Nannie Ridge is between the craggy peaks of Goat Rocks and the commanding presence of Mount Adams. The trail passes an old lookout site on its way to the meadows of Sheep Lake and Pacific Crest Trail. Understandably, Nannie Ridge is a popular trail in the Gifford Pinchot.

Beginning from the shores of Walupt Lake, Nannie Ridge Trail climbs steadily and steeply to the crest of the ridge. A social trail leads to Nannie Peak (2.5 miles, elevation 6,106), the first but not last opportunity for expansive views. The trail traverses the ridge beneath tall, rocky cliffs and over open meadows of heather. This is hot and dry country, demanding that hikers pack extra water and sunscreen. Nannie Ridge Trail ends at Sheep Lake, a favorite campsite and swimming hole for hikers passing through on PCT. If Sheep Lake doesn't tempt you into the water, Walupt Lake will.

User Groups: Hikers, leashed dogs, and hors-es. No mountain bikes are allowed. No wheelchair access.

Open Seasons: This trail is accessible June–October.

Permits: A federal Northwest Forest Pass is required to park here.

Maps: For a map of Gifford Pinchot National Forest, contact the Outdoor Recreation Information Center at the downtown Seattle REI. For a topographic map, ask Green Trails for No. 335, Walupt Lake, or ask the USGS for Walupt Lake.

Directions: From Randle, drive east 12 miles on Highway 12 to Forest Service Road 21. Turn right (south) and drive 18.5 miles to Forest Service Road 2160. Turn left and drive 5.5 miles to Walupt Lake Trailhead.

Contact: Gifford Pinchot National Forest, Cowlitz Valley Ranger Station, 10024 U.S. 12, Randle, WA 98377, 360/497-1100.

76 WALUPT CREEK
8.6–13.5 mi/4.5 hrs–2 days

south of White Pass in Goat Rocks Wilderness of Gifford Pinchot National Forest

Map 5.2, page 240

Short, easy, and not exceptionally scenic, Walupt Creek Trail is about more than just the creek.

The up-and-back along the trail is a great hike, with pleasant forest and meadows, and even a few high tarns thrown in at the end. But more importantly, Walupt Creek Trail provides two great loops along Pacific Crest Trail.

Walupt Creek Trail provides great access to PCT, gaining just 1,000 feet in more than four miles. The trail spends its first 1.5 miles along the shores of Walupt Lake. Good luck getting past here on a hot summer day without a quick dip to cool off. The trail briefly follows the creek before leaving it to climb out of the glacially shaped valley (notice the U shape) to a large, flat basin. Here are your open subalpine meadows and small tarns. Campsites are found along Walupt Creek and here, near the tarns and PCT.

Walupt Creek is the starting leg to a pair of great loops. From the end of Walupt Creek Trail, head north on PCT to Sheep Lake and along Nannie Ridge (see previous listing) to Walupt Lake (12.3 miles). This route has the most views, especially along Nannie Ridge. Or head south on PCT (13.5 miles), through a large basin and the meadows of Coleman Weedpatch. Both loops turn Walupt Creek from mundane into terrific.

User Groups: Hikers, leashed dogs, and horses. No mountain bikes are allowed. No wheelchair access.

Open Seasons: This trail is accessible June–October.

Permits: A federal Northwest Forest Pass is required to park here.

Maps: For a map of Gifford Pinchot National Forest, contact the Outdoor Recreation Information Center at the downtown Seattle REI. For a topographic map, ask Green Trails for No. 335, Walupt Lake, or ask the USGS for Walupt Lake.

Directions: From Randle, drive east 12 miles on Highway 12 to Forest Service Road 21. Turn right (south) and drive 18.5 miles to Forest Service Road 2160. Turn left and drive 5.5 miles to Walupt Lake Trailhead.

Contact: Gifford Pinchot National Forest, Cowlitz Valley Ranger Station, 10024 U.S. 12, Randle, WA 98377, 360/497-1100.

77 CLEAR FORK
19.2 mi/8.0 hrs

east of Packwood in Goat Rocks Wilderness of Gifford Pinchot National Forest

Map 5.2, page 240

Clear Fork Trail offers something rarely found south of the North Cascades: a long, undisturbed river valley hike up to Pacific Crest Trail. Although many river valleys in the area were logged long ago, the upper Clear Fork of Cowlitz River survived the ax and saw. That's a good thing, for the bubbling water of this stream makes for a serene scene. This is an ideal hike for families, with lots to see and very little elevation change in the first seven miles.

Clear Fork Trail begins on a level, timbered plateau above the river. Situated in an open meadow, Lily Lake (1.5 miles) makes a great swimming hole and turnaround for hikers seeking a shorter hike. Beyond, Clear Fork rambles through old-growth forest and meets the river (5.5 miles). Anglers will note that trout inhabit this wild, rarely fished water. The forests are full of deer and elk, and maybe even a black bear or two. The trail eventually fords the river (7 miles) and climbs to PCT (9.6 miles).

User Groups: Hikers, leashed dogs, and horses. No mountain bikes are allowed. No wheelchair access.

Open Seasons: This trail is accessible year-round.

Permits: A federal Northwest Forest Pass is required to park here.

Maps: For a map of Gifford Pinchot National Forest, contact the Outdoor Recreation Information Center at the downtown Seattle REI. For a topographic map, ask Green Trails for No. 303, White Pass, or ask the USGS for White Pass and Packwood.

Directions: From Randle, drive east 21 miles on Highway 12 to Forest Service Road 46. Turn right (south) and drive 9 miles to the trailhead at road's end.

Contact: Gifford Pinchot National Forest, Cowlitz Valley Ranger Station, 10024 U.S. 12, Randle, WA 98377, 360/497-1100.

78 BLUFF LAKE
3.0–13.2 mi/2.0–8.0 hrs

east of Packwood in Goat Rocks Wilderness of Gifford Pinchot National Forest

Map 5.2, page 240

On the map, Bluff Lake fails to muster much excitement, appearing as nothing more than a small body of water atop a low ridge. Once boots hit trail, however, it's apparent that a great trip is in store. Bluff Lake Trail climbs to its namesake and beyond, running 6.6 miles along the crest of Coal Creek Mountain. Old-growth forest gives way to subalpine meadows. No map mentions that your most likely traveling companions will be deer, elk, and mountain goats. And the map's biggest secret is huckleberries, acres of them.

Bluff Lake Trail gets under way in a mean way, quickly rising 1,000 feet to Bluff Lake (1.5 miles) in the forest atop the ridge. The lake is a good place to turn around for a short hike, but the best is yet to come. The trail maintains its ascent to the crest of Coal Creek Mountain and mellows out along the ridge. The forest grows increasingly sparse, giving way to meadows full of views and huckleberries. This is a good place to see the Goat Rocks, several miles to the southeast. At 6.6 miles, Bluff Lake Trail ends atop a high butte, at a junction with Clear Lost Trail (dropping to Lost Hat Lake, 1 mile) and Packwood Lake Trail (dropping to Lost Lake, 1.4 miles). Trips to these lakes can make your hike slightly longer. Other than Bluff Lake, there's no water to be found along the route.

User Groups: Hikers, leashed dogs, and horses. No mountain bikes are allowed. No wheelchair access.

Open Seasons: This trail is accessible mid-May–October.

Permits: A federal Northwest Forest Pass is required to park here.

Maps: For a map of Gifford Pinchot National Forest, contact the Outdoor Recreation Information Center at the downtown Seattle REI. For a topographic map, ask Green Trails

for No. 302, Packwood, or ask the USGS for Ohanapecosh.

Directions: From Randle, drive east 21 miles on Highway 12 to Forest Service Road 46. Turn right (south) and drive 2 miles to Forest Service Road 4610. Turn right and drive 2 miles to Forest Service Road 4612. Turn left and drive 3 miles to the trailhead at a sharp left turn in the road.

Contact: Gifford Pinchot National Forest, Cowlitz Valley Ranger Station, 10024 U.S. 12, Randle, WA 98377, 360/497-1100.

79 ROUND MOUNTAIN
5.0 mi/3.0 hrs

south of White Pass in Goat Rocks Wilderness of Gifford Pinchot National Forest

Map 5.2, page 240

Short but steep, Round Mountain Trail climbs to an abandoned lookout and onward over Twin Peaks to Pacific Crest Trail. This rugged trail shows few qualms about reaching its destination, gaining 1,600 feet in just 2.5 miles. Round Mountain Trail begins in open forest, but the timber gives way to rocky meadows near the top of Round Mountain. This is a good place to see elk and deer foraging in the forest. At the summit, 5,970 feet, stands an old, shuttered lookout no longer in use by the Forest Service. The views, looking out over miles of the Cascade Crest, are grand—north to Spiral Butte and Mount Rainier and south to Goat Rocks. Beyond the summit, Round Mountain Trail continues over Twin Peaks (4.5 miles) to PCT (6.5 miles). Be sure to carry plenty of water and sunscreen, as this is a hot and dry trail.

User Groups: Hikers, leashed dogs, and horses. No mountain bikes are allowed. No wheelchair access.

Open Seasons: This trail is accessible June–October.

Permits: A federal Northwest Forest Pass is required to park here.

Maps: For a map of Gifford Pinchot National Forest, contact the Outdoor Recreation Information Center at the downtown Seattle REI.

For a topographic map, ask Green Trails for No. 303, White Pass, or ask the USGS for Spiral Butte.

Directions: From White Pass, drive east 7.5 miles on Highway 12 to Tieton Road (Forest Service Road 1200). Turn right (south) and drive 3 miles to Forest Service Road 830. Turn right and drive 4.5 miles to the trailhead on the left side.

Contact: Wenatchee National Forest, Naches Ranger Station, 10237 Highway 12, Naches, WA 98937, 509/653-2205.

80 SHOE LAKE
13.5 mi/8.0 hrs

south of White Pass in Goat Rocks Wilderness of Gifford Pinchot National Forest

Map 5.2, page 240

Some of the best stretches of Pacific Crest Trail are here in Goat Rocks Wilderness. Though not as celebrated as the rocky crags of the Goat Rocks peaks, Shoe Lake is a scenic hike and certainly carries its own weight. Starting directly from Highway 12, PCT traverses seven miles of open forest and wide open meadows to reach refreshing Shoe Lake.

Pacific Crest Trail leaves White Pass and progressively climbs through open forest, passing small Ginette Lake (2.2 miles). PCT eventually finds itself swamped in meadows (5 miles) and awash in wildflower color in late June. For those who have made it this far, the best is still to come. Mount Rainier comes into view as PCT skirts Hogback Mountain and ascends to a high saddle (6.3 miles) overlooking the basin of Shoe Lake with Pinegrass Ridge in the distance. Reaching Shoe Lake requires a steep, short drop into the basin.

The hike to Shoe Lake is very hot and dry, especially during late summer. Until you reach the lake, water is nonexistent, an important consideration when packing before your trip. Camping is highly discouraged in Shoe Lake Basin because of heavy use in the past. Overnight hikers must continue to Hidden Spring (8.5 miles) or cross-country camp more than 200 yards from the trail.

User Groups: Hikers, leashed dogs, and horses. No mountain bikes are allowed. No wheelchair access.

Open Seasons: This trail is accessible June–October.

Permits: A federal Northwest Forest Pass is required to park here.

Maps: For a map of Gifford Pinchot National Forest, contact the Outdoor Recreation Information Center at the downtown Seattle REI. For a topographic map, ask Green Trails for No. 303, White Pass, or ask the USGS for White Pass.

Directions: From White Pass, drive east .7 mile on Highway 12 to the Pacific Crest Trailhead at White Pass Campground. Park here, on the north side of the highway. The trailhead is on the south side.

Contact: Wenatchee National Forest, Naches Ranger Station, 10237 Highway 12, Naches, WA 98937, 509/653-2205.

81 NORTH FORK TIETON
14.0 mi/1–2 days

south of White Pass in Goat Rocks Wilderness of Wenatchee National Forest

Map 5.2, page 240

North Fork Tieton Trail makes a terrific run up to Pacific Crest Trail and an amazing basin below the glaciers of Goat Rocks. This is one of the best ways to reach PCT, just before it climbs into the Goat Rocks. Although this isn't Mount Rainier, Goat Rocks still gets fairly crowded on a summer weekend. This northern side of Goat Rocks, however, sees a fraction of the use compared to the western side.

North Fork Tieton Trail climbs at a steady grade before making a steep rise to Tieton Pass (4.9 miles). Old-growth forests line the trail, with large timber despite being east of the Cascade Crest. Along the way are views of enormous Tieton Valley, ringed by tall, snowy peaks. Gilbert Peak and Old Snowy tower from the heart of the Goat Rocks, at the head of the basin. To the east stand the rugged, rocky slopes of Tieton Peak and Devils Horns.

Pacific Crest Trail runs north-south from Tieton Pass. Head south to reach a junction for McCall Basin (6.5 miles). Break south along McCall Basin Trail and wander into a subalpine wonderland. Acres of meadows run into rocky slopes. Large herds of mountain goats are regular visitors in the area. Since McCall Basin makes a long day hike, campsites are scattered about, ideal for Leave-No-Trace camping.

User Groups: Hikers, leashed dogs, and horses. No mountain bikes are allowed. No wheelchair access.

Open Seasons: This trail is accessible mid-June–mid-October.

Permits: A federal Northwest Forest Pass is required to park here.

Maps: For a map of Wenatchee National Forest, contact the Outdoor Recreation Information Center at the downtown Seattle REI. For a topographic map, ask Green Trails for No. 303, White Pass, or ask the USGS for Pinegrass Ridge and Old Snowy Mountain.

Directions: From White Pass, drive east 7.5 miles on Highway 12 to Tieton Road (Forest Service Road 1200). Turn right (south) and drive 3 miles to Forest Service Road 1207. Continue straight onto Road 1207 and drive 4.5 miles to the trailhead at road's end.

Contact: Wenatchee National Forest, Naches Ranger Station, 10237 Highway 12, Naches, WA 98937, 509/653-2205.

82 BEAR CREEK MOUNTAIN
12.8 mi/8.0 hrs

southeast of White Pass in Goat Rocks Wilderness of Wenatchee National Forest

Map 5.2, page 240

As far as forgotten and ignored trails in the Goat Rocks go, this is it. Bear Creek Mountain Trail makes a steep trip to the summit along the ridge dividing the North and South Fork Tieton Rivers. Because of an elevation gain of more than 3,000 feet, most hikers select other trails in the area. That's a shame, because high-country meadows full of wildflowers, maybe even mountain goats, reward those who make the trip.

Bear Creek Mountain Trail wastes little time before starting a steep ascent out of the South Fork Tieton Valley. The trees are big, but this being the east side of the Cascade Crest, the forest is open. Meadows begin to appear as the trail reaches a junction with Tieton Meadows Trail (5.4 miles). The views are grand from this north-facing vista, including Mount Rainier, which outshines any other peak.

To gain panoramic views, one must turn south and scramble nearly 1,000 feet in one mile to the summit of Bear Creek Mountain. To say the least, this is an impressive location from which to study Goat Rocks. Hikers who pack a pair of binoculars this far will be glad they did. Bear Creek Mountain Trail passes no water along the way, so plan to carry plenty.

User Groups: Hikers, leashed dogs, and horses. No mountain bikes are allowed. No wheelchair access.

Open Seasons: This trail is accessible July–October.

Permits: A federal Northwest Forest Pass is required to park here.

Maps: For a map of Wenatchee National Forest, contact the Outdoor Recreation Information Center at the downtown Seattle REI. For a topographic map, ask Green Trails for No. 303, White Pass, or ask the USGS for Pinegrass Ridge.

Directions: From White Pass, drive east 7.5 miles on Highway 12 to Tieton Road (Forest Service Road 1200). Turn right (south) and drive 12 miles to Forest Service Road 1000. Turn right and drive 12 miles to the trailhead at road's end.

Contact: Wenatchee National Forest, Naches Ranger Station, 10237 Highway 12, Naches, WA 98937, 509/653-2205.

83 SOUTH FORK TIETON RIVER
13.9 mi/1–2 days

southeast of White Pass in Goat Rocks Wilderness of Wenatchee National Forest

Map 5.2, page 240

Free from the crowds that pack much of the Goat Rocks Wilderness in summer, South Fork

Tieton River Trail offers access to one of the mountains' most beautiful basins. The trail follows the river upstream before splitting to make a loop around the top of the expansive basin. The beauty of this trail layout (it's shaped like a lasso) is that very little of the trail is walked twice. Rocky peaks of Gilbert Peak and Klickitat Divide loom over the loop, home to fields of wildflowers and herds of mountain goats.

South Fork Tieton Trail remains exceptionally level and easy for the first several miles. Open Conrad Meadows features some very large timber. Elk and deer are common. The trail comes to a junction (4.3 miles), where the loop begins. This is also where the climbing starts. Either side of the loop climbs quickly to the upper slopes of the basin before leveling out. Long, narrow Surprise Lake is truly a surprise along the forested slopes, and it makes a great place to pitch camp. Mountain goats are frequent along the rocky rim bordering the basin. Hikers can make great excursions among the rocky meadows to the crest of Klickitat Divide for views of the surrounding Goat Rocks.

User Groups: Hikers, leashed dogs, and horses. No mountain bikes are allowed. No wheelchair access.

Open Seasons: This trail is accessible July–October.

Permits: A federal Northwest Forest Pass is required to park here.

Maps: For a map of Wenatchee National Forest, contact the Outdoor Recreation Information Center at the downtown Seattle REI. For a topographic map, ask Green Trails for No. 303, White Pass, or No. 335, Walupt Lake, or ask the USGS for Jennies Butte and Pinegrass Ridge.

Directions: From White Pass, drive east 7.5 miles on Highway 12 to Tieton Road (Forest Service Road 1200). Turn right (south) and drive 12 miles to Forest Service Road 1000. Turn right and drive 12 miles to the trailhead at road's end.

Contact: Wenatchee National Forest, Naches Ranger Station, 10237 Highway 12, Naches, WA 98937, 509/653-2205.

84 CISPUS BRAILLE
0.5 mi/0.5 hr

south of Randle in Gifford Pinchot National Forest

Map 5.2, page 240

This nature trail at the Cispus Environmental Learning Center investigates a forest recovering from fire. The trail is level and easy to negotiate, an ideal outing for families or those using a wheelchair. Interpretive signs lead the way and describe the flora and fauna helping to recreate a forest. The folks at the Learning Center have also designed this trail to be accessible to the visually impaired, with Braille markings and roping to guide hikers around the loop. This is a wonderful place to find elk or deer grazing the understory, especially in the winter when the high country lies under several feet of wet snow.

User Groups: Hikers and leashed dogs. No horses or mountain bikes are allowed. The trail is wheelchair accessible.

Open Seasons: This trail is accessible year-round.

Permits: A federal Northwest Forest Pass is required to park here.

Maps: For a map of Gifford Pinchot National Forest, contact the Outdoor Recreation Information Center at the downtown Seattle REI. For a topographic map, ask Green Trails for No. 333, McCoy Peak, or ask the USGS for Tower Rock.

Directions: From Randle, drive south 1 mile on Highway 131 to Forest Service Road 23. Veer left and drive 8 miles to Forest Service Road 28. Turn right and drive 1.5 miles to Forest Service Road 76. Stay to the right and drive 1 mile to the Cispus Environmental Learning Center. The trailhead is on the opposite side of Road 76.

Contact: Gifford Pinchot National Forest, Cowlitz Valley Ranger Station, 10024 U.S. 12, Randle, WA 98377, 360/497-1100.

85 KLICKITAT TRAIL
17.1 mi one-way/9.0 hrs

south of Packwood in Gifford Pinchot National Forest

Map 5.2, page 240

Following an ancient Native American trail through the high country, Klickitat Trail makes an excellent ridge run. Bathed in summer sun, with miles of huckleberry bushes and mountain views, Klickitat Trail is an ideal day (or two) in the Gifford Pinchot. The length and orientation of the trail make an out-and-back hike very unappealing; a car-drop is best if it can be arranged. If not, the two trailheads are supplemented with several additional access points. Although the trail starts and ends high, the route encounters numerous ups and downs, making for some challenging elevation changes. Because much of the trail rides the crest of a ridge, snowfields are common on north slopes well into August.

From west to east, the trail skirts the rocky masses of Twin Sisters and Castle Butte. A side trail leads to the summit of Cispus Lookout (3.2 miles). Huckleberries and views of Mount Rainier dominate the scenery on the way to Horseshoe Point (7.5 miles), Cold Spring Butte (9 miles), and Mission Mountain (12.4 miles). The ridge (and trail) head south to the eastern trailhead, below Elk Peak (17.1 miles). The trail is dry except for Jackpot Lake (4.4 miles) and St. Michael Lake (off-trail below Cold Springs Butte).

User Groups: Hikers, leashed dogs, horses, and mountain bikes. No wheelchair access.

Open Seasons: This trail is accessible mid-July–October.

Permits: A federal Northwest Forest Pass is required to park here.

Maps: For a map of Gifford Pinchot National Forest, contact the Outdoor Recreation Information Center at the downtown Seattle REI. For a topographic map, ask Green Trails for No. 334, Blue Lake, or ask the USGS for Tower Rock, Hamilton Butte, and Blue Lake.

Directions: From Randle, drive south 1 mile on Highway 131 to Forest Service Road 25.

Stay to the right and drive 21 miles to Forest Service Road 28. Turn left and drive 2.5 miles to the signed trailhead.

Contact: Gifford Pinchot National Forest, Cowlitz Valley Ranger Station, 10024 U.S. 12, Randle, WA 98377, 360/497-1100.

86 HAMILTON BUTTES
5.6 mi/3.0 hrs

south of Randle in Gifford Pinchot National Forest

Map 5.2, page 240

Hamilton Buttes Trail features a pair of trailheads, one low and one high. Pick the starting location that's right for you, but the upper trailhead is 1.5 miles shorter and saves 1,000 feet of elevation gain. Hamilton Buttes Trail leads to the twin peaks on a route primarily cloaked in carpets of wildflower meadows and huckleberries.

From the upper trailhead, Hamilton Buttes Trail scales the side of a forested basin to reach a small ridgeline and junction (2.2 miles). Turning right drops to the lower trailhead, so don't do that. Head left, uphill, and climb to the top of the two peaks. This is divine country, with outstanding views of Goat Rocks and Mount Adams. August is the prime month to find ripe huckleberries. Carry plenty of water, as none is to be found once you leave the car.

User Groups: Hikers, leashed dogs, horses, mountain bikes, and motorcycles. No wheelchair access.

Open Seasons: This trail is accessible June–October.

Permits: A federal Northwest Forest Pass is required to park here.

Maps: For a map of Gifford Pinchot National Forest, contact the Outdoor Recreation Information Center at the downtown Seattle REI. For a topographic map, ask Green Trails for No. 334, Blue Lake, or ask the USGS for Hamilton Butte.

Directions: From Randle, drive south 1 mile on Highway 131 to Forest Service Road 23. Veer left and drive 12 miles to Forest Service

Road 22. Turn left and drive 6 miles to Forest Service Road 78. Turn right and drive 8.5 miles to the trailhead at the pass.

Contact: Gifford Pinchot National Forest, Cowlitz Valley Ranger Station, 10024 U.S. 12, Randle, WA 98377, 360/497-1100.

87 YOZOO
8.0 mi/4.0 hrs

south of Randle in Gifford Pinchot National Forest

Map 5.2, page 240

Don't ask where the name came from, just enjoy the huckleberries and views of Mount Rainier. That's easy enough, because Yozoo Trail spends a big chunk of its length in open meadows along the high ridge. Through large, old forest, the trail skirts a ridge and climbs through the small valley of Grouse Creek (1.5 miles). This is the last chance for water before Yozoo Trail enters the high country with open meadows of small trees and huckleberry bushes. The trail runs just below the rim of Yozoo Basin, where views of Mount Rainier are constant. Several peaks frame the basin and make great scrambles to even bigger views. Mountain goats, elk, and black bear are all regular visitors to this area during the summer and early fall. Just be mindful of the most annoying of beasts, roaring motorbikes. Yozoo Trail ends at Bishop Ridge Trail (4 miles), overlooking the sparkling and tempting water of Blue Lake.

User Groups: Hikers, leashed dogs, horses, mountain bikes, and motorcycles. No wheelchair access.

Open Seasons: This trail is accessible April–October.

Permits: A federal Northwest Forest Pass is required to park here.

Maps: For a map of Gifford Pinchot National Forest, contact the Outdoor Recreation Information Center at the downtown Seattle REI. For a topographic map, ask Green Trails for No. 334, Blue Lake, or ask the USGS for Hamilton Butte.

Directions: From Randle, drive south 1 mile on

Highway 131 to Forest Service Road 23. Veer left on Forest Service Road 23 and drive 12 miles to Forest Service Road 22. Turn left and drive 6 miles to Forest Service Road 78. Turn right and drive 5 miles to the signed trailhead.

Contact: Gifford Pinchot National Forest, Cowlitz Valley Ranger Station, 10024 U.S. 12, Randle, WA 98377, 360/497-1100.

88 LANGILLE RIDGE
8.4 mi/5.0 hrs

south of Randle in Gifford Pinchot National Forest

Map 5.2, page 240

In the heart of Gifford Pinchot National Forest, Langille Ridge stands as a lonely place. Because of a road washout at one end and a steep, rocky access trail, few hikers have the pleasure of hiking this high ridge. Thus the spoils of Langille Ridge are left to the few, a tantalizing prospect for hikers looking for solitude. The jagged ridge runs more than 10 miles from end to end, but the best spots are close to the car.

With the washout of the northern trailhead, Langille Ridge Trail is best reached via Rough Trail. Appropriately named, Rough Trail climbs 2,000 feet over a rocky path to Langille Ridge Trail (1.7 miles). This is the worst of it, however. From the junction, Langille Ridge Trail runs north and south, making some ups and downs along the jagged ridge. A hike south travels through rocky meadows, complete with huckleberries, to Boundary Trail (5.6 miles one-way).

The preferred option is to head north from the Rough Trail junction along Langille Ridge to McCoy Peak (4.2 miles) and Langille Peak (5.9 miles). Both peaks offer panoramic views of the surrounding countryside and forests. The northern half of Langille Ridge features uninterrupted views of Juniper Ridge and Mount Adams. This is a great place to see mountain goats along the rocky slopes and to hear elk bellowing from the basins below. Plan on packing plenty of water, as much of the ridge is exposed and dry.

User Groups: Hikers, leashed dogs, horses,

mountain bikes, and motorcycles. No wheel-chair access.

Open Seasons: This trail is accessible May–October.

Permits: A federal Northwest Forest Pass is required to park here.

Maps: For a map of Gifford Pinchot National Forest, contact the Outdoor Recreation Information Center at the downtown Seattle REI. For a topographic map, ask Green Trails for No. 333, McCoy Peak, or ask the USGS for Tower Rock and McCoy Peak.

Directions: From Randle, drive south 1 mile on Highway 131 to Forest Service Road 23. Veer left on Forest Service Road 23 and drive 8 miles to Forest Service Road 28. Turn right and drive 1.5 miles to Forest Service Road 29. Turn left and drive 12 miles to Forest Service Road 29-116. Turn right and drive .5 mile to the signed trailhead.

Contact: Gifford Pinchot National Forest, Cowlitz Valley Ranger Station, 10024 U.S. 12, Randle, WA 98377, 360/497-1100.

89 TONGUE MOUNTAIN
3.4 mi/2.0 hrs

south of Randle in Gifford Pinchot National Forest

Map 5.2, page 240

Standing slightly apart from Juniper Ridge, Tongue Mountain towers over lush Cispus River Valley. Although the peak looks as if it belongs to the neighboring ridge, Tongue Mountain is actually the remains of an old volcano. Tongue Mountain Trail makes a gentle climb through old-growth forest to an open saddle (1 mile). Folks interested in views but not a workout can enjoy looking out over the valley to Mount Adams and Mount Rainier from here. More determined hikers can make the sharp and steep ascent to the peak's summit (1.7 miles, elevation 4,838 feet). This section of trail is a tough climb, but it's over quickly and is certainly rewarding. Cascades volcanoes tower over the Gifford Pinchot, and the noisy Cispus River roars from below. Lucky hikers

will spot fluffy white mountain goats along the peaks' sheer cliffs.

User Groups: Hikers, leashed dogs, horses, and mountain bikes. No wheelchair access.

Open Seasons: This trail is accessible April–October.

Permits: A federal Northwest Forest Pass is required to park here.

Maps: For a map of Gifford Pinchot National Forest, contact the Outdoor Recreation Information Center at the downtown Seattle REI. For a topographic map, ask Green Trails for No. 333, McCoy Peak, or ask the USGS for Tower Rock.

Directions: From Randle, drive south 1 mile on Highway 131 to Forest Service Road 23. Veer left on Forest Service Road 23 and drive 8 miles to Forest Service Road 28. Turn right and drive 1.5 miles to Forest Service Road 29. Turn left and drive 4 miles to Forest Service Road 2904. Turn left and drive 4 miles to the signed trailhead.

Contact: Gifford Pinchot National Forest, Cowlitz Valley Ranger Station, 10024 U.S. 12, Randle, WA 98377, 360/497-1100.

90 BADGER PEAK
2.0 mi/1.5 hrs

south of Randle in Gifford Pinchot National Forest

Map 5.2, page 240

Such easy access to a former lookout point is hard to come by, but Badger Ridge Trail delivers. It's just one short mile to the summit of Badger Peak (elevation 5,664 feet), where a lookout stood until the 1960s. Even harder to find is a refreshing lake nearby to enjoy after the climb to the summit, but that is found here also. Badger Ridge Trail starts high and climbs to the crest of Badger Ridge (.6 mile). Already, the views of Mount St. Helens are grand. They have competition, however, from fields of huckleberries. The trail now splits, dropping slightly to Badger Lake or climbing to Badger Peak. From the summit, volcanoes new and old dominate the landscape. Mount

St. Helens, Mount Rainier, and Mount Adams represent the new school, still busy at building themselves up. Older, extinct volcanoes include craggy Pinto Rock, jagged Langille Ridge, and other surrounding peaks. Your best bet is to climb the summit before dipping into Badger Lake.

User Groups: Hikers, leashed dogs, horses, mountain bikes, and motorcycles. No wheelchair access.

Open Seasons: This trail is accessible May–October.

Permits: A federal Northwest Forest Pass is required to park here.

Maps: For a map of Gifford Pinchot National Forest, contact the Outdoor Recreation Information Center at the downtown Seattle REI. For a topographic map, ask Green Trails for No. 333, McCoy Peak, or ask the USGS for French Butte.

Directions: From Randle, drive south 1 mile on Highway 131 to Forest Service Road 25. Stay to the right and drive 21 miles to Forest Service Road 28. Turn left (east) and drive 2.5 miles to Forest Service Road 2816 (a bit rocky). Turn right and drive 5 miles to the trailhead at road's end.

Contact: Gifford Pinchot National Forest, Cowlitz Valley Ranger Station, 10024 U.S. 12, Randle, WA 98377, 360/497-1100.

91 JUNIPER RIDGE
6.4–8.8 mi/5.0 hrs

south of Randle in Gifford Pinchot National Forest

Map 5.2, page 240

High, open, and awash in huckleberries and views, Juniper Ridge Trail is a southern Washington favorite. The long ridge run follows the crest of Juniper Ridge over Juniper, Sunrise, and Jumbo Peaks. The hiker's reward is miles of huckleberries and views of Mount Adams, Mount Rainier, Mount St. Helens, and even Mount Hood. Between gazing and grazing, be sure not to bump into the numerous elk, mountain goats, deer, or bear that live here. Juniper

Ridge is tremendously scenic and wild (except for the occasional dirt bike roaring through).

Juniper Ridge Trail runs 11.4 miles along the crest of the high ridge. Fortunately, the trail is bisected by Sunrise Trail, a short access trail (1.4 miles) conveniently starting at 4,500 feet. From Sunrise, hikers have options to head north to two separate peaks or south to miles of huckleberry meadows. Backpackers thinking of spending the night here will need to pack extra water; the ridge is dry.

The southern half of Juniper Ridge is certainly the best. The route is one big meadow ramble. Huckleberries are ripest in August. Juniper Ridge Trail skirts Jumbo Peak (3.2 miles), a good turnaround, before dropping to Dark Meadows and Boundary Trail.

The northern half of Juniper Ridge Trail leaves Sunrise Trailhead and climbs Sunrise Peak (1.4 miles), a steep but manageable endeavor. This is Juniper Ridge's highest point. The trail follows the rocky ridge north to Juniper Peak (4.4 miles), a good turnaround, before dropping into clear-cuts.

User Groups: Hikers, leashed dogs, horses, mountain bikes, and motorcycles. No wheelchair access.

Open Seasons: This trail is accessible May–October.

Permits: A federal Northwest Forest Pass is required to park here.

Maps: For a map of Gifford Pinchot National Forest, contact the Outdoor Recreation Information Center at the downtown Seattle REI. For a topographic map, ask Green Trails for No. 333, McCoy Peak, and No. 334, Blue Lake, or ask the USGS for McCoy Peak and Tower Rock.

Directions: From Randle, drive south 1 mile on Highway 131 to Forest Service Road 23. Veer left on Forest Service Road 23 and drive 24 miles to Forest Service Road 2324. Turn right and drive 5 miles to Forest Service Road 2324-063. Turn left and drive .3 mile to the trailhead at road's end.

Contact: Gifford Pinchot National Forest,

Cowlitz Valley Ranger Station, 10024 U.S. 12, Randle, WA 98377, 360/497-1100.

92 YELLOWJACKET PASS/ HAT ROCK

5.4 mi/3.0 hrs

south of Randle in Gifford Pinchot National Forest

Map 5.2, page 240

Hat Rock is but one of many things to see or travel to from this trailhead. Yellowjacket Trail is merely a shortcut to other trails, heading in every direction through the high country. This is also known as a cheater trail; that is, quick and easy access to terrain normally approached by longer, more traditional routes. In this instance, Yellowjacket Trail provides a quick route to Boundary Trail's scenic eastern segment and Langille Ridge.

Yellowjacket Trail climbs sharply to Boundary Trail, gaining 800 feet in just one mile. Head left for Langille Ridge junction (1.2 miles from the trailhead) or to follow Boundary Trail to the huckleberry riches of Dark Meadow. Turning right from Yellowjacket Trail leads through open meadows with stunning views of Mount Adams to Hat Rock (2.4 miles from the trailhead) and Yellowjacket Pass (2.7 miles). A boot-beaten path leads to the top of Hat Rock (elevation 5,599 feet) and a remarkable view of Badger Peak, Craggy Peak, Langille Ridge, and Juniper Ridge. The flattened top of Mount St. Helens rises to the west. Although short, this is an exposed and dry hike; remember plenty of water.

User Groups: Hikers, leashed dogs, horses, mountain bikes, and motorcycles. No wheelchair access.

Open Seasons: This trail is accessible June–October.

Permits: A federal Northwest Forest Pass is required to park here.

Maps: For a map of Gifford Pinchot National Forest, contact the Outdoor Recreation Information Center at the downtown Seattle REI. For a topographic map, ask Green Trails

for No. 333, McCoy, or ask the USGS for McCoy Peak.

Directions: From Randle, drive south 1 mile on Highway 131 to Forest Service Road 23. Veer left on Forest Service Road 23 and drive 8 miles to Forest Service Road 28. Turn right and drive 11 miles to Forest Service Road 2810. Stay to the left and drive 9 miles to trailhead at road's end.

Contact: Gifford Pinchot National Forest, Mount St. Helens National Volcanic Monument, 42218 Northeast Yale Bridge Road, Amboy, WA 98601, 360/449-7871.

93 CRAGGY PEAK

8.8 mi/5.0 hrs

northeast of Cougar in Gifford Pinchot National Forest

Map 5.2, page 240

Craggy Peak Trail makes a great ridge run in the heart of the Gifford Pinchot, with meadow views to craggy peaks (including Craggy Peak!) and distant volcanoes. Enjoy the virgin forest shading the trail before it breaks out into spectacular meadows. Craggy Peak Trail also offers great access to Boundary Trail. With lots of campsites, this is a great day hike or an easy overnighter. Elk, deer, and mountain goats are frequent visitors to the area, and black bears appear in late summer to browse the huckleberries.

Craggy Peak Trail gets most of the climbing done early, ascending through an old forest of fir trees, dominated on the ground by bear grass. Quick glimpses of Mount Adams can be had through the trees, but the real views are reserved until the meadows (3 miles). The trail continues through prime huckleberry habitat to Boundary Trail, at the base of Craggy Peak (4.4 miles). Exploration along Boundary Trail is a meadow delight, north to Shark Rock or east to Yellowjacket Pass. The peaks tower over the deep, glaciated valleys, lush with old forests. Great campsites are situated along the trail, often down faint boot-worn paths to big views. Basin Camp is .5 mile east on Boundary Trail. Just be prepared for a dry trip with extra packed water.

User Groups: Hikers, leashed dogs, horses, mountain bikes, and motorcycles. No wheelchair access.

Open Seasons: This trail is accessible June–October.

Permits: A federal Northwest Forest Pass is required to park here.

Maps: For a map of Gifford Pinchot National Forest, contact the Outdoor Recreation Information Center at the downtown Seattle REI. For a topographic map, ask Green Trails for No. 333, McCoy Peak, and No. 365, Lone Butte, or ask the USGS for Spencer Butte, Quartz Creek, and McCoy Peak.

Directions: From Vancouver, drive north on I-5 to Highway 503 (Woodland, exit 21). Drive east 45 miles to Forest Service Road 25. Continue straight on Forest Service Road 25 and drive 6 miles to Forest Service Road 93, just beyond the Muddy River. Turn right and drive 13 miles to Forest Service Road 93-040. Turn left and drive .5 mile to the signed trailhead on the right.

Contact: Gifford Pinchot National Forest, Mount St. Helens National Volcanic Monument, 42218 Northeast Yale Bridge Road, Amboy, WA 98601, 360/449-7871.

94 SUMMIT PRAIRIE
17.8 mi/1–2 days

northeast of Cougar in Gifford Pinchot National Forest

Map 5.2, page 240

Miles from the nearest trailhead, Summit Prairie is isolated, to say the least. Access to the open meadows, chock-full of huckleberry bushes, requires a long climb of nearly 3,000 feet. That keeps the crowds out of Summit Prairie and the wildlife wild, despite the occasional motorbike (they're still allowed in this "roadless" area). Herds of elk and mountain goats live in Quartz Creek Ridge and Summit Prairie, one of the Gifford Pinchot's most remote places.

In honor of full disclosure, a cheater trail does offer access to Summit Prairie (Boundary Trail, via Table Mountain). It's a little shorter, but nowhere near as scenic. Better access is via Summit Prairie Trail, which climbs Quartz Creek Ridge and runs the long, open ridgeline to Summit Prairie. Leaving from Forest Service Road 90, Summit Prairie Trail climbs harshly to the ridgeline (4 miles). The only water on the route is found in this first segment. Open subalpine forest and frequent meadows cover the ridge to Summit Prairie (8.9 miles) and Boundary Trail.

This is a tough trip to complete in one day, but campsites are few and far between. Overnight campers should plan on cross-country camping without a water source. If you've made it this far, the best option is to turn the trip into a 20.7-mile loop on Boundary Trail, Quartz Creek Trail (see listing in this chapter), and Quartz Creek Butte Trail (a 1.5-mile trail that serves as connector between Summit Prairie and Quartz Creek Big Trees).

User Groups: Hikers, leashed dogs, horses, mountain bikes, and motorcycles. No wheelchair access.

Open Seasons: This trail is accessible mid-June–October.

Permits: A federal Northwest Forest Pass is required to park here.

Maps: For a map of Gifford Pinchot National Forest, contact the Outdoor Recreation Information Center at the downtown Seattle REI. For a topographic map, ask Green Trails for No. 334, Blue Lake, No. 365, Lone Butte, and No. 366, Mount Adams West, or ask the USGS for Steamboat Mountain and East Canyon Ridge.

Directions: From Vancouver, drive north on I-5 to Highway 503 (Woodland, exit 21). Drive east 45 miles to Pine Creek Information Center. Turn right and continue on Forest Service Road 90 for 25 miles to the signed trailhead on the left (1.5 miles before Forest Service Road 88).

Contact: Gifford Pinchot National Forest, Mount St. Helens National Volcanic Monument, 42218 Northeast Yale Bridge Road, Amboy, WA 98601, 360/449-7871.

95 DARK MEADOW
8.4 mi/4.5 hrs

south of Randle in Gifford Pinchot National Forest

Map 5.2, page 240

Yet another locale with an ill-fitting name, the only thing dark in Dark Meadows are black huckleberries, juicy and ripe in August. In fact, these open meadows are lit up with summer sun, revealing great views of Jumbo Peak, Langille Ridge, and Mount Adams. Dark Meadow Trail endures several miles of shady forest before emerging into the dueling glories of huckleberry fields and vistas.

Dark Meadow Trail begins by gently wandering up the level valley of Dark Creek. The forest here is old Douglas fir and western hemlock, a perfect home for elk. After one mile, the trail climbs steeply to a junction with Juniper Ridge Trail (3.2 miles). The forest opens occasionally to reveal views of the valleys below. A short mile south on Juniper Ridge Trail finds Dark Meadow. Black huckleberry bushes fill the open meadows, attracting hikers and black bears alike. A short footpath leads through the meadow to the summit of Dark Mountain for a panoramic viewpoint (Mount Adams, wow!).

User Groups: Hikers, leashed dogs, horses, mountain bikes, and motorcycles. No wheelchair access.

Open Seasons: This trail is accessible May–October.

Permits: A federal Northwest Forest Pass is required to park here.

Maps: For a map of Gifford Pinchot National Forest, contact the Outdoor Recreation Information Center at the downtown Seattle REI. For a topographic map, ask Green Trails for No. 333, McCoy Peak, and No. 334, Blue Lake, or ask the USGS for McCoy Peak and East Canyon Ridge.

Directions: From Randle, drive south 1 mile on Highway 131 to Forest Service Road 23. Veer left on Forest Service Road 23 and drive 25 miles to the signed trailhead on the right.

Contact: Gifford Pinchot National Forest, Cowlitz Valley Ranger Station, 10024 U.S. 12, Randle, WA 98377, 360/497-1100.

96 QUARTZ CREEK
21.2 mi/1–2 days

northeast of Cougar in Gifford Pinchot National Forest

Map 5.2, page 240

Lesser known for old-growth forests than other forests of Washington, Gifford Pinchot features forests as magnificent as any other. Quartz Creek Trail is a wonderful example of these ancient timberlands, where towering Douglas fir, western hemlock, and western red cedar grow to immense proportions. Quartz Creek Trail spends more than 10 miles wandering up the valley. Numerous streams enter Quartz Creek, including Straight Creek and its waterfalls. Regardless of how far one ventures up Quartz Creek Trail, the trip is sure to be grand.

Although Quartz Creek Trail gains 2,500 feet net elevation, numerous ups and downs make total elevation change more than twice that amount. The trail encounters Straight Creek (2 miles), home to a beautiful series of waterfalls. The occasional sections of logged forest are worth tolerating, balanced by the many miles of ancient old-growth forest. Campsites dot the trail as it wanders up the valley, passing Quartz Creek Butte Trail (a 1.5-mile connector between Summit Prairie and Quartz Creek Big Trees) junction at 4.5 miles. The upper section of the trail passes through forest burned long ago and now replaced by a subalpine setting. The trail connects to Boundary Trail (10.6 miles).

Folks who decide to hike the length of the trail are well advised to turn the trip into a loop. Summit Prairie Trail (see listing in this chapter) traverses Quartz Creek Ridge, awash in distant views and berry bushes. At the junction with Boundary Trail, hike east 2.3 miles to Summit Prairie Trail and turn south toward Quartz Creek Butte Trail, descending to Quartz Creek. Total mileage is 22 miles.

User Groups: Hikers, leashed dogs, horses, and mountain bikes. No wheelchair access.

Open Seasons: This trail is accessible mid-June–October.

Permits: A federal Northwest Forest Pass is required to park here.

Maps: For a map of Gifford Pinchot National Forest, contact the Outdoor Recreation Information Center at the downtown Seattle REI. For a topographic map, ask Green Trails for No. 333, McCoy Peak, No. 334, Blue Lake, No. 365, Lone Butte, and No. 366, Mount Adams West, or ask the USGS for Quartz Creek Butte, East Canyon Ridge, and Steamboat Mountain.

Directions: From Vancouver, drive north on I-5 to Highway 503 (Woodland, exit 21). Drive east 45 miles to Pine Creek Information Center. Turn right and continue on Forest Service Road 90 for 20 miles to the signed trailhead on the left (just beyond Forest Service Road 93).

Contact: Gifford Pinchot National Forest, Mount St. Helens National Volcanic Monument, 42218 Northeast Yale Bridge Road, Amboy, WA 98601, 360/449-7871.

97 HIGH LAKES
8.0 mi/3.5 hrs

south of Packwood in Gifford Pinchot National Forest

Map 5.2, page 240

Take much of what is great about the Gifford Pinchot, combine it into one trail, and High Lakes Trail is the result. The trail does indeed visit several high, meadow-rimmed lakes along the way. Views of Mount Adams make regular appearances along the route. And during the later summer, delicious, ripe huckleberries make this trip an appetizing day hike.

High Lakes Trail connects Olallie and Horseshoe Lakes. Save for a small segment in the middle, much of the route is easy to negotiate with little elevation gain. From the western end, the trail travels the dense forest around Olallie Lake to the open forest and meadows of Chain Lakes (1.3 miles). The trail crosses a large lava flow punctuating the valley of Adams Creek (2.8 miles) and climbs to Horseshoe

Lake and campground. August is usually the best month to harvest mouthfuls of huckleberries along the way. These juicy berries constitute a large part of the summer diets for local black bears.

User Groups: Hikers, leashed dogs, horses, mountain bikes, and motorcycles. No wheelchair access.

Open Seasons: This trail is accessible May–November.

Permits: A federal Northwest Forest Pass is required to park here.

Maps: For a map of Gifford Pinchot National Forest, contact the Outdoor Recreation Information Center at the downtown Seattle REI. For a topographic map, ask Green Trails for No. 334, Blue Lake, or ask the USGS for Green Mountain.

Directions: From Randle, drive south 1 mile on Highway 131 to Forest Service Road 23. Veer left on Forest Service Road 23 and drive 33 miles to Forest Service Road 2329. Turn left and drive 1 mile to the signed trailhead on the left.

Contact: Gifford Pinchot National Forest, Cowlitz Valley Ranger Station, 10024 U.S. 12, Randle, WA 98377, 360/497-1100.

98 TAKHLAKH LAKE AND MEADOWS
2.6 mi/1.5 hrs

north of Trout Lake in Gifford Pinchot National Forest

Map 5.2, page 240

Families on the lookout for an easy but scenic hike will want to pay attention here. Two trails combine to enjoy Takhlakh Lake, a 1.1-mile loop, and Takhlakh Meadows, a 1.5-mile loop situated off the first trail (imagine a figure eight). Both trails are flat and extremely level, perfect for hikers of any age. The trails are even barrier free, making them accessible for folks in wheelchairs, although in a few sections assistance will be appreciated. Both trails enjoy views of Mount Adams to the southeast. Takhlakh Lake Trail loops around the lake.

From the southeast part of this loop, Takhlakh Meadows Trail makes a separate loop. In August, these open meadows are full of delicious, ripe huckleberries.

User Groups: Hikers and leashed dogs. No horses or mountain bikes are allowed. These trails are wheelchair accessible.

Open Seasons: This trail is accessible May–November.

Permits: A federal Northwest Forest Pass is required to park here.

Maps: For a map of Gifford Pinchot National Forest, contact the Outdoor Recreation Information Center at the downtown Seattle REI. For a topographic map, ask Green Trails for No. 334, Blue Lake, or ask the USGS for Green Mountain.

Directions: From Randle, drive south 1 mile on Highway 131 to Forest Service Road 23. Veer left on Forest Service Road 23 and drive 33 miles to Forest Service Road 2329. Turn left and drive 2 miles to the signed trailhead at road's end.

Contact: Gifford Pinchot National Forest, Mount Adams Ranger District, 2455 Highway 141, Trout Lake, WA 98650, 509/395-3400.

99 SPENCER BUTTE
3.8 mi/2.0 hrs

north of Cougar in Gifford Pinchot National Forest

Map 5.2, page 240

Spencer Butte Trail leads to one of the most beautiful views of a volcano you're likely to find anywhere. From atop Spencer Butte, a natural rock arch frames Mount St. Helens, a memorable and picturesque view. Short and accessible, with trailheads at either end of the three-mile route, Spencer Butte is a great trip for folks looking for views on a quick day hike.

The best access is from the upper (north) trailhead in Spencer Meadows. It's not unlikely that you'll spot a herd of elk before you've even hit the trail. Spencer Butte Trail climbs steadily from the open meadows along a wide ridge. White pines give way to noble fir as the trail

ascends through an open forest with regular views of the surrounding valleys. The trail crests atop Spencer Butte (elevation 4,247 feet). On the south side, a side trail drops slightly to a cold-water spring and the natural archway. Bring a camera, and you'll have a picture to display for years.

User Groups: Hikers, leashed dogs, horses, mountain bikes, and motorcycles. No wheelchair access.

Open Seasons: This trail is accessible May–November.

Permits: A federal Northwest Forest Pass is required to park here.

Maps: For a map of Gifford Pinchot National Forest, contact the Outdoor Recreation Information Center at the downtown Seattle REI. For a topographic map, ask Green Trails for No. 365, Lone Butte, or ask the USGS for Spencer Butte.

Directions: From Vancouver, drive north on I-5 to Highway 503 (Woodland, exit 21). Drive east 45 miles to Forest Service Road 25. Continue straight on Forest Service Road 25 and drive 6 miles to Forest Service Road 93, just beyond the Muddy River. Turn right and drive 9 miles to the signed trailhead on the left. This road is accessible for a passenger car but a high-clearance vehicle is recommended.

Contact: Gifford Pinchot National Forest, Mount St. Helens National Volcanic Monument, 42218 Northeast Yale Bridge Road, Amboy, WA 98601, 360/449-7871.

100 BIG CREEK FALLS
1.4 mi/0.5 hr

north of Cougar in Gifford Pinchot National Forest

Map 5.2, page 240

This is one of the best and easiest trails in the Gifford Pinchot National Forest. Big Creek Falls Trail follows the steep cliffs alongside Big Creek to an overlook with an excellent view of the 110-foot cascade. Big Creek is exactly that, a thunderous gusher of a stream. The sound alone of Big Creek dropping into a pool beside the Lewis

River is impressive, not to say anything of the enormous cloud of mist the fall generates. The trail has some interpretive signs discussing the old-growth forest through which the trail travels. Granddaddy Douglas firs and western hemlocks dominate the forest, draped in shrouds of ferns and mosses. The trail ends at a viewpoint over the falls, overlooking the Lewis River and Hemlock Falls on the opposite side. This is an ideal trail for young hikers-in-training.

User Groups: Hikers and leashed dogs. No horses or mountain bikes are allowed. Part of this trail (a loop to a viewpoint) is wheelchair accessible.

Open Seasons: This trail is accessible year-round.

Permits: A federal Northwest Forest Pass is required to park here.

Maps: For a map of Gifford Pinchot National Forest, contact the Outdoor Recreation Information Center at the downtown Seattle REI. For a topographic map, ask Green Trails for No. 365, Lone Butte, or ask the USGS for Burnt Peak.

Directions: From Vancouver, drive north on I-5 to Highway 503 (Woodland, exit 21). Drive east 45 miles to Pine Creek Information Center. Turn right and continue on Forest Service Road 90 for 11 miles to the signed trailhead on the left.

Contact: Gifford Pinchot National Forest, Mount St. Helens National Volcanic Monument, 42218 Northeast Yale Bridge Road, Amboy, WA 98601, 360/449-7871.

101 THOMAS LAKE
6.6 mi/3.0 hrs

north of Carson in Indian Heaven Wilderness of Gifford Pinchot National Forest

Map 5.2, page 240

The high country of Indian Heaven is covered by small lakes in beautiful subalpine settings. Thomas Lake Trail encounters more of these lakes than any other trail in Indian Heaven Wilderness. It's also one of the easiest trails here, gaining just 600 feet in three miles. That makes Thomas Lake Trail a popular route into the huckleberry fields and wildflower meadows that characterize this high, volcanic plateau.

Thomas Lake Trail gets much of the work out of the way early, quickly climbing through dense forest to Thomas, Dee, and Heather Lakes (.6 mile). The forest begins to break frequently, revealing meadows full of lupine and huckleberries in August. Elk and deer are frequently seen in this area, grazing in the meadows or wallowing in the small lakes and tarns. The trail ascends gently through meadows, passing yet more lakes. It crests at Rock Lake before dropping slightly to Blue Lake and Pacific Crest Trail. Although the trail is easily accomplished in a morning, it's advisable to plan on spending a full day exploring the many meadows and lakes. Just remember a fly rod or swimsuit.

User Groups: Hikers, leashed dogs, and horses. No mountain bikes are allowed. No wheelchair access.

Open Seasons: This trail is accessible May–October.

Permits: A federal Northwest Forest Pass is required to park here.

Maps: For a map of Gifford Pinchot National Forest, contact the Outdoor Recreation Information Center at the downtown Seattle REI. For a topographic map, ask Green Trails for No. 365S, Indian Heaven, or ask the USGS for Gifford Peak and Lone Butte.

Directions: From Vancouver, drive east 55 miles on Highway 14 to the town of Carson. Turn north on Wind River Road and drive 5 miles to Forest Service Road 65. Turn right and drive 17 miles to the signed trailhead on the right.

Contact: Gifford Pinchot National Forest, Mount Adams Ranger District, 2455 Highway 141, Trout Lake, WA 98650, 509/395-3400.

102 HIDDEN LAKES
0.4 mi/0.5 hr

west of Trout Lake in Indian Heaven Wilderness of Gifford Pinchot National Forest

Map 5.2, page 240

Hidden Lakes is a short and easy hike for everyone. Traveling around several small subalpine lakes, Hidden Lakes Trail provides a great sampler of this scenic area. On the northeast side of Indian Heaven Wilderness, the lakes are home to a primitive car campground. Small forest and open meadows dominate this area of the Gifford Pinchot National Forest, famous for its berry fields. Hidden Lakes is no different, basking in large fields of huckleberries, with peak season typically arriving in early August. Enjoy the berries, but leave some for others. A view of Mount Adams completes the scene.

User Groups: Hikers, leashed dogs, mountain bikes, and horses. No wheelchair access.

Open Seasons: This trail is accessible June–October.

Permits: A federal Northwest Forest Pass is required to park here.

Maps: For a map of Gifford Pinchot National Forest, contact the Outdoor Recreation Information Center at the downtown Seattle REI. For a topographic map, ask Green Trails for No. 365S, Indian Heaven, or ask the USGS for Sleeping Lady.

Directions: From Vancouver, drive east 70 miles on Highway 14 to Highway 141. Turn north and drive 22 miles to Trout Lake. Continue north on Highway 141 as it becomes Forest Service Road 24 for 16 miles (past Little Goose Campground) to the trailhead on the right.

Contact: Gifford Pinchot National Forest, Mount Adams Ranger District, 2455 Highway 141, Trout Lake, WA 98650, 509/395-3400.

103 INDIAN HEAVEN
6.6 mi/3.5 hrs

west of Trout Lake in Indian Heaven Wilderness of Gifford Pinchot National Forest

Map 5.2, page 240

Strewn with high country lakes and subalpine meadows, Indian Heaven is heavenly indeed. A visit to this volcanic highland in August is divine, when ripe black huckleberries are ubiquitous. Indian Heaven Trail is the best way to the meadows and lakes of this subalpine playground. The short and accessible trail delivers

every step of the way, whether it be old-growth forest, wildflower meadows, or scenic vistas.

Indian Heaven Trail wastes no time in reaching the high plateau of Indian Heaven. The trail climbs steadily through superb old-growth forest of subalpine fir, mountain hemlock, Englemann spruce, and white pine. Peek-a-boo views of Mount Adams whet the appetite for the meadows to come. The arrival into the high country is signaled when the trail reaches Cultus Lake, directly next to the trail (2.3 miles). A signed side trail leads a few hundred yards to Deep Lake. The trail junctions with Lemei Trail (2.5 miles) and bypasses Clear Lake before continuing to Pacific Crest Trail (3.3 miles). Rambling along any of these trails is well recommended.

Hikers looking for a little variety can turn Indian Heaven Trail into part of a great loop. The 6.7-mile loop uses PCT to encircle Bird Mountain, passing numerous lakes along the way. Hike east on Indian Heaven Trail to PCT (3.3 miles). Turn north and hike to Cultus Creek Trail (5.2 miles), which quickly descends back to Cultus Creek Campground and trailhead.

User Groups: Hikers, leashed dogs, and horses. No mountain bikes are allowed. No wheelchair access.

Open Seasons: This trail is accessible June–October.

Permits: A federal Northwest Forest Pass is required to park here.

Maps: For a map of Gifford Pinchot National Forest, contact the Outdoor Recreation Information Center at the downtown Seattle REI. For a topographic map, ask Green Trails for No. 365S, Indian Heaven, or ask the USGS for Lone Butte.

Directions: From Vancouver, drive east 70 miles on Highway 14 to Highway 141. Turn north and drive 22 miles to Trout Lake. Continue north on Highway 141 as it becomes Forest Service Road 24 for 18 miles to the signed trailhead within Cultus Creek Campground.

Contact: Gifford Pinchot National Forest, Mount Adams Ranger District, 2455 Highway 141, Trout Lake, WA 98650, 509/395-3400.

104 LEMEI

10.6 mi/5.0 hrs

**west of Trout Lake in Indian Heaven
Wilderness of Gifford Pinchot National Forest**

Map 5.2, page 240

Lemei Trail provides a scenic route to the volcanic plateau of Indian Heaven Wilderness. The trail is a decent workout, ascending through much of its length. Views, huckleberries, and lakes are ample reward for the effort. After enjoying the meadows teeming with wildflower displays and feasting on August-ripe huckleberries, hikers will find that the waters of Lake Wapiki make a refreshing dip. One of the prettiest lakes in the high country of Indian Heaven, Lake Wapiki is enclosed by the area's tallest peak, jagged Lemei Rock.

Lemei Trail spends its first mile in dense second-growth forest. As the trail enters the wilderness (1 mile), the timber becomes old and large, in a more open forest. An understory of huckleberry bushes helps to ease the sting of the continuous climb. A side trail (3 miles) leads .5 mile to Lake Wapiki in the basin of Lemei Rock. Small forest and meadow fill the basin under craggy Lemei Rock. Lemei Trail continues beyond the junction to Indian Heaven Trail (5.3 miles) and miles of meadow exploration.

User Groups: Hikers, leashed dogs, and horses. No mountain bikes are allowed. No wheelchair access.

Open Seasons: This trail is accessible June–October.

Permits: A federal Northwest Forest Pass is required to park here.

Maps: For a map of Gifford Pinchot National Forest, contact the Outdoor Recreation Information Center at the downtown Seattle REI. For a topographic map, ask Green Trails for No. 365S, Indian Heaven, or ask the USGS for Sleeping Beauty and Lone Butte.

Directions: From Vancouver, drive east 70 miles on Highway 14 to Highway 141. Turn north and drive 22 miles to Trout Lake. Continue north on Highway 141 as it becomes Forest Service Road 24 for 13 miles to the trailhead on the left (before Little Goose Campground).

Contact: Gifford Pinchot National Forest, Mount Adams Ranger District, 2455 Highway 141, Trout Lake, WA 98650, 509/395-3400.

105 RACE TRACK

6.2 mi/3.5 hrs

**west of Trout Lake in Indian Heaven
Wilderness of Gifford Pinchot National Forest**

Map 5.2, page 240

Huckleberries and history are the story of this trail. Race Track Trail delves into the southern section of Indian Heaven Wilderness, a former meeting place for Native Americans. Each year, thousands of people from Yakama, Klickitat, and Columbia River nations gathered here during the height of the berry-harvesting season (August). The huckleberry bushes that flourish in this volcanic soil were a major source of food for Native Americans. And as it's situated along an important cross-Cascades trade route, it's easy to see how this area came to be known as an "Indian Heaven." During their time here, Native Americans entertained themselves by staging pony races, hence the name Race Track. The dirt track used is still visible today within an open meadow.

A popular trail into the wilderness, Race Track Trail climbs steadily but gently, emerging from large timber to open subalpine meadows. During August, huckleberries will be sure to be the main attraction. But don't let them keep you from spotting the abundant wildlife, including deer, elk, hawk, and even black bear. Race Track Trail reaches Race Track Lake (2.3 miles), where the dirt track can be seen, and then ascends to the peak of Red Mountain. This lofty peak with big views is home to one of Gifford Pinchot's three remaining fire lookouts.

User Groups: Hikers, leashed dogs, and horses. No mountain bikes are allowed. No wheelchair access.

Open Seasons: This trail is accessible June–October.

Permits: A federal Northwest Forest Pass is required to park here.

Maps: For a map of Gifford Pinchot National Forest, contact the Outdoor Recreation Information Center at the downtown Seattle REI. For a topographic map, ask Green Trails for No. 365S, Indian Heaven, or ask the USGS for Gifford Peak.

Directions: From Vancouver, drive east 55 miles on Highway 14 to the town of Carson. Turn north on Wind River Road and drive 5 miles to Forest Service Road 65. Turn right and drive 13 miles to the signed trailhead at Falls Creek Horse Camp.

Contact: Gifford Pinchot National Forest, Mount Adams Ranger District, 2455 Highway 141, Trout Lake, WA 98650, 509/395-3400.

106 SLEEPING BEAUTY
2.8 mi/2.0 hrs

north of Trout Lake in Gifford Pinchot National Forest

Map 5.2, page 240

As close to Mount Adams as one can be without actually scaling its slopes, Sleeping Beauty offers a grand view of the mountain. A tall outcrop of craggy rock sticking out above the surrounding forest, Sleeping Beauty gazes at the mass of Mount Adams from just eight miles distant. Access to the rocky peak is a steep but quick trip through dense second-growth forest. The trail finds the edge of logging and enjoys old timber for a short time. Any views are reserved until the very end.

Sleeping Beauty is so named because it apparently resembles the profile of a sleeping woman; we'll let you decide. All personifications aside, the view from the top is spectacular. Rainier, St. Helens, and Hood dot the distant horizons. The peaks of Indian Heaven rise on the western skyline. The peak was formerly home to a Forest Service lookout.

User Groups: Hikers and leashed dogs. No horses or mountain bikes are allowed. No wheelchair access.

Open Seasons: This trail is accessible May–November.

Permits: A federal Northwest Forest Pass is required to park here.

Maps: For a map of Gifford Pinchot National Forest, contact the Outdoor Recreation Information Center at the downtown Seattle REI. For a topographic map, ask Green Trails for No. 366, Mount Adams West, or ask the USGS for Sleeping Beauty.

Directions: From Vancouver, drive east 70 miles on Highway 14 to Highway 141. Turn north and drive 22 miles to Forest Service Road 88, just beyond the town of Trout Lake. Turn right on Forest Service Road 88 and drive 5 miles to Forest Service Road 8810. Turn right and drive 5 miles to Forest Service Road 8810-040. Turn right and drive .5 mile to the trailhead on the left.

Contact: Gifford Pinchot National Forest, Mount Adams Ranger District, 2455 Highway 141, Trout Lake, WA 98650, 509/395-3400.

107 STAGMAN RIDGE
8.0–12.8 mi/4.0–7.0 hrs

north of Trout Lake in Mount Adams Wilderness of Gifford Pinchot National Forest

Map 5.2, page 240

Stagman Ridge Trail provides great access to the high-country meadows flanking the western slopes of Mount Adams. The trail steadily but gently climbs to Horseshoe Meadows, home of juicy huckleberries, roaming mountain goats, and some pretty spectacular views. A trip to Horseshoe Meadows is indeed a great day, but hikers looking to throw in a subalpine lake (think refreshing swim) can continue an extra 2.4 miles to Lookingglass Lake.

Stagman Ridge Trail begins at a lofty elevation of 4,200 feet and gains about 1,600 feet over four miles. The forested trail quickly opens to reveal tremendous views of the mountain. It crosses several small streams, and Stagman Ridge Trail intersects PCT (4 miles) on the lower slopes of Horseshoe Meadows. Although you could turn around here, hikers are well advised to continue on PCT in either direction for at least a mile; the meadows are full of huckleberries in late summer and offer outstanding views year-round.

If the cold and refreshing water of Lookingglass Lake entices you to continue (it's well worth it), turn right on PCT, turn right again on Round the Mountain Trail (4.4 miles), and one more right turn onto Lookingglass Trail (5.5 miles). The lake (6.4 miles) is situated within high meadows, underneath the mountain.

User Groups: Hikers, leashed dogs, and horses. No mountain bikes are allowed. No wheelchair access.

Open Seasons: This trail is accessible June–October.

Permits: A federal Northwest Forest Pass is required to park here.

Maps: For a map of Gifford Pinchot National Forest, contact the Outdoor Recreation Information Center at the downtown Seattle REI. For a topographic map, ask Green Trails for No. 367S, Mount Adams, or ask the USGS for Mount Adams West.

Directions: From Vancouver, drive east 70 miles on Highway 14 to Highway 141. Turn north and drive 22 miles to Forest Service Road 23 (Buck Creek Road), near the town of Trout Lake. Turn right and drive 8 miles to Forest Service Road 8031. Turn right and drive .5 mile to Forest Service Road 070. Turn left and drive 3.5 miles to Forest Service Road 120. Turn right and drive .5 mile to the trailhead at road's end.

Contact: Gifford Pinchot National Forest, Mount Adams Ranger District, 2455 Highway 141, Trout Lake, WA 98650, 509/395-3400.

108 ROUND-THE-MOUNTAIN
22.2 mi one-way/2 days 🥾 🔟

north of Trout Lake in Mount Adams Wilderness of Gifford Pinchot National Forest

Map 5.2, page 240

Like Washington's other big volcanoes, Mount Adams is circumnavigated by a long, demanding trail. Set high in the subalpine meadows

gracing the slopes of Mount Adams, Round-the-Mountain Trail is the best way to fully experience Washington's second-tallest peak. Here's the catch. The east side of Mount Adams is managed by the Yakima Indian Nation, and special permits are required to hike within the reservation (a vexing process). Additionally, this section of trail is extremely difficult. East-side streams turn into dangerous glacial torrents during the summer, and no maintained trail exists over enormous lava fields. Thus, Round-the-Mountain is best completed as a through-hike, along the western side of Mount Adams.

Round-the-Mountain Trail is best begun from Cold Springs on the south side of Mount Adams. Hike South Climb Trail to Round-the-Mountain Trail (1.3 miles) and turn north. The scenery is supreme every step of the way, with alpine meadows and distant mountain views the norm. Expect to see an abundance of wildflowers in midsummer and huckleberries in early fall. The trail encounters Pacific Crest Trail (7 miles) and follows it to Muddy Meadows Trail (19.8 miles). Turn north to reach the northern trailhead at Keenee Campground (22.2 miles).

Highlights along the way include Lookingglass Lake (5.9 miles), Horseshoe Meadows (7 miles), Sheep Lake (11 miles), and Adams Meadows (14.5 miles, below Adams Glacier). Campsites are frequent along the route; stick to already established sites to minimize damage to fragile meadows. The views of Mount Adams improve with progress around the peak, with great looks at the glaciers. If a true circumnavigation of the mountain is an unshakable goal, please contact the Mount Adams Ranger Station for full details on trail conditions.

User Groups: Hikers, leashed dogs, and horses. No mountain bikes are allowed. No wheelchair access.

Open Seasons: This trail is accessible July–mid-October.

Permits: A federal Northwest Forest Pass is required to park here.

Maps: For a map of Gifford Pinchot National Forest, contact the Outdoor Recreation Information Center at the downtown Seattle REI. For a topographic map, ask Green Trails for No. 367S, Mount Adams, or ask the USGS for Mount Adams West, Mount Adams East, and Green Mountain.

Directions: From Vancouver, drive east 70 miles on Highway 14 to Highway 141. Turn north and drive 22 miles to Forest Service Road 23 (Buck Creek Road), near the town of Trout Lake. Turn right and drive 3 miles to Forest Service Road 82. Turn right and drive .5 mile to Forest Service Road 80. Turn left and drive 4 miles to Forest Service Road 8040. Continue 5 miles on Road 8040 to Morrison Creek Campground and Forest Service Road 500. Turn right and drive 2 miles to the trailhead at road's end.

Contact: Gifford Pinchot National Forest, Mount Adams Ranger District, 2455 Highway 141, Trout Lake, WA 98650, 509/395-3400.

109 KILLEN CREEK
6.2 mi/4.0 hrs

north of Trout Lake in Mount Adams Wilderness of Gifford Pinchot National Forest

Map 5.2, page 240

By the time the first views of Mount Adams emerge (which is quickly), hikers on Killen Creek Trail know they've selected a beauty of a hike. This popular route on the north side of Mount Adams climbs steadily through open forest to wide open meadows beneath towering glaciers. This is undoubtedly great rambling country, where the hike gets better every step of the way. Day hikes this grand are hard to come by in Southern Washington, and this is one of the best in the state.

Killen Creek Trail starts high (4,600 feet) and climbs slowly but steadily to Pacific Crest Trail (3.1 miles). Much of the trail traverses open forest with repeated views of Mount Adams, but the last mile or so revels in meadows. Wildflowers take turns blooming throughout the summer. Rambling in either direction along PCT is highly recommended to soak up the scenery. Hikers hoping to approach even

closer to the mountain are welcome to do so along High Camp Trail, a continuation of Killen Creek Trail on the uphill side of PCT. This is a one-mile trail to High Camp, one of Adams' best, among rocky meadows and glacier moraine.

User Groups: Hikers, leashed dogs, and horses. No mountain bikes are allowed. No wheelchair access.

Open Seasons: This trail is accessible mid-June–October.

Permits: A federal Northwest Forest Pass is required to park here.

Maps: For a map of Gifford Pinchot National Forest, contact the Outdoor Recreation Information Center at the downtown Seattle REI. For a topographic map, ask Green Trails for No. 367S, Mount Adams, or ask the USGS for Green Mountain and Mount Adams West.

Directions: From Vancouver, drive east 70 miles on Highway 14 to Highway 141. Turn north and drive 22 miles to Forest Service Road 23 (Buck Creek Road), near the town of Trout Lake. Turn right and drive about 30 miles to Forest Service Road 2329. Turn right and drive 5 miles (around Takhlakh Lake) to the trailhead on the right.

Contact: Gifford Pinchot National Forest, Mount Adams Ranger District, 2455 Highway 141, Trout Lake, WA 98650, 509/395-3400.

110 SOUTH CLIMB
6.8 mi/4.5 hrs

north of Trout Lake in Mount Adams Wilderness of Gifford Pinchot National Forest

Map 5.2, page 240

Not for the faint of heart, South Climb is exactly what the name implies: an ascent of Mount Adams from the south side. The summit needn't be one's goal to embark on this beautiful trail, but well-conditioned legs certainly are always helpful. South Climb Trail assaults the mountain straight on and reaches 8,500 feet of elevation before petering out beside Crescent Glacier. From here, it's a mad scramble to the top. Stopping at Crescent Glacier reveals spectacular views of the surrounding valleys, forests, and distant mountain ridges. If the wildflower meadows alongside the trail and beautiful views don't take your breath away, the steep pitch of South Climb will.

Should a summit of Mount Adams be on your wish list, keep several things in mind. One, it's steep as hell and strenuous. Experienced climbers take at least 6–8 hours to reach the summit from Cold Springs, an elevation gain of 6,700 feet. Visibility decreases after early morning, so smart mountaineers camp at Cold Springs Car Campground and hit the trail by 3 A.M. That's 3 o'clock in the morning. And the climb requires permits from the ranger station in Trout Lake. The summit is certainly achievable and is relatively easy compared to Mount Hood or Mount Rainier. Novices frequently reach the peak. At the top are views conceivable only if you've been there.

User Groups: Hikers, leashed dogs, and horses. No mountain bikes are allowed. No wheelchair access.

Open Seasons: This trail is accessible July–September.

Permits: A federal Northwest Forest Pass is required to park here. Climbing permits are required for summits of Mount Adams. The $15 permits are available at Trout Lake Ranger Station.

Maps: For a map of Gifford Pinchot National Forest, contact the Outdoor Recreation Information Center at the downtown Seattle REI. For a topographic map, ask Green Trails for No. 367S, Mount Adams, or ask the USGS for Mount Adams West.

Directions: From Vancouver, drive east 70 miles on Highway 14 to Highway 141. Turn north and drive 22 miles to Forest Service Road 23 (Buck Creek Road), near the town of Trout Lake. Turn right and drive 3 miles to Forest Service Road 82. Turn right and drive .5 mile to Forest Service Road 80. Turn left and drive 4 miles to Forest Service Road 8040. Continue 5 miles on Road 8040 to Morrison Creek Campground and Forest Service Road 500. Turn right and drive 2 miles to the trailhead at road's end.

Contact: Gifford Pinchot National Forest, Mount Adams Ranger District, 2455 Highway 141, Trout Lake, WA 98650, 509/395-3400.

111 BATTLE GROUND LAKE LOOP
7.0 mi/3.5 hrs

north of Vancouver in Battle Ground Lake State Park

Map 5.3, page 241

There's no need to drive all the way to southern Oregon to see Crater Lake. Washington has its own miniature version here in Battle Ground Lake. Like Crater Lake, Battle Ground Lake was created by a massive volcanic explosion. The resulting crater filled with spring water and created Battle Ground Lake. Today, conifer forests of Douglas fir and western hemlock surround the lake, creating peaceful and quiet surroundings. The trail circles the lake within the shady forest, never venturing far from the lakeshore. Anglers will appreciate the access to solitary fishing holes, where monster trout hide out. The state park has a large car campground, but it fills quickly on summer weekends.

User Groups: Hikers, leashed dogs, and horses. No mountain bikes are allowed. No wheelchair access.

Open Seasons: This trail is accessible year-round.

Permits: A $5 day-use fee is required to park here and is payable at the trailhead, or you can get an annual State Parks Pass for $30; contact Washington State Parks and Recreation, 360/902-8500.

Maps: For a topographic map, ask the USGS for Battleground and Wacolt.

Directions: From Vancouver, drive north on I-5 to Exit 14. Turn right on Northeast 179th Street and drive to the city of Battle Ground. Drive to the east end of town and turn left on Grace Avenue. Drive three miles to Battle Ground Lake State Park. The signed trailhead is near the day-use area within the park.

Contact: Battle Ground Lake State Park, 18002

Northeast 249th Street, Battle Ground WA, 98604, 360/687-4621.

112 BEACON ROCK
2.0 mi/2.0 hrs

east of Vancouver in Beacon Rock State Park

Map 5.3, page 241

Visible from miles away and towering over the Columbia River, Beacon Rock offers an unbeatable view of the Columbia River Gorge. Geologically speaking, Beacon Rock is a true rock. That is, it's one solid piece of rock, not a conglomeration of different types of rock like many mountains are. That makes Beacon Rock the second tallest "rock" in the world! Beacon Rock is actually the core of an old volcano, exposed when the Missoula Floods eroded softer rock encasing it. The resulting hulk towers 848 feet over the mighty Columbia. It's quite a perch from the top.

Beacon Rock State Park offers nearly 20 miles of trail and road to explore, but the most popular and scenic is the trail to the summit. It's a little under one mile to the top, but don't let the short distance fool you. It's a steep climb every step of the way. Old forest shades the trail where trees can find a small ledge to grow, but many areas are on steep, exposed cliffs. Boardwalks, stairways, and handrails have been installed to present a safer experience. The summit is an ideal picnic spot, with great views of the gorge and Mount Hood.

User Groups: Hikers and leashed dogs. No horses or mountain bikes are allowed. No wheelchair access.

Open Seasons: This trail is accessible March–November.

Permits: A $5 day-use fee is required to park here and is payable at the trailhead, or you can get an annual State Parks Pass for $30; contact Washington State Parks and Recreation, 360/902-8500.

Maps: For a topographic map, ask the USGS for Bonneville Dam and Tanner Butte.

Directions: From Vancouver, drive east on Highway 14 to Beacon Rock State Park (near Mile Marker 35). The trailhead is on the right side of the highway.

Contact: Beacon Rock State Park, Highway 14, Skamania, WA, 509/427-8265.

113 SIOUXON
8.0 mi/4.0 hrs

east of Cougar in Gifford Pinchot National Forest

Map 5.3, page 242

Deep within old forest, Siouxon Trail journeys alongside the noisy creek. Waterfalls and deep pools are regular highlights, making this a great winter hike when higher routes are closed by snow. Siouxon Trail quickly descends from the trailhead to the creek. Large and gushing West Creek is crossed by a large wooden bridge (.5 mile). Peer downstream to see the first of many waterfalls. The trail encounters another cascade on Siouxon Creek (4 miles), where the creek empties into a large emerald pool. During the summer, good luck avoiding the urge for a quick dip in the cold water. This is a common turnaround for many day hikers, but Siouxon Trail travels along the creek for a total of 5.5 miles through grand forest the entire length. This is a great place to spend a night with little ones or first-time backpackers. Numerous campsites are on the stream banks, where the noisy stream lulls one to sleep.

User Groups: Hikers, leashed dogs, horses, and mountain bikes. No wheelchair access.

Open Seasons: This trail is accessible year-round.

Permits: A federal Northwest Forest Pass is required to park here.

Maps: For a map of Gifford Pinchot National Forest, contact the Outdoor Recreation Information Center at the downtown Seattle REI. For a topographic map, ask Green Trails for No. 396, Lookout Mountain, or ask the USGS for Siouxon Peak and Bear Mountain.

Directions: From Vancouver, drive north on I-5 to Highway 503 (Woodland, exit 21). Drive east 45 miles to Pine Creek Information Center. Turn right and continue on Forest Service

Road 90 to Northeast Healy Road, in the town of Clehatchie. Turn right and drive 10 miles to Forest Service Road 57. Turn left and drive 1.5 miles to Forest Service Road 5701. Turn left and drive 4 miles to the trailhead at road's end.
Contact: Gifford Pinchot National Forest, Mount Adams Ranger District, 2455 Highway 141, Trout Lake, WA 98650, 509/395-3400.

114 LOWER FALLS CREEK
3.4 mi/2.0 hrs

north of Carson in Gifford Pinchot
National Forest
Map 5.4, page 242

About the only thing keeping the masses from Lower Falls Creek is the short length of the trail. It's not a destination in itself. But anyone visiting the town of Carson should certainly spend the time to visit Lower Falls Creek. The trail follows this beautiful stream as it passes through a narrow gorge and ends at the base of a large waterfall. On hot summer days, the forest is cool and shady, and the water of Falls Creek is especially appealing.

Lower Falls Creek Trail climbs gently throughout its short length. Deer and elk are frequently seen browsing in the forest, filled with the sounds of woodpeckers and wrens. The trail crosses Falls Creek as it gushes through a rock gorge; fortunately, a suspension bridge spans the gap. Falls Creek Trail ends at the base of a large waterfall, where Falls Creek cascades down a steep wall.

User Groups: Hikers, leashed dogs, and mountain bikes. No horses are allowed. No wheelchair access.

Open Seasons: This trail is accessible year-round.

Permits: A federal Northwest Forest Pass is required to park here.

Maps: For a map of Gifford Pinchot National Forest, contact the Outdoor Recreation Information Center at the downtown Seattle REI. For a topographic map, ask Green Trails for No. 397, Wind River, or ask the USGS for Termination Point.

Directions: From Vancouver, drive east 55 miles on Highway 14 to the town of Carson. Turn north on Wind River Road and drive 9 miles to Forest Service Road 30. Turn right and drive 3 miles to the signed trailhead on the right.
Contact: Gifford Pinchot National Forest, Mount Adams Ranger District, 2455 Highway 141, Trout Lake, WA 98650, 509/395-3400.

115 TRAPPER CREEK
9.5 mi/4.5 hrs

north of Carson in Trapper Creek Wilderness
of Gifford Pinchot National Forest
Map 5.4, page 242

Any opportunity to hike in old-growth forest should be seized, sooner rather than later. Trapper Creek, one of the least-known wildernesses in the state of Washington, preserves a small chunk of ancient timberland just north of the Columbia River Gorge. Trapper Creek Trail makes a full immersion into the wilderness, following the beautiful, restless creek to its headwaters as it flows over waterfalls and through narrow gorges. Trapper Creek Trail connects to Observation Trail (see next listing), so if you're itching for views, you can have them by making a large loop.

Trapper Creek Trail spends much of its length alongside the noisy creek. The forest is a diverse mix of giants, with Douglas fir, western hemlock, and western red cedar, all draped with mosses and lichens, growing to immense proportions. Trapper Creek Trail junctions with Observation Peak Trail (1 mile) but continues alongside the creek. The creek is a long sequence of cascades and pools, but Trapper Creek Falls (4.5 miles) are the highlight of the trip and a good turnaround point. The trail ends at another junction with Observation Trail, the option for a loop trip (about 12 miles).

User Groups: Hikers, leashed dogs, and horses. No mountain bikes are allowed. No wheelchair access.

Open Seasons: This trail is accessible year-round.

Permits: A federal Northwest Forest Pass is required to park here.

Maps: For a map of Gifford Pinchot National Forest, contact the Outdoor Recreation Information Center at the downtown Seattle REI. For a topographic map, ask the USGS for Bare Mountain.

Directions: From Vancouver, drive east 55 miles on Highway 14 to the town of Carson. Turn north on Wind River Road and drive 10 miles to Forest Service Road 3065. Turn left and drive 1.5 miles to the signed trailhead at Government Mineral Springs.

Contact: Gifford Pinchot National Forest, Mount Adams Ranger District, 2455 Highway 141, Trout Lake, WA 98650, 509/395-3400.

116 OBSERVATION PEAK
6.0–13.0 mi/3.0–7.0 hrs

north of Carson in Trapper Creek Wilderness of Gifford Pinchot National Forest

Map 5.4, page 242

Options, options, options. Observation Peak provides great views from the heart of Trapper Creek Wilderness, over lush, green valleys out to several snowcapped volcanic peaks. Best of all, there are several ways to enjoy this pristine and unlogged section of the Gifford Pinchot. A trip to Observation Peak can be a short hike (5.6 miles), a long up and down (13 miles), or one of two loop trips (12 miles). These loops are by far the best way to experience the wilderness, where misty forests are full of ancient timber.

Observation Trail runs from the valley bottom up along a high ridge to Observation Peak and out to Forest Service Road 58. For a short hike, park on Forest Service Road 58 and hike south through Sister Rocks Natural Area (big trees!) to the peak (2.8 miles). Reaching Observation Peak from the south is certainly longer and more strenuous, but remember that rule: no pain, no gain.

From Government Mineral Springs, Observation Trail climbs steadily from old-growth lowland forest into a mix of subalpine trees. Views are frequent along the lightly forested

ridge, as are huckleberries and deer. Hearty hikers can pass the peak and descend back to the trailhead via Trapper Creek Trail (see previous listing) or Dry Creek (Big Hollow Trail, another big tree and beautiful creek route).

User Groups: Hikers, leashed dogs, and horses. No mountain bikes are allowed. No wheelchair access.

Open Seasons: This trail is accessible April–November.

Permits: A federal Northwest Forest Pass is required to park here.

Maps: For a map of Gifford Pinchot National Forest, contact the Outdoor Recreation Information Center at the downtown Seattle REI. For a topographic map, ask Green Trails for No. 396, Lookout Mountain, and No. 397, Wind River, or ask the USGS for Bare Mountain.

Directions: From Vancouver, drive east 55 miles on Highway 14 to the town of Carson. Turn north on Wind River Road and drive 10 miles to Forest Service Road 3065. Turn left and drive 1.5 miles to the signed trailhead at Government Mineral Springs.

Contact: Gifford Pinchot National Forest, Mount Adams Ranger District, 2455 Highway 141, Trout Lake, WA 98650, 509/395-3400.

117 BUNKER HILL
3.6 mi/1.5 hrs

north of Carson in Gifford Pinchot National Forest

Map 5.4, page 242

Great for folks in Carson with a couple of hours to kill, Bunker Hill Trail is a quick but strenuous climb to the summit. The first .5 mile of the route follows Pacific Crest Trail north. Most folks on PCT are through-hikers coming from Oregon and on their way to big, grand country in the coming months. Turn left onto Bunker Hill Trail and do the switchback shuffle up to the summit. Views are reserved until the very top, where a fire lookout once stood. Views of the Wind River Valley are revealed, as are numerous surrounding ridges.

User Groups: Hikers and leashed dogs. No

horses or mountain bikes are allowed. No wheel-chair access.

Open Seasons: This trail is accessible April–December.

Permits: A federal Northwest Forest Pass is required to park here.

Maps: For a map of Gifford Pinchot National Forest, contact the Outdoor Recreation Information Center at the downtown Seattle REI. For a topographic map, ask Green Trails for No. 397, Wind River, or ask the USGS for Stabler.

Directions: From Vancouver, drive east 55 miles on Highway 14 to the town of Carson. Drive north 5.5 miles on Wind River Road to Hemlock Road. Turn left and drive 1.5 miles to Forest Service Road 43. Turn right and drive .5 mile to Forest Service Road 43-417. Turn right and drive .2 mile to the Pacific Crest Trail-head. Head to the right (north) on the PCT.

Contact: Gifford Pinchot National Forest, Mount Adams Ranger District, 2455 Highway 141, Trout Lake, WA 98650, 509/395-3400.

118 LITTLE HUCKLEBERRY
5.0 mi/3.0 hrs

west of Trout Lake in Gifford Pinchot National Forest

Map 5.4, page 242

One of the more accessible viewpoints from Highway 14, Little Huckleberry Trail makes a quick and at times steep trip to an old lookout site. Views of Mount Adams and Mount Hood, across the Columbia River, are quite nice. And a feast of huckleberries along the way sweetens the deal on August trips to the mountain. This is a nice trail for a weekend morning, if you're coming from Vancouver or Portland.

Little Huckleberry Trail gains 1,800 feet in just 2.5 miles, a steady and soon tiring ascent within a small draw. Enjoy the old forest and take your time. Early in the summer, a cold-water spring runs (2 miles), offering a great place to break. The final .5 mile climbs through open berry fields and rock slopes to the summit. A lookout once stood atop this rounded

top, perched over a wide expanse of the Gifford Pinchot. With room for a tent, this is a fun overnighter for beginning backpackers (think of the stars).

User Groups: Hikers, leashed dogs, horses, and mountain bikes. No wheelchair access.

Open Seasons: This trail is accessible April–November.

Permits: A federal Northwest Forest Pass is required to park here.

Maps: For a map of Gifford Pinchot National Forest, contact the Outdoor Recreation Information Center at the downtown Seattle REI. For a topographic map, ask Green Trails for No. 398, Willard, or ask the USGS for Sleeping Beauty.

Directions: From Vancouver, drive east 70 miles on Highway 14 to Highway 141. Turn north and drive 22 miles to Trout Lake. Continue north on Highway 141 as it becomes Forest Service Road 24 for 10 miles to Forest Service Road 66. Turn left (south) and drive 5 miles to the trailhead on the left.

Contact: Gifford Pinchot National Forest, Mount Adams Ranger District, 2455 Highway 141, Trout Lake, WA 98650, 509/395-3400.

119 DOG MOUNTAIN
6.0 mi/3.5 hrs

east of Carson in Gifford Pinchot National Forest

Map 5.4, page 242

Getting to Dog Mountain, with a trailhead directly on Highway 14, is no problem. Getting up Dog Mountain is a bit more of a workout, however. Dense forest mixes with open wildflower meadows along the trail, cresting at the open summit of Dog Mountain. The views of the Columbia River Gorge are outstanding, with snowcapped Mount Hood standing across the way. This is a very popular hike with folks coming from Vancouver or Portland, especially on the weekends. Expect to see a neighbor or two.

Dog Mountain Trail makes the best of what it has been given, forming a loop instead of a straight up and down. The loop is arranged like a lasso. Climb steeply to the loop junction (.5 mile). Head to the right for a more gradual and scenic route to the top. Regular breaks in the forest provide room for open meadows of wildflowers (May is a great month here). This is dry country, meaning water is nonexistent; pack plenty, because overall elevation gain is 2,700 feet. Do be on the lookout for poison oak and rattlesnakes, things that most hikers don't care to mess with. The summit is the former home to a Forest Service lookout. The loop returns to the junction via a steep, densely forested route.

User Groups: Hikers and leashed dogs. No horses or mountain bikes are allowed. No wheelchair access.

Open Seasons: This trail is accessible March–December.

Permits: A federal Northwest Forest Pass is required to park here.

Maps: For a map of Gifford Pinchot National Forest, contact the Outdoor Recreation Information Center at the downtown Seattle REI. For a topographic map, ask the USGS for Mount Defiance.

Directions: From Vancouver, drive east on Highway 14 to Mile Marker 53 and the signed trailhead.

Contact: Gifford Pinchot National Forest, Mount Adams Ranger District, 2455 Highway 141, Trout Lake, WA 98650, 509/395-3400.

Chapter 6

© SCOTT LEONARD

Southeast Washington

Southeast Washington

What's that? You didn't know that there was any hiking in the southeast portion of our state? There surely is, and most of it is unlike anything else found in a state famous for cloudy and rainy days. Better known for its agricultural base, this region offers up some beautiful and wild places for hiking, although not much. This is the sparsest region for trails, and most of them are concentrated in the very southeastern corner of the state in the Blue Mountains. That's a long drive for most Washington residents, especially those living on the west side of the Cascades. Still, thanks to the warm weather that makes wheat, hops, and wine grapes major crops in the region, some great trails exist for spring hiking, when snow still blankets the high country of the Cascades.

Near Yakima, the Cascades devolve into a mass of rolling foothills. Just a few dozen miles from the rain forests on the west side of the Cascades, this is dry country for sure. Much of this region receives just 20 inches or less of rain each year, so you can almost always count on sunny skies. Yakima Rim Trail is a hike for the first outing of the year. While snow measured by the foot still lingers in the Cascades, wildflowers are beginning to blossom in this desert-steppe environment. Yakima Rim runs along Umtanum Ridge, delivering views of the snow-capped Stuart Range on the horizon, colorful blossoms, and dry, moderate temperatures in April and May. Umtanum Creek Trail wanders up a low valley, one of the few places to find water year-round. Each of these hikes is located on the Yakima River, a world-class trout river and a pretty good river raft, too.

Spread amidst miles of agricultural land are several unlikely environments for Washington. Potholes Sand Dunes are an expansive landscape in the middle of our state. Countless small lakes and the larger Potholes reservoir break up large dunes of sand. Near the Tri-Cities are Juniper Dunes Wilderness, another desertlike landscape seemingly out of place in Washington. In fact, it's so unusual that it is affectionately known as "Washington's Sahara," and vast dunes spread out over the high desert, dotted by small shrubs and the occasional tree. You may even find the grove of ancient juniper trees, many of them centuries old and subsisting on just inches of rain each year. Coyotes, deer, and owls far outnumber bipeds in this area. This is one of the region's best places to set out and explore cross-country. Folks who don't want to venture far from the car will love the easy access to Palouse Falls, Washington's version of Niagara Falls. Smack dab in the middle of nowhere (ever heard of Washtucna?), the Palouse River makes a mighty and vociferous drop into a large bowl. The falls are just one of the many land features left by the Missoula Glacial Floods, when billions of gallons of water rushed from Montana to the Pacific, scouring eastern Washington along the way.

The jackpot of hiking in southeast Washington is the Wenaha-Tucannon Wilderness. This federally protected wilderness envelops more than 177,000 acres of the Blue Mountains, stretching across the border of Washington and Oregon. The Blue Mountains are an untamed, rarely visited place, where bighorn sheep, deer, and elk are plentiful and draw hundreds of hunters in the fall. The Wenaha-Tucannon Wilderness is unique in that access points start from on high, usually around 5,000 feet, and require hikers to drop down into the vast canyons and gorges to explore. The lookout atop Oregon Butte is a popular (and easy) place to visit here, where you can get a panoramic view of the arid mountains and valleys. Longer trips can be made along Crooked Creek or Smooth Ridge down to the Wenaha River, an excellent trout and salmon river. Despite its remote location, the Wenaha-Tucannon Wilderness is a beautiful Washington landscape and should be visited at least once by all devout hikers.

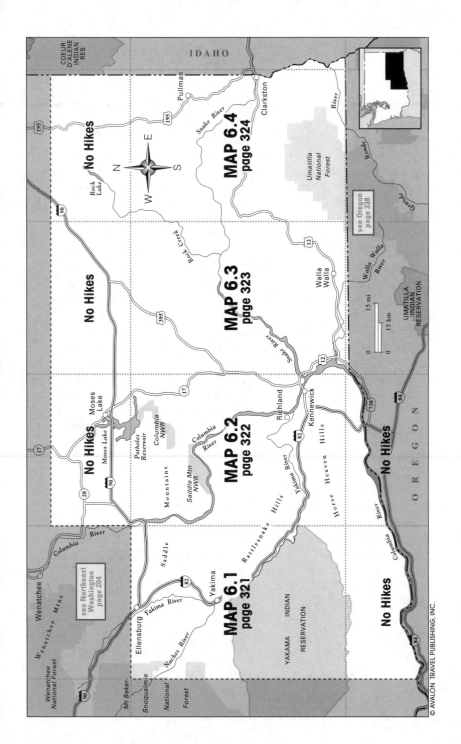

Customer Orders (B0191)

From:
To: onlinereservations
Cc: Customer Orders (B0191)
Subject: RESERVE: Perez/Designing the Obvious: A Common Ser
Attachments:

Online Reserve

Title: Designing the Obvious: A Common Sense Approach to Web A
Author: Robert Hoekman
BINC: 8715034
ISBN: 032145345X
Format: Paperback
Type: Paperback
Quantity: 1   Title

Customer Name: Janete Perez
Customer Email: janete.perez@gmail.com   quantity:1   title informa

Map 6.1

Hikes 1–2
Page 325

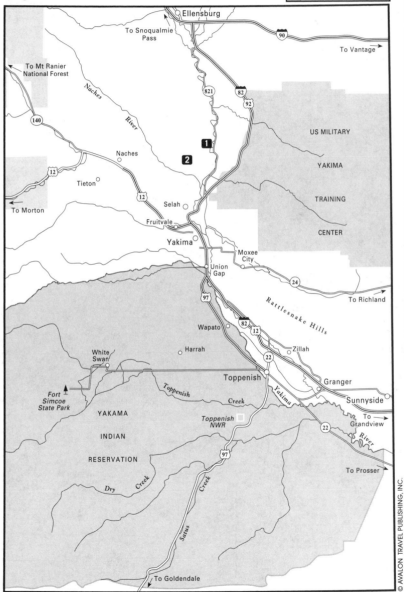

© AVALON TRAVEL PUBLISHING, INC.

Map 6.2

Hike 3
Page 326

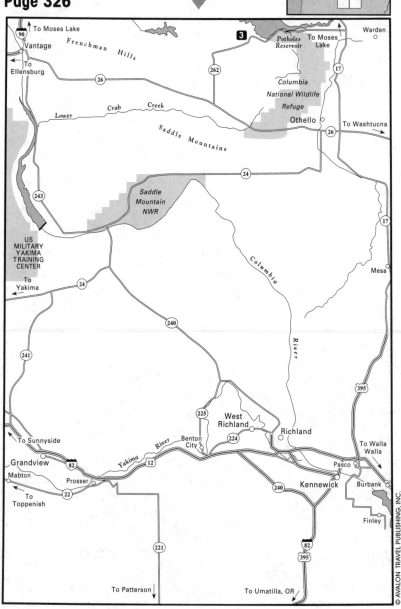

To Moses Lake

Vantage

Frenchman Hills

To Ellensburg

3

Potholes Reservoir

To Moses Lake

Warden

Columbia National Wildlife Refuge

Othello

To Washtucna

Lower Crab Creek

Saddle Mountains

Saddle Mountain NWR

US MILITARY YAKIMA TRAINING CENTER

To Yakima

Columbia River

Mesa

To Sunnyside

West Richland

Richland

To Walla Walla

Grandview

Mabton

Prosser

Benton City

Yakima River

Pasco

Burbank

Kennewick

To Toppenish

Finley

To Patterson

To Umatilla, OR

© AVALON TRAVEL PUBLISHING, INC.

Map 6.3

Hikes 4–5
Pages 327-328

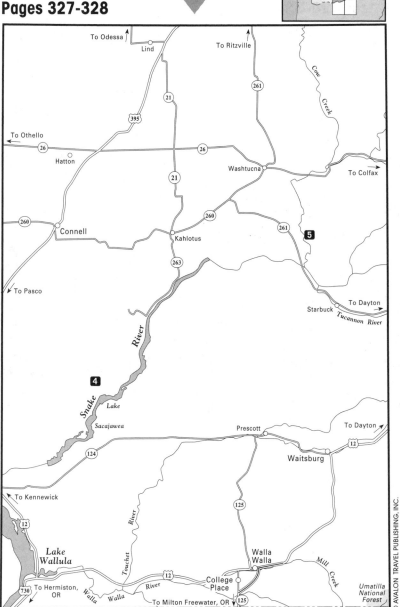

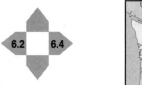

Map 6.4

Hikes 6–19
Pages 328–336

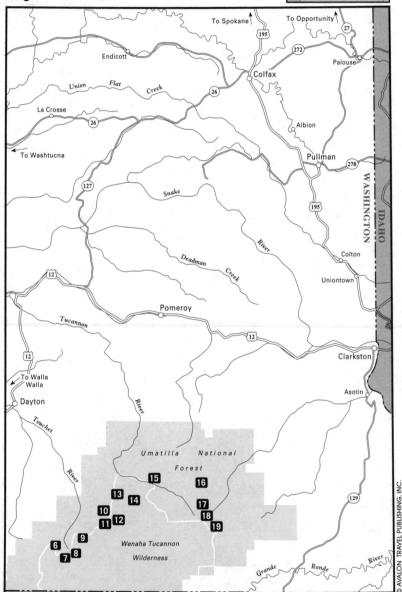

1 UMTANUM CREEK
4.0 mi/2.0 hrs

**north of Yakima in L. T. Murray
Wildlife Refuge**

Map 6.1, page 321

Umtanum Creek offers the ideal early season hike. You know that time of year, when Cle Elum and Yakima are hitting 75°F but Seattle is still mired in May showers, and snow blankets the Cascades. This is the trail to hit. Umtanum Creek Trail begins within one of Washington's most beautiful canyons, home to the Yakima River. Basalt cliffs and large rounded mountains dominate the valley, with small creek drainages running in between. Umtanum Creek Trail follows the creek through rarely experienced east-side meadows, a rich habitat for wildlife. Spring is the best season to hike here, especially in May, when wildflowers smother the hillsides in color.

The trail begins by crossing the Yakima River on a suspension bridge and quickly crosses railroad tracks, entering the L. T. Murray Wildlife Refuge. Although it gets extremely dry in summer, this area is home to an array of wildlife, including deer, eagles, hawks, coyotes, amphibians, snakes, and, some say, bighorn sheep. Umtanum Creek Trail follows the gently flowing creek up the valley. Willows and cottonwoods mark the creek, a sharp contrast to the meadows on the hillsides. The maintained trail ends about two miles upstream. If a longer hike is your intention, it's only a short scramble to the top of the bordering ridges. From on top, views stretch from the valley below to the Stuart Range.

User Groups: Hikers, leashed dogs, horses, and mountain bikes. No wheelchair access.

Open Seasons: This trail is accessible March–November.

Permits: The Washington Department of Fish and Wildlife requires an annual Vehicle Use Permit to park here. Permits are issued free with the purchase of a hunting or fishing license; additional permits are $10 each. Permits are available anywhere hunting or fishing

licenses are sold, by telephone at 866/246-9453, or online at website: fishhunt.dfw.wa.gov.

Maps: For topographic maps, ask the USGS for Wymer and The Cottonwoods.

Directions: From Ellensburg, drive south 16.5 miles on Highway 821 to the signed trailhead and parking area on the right (west) side of the road.

Contact: Washington Department of Fish and Wildlife, 201 North Pearl Street, Ellensburg, WA 98926, 509/925-6746.

2 YAKIMA RIM
4.0–18.0 mi/2.0 hrs–2 days

**north of Yakima in L. T. Murray
Wildlife Refuge**

Map 6.1, page 321

When snow still blankets the high country and the rains are still drenching the west side (that is, much of the spring), there is no better trail than Yakima Rim. It's an east-side gem, especially considering that you can tally on one hand the number of trees you encounter. The route traverses a high, rolling ridge with views of the surrounding countryside and far-off mountains. Wildflowers are everywhere, bringing much-needed life to a normally brown and dry terrain. It's a completely different world from the forests of the Cascades and every bit as beautiful.

Yakima Rim Trail is more of a route than a trail. Often following an old road through the L. T. Murray Wildlife Refuge, the trail makes a long loop, with half along a high ridge and the other half through a narrow valley. From the lower trailhead, head to the left and climb along the old, abandoned, but signed Jacob Durr Road to the crest of the ridge, about 4.5 miles, and an upper trailhead. Mount Rainier pokes up from the southwest while the Stuart Range is visible in all its glory to the north. A closed dirt road heads east along the ridge, dropping to the Yakima River in about 10 miles. The way back to the trailhead is 4 miles through the lush Rosa Creek Valley, full of grasses, willows, snakes, and deer.

Yakima Rim Trail, the chapter's most accessible hike from Seattle

© SCOTT LEONARD

Spring is by far the best time to visit, when the daytime air is still cool. Be sure to carry water, especially on the ridge, as water is found only in Rosa Creek. The best campsite is on Rosa Creek 1.5 miles from the Yakima River at Birdsong Tree, an old locust tree planted nearly 150 years ago by homesteaders. For a shorter and less demanding trip, head to the left from the trailhead to find Birdsong Tree (2.0 miles). Deer are a frequent companion within the willow groves alongside Rosa Creek.

User Groups: Hikers, leashed dogs, horses, and mountain bikes. No wheelchair access.

Open Seasons: This trail is accessible March–November.

Permits: The Washington Department of Fish and Wildlife requires an annual Vehicle Use Permit to park here. Permits are issued free with the purchase of a hunting or fishing license; additional permits are $10 each. Permits are available anywhere hunting or fishing licenses are sold, by telephone at 866/246-9453, or online at website: fishhunt.dfw.wa.gov.

Maps: For topographic maps, ask the USGS for Wymer and The Cottonwoods.

Directions: From Selah, drive 5 miles on Wenas Road to Sheep Company Road. Turn right and drive 5 miles (enter the wildlife refuge at Mile

2.6) to the unsigned trailhead. The key to finding the start of the trail is a small sign at a junction naming the Jacob Durr Road. Head left on the road to reach the ridge. Head right to find Rosa Creek Valley.

Contact: Washington Department of Fish and Wildlife, 201 North Pearl Street, Ellensburg, WA 98926, 509/925-6746.

3 POTHOLES SAND DUNES
3.0–6.0 mi/1.5–3.0 hrs

south of Moses Lake in South Columbia Basin Wildlife Area

Map 6.2, page 322

Don't show up expecting to find any trails at Potholes Sand Dunes, because you're unlikely to find any. Instead, this is true cross-country hiking, setting out over miles of sand dunes spread out among a number of small lakes, or potholes. They seem oddly out of place here in the middle of eastern Washington, a sort of desert oasis. The small lakes and larger Potholes Reservoir were created when the lengthy O'Sullivan Dam was built in the 1940s; the low, flat land was flooded, creating a sort of wetland among sand dunes. Grasses and juniper grow thickly, supporting a rich population of wildlife—mule deer, coyotes, and a vast abundance of birds. As there are no trails, an excursion of any size is possible. The best bet is to head out north from the parking area (crossing Winchester Wasteway via bridge) and hike roughly 1.5 miles to the edge of Potholes Reservoir. Since there aren't any trails to follow, other than faint game trails, it's ideal to bring a map and compass to help you find your way back to the car. If you can't, civilization and help are never far away. Bring water, as the area is quite hot during summer, and the potholes aren't recommended for drinking. Wide open horizons make this a great place for a night hike. Set out under a full moon and witness the night shift of wildlife do business.

User Groups: Hikers, leashed dogs, horses, and mountain bikes. No wheelchair access.

Open Seasons: This area is accessible year-round.

Permits: The Washington Department of Fish and Wildlife requires an annual Vehicle Use Permit to park here. Permits are issued free with the purchase of a hunting or fishing license; additional permits are $10 each. Permits are available anywhere hunting or fishing licenses are sold, by telephone at 866/246-9453, or online at website: fishhunt.dfw.wa.gov.

Maps: For topographic maps, ask the USGS for Royal Camp and Mae.

Directions: From Royal City, drive east 9 miles on Highway 26 to Highway 262. Turn left (north) and drive 8.5 miles to C Street Southeast. Turn left (north) and drive 1.5 miles to road's end and signed parking area.

Contact: Washington Department of Fish and Wildlife, 6653 Road K Northeast, Moses Lake, WA 98837, 509/765-6641.

◼ JUNIPER DUNES
5.5 mi/4.0 hrs

northeast of Pasco in Juniper Dunes Wilderness

Map 6.3, page 323

One of Washington's smallest and certainly most isolated wildernesses, Juniper Dunes promises to be unique. Covering more than

7,100 acres of pristine high desert, the Juniper Dunes preserve what once was and still is a small gem in the middle of eastern Washington. Sagebrush and desert grasses do their best to hold together the large mounds of sand, some more than 100 feet high. This layer of vegetation keeps the dunes in place and provides habitat for wildlife. Mule deer, coyotes, porcupines, and mice do their business on the ground while red-tailed hawks and owls work from the skies. The highlight of a trip to Juniper Dunes is surely the six small groves of juniper trees found near the center of the wilderness. From the trailhead, walk the road roughly 1.5 miles before turning due north for one mile. These groves of juniper trees have existed here in relative isolation for thousands of years, with many individual trees having grown for two or three centuries. The trees are surprisingly big and seem fairly out of place, in light of the fact that the region receives on average only 12 inches of rain a year. Special considerations include water (there is none to be found here) and a map and compass (other than the jeep trail bisecting the wilderness, there are no discernable trails). A field guide and binoculars will also prove helpful, for wildlife is sure to be a part of your trip to Juniper Dunes.

User Groups: Hikers, leashed dogs, and horses. No mountain bikes are allowed. No wheelchair access.

Open Seasons: This trail is accessible year-round.

Permits: No permits are needed. Parking and access are free.

Maps: For topographic maps, ask the USGS for Levey, Levey SW, and Levey NE.

Directions: From Pasco, drive east 2 miles on Highway 12 to Pasco/Kahlotus Highway. Turn left and drive 5.5 miles to Peterson Road. Turn left and drive 4.5 miles to a large sandy parking area, where the jeep trail starts.

Contact: Bureau of Land Management, Spokane District Office, 1103 North Fancher Street, Spokane, WA 99212-1275, 509/536-1200.

5 PALOUSE FALLS
0.2 mi/0.5 hr

north of Walla Walla on the Palouse River

Map 6.3, page 323

The trail may be short, but the falls are big. From a high viewpoint, watch the Palouse River make a thunderous plummet nearly 200 feet into a large bowl before rolling downstream to the Snake River. Adding to the scenic beauty are enormous cliffs and columns of basalt stationed around the falls. The enormous falls were created by the Missoula Floods more than 15,000 years ago. Mile-thick sheets of ice in Montana blocked glacial meltwater, creating an enormous lake. When the dams eventually broke (dozens of times through thousands of years), the released torrents raced from Montana down through the Columbia Basin of Washington. Much of eastern Washington was scoured and altered, as were eastern Oregon and the Willamette Valley. Palouse Falls is just one of the more interesting and noisy changes the floods left behind. The heavy flows of water quickly eroded the basalt, producing the falls. The official trail is short, but there are several nonofficial side trails leading (safely) to viewpoints upriver from the parking lot. A trail is visible down around the falls, but it is dangerous and should not be attempted. It's not a destination hike (don't drive from Seattle just to see it), but Palouse Falls is a good stopover when passing through the area. A number of trees provide welcome shade for picnics and lounging. The only safety consideration is an important one: This is rattlesnake country, so be cautious at all times. Rattlers enjoy basking on side trails, in the grass, or even in the parking lot.

User Groups: Hikers and leashed dogs. No horses or mountain bikes are allowed. This trail is wheelchair accessible.

Open Seasons: This trail is accessible year-round.

Permits: A $5 day-use fee is required to park here and is payable at the trailhead, or you can get an annual State Parks Pass for $30; contact Washington State Parks and Recreation, 360/902-8500.

Maps: For a topographic map, ask the USGS for Palouse Falls.

Directions: From Kennewick, drive north on U.S. 395 to Highway 260. Head east for 25 miles to Highway 261. Turn north and drive 14.5 miles to Palouse Falls Road. Turn left and drive 2 miles to the parking area where the trail starts.

Contact: Palouse Falls State Park, Highway 261, Washtucna, WA, 509/549-3551.

6 SAWTOOTH RIDGE
28.0 mi/3–4 days

east of Walla Walla in the Wenaha-Tucannon Wilderness of Umatilla National Forest

Map 6.4, page 324

The trail along Sawtooth Ridge is the epitome of the Wenaha-Tucannon Wilderness—long and high, dry and secluded, but chock-full of gorgeous views of the surrounding country. The trail makes a long traverse of Sawtooth Ridge, passing in and out of forests and meadows on its way into Oregon and down to the Wenaha River. The trail's placement along the ridge means that you shouldn't expect to find any water until the Wenaha. On such a long trail, it's necessary to plan carefully and carry plenty of extra fluids. Much of the path is rocky and difficult, not surprising for a ridge named Sawtooth. As far as camping is concerned, set up camp in the scenic meadow of your choice, as long as it's low impact. Wildlife in the forms of deer, bighorn sheep, and elk abound, while other hikers certainly do not (save for hunting seasons). In May and early June, Sawtooth Ridge will pleasantly surprise hikers with a grand display of wildflowers.

User Groups: Hikers, leashed dogs, and horses. No mountain bikes are allowed. No wheelchair access.

Open Seasons: This trail is accessible mid-June–October.

Permits: A federal Northwest Forest Pass is required to park here.

Maps: For a map of Umatilla National Forest, contact the Outdoor Recreation Information Center at the downtown Seattle REI. For topographic maps, ask the USGS for Godman Spring and Wenaha Forks.

Directions: From Dayton, drive south on North Fork Touchet River Road (following signs toward Bluewood Ski Area). This road becomes Forest Service Road 64 and eventually intersects Forest Service Road 46. Turn left on Forest Service Road 46 and drive .5 mile to the signed trailhead on the right side of the road.

Contact: Umatilla National Forest, Pomeroy Ranger District, 71 West Main Street, Pomeroy, WA 99347, 509/843-1891.

7 SLICK EAR
12.0 mi/7.0 hrs

east of Walla Walla in the Wenaha-Tucannon Wilderness of Umatilla National Forest

Map 6.4, page 324

More than half of this trail actually lies within Oregon, but it would be a shame to omit such a beautiful route to the Wenaha River. Heavily used by hunters in the fall but rarely during other times of the year, Slick Ear offers hikers outstanding views of the surrounding landscape before dramatically dropping into a beautiful forested canyon ending at the Wenaha. Don't expect to find much water along the first two miles, where the trail rides the ridge top. At that point (a good turnaround for less serious excursions), the trail drops steeply into the canyon containing Slick Ear Creek. Down here is where you'll find water, campsites, and, unfortunately, rattlesnakes too. The trail ends at the Wenaha River, a prime spot for both trout and salmon fishing (Wenaha salmon are endangered and federally protected, so be sure to check Oregon fishing regulations). The trail works especially well as a loop if hikers travel east on the Wenaha River Trail to Grizzly Bear Trail, a total of 18.2 miles.

User Groups: Hikers, leashed dogs, and horses. No mountain bikes are allowed. No wheelchair access.

Open Seasons: This trail is accessible June–October.

Permits: A federal Northwest Forest Pass is required to park here.

Maps: For a map of Umatilla National Forest, contact the Outdoor Recreation Information Center at the downtown Seattle REI. For topographic maps, ask the USGS for Godman Spring and Wenaha Forks.

Directions: From Dayton, drive south on North Fork Touchet River Road (following signs toward Bluewood Ski Area). This road becomes Forest Service Road 64 and eventually intersects Forest Service Road 46. Turn left on Forest Service Road 46 and drive 3 miles to Forest Service Road 46-300. Turn right and drive 5 miles to Twin Buttes Trailhead at road's end.

Contact: Umatilla National Forest, Pomeroy Ranger District, 71 West Main Street, Pomeroy, WA 99347, 509/843-1891.

8 GRIZZLY BEAR RIDGE
15.0 mi/2 days

east of Walla Walla in the Wenaha-Tucannon Wilderness of Umatilla National Forest

Map 6.4, page 324

This is one more of the many great ridge hikes in the wilderness. Putting it near the top of the list is a pair of cold-water springs supplying much-needed refreshment on hot summer days and panoramic views leading to the Wenaha River. The Wenaha is an outstanding river for trout fishing with Grizzly Bear offering access to one of the most remote sections. The trail follows an old road for about two miles, at which point Coyote Spring can be found on the south side. The trail then follows the ridge into Oregon, slowly losing elevation for four miles to Meadow Spring (on the north side of the trail). Meadow Spring is a good turnaround point for folks out for just a day hike. The descent continues as the trail makes its way to the Wenaha River. Camps are best made near Meadow Spring or preferably at the Wenaha. Hikers can make a great loop by combining Grizzly Bear Ridge with

Slick Ear, a total of 18.2 miles. Grizzly bears may be gone in this area, but a lot of other wildlife still lives in this place. Black bears roam the meadows, as do mule deer, elk, and bighorn sheep. Hawks and ravens soar in the skies, while trout and salmon ply the the Wenaha.

User Groups: Hikers, leashed dogs, and horses. No mountain bikes are allowed. No wheelchair access.

Open Seasons: This trail is accessible June–October.

Permits: A federal Northwest Forest Pass is required to park here.

Maps: For a map of Umatilla National Forest, contact the Outdoor Recreation Information Center at the downtown Seattle REI. For topographic maps, ask the USGS for Godman Spring, Oregon Butte, and Elbow Creek.

Directions: From Dayton, drive south on North Fork Touchet River Road (following signs toward Bluewood Ski Area). This road becomes Forest Service Road 64 and eventually intersects Forest Service Road 46. Turn left on Forest Service Road 46 and drive 3 miles to Forest Service Road 46-300. Turn right and drive 5 miles to Twin Buttes Trailhead at road's end.

Contact: Umatilla National Forest, Pomeroy Ranger District, 71 West Main Street, Pomeroy, WA 99347, 509/843-1891.

❾ WEST BUTTE CREEK
16.0 mi/2 days

east of Walla Walla in the Wenaha-Tucannon Wilderness of Umatilla National Forest

Map 6.4, page 324

West Butte Creek has a bit of everything. After spending several miles along a high open ridge with panoramic views of the wilderness, the trail drops through the Rainbow Creek Natural Research Area. Wildlife is extremely abundant along this route. Mule deer, elk, bighorn sheep, and black bear are frequent sightings in this wild area.

The trail begins from Godman, a Forest Service station on the edge of Wenaha-Tucannon Wilderness. Soak in the views as you slowly traverse the ridge for two miles. The trail then steeply drops to Rainbow Creek and campsites (4 miles). This is in the heart of the Rainbow Creek Natural Research Area, a large section of wilderness devoted to the study of this unique and natural ecosystem. Large Douglas and grand firs provide welcome shade and lower the temperature significantly during the summer. The route ends at a junction with East Butte and Twin Buttes Trails, two primitive and rarely maintained routes back up to high ridge trailheads that would require car-drops. The trail is hot and dry along the ridge but water is available year-round from Rainbow Creek.

User Groups: Hikers, leashed dogs, and horses. No mountain bikes are allowed. No wheelchair access.

Open Seasons: This trail is accessible June–October.

Permits: A federal Northwest Forest Pass is required to park here.

Maps: For a map of Umatilla National Forest, contact the Outdoor Recreation Information Center at the downtown Seattle REI. For topographic maps, ask the USGS for Godman Spring and Oregon Butte.

Directions: From Dayton, drive 1 mile south on 4th Street to Mustard Hollow Road. Turn left and drive 28 miles (as the road turns to Eckler Mountain Road, Skyline Drive, and Forest Service Road 46) to the Godman Guard Station. The trailhead is on the left immediately after the guard station.

Contact: Umatilla National Forest, Pomeroy Ranger District, 71 West Main Street, Pomeroy, WA 99347, 509/843-1891.

❿ SMOOTH RIDGE
28.0 mi one-way/3 days

east of Walla Walla in the Wenaha-Tucannon Wilderness of Umatilla National Forest

Map 6.4, page 324

Smooth Ridge is the chief high route through the Wenaha-Tucannon Wilderness, offering constant views of mountains near and far. No route through the wilderness is as scenic or as likely to provide wildlife sightings as Smooth Ridge. Numerous cold-water springs along the route provide water well into summer, and campsites are found regularly along the way, making the long journey easy. Smooth Ridge is a trekker's dream, either as an excellent through-hike or an outstanding (but extremely long) loop hike.

The best access to Smooth Ridge is via Mount Misery Trail out of Teepee Trailhead. After 2.5 miles, the trail intersects Smooth Ridge below the north slope of Oregon Butte, a quick, must-see side trip. Smooth Ridge Trail heads south over Danger Point and encounters the first set of springs at about five miles. From here, the trail follows the ridge through forest and meadow up to Weller Butte at 10 miles and slowly drops to the Wenaha River and the state of Oregon (18 miles). On clear days (which is nearly every day during summer), the Wallowa Range in Oregon and the Seven Devils Range in Idaho are plainly visible.

It's highly recommended to carry a map on this trip to help find the many springs (usually just off the main trail). Most springs provide water well into August, unless it's been a very dry spring. Campsites are situated throughout the route, with the best ones found next to the springs. From the Wenaha River, hike nine miles east to Troy, Oregon, and the logical drop-off for your return ride. Another option is to hike Crooked Creek north and return via Indian Corral, a long, tiring, and beautiful loop of more than 50 miles.

User Groups: Hikers, leashed dogs, and horses. No mountain bikes are allowed. No wheelchair access.

Open Seasons: This trail is accessible June–October.

Permits: A federal Northwest Forest Pass is required to park here.

Maps: For a map of Umatilla National Forest, contact the Outdoor Recreation Information Center at the downtown Seattle REI. For topographic maps, ask the USGS for Oregon Butte, Eden, and Diamond Peak.

Directions: From Dayton, drive 1 mile south on 4th Street to Mustard Hollow Road. Turn left and drive 28 miles (as the road turns to Eckler Mountain Road, Skyline Drive, and Forest Service Road 46) to the Godman Guard Station. Turn left onto Forest Service Road 4608 and drive 5 miles to Teepee Trailhead at road's end.

Contact: Umatilla National Forest, Pomeroy Ranger District, 71 West Main Street, Pomeroy, WA 99347, 509/843-1891.

11 TURKEY CREEK
8.0 mi/4.5 hrs

east of Walla Walla in the Wenaha-Tucannon Wilderness of Umatilla National Forest

Map 6.4, page 324

While much of Southeastern Washington receives little rain or snow, Turkey Creek is an exception. Turkey Creek drains to the north, meaning much of the valley gets less sunshine than other valleys. That results in Turkey Creek's holding on to a hefty snowpack well into May. With a source of water lasting so long, the creek supports a more lush forest. And that makes for great hiking scenery: many large trees with a thick, green understory. Water also means an abundance of wildlife, with deer and elk finding Turkey Creek a cool refuge from the area's dry, hot ridges.

Turkey Creek Trail drops from Teepee Trailhead, the one and only vista along the route (in the opposite direction, no less). The trail descends sharply into a valley of enormous Douglas firs and western larches. The strongly flowing creek is never out of ear's reach as the trail travels four miles to the confluence with Panjab Creek. Several camps lie along the route (mainly used by hunters in the fall), including a pair near the midpoint and the best site at the junction with Panjab Trail. Turkey Creek flows year-round, meaning water is readily available, even on hot summer days. Good on its own, the trail works especially well as part of a 16-mile loop with Panjab and Oregon Butte Trails.

User Groups: Hikers, leashed dogs, and horses. No mountain bikes are allowed. No wheelchair access.

Open Seasons: This trail is accessible June–November.

Permits: A federal Northwest Forest Pass is required to park here.

Maps: For a map of Umatilla National Forest, contact the Outdoor Recreation Information Center at the downtown Seattle REI. For topographic maps, ask the USGS for Panjab Creek and Oregon Butte.

Directions: From Dayton, drive 1 mile south on 4th Street to Mustard Hollow Road. Turn left and drive 28 miles (as the road turns to Eckler Mountain Road, Skyline Drive, and Forest Service Road 46) to the Godman Guard Station. Turn left onto Forest Service Road 4608 and drive 5 miles to Teepee Trailhead at road's end.

Contact: Umatilla National Forest, Pomeroy Ranger District, 71 West Main Street, Pomeroy, WA 99347, 509/843-1891.

12 OREGON BUTTE
5.5 mi/3.0 hrs

east of Walla Walla in the Wenaha-Tucannon Wilderness of Umatilla National Forest

Map 6.4, page 324

Where there are fire lookouts, there are views. Oregon Butte is no exception to this high-country rule. With easy access and knockout vistas, Oregon Butte is undoubtedly the most beautiful day hike in the Wenaha-Tucannon Wilderness. The high, open mountaintop reveals all of the surrounding wilderness, and on clear days, the jagged, snowy peaks of the Wallowa Range in Oregon and Seven Devils Range in Idaho are readily visible. And to top it off, mule deer and bighorn sheep are frequently seen along the route.

The trip to Oregon Butte follows Mount Misery Trail east out of Teepee Trailhead. At 2.5 miles, the trail passes Oregon Butte Spring, the route's only source of water. Just beyond is the junction for Smooth Ridge, along with several campsites. An easily found side trail heads straight up to the summit of Oregon Butte and the fire lookout, still staffed by the Forest Service during the summer. The views extend in every direction, with most of the wilderness's drainages easily traced back to their sources. The trail is easy to follow at all times and fairly gentle and easy. It's important to know that Mount Misery Trail lies on the north side of a ridge, meaning snow can linger along the trail well into June.

User Groups: Hikers, leashed dogs, and horses. No mountain bikes are allowed. No wheelchair access.

Open Seasons: This trail is accessible June–October.

Permits: A federal Northwest Forest Pass is required to park here.

Maps: For a map of Umatilla National Forest, contact the Outdoor Recreation Information Center at the downtown Seattle REI. For a topographic map, ask the USGS for Oregon Butte.

Directions: From Dayton, drive 1 mile south on 4th Street to Mustard Hollow Road. Turn left and drive 28 miles (as the road turns to Eckler Mountain Road, Skyline Drive, and Forest Service Road 46) to the Godman Guard Station. Turn left onto Forest Service Road 4608 and drive 5 miles to Teepee Trailhead at road's end.

Contact: Umatilla National Forest, Pomeroy Ranger District, 71 West Main Street, Pomeroy, WA 99347, 509/843-1891.

13 PANJAB
11.2 mi/6.0 hrs

east of Walla Walla in the Wenaha-Tucannon Wilderness of Umatilla National Forest

Map 6.4, page 324

Panjab provides the best access to Indian Corral, the Wenaha-Tucannon Wilderness's largest and most popular high-country camp. Indian Corral is an intersection for several long, highly scenic trails spreading into the far reaches of the wilderness. Having such a crossroads as a end makes Panjab useful as a starting point for long treks. With wide expansive meadows, Panjab is also a great day hike.

The trail starts from large Panjab Trailhead and gently climbs alongside Panjab Creek through cool forests for 1.5 miles to an intersection with Turkey Creek Trail and the route's only camp. Notice the diverse forests, full of Douglas fir, yews, grand fir, ponderosa pine, and western larch. This a good turnaround for casual hikers, as the trail only gets steeper. The next 2.5 miles climb steadily through the forest to Indian Corral and wide meadows of wildflowers. Water is common along the route, important on those hot summer days. Numerous camps are available at Indian Corral, and for water Dunlap Springs is just a few hundred yards down Crooked Creek Trail. Except in the fall, during hunting season, don't expect to see many people; the Wenaha-Tucannon is desolate country.

User Groups: Hikers, leashed dogs, and horses. No mountain bikes are allowed. No wheelchair access.

Open Seasons: This trail is accessible June–October.

Permits: A federal Northwest Forest Pass is required to park here.

Maps: For a map of Umatilla National Forest, contact the Outdoor Recreation Information Center at the downtown Seattle REI. For topographic maps, ask the USGS for Panjab Creek.

Directions: From Dayton, drive east 12 miles on Highway 12 to Tucannon River Road. Turn right and drive 35 miles to a fork. Stay to the right as the road turns into Forest Service Road 4713 and drive 3 miles to the well-signed trailhead.

Contact: Umatilla National Forest, Pomeroy Ranger District, 71 West Main Street, Pomeroy, WA 99347, 509/843-1891.

14 CROOKED CREEK

29.2 mi one-way/2–3 days

east of Walla Walla in the Wenaha-Tucannon Wilderness of Umatilla National Forest

Map 6.4, page 324

This is the trail for those seeking a long trek through the heart of the Wenaha-Tucannon Wilderness. Starting high at Indian Corral, overlooking the surrounding Blue Mountains,

Crooked Creek Trail drops into cool, shady forests and travels 18 miles to the Wenaha River. By the time you're done, you'll be in Oregon. And you'll likely be tired. Crooked Creek Valley is full of life, passing through prime wildlife country where deer, elk, bighorn sheep, and black bears are common residents.

The route begs for a car-drop, with one vehicle stationed at Panjab Trailhead and another in Troy, Oregon. Otherwise, it's a long trip back to your car, either via the same route or via Smooth Ridge (a 52-mile loop). Start at Panjab Trailhead and hike to Indian Corral (5.6 miles). Crooked Creek Trail drops beside Trout Creek, which runs into Third Creek (12 miles), which runs into Crooked Creek (18 miles). Another five miles brings hikers to the Wenaha River; Troy is six miles to the east.

Much of the route is well forested, a big plus in this hot, dry region. Frequent breaks in the trees, however, reveal the high open ridges that define this wilderness. Water is never a problem since the creeks run year-round. Camps are situated regularly along the trail as well. A fishing pole is a nice luxury, as Crooked Creek and the Wenaha are prime fishing streams. Solitude seekers will be in heaven here; except during the fall hunting seasons, you likely won't encounter another soul.

User Groups: Hikers, leashed dogs, and horses. No mountain bikes are allowed. No wheelchair access.

Open Seasons: This trail is accessible June–October.

Permits: A federal Northwest Forest Pass is required to park here.

Maps: For a map of Umatilla National Forest, contact the Outdoor Recreation Information Center at the downtown Seattle REI. For topographic maps, ask the USGS for Diamond Peak, Eden, Oregon Butte, and Panjab Creek.

Directions: From Dayton, drive east 12 miles on Highway 12 to Tucannon River Road. Turn right and drive 35 miles to a fork in the road. Veer to the left onto Forest Service Road 4712 and drive 5 miles to the well-signed trailhead at road's end.

Contact: Umatilla National Forest, Pomeroy Ranger District, 71 West Main Street, Pomeroy, WA 99347, 509/843-1891.

15 TUCANNON RIVER
8.2 mi/4.5 hrs

east of Walla Walla in Umatilla National Forest

Map 6.4, page 324

The Tucannon River provides the setting for the area's most laid-back hike, a gentle walk through a striking canyon among surprisingly large trees. The route gains little elevation over its five-mile length, making it great for families and casual hikers. Though after 4.1 miles in, the trail begins a steep climb out of the valley. For a more relaxed hike, turn back after 4.1 miles. The Tucannon is well stocked with trout, making it an angler's dream. Although the trail isn't within the wilderness boundaries, there's little trace of people other than the easy-to-follow footpath. The narrow valley of the Tucannon is made of steep cliffs giving way to rounded ridges, with thick forests in the valley bottom. Ponderosa pine, yew, Douglas fir, and grand fir grow quite large here, creating a forest as impressive as those of the West Cascades, at least in light of what little precipitation the area receives. The trail ends at a junction with Jelly Springs Trail (a steep ascent to Diamond Peak) and Bear Creek (a steep ascent to Hunter's Spring). The Tucannon is a protected stream, so anglers will want to check state fishing regulations on the way in. Also keep in mind that this is rattlesnake country. They're most often found in sunny, rocky sections of the trail and are likely to warn you of their presence with a few shakes of their tails. Nevertheless, keep your eyes and ears peeled.

User Groups: Hikers, leashed dogs, and horses. No mountain bikes are allowed. No wheelchair access.

Open Seasons: This trail is accessible April–November.

Permits: A federal Northwest Forest Pass is required to park here.

Maps: For a map of Umatilla National Forest, contact the Outdoor Recreation Information Center at the downtown Seattle REI. For a topographic map, ask the USGS for Stentz Spring.

Directions: From Dayton, drive east 12 miles on Highway 12 to Tucannon River Road. Turn right and drive 35 miles to a fork in the road. Veer to the left onto Forest Service Road 4712 and drive 5 miles to the well-signed trailhead at road's end.

Contact: Umatilla National Forest, Pomeroy Ranger District, 71 West Main Street, Pomeroy, WA 99347, 509/843-1891.

16 BEAR CREEK
6.0 mi/4.0 hrs

east of Walla Walla in Umatilla National Forest

Map 6.4, page 324

Bear Creek serves as a route to the wildest parts of the Tucannon River. The trail drops from Hunter's Spring atop a high ridge into a rough canyon encasing the Tucannon River. This section of the river is at least three miles from any road, making visitors scarce. Few visitors means even fewer anglers. Which in turn means these parts are mostly unfished water, otherwise known as a trout angler's dream. The hike down is not easy, though, losing more than 1,600 feet along a steep and rocky descent. Although the trail is rough, the view is great. Pine, spruce, and larch create an open parkland forest with plenty of views of the rocky canyon below. The rustling in the bushes is probably mule deer or elk, both of which are plentiful in this wild area. Also present in the area are rattlesnakes, so be sure to keep eyes and ears alert. The trail empties on the valley floor at the shores of the Tucannon River. A couple of campsites can be found here at this junction, where trails lead down the river or up the other side of the canyon to Jelly Springs.

User Groups: Hikers, leashed dogs, and horses. No mountain bikes are allowed. No wheelchair access.

Open Seasons: This trail is accessible June–November.

Permits: A federal Northwest Forest Pass is required to park here.

Maps: For a map of Umatilla National Forest, contact the Outdoor Recreation Information Center at the downtown Seattle REI. For a topographic map, ask the USGS for Stentz Spring.

Directions: From Pomeroy, drive south 10 miles on County Road 128 to Mountain Road 40. Stay to the right and drive about 16 miles to Blue Mountain Trail sign. Turn right and drive .25 mile to the signed trailhead.

Contact: Umatilla National Forest, Pomeroy Ranger District, 71 West Main Street, Pomeroy, WA 99347, 509/843-1891.

⒘ JELLY SPRINGS
9.0 mi/5.0 hrs

east of Walla Walla in Umatilla National Forest

Map 6.4, page 324

Within the Blue Mountains just north of the Wenaha-Tucannon Wilderness, Jelly Springs Trail offers a unique perspective on the area. The trail is one of the few to bear due north from the wilderness, offering views not seen from the region's other trails. From Diamond Peak Trailhead, the route makes an easy traverse of a high ridge (over 6,000 feet in elevation) for three miles. Hawks frequently patrol the skies in search of a meal while Rocky Mountain elk and mule deer graze within the high meadows. Jelly Springs, a cold-water spring that runs well into August, serves as a good turnaround point for those not interested in making the sharp, steep descent to the Tucannon River. The trail encounters the Tucannon River Trail at 4.5 miles, a potential route for a through-hike. While most of the trail lies outside the wilderness boundary, the uppermost section is protected, keeping out noisy motorbikes.

User Groups: Hikers, leashed dogs, and horses. Motorcycles are allowed on the lower section of the trail and must turn around at the wilderness boundary. No mountain bikes are allowed. No wheelchair access.

Open Seasons: This trail is accessible June–October.

Permits: A federal Northwest Forest Pass is required to park here.

Maps: For a map of Umatilla National Forest, contact the Outdoor Recreation Information Center at the downtown Seattle REI. For topographic maps, ask the USGS for Stentz Spring and Diamond Peak.

Directions: From Pomeroy, drive south 10 miles on County Road 128 to Mountain Road (Forest Service Road 40). Continue straight (on Forest Service Road 40) for 24 miles to Forest Service Road 4030. Turn right and drive 5 miles to Diamond Trailhead at road's end. Jelly Springs Trail begins 1.5 miles west on Mount Misery Trail.

Contact: Umatilla National Forest, Pomeroy Ranger District, 71 West Main Street, Pomeroy, WA 99347, 509/843-1891.

⒙ MOUNT MISERY
14.7 mi one-way/2 days

east of Walla Walla in the Wenaha-Tucannon Wilderness of Umatilla National Forest

Map 6.4, page 324

It may be known as Mount Misery Trail, but in fact, it has little to do with its namesake. Mount Misery is quickly skirted in the first few miles and soon forgotten. Instead, the trail continues to Diamond Peak, the Wenaha-Tucannon Wilderness's highest point, and onward for 12 miles through exceptional meadows packed full of far-flung vistas. This is some of the area's best hiking along a trail that starts high and stays there. Throw in a number of cold-water springs and scenic camps, and you have yourself a wonderful trip.

The trail is best completed as a through-hike, with a start at Diamond Peak Trailhead and ending at Teepee Trailhead. Pass on the side trip to Mount Misery (although it isn't a miserable view) and make a short side trip up

Diamond Peak (at 2.5 miles) and big-time views. From there the trail travels seven miles to Indian Corral, wandering in and out of meadows along Horse Ridge. Views extend over the whole of the Wenaha-Tucannon Wilderness, all the way to the Wallowa Range in Oregon and Seven Devils Range in Idaho. The route passes five springs along the way and campsites are plentiful, with the best spots usually near the springs. From Indian Corral, the trail heads south three miles to Oregon Butte (another great, short side trip) then east two miles to Teepee Trailhead. Expect to encounter a fair amount of wildlife, including mule deer, Rocky Mountain elk, and bighorn sheep. Don't expect to run into many other hikers, save for during the fall hunting seasons.

User Groups: Hikers, leashed dogs, and horses. No mountain bikes are allowed. No wheelchair access.

Open Seasons: This trail is accessible June–October.

Permits: A federal Northwest Forest Pass is required to park here.

Maps: For a map of Umatilla National Forest, contact the Outdoor Recreation Information Center at the downtown Seattle REI. For topographic maps, ask the USGS for Panjab Creek, Diamond Peak, and Stentz Spring.

Directions: From Pomeroy, drive south 10 miles on County Road 128 to Mountain Road (Forest Service Road 40). Continue straight (on Forest Service Road 40) for 24 miles to Forest Service Road 4030. Turn right and drive 5 miles to Diamond Trailhead at road's end.

Contact: Umatilla National Forest, Pomeroy Ranger District, 71 West Main Street, Pomeroy, WA 99347, 509/843-1891.

19 MELTON CREEK
19.4 mi/2 days

east of Walla Walla in the Wenaha-Tucannon Wilderness of Umatilla National Forest

Map 6.4, page 324

It's a shame that so few people travel Melton Creek Trail, for it's packed full of exceptional views and awe-inspiring terrain. The first five miles traverse a high ridge immersed in panoramic views of the surrounding wilderness. There are loads of opportunities to see bighorn sheep and Rocky Mountain elk in this country. As if that weren't good enough, the trail then drops to the shady forest of Melton Creek, which flows through a stunning canyon. This is one of the more secluded spots within the Wenaha-Tucannon Wilderness, an attractive consideration for those seeking a little solitude. Water is nonexistent along the ridge but Melton Creek flows year-round. The trail intersects Crooked Creek Trail at the 10-mile mark, a decent day's travel (day hikers will want to turn around before the trail drops to Melton Creek). A few camps are spread out along the route, with the best ones in the valley. The few who set out on this trail will surely not be disappointed.

User Groups: Hikers, leashed dogs, and horses. No mountain bikes are allowed. No wheelchair access.

Open Seasons: This trail is accessible June–October.

Permits: A federal Northwest Forest Pass is required to park here.

Maps: For a map of Umatilla National Forest, contact the Outdoor Recreation Information Center at the downtown Seattle REI. For a topographic map, ask the USGS for Diamond Peak.

Directions: From Pomeroy, drive south 10 miles on County Road 128 to Mountain Road (Forest Service Road 40). Continue straight (on Forest Service Road 40) for 24 miles to Forest Service Road 4030. Turn right and drive 5 miles to Diamond Trailhead at road's end. Melton Creek Trail begins 1.5 miles west on Mount Misery Trail.

Contact: Umatilla National Forest, Pomeroy Ranger District, 71 West Main Street, Pomeroy, WA 99347, 509/843-1891.

Oregon

OREGON REGIONS

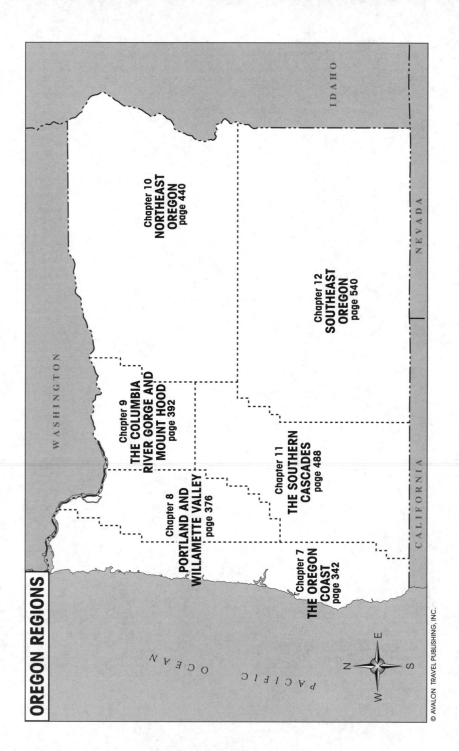

WASHINGTON

IDAHO

Chapter 10
NORTHEAST OREGON
page 440

NEVADA

Chapter 12
SOUTHEAST OREGON
page 540

Chapter 9
THE COLUMBIA RIVER GORGE AND MOUNT HOOD
page 392

Chapter 8
PORTLAND AND WILLAMETTE VALLEY
page 376

Chapter 11
THE SOUTHERN CASCADES
page 488

CALIFORNIA

Chapter 7
THE OREGON COAST
page 342

PACIFIC OCEAN

N
W   E
S

© AVALON TRAVEL PUBLISHING, INC.

The Oregon Coast

The Oregon Coast

et's face it: Oregon isn't about to be nicknamed "the Sunshine State" anytime soon. You won't find MTV filming a spring-break beach party here, and you'd be hard-pressed to find a bikini anywhere. That is precisely its appeal. Instead, you'll find windswept beaches, majestic rocky bluffs, lighthouses, and the Oregon Dunes along famous U.S. 101. We know, it all sounds clichéd—and it is, in a way. Don't be surprised if you feel a weird sense of déjà vu when you explore the coast—it's just because of the many postcards and ads that have been shot here.

The entire Oregon coast is public property, which means you can hike from one end to the other—literally. The 360-mile Oregon Coast Trail (OCT) extends from the northern tip in Astoria to the California border at Brookings-Harbor; many of the hikes in this chapter join the OCT. The coast is broken up by locals into three categories: the north coast (including the towns of Astoria, Seaside, Cannon Beach, and Tillamook), the central coast (including Lincoln City, Depoe Bay, Newport, Waldport, Yachats, and Florence), and the south coast (including Coos Bay, North Bend, Port Orford, Bandon, Gold Beach, and Brookings-Harbor).

But the ocean isn't the only hot spot in the coastal region: The Tillamook State Forest in the north coast, the Siuslaw National Forest in the north and central coast, and the Siskiyou National Forest in the south coast round out the area and offer some of the tougher hikes and peaks for great views of the coast. One side note: The Biscuit Fire in 2002, estimated to be one of Oregon's largest wildfires in recorded history, burned 499,965 acres in southern Oregon and northern California.

It swept through most of the Kalmiopsis Wilderness in the Siskiyou National Forest, which means that many trails at this writing have not bounced back enough to travel through (although many have been maintained and are included in this chapter).

Unlike some of the higher-elevation trails in other regions of the state, which are covered by snow sometimes through July, the coast is hikeable year-round. In fact, it's a popular destination in the winter months, as it's a top whale-watching spot from December to February and from March to May. During whale-watching weeks in December and March, trained volunteers will help you spot the spouts at 29 locations along the coast.

There are more short hikes in this chapter than in others, and there's a reason for that. We just couldn't leave out some of the gorgeous lighthouse jaunts. One idea is to plan several hikes in one day as you drive down the coast—a perfect way to gently introduce kids to hiking.

Of course, you'll want to check out the local flavors while you're here: Moe's Clam Chowder is famous; it originated in Newport and has five locations along the coast. The entire coast is lined with fishing villages and cute coastal towns—Cannon Beach in particular (in the north coast) is popular with bed-and-breakfast types. If you're more of a tent person, there are plenty of year-round sites all along the coast. Just hit the road down U.S. 101 and see all the signs lined up pointing you to beachside camping.

Whether you decide to hit a few small hikes in a day or want a lung-busting peak, you'll find it all here. In fact, the only thing you won't find is a teeny-weeny bikini.

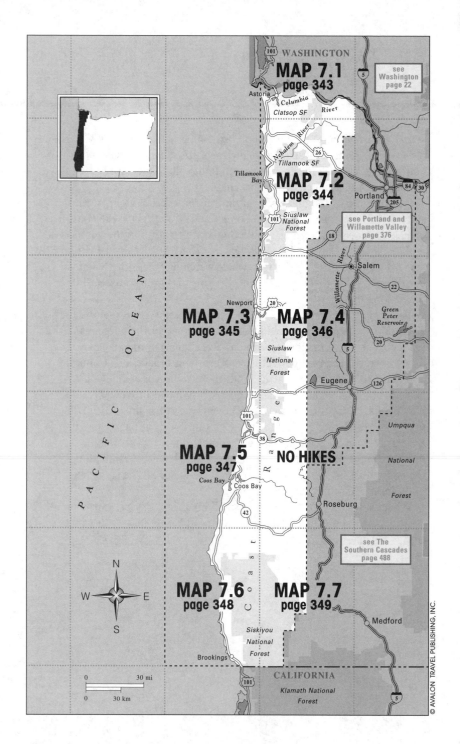

Map 7.1

Hike 1
Page 350

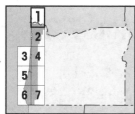

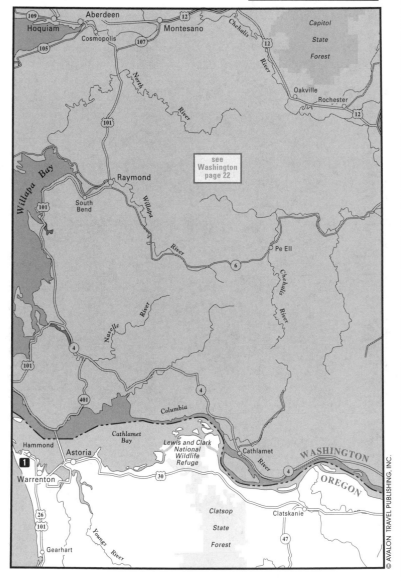

Map 7.2

Hikes 2–14
Pages 350–357

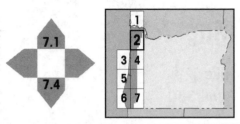

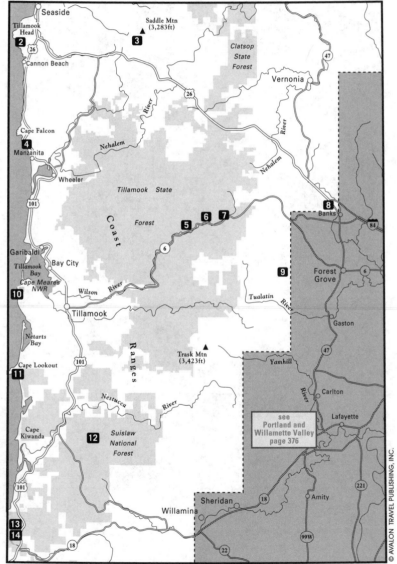

© AVALON TRAVEL PUBLISHING, INC.

Map 7.3

Hikes 15–19
Pages 357–359

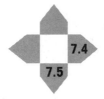

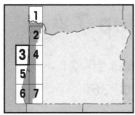

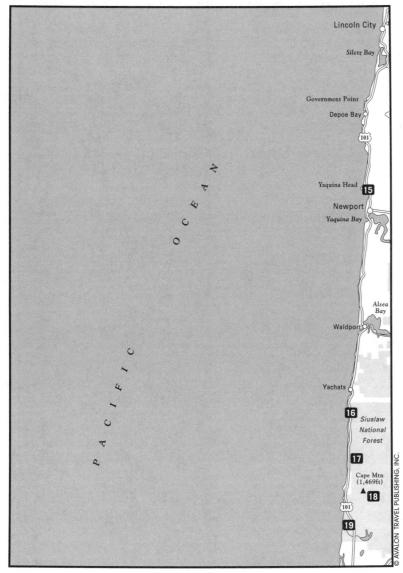

Map 7.4

Hikes 20–21
Page 360

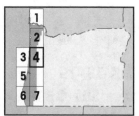

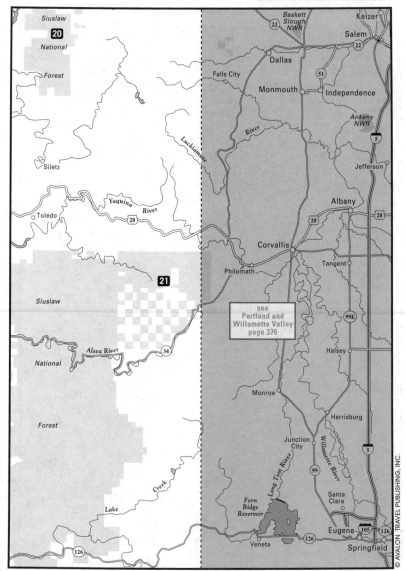

see
Portland and
Willamette Valley
page 376

© AVALON TRAVEL PUBLISHING, INC.

Map 7.5

Hikes 22–25
Pages 361–362

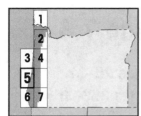

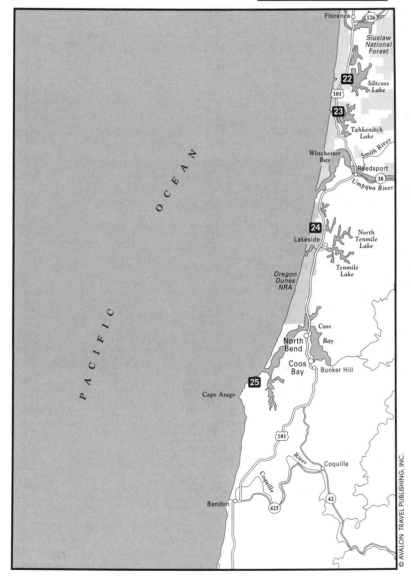

Map 7.6

Hikes 26–37
Pages 363–368

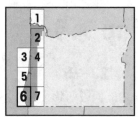

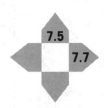

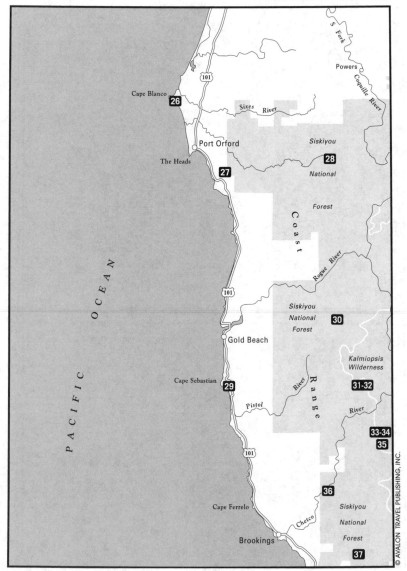

Map 7.7

Hikes 38–43
Pages 369–371

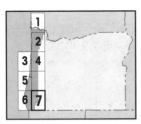

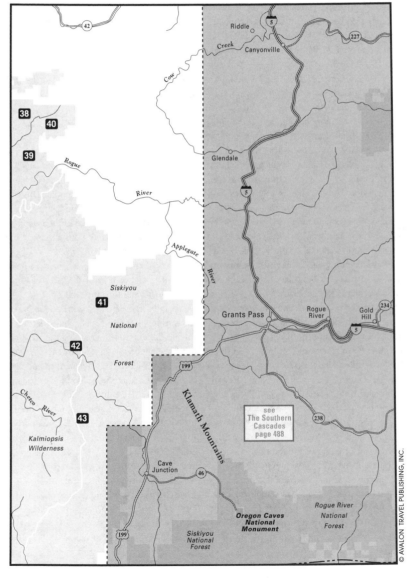

1 FORT STEVENS STATE PARK
1.0–9.0 mi/5.0 hrs

west of Astoria on the northwestern point of Oregon

Map 7.1, page 343

This state park has an interesting set of claims to fame within its 3,700 acres. The site originally served as the primary military defense installation in the Harbor Defense System, at the mouth of the Columbia River. There it stood for 84 years, from the Civil War until the end of World War II. Although some relics remain—you can explore the abandoned gun batteries, climb to the commander's station for a view, and visit the military museum on the property—it now primarily serves more civilian needs. The Oregon Coast Trail starts here, and in addition to the historical artifacts, there are also six miles of hiking trails and nine miles of paved biking paths. Swing by the information kiosk at the park entrance before planning your attack, because there's plenty to choose from. An easy-to-follow 2.4-mile path around Coffenbury Lake is a good way to start your day. Then hit the Peter Iredale shipwreck and follow the two-mile beachside bike path for great ocean views. No matter how you decide to spend your day, you can't really go wrong in this jam-packed park.

User Groups: Hikers, dogs, and mountain bikes. No horses are allowed. Wheelchair access is available on paved portions of trails.

Permits: Permits are not required. A $3 day-use fee is collected at the park entrance, or you can get an annual Oregon Parks and Recreation pass for $25; contact Oregon Parks and Recreation, 800/551-6949. Another option is to buy the Oregon Pacific Coast Passport, which is valid at 17 locations along the coast; it costs $35 for a year or $10 for a five-day pass and is available at local vendors and through the Oregon Parks and Recreation Department.

Maps: For a free park brochure and map, contact Oregon Parks and Recreation Department, 800/551-6949, www.oregonstateparks.org. For a topographic map, ask the USGS for Warrenton.

Directions: From Astoria, drive four miles south on U.S. 101 to Fort Stevens State Park. (From Seaside, drive nine miles north.) Follow signs for 4.5 miles into the park and continue to the campground entrance and picnic area A, where Coffenbury Lake is located.

Contact: Oregon Parks and Recreation Department, 1115 Commercial Street Northeast, Salem, OR 97301, 800/551-6949, www.oregonstateparks.org.

2 TILLAMOOK HEAD
4.0 mi/2.0 hrs

two miles north of Cannon Beach on the Oregon Coast

Map 7.2, page 344

This is quintessential Oregon coast—you've got massive jutting rocks, a distant lighthouse, and scenic viewpoints. What else do you need? A camera and binoculars, to capture the beauty and to watch out for whale spouts. This is a popular whale-watching spot in the months of December and March. In fact, Ecola State Park, where the trail is located, takes it name from the Chinook word for "whale." While Tillamook Head Trail extends for eight miles point to point—which is part of the Oregon Coast Trail, not to mention the trail of choice for Lewis and Clark explorers—a great loop option starts from the Indian Creek parking lot. Look for the outhouse in the parking lot; the trailhead begins there with a handy map to show you what's in store. This well-marked and well-mapped trail leads to mind-blowing viewpoints, including an old military bunker viewpoint (great news for view-lovers, but not for height-haters) where you can see the Tillamook Rock Lighthouse, nicknamed "Terrible Tilly" for its exposure to harsh winds and storms. The breeze and white noise from the ocean provide a refreshing backdrop for this scenic trail.

User Groups: Hikers and dogs. No mountain bikes or horses are allowed. No wheelchair facilities.

Permits: Permits are not required. A $3 day-use fee is collected at the park entrance, or you can get an annual Oregon Parks and Recreation pass for $25; contact Oregon Parks and Recreation, 800/551-6949. Another option is to buy the Oregon Pacific Coast Passport, which is valid at 17 locations along the coast; it costs $35 for a year or $10 for a five-day pass and is available at local vendors or through the Oregon Parks and Recreation Department.

Maps: For a free park brochure and map, contact Oregon Parks and Recreation Department, 800/551-6949, www.oregonstateparks.org. For a topographic map, ask the USGS for Tillamook Head.

Directions: At the north end of Cannon Beach, follow signs for two miles to the park entrance. Drive through the park to the Indian Creek picnic area (closed in winter).

Contact: Oregon Parks and Recreation Department, 1115 Commercial Street Northeast, Salem, OR 97301, 800/551-6949, www.oregon stateparks.org.

🔳 SADDLE MOUNTAIN
6.0 mi/4.0 hrs

east of Seaside in Saddle Mountain State Natural Area

Map 7.2, page 344

When you're driving in on the windy road, you may wonder if you're headed directly to the summit, since it's such a long road—seven miles, to be exact. Suddenly, you'll round a bend and see it looming before you, a great craggy peak towering over the parking lot. It's an impressive sight, as are the many viewpoints along the way. The well-marked trailhead starts off with gentle switchbacks, but the final mile can be a little treacherous, with rocky crossings, so make sure your soles have traction—and your nerves are height-proof. There's just one, easy-to-navigate trail to the top of this 3,283-foot mountain, which is shaped like a saddle, hence the name. The trail can still be covered in snow through May, so it's best to check the weather beforehand. On a clear, sunny day, it offers one of the best views around of the Tillamook Forest and the coastal range.

User Groups: Hikers and dogs. No mountain bikes or horses are allowed. No wheelchair facilities.

Permits: Permits are not required. Parking and access are free.

Maps: For a free brochure and map, contact Oregon State Parks, 800/551-6949, www.oregonstateparks.org. For a topographic map, ask the USGS for Saddle Mountain.

Directions: From Portland, drive about 65 miles west on U.S. 26 (or 10 miles east from Seaside) and turn north at the Saddle Mountain State Park road sign. Drive seven miles to the trailhead.

Contact: Oregon Parks and Recreation Department, 1115 Commercial Street Northeast, Salem, OR 97301, 800/551-6949, www.oregon stateparks.org.

🔳 NEAHKAHNIE MOUNTAIN
3 mi/1.5 hrs

in Oswald West State Park on the north coast

Map 7.2, page 344

If you're hiking with a canine companion who stops to paw and sniff at the ground, take a closer look: You may have happened upon the buried treasure that local legend claims is hidden on this mountain (just make sure to reward your buddy with a nice jeweled collar or something). But be careful, because it's also rumored to be haunted by the ghosts of shipwrecked Spanish pirates who guard their lost treasure, and you know how testy Spanish pirates can get! The name of this popular mountain means "home of the Gods," and on your hike you'll wonder whether you're going straight to the heavens—not only because of the steep ascent, but because of the ocean views that await you at the top. Keep in mind that it's easy to miss the summit when you reach it; if you find yourself starting to go downhill, you've gone too far. Instead, look up to find the rocky summit that you'll need to scramble (it's worth it for the views). Return the way you came once you bag the peak—and if you find yourself sans treasure, pick a few treasures of your own: Thimbleberries, tasty morsels when they're in season (mid-July to late August), line the route. Stick around for some excellent beachside walks as well (before you go, pick up a brochure for trail maps). For a longer hike, you can start on the Oregon Coast Trail (for seven miles round trip) from the campground at Oswald West State Park.

User Groups: Hikers and dogs. No horses or mountain bikes are allowed. No wheelchair access.

Permits: Permits are not required. Parking and access are free.

Maps: For a free Oswald West State Park brochure and trail map, contact Oregon Parks and Recreation Department, 800/551-6949, www.oregonstateparks.org. For a topographic map, ask the USGS for Arch Cape and Nehalem.

Directions: From Cannon Beach, drive 10 miles south on U.S. 101 to Oswald West State Park. Drive past the park, and between mile markers 41 and 42, turn left (east) onto gravel Road 38555 and drive .4 mile to the trailhead. Park on the side of the road, and look for the brown trail sign on the left side of the road. For a shuttle hike or the longer option, park in Oswald West State Park campground parking lot and start your hike on the Oregon Coast Trail.

Contact: Oregon Parks and Recreation Department, 1115 Commercial Street Northeast, Salem, OR 97301, 800/551-6949, www.oregon stateparks.org.

5 KINGS MOUNTAIN
5.0 mi/3.5 hrs

in Tillamook State Forest north of Highway 6

Map 7.2, page 344

Like neighboring Elk Mountain, this 3,226-foot peak is a rocky adventure. You'll gain 2,700 feet on your way up to a great scenic view of the coastal range (and even Mount Hood on a clear day), but you have to work to get there. Be careful on your way up, as the

route is rocky and steep, and can be snow-covered through May. If you think you have it bad, here are some facts to ponder to take your mind off your aching legs: The Tillamook Forest went through a run of bad luck from the 1930s through the 1950s, when a series of logging fires decimated trees within a combined total area of 355,000 acres, enough timber to build one million five-room homes. Today, the second-growth forest shows barely any signs of the destruction, thanks to the determined efforts of the locals, who went on a planting frenzy, armed with 72 million seedlings (don't mess with Oregonians and their trees!). If the climb isn't enough of a challenge for you, you can combine this trail with Elk Mountain summit for a loop hike (see the Elk Mountain listing for directions).

User Groups: Hikers and dogs. No mountain bikes or horses are allowed. No wheelchair access.

Permits: Permits are not required. Parking and access are free.

Maps: For a Tillamook Forest Visitor Map & Guide, contact the Forest Grove District Office, 503/357-2191, www.odf.state.or.us/tsf. For a topographic map, ask the USGS for Rogers Peak.

Directions: From Portland, drive 42 miles west on U.S. 26 and Highway 6 to the trailhead and parking area near milepost 25, on the right (north) side of the road.

Contact: Tillamook State Forest, Forest Grove District Office, 801 Gales Creek Road, Forest Grove, OR 97116, 503/357-2191, www.odf.state.or. us/tsf.

6 ELK MOUNTAIN
3.0 mi/2.5 hrs

in Tillamook State Forest north of Highway 6

Map 7.2, page 344

Why trudge up miles and miles of switchbacks slowly inching their way up to the summit? This trail doesn't mess around; instead, it cuts a path 1.5 miles directly up to the 2,788-

foot peak. Or at least it will feel this way when you're climbing it. Bring along some gloves for this one, as you'll be scrambling up plenty of rocks on the steep ascent. It's not for the faint of heart—or of leg muscle—but at least it gets you to your destination faster, with plenty of gorgeous views of the Tillamook Forest and surrounding coastal mountains. Head back the way you came for a steep but relatively short descent. This trail can also be combined with Kings Mountain for a tough 11.5-mile loop by continuing past the summit of Elk Mountain to the junction with Kings Mountain Trail (take a left at the junction). Descend Kings Mountain, continuing until you nearly reach the trailhead, and take a left onto the 3.5-mile Wilson River Trail back to the Elk Mountain trailhead.

User Groups: Hikers and dogs. Mountain bikes and horses are not allowed. No wheelchair facilities.

Permits: Permits are not required. Parking and access are free.

Maps: For a Tillamook Forest Visitor Map & Guide, contact the Forest Grove District Office, 503/357-2191, www.odf.state.or.us/tsf. For a topographic map, ask the USGS for Cochran.

Directions: From Portland, drive 44 miles west on U.S. 26 and Highway 6 to the Elk Creek Campground, near milepost 28. Parking and the trailhead are on the right (north) side of the road.

Contact: Tillamook State Forest, Forest Grove District Office, 801 Gales Creek Road, Forest Grove, OR 97116, 503/357-2191, www.odf.state.or.us/tsf.

7 GALES CREEK
4.0 mi/2.0 hrs

in Tillamook State Forest north of Highway 6

Map 7.2, page 344

The initial descent isn't exactly knee-friendly, but Gales Creek makes up for it by being convenient and straightforward (read: no heavy-duty navigation is required). After the short but steep downhill trek to the creek bed, it's a

pleasant stroll through a surreal mixture of ferns and tall Douglas firs, making you feel as if you've just stepped onto a movie set. You might share the trail with mountain bikers, who like the screaming descent and twisty trail, so keep your head up. Pack a lunch to enjoy when you hit the campground, where picnic tables line the creek. Head back the way you came for a pleasant but heart rate-raising hike back up to your car. To make a loop (6.5 miles total from the trailhead), continue past the campground for almost a mile, turn left on Storey Burn Trail at the T-junction, and continue to the Storey Burn Road, turning left to hike two miles back to the car on the gravel road.

User Groups: Hikers, dogs, and mountain bikes. Horses allowed only on Storey Burn Trail. No wheelchair facilities.

Permits: Permits are not required. Parking and access are free.

Maps: For a Tillamook Forest Visitor Map & Guide, contact the Forest Grove District Office, 503/357-2191, www.odf.state.or.us/tsf. For a topographic map, ask the USGS for Timber and Cochran.

Directions: From Portland, drive 39 miles west on U.S. 26 and Highway 6 to the Gales Creek trailhead signpost and parking area near milepost 33, on the right (north) side of the highway.

Contact: Tillamook State Forest, Forest Grove District Office, 801 Gales Creek Road, Forest Grove, OR 97116, 503/357-2191, www.odf.state.or.us/tsf.

8 BANKS-VERNONIA STATE TRAIL
2.0–21.0 mi one-way/ 1.0 hr–1.0 day

between the towns of Banks and Vernonia off Highway 47

Map 7.2, page 344

If you're tired of the old switchback routine up a never-ending slope and just want to lose yourself in nature without, well, getting *lost,* this old Rails to Trails hike is calling your name (well, not literally—that would be creepy, but you know what I mean). The old railway trail was the first linear state park in Oregon, and what it may lack in scenery it makes up for in a feeling of Serenity Now, as you pass through meadows, past streams, and over bridges. Although it starts in Vernonia, where the path offers a paved portion for hikers and cyclists, and a separate gravel path for horses, another popular setting-off point is Buxton, where you can walk over the train trestle. There are also three other parking spots along the way, so pick your pleasure. Wherever you start, you can be sure of a peaceful stroll; even when others are around, the wide path makes room for everyone, so you're not bumping elbows with other peace-seekers.

User Groups: Hikers, mountain bikes, horses, and dogs. Wheelchair facilities at the paved portions and parks.

Permits: Permits are not required. Parking and access are free.

Maps: For a free trail map and brochure, contact Oregon State Parks, 800/551-6949. For a topographic map, ask the USGS for Vernonia and Buxton.

Directions: From Portland, drive approximately 28 miles west on U.S. 26 to Banks and turn right on Highway 47. Several trailheads line this route, all directly off Highway 47: Banks, Manning (4 miles from Banks), Buxton (6 miles from Banks), Top Hill (12 miles from Banks), and Beaver Creek (16 miles from Banks). The northern section is located at Anderson Park in Vernonia, 20 miles from Banks, off Highway 47.

Contact: Oregon Parks and Recreation Department, 1115 Commercial Street Northeast, Salem, OR 97301, 800/551-6949, www.oregonstateparks.org.

9 HAGG LAKE LOOP
15.4 mi/7.5 hrs

south of Forest Grove off Highway 47

Map 7.2, page 344

This lakeside trail is popular with Portland-area triathletes, who take advantage of the three types of training terrain: swimming in the lake,

running on the trail, and biking the paved bike route surrounding the lake. In fact, many running, biking, and triathlon races are held at this lake, so it's a good idea to check ahead of time to make sure the schedule is clear (unless spectating sweaty bodies is your thing). The 15.4-mile loop is popular with mountain bikers, so keep your eye out for two-wheeled types, and keep your pets on a leash. Throughout the lake loop, you get a change of scenery almost every time you round a bend—from open wildflower meadows to old-growth forest. For those who don't like to navigate much on their hike, you'll like this one because it's practically impossible to get lost since it parallels the surrounding paved road the whole time. Although it's a quick getaway for those who live nearby, it can get a bit crowded with all the different types of users (it's also popular for fishing and boating). Also, steer clear on a day after a big rain, when it can be a sogfest here, especially in the spring and fall. Occasional washouts on the path mean you'll have to sometimes walk on the road.

User Groups: Hikers, dogs, and mountain bikes. Horses are not allowed. There is wheelchair access at the boat ramps and picnic areas.

Permits: Permits are not required. A $5 day-use fee is collected at the park entrance.

Maps: For a map, contact Washington County Facilities Management, 169 North 1st Avenue, MS 42, Hillsboro, OR 97124. For a topographic map, ask the USGS for Gaston.

Directions: From Portland, drive about 20 miles west on Highway 26 to Forest Grove Exit/Glencoe Road, following Glencoe Road/Highway 8 for five miles into Hillsboro. From Hillsboro, turn left (south) onto Highway 47, and drive 5.9 miles to the yellow flashing light and signs for Hagg Lake/Scoggins Valley Park. Turn right and drive 3.7 miles to the park entrance. There is no official trailhead, so you can park at any of the three boat ramps or two picnic areas surrounding the lake.

Contact: Washington County Facilities Management, 169 North 1st Avenue, MS 42, Hillsboro, OR 97123, 503/359-5732 (for trail and weather conditions) or 503/846-8715 (for all other questions).

10 CAPE MEARES
0.5–4.0 mi/0.5–2.0 hrs

northwest of Tillamook in Cape Meares State Park

Map 7.2, page 344

This area's trails offer a taste of everything—a lighthouse, a giant tree, tidbits on local wildlife, and great views. Plaques line the route, helping hikers spot different seabirds on the nearby Three Arches Rocks, where common murres and tufted puffins like to rest their little feet. The area is a conglomeration of mini-hikes, so here's a guide: At the park entrance, you can pick up a short trail to a big spruce—you'll know it when you come across, well, a big spruce—and the beach. Then drive into the parking area, where you can visit the lighthouse. On your way back up the path, pick up Octopus Tree Trail, where you'll find a giant Sitka spruce appropriately called the "Octopus Tree" because its limbs extend out to form multiple trunks. Strong coastal winds sculpted its unusual shape. The Octopus Tree's base has a circumference of about 50 feet. If you want to walk farther, continue on the trail until you hit the road, then turn back the way you came.

User Groups: Hikers and dogs. No mountain bikes or horses are allowed. Parts of the paved trail are wheelchair accessible.

Permits: Permits are not required. Parking and access are free.

Maps: For a free park brochure, contact the Oregon Parks and Recreation Department, 800/551-6949, www.oregonstateparks.org. For a topographic map, ask the USGS for Netarts.

Directions: From U.S. 101 at Tillamook, drive 10 miles west on the Three Capes Scenic Highway to the park entrance, on the right side of the road. The first trailhead is at the front entrance, while the lighthouse and other trails are at the end of the road.

Contact: Oregon Parks and Recreation Department, 1115 Commercial Street Northeast,

Salem, OR 97301, 800/551-6949, www.oregon stateparks.org.

11 CAPE LOOKOUT
5.0 mi/3.0 hrs

southwest of Tillamook off U.S. 101

Map 7.2, page 344

On a scenic coast with views, views, and more views, it's hard to stand out from the crowd—and yet Cape Lookout does it well. You gotta admire a trail that doesn't mince words—Lookout Trail just says it like it is, plain and simple. The 2.4-mile trail travels through the forest down the length of the peninsula, where you'll be hit with a hard-to-beat southern view of the sea 400 feet below, and maybe even a whale or two. Along the way, you'll find a plaque that memorializes a plane crash site from the '40s. At the tip of the cape, you can rest on a bench that looks out over the sea—that is, if you get there on a not-so-crowded day, as it can get a smidge packed on a sunny weekend. And you'll be lucky if you see some rays, as Cape Lookout is the proud recipient of 100 inches of rain a year. Two other trails also take off from the parking area; one heads down to a secluded beach, the other to a campground, so if you have extra energy to burn, you can make a day out of it.

User Groups: Hikers and dogs. No mountain bikes or horses are allowed. No wheelchair facilities.

Permits: Permits are not required. A $3 day-use fee is collected at the park entrance, or you can get an annual Oregon Parks and Recreation pass for $25; contact Oregon Parks and Recreation, 800/551-6949. Another option is to buy the Oregon Pacific Coast Passport, which is valid at 17 locations along the coast; the cost is $35 for a year or $10 for a five-day pass. It is available at local vendors or through the Oregon Parks and Recreation Department.

Maps: For a free brochure, contact the Oregon Parks and Recreation Department, 800 /551-6949, www.oregonstateparks.org. For a topographic map, ask the USGS for Sand Lake.

Directions: From Tillamook, drive west on Three Capes Scenic Highway for 13 miles. The trailhead is on the right side of the road (2.5 miles past the campground).

Contact: Oregon Parks and Recreation Department, 1115 Commercial Street Northeast, Salem, OR 97301, 800/551-6949, www.oregon stateparks.org.

12 PIONEER-INDIAN TRAIL TO MOUNT HEBO

6.5 mi/4.0 hrs

between Tillamook and Lincoln City in Siuslaw National Forest

Map 7.2, page 344

This trail was the first developed transportation route between the Willamette and Tillamook Valleys. It travels through Sitka spruce (second-growth, courtesy of the infamous Tillamook Burn, which destroyed 355,000 acres of forest from the '30s through the '50s) and operates like a little nature museum, with plaques along the trail detailing fun facts about the area's plant life. Here's one: Did you know that braken fern, which lines the trail and can grow to five feet tall, is edible when it first sprouts in spring? Now you do. The trail markings are somewhat sporadic because new loop trails are currently under construction, so keep to the main trail. When you hit Road 14, turn right to take the side trip to the summit of 3,164-foot Mount Hebo. When you've had your fill of the view, head back the way you came for a 6.5-mile round-trip. (The full length of Pioneer-Indian Trail is eight miles one-way, so shoot for a turning-around point when you've had enough history and nature lessons.)

User Groups: Hikers, dogs, and horses. Mountain bikes are not allowed. No wheelchair facilities.

Permits: A federal Northwest Forest pass is required to park here; the cost is $5 for a day pass or $30 for an annual pass. You can buy a day pass at the trailhead, at ranger stations, through private vendors, or through Nature of the Northwest Information Center. Another option is to buy the Oregon Pacific Coast Passport, which is valid at 17 locations along the coast; the cost is $35 for a year or $10 for a five-day pass. It is available at local vendors or through the Oregon Parks and Recreation Department.

Maps: For a map of the Siuslaw National Forest, contact the Nature of the Northwest Information Center. For a topographic map, ask the USGS for Hebo and Niagara Creek.

Directions: From Tillamook, travel 20 miles south on Highway 101 to Hebo, and turn left (east) on Highway 22. Following signs to Hebo Lake, turn left on Highway 14 and continue four miles to the Hebo Lake Campground and the trailhead.

Contact: Siuslaw National Forest, Hebo Ranger District, 31525 Highway 22, Hebo, OR 97122, 503/392-3161.

13 HART'S COVE

5.4 mi/2.5 hrs

north of Lincoln City in Cascade Head Scenic Area

Map 7.2, page 344

Hart's Cove stands out from the crowd in many ways. Whereas most trails like to climb to a viewpoint, this spectacular cove isn't content to conform to the normal trail format. Instead, you'll encounter an original steep descent on the 2.7-mile journey down to the scenic spot. Rest up and take in the sweeping views of the ocean, a waterfall, and surrounding capes before climbing back through the spruce forest where you came from. Note: This trail is closed from January 1 to July 15.

User Groups: Hikers and dogs. No mountain bikes or horses are allowed.

Permits: Permits are not required. Parking and access are free.

Maps: For a map of the Siuslaw National Forest, contact the Nature of the Northwest Information Center. For a topographic map, ask the USGS for Neskowin.

Directions: From Lincoln City, drive north on U.S. 101 for six miles to Forest Service Road

1861. Turn left and drive four miles to the end of the road and the trailhead, on the left side of the road.

Contact: Siuslaw National Forest, Hebo Ranger District, 31525 Highway 22, Hebo, OR 97122, 503/392-3161.

14 CASCADE HEAD NATURE CONSERVANCY TRAIL

4.5–6.0 mi/2.0–4.0 hrs

North of Lincoln City in Cascade Head Scenic Area

Map 7.2, page 344

The Cascade Head Scenic Area is home to my favorite rare plant name: the hairy checkermallow. The "mallow," as we've nicknamed it, also shares digs with other rare species, like the Cascade Head catchfly and the Oregon silverspot butterfly. No wonder the Nature Conservancy has gotten their hands on this treasure trove of plants and wildlife; they like to gently remind hikers to keep their feet on the trail and their furry friends at home. Don't let the term "nature trail" mislead you into thinking this trail is a snap—you'll climb 1,200 feet on the 4.5-mile round-trip. The views are worth it as you wind your way along the grasslands to the top of the headland. Turn back at the unmarked upper viewpoint (you can also drive from the other side to hit the upper view for a one-mile level hike, but that's not as much fun, right?). Along with the good news comes the bad, though: While the lack of tree coverage means stellar views, this trail is best enjoyed on a day that is light in the wind category. Trust me.

Two other trails lead from this area: Hart's Cove (see listing in this chapter) and Cascade Head Trail, which runs six miles through rainforest from Falls Creek to Three Rocks Road.

User Groups: Hikers and horses. Dogs and mountain bikes are not allowed. No wheelchair facilities.

Permits: Permits are not required. Parking and access are free.

Maps: For a map of the Siuslaw National Forest, contact the Nature of the Northwest Information Center. For a topographic map, ask the USGS for Neskowin.

Directions: From Lincoln City, drive three miles north on U.S. 101 to Three Rocks Road. Turn left, drive two miles, and park at Knight Park. To reach Cascade Head Trail, turn right to a parking area and trailhead immediately after turning onto Three Rocks Road.

Contact: Siuslaw National Forest, Hebo Ranger District, 31525 Highway 22, Hebo, OR 97122, 503/392-3161.

15 YAQUINA HEAD LIGHTHOUSE

0.5–4.0 mi/0.5–2.0 hrs

north of Newport off U.S. 101

Map 7.3, page 345

Don't you hate it when you get to your hard-earned destination hoping to find a shiny plaque declaring that you've arrived, with maybe a few bits of trivia thrown in for good measure, and you find nothing? Well, you'll be in plaque heaven at Yaquina Head Lighthouse, and you won't have to hike far to reach one. This area includes a variety of trails. Choose among the tallest lighthouse in Oregon (complete with a 93-foot spiral staircase), a half-mile jaunt up to Salal Hill ("the big hill"), a stroll down to Cobble Beach (which, as the name suggests, is filled with naturally formed basalt cobbles), or Quarry Cove Trail to view the tidepools. With any destination you choose, you're guaranteed a good view and some facts to fill your head. This is also a hot spot for watching migrating whales. Harbor seals and common murres (which look like a beach version of penguins) take up residence on the rocks nearby.

User Groups: Hikers and mountain bikes. No dogs or horses are allowed. There is wheelchair access.

Permits: Permits are not required. There is a $5 parking fee collected at the park entrance, or you can get an annual Oregon Parks and Recreation pass for $25; contact Oregon Parks and Recreation, 800/551-6949. Another option is to buy the Oregon Pacific Coast Passport, which is valid at 17 locations along the coast; the cost is $35 for a year or $10 for a five-day pass. It is available at local vendors or through the Oregon Parks and Recreation Department.

Maps: For a brochure and map, contact the Bureau of Land Management, 541/574-3100. For a topographic map, ask the USGS for Newport North.

Directions: From Newport, drive two miles north on U.S. 101 to the park entrance. All the trailheads start from the parking area and are well marked and easy to find.

Contact: Bureau of Land Management, 1717 Fabry Road Southeast, Salem OR, 541/574-3100.

16 CAPE PERPETUA
1.0–6.25 mi/0.5–3.5 hrs

south of Yachats off U.S. 101

Map 7.3, page 345

Ten trails lead from Cape Perpetua Scenic Area, and the trail names don't mess around—they tell it like it is here. My favorite trail name is Trail of the Restless Waters, which leads to Devil's Churn, where waves crash across the rocks. Check the map (available at the visitors center) and take your pick. If you feel like a climb, try Cape Perpetua Trail to the summit—worth the 1.3-mile push. Once you're up there, wind your way around .25-mile Whispering Spruce Trail, which encircles the summit and offers great views from all sides of the neighboring capes and Heceta Head Lighthouse below. Once you head back down, a mile on Giant Spruce Trail leads to a hefty member of the spruce family (what did you expect, a giant fern?). Not enough? There's more, including the 6.25-mile Cummins Creek Loop and the one-mile Discovery Loop Trail.

User Groups: Hikers and dogs. No mountain bikes or horses are allowed. Part of Whispering Spruce Trail is wheelchair accessible.

Permits: A federal Northwest Forest pass is required to park here. The cost is $5 for a day pass or $30 for an annual pass. You can buy a day pass at the trailhead, at ranger stations, from private vendors, or through Nature of the Northwest Information Center. Another option is to buy the Oregon Pacific Coast Passport, which is valid at 17 locations along the coast; the cost is $35 for a year or $10 for a five-day pass and is available at local vendors or through the Oregon Parks and Recreation Department.

Maps: For a map of the Siuslaw National Forest, contact the Nature of the Northwest Information Center. For a topographic map, ask the USGS for Yachats.

Directions: From Waldport, drive 11 miles south on U.S. 101 to the Cape Perpetua Visitors Center parking area on the left (east) side of the road. All the well-marked trailheads start from this parking area.

Contact: Siuslaw National Forest, Waldport Ranger District, 1094 Southwest Pacific Highway, Waldport, OR 97394, 541/563-3211.

17 CARL WASHBURNE STATE PARK TO HECETA HEAD LIGHTHOUSE
6.0 mi/3.0 hrs

between Florence and Yachats off U.S. 101

Map 7.3, page 345

Washburne State Park is more of a jumping-off point than a destination in and of itself (no offense, Carl). One option is to start from the campground and head to the scenic lighthouse. First, park at the day-use area and then scurry across the road to the trailhead, on the right side of the campground entrance road. Take Valley Trail, a shady forested path, south along China Creek for a good change of pace from the windblown coast. Hikers can either do an out-and-back, or if you're someone who likes a destination hike, keep on keepin' on until the trail reaches the highway (just under two miles down), cross the highway, and take the steep climb on Heceta Head Trail to the lighthouse.

Heceta Head, shining proudly since 1894, boasts the brightest light on the coast. You can also drive directly to the lighthouse, but hey, this book is all about hiking, right? After checking out the view, you can head back the way you came or turn left on the interesting Hobbit Trail and walk down to the beach for scenery and an easy 1.5-mile stroll along the beach back to the day-use parking lot.

User Groups: Hikers, dogs, and horses. No mountain bikes are allowed. No wheelchair facilities.

Permits: Permits are not required. Parking and access are free.

Maps: For a free park brochure, contact Oregon State Parks, 800/551-6949, www.oregonstateparks.org. For a topographic map, ask the USGS for Heceta Head.

Directions: From Florence, drive 14 miles north on U.S. 101 to the day-use area of Washburne State Park, on the west side of the highway. Park here and cross the highway to the campground entrance. The Valley Trail trailhead is on the right side of the campground entrance road.

Contact: Oregon Parks and Recreation Department, 1115 Commercial Street Northeast, Salem, OR 97301, 800/551-6949.

18 CAPE MOUNTAIN
2.0 mi/1.0 hr

north of Florence in the Siuslaw National Forest

Map 7.3, page 345

History lovers, rejoice—Cape Mountain is the site of an old fire lookout built in 1932, and photos of what it used to look like await you on the summit. The vista is rarely crowded, so you'll probably get to enjoy the view of the ocean below all by yourself. Hikers who are directionally challenged will appreciate this trail, as it's got to be the best-marked trail in the entire state. However, first you have to find the trailhead, which, ironically, is hard to find. From the parking lot, look to the left of the restrooms, where a posted map will help you get your bear-

ings. You'll start off on the Princess Tasha trail, and then fork left to reach the summit, returning the way you came (all junctions are ridiculously well marked). This trail is actually made for horses, so keep an eye out for hooved creatures.

User Groups: Hikers, dogs, mountain bikes, and horses. No wheelchair facilities.

Permits: None required. Parking and access are free.

Maps: For a map of the Siuslaw National Forest, contact the Nature of the Northwest Information Center. For a topographic map, ask the USGS for Mercer Lake.

Directions: From Florence, drive seven miles north on U.S. 101 and turn right on Herman Peak Road. Drive three miles to Dry Lake parking area.

Contact: Siuslaw National Forest, Mapleton Ranger District, 4480 Highway 101, Building G, Florence, OR 97439, 541/902-8526.

19 SUTTON CREEK DUNES
5.0 mi/2.5 hrs

south of Florence off U.S. 101

Map 7.3, page 345

If you want to get some sand—and water—in your shoes, try the hike to Sutton Creek dunes. Choose from three loops along and in the dunes, for five miles total. Our suggestion: First, head up to the Holman Vista viewing deck (right by the parking area) to get your bearings, then try the longer three-mile loop, which starts at the parking area and follows Sutton Creek. Once you hit the campground, you'll have to ford the creek, so take your sandals along. The trail then enters the dunes, so prepare to add some sand to your wet shoes. If you're ready for more after you get back to your car, try one of the smaller one-mile loops or head to the beach to frolic in the sand (you'll have to ford the creek again, but by now you're a creek-crossing pro).

User Groups: Hikers, dogs, and horses. No mountain bikes allowed. The Holman Vista viewing deck is wheelchair accessible.

Permits: A federal Northwest Forest pass is required to park here. The cost is $5 for a day pass or $30 for an annual pass. You can buy a day pass at the trailhead, at ranger stations, from private vendors, or through Nature of the Northwest Information Center. Another option is to buy the Oregon Pacific Coast Passport, which is valid at 17 locations along the coast; the cost is $35 for a year or $10 for a five-day pass, and it is available at local vendors or through the Oregon Parks and Recreation Department.

Maps: For a map of the Siuslaw National Forest, contact the Nature of the Northwest Information Center. For a topographic map, ask the USGS for Mercer Lake.

Directions: From Florence, drive five miles north on U.S. 101 to Sutton Road. Turn left (west) and drive two miles to the end of the road. Park in the Holman Vista day-use area to find the well-marked trailheads.

Contact: Siuslaw National Forest, Mapleton Ranger District, 4480 Highway 101, Building G, Florence, OR 97439, 541/902-8526.

20 DRIFT CREEK FALLS
3.0 mi/1.5 hrs

south of Lincoln City in the Siuslaw National Forest

Map 7.4, page 346

As you drive on the 10-mile stretch of twisting road you may be muttering to yourself, "This better be worth it!" It is. Perhaps the most awe-inspiring part of Drift Creek Falls Trail is not the beautiful 75-foot waterfall, but the suspension bridge that hovers 100 feet over the creek (acrophobes would be wise to look straight ahead while crossing the 240-foot-long bridge). It is an exhilarating walk to the other side, where a tree trunk/picnic bench awaits. Have a seat for a stellar view of the waterfall and bridge.

User Groups: Hikers and dogs. No horses or mountain bikes allowed. No wheelchair facilities.

Permits: A federal Northwest Forest pass is required to park here. The cost is $5 for a day pass

or $30 for an annual pass. You can buy a day pass at the trailhead, at ranger stations, from private vendors, or through Nature of the Northwest Information Center. Another option is to buy the Oregon Pacific Coast Passport, which is valid at 17 locations along the coast; the cost is $35 for a year or $10 for a five-day pass, and it is available at local vendors or through the Oregon Parks and Recreation Department.

Maps: For a map of the Siuslaw National Forest, contact the Nature of the Northwest Information Center. For a topographic map, ask the USGS for Stott Mountain.

Directions: From Lincoln City, drive on U.S. 101 to the south edge of town and turn east onto Drift Creek Road (Road 17) for 10 miles to the small parking area and the well-marked trailhead.

Contact: Siuslaw National Forest, Hebo Ranger District, 31525 Highway 22, Hebo, OR 97122, 503/392-3161.

21 MARY'S PEAK
5.8–11.0 mi/3.0–6.0 hrs

west of Philomath in the Oregon Coastal Range

Map 7.4, page 346

There are two ways to get to the highest peak in the Coastal Range: East Ridge Trail (5.8 miles round-trip, gaining 1,500 feet in elevation) and North Ridge Trail (11 miles round-trip, gaining 2,300 feet). Okay, actually there's a third route to the summit—you can drive directly to it—but that's not much fun, now is it? Whatever route you choose, you end up at the top of the 4,097-foot peak with great views of Mount Hood, Mount Adams, Mount St. Helens, Mount Rainier, Sisters, and the college town of Corvallis (home of Oregon State University). You'll be sharing the view with many softer souls who have driven to the top, but you'll know you earned the view. Bask in the glory of a job well done—or try the two-mile Meadow Edge loop up top—before you head back down the route you came from.

User Groups: Hikers, dogs, mountain bikes,

and horses. The top of the summit is wheelchair accessible.

Permits: A federal Northwest Forest pass is required to park here. The cost is $5 for a day pass or $30 for an annual pass. You can buy a day pass at the trailhead, at ranger stations, from private vendors, or through Nature of the Northwest Information Center. Another option is to buy the Oregon Pacific Coast Passport, which is valid at 17 locations along the coast; the cost is $35 for a year or $10 for a five-day pass, and it is available at local vendors or through the Oregon Parks and Recreation Department.

Maps: For a map of the Siuslaw National Forest, contact the Nature of the Northwest Information Center. For a topographic map, ask the USGS for Mary's Peak and Alsea.

Directions: From Corvallis to the North Ridge trailhead, drive west on U.S. 20 through Philomath to the U.S. 34 junction. Continue on U.S. 20 about two miles to Woods Creek Road, drive six miles to the trailhead, and park at the side of the road. From Corvallis to the East Ridge trailhead, drive west on U.S. 20 through Philomath to the U.S. 34 junction. Drive west on U.S. 34 for nine miles, and turn right on Mary's Peak Road. The trailhead and small parking area are 5.5 miles in, on the right.

Contact: Siuslaw National Forest, Waldport Ranger District, 1094 Southwest Pacific Highway, Waldport, OR 97394, 541/563-3211.

22 SILTCOOS LAKE
4.0 mi/2.0 hrs

south of Florence in the Oregon Dunes National Recreation Area

Map 7.5, page 347

If you're one of those goal-oriented people who likes to have a destination when hiking, try this relatively easy stroll through the forest. Enjoy the trip out to the lake, because the lake itself is not the most scenic in the state. It's a shady trail through second-growth Sitka spruce and Douglas fir forest, and is refreshing on a hot day. About one mile in, the trail splits into

north and south routes, appropriately named North and South Trails, both of which end at the lake. Once you reach the lake, head back on the other trail to complete the loop. At the lake, there are five campsites where you can hang out for a picnic or simply rest your soles (the lake is also renowned for fishing).

User Groups: Hikers, dogs, and mountain bikes. No horses are allowed. No wheelchair facilities.

Permits: A federal Northwest Forest pass is required to park here. The cost is $5 for a day pass or $30 for an annual pass. You can buy a day pass at the trailhead, at ranger stations, from private vendors, or through Nature of the Northwest Information Center. Another option is to buy the Oregon Pacific Coast Passport, which is valid at 17 locations along the coast; the cost is $35 for a year or $10 for a five-day pass, and it is available at local vendors or through the Oregon Parks and Recreation Department.

Maps: For a map of the Siuslaw National Forest, contact the Nature of the Northwest Information Center. For a topographic map, ask the USGS for Goose Pasture, Florence, Tahkenitch Creek, and Fivemile Creek.

Directions: From Florence, drive seven miles south on U.S. 101 to the Siltcoos Lake sign on your left, and turn into the parking area and trailhead.

Contact: Oregon Dunes National Recreation Area, 855 Highway 101, Reedsport, OR 97467, 541/271-3611.

23 TAHKENITCH DUNES
6.0 mi/3.0 hrs

south of Florence in the Oregon Dunes National Recreation Area

Map 7.5, page 347

If you like a change of scenery while you hike, try this interesting loop: The first .5 mile is through a forest before you reach the sand, then it's another 1.5 mile through dunes to the water. Hang a left when you reach the ocean, and walk along the water for about a mile until you hit Threemile Lake Trail, which handily suggests its length: three miles. This trail travels past the freshwater Threemile Lake and offers up a few good vistas of the sea before slipping into a second-growth forest with spruce and ferns and heading back to the parking lot.

User Groups: Hikers, dogs, and horses. No mountain bikes allowed. No wheelchair facilities.

Permits: A federal Northwest Forest pass is required to park here. The cost is $5 for a day pass or $30 for an annual pass. You can buy a day pass at the trailhead, at ranger stations, from private vendors, or through Nature of the Northwest Information Center. Another option is to buy the Oregon Pacific Coast Passport, which is valid at 17 locations along the coast; the cost is $35 for a year or $10 for a five-day pass, and it is available at local vendors or through the Oregon Parks and Recreation Department.

Maps: For a map of the Oregon Dunes National Recreation Area, contact the Nature of the Northwest Information Center. For a topographic map, ask the USGS for Tahkenitch Creek.

Directions: From Reedsport, drive 7.5 miles north (or 12.5 miles south from Florence) on U.S. 101 to the Tahkenitch Lake Campground. Park in the day-use area and walk to the well-marked trailhead.

Contact: Oregon Dunes National Recreation Area, 855 Highway 101, Reedsport, OR 97467, 541/271-3611.

24 UMPQUA DUNES
5.0 mi/3.0 hrs

south of Reedsport in the Umpqua Dunes Scenic Area

Map 7.5, page 347

Have you ever wanted to get a picture of yourself in the middle of the desert, crawling on hands and knees with nothing in sight, but don't have the time or resources to high-tail it to the Sahara? Here's your chance (not that I've ever participated in such a silly display, you understand). The Oregon Dunes are a must-see area of the coastal region, and Umpqua Dunes is perhaps the most impressive of them all. Be prepared for sand in your shoes, because most of the six-mile trail is actually in the dunes. You'll

start off on a well-marked, .5-mile interpretive trail before you hit the sandy stuff. Now the fun begins. Using the ocean as your beacon, either climb up on the large dune to your left (you can't miss it) or keep just to the right of it, looking for the blue trail blazes in the distance. It's like a beach treasure hunt to find the next blue marker in the middle of what seems like a never-ending desert (now's your chance to snap the aforementioned picture). The trail leads to the beach and then returns the way it came.

User Groups: Hikers, dogs, and horses. Mountain bikes are not allowed. No wheelchair facilities.

Permits: A federal Northwest Forest pass is required to park here. The cost is $5 for a day pass or $30 for an annual pass. You can buy a day pass at the trailhead, at ranger stations, from private vendors, or through Nature of the Northwest Information Center. Another option is to buy the Oregon Pacific Coast Passport, which is valid at 17 locations along the coast; the cost is $35 for a year or $10 for a five-day pass, and it is available at local vendors or through the Oregon Parks and Recreation Department.

Maps: For a map of the Oregon Dunes National Recreation Area, contact the Nature of the Northwest Information Center. For a topographic map, ask the USGS for Lakeside.

Directions: From Reedsport, drive 10.5 miles south on U.S. 101 to the Umpqua Dunes Trail signpost. Turn west (right) into the parking area and the trailhead.

Contact: Oregon Dunes National Recreation Area, 855 Highway 101, Reedsport, OR 97467, 541/271-3611.

25 SUNSET BAY TO CAPE ARAGO
8.0 mi/4.0 hrs

west of Coos Bay between Sunset Bay State Park and Cape Arago

Map 7.5, page 347

You'll be kicking yourself if you didn't bring your camera on this hike. A four-mile stretch of the Oregon Coast Trail, this unique trail is a prime whale-watching spot. Sir Francis Drake first spotted this cape in the 1500s, and modern visitors have been flocking ever since. A fun fact: On October 4, 1973, the first transcontinental hot-air balloon crossing started from this spot. The balloonist landed a month later on Chesapeake Bay, on the East Coast. You don't need to reach magical heights to glimpse some great views of the water below, though— the cliffside path is filled with views the whole way. Starting from Sunset Bay, stroll for two miles to an observation deck, then continue south along the coast for stellar views of the cape, plus a sea lion viewpoint (you can hear their calls from the water below). You need to walk along the road for .5 mile at the southern end to reach Cape Arago, but it's well worth it, as another observation deck awaits. (For a shuttle hike, you can leave one car at the cape itself and another at Sunset Bay.)

User Groups: Hikers and dogs. No horses or mountain bikes are allowed.

Permits: Permits are not required. Parking and access are free.

Maps: For a free brochure, contact the Oregon Parks and Recreation Department at 800/551-6949. For a topographic map, ask the USGS for Charleston and Cape Arago.

Directions: From Coos Bay, drive south 12 miles on Cape Arago Highway, following signs to Sunset Bay State Park. Park in the day-use picnic area to the right; the trailhead is located to the right of the restrooms and is marked as the Oregon Coast Trail.

Contact: Oregon Parks and Recreation Department, 1115 Commercial Street Northeast, Salem, OR 97301, 800/551-6949, www.oregon stateparks.org.

26 CAPE BLANCO
2.6 mi/1.5 hrs

northwest of Port Orford in Cape Blanco State Park

Map 7.6, page 348

With a campground on the premises, including four beachside log cabins, you can while

away an entire weekend at Cape Blanco State Park. Cape Blanco is the westernmost point of Oregon, and its lighthouse has a few claims to fame: The oldest continuously operating lighthouse, it stands taller than any others on the coast, at 245 feet. There are a few short trails (less than .5 mile) that take you to the lighthouse or along the beach, but we've chosen to spotlight the Hughes House trail. This 2.6-mile round-trip leads to an 11-room historic house built in 1898 that you can tour. (Visitors can also drive directly to the house, open Thursday through Monday, 10 A.M. to 3:30 P.M. from April to October). After touring the house, return the way you came and explore the great views of the beach, or head to the lighthouse.

User Groups: Hikers and dogs. Mountain bikes are allowed only on roads. Horses are allowed only on designated horse trails. There is wheelchair access on paved portions.

Permits: Permits are not required. Parking and access are free.

Maps: For a free map, contact Oregon Parks and Recreation Department, 800/551-6949, www.oregonstateparks.org. For a topographic map, ask the USGS for Cape Blanco.

Directions: From Port Orford, drive four miles north on U.S. 101 and turn left (west) onto Cape Blanco Highway. Drive five miles and park at the lighthouse entrance parking area, where the trails start. For the Hughes House Trail, backtrack along the road; the trailhead is on the left (north) side of the road, roughly .2 mile down.

Contact: Oregon Parks and Recreation Department, 1115 Commercial Street Northeast, Salem, OR 97301, 800/551-6949, www.oregon stateparks.org.

27 HUMBUG MOUNTAIN
5.5 mi/2.5 hrs

south of Port Orford off U.S. 101

Map 7.6, page 348

If you want to enjoy this trail with elbow room, get there early, as the parking lot quickly fills up on a sunny weekend day—especially since there's a campground nearby. From the conveniently located trailhead right off Highway 101, you'll quickly leave the traffic noise behind as you start your ascent; suddenly you'll round a bend and find yourself in the middle of the fern and Douglas fir forest, serenaded by birdsong and the rushing creek below. Although we like the fact that every .5 mile is marked, it can also evoke feelings of "what, we've only gone a half mile?" because the trail gains over 1,700 feet in elevation. Catch your breath at a bench and look out over at Cape Blanco to the north. After a mile, the trail splits: The steeper West Trail tops out at the summit in 1.5 miles, while East Trail takes its time, reaching the top in 2 miles. Take your pick, then choose the other trail for the return trip. At the top, a short trail leads to a bench facing south, a prime place to enjoy a picnic. Although there's a clearing where you can view the ocean in the distance, trees partially block the full view.

User Groups: Hikers and dogs. No mountain bikes or horses are allowed. No wheelchair access.

Permits: Permits are not required. Parking and access are free.

Maps: For a free map, contact Oregon Parks and Recreation Department, 800/551-6949, www.oregonstateparks.org. For a topographic map, ask the USGS for Port Orford.

Directions: From Port Orford, drive six miles south on U.S. 101. The parking area and trailhead are on the right side of the highway.

Contact: Oregon Parks and Recreation Department, 1115 Commercial Street Northeast, Salem, OR 97301, 800/551-6949, www.oregon stateparks.org.

28 BARKLOW MOUNTAIN TRAIL
2.0 mi/1.0 hr

northeast of Gold Beach in the Siskiyou National Forest

Map 7.6, page 348

Attention to those of you who love off-road adventuring: Here's your chance to test your tires, brakes, obstacle-maneuvering skills—and your new paint job. If you're the type who winces at

each and every bump in the road ("Ack, did I just lose my muffler?"), you may want to skip this trail. But once you've reached your destination, you'll most likely be able to enjoy the scenery solo. After you've unclenched your fingers from the steering wheel and done a quick once-over to make sure your car is still intact, start on the trailhead. You can choose between a lookout site to the right or travel to the left toward a deserted Forest Service shelter. Try the old fire lookout first, which takes you to the highest point on 3,579-foot Barklow Mountain for views of the Siskiyou mountain range. Then return back to the junction and head across a slope, where you can revel in more peaceful views before heading into the forest to the shelter, where old relics remain. The trail is short and sweet, but it's perfect if you like peace and quiet and believe that "part of the fun is getting there."

User Groups: Hikers and dogs. No mountain bikes or horses are allowed. No wheelchair facilities.

Permits: Permits are not required. Parking and access are free.

Maps: For a map of the Siskiyou National Forest, contact the Nature of the Northwest Information Center. For a topographic map, ask the USGS for Barklow Mountain.

Directions: From Port Orford, turn right (east) onto Elk River Road. Drive on Highway 208 for 18.8 miles, then turn right onto Forest Service Road 5325. Continue nine miles and turn left onto Forest Service Road 3353. After 9.5 miles, turn left on bumpy, dirt Spur Road 220 and go one mile to the end of the road and the trailhead.

Contact: Siskiyou National Forest, Powers Ranger District, Powers, OR 97466, 541/439-3011.

29 CAPE SEBASTIAN
3.0 mi/1.0 hr

south of Gold Beach off U.S. 101

Map 7.6, page 348

You don't even need to get out of your car

to witness the picture-perfect scenery of Cape Sebastian, since the parking lot sits 200 feet above sea level. The 1.5-mile trail starts from the south parking lot, turning from a paved walkway into a path through Sitka spruce forest, ending at the cape's edge. You'll want to linger here, and the Oregon State Parks Department has read your mind: Plenty of benches line the path, so you can take your time strolling the area and lining up that perfect shot. Bring warm clothes, because the wind can take the temperature down several notches, even on a sunny day. Another packing must: binoculars. The views extend 50 miles north to Humbug Mountain and 50 miles south to Crescent City, California and the Point Saint George lighthouse.

User Groups: Hikers, dogs, and mountain bikes. No horses are allowed. The first section of the trail is paved for wheelchair access.

Permits: Permits are not required. Parking and access are free.

Maps: For a topographic map, ask the USGS for Cape Sebastian.

Directions: From Gold Beach, drive 4.5 miles south on U.S. 101 to the park entrance on the right (west) side of the highway. Drive .5 mile to the south parking lot.

Contact: Oregon Parks and Recreation Department, 1115 Commercial Street Northeast, Salem, OR 97301, 800/551-6949, www.oregon stateparks.org.

30 SNOW CAMP LOOKOUT
7.0 mi/3.5 hrs

northeast of Brookings in the Kalmiopsis Wilderness of Siskiyou National Forest

Map 7.6, page 348

This popular lookout cabin, perched 4,223 feet on Snow Camp Mountain, was unfortunately destroyed in the 2002 Biscuit Fire (plans are currently under way to rebuild it as a rental cabin). The good news is, the views remain, as does the steep climb to get here. The trail first gives you a break by descending into the Windy Valley meadow, where you cross the stream. Then the

real climbing begins, a steep 1,500-foot hoof up to the mountain, where you can see remnants of the lookout cabin. As with all trails affected by the fire, it's a good idea to check with the Forest Service for current conditions.

User Groups: Hikers, dogs, and horses. No mountain bikes are allowed. No wheelchair access.

Permits: A federal Northwest Forest pass is required to park here. The cost is $5 for a day pass or $30 for an annual pass. You can buy a day pass at ranger stations, from private vendors, or through Nature of the Northwest Information Center.

Maps: For a map of the Siskiyou National Forest, contact the Nature of the Northwest Information Center. For a topographic map, ask the USGS for Collier Butte.

Directions: From Brookings, drive east on County Road 784 (marked as Constitution Avenue) for 16 miles (it becomes Forest Service Road 1376 at the forest boundary). Turn left at the T-junction to continue on gravel Road 1376 for 14.5 miles. The trailhead and parking are on the left side of the road.

Contact: Siskiyou National Forest, Chetco Ranger District, P.O. Box 4580, 539 Chetco Avenue, Brookings, OR 97415, 541/412-6000.

31 MISLATNAH TRAIL
6.6 mi/3.5 hrs

northeast of Brookings in the Kalmiopsis Wilderness of Siskiyou National Forest

Map 7.6, page 348

Mislatnah Trail, sharing Tincup Trail for more than a mile, starts off as a gentle descent to Mislatnah Creek. Then it says "later" to Tincup (take the left junction) to climb to 3,124-foot Mislatnah Peak, where great views from the former lookout site await and the trail ends. Look out over the deep canyons of the Big Craggies Botanical Area, the only view of the area that is accessible by trail. You'll have to ford the creek, and, as water levels can get high in the winter and early spring, it's best to tackle this one in the late spring or summer. As this trail is within the 2002 Biscuit Fire region, it's a good idea to check current conditions before you head out.

User Groups: Hikers, dogs, and horses. No mountain bikes are allowed. No wheelchair access.

Permits: A federal Northwest Forest pass is required to park here. The cost is $5 for a day pass or $30 for an annual pass. You can buy a day pass at the trailhead, at ranger stations, from private vendors, or through Nature of the Northwest Information Center.

Maps: For a map of the Siskiyou National Forest, contact the Nature of the Northwest Information Center. For a topographic map, ask the USGS for Big Craggies.

Directions: From Brookings, drive 25.3 miles on County Road 784 (marked as Constitution Avenue in town), which becomes Forest Service Road 1376 at the forest boundary to the junction with Forest Service Road 360. Turn right on 360 and drive 1.5 miles to Forest Service Road 365. Turn right and drive .8 mile to the end of the road and the trailhead.

Contact: Siskiyou National Forest, Chetco Ranger District, P.O. Box 4580, 539 Chetco Avenue, Brookings, OR 97415, 541/412-6000.

32 TINCUP TRAIL
19.4 mi/1.0–2.0 days

northeast of Brookings in the Kalmiopsis Wilderness of Siskiyou National Forest

Map 7.6, page 348

Don't you hate it when you've hiked for miles and finally feel like you're in the middle of nowhere, only to come across a Boy Scout troop who just hiked in one mile from a road nearby? Well, that won't happen when you do Tincup Trail, because it leads into the edge of the Kalmiopsis Wilderness, where no other trails connect to it. It's best to try this in the late spring and summer, because you have to ford Mislatnah Creek, a tributary of the Chetco River, and the water level can't be safely crossed during the winter and early spring. The trail starts off above the water and dips down to a ford of the creek, then follows the Wild and Scenic portions of the Chetco River.

Since this trail is in the 2002 Biscuit Fire region, it's a good idea to check conditions beforehand.

User Groups: Hikers, dogs, and horses. No mountain bikes are allowed. No wheelchair access.

Permits: A federal Northwest Forest pass is required to park here. The cost is $5 for a day pass or $30 for an annual pass. You can buy a day pass at the trailhead, at ranger stations, from private vendors, or through Nature of the Northwest Information Center.

Maps: For a map of the Siskiyou National Forest, contact the Nature of the Northwest Information Center. For a topographic map, ask the USGS for Big Craggies.

Directions: From Brookings, drive 25.3 miles on County Road 784 (marked as Constitution Avenue in town), which becomes Forest Service Road 1376 at the forest boundary to the junction with Forest Service Road 360. Turn right on 360 and drive 1.5 miles to Forest Service Road 365. Turn right and drive .8 mile to the end of the road and the trailhead.

Contact: Siskiyou National Forest, Chetco Ranger District, P.O. Box 4580, 539 Chetco Avenue, Brookings, OR 97415, 541/412-6000.

33 JOHNSON BUTTE
12.6 mi/6.5 hrs

northeast of Brookings in the Kalmiopsis Wilderness of Siskiyou National Forest

Map 7.6, page 348

May and June are the best months to hike this scenic ridgeline trail, when the pink, saucer-shaped Kalmiopsis (pronounced kal-mee-OP-sis) plant is in bloom, the namesake of this wilderness area. The trail starts on an abandoned road for the first two miles, then passes two small lakes—Salamander and Valen Lakes—before ending at the junction with the Chetco trail system. This trail was affected by the 2002 Biscuit Fire, so you may have to cross some downed tree trunks. As with all trails affected by the fire, it's a good idea to check with the Forest Service beforehand for up-to-date conditions.

User Groups: Hikers, dogs, and horses. No mountain bikes are allowed. No wheelchair access.

Permits: A federal Northwest Forest pass is required to park here. The cost is $5 for a day pass or $30 for an annual pass. You can buy a day pass at ranger stations, from private vendors, or through Nature of the Northwest Information Center.

Maps: For a map of the Siskiyou National Forest, contact the Nature of the Northwest Information Center. For a topographic map, ask the USGS for Chetco Peak and Tincup Peak.

Directions: From Brookings, drive east on County Road 784 (marked as Constitution Avenue) for 16 miles (it becomes Forest Service Road 1376 at the forest boundary). Turn right onto Forest Service Road 1909 and drive 13.4 miles, then turn left, continuing on Forest Service Road 1909 for 1.7 bumpy miles to the end of the road and the trailhead.

Contact: Siskiyou National Forest, Chetco Ranger District, P.O. Box 4580, 539 Chetco Avenue, Brookings, OR 97415, 541/412-6000.

34 VULCAN PEAK
2.2 mi/1.5 hrs

northeast of Brookings in the Kalmiopsis Wilderness of Siskiyou National Forest

Map 7.6, page 348

It's only 1.1 miles to the top of this 4,655-foot peak, but it's a steep and rocky climb that will leave you breathless at the top. Starting on an abandoned road, you'll soon fork left to hit the top. Stick around for a while, because the views are worth it (and you're likely to have them all to yourself). It's fitting that this is an old fire lookout: It's a perfect perch from which to view the pattern of the Biscuit Fire, which whipped through this area in 2002. Rest here before returning on the rocky descent back to your car.

User Groups: Hikers, dogs, and horses. No mountain bikes are allowed. No wheelchair facilities.

Permits: A federal Northwest Forest pass is required to park here. The cost is $5 for a day pass or $30 for an annual pass. You can buy a day pass at ranger stations, from private vendors, or through Nature of the Northwest Information Center.

Maps: For a map of the Siskiyou National Forest, contact the Nature of the Northwest Information Center. For a topographic map, ask the USGS for Chetco Peak.

Directions: From Brookings, drive east on County Road 784 (marked as Constitution Avenue) for 16 miles (it becomes Forest Service Road 1376 at the forest boundary). Turn right onto Forest Service Road 1909 and drive 13.4 miles, then turn right for less than .1 mile to the end of the road and the trailhead.

Contact: Siskiyou National Forest, Chetco Ranger District, P.O. Box 4580, 539 Chetco Avenue, Brookings, OR 97415, 541/412-6000.

35 VULCAN LAKE
2.8 mi/2.0 hrs

northeast of Brookings in the Kalmiopsis Wilderness of Siskiyou National Forest

Map 7.6, page 348

Desperately seeking solitude? Your search is over. The long, bumpy drive in practically guarantees that you will be on your own, or among only a brave few. The 2002 Biscuit Fire swept through this area, producing an interesting mix of burnt limbs and trunks coexisting peacefully with new and undamaged trees. The trail starts at an elevation of 3,750 feet, which means you'll have views galore as you hike. The path starts on a windswept hill, where you can glimpse the Siskiyou mountain range to the north, and then switchbacks up a hot and dusty trail to a fantastic lookout, where you can view the ocean to the west in the distance. Make sure to watch your step as you take in the view: You'll most likely be hopping over a burnt trunk or three, and the path also has some rocky portions. Keep on truckin', the best is yet to come. Rounding a bend, you'll have yet another view, this time of Little Vulcan Lake and Vulcan Lake, glistening in the sun. The trail descends from here to Vulcan Lake. Stick around to enjoy the solitude before you retrace your steps.

User Groups: Hikers and dogs. No mountain bikes or horses are allowed. No wheelchair access.

Permits: A federal Northwest Forest pass is required to park here. The cost is $5 for a day pass or $30 for an annual pass. You can buy a day pass at the trailhead, at ranger stations, from private vendors, or through Nature of the Northwest Information Center.

Maps: For a map of the Siskiyou National Forest, contact the Nature of the Northwest Information Center. For a topographic map, ask the USGS for Chetco Peak.

Directions: From Brookings, drive east on County Road 784 (marked as Constitution Avenue) for 16 miles (it becomes Forest Service Road 1376 at the forest boundary). Turn right onto Forest Service Road 1909 and drive 13.4 miles, then turn left, continuing on Forest Service Road 1909 for 1.7 bumpy miles to the end of the road and the trailhead.

Contact: Siskiyou National Forest, Chetco Ranger District, P.O. Box 4580, 539 Chetco Avenue, Brookings, OR 97415, 541/412-6000.

36 REDWOOD NATURE LOOP
1.2 mi/0.5 hr

northeast of Brookings in Siskiyou National Forest

Map 7.6, page 348

You don't need to head south to Oregon's neighboring state to see these famous trees—we've got a few of our own to show off. This flat, well-marked loop is lined with interpretive signs (pick up a brochure at the trailhead) so you'll know what you're looking at. Old-growth redwoods up to 250 feet tall and 10 feet in diameter join forces with Oregon staples such as Douglas fir, bigleaf maple, Oregon myrtle, and red alder to make you feel like you're walking through a tree museum. This is a great one for kids, or for those who have always wondered how to tell the difference between a fir and a pine.

User Groups: Hikers and dogs. No mountain bikes or horses are allowed. No wheelchair access.

Permits: A federal Northwest Forest pass is required to park here. The cost is $5 for a day pass or $30 for an annual pass. You can buy a day pass at the trailhead, at ranger stations, from private vendors, or through Nature of the Northwest Information Center.

Maps: For a map of the Siskiyou National Forest, contact the Nature of the Northwest Information Center. For a topographic map, ask the USGS for Mount Emily.

Directions: From Brookings, drive east on County Road 784 (marked as Constitution Avenue). Continue 8.1 miles; parking and the trailhead are on the left (north) side of the road.

Contact: Siskiyou National Forest, Chetco Ranger District, P.O. Box 4580, 539 Chetco Avenue, Brookings, OR 97415, 541/412-6000.

37 OREGON REDWOODS TRAIL
1.6 mi/1.0 hr

southeast of Brookings in Siskiyou National Forest

Map 7.6, page 348

Hey, who says California has all the big guys? Redwoods are alive and well in southern Oregon, too, but there are only a couple places to view them (see also the Redwood Nature Loop listing in this chapter). In fact, the Siskiyou National Forest has a monopoly on these giants, hosting the only redwoods in the Pacific Northwest. This trail starts out flat and easy, complete with a .8-mile wheelchair-accessible loop. The trail is 1.2 miles one-way, but for an interesting return journey, try the barrier-free route on the return trip for a 1.6-mile loop. Bring your camera; you'll want to get a pic of your hiking partner in the hollowed-out redwoods on this gentle route.

User Groups: Hikers and dogs. No mountain bikes or horses are allowed. This trail includes a wheelchair-accessible loop.

Permits: A federal Northwest Forest pass is

required to park here. The cost is $5 for a day pass or $30 for an annual pass. You can buy a day pass at the trailhead, at ranger stations, from private vendors, or through Nature of the Northwest Information Center.

Maps: For a map of the Siskiyou National Forest, contact the Nature of the Northwest Information Center. For a topographic map, ask the USGS for Mount Emily.

Directions: From Brookings, drive five miles south on U.S. 101 and turn left on Winchuck Road. Drive 1.5 miles, then turn right on Peavine Ridge Road and drive 4.1 miles to the end of the road and the trailhead.

Contact: Siskiyou National Forest, Chetco Ranger District, P.O. Box 4580, 539 Chetco Avenue, Brookings, OR 97415, 541/412-6000.

38 ELK CREEK FALLS AND BIG TREE
2.6 mi/1.5 hrs

northeast of Gold Beach in Siskiyou National Forest

Map 7.7, page 349

Two short and aptly named trails lead from this trailhead, Elk Creek Falls and Big Tree. For a short and sweet hike to a scenic falls, hit the left trail first for the .2-mile round-trip. Back at the trailhead, take the right trail for a pleasant climb through a lush fern forest as you seek out the largest Port Orford cedar in the world. The trail will seem longer than its 1.2 miles, and at every turn the trees get bigger and bigger. But those are only the bridesmaids—the bride stands tall at 219 feet, measuring in at over 12 feet in diameter. Our favorite part is a viewing platform, made solely so you can behold the Big Tree.

User Groups: Hikers and dogs. No mountain bikes or horses allowed. No wheelchair access.

Permits: Permits are not required. Parking and access are free.

Maps: For a map of the Siskiyou National Forest, contact the Nature of the Northwest Information Center. For a topographic map, ask the USGS for China Flat.

Directions: From Powers, drive south for six miles on Powers South Road/Highway 90 (which turns into Highway 33); the trailhead is 1.7 miles after entering Highway 33. The trailhead and parking area are on the left (east) side of the highway.

Contact: Siskiyou National Forest, Powers Ranger District, Powers, OR 97466, 541/439-3011.

39 PANTHER RIDGE/ HANGING ROCK
14.4 mi/8.0 hrs

northeast of Gold Beach in Siskiyou National Forest

Map 7.7, page 349

Solitude-seekers will enjoy this trail, as it's a long and winding—though thankfully paved—drive up to the ridge. Although the trail is 7.2 miles one-way, one of the highlights is majestic Hanging Rock, roughly two miles in. The rest of the trail is not nearly so scenic, so you may want to call it a day after hitting this giant boulder situated on top of a sheer cliff. Height-lovers who dare take a peek below will be rewarded with a superb view of Eden Valley and the distant Rogue River Canyon. This is definitely one of those "I was here!" moments that cameras are made for.

User Groups: Hikers and dogs. No mountain bikes or horses are allowed. No wheelchair access.

Permits: Permits are not required. Parking and access are free.

Maps: For a map of the Siskiyou National Forest, contact the Nature of the Northwest Information Center. For a topographic map, ask the USGS for Eden Valley, Illahe, and Marial.

Directions: From Powers, drive south on Forest Service Road 33 for 12.2 miles to paved Forest Service Road 3348, then turn left. Drive nine miles to Forest Service Road 5520 (ignore the first sign for 5520), turn right and continue 1.1 miles, then turn left onto Spur Road 230 and go .5 mile to the end of the road and the trailhead.

Contact: Siskiyou National Forest, Powers Ranger District, Powers, OR 97466, 541/439-3011.

40 MOUNT BOLIVAR
2.8 mi/2.0 hrs

south of Powers in Siskiyou National Forest

Map 7.7, page 349

If you're the type who likes to see where you're going, you'll appreciate Mount Bolivar. From the trailhead, you can glimpse your destination, so you can use it as a beacon as you start your ascent. As with many of this area's hikes, you'll feel as if you're getting away from it all as you trudge through the old-growth timber and scrub oak trail—mostly because the drive there is never-ending (although thankfully paved). Since you'll be likely to have the 4,319-foot summit to yourself, sit and enjoy the stellar view of Rogue River Valley and Eden Valley below. Also, take in a bit of history while you're there: At the top, a plaque gives a well-deserved nod to Simón Bolívar, who wrested Venezuela away from those pesky Spaniards.

User Groups: Hikers and dogs. No mountain bikes or horses are allowed. No wheelchair facilities.

Permits: Permits are not required. Parking and access are free.

Maps: For a map of the Siskiyou National Forest, contact the Nature of the Northwest Information Center. For a topographic map, ask the USGS for Mount Bolivar.

Directions: From Powers, drive south on Forest Service Road 33 for 12.2 miles, and turn left on paved Forest Service Road 3348. Continue almost 20 miles to the parking area and trailhead, on the right side of the road.

Contact: Siskiyou National Forest, Powers Ranger District, Powers, OR 97466, 541/439-3011.

41 BIG PINE INTERPRETIVE LOOP TRAIL
1.1 mi/0.5 hr

west of Grants Pass in Siskiyou National Forest

Map 7.7, page 349

Four teeny loops make up this homage to the wide world of pines: Creek Loop is .2 mile, Challenge Loop is .75 mile, Sunshine Loop is .5 mile, and, last but not least, Big Pine Loop measures in at a cute .3 mile. The big guy himself stands over 250 feet tall, a height he can lord over all the other ponderosa pines in the world. With benches on which to sit and soak up the essence of all things pine, and eight interpretive signs, this easy and flat stroll through old-growth forest just screams "family outing". It's located conveniently in the Big Pine Campground, so if you're camping, you can make this a short morning walk before hitting other trails nearby.

User Groups: Hikers and dogs. No horses or mountain bikes are allowed. The path is wheelchair accessible.

Permits: A federal Northwest Forest pass is required to park here. The cost is $5 for a day pass or $30 for an annual pass. You can buy a day pass at the trailhead, at ranger stations, from private vendors, or through Nature of the Northwest Information Center.

Maps: For a map of the Siskiyou National Forest, contact the Nature of the Northwest Information Center. For a topographic map, ask the USGS for Chrome Ridge.

Directions: From Grants Pass, drive five miles north on I-5 to the Merlin Exit 61. Drive 12.2 miles on Merlin-Galice Road and turn left on Briggs Creek Road/Forest Service Road 25 (a one-lane paved road). Drive 12.4 miles and turn right into Big Pine Campground. The trailhead is straight ahead as you're driving in.

Contact: Siskiyou National Forest, Galice Ranger District, 200 Northeast Greenfield Road, P.O. Box 440, Grants Pass, OR 97526, 541/471-6500.

42 BRIGGS CREEK
19.0 mi/2.0 days

west of Grants Pass in Siskiyou National Forest

Map 7.7, page 349

If you like to get your feet wet or want to take a mid-hike dip, try this creekside trail. You'll have to ford the creek a few times, so the summer and early fall are the best bets for this history-rich area. The Briggs Creek area used to be mining country, and some mining operations are still running today. Four miles in, you'll find the Courier Mine Historic Cabin, a handy destination for the day, or you can continue along the 9.5-mile (one-way) trail and camp along the way (there's a campsite five miles in). It's a relatively view-free hike, but if you want some solo adventuring along the creek, with a little history thrown in for good measure, check this one out.

User Groups: Hikers, dogs, mountain bikes, and horses. No wheelchair access.

Permits: Permits are not required. Parking and access are free.

Maps: For a map of the Siskiyou National Forest, contact the Nature of the Northwest Information Center. For a topographic map, ask the USGS for Chrome Ridge and York Butte areas.

Directions: From Grants Pass, drive five miles north on I-5 to the Merlin Exit 61. Drive 12.2 miles on Merlin-Galice Road and turn left on Briggs Creek Road/Forest Service Road 25 (a one-lane paved road). Turn left and drive 13.1 miles to Forest Service Road 2512. Turn right and drive .5 mile, then turn left into Sam Brown Campground. Turn right before the day-use sign and drive to the parking area and trailhead.

Contact: Siskiyou National Forest, Galice Ranger District, 200 Northeast Greenfield Road, P.O. Box 440, Grants Pass, OR 97526, 541/471-6500.

43 BABYFOOT LAKE
2.0 mi/1.0 hr

west of Cave Junction in Kalmiopsis Wilderness of Siskiyou National Forest

Map 7.7, page 349

While many surrounding trails were destroyed in the 2002 Biscuit Fire, Babyfoot Lake Trail is still ticking, and new signs have been erected to show you the way. It's an interesting walk through the remnants of bare tree trunks still singed black, and you can see signs of life slowly returning to the trail as stubborn plants poke their way out

of the soil. Despite this, or actually because of it, this burned trail makes for a peaceful walk. When you come to a junction .25 mile in with Babyfoot Lake Rim Trail, turn right to head to the clear green lake, which is an oasis in this wasteland of dead trees. It's one mile total to the lake itself, worth a visit if you're interested in solitude and a bit of natural history along the way.

User Groups: Hikers and dogs. No horses or mountain bikes are allowed. No wheelchair facilities.

Permits: Permits are not required. Parking and access are free.

Maps: For a map of the Siskiyou National Forest, contact the Nature of the Northwest Information Center. For a topographic map, ask the USGS for Josephine Mountain.

Directions: From Cave Junction, drive 4.5 miles north on U.S. 199 and turn left onto Eight Dollar Road, which becomes Forest Service Road 4201. Drive 11 miles to Forest Service Road 141, then turn left. Continue for 14.6 miles (3 miles of which is paved) to Forest Service Road 140, then turn left and drive .6 mile to the trailhead and parking area, on the right.

Contact: Siskiyou National Forest, Illinois Valley Ranger District, 26568 Redwood Highway, Cave Junction, OR 97523, 541/592-2166.

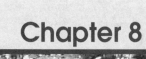

Portland and Willamette Valley

Portland and
Willamette Valley

I n most cities, you have to plan a three-day weekend to get to trails.
Not so with Portland (or PDX for short, a nickname it snagged from
the airport). A two-hour cruise to the west takes you to the coast,
and most of the trails within the Columbia River Gorge and on Mount
Hood are within an easy hour's drive. But there's also plenty in the
heart of Portland itself and the Willamette Valley (the pronunciation
stumps many a visitor: It's will-AM-et).

First, let's clear up a little something about the rain. Although Portland gets a bad rap for its wet stuff, consider this: The City of Roses
gets less annual rainfall than Atlanta, Houston, Indianapolis, or Seattle. How so? Precipitation in Portland tends to be a light daily mist
during the October-through-May rainy season, rather than all-out
downpours. Consider it a small price to pay for the area's lush green
scenery.

Portland is proud of Forest Park, and why not? The biggest city park
in the United States within city limits, 5,000-acre Forest Park is an
urban trail runner's dream. (Portland also boasts the nation's smallest
park, Mills End Park on Front Street along the Willamette River, but
its two-foot length would make for a mighty short hike.) When you
enter the wilder, northern areas of 30.2-mile Wildwood Trail, you
would never know that coffeehouses and brewpubs are just a stone's
throw away on ever-trendy Northwest 23rd Avenue. Tryon Creek, Oregon's only state park that is located in a major metropolitan area, is
the second-largest hiking area, with eight miles of trails popular with
runners and hikers. You can easily never leave the city and still have
more trails at your disposal than you'll know what to do with.

Traveling south down the I-5 corridor beyond Portland, there are two state parks that offer some interesting history to ponder as you hike. Willamette Mission Park is the site of the first mission for Native Americans, as well as the landing for the first ferry to carry a covered wagon across the Willamette River; the Champoeg (pronounced sham-POO-ey) State Heritage Area marks the spot where the West Coast's first provisional government was formed, in 1843. Both parks are perfect for families, with easy strolls lined with historical plaques. Farther south is Silver Falls State Park, the largest park in the Oregon state parks system; popular Trail of Ten Falls is just one of its many attractions.

Moseying on down through the state capital of Salem and the Willamette Valley, which is unofficially edging out Napa Valley as a prime winery hot spot, you'll arrive at Eugene and the University of Oregon, famous for being the Running Capital of the World. Legendary U. of O. track star Steve Prefontaine returned from track meets with visions of bark chip-lined trails, and Pre's Trail was born (sadly, he died before he ever saw his dream come true, but the trail lives on in his honor). On the outskirts of Eugene, there are several worthy hikes at Mount Pisgah, Falls Creek, and Elijah Bristow State Park.

This area is more urban than those covered in the other chapters, but don't let that term fool you. Oregon is renowned for liveable big cities that are clean and outdoors-oriented, and most cities have strict urban-growth boundaries—which means you get to enjoy the wilds surrounding the cities for years to come.

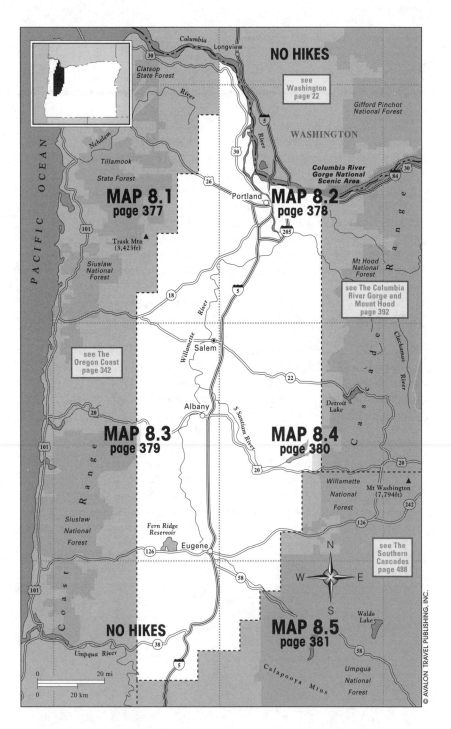

Map 8.1

Hike 1
Page 382

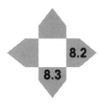

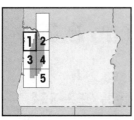

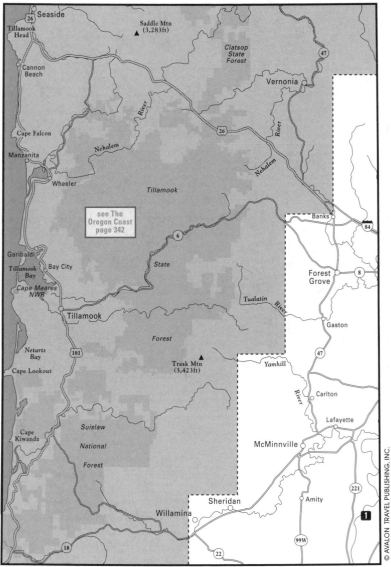

© AVALON TRAVEL PUBLISHING, INC.

Map 8.2

Hikes 2–5
Pages 382–384

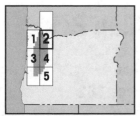

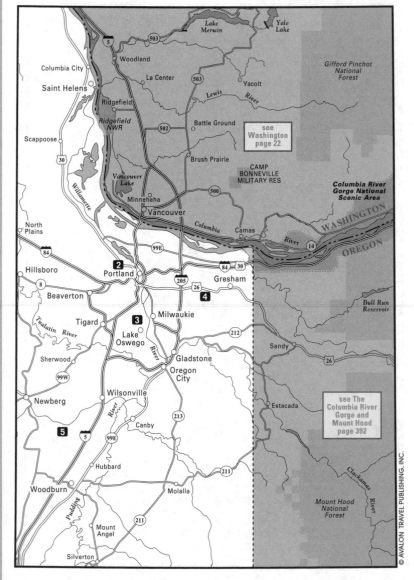

Map 8.3

Hikes 6–7
Pages 384–385

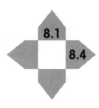

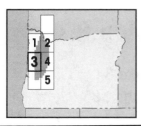

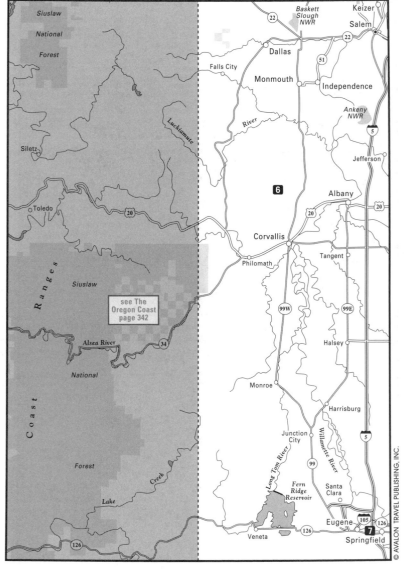

Map 8.4

Hike 8
Page 385

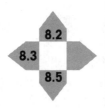

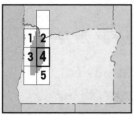

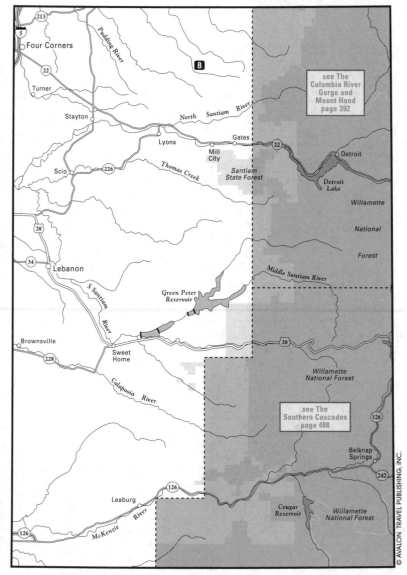

Map 8.5

Hikes 9–11
Pages 386–387

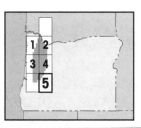

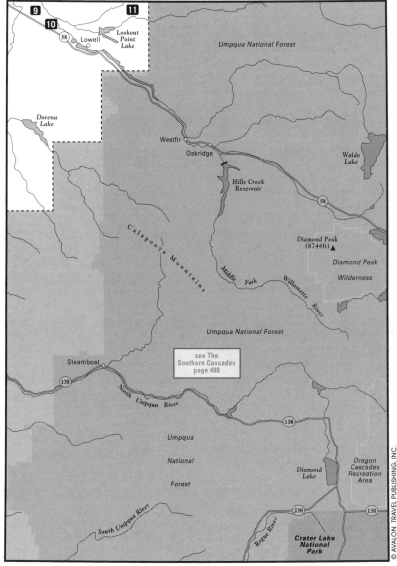

■ WILLAMETTE MISSION STATE PARK
2.7 mi/1.5 hrs

north of Salem on the Willamette River

Map 8.1, page 377

Ever wonder where the largest black cottonwood rests its roots? Wonder no more: Willamette Mission State Park is the proud soil provider for this thick trunk, measuring in at 26 feet, three inches in circumference. Throw in a free ferry ride, prime picnic spots, and a few history tidbits, and this state park can keep you occupied all day. The loop starts at the Filbert Grove day-use area. It then travels on a biking trail along the Willamette River straight up to the Wheatland ferry landing, which hauled the first covered wagon across the Willamette River in 1844. After your thrill ride, backtrack about a half mile, and hang a left on the hiking trail to hug the side of Mission Lake, passing the Jason Lee Mission monument, a nod to the reverend who in 1834 founded the first mission for Native Americans. The trail ends at the mighty cottonwood itself. Stand and admire its sturdy trunk before continuing straight on the paved road back to your car.

User groups: Hikers, dogs, mountain bikes, and horses. Paved portions are wheelchair accessible.

Permits: Permits are not required. A $3 day-use fee is collected at the park entrance, or you can get an annual Oregon Parks and Recreation pass for $25; contact Oregon Parks and Recreation, 800/551-5949.

Maps: For a free park brochure, contact Oregon Parks and Recreation, 800/551-6949, www.oregonstateparks.org. For a topographic map, ask the USGS for Mission Bottom.

Directions: From Portland, drive on I-5 South for 35 miles to Exit 263, toward Brooks/Gervais. Turn right onto Brooklake Road Northeast and drive 1.7 miles, then turn right onto Wheatland Road North for 2.4 miles to the park entrance. Drive to the Filbert Grove day-use area; the trailhead starts from there.

Contact: Oregon Parks and Recreation Department, 1115 Commercial Street Northeast, Salem, OR 97301, 800/551-6949, www.oregonstateparks.org.

■ WILDWOOD NATIONAL RECREATION TRAIL
30.2 mi/.5 hr–1.0 day

in Portland's Washington and Forest Parks

Map 8.2, page 378

This is without a doubt the best urban hike you'll find in the entire state, if not the country. Starting in Washington Park and zigzagging through 5,000-acre Forest Park—the largest city park in the United States—Wildwood Trail is a great escape from the city. Sure, you'll hear highway traffic now and then, and you'll see plenty of other hikers and runners, but scenery-wise it's like you just stepped into a national forest. The 30.2-mile trail starts in Washington Park at the Veterans Memorial at the zoo, then travels through Hoyt Arboretum, past the Japanese gardens (check out the Rose Garden while you're here), and then continues north, crossing busy Burnside Street to enter Forest Park. A steep two-mile climb leads you to Pittock Mansion, where you can take a well-deserved break and view the city below. In the northern sections, the trail parallels the Leif Erickson fire road, popular with bikers and runners. Plenty of well-marked side trails branch out from Wildwood, so you can choose loops or just do an out-and-back. The possibilities are endless in this park that just refuses to act like it's in city limits.

User groups: Hikers and dogs. No mountain bikes or horses.

Permits: Permits are not required. Parking and access are free.

Maps: For a free trail map, contact Portland Parks and Recreation, 503/823-PLAY (503/823-7529). For a topographic map, ask the USGS for Portland and Linnton.

Directions: There are many points of access to Wildwood Trail. To get to the southern trailhead from downtown Portland, drive west on

U.S. 26 to Exit 72/Canyon Road. Turn right to enter the Oregon Zoo entrance and the large parking lot. The trail starts to the right of the Vietnam Veterans Memorial. To reach the northern trailhead, drive on U.S. 30/St. Helen's Road to Newberry Road, turn left and drive several miles to the trailhead on the left. Another popular northern trailhead is from the Germantown Road exit off U.S. 30 (trailhead and parking area are on left).

Contact: Portland Parks and Recreation, 1120 Southwest 5th Avenue, Suite 1302, Portland, OR 97204, 503/823-PLAY (503/823-7529).

3 TRYON CREEK
2.0–8.0 mi/1.0–4.0 hrs

in southwest Portland's Tryon Creek State Park

Map 8.2, page 378

Yet another example of a park-within-the-city that feels worlds away, Tryon Creek offers a perfect escape from the city when you don't feel like driving hours to get there. The 645-acre state park is popular with runners and has eight miles of trails to explore through old-growth forest of red alder, Douglas fir, bigleaf maple, and western red cedar. Before you set out, pick up a trail brochure at the nature center, or check out the handy trail map on the wall nearby. It's pretty tough to get lost here, even if you are directionally challenged, but there are many short, interconnecting trails, all with different names, so you'll want to come up with a game plan before you start your trek. The 1.25-mile Upper Loop connects to many other trails that can extend your trip.

User groups: Hikers and dogs. Mountain bikes and horses are allowed only on certain trails. The .35-mile Trillium Trail is paved and wheelchair accessible.

Permits: Permits are not required. Parking and access are free.

Maps: For a free map, contact Oregon Parks and Recreation, 800/551-6949, www.oregon stateparks.org. For a topographic map, ask the USGS for Lake Oswego.

Directions: From Portland, drive south on I-5 to Exit 297/Terwilliger Boulevard. Keep right at the fork in the ramp, and turn right onto Southwest Barbur Boulevard, then take a slight right onto Southwest Terwilliger Boulevard. Drive 2.3 miles to the park entrance and the large parking area.

Contact: Tryon Creek State Natural Area, 11321 Southwest Terwilliger Boulevard, Portland, OR 97219, 503/636-9886.

4 POWELL BUTTE
3.0 mi/1.5 hrs

between Portland and Gresham south of U.S. 26

Map 8.2, page 378

It may not win the prize for biggest park in Portland (but it is runner-up to the overall winner, Forest Park), but Powell Butte has its own claim to fame: It's an extinct volcano, and just steps from your car you can stand on its top to witness commanding views of five mountains on a clear day. The park contains nine miles of trails, but keep in mind that many are open to horses and it's a popular mountain-biking spot, so watch the signs. For a quick three-mile loop, start on the appropriately named Mountain View Trail, where a plaque points out the various peaks to spot. Then keep straight onto Mount Hood Trail, which heads into the woods (with the steep descent, you can see why it's popular with mountain bikers). Hang a right when you reach the T intersection to return on Cedar Grove Trail, and then turn left onto Meadowland Trail. Don't worry, it's not as confusing as it sounds. Besides, it's pretty difficult to get lost in a city park.

User groups: Hikers, dogs, horses, and mountain bikes. Part of Mountain View Trail is paved and wheelchair accessible.

Permits: Permits are not required. Parking and access are free.

Maps: For a free brochure and map, contact the Portland Parks and Recreation Department, 503/823-PLAY (503/823-7529). For a topographic map, ask the USGS for Gladstone.

Directions: From Portland, drive on I-205 south to Exit 19. Follow Southeast Powell Boulevard three miles south and turn right onto Southeast 162nd Avenue to the park entrance and the parking area. The trail starts on the west side of the parking area.

Contact: Portland Parks and Recreation, 1120 Southwest 5th Avenue, Suite 1302, Portland, OR 97204, 503/823-PLAY (503/823-7529).

5 CHAMPOEG STATE PARK LOOP
3.0 mi/1.5 hrs

east of Newberg on the south banks of the Willamette River

Map 8.2, page 378

Hikers who like a little history thrown in with their hiking will appreciate this state park. Pronounced sham-POO-ey, the park is the old stomping grounds of Native Americans who found the Willamette River ideal for hunting and fishing. The first provisional government on the West Coast was established on this site in 1843, and in Champoeg's heyday it was a popular stop for stagecoaches and steamboats. Alas, the riverfront location that contributed to its popularity was also its downfall: In 1861, the largest flood ever recorded on the Willamette River submerged the busy town in 23 feet of water, which put a damper on business, to say the least. Although the town was partly rebuilt, it never stood a chance, as floods returned in 1890. Hikers can check out the whole story at the visitors center and at two museums on the state park property. Although the park's scenery isn't exactly mind-blowing, it's the idea that you never know what's around the bend that makes this area a must-visit. The trail passes historical monuments, the Pioneer Mother's cabin museum, and Robert Newell House; strolls down the riverfront (check out the waterfront homes across the river); and winds around a Frisbee Golf course, so your eyes and mind are constantly engaged. A .25-mile nature trail starts from the campground (where you can rent a yurt or cabin), and a paved bike trail extends to the town of Butteville. Pick up a park brochure before you set out to make sure you don't miss any sights.

User groups: Hikers and dogs. Mountain bikes are allowed only on the biking trails. No horses are allowed. Paved portions of the park are wheelchair accessible.

Permits: Permits are not required. A $3 day-use fee is collected at the park entrance, or you can get an annual Oregon Parks and Recreation pass for $25; contact Oregon Parks and Recreation, 800/551-5949.

Maps: For a free park brochure, contact Oregon Parks and Recreation, 800/551-6949, www .oregonstateparks.org. For a topographic map, ask the USGS for Newberg.

Directions: From Portland, drive south on I-5 for 20 miles to Exit 278 for Donald/Aurora. Turn right (west) and drive about six miles to the park entrance. Park in the Riverside Day-Use Area.

Contact: Oregon Parks and Recreation Department, 1115 Commercial Street Northeast, Salem, OR 97301, 800/551-6949, www.oregon stateparks.org.

6 MCDONALD RESEARCH FOREST LOOP
3.5 mi/2.0 hrs

north of Corvallis off Highway 99W

Map 8.3, page 379

This is a college hangout, minus the frat parties. Instead, a different type of celebration is going on here—a festival of forestry. It's a research forest for nearby Oregon State University, with over 60 projects going on at once in this eclectic ecosystem, where even-age, uneven-age, and new-growth stand side by side. Don't know what that means? Don't worry, it makes for an interesting hike anyway. Along the way, you can look out for flags marking various projects (it's like walking through a petri dish). The trails, popular with mountain bikers, also host the locally famous McDonald 50K run every April. You don't need to be in marathon shape or a forestry buff to take advantage of the scenery, though: Within these 11,000 acres, there are several short nature trails, including 1.4-mile Forest Discovery Trail, a loop that features a tree once used to cure malaria, and trees used to build temples in China. A popular loop is the Section 36/Powder House loop, which offers a good gaze at Soap Creek Valley and a meander near Cronemiller Lake. Pick up a brochure at the Forestry Club Cabin, or check out the detailed map at the trailhead. Not that you good citizens would ever need a reminder, of course, but remember to stick to the trail so as not to disturb the research projects.

User groups: Hikers, dogs, mountain bikes, and horses. (The Section 36/Power House loop is for hikers only, but other trails in the forest allow bikes and horses.) No wheelchair access.

Permits: Permits are not required. Parking and access are free.

Maps: A trail map is available at local outdoor vendors like the Oregon State University bookstore in Corvallis. A brochure is available at the Peavy Arboretum offices in the forest, or online at www.cof.orst.edu. For a topographic map, ask the USGS for Airlie South.

Directions: From Corvallis, drive north on Highway 99W for five miles, and turn left (west) onto Arboretum Road to the park entrance. Park at the day-use parking area.

Contact: Oregon State University, College of Forestry, 8692 Peavy Auditorium Road, Corvallis, OR 97330, www.cof.orts.edu.

⁊ PRE'S TRAIL
3.8 mi/1.5 hrs

in Eugene's Alton Baker Park

Map 8.3, page 379

Okay, okay, this isn't exactly in the wilderness, but any trail book just isn't complete without a nod to Eugene's famous Pre's Trail. Here's the story: Legendary University of Oregon track star Steve Prefontaine, while traveling in Europe to attend meets, developed a soft spot for

European tracks made of bark chip. He dreamed of making a similar surface on his training ground, Alton Baker Park (named after the publisher of Lane County's daily newspaper, the *Register-Guard*). Sadly, Prefontaine died before he got to see his dream realized, but a day after his untimely death in May 1975, the park gave his idea the green light. One trail just doesn't do justice to a guy like Pre, so they decided to give him three short loops in this system, with a total of 3.8 miles. Arrive extra early on a weekend morning to watch locals venturing out of their cars in the still-dark hours, ready to run on the flat, popular trails that meander near the McKenzie River. The trails offer a good way to see some of the campus, too, but avoid game days, when the mighty Ducks take over the park.

User groups: Hikers, dogs, and mountain bikes. No horses allowed. Paved portions of the park are wheelchair accessible.

Permits: Permits are not required. Parking and access are free.

Maps: For a free map online, go to www.oregontrackclub.org. For a topographic map, ask the USGS for Eugene East.

Directions: From downtown Eugene, drive north across the Ferry Street Bridge and turn right onto Centennial Boulevard. Turn right again at the first light and drive a short distance to the Alton Baker Park entrance and the large parking lot.

Contact: City of Eugene Parks and Open Space, Recreation Services Division, 99 West 10th Avenue, Suite 340, Eugene, OR 97401, 541/682-5333.

⁊ TRAIL OF TEN FALLS/ CANYON TRAIL
7.0 mi/3.5 hrs

east of Salem in Silver Falls State Park

Map 8.4, page 380

Not only is this the Trail of Ten Falls, but it's the Trail of Two Names. Apparently, the name-givers couldn't choose between the glorious falls and the Silver Creek Canyon as the trail's main feature (perhaps an arm-wrestling match ensued, with no clear winner? Just a guess . . .). Like its name suggests, this trail takes you past not one, not two, but—all together now—ten waterfalls before it calls it a loop and heads back to your car. Ranging in height from cute 27-footers to awesome 178-footers you can walk underneath, all the falls come proudly equipped with a handy plaque. Benches along the way invite you to sit and soak (no pun intended) up the scenery of this state park, Oregon's largest. Besides this trail, Silver Falls State Park features camping, cabins, horse trails (and horse rentals), and paved biking trails. Another tidbit of interest: This park was the location of the outdoor scenes in the film *The Hunted,* starring Tommy Lee Jones, where Benicio del Toro played a trained killer gone haywire, killing hunters to save the animals. (Don't worry, hunting isn't allowed here in real life.) Although the scenery is astounding, you're not far from civilization, so those who like post-hike lattes will enjoy the gift shop and café, conveniently located next to the parking lot.

User groups: Hikers only. No dogs, mountain bikes, or horses allowed. The trail is not wheelchair accessible, although there are paved parts of the park that are wheelchair friendly.

Permits: Permits are not required. A $3 day-use fee is collected at the park entrance, or you can get an annual Oregon Parks and Recreation pass for $25; contact Oregon Parks and Recreation, 800/551-5949.

Maps: For a free trail and park brochure, contact Oregon Parks and Recreation, 800/551-6949, www.oregonstateparks.org. For a topographic map, ask the USGS for Drake Crossing.

Directions: From Salem, drive on U.S. 22 five miles to Highway 214. Turn left and drive 15 miles to the park entrance and the large parking lot. The trail starts from behind the lodge.

Contact: Oregon Parks and Recreation Department, 1115 Commercial Street Northeast, Salem, OR 97301, 800/551-6949, www.oregon stateparks.org.

9 MOUNT PISGAH SUMMIT
3.0 mi/1.5 hrs

southeast of Eugene in the Howard Buford Recreation Area

Map 8.5, page 381

If you live in or are visiting Eugene and you want a quick getaway, Mount Pisgah is the place to do it. Local legend has it that the earliest Lane County settlers saw the view and named it after the Biblical summit from which Moses himself viewed the Promised Land. In any case, Pisgah is certainly divine. It's a short and sweet climb, gaining 1,000 feet in elevation, and you'll be rewarded with a 360-degree view of the rolling Willamette Valley below, and even the Cascade peaks if you catch it on a clear day. You'll also glimpse plenty of fellow urban-escapers out for a quick jaunt before brunch or football games at nearby University of Oregon. There are many offshoot trails that will take hikers up a more meandering route, but stick to the main summit trail for a well-marked route, which even gives you progress reports on your climb. You won't exactly feel like you're getting away from it all—what with the power lines and fellow hikers—but for a speedy, sweat-inducing jaunt with a view at the top, it's a great pick if you're already in the area.

User groups: Hikers and dogs. No mountain bikes or horses are allowed.

Permits: Permits are not required. From May through August, a $2 parking fee is collected at the park entrance.

Maps: For a free map, contact the Lane County Parks Division, Armitage Park, 90064 Coburg Road, Eugene, OR 97408, 541/682-2000. For a topographic map, ask the USGS for Springfield.

Directions: From the south end of Eugene, take I-5 to the 30th Avenue exit. At the second light, turn left to travel over I-5, and at the stop sign turn left, then turn right onto Franklin Road. In less than .25 mile, turn left onto Seavey Loop Road. Drive 1.5 miles and turn right to the park entrance. Parking is at the end of the road, at the arboretum entrance.

Contact: Lane County Parks Division, Armitage Park, 90064 Coburg Road, Eugene, OR 97408, 541/682-2000.

⑩ ELIJAH BRISTOW STATE PARK
2.0 mi/1.0 hr

southeast of Eugene on the Middle Fork Willamette River

Map 8.5, page 381

If you're in the mood for a simple Sunday stroll or a picnic with the whole family, Elijah Bristow State Park is a perfect place to spend an afternoon. The riverside park is named after one Elijah Bristow, a pioneer from Virginia who apparently went first to California, which didn't suit this mountain man, and then came north to Lane County, where he raised his hat and exclaimed, "This is my claim! Here I will live, and when I die, here I shall be buried!" (You gotta love the guy's enthusiasm for this great state, no?) Well, at least he got a park out of the deal, with plenty of hiking loops to choose from. A big map will greet you with your choices as you enter the park, so you can take your pick. One option is taking the two-mile Lost Creek Trail, where the easy-to-follow signposts will lead you on your way up Lost Creek and turning right at the junction to reach the Willamette River. (Or, to add a third mile to your hike, continue straight at the intersection to reach the river). The 847-acre park consists of meadows, woodlands, and wetlands, and do we ever mean wet: This is definitely a summer picnicking spot, as the rainy season turns everything into a massive sogfest (let's just say we learned this the hard way, shall we?). Home to several threatened animal species such as the Western pond turtle and the Oregon chub, tree-lovers will be in leafy heaven among the cottonwood, bigleaf maple, western red cedar, Douglas fir, western hemlock, Oregon ash, and white oak. It won't necessarily satisfy the hardy-hiker crowd, and the picnic areas scream "family reunion," but if you are looking for some interesting scenery for your next gathering, Bristow won't disappoint.

User groups: Hikers, dogs, horses, and mountain bikes. No wheelchair facilities.

Permits: Permits are not required. Parking and access are free.

Maps: For a free park brochure, contact the Oregon Parks and Recreation Department, 800/551-6949, www.oregonstateparks.org. For a topographic map, ask the USGS for Lowell.

Directions: From Eugene, drive seven miles on Willamette Highway/Highway 58 and turn left into the park entrance. The trailhead is to the left past the first parking lot, just past the small bridge.

Contact: Oregon Parks and Recreation Department, 1115 Commercial Street Northeast, Salem, OR 97301, 800/551-6949, www.oregon stateparks.org.

⑪ FALL CREEK NATIONAL RECREATION TRAIL
13.7 mi one-way/6.0 hrs

southeast of Eugene near the Middle Fork Willamette River

Map 8.5, page 381

You may feel like you've just entered a Dr. Suess book with all the dripping, mossy tentacles of the Douglas fir and maple trees along this scenic route. The undulating trail—mostly flat, except for a healthy climb near the Bedrock campground—is easy to follow. You'll have plenty of company along the way: This is a popular stomping ground on sunny weekends, especially because it crosses Forest Service Road 18 several times, providing several access points. Trails lead down to the clear, green Fall Creek for fishing, swimming, and picnic spots. Seasonal camping is provided nearby, so you can take full advantage of this scenic spot.

User groups: Hikers and dogs. No horses or mountain bikes are allowed. No wheelchair facilities.

Permits: A federal Northwest Forest pass is required to park here. The cost is $5 for a day pass or $30 for an annual pass. You can buy a day pass at ranger stations, from private vendors, or through Nature of the Northwest Information Center.

Maps: For a map of the Willamette National Forest, contact the Nature of the Northwest Information Center. For a topographic map, ask the USGS for Fall Creek Lake, Saddleback Mountain, and Sinker Mountain.

Directions: From Eugene, drive 15 miles east on Willamette Highway/Highway 58, and turn left on Lowell-Jasper Road (you'll cross the Dexter Reservoir on the bridge towards Lowell). Drive two miles through the town of Lowell and turn right on Fall Creek Road/Forest Service Road 18. Continue 11 miles to the trailhead on the right, just before Dolly Varden campground. If you want to arrange a car shuttle, continue on Forest Service Road 18 for 12 miles to the junction with Forest Service Road 1833. Turn right and cross the bridge over Fall Creek to the trailhead and parking area, on the left.

Contact: Willamette National Forest, Middle Fork Ranger District, Lowell Office, 60 South Pioneer Street, Lowell, OR 97452, 541/937-2129.

Chapter 9

© MEGAN MCMORRIS

The Columbia River Gorge and Mount Hood

The Columbia River Gorge and Mount Hood

L ooming large as a constant presence for Portlanders (and, on clear days, for those living to the south as well), 11,239-foot Mount Hood is the tallest peak in Oregon and is the second-most climbed mountain in the world (after Mount Fuji in Japan). Although scaling its heights requires mountaineering skills and equipment, you can easily access its slopes and foothills for seemingly endless miles. Mount Hood's Timberline Ski Resort offers the only year-round ski season in North America, and many elite skiers and snowboarders use Mount Hood's slopes for training. Mount Hood has an unbelievable number of trails within its boundaries, most of which are right off Highways 26 and 35. Timberline Trail is the mightiest of them all, a strenuous 40.7-mile loop circling Mount Hood. And though many of the higher-elevation trails remain snow-covered until July, there are plenty of lower trails you can explore year-round.

Just north of Mount Hood is the Columbia River Gorge National Scenic Area, which slices the border between Oregon and Washington. The Gorge, as the locals call it, is lined with trails right off I-84. (Drive down the highway on a summer weekend and you'll see cars with license plates from all over the country packed into parking areas.) The Pacific Crest Trail makes its Oregon debut in the Gorge, extending from the Bridge of the Gods in Cascade Locks to Timberline Lodge in Mount Hood. Popular for its easy access to trails and cliffside scenery, the area is known for its waterfalls and tough peak climbs, with 4,960-foot Mount Defiance being the toughest of the bunch. But by far, the hot tamale of the Gorge is Multnomah Falls, the fourth-largest waterfall in the country. The area is also known for stiff breezes: The wind rushing through the Gorge has turned the area into "the windsurfing capital of the world." On a summer day, you'll see sail- and kiteboarders zipping through the water.

The Columbia Gorge Scenic Area extends 70 miles from Corbett to Cascade Locks to The Dalles, with outdoors hub Hood River being the unofficial capital of it all. Bed-and-breakfasts, historic hotels, upscale restaurants, and downscale brewpubs offer great stopping points after a long day of hiking. (Treat yourself to a swirl cone at the East Wind Drive-In, in Cascade Locks—just look for the ever-present line snaking in front of the walk-up window.)

Water is also a big selling point of this area, from the white-water Clackamas River west of Mount Hood—popular with rafters and kayakers—to the Columbia River itself, to plenty of waterfalls, mountain lakes, and smaller creeks. Speaking of water, the rainy season tends to be October through May, so come prepared if you want to head out on the trails during the wet months.

Extending to the south, this chapter also includes the northern sections of Willamette National Forest and the Mount Jefferson Wilderness Area. At 10,497 feet, Mount Jefferson is the second-highest peak in Oregon, adding wildflower meadows and backcountry wilderness to this fine mix, while nearby Detroit Reservoir is a campground mecca for day hikers.

Overall, the hikes in this chapter range from many short waterfall and riverfront strolls right off the highway to tough day hikes up a cliff, to backpacking adventures in the backcountry. There are so many loops and interconnecting trails, the hiking possibilities truly seem endless. All this within an easy drive of Portland and surrounding cities! Seem too good to be true? It isn't.

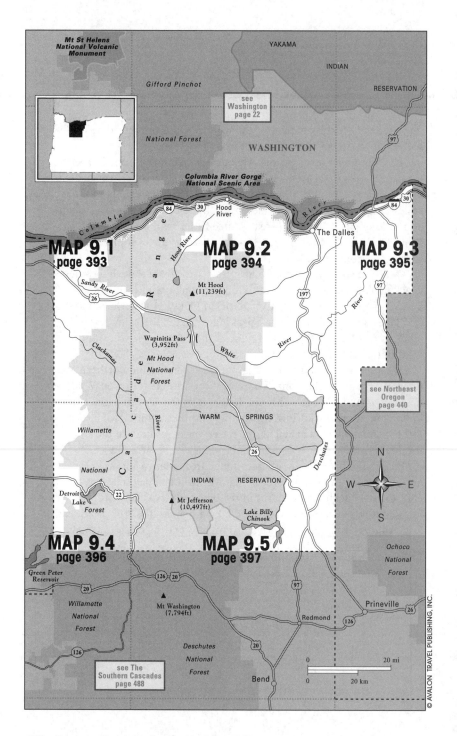

Mt St Helens
National Volcanic
Monument

YAKAMA

INDIAN

RESERVATION

Gifford Pinchot

see
Washington
page 22

National Forest

WASHINGTON

Columbia River Gorge
National Scenic Area

Columbia

84   30   Hood
River

Hood River

The Dalles

MAP 9.1
page 393

MAP 9.2
page 394

MAP 9.3
page 395

Sandy River

26

Mt Hood
▲(11,239ft)

197

River

Wapinitia Pass
(3,952ft)

Clackamas

White   River

Mt Hood
National
Forest

River

see Northeast
Oregon
page 440

WARM   SPRINGS

Willamette

26

Deschutes

INDIAN   RESERVATION

National

Detroit
Lake

22

▲ Mt Jefferson
(10,497ft)

Lake Billy
Chinook

Forest

Green Peter
Reservoir

MAP 9.4
page 396

MAP 9.5
page 397

Ochoco

National

Forest

N

W   E

S

126   20

20

Willamette

National

Forest

▲
Mt Washington
(7,794ft)

97

Redmond

Prineville

26

126

126

see The
Southern Cascades
page 488

Deschutes

National

Forest

20

Bend

0   20 mi

0   20 km

© AVALON TRAVEL PUBLISHING, INC.

Map 9.1

Hikes 1–11
Pages 398–403

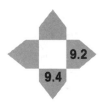

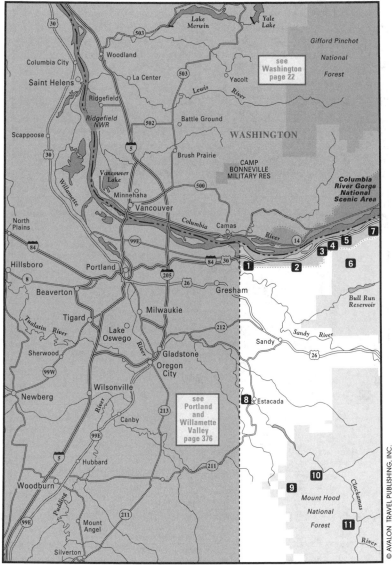

Map 9.2

Hikes 12–48
Pages 403–425

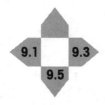

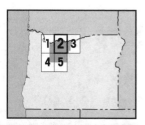

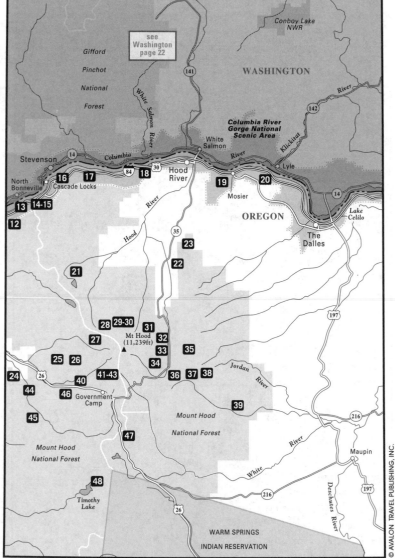

Map 9.3

Hike 49
Page 425

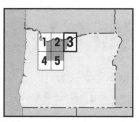

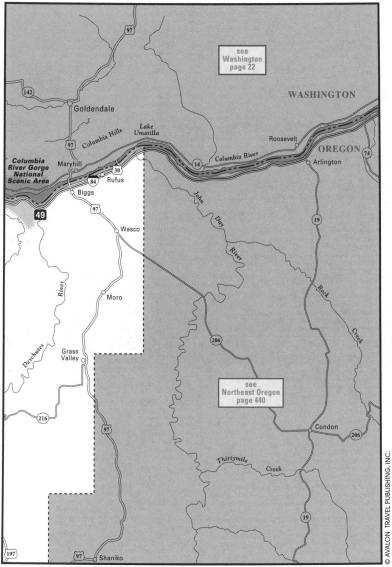

© AVALON TRAVEL PUBLISHING, INC.

Map 9.4

Hikes 50–59
Pages 426–431

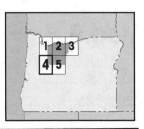

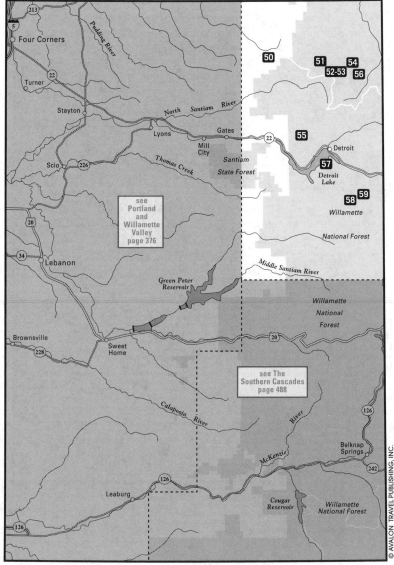

Map 9.5

Hikes 60–67
Pages 431–435

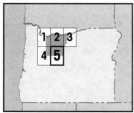

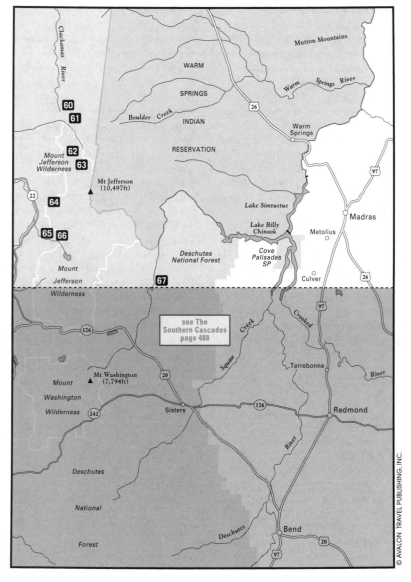

1 LEWIS AND CLARK NATURE TRAIL
4.0 mi/2.0 hrs

in Lewis & Clark State Park on the west side of the Columbia River Gorge

Map 9.1, page 393

In an area that's filled with references to intrepid explorers Lewis and Clark, this is the ultimate trail, where they ended their journey. Clark reportedly attempted to wade across the Sandy River here but found the bottom was quicksand, so they named it Quicksand River. (Thankfully, that name has changed!) This two-mile nature trail is lined with interpretive signs, courtesy of a local Girl Scout troop. Botanical highlights of the trail include Oregon grape (the state flower), wild ginger, Oregon white oak, bigleaf maple, and Oregon crabapple. Detect a theme? Oregonians are notorious for their pride in native status, and local plants are included in the glory. After a flat nature exhibit, the trail heads into the forest before flattening out again. Another short but rocky trail in this state park leads up to Broughton's Bluff, a popular climbing spot. The trail is short but requires some scrambling on the rocks, so skip it on a wet day. Although this is probably the least scenic trail in the Gorge, it's a good leg-stretcher if you're already in the area, are bringing the kids along, or want to work off that potato salad after a picnic.

User Groups: Hikers and dogs. No mountain bikes or horses are allowed. No wheelchair access.

Permits: Permits are not required. Parking and access are free.

Maps: For a map of the Columbia River Gorge, contact Nature of the Northwest Information Center. For a topographic map, ask the USGS for Washougal.

Directions: From Portland, drive east on I-84 for 20 miles to Exit 18 and follow signs less than .1 mile to Lewis & Clark State Park and the parking lot. The trail starts on the southwest side of the parking lot.

Contact: Oregon Parks and Recreation Department, 1115 Commercial Street Northeast, Salem, OR 97301, 800/551-6949, www.oregon stateparks.org.

2 LATOURELL FALLS
2.1 mi/1.0 hr

east of Crown Point in the Columbia River Gorge

Map 9.1, page 393

Latourell Falls is so easygoing: It doesn't make you drive far (it's the closest of the Gorge falls to Portland) or walk far (it's an easy two-mile loop). So do it a favor and pay it a visit. Starting from the parking lot, you'll climb up a short paved trail for about .5 mile to a lookout over the falls, then the pavement ends and a path continues to Upper Latourell Falls, where a footbridge spans Latourell Creek right in front of the falls, a perfect place to snap some shots. Great viewpoints line this short and sweet trip. Add in the nearby Bridal Veil (a popular one-mile round-trip) waterfall for another short and scenic hike. Be warned, though: Because they are so convenient to the highway and close to Portland, these easy trails can get packed with families and tourists on summer weekends.

User Groups: Hikers and dogs. No mountain bikes or horses are allowed. No wheelchair access.

Permits: Permits are not required. Parking and access are free.

Maps: For a map of the Columbia River Gorge, contact Nature of the Northwest Information Center. For a topographic map, contact Green Trails, Inc. (ask for Bridal Veil, map number 428), 206/546-MAPS (206/546-6277), www.green trails.com; or ask the USGS for Bridal Veil.

Directions: From Portland, drive about 25 miles east on I-84 to Bridal Veil Falls/Exit 28. Turn right onto the historic Columbia River Scenic Highway, and drive 2.5 miles to the trailhead and parking area on the left.

Contact: Columbia River Gorge National Scenic Area, 902 Wasco Avenue, Suite 200, Hood River, OR 97031, 541/386-2333.

3 ANGEL'S REST
4.5 mi/2.5 hrs

on the Columbia River Scenic Highway in the Columbia River Gorge

Map 9.1, page 393

This would rate a higher score scenery-wise if it weren't for the fact that it's such a popular spot. You'll also hear highway traffic pretty much the whole way, so it's not exactly back-country solitude. Still, if you have visitors—or are a visitor yourself—you should definitely check this one out. It offers great views of the Gorge, a waterfall, friendly Oregonians (you'll encounter a lot), and offshoot lookout trails. About a half mile in, you'll come across 150-foot Coopey Falls, and then the true switch-backing continues up to the 1,600-foot viewpoint. When you reach a rock field at the top, don't stop: Continue straight across the rock field and climb on. At the top, pick your pleasure of rock formations for a picnic spot and a rest before heading back down the way you came. This trail also continues for 1.8 miles to Wah-keena Falls (see listing in this chapter) and another 1.6 miles to Devil's Rest Viewpoint so you can keep on pushing if you want to make a day of it.

User Groups: Hikers and dogs. No mountain bikes or horses are allowed. No wheelchair access.

Permits: Permits are not required. Parking and access are free.

Maps: For a map of the Columbia River Gorge, contact Nature of the Northwest Information Center. For a topographic map, contact Green Trails, Inc. (ask for Bridal Veil, map number 428), 206/546-MAPS (206/546-6277), www.greentrails.com; or ask the USGS for Bridal Veil.

Directions: From Portland, drive about 25 miles east on I-84 to Exit 28/Bridal Veil. Drive off the exit to the junction with Columbia River Scenic Highway. The trailhead starts on the south side of the junction.

Contact: Columbia River Gorge National Scenic Area, 902 Wasco Avenue, Suite 200, Hood River, OR 97031, 541/386-2333.

4 WAHKEENA FALLS LOOP
4.7 mi/2.5 hrs

west of Multnomah Falls in the Columbia River Gorge

Map 9.1, page 393

Most people just saunter up to the falls and then return to their cars, but they're missing out on the good stuff. For a true waterfall fiesta, you can hit several falls on this loop hike and escape the crowds, to boot. Start on the short .5-mile trip up to pleasant Wahkeena Falls, and then continue up the trail another mile to Wahkeena Springs. Take a left (east) when you hit the springs for .5 mile on Wahkeena Trail. If you have enough juice, try the switchbacks up to the viewpoint at 2,400 feet by turning right at the junction at this point. Or continue straight for another 1.2 miles, then turn left for the return trip home on Larch Mountain Trail (see listing in this chapter), which descends past upper Multnomah Falls areas, like Ecola Falls and Weisendanger Falls, before reaching the dizzying Multnomah Falls overlook on a short side trail. Continue back to the Multnomah Falls lodge and return along the highway to find the .6-mile return trail back to the parking area.

User Groups: Hikers and dogs. No mountain bikes or horses are allowed.

Permits: Permits are not required. Parking and access are free.

Maps: For a map of the Columbia River Gorge, contact Nature of the Northwest Information Center. For a topographic map, contact Green Trails, Inc. (ask for Bridal Veil, map number 428), 206/546-MAPS (206/546-6277), www.greentrails.com; or ask the USGS for Bridal Veil and Multnomah Falls.

Directions: From Portland, drive about 25 miles east on I-84 to Bridal Veil Falls/Exit 28. Turn left on the historic Columbia River Scenic Highway for 2.5 miles to the parking area on the left; the trailhead is across the highway on the right.

Contact: Columbia River Gorge National Scenic Area, 902 Wasco Avenue, Suite 200, Hood River, OR 97031, 541/386-2333.

5 MULTNOMAH FALLS
2.4 mi/1.5 hrs

on the Columbia River Scenic Highway in the Columbia River Gorge

Map 9.1, page 393

If you were the second-highest year-round waterfall in the country, wouldn't you want a nice shiny plaque proudly proclaiming the fact? I guess they figure the 620-foot falls speak for themselves, but still. Multnomah does receive plenty of attention, though, so here's a word to the wise: Don't even think about visiting Multnomah Falls on a sunny weekend. It's the number-one tourist attraction in the state, and the parking lot fills quickly. Better to hit some of the lesser-known falls in this chapter, and save the Big One for a weekday if you can swing it. (I know, the job does tend to get in the way of such outings, but it's worth it.) The paved trail leads up to a viewpoint at Benson Bridge, just .5 mile up, to behold the falls (those prone to dizziness should skip this). You can also continue to the top of the trail for an overlook above the falls, for a 2.4-mile round-trip hike. The trail also continues another five miles up to Larch Mountain and connects with Wahkeena Falls Trail for a five-mile loop (see listings in this chapter).

User Groups: Hikers and dogs. No mountain bikes or horses are allowed.

Permits: Permits are not required. Parking and access are free.

Maps: For a map of the Columbia River Gorge, contact Nature of the Northwest Information Center. For a topographic map, contact Green Trails, Inc. (ask for Bridal Veil, map number 428), 206/546-MAPS (206/546-6277), www.greentrails.com; or ask the USGS for Multnomah Falls.

Directions: From Portland, drive about 30 miles east on I-84 to Multnomah Falls/Exit 31. Park in the large parking lot and go under a short tunnel to the falls and the well-marked trailhead.

Contact: Columbia River Gorge National Scenic Area, 902 Wasco Avenue, Suite 200, Hood River, OR 97031, 541/386-2333.

6 LARCH MOUNTAIN LOOP
5.4 mi/3.0 hrs

above Multnomah Falls in the Columbia River Gorge

Map 9.1, page 393

You can walk 6.8 miles one-way up to Larch Mountain from Multnomah Falls, but there's a better way to get there: Start from the top of the mountain itself for great Gorge views right off the bat (check out the .25-mile trail to scenic Sherrard's Point from the parking lot first), then descend into the Gorge for 1.5 miles. Head east (right) at a junction onto Multnomah Creek Way to cross the creek, and then head north (right) to let the climbing begin, for 2.5 miles. Take another right on Oneonta Trail to complete the loop. Alternatively, keep going straight when you come upon the junction to reach Multnomah Falls, and make it a shuttle hike.

User Groups: Hikers, dogs, and mountain bikes. No horses are allowed. No wheelchair access.

Permits: A federal Northwest Forest pass is required to park here. The cost is $5 for a day pass or $30 for an annual pass. You can buy a day pass at ranger stations, from private vendors, or through Nature of the Northwest Information Center.

Maps: For a map of Mount Hood National Forest, contact Nature of the Northwest Information Center. For a topographic map, contact Green Trails, Inc. (ask for Bridal Veil, number 428), 206/546-MAPS (206/546-6277), www.greentrails.com; or ask the USGS for Multnomah Falls.

Directions: From Portland, drive east for about 20 miles on I-84 to Exit 22/Corbett. Drive up the Corbett hill for 1.3 miles, then turn left on the historic Columbia River Highway for two miles, and turn right on Larch Mountain Road for 14 miles to the end of the road, parking area and well-marked trailhead.

Contact: Columbia River Gorge National Scenic Area, 902 Wasco Avenue, Suite 200, Hood River, OR 97031, 541/386-2333.

7 ONEONTA/HORSETAIL FALLS LOOP

2.7 mi/1.5 hrs

east of Multnomah Falls in the Columbia River Gorge

Map 9.1, page 393

Dare I say there are cooler falls than Multnomah? I dare. Although they may not be as large as their flashier sister next door, these falls are more scenic simply because the crowds are busy ooh-ing and ah-ing at the Big M. This trail hits three lesser-known falls (add 2.4 miles to your hike to throw in an extra one for good measure). Start off beside Horsetail Falls and then take a right (west) after .2 mile onto Horsetail Falls Trail to arrive at Bachelor Number Two: Upper Horsetail Falls, a.k.a. Ponytail Falls. Here you can actually walk behind the falls in a cavern before continuing on for more than a mile to Oneonta Trail, which heads into the Oneonta Gorge and spits you out at Oneonta Falls. If you want to reach Triple Falls (which sounds like the name suggests and is worth the trip), 1.2 miles down, take a left at Oneonta Falls. Otherwise, turn right here to complete the loop back to the highway and a .5-mile walk back to your car.

User Groups: Hikers and dogs. No mountain bikes or horses are allowed. No wheelchair access.

Permits: Permits are not required. Parking and access are free.

Maps: For a map of the Columbia River Gorge, contact Nature of the Northwest Information Center. For a topographic map, contact Green Trails, Inc. (ask for Bridal Veil, map number 428), 206/546-MAPS (206/546-6277), www.greentrails.com, or ask the USGS for Multnomah Falls.

Directions: From Portland, drive about 35 miles east on I-84 to Ainsworth State Park/Exit 35. Follow the historic Columbia River Scenic Highway west, and drive 1.5 miles to the large parking area on the right (north) side of the highway. The trail starts across the road.

Contact: Columbia River Gorge National Scenic Area, 902 Wasco Avenue, Suite 200, Hood River, OR 97031, 541/386-2333.

8 MILO MCIVER STATE PARK

4.5 mi/2.0 hrs

northwest of Estacada off Highway 211

Map 9.1, page 393

A remote wilderness excursion this is not. Between the Frisbee golf, fish hatchery, horseback riding, fishing, massive campground, and even a model-airplane field, this is a mecca for the whole family. The "main drag" is a 4.5-mile loop, but the trail markings aren't exactly bountiful, if even present. Still, even if you're not quite the wizard with directions, you'll be hard-pressed to stray far, as all the paths connect. A scenic riverside stroll along the Clackamas River and a one-mile nature trail round out the trails in the park, where you'll spot trillium and purple foxglove, and maybe even a curious deer wondering what all the ruckus is about. Pick up a map at the park entrance to plan your route. A word to the wise: Make advance camping reservations because the campground fills up fast.

User Groups: Hikers, dogs, and horses. Mountain bikes are not allowed. Wheelchair access is on paved portions of the trail.

Permits: A $3 day-use fee is collected at the park entrance, or you can get an annual Oregon Parks and Recreation pass for $25; contact Oregon Parks and Recreation, 800/551-6949, www.oregonstateparks.org.

Maps: Free brochures are available at the park entrance and through Oregon Parks and Recreation Department, 800/551-6949, www.oregonstateparks.org. For a topographic map, ask the USGS for Estacada.

Directions: From Portland, drive 25 miles east on U.S. 26 to Highway 211 (two miles past Estacada). Turn right (south) on Highway 211 to Hayden Road. After one mile, turn right on Spring Water Road and continue 1.2 miles to the well-marked park entrance. The loop starts in the southern day-use area; the nature and riverside trails start in the northern day-use area.

Contact: Oregon Parks and Recreation Department, 1115 Commercial Street Northeast, Salem, OR 97301, 800/551-6949, www.oregonstateparks.org.

9 MEMALOOSE LAKE
2.6 mi/1.5 hrs

southeast of Estacada in the Clackamas River area of Mount Hood National Forest

Map 9.1, page 393

This easy stroll follows Memaloose Creek to a pretty lake at 4,100 feet (elevation gain is 500 feet). You'll walk through beautiful old-growth forest on your way to the lake, and you'll feel like you're miles from anywhere (even though you're only about an hour's drive from Portland). Keep in mind that the trail can be snowy through the end of June, so it's best to try this trail later in the season if you don't want to drive—or walk—through the white stuff.

User Groups: Hikers, dogs, mountain bikes, and horses. No wheelchair access.

Permits: Permits are not required. Parking and access are free.

Maps: For a map of Mount Hood National Forest, contact Nature of the Northwest Information Center. For a topographic map, contact Green Trails, Inc. (ask for Fish Creek Mountain, map number 492), 206/546-MAPS (206/546-6277), www.greentrails.com; or ask the USGS for Wanderers Peak.

Directions: From Estacada, drive southeast on Highway 224 for nine miles to Memaloose Road/Forest Service Road 45. Turn right and drive 11.2 miles until the pavement ends, then keep right to drive on a gravel road for another .9 mile to a small parking pullout and the trailhead on the left.

Contact: Mount Hood National Forest, Clackamas River Ranger District, Estacada Ranger Station, 595 Northwest Industrial Way, Estacada, OR 97023, 503/630-6861.

10 CLACKAMAS RIVER
7.8 mi one-way/3.5 hrs

on the Clackamas River between Fish Creek and Indian Henry Campgrounds in Mount Hood National Forest

Map 9.1, page 393

This trail winds along the scenic Clackamas River, which makes for a great and simple getaway from Portland. The river is popular with white-water kayakers and rafters, so you may glimpse a few along the way. Extending from Fish Creek campground to Indian Henry campground, the trail travels through old-growth forest and passes by beaches and waterfalls. You can do this hike as a shuttle, or for a seven-mile round-trip, hike from the lower trailhead (from Fish Creek Campground) to Pup Creek Falls, a 100-foot waterfall with a half-cave you can hike through. Plenty of fishing and picnic spots line the way, for a perfect year-round weekend escape.

User Groups: Hikers and dogs. No mountain bikes or horses are allowed. No wheelchair access.

Permits: A federal Northwest Forest pass is required to park here. The cost is $5 for a day pass or $30 for an annual pass. You can buy a day pass at ranger stations, from private vendors, or through Nature of the Northwest Information Center.

Maps: For a map of Mount Hood National Forest, contact Nature of the Northwest Information Center. For a topographic map, contact Green Trails, Inc. (ask for Fish Creek Mountain, map number 492), 206/546-MAPS (206/546-6277), www.greentrails.com; or ask the USGS for Beford Point, Three Lynx, and Fish Creek Mountain.

Directions: From Estacada, drive 15 miles southeast on Highway 224 to Fish Creek Road/Forest Service Road 54. Turn right and drive .2 mile to the parking lot on the right. The trail starts from the far end of the parking lot and crosses the road to the actual trailhead.

Contact: Mount Hood National Forest, Clackamas River Ranger District, Estacada Ranger

Station, 595 Northwest Industrial Way, Estacada, OR 97023, 503/630-6861.

🈁 RIVERSIDE NATIONAL RECREATION TRAIL
4.0 mi one-way/2.0 hours

on the Clackamas River between Rainbow and Riverside Campgrounds in Mount Hood National Forest

Map 9.1, page 393

No fancy monikers here: Riverside Trail's name is plain Jane and it likes it that way, thanks very much. If you want an easy stroll but don't feel like dealing with other pleasure-seekers, paved paths, or super-short hikes, this riverside amble along the mighty shores of the Clackamas River aims to please. The river provides white noise, and the cool forest air and river breeze refreshes on a scorching day. Mossy trees and ferns line the route, and it's a shade of green you can't get in a box of crayons. You can access the river at several spots, so bring along lunch—you probably won't have to share your spot with others, since it's not nearly as crowded as other area trails. A relatively flat trail extending from Rainbow camp to Riverside camp, it's a good way to put in some mileage without having to climb too much. You can do this as a four-mile one-way hike, an eight-mile round-trip, or anything in between.

User Groups: Hikers, dogs, mountain bikes, and horses. No wheelchair access.

Permits: A federal Northwest Forest pass is required to park here. The cost is $5 for a day pass or $30 for an annual pass. You can buy a day pass at the trailhead, at ranger stations, from private vendors, or through Nature of the Northwest Information Center.

Maps: For a map of Mount Hood National Forest, contact Nature of the Northwest Information Center. For a topographic map, contact Green Trails, Inc. (ask for Fish Creek Mountain, map number 492), 206/546-MAPS (206/546-6277), www.greentrails.com; or ask the USGS for Fish Creek Mountain.

Directions: From Estacada, drive southeast on Highway 224 for 25.5 miles to Rainbow Camp on the right, at the junction with Forest Service Road 46. Drive in the campground entrance and park to the left of site 14 in the small parking area. The trailhead isn't noticeable as you're driving in, so park here and walk a short distance to the sign straight ahead. To reach the trailhead from Riverside Campground, continue on Forest Service Road for four miles; the campground and trailhead are on the right side of the road.

Contact: Mount Hood National Forest, Clackamas River Ranger District, Estacada Ranger Station, 595 Northwest Industrial Way, Estacada, OR 97023, 503/630-6861.

🈁 NESMITH POINT
9.2 mi/6.5 hrs

between Multnomah Falls and Bonneville in the Columbia River Gorge

Map 9.2, page 394

Feel like climbing a few feet? How about 3,800? Then check out Nesmith Point, the highest point along the Gorge cliffs (it doesn't snag the Gorge's ultimate highest title, though—Mount Defiance has that glory). It's a great escape from crowds, as it's a tough one and not as well known as other trails in the Gorge. The switchbacks through this box canyon are steep, but most of the climbing is in the first three miles, then you'll reach the top of the canyon and gradually ascend the ridgeline to the former lookout site. Keep right at the intersection with an abandoned road to reach the lookout. Once on top, give a friendly wave to Oregon's next-door neighbor, Washington, and its Beacon Rock and Mount Adams. This trail also connects to Horsetail Falls and Oneonta Trails (see listing in this chapter) by turning left (west) .3 mile before the summit when you reach the abandoned road.

User Groups: Hikers and dogs. No mountain bikes or horses are allowed. No wheelchair access.

Permits: Permits are not required. Parking and access are free.

Maps: For a map of the Columbia River Gorge,

contact Nature of the Northwest Information Center. For a topographic map, contact Green Trails, Inc. (ask for Bridal Veil, map number 428), 206/546-MAPS (206/546-6277), www.greentrails.com; or ask the USGS for Bridal Veil.

Directions: From Portland, drive east on I-84 for 35 miles to Exit 35/Ainsworth State Park. Turn left toward Dodson for a short distance, then turn right onto Frontage Road and drive two miles to Yeon Park trailhead and the parking area.

Contact: Columbia River Gorge National Scenic Area, 902 Wasco Avenue, Suite 200, Hood River, OR 97031, 541/386-2333.

13 WAHCLELLA FALLS
1.8 mi/1.0 hr

near Bonneville Dam in the Columbia River Gorge

Map 9.2, page 394

The trail may not get off to a great start—it begins on an old gated road—but it makes up for it later on. You'll pass by a small dam for the Bonneville Fish Hatchery before entering a canyon to arrive at this spectacular two-tiered, 350-foot waterfall, which shows off for you and thanks you for visiting it by splashing dramatically into a pool below. After .7 mile, the trail forks—it's a loop, so take your pick. Once you arrive at the falls, you'll cross a bridge at Tanner Creek with a good view of the water display before returning to complete the loop.

User Groups: Hikers and dogs. No mountain bikes or horses are allowed. No wheelchair access.

Permits: A federal Northwest Forest pass is required to park here. The cost is $5 for a day pass or $30 for an annual pass. You can buy a day pass at ranger stations, from private vendors, or through Nature of the Northwest Information Center.

Maps: For a map of the Columbia River Gorge, contact Nature of the Northwest Information Center. For a topographic map, contact Green Trails, Inc. (ask for Bonneville Dam, map num-

ber 429), 206/546-MAPS (206/546-6277), www.greentrails.com; or ask the USGS for Tanner Butte.

Directions: From Portland, drive about 40 miles east on I-84 to Bonneville Dam/Exit 40 and drive south (away from the dam) a short distance to the parking area and trailhead.

Contact: Columbia River Gorge National Scenic Area, 902 Wasco Avenue, Suite 200, Hood River, OR 97031, 541/386-2333.

14 WAUNA VIEWPOINT
3.6 mi/2.0 hrs

near Bonneville Dam in the Columbia River Gorge

Map 9.2, page 394

It's a short climb up 950 feet to the Wauna Viewpoint, where you can gaze down at the Bonneville Dam and the Gorge in all its glory. You'll cross a 200-foot suspension bridge at the start of the trail before switchbacking through Douglas fir forest to the bluff, where you can pretend the power lines don't exist. A mile down, the trail reaches a junction with Gorge Trail, where you should fork left for the last push uphill. Once on top, enjoy the scenery and check out the wildflowers (in spring and summer), such as red paintbrush and orange tiger lily.

User Groups: Hikers and dogs. No mountain bikes or horses are allowed. No wheelchair access.

Permits: A federal Northwest Forest pass is required to park here. The cost is $5 for a day pass or $30 for an annual pass. You can buy a day pass at ranger stations, from private vendors, or through Nature of the Northwest Information Center.

Maps: For a map of the Columbia River Gorge, contact Nature of the Northwest Information Center. For a topographic map, contact Green Trails, Inc. (ask for Bonneville Dam, map number 429), 206/546-MAPS (206/546-6277), www.greentrails.com; or ask the USGS for Bonneville Dam and Tanner Butte.

Directions: From Portland, drive about 40 miles

east on I-84 to Eagle Creek/Exit 41. Turn right (south) and drive past the Bonneville Fish Hatchery, parking on the left by the picnic area.

Contact: Columbia River Gorge National Scenic Area, 902 Wasco Avenue, Suite 200, Hood River, OR 97031, 541/386-2333.

15 EAGLE CREEK TO TUNNEL FALLS
12.0 mi/7.0 hrs

east of Bonneville Dam in the Columbia River Gorge

Map 9.2, page 394

Eagle Creek is a popular out-and-back trail for runners, backpackers, and those who are just out for a short stroll. Like the name suggests, it travels along Eagle Creek for 13.2 miles to Wahtum Lake, where there are campsites if you want to make this a two-day trip. For day hikers, there is plenty to see along the way. First on the itinerary is Punchbowl Falls, a 25-foot fall plunging into a blue-green pool. That's the turn-around point for many people, for a 4.2-mile round-trip. Three words if you're thinking about doing the same: Don't do it! Hike another mile and you'll cross High Bridge, a suspension bridge 150 feet over the Gorge. The scenery gets better the more you hike in, and at times you'll be tempted to hold on to the wall because it's a long drop below (at precarious points, there are handrails to grasp onto). The coolest part on the trail is the amazing Tunnel Falls, named for the tunnel you walk through underneath the falls. Even if you're cool as a cucumber with heights, you may find yourself holding on a little too tightly to the handrails once you get to the falls, and it's an exhilarating experience. The total elevation gain is about 1,000 feet, parceled out gently on the six-mile stretch.

User Groups: Hikers and dogs. No mountain bikes or horses are allowed. No wheelchair access.

Permits: A federal Northwest Forest pass is required to park here. The cost is $5 for a day

pass or $30 for an annual pass. You can buy a day pass at ranger stations, from private vendors, or through Nature of the Northwest Information Center.

Maps: For a map of the Columbia River Gorge, contact Nature of the Northwest Information Center. For a topographic map, contact Green Trails, Inc. (ask for Bonneville Dam, map number 429), 206/546-MAPS (206/546-6277), www.greentrails.com; or ask the USGS for Wahtum Lake.

Directions: From Portland, drive about 40 miles east on I-84 to Eagle Creek/Exit 41 and turn right to drive a mile to the large parking area and the well-marked trailhead.

Contact: Columbia River Gorge National Scenic Area, 902 Wasco Avenue, Suite 200, Hood River, OR 97031, 541/386-2333.

16 HERMAN CREEK/ NICK EATON RIDGE LOOP
8.0 mi/5.0 hrs

between Cascade Locks and Wyeth in the Columbia River Gorge

Map 9.2, page 394

The Herman Creek area has tons of intersecting trails and options, and unlike some of the Gorge trails to the west, the area typically isn't as crowded. For both of these reasons, it can be helpful to bring along a map to check your progress if you don't like to spend your time scratching your head and wondering if you're on the right trail. In any case, here's one option for a tough climb up to Indian Point: At the first junction, at .7 mile, keep to the left, climbing up an old road for another mile to Herman Camp and a clearing. Stay to the left to pick up Gorton Creek Trail (Herman Creek Trail, to the right, heads eight miles to Wahtum Lake for an overnight option). Gorton Creek Trail climbs for another three miles up some tough switchbacks; elevation gain on the entire trail is about 2,700 feet. Enjoy the scenery of the Douglas fir forest, but keep your head up, because the Ridge Cut-Off Trail junction can be hard to miss. You'll turn right about

3.5 miles after the last junction to climb about 100 feet, then you'll descend two miles back to the Herman Camp clearing, where you first took Gorton Creek Trail, and return from there the way you came. It's a tough climb with great views, and you're likely to encounter few people on the way.

User Groups: Hikers, dogs, and horses. No mountain bikes are allowed. No wheelchair access.

Permits: A federal Northwest Forest pass is required to park here. The cost is $5 for a day pass or $30 for an annual pass. You can buy a day pass at ranger stations, from private vendors, or through Nature of the Northwest Information Center.

Maps: For a map of the Columbia River Gorge, contact Nature of the Northwest Information Center. For a topographic map, contact Green Trails, Inc. (ask for Bonneville Dam, map number 429), 206/546-MAPS (206/546-6277), www.greentrails.com; or ask the USGS for Carson and Wahtum Lake.

Directions: From Portland, drive about 45 miles east on I-84 to Cascade Locks/Exit 44. Drive under the highway and through Cascade Locks for 1.8 miles to the eastbound entrance ramp. At the stop sign, cross the road and drive 1.6 miles toward Oxbow Fish Hatchery, and turn right into the Herman Creek Campground. Drive through the campground to the parking area and the trailhead a short distance down at the end of the road.

Contact: Columbia River Gorge National Scenic Area, 902 Wasco Avenue, Suite 200, Hood River, OR 97031, 541/386-2333.

17 MOUNT DEFIANCE/ STARVATION RIDGE

11.4 mi/1.0 day

at Starvation Creek rest area east of Wyeth in the Columbia River Gorge

Map 9.2, page 394

Even its name is bold: Mount Defiance is the tallest peak in the Gorge, standing proud over all the little people. This renowned sweat bonanza requires climbing almost 5,000 feet in five miles (no, that's not a typo). Be prepared for a heart-pounding trip—the view up top is worth the aching in your quads (just pretend those TV antennas don't exist). If the climb doesn't get to you, the poison oak that grows along the trail might, so be careful.

Right after leaving your car, you'll pass by Cabin Creek Falls, just 200 feet from the trailhead. Stop here to enjoy the scenery before tackling the climb ahead. If the falls look familiar, it's because they are—they're the image on the cover of this book.

There are two ways to reach the top: the rockier, steeper Starvation Ridge and the well-maintained but still steep Mount Defiance Trail. (There's no way to get around that elevation gain, unless you drive directly to the top, which is possible, by the way.) It's a good idea to climb up the Starvation Ridge route, because all the loose rock makes for a nasty descent. If you value the cartilage in the ol' knees, try it this way: After reaching the summit, and stopping to catch your breath, of course, head east past Warren Lake to reach Mount Defiance Trail, turning right for the 5.5-mile return trip to your car. There are several good camping spots at Warren Lake if you want to make it an overnight trip, although one could think of easier things to do than hauling a heavy pack up this ridge.

User Groups: Hikers and dogs. No mountain bikes or horses are allowed. No wheelchair access.

Permits: Permits are not required. Parking and access are free.

Maps: For a map of the Columbia River Gorge, contact Nature of the Northwest Information Center. For a topographic map, contact Green Trails, Inc. (ask for Hood River, map number 430), 206/546-MAPS (206/546-6277), www .greentrails.com; or ask the USGS for Mount Defiance.

Directions: From Portland, drive about 50 miles to Starvation Creek State Park exit, just after Wyeth Exit 51. Turn into the rest area;

the trailheads are on the right (west) side of the parking lot.

Contact: Columbia River Gorge National Scenic Area, 902 Wasco Avenue, Suite 200, Hood River, OR 97031, 541/386-2333.

18 WYGANT POINT
8.0 mi/5.5 hrs

between Viento State Park and Hood River in the Columbia River Gorge

Map 9.2, page 394

Wygant Point is the often-overlooked middle child of the Columbia River Gorge—not as mighty as its neighbor Mount Defiance, not as flashy as Multnomah Falls. But Wygant Point is proud of its understated, strong and silent status. You'll huff and puff up this switchback-happy trail to the 2,200-foot summit. Just when you feel like you're getting the hang of this switchback thing, the trail flattens for a bit before the real climbing begins. Outstanding viewpoints of the Gorge await you along the way, and you'll discover see why the area is sometimes called "the windsurfing capital of the world." (Hold on to anything that isn't attached to your body or it will be gone with the wind.) You've probably been wringing your hands in anticipation of the grand finale of views at the point, but it's kind of a buzz-kill when you finally reach it. A bunch of rocks marks the spot (I'd prefer a plaque myself, but that's just me). You can return the way you came or on Chetwoot Trail, which goes through the Perham Creek area (and lacks the great viewpoints). Keep in mind that poison oak grows rampant in this area, so be forewarned and wear long pants.

User Groups: Hikers and dogs. No mountain bikes or horses are allowed. No wheelchair access.

Permits: Permits are not required. Parking and access are free.

Maps: For a map of the Columbia River Gorge, contact Nature of the Northwest Information Center. For a topographic map, contact Green Trails, Inc. (ask for Hood River, map number 430), 206/546-MAPS (206/546-6277), www

.greentrails.com; or ask the USGS for Hood River and Mount Defiance.

Directions: From Portland, drive east on I-84 for about 55 miles to Exit 58/Mitchell Point Overlook. Park in the large parking area at the well-marked trailhead, which starts to the right as you're driving in (along an abandoned road at first). Note: This exit is accessible only to eastbound traffic. If you're coming from Hood River, travel 5.5 miles to Exit 56/Viento State Park and re-exit the highway going east.

Contact: Oregon Parks and Recreation Department, 1115 Commercial Street Northeast, Salem, OR 97301, 800/551-6949, www.oregonstateparks.org.

19 MOSIER TWIN TUNNELS
4.5 mi one-way/2.0 hrs

between Mosier and Hood River

Map 9.2, page 394

Traveling along historic Old Columbia River Highway, the first complete road built though the Columbia Gorge, this bike and hike path has a lot of history behind it, although the restoration of the trail itself didn't start until 1995. The trail extends from Mosier to Hood River for 4.5 miles, but the best part is the Mosier Twin Tunnels, just .9 mile from the trailhead outside of Mosier. Construction of the tunnels began in 1919 and took—appropriately enough—two long years to complete. The whole trail is paved and wide, making it a hit with bikers. It's a great way to take in spectacular views without having to exert a lot (or really any) effort to reach the vantage point, since you start high above the river. Stop and watch for sail- and kiteboarders slicing across the river—this area is "the windsurfing capital of the world." You'll find out why it's such a popular watersports place when you reach the blustery tunnels (bring warm clothes, even on a hot day).

User Groups: Hikers, dogs, and mountain bikes. No horses are allowed. The entire trail is wheelchair accessible, and there is a separate parking area for wheelchair users.

Permits: Permits are not required. A $3 day-use fee is collected at the park entrance, or you can get an annual Oregon Parks and Recreation pass for $25; contact Oregon Parks and Recreation, 800/551-6949.

Maps: For a map of the Historic Columbia River Highway State Trail, contact Oregon Parks and Recreation Department, 800/551-6949, www.oregonstateparks.org. For a topographic map, ask the USGS for White Salmon and Hood River.

Directions: From Hood River, travel five miles east on I-84 to Exit 69. Before you hit the town of Mosier, turn left onto Rock Creek Road and drive one mile to the Mark O. Hatfield parking entrance, on the left. Follow the well-marked path along paved Rock Creek Road, and then cross the street to the wheelchair parking area, where the trail officially begins.

Contact: Oregon Parks and Recreation Department, 1115 Commercial Street Northeast, Salem, OR 97301, 800/551-6949, www.oregonstateparks.org.

20 TOM MCCALL PRESERVE
5.0 mi/3.0 hrs

east of Hood River at the Rowena Crest Viewpoint in the Columbia River Gorge

Map 9.2, page 394

Named after a former Oregon governor, Tom McCall Preserve offers something different than other Gorge trails. Two trails leave from Rowena Crest: One is an easy one-mile stroll out past two lakes before ending at a cliffside viewpoint; the other leads up to McCall Point (open May through November), gaining 1,000 feet in elevation to a view of the Gorge and the wildflowers that cover the area in the spring and summer. More than 300 plant species live here, and you can't blame them for setting up camp at this scenic spot. Although this is a good place to bring the kids, you should leave your furry friends at home.

User Groups: Hikers only. No dogs, mountain bikes, or horses are allowed. No wheelchair access.

Permits: Permits are not required. Parking and access are free.

Maps: Brochures are available (when supplies last) at the trailhead. For a topographic map, ask the USGS for White Salmon.

Directions: From Portland, drive 65 miles east on I-84 to Mosier/Exit 69 and follow signs for 6.5 miles to Rowena Crest Viewpoint. Park at the Rowena Viewpoint parking area, where both trails start.

Contact: The Nature Conservancy of Oregon, 821 Southeast 14th Avenue, Portland, OR 97214, 503/230-1221.

21 LOST LAKE LOOP
3.2 mi/1.5 hrs

southwest of Hood River in Mount Hood National Forest

Map 9.2, page 394

Lost Lake doesn't seem to mind that it's lost, sitting in such a beautiful area. With Mount Hood as the backdrop, this trail follows the lakeshore for an easy loop that everyone can—and will want to—do. The lake is a happenin' place, with a store, a huge campground, canoe rental, and, of course, hiking. Pick up a self-guided nature tour brochure at the store before you head out. If you want to put a little more legwork and add some even cooler scenery into the whole affair, you can add four miles to the trip by heading to 4,468-foot Lost Lake Butte (the trailhead starts from the northeast corner of the lake). Since the lake's elevation is 3,100 feet, it's best to hit this area from June through September, as it can be snowbound the rest of the year.

User Groups: Hikers and dogs. Mountain bikes are not allowed. Horses are not allowed.

Permits: Permits are not required. Parking and access are free.

Maps: For a map of Mount Hood National Forest, contact Nature of the Northwest Information Center. For a topographic map, contact Green Trails, Inc. (ask for Government Camp, map number 461), 206/546-MAPS (206/546-6277), www.greentrails.com; or ask the USGS for Bull Run Lake.

Directions: From Portland, drive about 40 miles east on Highway 26 to Zigzag, and turn left onto East Lolo Pass Road/Forest Service Road 18. After 10.5 miles, turn right onto McGee Creek Road/Forest Service Road 1810 for 7.5 miles until it rejoins Forest Service Road 18. Continue another seven miles and turn left onto Forest Service Road 13 to the Lost Lake entrance. The trailhead starts at the picnic area near the parking lot.

Contact: Mount Hood National Forest, Hood River Ranger District, 6780 Highway 35, Mount Hood-Parkdale, OR 97041, 541/352-6002.

22 OAK RIDGE TO BALD BUTTE/RIMROCK

8.2–9.2 mi/5.0–6.0 hrs

east of Highway 35 in Mount Hood National Forest

Map 9.2, page 394

Robert Frost knew a thing or two when he wrote "The Road Not Taken." He took the lesser-known path when encountering two roads diverging in the woods, and look what happened to him—he's famous! You'll have a chance to solve the same dilemma when you encounter two paths here, each to a viewpoint. There are no guarantees that either path will necessarily be less traveled, as they hit the popular Surveyor's Ridge (see listing in this chapter). Starting at an open grassy area, the trail soon enters the oak and fir forest, and then you start to climb up switchbacks. At 2.3 miles, Oak Ridge Trail officially ends, but your trip has only begun: Turn right for another 2.3 miles south to hit 4,300-foot Rimrock, or head left to reach the 3,779-foot Bald Butte, to the north. Take your pick, or do them both if one viewpoint just isn't enough for you. Clear views of Mount Hood, Mount Adams, Mount St. Helens, Mount Rainier, and the Hood River Valley are your reward for the tough climb up.

User Groups: Hikers, dogs, mountain bikes, and horses. No wheelchair access.

Permits: Permits are not required. Parking and access are free.

Maps: For a map of Mount Hood National Forest, contact Nature of the Northwest Information Center. For a topographic map, contact Green Trails, Inc. (ask for Hood River, map number 430), 206/546-MAPS (206/546-6277), www.greentrails.com; or ask the USGS for Parkdale.

Directions: From Hood River, drive 15 miles south on Highway 35 and turn left on Smullin Road. Drive .2 mile to an unmarked gravel road, turn left, and drive less than .1 mile to the small parking area and well-marked trailhead, on the right.

Contact: Mount Hood National Forest, Hood River Ranger District, 6780 Highway 35, Mount Hood-Parkdale, OR 97041, 541/352-6002.

23 SURVEYOR'S RIDGE

13.0 mi one-way/
1.0–2.0 days

east of Highway 35 in Mount Hood National Forest

Map 9.2, page 394

The name says it all: This is a ridgeline trail from which to survey the land below. And what a land it is. From this popular trail, you can spy on Mount Hood, Mount St. Helens, Mount Rainier, Mount Adams, and the upper Hood River Valley. This trail has an interesting weather pattern, as it's the dividing line between the wet weather of the Columbia River Gorge and Hood River Valley to the west and the dry climate of the desert to the east. Surveyor's Ridge is well known in the area, especially to mountain bikers, so expect some company along the way. The path also hits Gibson Prairie Horse Camp five miles down the way, so you may also see some four-legged friends. There are several access points and campsites along the way, so you can do this as a shuttle or an out-and-back overnight trip. The trail also hits Bald Butte and intersects Oak Ridge Trail (see listing in this chapter).

User Groups: Hikers, dogs, horses, and mountain bikes. No wheelchair access.

Permits: A federal Northwest Forest pass is required to park here. The cost is $5 for a day pass or $30 for an annual pass. You can buy a day pass at ranger stations, from private vendors, or through Nature of the Northwest Information Center.

Maps: For a map of Mount Hood National Forest, contact Nature of the Northwest Information Center. For a topographic map, contact Green Trails, Inc. (ask for Hood River and Mount Hood, map numbers 430 and 462), 206/546-MAPS (206/546-6277), www.greentrails.com; or ask the USGS for Parkdale and Dog River.

Directions: From Hood River, drive south on Highway 35 for 15 miles to Pinemont Drive/Forest Service Road 17. Turn left and drive six miles to Spur Road 630. Turn right and drive four miles to the parking area on the left, a short distance past the fork in the road; take the right fork. (Before the road forks, you'll pass another small parking area; keep going until you come to the small parking area on the left, under the power lines.) To reach the south trailhead, drive south on Highway 35 from Hood River for 25 miles. Between mileposts 70 and 71, turn left onto paved Forest Service Road 44. Drive for 3.5 miles to the junction with Road 620. Park on the side of the road; the trailhead is on the left.

Contact: Mount Hood National Forest, Hood River Ranger District, 6780 Highway 35, Mount Hood-Parkdale, OR 97041, 541/352-6002.

24 HUCKLEBERRY MOUNTAIN
10.5 mi/6.0 hrs 🥾 ⓼

south of Highway 26 in the Salmon Huckleberry Wilderness of Mount Hood National Forest

Map 9.2, page 394

A popular stomping ground for Portlanders, Huckleberry Mountain offers choices on how to visit it. Most people access the 4,000-foot summit from Wildwood Recreation Area, which means that it can get crowded—but not too crowded, as the trail is a hefty hike. Starting from Boulder Ridge Trail, the path switchbacks up through Douglas fir forest, where views get better with each step (remember to look behind you once in a while to glimpse Mount Hood). At the 4.2-mile mark, turn right onto Plaza Trail for another mile to reach the summit. Return the same way, or continue along the mountain's ridge to turn right at Bonanza Mine Trail for five miles to the eastern trailhead (arrange a pick-up if you take this route, as parking can be tough at the trailhead).

User Groups: Hikers, dogs, and horses. No mountain bikes are allowed. No wheelchair access.

Permits: A federal Northwest Forest pass is required to park here. The cost is $5 for a day pass or $30 for an annual pass. You can buy a day pass at ranger stations, from private vendors, or through Nature of the Northwest Information Center.

Maps: For a map of Mount Hood National Forest and Salmon Huckleberry Wilderness, contact Nature of the Northwest Information Center. For a topographic map, contact Green Trails, Inc. (ask for Cherryville and Government Camp, map numbers 460 and 461), 206/546-MAPS (206/546-6277), www.greentrails.com; or ask the USGS for Wildcat Mountain and Rhododendron.

Directions: From Portland, drive about 40 miles east on U.S. 26 to Zigzag. Just past the town, turn right (south) on Salmon River Road and drive 6.7 miles (paved for the first 5.1 miles) to the small parking area on the left. The trailhead starts across the street on an unmarked spur road.

Contact: Mount Hood National Forest, Zigzag Ranger District, 70220 East Highway 26, Zigzag, OR 97049, 503/622-3191.

25 ZIGZAG MOUNTAIN LOOP
11.0 mi/8.0 hrs 🥾 ⓽

west of Mount Hood in the Mount Hood Wilderness

Map 9.2, page 394

One peak not enough for you? Double your pleasure (and pain) with this challenging mountain loop that hits both East and West Zigzag summits. Starting from Burnt Lake Trail (from the other direction than the one in this chapter's listing), the trail starts off on an abandoned road up through Devil's Meadow, filled with wildflowers in the summer. For a shorter loop that shaves 2.5 miles from your trip, you can take the first junction you come across, the Devil's Tie Trail, but then you'd be missing out on the East Zigzag peak. Instead continue straight for another 1.3 miles, turning left to head up the ridge to the peak (4,980 feet) for a peek down into Burnt Lake and, of course, across to Mount Hood. Continue downhill and consider how you're feeling: If you want to take your time, you can add another mile round-trip by heading to Cast Lake for a rest stop. Otherwise, continue just past the lake junction and turn right (west) on Zigzag Mountain Trail another 3.8 miles to the West Zigzag Mountain lookout, passing Horseshoe Ridge Trail to your second lookout. The beauty of this trail is that you're not locked into your distance—if you've had enough, you can always continue straight to return three miles back to your car at this point, turning right at Burnt Lake Trail for an eight-mile loop. If you want to say you bagged two peaks in one day, though, and you're up for a challenge, the entire loop is worth the trip. After reaching the summit of West Zigzag (passing the return trail to your left about .1 mile from the summit), backtrack to West Zigzag Trail for a 2.3-mile descent.

User Groups: Hikers, dogs, and horses. No mountain bikes are allowed. No wheelchair access.

Permits: A federal Northwest Forest pass is required to park here. The cost is $5 for a day pass or $30 for an annual pass. You can buy a day pass at ranger stations, from private vendors, or through Nature of the Northwest Information Center.

Maps: For a map of Mount Hood Wilderness and Mount Hood National Forest, contact Nature of the Northwest Information Center. For a topographic map, contact Green Trails, Inc. (ask for Government Camp, map number 461), 206/546-MAPS (206/546-6277), www.greentrails.com; or ask the USGS for Government Camp.

Directions: From Portland, drive east on U.S. 26 for about 45 miles, passing through the town of Rhododendron. Turn left on Forest Service Road 27, and drive .5 mile to Forest Service Road 207. Turn left and drive 4.5 rough miles to the trailhead and the parking area at the end of the road.
Contact: Mount Hood National Forest, Zigzag Ranger District, 70220 East Highway 26, Zigzag, OR 97049, 503/622-3191.

26 BURNT LAKE
6.0 mi/3.0 hrs

west of Mount Hood in Mount Hood National Forest

Map 9.2, page 394

Burnt Lake sure got the short end of the stick when it came to naming. But there's a good reason for the unfortunate moniker: an old fire that left an interesting display of burned tree trunks you can step inside. A couple miles in, look for a short side trail to the left to find Lost Creek Falls before continuing the climb. You'll get a good workout on the way up, as the trail ascends about 1,500 feet through a mixture of old- and new-growth forest to the lake with a great view of Mount Hood. This trail also continues past the lake less than a mile to Zigzag Mountain Trail (see listing in this chapter).

User Groups: Hikers and dogs. No horses or mountain bikes are allowed. No wheelchair access.

Permits: A federal Northwest Forest pass is required to park here. The cost is $5 for a day pass or $30 for an annual pass. You can buy a day pass at ranger stations, from private vendors, or through Nature of the Northwest Information Center.

Maps: For a map of Mount Hood National Forest, contact Nature of the Northwest Information Center. For a topographic map, contact Green Trails, Inc. (ask for Government Camp, map number 461), 206/546-MAPS (206/546-6277), www.greentrails.com; or ask the USGS for Government Camp.

Directions: From Portland, drive east on Highway 26 for about 40 miles to the town of Zigzag.

Turn left onto East Lolo Pass Road/Forest Service Road 18 and drive 4.2 miles to a fork in the road. Stay to the right, turning onto Forest Service Road 1825. Drive 2.5 miles, and just past the Lost Creek Campground entrance, turn left onto a gravel road for 1.3 miles to the small parking area and well-marked trailhead at the end of the road.

Contact: Mount Hood National Forest, Zigzag Ranger District, 70220 East Highway 26, Zigzag, OR 97049, 503/622-3191.

27 RAMONA FALLS
7.1 mi/3.0 hrs

south of Bald Mountain in Mount Hood National Forest

Map 9.2, page 394

For a well-marked loop to remarkable falls, this is a pleasant day trip. It can get a smidge crowded, though, as the falls are a popular destination. Rhododendron blooms here in the summer, keeping you company as you stroll down this relatively easy path to the falls. Travel one mile to a bridge (which is removed every fall to prevent damage from the high water levels, then reinstalled in the spring), and you'll come to a fork. The right fork is slightly shorter and easier, reaching Ramona in two miles, but it's a sandy trail popular with horses. The left fork wants to be fashionably late, arriving at the falls in 2.3 miles. When you get there, you can see why it's such a popular place. Unlike other waterfalls, which show off with one giant explosion of water, Ramona takes a more dainty approach: Trickling cascades of water rush down the entire rock wall. It's a sight worth seeing, despite the crowds. Complete the loop to travel back to the trailhead. You can lengthen the hike by adding a six-mile loop to Bald Mountain: When you reach the falls, turn north onto Pacific Crest Trail for 4.8 miles, then keep left at the junction to return back to Ramona Falls Trail. You'll have to cross Muddy Fork River, which is lower earlier in the day, so keep that in mind when you arrange your trip.

User Groups: Hikers and horses. No mountain bikes are allowed. No wheelchair access.

Permits: A federal Northwest Forest pass is required to park here. The cost is $5 for a day pass or $30 for an annual pass. You can buy a day pass at ranger stations, from private vendors, or through Nature of the Northwest Information Center.

Maps: For a map of Mount Hood National Forest, contact Nature of the Northwest Information Center. For a topographic map, contact Green Trails, Inc. (ask for Government Camp, map number 461), 206/546-MAPS (206/546-6277), www.greentrails.com; or ask the USGS for Government Camp.

Directions: From Portland, drive east on Highway 26 for about 40 miles to the town of Zigzag. Turn left onto East Lolo Pass Road/Forest Service Road 18 and drive 4.2 miles to a fork in the road. Stay to the right, turning onto Forest Service Road 1825. Continue another 2.4 miles, turning left at the sign for Ramona Falls, and drive .4 mile to the large parking area and the well-marked trailhead.

Contact: Mount Hood National Forest, Zigzag Ranger District, 70220 East Highway 26, Zigzag, OR 97049, 503/622-3191.

28 VISTA RIDGE TO EDEN PARK, CAIRN, AND WY'EAST BASINS
8.0 mi/5.0 hrs

on the northwest slope of Mount Hood

Map 9.2, page 394

The scenic ridgeline (yep, the trail is aptly named) is an easy way to access Timberline Trail to three wildflower meadows: Eden Park, Cairn, and Wy'east Basins. It starts on an old road for a few hundred feet before heading into the hemlock forest, with views of Mount Hood peeking out here and there when you least expect it. It climbs to 5,700 feet (total elevation gain is 900 feet) for 2.5 miles and then comes to the Timberline Trail junction. From here, you can do a three-mile loop to access the attractions. First, head right (west) to Eden Park and Cairn Basin, turning left at both junctions as you head back to Wy'east Basin, and turn left again to complete the loop (remember, when in doubt after that first right, take a left). These meadows afford stellar views of mighty Mount Hood and are worth the trip in. The trail also connects to Elk Cove, two miles to the east (to the left when you first hit Timberline Trail; see listing in this chapter), so you can add another four miles to your trip if you're a fool for alpine beauty.

User Groups: Hikers and dogs. No mountain bikes or horses are allowed.

Permits: A federal Northwest Forest pass is required to park here. The cost is $5 for a day pass or $30 for an annual pass. You can buy a day pass at ranger stations, from private vendors, or through Nature of the Northwest Information Center.

Maps: For a map of Mount Hood National Forest, contact Nature of the Northwest Information Center. For a topographic map, contact Green Trails, Inc. (ask for Mount Hood, map number 462), 206/546-MAPS (206/546-6277), www.greentrails.com; or ask the USGS for Mount Hood North.

Directions: From Portland, drive about 40 miles east on U.S. 26 to East Lolo Pass Road/Forest Service Road 18 and drive 10.5 miles to McGee Creek Road/Forest Service Road 1810. Turn right and drive until the road rejoins Forest Service Road 18, 7.5 miles down, and continue another 3.5 miles and turn right on Forest Service Road 16. Drive 5.5 miles and turn left onto Forest Service Road 1650, following signs another four miles to the end of the rough road and the trailhead.

Contact: Mount Hood National Forest, Hood River Ranger District, 6780 Highway 35, Mount Hood-Parkdale, OR 97041, 541/352-6002.

29 TIMBERLINE TRAIL TO ELK COVE
9.8 mi/6.0 hrs

on the north slope of Mount Hood

Map 9.2, page 394

Ready for a close-up of Mount Hood? Try this 4.9-mile stretch of Timberline Trail to Elk Cove, a meadowed basin of "Da Hood" itself. Along

the challenging and exhilarating hike, you'll cross several streams then descend before the steep, rocky climb to the cove. You'll know you've arrived when you hit the remains of a stone shelter. Wildflowers complete the photo op-filled hike in July and August (it can be snowbound through July, so it's best to hit this one later in the season).

User Groups: Hikers and dogs. No mountain bikes or horses are allowed.

Permits: A federal Northwest Forest pass is required to park here. The cost is $5 for a day pass or $30 for an annual pass. You can buy a day pass at ranger stations, from private vendors, or through Nature of the Northwest Information Center.

Maps: For a map of Mount Hood National Forest, contact Nature of the Northwest Information Center. For a topographic map, contact Green Trails, Inc. (ask for Mount Hood, map number 462), 206/546-MAPS (206/546-6277), www.greentrails.com; or ask the USGS for Mount Hood North.

Directions: From Hood River, drive 23 miles south on Highway 35. At the sign for Cooper Spur Ski Area, turn right onto Cooper Spur Road. Drive 2.3 miles and turn left at the sign for Cloud Cap, onto Forest Service Road 3512. Drive 10.2 miles up the narrow, winding road (paved road turns into gravel after 1.4 miles) to the end of the road and the large parking pullout by the restroom. The trailhead is on the right as you're driving in. Look for the sign to Timberline Trail, and take the right fork heading west.

Contact: Mount Hood National Forest, Hood River Ranger District, 6780 Highway 35, Mount Hood-Parkdale, OR 97041, 541/352-6002.

30 COOPER SPUR
6.8 mi/4.0 hrs

on the north slope of Mount Hood

Map 9.2, page 394

One of the highest trails on Mount Hood, Cooper Spur Trail climbs to 8,514 feet, gaining almost 2,000 feet in elevation. Remember to pack along warm clothes, since it can get a bit nippy at that altitude. You'll walk on Timberline Trail (ignore the right fork heading to Eliot Glacier) for more than a mile before reaching a rock shelter and the junction with Cooper Spur Trail, and then the true climbing begins. Continue until you've reached Tie-In Rock, your beacon in this lonely and beautiful alpine wilderness. The trail is usually snowed in through late July, so it's best to tackle the grueling route later in the season (which will give you all summer to get in shape for it).

User Groups: Hikers and dogs. No mountain bikes or horses are allowed. No wheelchair access.

Permits: A federal Northwest Forest pass is required to park here. The cost is $5 for a day pass or $30 for an annual pass. You can buy a day pass at ranger stations, from private vendors, or through Nature of the Northwest Information Center.

Maps: For a map of Mount Hood National Forest, contact Nature of the Northwest Information Center. For a topographic map, contact Green Trails, Inc. (ask for Mount Hood, map number 462), 206/546-MAPS (206/546-6277), www.greentrails.com; or ask the USGS for Mount Hood North.

Directions: From Hood River, drive 23 miles south on Highway 35. At the sign for Cooper Spur Ski Area, turn right onto Cooper Spur Road. Drive 2.3 miles and turn left at the sign for Cloud Cap, onto Forest Service Road 3512. Drive 10.2 miles up the narrow, winding road (paved road turns into gravel after 1.4 miles) to the end of the road and the large parking pullout by the restroom. The trailhead is on the right as you're driving in.

Contact: Mount Hood National Forest, Hood River Ranger District, 6780 Highway 35, Mount Hood-Parkdale, OR 97041, 541/352-6002.

31 TILLY JANE SKI TRAIL/ POLALLIE RIDGE TO CLOUD CAP

6.0 mi/3.5 hrs

between Cooper Spur Ski Area and Cloud Cap on the northeastern slope of Mount Hood

Map 9.2, page 394

Want to say you've climbed up to the country's oldest alpine ski cabin? (You can also say you drove to it, but that doesn't have quite the same ring to it.) Cloud Cap cabin was built in 1889, and a large section of this area has been listed on the National Registry of Historic Places since 1981. Tilly Jane Ski Trail was nominated in August 2003 for a place of her own on the list. The historic ski trail extends 2.5 miles up to the Tilly Jane shelter and old amphitheater, which was first used in 1920, and then continues for another .5 mile to Cloud Cap. Tilly Jane Ski Trail is one of those continuous, sneaky ascents where, if it weren't for your racing heart, you might not realize you're going uphill. The trail is popular in the winter—all the more reason to hike it in the summer, when you may have it all to yourself. Close to the top, you'll come to a clearing with wildflowers where you can view the valley spread out before you. After exploring Cloud Cap, return to the Tilly Jane shelter and follow the sign marked "Tilly Jane Trail #600A," taking that trail back to Polallie Ridge Trail for the return loop back.

User Groups: Hikers, dogs, mountain bikes, and horses. No wheelchair access.

Permits: A federal Northwest Forest pass is required to park here. The cost is $5 for a day pass or $30 for an annual pass. You can buy a day pass at ranger stations, from private vendors, or through Nature of the Northwest Information Center.

Maps: For a map of Mount Hood National Forest, contact Nature of the Northwest Information Center. For a topographic map, contact Green Trails, Inc. (ask for Mount Hood, map number 462), 206/546-MAPS (206/546-6277), www.greentrails.com; or ask the USGS for Mount Hood North.

Directions: From Hood River, drive 23 miles south on Highway 35. At the sign for Cooper Spur Ski Area, turn right onto Cooper Spur Road. Drive 2.3 miles to Cloud Cap Road, following signs to the Cooper Spur Ski Area for 1.4 miles. Park in the small parking area on the right; the trailhead is across the road on the left.

Contact: Mount Hood National Forest, Hood River Ranger District, 6780 Highway 35, Mount Hood-Parkdale, OR 97041, 541/352-6002.

32 TAMANAWAS FALLS
4.0 mi/2.0 hrs

off Highway 35 north of Sherwood campground in Mount Hood National Forest

Map 9.2, page 394

 You'll get tongue-tied pronouncing the name (ta-MA-na-was, a Native American word meaning "spiritual guardian"), but you'll be speechless when you reach the 100-foot falls. Starting from the East Fork trailhead, the trail starts by crossing a log bridge over East Fork Hood River and then following the creek to the falls (total elevation gain: about 450 feet). A canopy of Douglas fir cools your route, and the flowing creek drowns out all other sounds. You'll be tempted to stop for a picnic and soak up the scenery, but hold your hunger: The best is yet to come. When you finally round a bend and see the falls (two miles in), remember not to gape and walk at the same time—you'll need to watch where you're going. It's a sketchy final climb through boulder fields to the falls, but it's worth the effort: Standing under the cave as water pours down in front of you is like having a slice of your own private Oregon. Well, kind of, as the trail can get crowded. After lingering in the cool mist, return on the same route. Feeling extra energetic? Add 1.5 miles for a loop off the beaten path: Turn left after the second boulder field on your return trip, which takes you up to Polallie Overlook, where you can view the 1980 flood's path of destruction. Return along East Fork Trail, following the signs back to Tamanawas Trail.

User Groups: Hikers and dogs. No horses or mountain bikes are allowed. No wheelchair access.

Permits: A federal Northwest Forest pass is required to park here. The cost is $5 for a day pass or $30 for an annual pass. You can buy a day pass at ranger stations, from private vendors, or through Nature of the Northwest Information Center.

Maps: For a map of Mount Hood National Forest, contact Nature of the Northwest Information Center. For a topographic map, contact Green Trails, Inc. (ask for Mount Hood, map number 462), 206/546-MAPS (206/546-6277), www.greentrails.com; or ask the USGS for Dog River.

Directions: From Hood River, drive 25 miles south on Highway 35 to the trailhead on the right side of the highway, just before Sherwood Campground.

Contact: Mount Hood National Forest, Hood River Ranger District, 6780 Highway 35, Mount Hood-Parkdale, OR 97041, 541/352-6002.

33 EAST FORK TRAIL
6.0 mi one-way/3.0 hrs

west of Highway 35 along the East Fork Hood River

Map 9.2, page 394

Traveling along the East Fork Hood River, this trail is a popular one with mountain bikers for the rolling hills and great single-track trail. Although the entire length is six miles, the trail gets extremely sandy from a washout leading up to Robinhood Campground (the southern trailhead), so unless you feel like a sandy stroll, you should turn around at this point. Still, most of the trail is a scenic walk along the rushing waters of Hood River, and there are plenty of top-notch campsites across the river. The beauty of this camping spot is that it's convenient, right by the highway, but the water drowns out the highway traffic, so you feel as if you're in the middle of the wilderness. Also, it's not nearly as crowded as nearby Tamanawas Falls, where the northern trailhead is located, making it a good choice after hitting the falls to see more of this beautiful area.

User Groups: Hikers, dogs, and mountain bikes. Horses are not allowed. No wheelchair access.

Permits: A federal Northwest Forest pass is required to park here. The cost is $5 for a day pass or $30 for an annual pass. You can buy a day pass at ranger stations, from private vendors, or through Nature of the Northwest Information Center.

Maps: For a map of Mount Hood National Forest and Salmon Huckleberry Wilderness, contact Nature of the Northwest Information Center. For a topographic map, contact Green Trails, Inc. (ask for Mount Hood, map number 462), 206/546-MAPS (206/546-6277), www.greentrails.com; or ask the USGS for Dog River and Badger Lake.

Directions: From Hood River, drive 25 miles south on Highway 35 to the trailhead on the right side of the highway, just before Sherwood Campground.

Contact: Mount Hood National Forest, Hood River Ranger District, 6780 Highway 35, Mount Hood-Parkdale, OR 97041, 541/352-6002.

34 ELK MEADOWS LOOP
7.8 mi/4.0 hrs

on the southeast side of Mount Hood

Map 9.2, page 394

Leading up to a wildflower meadow, this trail is popular with not only other hikers but also with other trails, as many other routes connect to it. The route starts in Clark Creek Sno-Park, leading into a fir forest. At the one-mile point, hikers reach a junction with Newton Creek Trail. Keep going straight, crossing the creek over logs and rocks (it's best to hit this early in the day, when water levels are lower). Then the switchbacks begin, gaining 1,500 feet in elevation en route to the 5,900-foot meadows. Once at the top, you'll arrive at a four-way junction, where you have plenty of options. You can either do a loop around the meadows by heading straight, or turn left (west) to tackle Gnarl Ridge and a tough climb up to 6,500-foot Lamberson Butte. This op-

tion will pile five more miles on to your trip. Otherwise, circle the meadows and return the way you came for a long and exhilarating downhill hike.

User Groups: Hikers, dogs, and horses. No mountain bikes are allowed. No wheelchair access.

Permits: A federal Northwest Forest pass is required to park here. The cost is $5 for a day pass or $30 for an annual pass. You can buy a day pass at ranger stations, from private vendors, or through Nature of the Northwest Information Center.

Maps: For a map of Mount Hood National Forest, contact Nature of the Northwest Information Center. For a topographic map, contact Green Trails, Inc. (ask for Mount Hood, map number 462), 206/546-MAPS (206/546-6277), www.greentrails.com; or ask the USGS for Mount Hood South and Badger Lake.

Directions: From Hood River, drive 35 miles on Highway 35 to Clark Creek Sno-Park, on the right. (Note: You can also start from Hood River Meadows, which is another mile down Highway 35 on the right.)

Contact: Mount Hood National Forest, Hood River Ranger District, 6780 Highway 35, Mount Hood-Parkdale, OR 97041, 541/352-6002.

35 HIGH PRAIRIE TRAIL TO LOOKOUT MOUNTAIN
2.4 mi/2.0 hrs

east of Mount Hood in Mount Hood National Forest

Map 9.2, page 394

So many trailheads lead to Lookout Mountain that it would almost take a book to cover all of them. One longer route starts from Highway 35 and ascends steeply up 2.4 long miles to Gumjuwac Saddle, then another 2.2 miles on Divide Trail up to Lookout Mountain. Another route starts from Fifteenmile Campground and treks for 2.1 miles before hitting Divide Trail for another 1.5 miles. But why mess around with switchbacks? To cut to the chase, take High Prairie Trail for a gentle 600-climb to the top, after which you can check out the surrounding areas. The trail starts on the not-so-scenic old summit road, which can be snow-covered through July, so it's best to leave this one until later in the season. After 1.2 miles you'll reach a junction with Divide Trail; turn left for the summit, just 200 yards away. The views extend as far as Mount Rainier and the Three Sisters. Stick around once you've reached the ridge to explore other attractions, like Oval Lake (about 1.5 miles past the summit, off a short side trail to the left), Palisade Point (another great viewpoint, just past Oval Lake), and Flag Point (about two more miles from Palisade Point). You can just line up your attractions in a row and decide how many you have the energy to hit in one day.

User Groups: Hikers, dogs, and horses. No mountain bikes are allowed. No wheelchair access.

Permits: A federal Northwest Forest pass is required to park here. The cost is $5 for a day pass or $30 for an annual pass. You can buy a day pass at ranger stations, from private vendors, or through Nature of the Northwest Information Center.

Maps: For a map of Mount Hood National Forest, contact Nature of the Northwest Information Center. For a topographic map, contact Green Trails, Inc. (ask for Mount Hood, map number 462), 206/546-MAPS (206/546-6277), www.greentrails.com; or ask the USGS for Badger Lake.

Directions: From Hood River, drive south on Highway 35 for about 30 miles to paved Dufur Mill Road/Forest Service Road 44, between mileposts 70 and 71. Turn left (east) and drive 3.8 miles to High Prairie Road/Forest Service Road 4410. Turn right and go 4.7 miles to a T-junction. Turn left and continue .1 mile to the small parking area on the left. The trailhead is across the road from the parking area.

Contact: Mount Hood National Forest, Hood River Ranger District, 6780 Highway 35, Mount Hood-Parkdale, OR 97041, 541/352-6002.

🖼 GUMJUWAC SADDLE/ GUNSIGHT BUTTE/DIVIDE TO BADGER LAKE

5.4–9.2 mi/3.0–5.0 hrs

east of Highway 35 in the Badger Creek Wilderness of Mount Hood National Forest

Map 9.2, page 394

There are approximately 9,845 routes to Badger Lake (give or take). Okay, there are really only four, if you count the bumpy and often snowy road that leads directly to the lake, but once you're up there it seems like the possibilities are endless. Here are your options: Divide Trail, the easiest path and gentlest on your knees, leads 2.7 miles and 600 feet directly down to the lake. In the middle-of-the-road category with a view to kill, there's Gunsight Trail, which follows the ridgeline for 3.3 miles to Gunsight Butte, which then connects with Badger Creek Trail for 1.3 miles to the lake (elevation loss is also 600 feet but it's a longer route). For the final option, tougher Gumjuwac Saddle Trail offers a challenge, shooting down 1,300 feet in 2.2 miles, then connecting with Badger Creek Trail for two miles to the lake. If you want to get to the lake directly and get a workout hiking back up, try Divide Trail down to the lake and return on Gumjuwac Saddle Trail via Badger Creek Trail for a 6.9-mile loop. (Don't try the loop around the lake itself, though, as it's not maintained.) You can make this an overnight trip by camping at the lake, where there are developed campsites. It's a good idea to get a map of this area before you start off; although the trails are usually marked, it can get confusing at times with all the options. Also, be warned that the road to this trail is rough and often snowed in through July, so check ahead of time to make sure it's clear.

User Groups: Hikers, dogs, and horses. Mountain bikes are allowed only on Gunsight Trail. No wheelchair access.

Permits: Permits are not required. Parking and access are free.

Maps: For a map of Mount Hood National Forest and Badger Creek Wilderness, contact

Nature of the Northwest Information Center. For a topographic map, contact Green Trails, Inc. (ask for Mount Hood, map number 462), 206/546-MAPS (206/546-6277), www.greentrails.com; or ask the USGS for Badger Lake.

Directions: From Hood River, drive about 30 miles south on Highway 35 to Dufur Mill Road/Forest Service Road 44, between mileposts 70 and 71. Turn left (east) and drive 3.8 miles to High Prairie Road/Forest Service Road 4410. Turn right and drive 4.5 miles and then turn right on the rough, dirt Bennett Pass Road/Forest Service Road 3350 for 3.5 miles to the trailheads. Gunsight Trail starts on the right side of the road, while Gumjuwac Saddle and Divide Trails start from the left side of the road.

Contact: Mount Hood National Forest, Barlow Ranger District, Dufur Ranger Station, 780 Northeast Court Street, Dufur, OR 97021, 541/467-2291.

37 FLAG POINT/ GORDON BUTTE

7.0 mi/3.5 hrs

east of Highway 35 in the Badger Creek Wilderness of Mount Hood National Forest

Map 9.2, page 394

Your car does most of the work on the bumpy ride in to this 5,651-foot lookout tower, but it's worth the effort: You can climb up stairs to the top of Flag Point Lookout (which is available for rental), where northern views extend to Mount Rainier and Mount Adams in Washington. For a sweeping southern view, head to the south of the A-frame building to pick up the .5-mile round-trip West Point Trail, where the ranger on duty takes a daily pilgrimage to check out how the south side is faring. Once you've seen both sides of the picture, return to the lookout and pick up Douglas Cabin Trail. It leads 3.5 miles down 800 feet to 4,820-foot Gordon Butte for more southern exposure (there may be some logs on the route; check to see if it's clear if you don't want to hop the obstacles). Be warned: The road leading to this trail is often snowed in through July, so unless you enjoy

plowing through snow on a bumpy road with a cliff on one side—which, I found out while driving through this area, some people actually do enjoy—you'd be wise to steer (no pun intended) clear until it's snow-free. Check conditions with the Forest Service before heading out.

User Groups: Hikers, dogs, and horses. No mountain bikes are allowed. No wheelchair access.

Permits: Permits are not required. Parking and access are free.

Maps: For a map of Mount Hood National Forest and Badger Creek Wilderness, contact Nature of the Northwest Information Center. For a topographic map, contact Green Trails, Inc. (ask for Flag Point, map number 463), 206/546-MAPS (206/546-6277), www.greentrails.com; or ask the USGS for Flag Point.

Directions: From Hood River, drive 30 miles south on U.S. 35. Turn left (east) on Forest Service Road 44/Dufur Mill Road, between mileposts 70 and 71. Drive 8.5 miles to Forest Service Road 4420. Turn right and continue two miles to a fork, turning left onto Forest Service Road 2730, which turns into a narrow, one-lane paved road. Drive 3.4 miles to Forest Service Road 200 and turn right. Continue 3.1 miles to the Flag Point trailhead at the end of the road. (Note: Road 200 is bumpy and often snowed in through July.)

Contact: Mount Hood National Forest, Barlow Ranger District, Dufur Ranger Station, 780 Northeast Court Street, Dufur, OR 97021, 541/467-2291.

38 SCHOOL CANYON/ BALL POINT

6.5 mi/3.5 hrs

east of Highway 35 in the Badger Creek Wilderness of Mount Hood National Forest

Map 9.2, page 394

Walking up the dusty old road that starts off School Canyon Trail, you get a sneaking suspicion that you've just stepped out of the Mount Hood area. You have, kind of. The Badger Creek Wilderness area is typically drier than its brethren to the west, and you'll notice a change in the scenery, with scrub alpine hinting at the desert landscape just east. You'll know you're still in the Mount Hood area, though, because of the views. They begin almost as soon as you leave your car, extending to Mount Jefferson to the south. Leading up a mile just before 3,959-feet Ball Point summit, the trail goes on another three miles to amazing views on a cliff just past the junction with Little Badger Creek Trail. Turn around here, or return on Little Badger Creek Trail for a shuttle hike just three miles down from where you started.

User Groups: Hikers, dogs, and horses. No mountain bikes are allowed. No wheelchair access.

Permits: A federal Northwest Forest pass is required to park here. The cost is $5 for a day pass or $30 for an annual pass. You can buy a day pass at ranger stations, from private vendors, or through Nature of the Northwest Information Center.

Maps: For a map of Mount Hood National Forest and Badger Creek Wilderness, contact Nature of the Northwest Information Center. For a topographic map, contact Green Trails, Inc. (ask for Flag Point, map number 463), 206/546-MAPS (206/546-6277), www.green trails.com; or ask the USGS for Flag Point and Friend.

Directions: From the intersection of U.S. 26 and U.S. 35 (about three miles east of Government Camp), drive 3.5 miles north on U.S. 35 toward Hood River. Turn right on Forest Service Road 48 at the sign for Rock Creek Reservoir. Drive 24.5 miles on paved Forest Service Road 48 and turn left on Forest Service Road 4810 at the sign for Bonney Creek Crossing (keeping to the right when the road veers left); drive two miles to Forest Service Road 4811. Continue 1.2 miles to Forest Service Road 2710 and turn right, continuing 5.7 miles to a junction. Turn right and stay on the gravel road for three miles to Forest Service Road 27. Turn left and drive two miles to the trailhead and parking pullout on the left.

Contact: Mount Hood National Forest, Barlow Ranger District, Dufur Ranger Station, 780 Northeast Court Street, Dufur, OR 97021, 541/467-2291.

39 BADGER CREEK TRAIL
12.2 mi one-way/2.0 days

between Badger Lake and Bonney Crossing Campground in the Badger Creek Wilderness of Mount Hood National Forest

Map 9.2, page 394

This is the longest and probably the most popular trail in the Badger Creek Wilderness, connecting with plenty of other trails, so you can choose to shorten the route or make it an overnight trip; there are prime creekside camping spots along the way. The east side of Mount Hood can get hot and dry in the summer (look out for rattlesnakes), so the creekside access is refreshing on a scorching day. This is also a longer and, for the most part, gentler access route to Badger Lake (although there are some steep climbs along the way on the upper part of the route). Badger Lake is about 11 miles down the trail.

User Groups: Hikers, dogs, and horses. No mountain bikes are allowed. No wheelchair access.

Permits: A federal Northwest Forest pass is required to park here. The cost is $5 for a day pass or $30 for an annual pass. You can buy a day pass at ranger stations, from private vendors, or through Nature of the Northwest Information Center.

Maps: For a map of Mount Hood National Forest and Badger Creek Wilderness, contact Nature of the Northwest Information Center. For a topographic map, contact Green Trails, Inc. (ask for Mount Hood and Flag Point, map numbers 462 and 463), 206/546-MAPS (206/ 546-6277), www.greentrails.com; or ask the USGS for Flag Point and Badger Lake.

Directions: From the U.S. 26/Highway 35 intersection (about three miles east of Government Camp), drive 3.5 miles north on U.S. 35 toward Hood River. Turn right on paved Forest Service

Road 48 at the sign for Rock Creek Reservoir. Drive 24.5 miles and turn left on Forest Service Road 4810 at the sign for Bonney Creek Crossing, staying to the right when the road forks. Drive two miles to Forest Service Road 4811 and turn right. Continue 1.2 miles to gravel Forest Service Road 2710. Turn right and drive 1.8 miles to the trailhead at Bonney Crossing campground. The small parking lot and trailhead begin just after you drive across the bridge on the left side of the road.

Contact: Mount Hood National Forest, Barlow Ranger District, Dufur Ranger Station, 780 Northeast Court Street, Dufur, OR 97021, 541/467-2291.

40 HIDDEN LAKE

4.0 mi/2.5 hrs

north of Government Camp in the Mount Hood Wilderness of Mount Hood National Forest

Map 9.2, page 394

It's hidden all right, and views are hidden from it. It's not the most scenic lake you'll ever come across, but the pink rhododendrons lining the trail in June make up for it. You also won't be hidden from the sound of highway traffic, which accompanies you for about half of the hike. It's a gentle switchbacking trail that will give you some exercise without leaving you a sweating mess. Once you reach the lake, you can take a rest and turn around from here, or you can continue on for a super-challenging 13-mile loop: Continue past the lake for three miles, then turn left when you reach Pacific Crest Trail. Wind through Zigzag Canyon for 2.5 miles until you reach Paradise Park Trail, then return the five miles back to the road and the trailhead, which ends on Kiwanis Camp Road, about a mile from the trailhead you started from.

User Groups: Hikers, dogs, and horses. No mountain bikes are allowed. No wheelchair access.

Permits: A federal Northwest Forest pass is required to park here. The cost is $5 for a day pass or $30 for an annual pass. You can buy a day pass at ranger stations, from private vendors, or through Nature of the Northwest Information Center.

Maps: For a map of Mount Hood National Forest, contact Nature of the Northwest Information Center. For a topographic map, contact Green Trails, Inc. (ask for Mount Hood and Government Camp, map numbers 461 and 462), 206/546-MAPS (206/546-6277), www.greentrails.com; or ask the USGS for Mount Hood South and Government Camp.

Directions: From Portland, drive about 50 miles east on Highway 26 to about two miles past Rhododendron. Turn left onto Kiwanis Camp Road/Forest Service Road 2639 and drive two miles to the large parking area and trailhead on the left.

Contact: Mount Hood National Forest, Zigzag Ranger District, 70220 East Highway 26, Zigzag, OR 97049, 503/622-3191.

41 TIMBERLINE LODGE TO ZIGZAG CANYON/PARADISE PARK

4.4–12.3 mi/2.5–8.0 hrs

west of Mount Hood's Timberline Lodge in Mount Hood National Forest

Map 9.2, page 394

Simply put, this section of Pacific Crest Trail is a beaut, but don't let her looks fool you: She's also out to kill (or maybe just maim a little). It's a tough climb through Zigzag Canyon and up through Paradise Park, but it's well worth the grunts and curses. The views of Mount Hood can't be beat, and you'll feel like you're walking through a vast expanse all to yourself. You may encounter a few other people along the way, but overall it's surprisingly uncrowded. If you just want a taste of the scenery without too much effort, you can turn around when you hit the Zigzag Canyon viewpoint, 2.2 miles down the trail (you'll know it when you see it; the zigging and zagging is impossible to miss). If you want to keep on going, you'll have to descend into the canyon and climb up the other side, which is no easy feat. When you reach Paradise Park Trail, about 3.5 miles in, turn

right to continue the scenic tour of alpine wild-flower meadows. The trail starts and ends at the massive yet cozy Timberline Lodge, where you can end your day with a meal. Locals know it as the place where exterior shots in *The Shining* were filmed (the interior and other exterior shots were filmed in Colorado and England), but the lodge itself doesn't broadcast this information. Maybe they think it would spook overnight guests? Anyway, the lodge is a great destination in and of itself, so if camping isn't your thing, treat yourself to a night of luxury.
User Groups: Hikers, dogs, and horses. No mountain bikes are allowed. No wheelchair access.
Permits: Permits are not required. Parking and access are free.
Maps: For a map of Mount Hood National Forest, contact Nature of the Northwest Information Center. For a topographic map, contact Green Trails, Inc. (ask for Mount Hood, map number 462), 206/546-MAPS (206/546-6277), www.greentrails.com; or ask the USGS for Mount Hood South.
Directions: From Portland, drive about 55 miles east on Highway 26 to Government Camp. Following signs to Timberline Lodge, turn left onto Timberline Road, and drive six miles to the road's end and the large parking lot. The trail starts from behind the lodge; look for signs for Timberline Trail, and head west (left) as it travels under a chairlift to start the trail.
Contact: Mount Hood National Forest, Zigzag Ranger District, 70220 East Highway 26, Zigzag, OR 97049, 503/622-3191.

42 MOUNTAINEER TRAIL TO SILCOX HUT

2.0 mi/1.5 hrs

from Timberline Lodge to Silcox Hut on the south slope of Mount Hood

Map 9.2, page 394

Built in 1939, Silcox Hut was named after Ferdinand Silcox, who reigned supreme as chief of the National Forest Service in the 1930s. In its infancy, it was used as a warming hut for the ski area's original Magic Mile chairlift, the sec-

ond chairlift in the country. It was brushed aside for a fancier, shinier Magic Mile chairlift and a new warming hut, but it wasn't entirely left out in the cold: The 13-room hut with sleeping bunks is now available for rent, with your own chef and bartender for group parties. The trail heads straight up for 1,000 feet (you may wonder why you're breathless so quickly; remember, you're *starting* at 6,000 feet). The mile-long trail is mostly on a Snowcat road, but the trail is not the main attraction here. It's worth the trip just to be hiking alongside skiers and snowboarders in the middle of the summer (Mount Hood is renowned for offering year-round snow, and the national teams often flock here because of that). Once you reach the hut, park yourself on the picnic bench and enjoy the ridiculously cool views of the Mount Hood area. You really have to see it to believe it, and all that for chump change, as far as mileage goes! Return the way you came, or continue west just past the hut to return on a Snowcat road back down to the lodge. It's hard to get lost on this one. Use the hut as your beacon to the top and the lodge as your beacon to the bottom. Pack warm clothes—it can get gusty at the top.
User Groups: Hikers and dogs. No mountain bikes or horses are allowed. No wheelchair access.
Permits: Permits are not required. Parking and access are free.
Maps: For a map of Mount Hood National Forest, contact Nature of the Northwest Information Center. For a topographic map, contact Green Trails, Inc. (ask for Mount Hood, map number 462), 206/546-MAPS (206/546-6277), www.greentrails.com; or ask the USGS for Mount Hood South.
Directions: From Portland, drive about 55 miles east on Highway 26 to Government Camp. Following signs to Timberline Lodge, turn left onto Timberline Road and drive six miles to the road's end and the large parking lot. The trail starts from the east (right) side of the lodge. Look for signs to Mountaineer Trail.
Contact: Mount Hood National Forest, Zigzag

Ranger District, 70220 East Highway 26, Zigzag, OR 97049, 503/622-3191.

43 TIMBERLINE TRAIL
40.7 mi/4.0–5.0 days

around the rim of Mount Hood

Map 9.2, page 394

Mighty Timberline Trail is a famous notch in any backpacker's belt. Circling Mount Hood, the path travels partly on Pacific Crest Trail. If you're looking for the Ultimate Experience, you should try this trail. Keep several things in mind, though: It's not for the novice, the faint of heart, the faint of lungs, or the directionally challenged. Absolutely bring along a map and compass (and know how to use them), and realize that conditions change quickly on the mountain. Come prepared with plenty of warm clothes and emergency survival equipment. It can still be snowy through July, so plan accordingly. If you're tough enough, you'll be rewarded with amazing views the whole way, not to mention bragging rights. The average elevation on the trail is 5,000 feet, with ranges from 3,000 to 7,000 feet, so you'll be doing a lot of climbing and descending along the way—and that's why you get to brag about it when all is said and done.

User Groups: Hikers and dogs. No mountain bikes. Horses are allowed only on Pacific Crest Trail portions of the trail. No wheelchair access.

Permits: No permits are required at Timberline Lodge. At other trailheads, a federal Northwest Forest pass is required to park there; the cost is $5 for a day pass or $30 for an annual pass. You can buy a day pass at ranger stations, from private vendors, or through Nature of the Northwest Information Center.

Maps: For a map of Mount Hood National Forest, contact Nature of the Northwest Information Center. For a topographic map, contact Green Trails, Inc. (ask for Government Camp and Mount Hood, map numbers 461 and 462), 206/546-MAPS (206/546-6277), www.greentrails.com; or ask the USGS for Mount Hood North, Mount Hood South, and Bull Run Lake.

Directions: There are several access points. The most popular starting point from the south is Timberline Lodge: From Portland, drive about 55 miles east on Highway 26 to Government Camp. Following signs to Timberline Lodge, turn left onto Timberline Road, and drive six miles to the road's end and the large parking lot. The trail starts behind the lodge and is marked as the Pacific Crest Trail. The most popular starting point from the north is Cloud Cap (see listing in this chapter for directions).

Contact: Mount Hood National Forest Information Center, 65000 East Highway 26, Welches, OR 97067, 503/622-7674.

44 OLD SALMON RIVER/ DEVIL'S PEAK
16.0 mi one-way/ 1.0–2.0 days

south of Highway 26 in the Salmon Huckleberry Wilderness of Mount Hood National Forest

Map 9.2, page 394

Plenty of spots access the scenic shores of the Old Salmon River, and plenty of people do just that. Traveling the river for almost its entirety, minus a slight climb in the northern region to cliffside views, the riverside trail is a good one for the whole family. Be warned: Because it's so easy to get to, it can get crowded on sunny weekends. The trail follows the road for almost three miles, then leaves civilization behind to pass by waterfalls and deep canyons, with plenty of camping sites along the way. You can also get some climbing in on this trail, if the flat route just isn't putting enough strain on your hamstrings. About 10 miles from the original trailhead, the trail forks to the left to climb 3.5 miles to 5,045-foot Devil's Peak Lookout, where there are views of the Cascade peaks and the Salmon River Valley. One option is to start from the Upper Salmon River trailhead (see directions, below) and hike in about five miles to one of the many riverside camp spots, then tackle Devil's Peak on the next day. (Or do it all in one day if you have to be like that.) Unlike many of the trails in the

Mount Hood area, this one is quite simple to follow: Keep the river at your side and you can't go wrong. If you want a simple yet scenic stroll, Old Salmon has got your back.

User Groups: Hikers and dogs. Mountain bikes are allowed on the lower portion of the trail. No horses are allowed. No wheelchair access.

Permits: A federal Northwest Forest pass is required to park here. The cost is $5 for a day pass or $30 for an annual pass. You can buy a day pass at ranger stations, from private vendors, or through Nature of the Northwest Information Center.

Maps: For a map of Mount Hood National Forest and Salmon Huckleberry Wilderness, contact Nature of the Northwest Information Center. For a topographic map, contact Green Trails, Inc. (ask for Government Camp and High Rock, map numbers 461 and 493), 206/546-MAPS (206/546-6277), www.greentrails.com; or ask the USGS for Rhododendron, High Rock, and Wolf Peak.

Directions: From Portland, drive about 40 miles east on U.S. 26 to Zigzag. Just past the town, turn right (south) on Salmon River Road. The first trailhead and parking area is 2.7 miles down the road on the right. Other access points are farther down the road and tend to be less crowded: Continue another two miles down Salmon River Road to the Upper Salmon River Bridge, where parking and the trail are on the left.

Contact: Mount Hood National Forest, Zigzag Ranger District, 70220 East Highway 26, Zigzag, OR 97049, 503/622-3191.

leads you to the 4,877-foot summit for views of Mount Hood, Mount Jefferson, Mount St. Helens, and the Salmon River Valley below. The trailhead can be a little confusing: You first walk on an old road for .25 mile, and when you come to a clearing, the trailhead is on the left. It's typically not as crowded as other trails in the area, so you may have a view for one (or two, if you bring a friend to share the glory with).

User Groups: Hikers, dogs, and horses. No mountain bikes are allowed. No wheelchair access.

Permits: A federal Northwest Forest pass is required to park here. The cost is $5 for a day pass or $30 for an annual pass. You can buy a day pass at ranger stations, from private vendors, or through Nature of the Northwest Information Center.

Maps: For a map of Mount Hood National Forest and Salmon Huckleberry Wilderness, contact Nature of the Northwest Information Center. For a topographic map, contact Green Trails, Inc. (ask for Government Camp and High Rock, map numbers 461 and 493), 206/546-MAPS (206/546-6277), www.greentrails.com; or ask the USGS for Rhododendron and High Rock.

Directions: From Portland, drive about 40 miles east on U.S. 26 to Zigzag. Just past the town, turn right (south) on Salmon River Road and drive 6.7 miles (paved for the first 5.1 miles) to the small parking area on the left. The trailhead starts across the street on an unmarked spur road.

Contact: Mount Hood National Forest, Zigzag Ranger District, 70220 East Highway 26, Zigzag, OR 97049, 503/622-3191.

45 SALMON BUTTE
8.4 mi/5.0 hrs

south of Highway 26 in the Salmon Huckleberry Wilderness of Mount Hood National Forest

Map 9.2, page 394

When the snow is away, the flowers will play: In June, when the snow typically melts from the area, the rhododendrons are in bloom as you hike up to the former lookout site. At about four miles, the trail connects to an old road that

46 MIRROR LAKE
3.2 mi/2.0 hrs

west of Government Camp off U.S. 26 in Mount Hood National Forest

Map 9.2, page 394

Convenience is the spice of life (or something like that), and this trail is made for those who want to get in and out quickly. Starting right off the highway on a narrow footbridge, the wide and well-maintained trail switchbacks gently for 1.4 miles, just enough to make you feel like you're getting a workout. There are campsites along the picturesque lakeshore, and plenty of picnic stops and access points. Although it's just a stone's throw from the highway, you may as well have hiked in 10 miles, because it seems so remote. The only clue that it's a short hike is the number of other people who are also attracted to this hot spot. Take a .4-mile loop around the lake and head back the way you came for a quick and easy hike to a grand locale. If that wasn't enough, you can also visit your three buds Tom, Dick, and Harry: As you start to circle the lake, take a right onto Wind Creek Trail when the trail forks, continuing 1.8 miles up to a viewpoint on Tom, Dick, and Harry Mountain (which has to win the "weirdest mountain name" contest) and views of Mount Hood. Return the way you came, continue circling the lake, and head back to the trailhead.

User Groups: Hikers and dogs. No mountain bikes or horses are allowed. No wheelchair access.

Permits: A federal Northwest Forest pass is required to park here. The cost is $5 for a day pass or $30 for an annual pass. You can buy a day pass at ranger stations, from private vendors, or through Nature of the Northwest Information Center.

Maps: For a map of Mount Hood National Forest, contact Nature of the Northwest Information Center. For a topographic map, contact Green Trails, Inc. (ask for Government Camp, map number 461), 206/546-MAPS (206/546-6277), www.greentrails.com; or ask the USGS for Government Camp.

Directions: From Portland, drive about 50 miles east on Highway 26, between mileposts 51 and 52, about two miles west of Government Camp. The small parking area and the well-marked trailhead are on the right side of the highway.

Contact: Mount Hood National Forest, Zigzag Ranger District, 70220 East Highway 26, Zigzag, OR 97049, 503/622-3191.

47 TWIN LAKES
5.0 mi/2.5 hrs

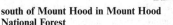

south of Mount Hood in Mount Hood National Forest

Map 9.2, page 394

As with many trails that lead directly from the highway, this trail tends to be busy, especially to the lower lake. It's an easy hike to two clear, pristine lakes, and you can also include Palmateer Point to add four more miles to your trip. From the trailhead, start off on Pacific Crest Trail for the first 1.5 miles, turning right at the junction to the lower lake. Circle the one-mile perimeter, and if you want to escape the crowds, continue around the lake to turn right and hit the upper lake after another .5 mile. If you're looking for a good swimming spot, this is the place to stop for a while. After you've had your fill, continue on the trail you started from, turning left and hiking .5 mile to the junction with Pacific Crest Trail; then turn left again to complete the loop. If you want to add some views of Mount Hood and some muscle power to your trip, continue on past the upper lake for a steep, rocky climb on Palmateer Trail another mile to the crest, then return the way you came, or continue past the point for a mile to the Pacific Crest Trail junction, turning left to complete the loop.

User Groups: Hikers, dogs, and horses. No mountain bikes are allowed. No wheelchair access.

Permits: A federal Northwest Forest pass is required to park here. The cost is $5 for a day pass or $30 for an annual pass. You can buy a day pass at ranger stations, from private vendors, or through Nature of the Northwest Information Center.

Maps: For a map of Mount Hood National Forest, contact Nature of the Northwest Information Center. For a topographic map, contact Green Trails, Inc. (ask for Mount Hood and Mount Wilson, map numbers 462 and 494), 206/546-MAPS (206/546-6277), www.green trails.com; or ask the USGS for Mount Hood South.

Directions: From Portland, drive about 60 miles east on U.S. 26, about eight miles past Government Camp, and turn into the Frog Lake Sno-Park parking area on the right. The trailhead, marked as the Pacific Crest Trail, is on the left side of the parking lot.

Contact: Mount Hood National Forest, Hood River Ranger District, 6780 Highway 35, Mount Hood-Parkdale, OR 97041, 541/352-6002.

48 TIMOTHY LAKE LOOP
12.0 mi/6.5 hrs

around Timothy Lake south of Mount Hood in Mount Hood National Forest

Map 9.2, page 394

Tired of sweet little two-mile saunters around cute little lakes? Timothy is your man! As far as lakes go in the Mount Hood area, this is the Master of the Loops, the Big Loop-ola, the Loop to End Them All. This 12-mile flat loop circles this scenic lake with Mount Hood as a backdrop. You'll travel on Timothy Lake Trail and catch the Pacific Crest Trail; it's all straightforward, no navigation required. The lake is popular for camping and fishing, with several campgrounds on the shores. Hiking the well-maintained trail, you can actually feel like you've gotten some exercise for the day (and have earned that cold beverage at your campsite). What else do you need? Well, maybe to have it to yourself, but 'dems the breaks.

User Groups: Hikers, dogs, mountain bikes, and horses. There is wheelchair access at several points.

Permits: A federal Northwest Forest pass is required to park here. The cost is $5 for a day pass or $30 for an annual pass. You can buy a day pass at ranger stations, from private vendors, or through Nature of the Northwest Information Center.

Maps: For a map of Mount Hood National Forest, contact Nature of the Northwest Information Center. For a topographic map, contact Green Trails, Inc. (ask for High Rock and Mount Wilson, numbers 493 and 494), 206/546-MAPS (206/546-6277), www.greentrails.com; or ask the USGS for Wolf Peak and Timothy Lake.

Directions: From Portland, drive east on U.S. 26 past Mount Hood, between mileposts 65

and 66. Turn right at the sign for Timothy Lake onto Skyline Road, and continue for four miles. Turn right onto Abbott Road/Forest Service Road 58, and drive 1.5 miles to the trailhead at the eastern end of the campground loop at Little Crater Campground.

Contact: Mount Hood National Forest, Zigzag Ranger Station, 70220 East Highway 26, Zigzag, OR 97049, 503/622-3191.

49 LOWER DESCHUTES RIVER
4.0 mi/2.0 hrs

at the confluence of the Columbia and Deschutes Rivers in the eastern Columbia River Gorge

Map 9.3, page 395

Commonly known as the Gateway to the Desert (okay, I actually just made that up—but I did see a tumbleweed as I drove in), this area is where the Deschutes meets the Columbia River. (Deschutes, meet Columbia. Columbia, meet Deschutes.) It's also the beginning of the desert environment, a stark contrast to the lush forest areas of the western Gorge trails. Between the campground and fishing spots and horseback riding, there's a lot going on in Deschutes State Park, where the trail is located, but keep your focus to find the easy-to-miss trailhead. The first part of the trail is just a faint path through the grass directly in front of the second day-use parking area (on the south end of the campground). Just trod on through to spot the trail sign, visible across the meadow. There are two trails that connect for a four-mile loop. Start on the lower trail along the Deschutes River for a pleasant riverside saunter, then head back on the easy-to-find middle trail for a two-mile trek back through the desert shrubs and a view of the bald peaks on the Washington side of the Gorge. Hikers can also share the 16 miles of biking trails here.

User Groups: Hikers and dogs. Horses and mountain bikes are allowed on separate trails in the park. No wheelchair access.

Permits: Permits are not required. Parking and access are free.

Maps: For a free brochure, contact Oregon Parks and Recreation Department, 800/551-6949, www.oregonstateparks.org. For a topographic map, ask the USGS for Emerson.

Directions: From The Dalles (85 miles east of Portland), drive east on I-84 for 12 miles to Exit 97/Deschutes Park, following signs for three miles to the park entrance. Drive past the campground (you'll pass one day-use parking area on your right), and park in the southern end of the campground in the day-use parking area, to the left of the tent camping spot. The trailhead is straight ahead, across the meadow.

Contact: Oregon Parks and Recreation Department, 1115 Commercial Street Northeast, Salem, OR 97301, 800/551-6949, www.oregon stateparks.org.

50 TABLE ROCK
7.6 mi/3.5 hrs

east of Salem off Highway 22 in the Table Rock Wilderness

Map 9.4, page 396

Since it's the highest point in the Table Rock Wilderness, the 4,881-foot sheer granite wall gets a wilderness named after it. As well it should. The sweeping view from the top peeks into California and Washington, and surveys the Cascade range. The trail starts off gently on a gravel road, with buttercups, Indian paintbrush, and rhododendrons lining the way. It climbs steeper in the last .5 mile, when you turn left to switchback and scramble up a rocky scree slope to reach the summit (the overall elevation gain along the trail is 1,200 feet). A landslide now covers part of the road, but determined hikers have beaten a path through the forest; take that trail, to the right, hike around the slide, and continue up the main road again before reaching the trail to the right again after a mile. Because the route can be confusing at times, get a trail map before you set out. Once you reach the summit, backtrack to the main trail again, and head over to Table Rock's runner-up in the tallest-peak division:

Rooster Rock, standing proud at 4,663 feet. Return to the saddle junction and continue straight across the saddle to add three miles to your trip.

User Groups: Hikers, dogs, and horses. No mountain bikes are allowed. No wheelchair access.

Permits: Permits are not required. Parking and access are free.

Maps: For a map of the Table Rock Wilderness, contact Nature of the Northwest Information Center. For a topographic map, ask the USGS for Rooster Rock.

Directions: From Molalla, drive .5 mile east on Highway 211 to South Mathias Road. Turn right and drive .2 mile to South Feyrer Park Road, taking a slight left. Drive 1.6 miles to South Dickie Prairie Road, and then turn right. Continue 5.3 miles and turn right to cross a bridge over the Molalla River. Drive 12.8 miles to a fork and veer left onto gravel Middle Fork Road. Go another 2.6 miles and turn right on Table Rock Road. The road dead-ends at a landslide at 4.3 miles. Park on the side of the road and hike up the road.

Contact: Bureau of Land Management, Salem District, 1717 Fabry Road Northeast, Salem, OR 97306, 503/375-5646.

51 BAGBY HOT SPRINGS
3.0 mi/1.5 hrs

on the Hot Springs Fork of the Collawash River in the Bull of the Woods Wilderness in Mount Hood National Forest

Map 9.4, page 396

As the Monty Python saying goes, "And now for something completely different." This is definitely a different type of hike than any others, which you'll notice as soon as you reach the trailhead. That's because the main gig here isn't the hike itself, but the Bagby Hot Springs. Soooo, let's just say you'll encounter all types on this gentle hike: couples, groups of teenagers, and folks who look like they are quite comfy on the back of a Harley. Here, backpacks are swapped for towels and loungewear—or no wear at all. Check your modesty at the trailhead: These are hot springs, after all, and people don't necessarily wear clothing when bathing in them. The path is amazingly well maintained, with logs on either side of the mostly gravel path and mini-bridges spanning each and every steam, lest your dainty feet get soaked. Kinda defeats the purpose, seeing as you're about to dip into the springs, but what the heck. You'll cross a bridge over a little waterfall when you're almost there, and you can see the clear, green water, a glimpse of things to come. If you're interested in taking a dip in the springs, which are all enclosed in little cabins, you may have to wait in line on a weekend, because it can get packed. The trail also leads six miles to Silver King Mountain, connecting to the Whetstone Mountain trail system for endless loop and backpacking options if you want to use the hot springs as a setting-off point further into the Bull of the Woods Wilderness.

User Groups: Hikers and dogs. Mountain bikes and horses are not allowed. No wheelchair access.

Permits: A federal Northwest Forest pass is required to park here. The cost is $5 for a day pass or $30 for an annual pass. You can buy a day pass at ranger stations, from private vendors, or through Nature of the Northwest Information Center.

Maps: For a map of the Bull of the Woods Wilderness, contact Nature of the Northwest Information Center. For a topographic map, contact Green Trails, Inc. (ask for Battle Ax, map number 524), 206/546-MAPS (206/546-6277), www.greentrails.com; or ask the USGS for Bagby Hot Springs.

Directions: From Estacada, drive 25.5 miles southeast on Highway 224 to the junction with Forest Service Road 46 (Highway 224 ends here). Turn right (south) and drive 3.5 miles, then turn right on Forest Service Road 63. Go 3.5 miles, then turn right on Forest Service Road 70. Continue for six miles to the trailhead and large parking area, to the left.

Contact: Mount Hood National Forest, Clackamas River Ranger District, Estacada Ranger Station, 595 Northwest Industrial Way, Estacada, OR 97023, 503/630-6861.

52 PANSY LAKE
4.0 mi/2.0 hrs

in the Bull of the Woods Wilderness in Mount Hood National Forest

Map 9.4, page 396

An easy lake stroll means it's popular on a sunny weekend, but don't rule it out: It's worth a trip, and you can turn this into a challenging loop up to Bull of the Woods Lookout if you want to escape the crowds. Start with a 500-foot elevation climb up to the lake, ignoring a junction to the right, which leads down an abandoned trail. Continue to the lake, which will be on your right, and stop here to decide your attack plan. If the lake is your thing, stick around and then return the way you came. If you want more, continue 1.3 miles to the junction with Mother Lode Trail, then turn left and climb about 1.3 miles to reach the Bull of the Woods Lookout for views of Mount Hood, Mount Jefferson, Three Sisters, and Three Fingered Jack from the 5,523-foot summit. Total elevation gain for this loop is about 2,000 feet. After enjoying the view from the top, continue down Bull of the Woods Trail to reach a junction with the return route; turn left here to return to the trailhead.

User Groups: Hikers, dogs, and horses. No mountain bikes are allowed. No wheelchair access.

Permits: A free wilderness permit is required to hike here, available shortly after entering the trailhead. In addition, a federal Northwest Forest pass is required to park here. The cost is $5 for a day pass or $30 for an annual pass. You can buy a day pass at ranger stations, from private vendors, or through Nature of the Northwest Information Center.

Maps: For a map of the Bull of the Woods Wilderness, contact Nature of the Northwest Information Center. For a topographic map, contact Green Trails, Inc. (ask for Battle Ax, map number 524), 206/546-MAPS (206/546-6277), www.greentrails.com; or ask the USGS for Bull of the Woods.

Directions: From Estacada, drive 27 miles southeast on Highway 224, which becomes Forest Service Road 46. Continue on Forest Service Road 46 for three miles to paved Forest Service Road 63. Turn right and drive six miles, then turn right on gravel Forest Service Road 6340. Drive 9.5 miles to the trailhead and the parking pullout, on the right side of the road.

Contact: Mount Hood National Forest, Clackamas River Ranger District, Estacada Ranger Station, 595 Northwest Industrial Way, Estacada, OR 97023, 503/630-6861.

53 BULL OF THE WOODS LOOKOUT

6.4 mi/3.5 hrs

in the Bull of the Woods Wilderness in Mount Hood National Forest

Map 9.4, page 396

This relatively easy hike gains just 900 feet in elevation to the Bull of the Woods Lookout, where you can mosey on up to spend some quality time with the Indian paintbrush and rhododendrons, along with views of Mount Hood, Mount Jefferson, Three Sisters, and Three Fingered Jack along the trail and at the 5,523-foot summit. This trail can also be combined with Pansy Lake for a loop (see listing in this chapter), starting at the Pansy Lake trailhead. If you see hikers traveling up from that more strenuous side, try not to be too smug about your easier route.

User Groups: Hikers, dogs, and horses. No mountain bikes are allowed. No wheelchair access.

Permits: A federal Northwest Forest pass is required to park here. The cost is $5 for a day pass or $30 for an annual pass. You can buy a day pass at ranger stations, from private vendors, or through Nature of the Northwest Information Center.

Maps: For a map of the Bull of the Woods Wilderness, contact Nature of the Northwest Information Center. For a topographic map, contact Green Trails, Inc. (ask for Battle Ax, map number 524), 206/546-MAPS (206/546-

6277), www.greentrails.com; or ask the USGS for Bull of the Woods.

Directions: From Estacada, drive 27 miles southeast on Highway 224, which becomes Forest Service Road 46. Continue on Forest Service Road 46 for three miles to paved Forest Service Road 63. Turn right and drive six miles, then turn right on gravel Forest Service Road 6340. Drive 9.5 miles to the trailhead and parking pullout on the right side of the road.

Contact: Mount Hood National Forest, Clackamas River Ranger District, Estacada Ranger Station, 595 Northwest Industrial Way, Estacada, OR 97023, 503/630-6861.

54 DICKEY CREEK TO BIG SLIDE LAKE

11.0 mi/5.5 hrs

north of Bull of the Woods Wilderness in Mount Hood National Forest

Map 9.4, page 396

This trail has it all: a forested valley, sweeping valley views, and a lake. Oh, yeah, and switchbacks. After an initial descent, the trail levels out and then the climbing begins, topping out at Big Slide Lake (total elevation gain is 2,200 feet). You can also access the Bull of the Woods Lookout or Big Slide Mountain by taking Schreiner Peak Trail about four miles round-trip for each option (as if 11 miles weren't enough): For the mountain, turn left onto Schreiner Peak Trail, and for the lookout, keep right at all junctions. Keep in mind that Schreiner Peak may not be maintained, so you should check before you go if you want to try the longer route. It's not as crowded as other nearby trails, so if you want some solitude, this is a good choice.

User Groups: Hikers, dogs, and horses. No mountain bikes are allowed. No wheelchair access.

Permits: Permits are not required. Parking and access are free.

Maps: For a map of Mount Hood National Forest and Bull of the Woods Wilderness, contact Nature of the Northwest Information Center. For a topographic map, contact Green Trails, Inc. (ask for Battle Ax, map number 524), 206/

546-MAPS (206/546-6277), www.greentrails.com; or ask the USGS for Bull of the Woods.

Directions: From Estacada, drive southeast on Highway 224 for 27 miles. When it turns into Forest Service Road 46, continue three more miles to paved Forest Service Road 63. Turn right and drive six miles to gravel Forest Service Road 6340. Turn right and drive three miles to dirt Spur Road 140. Turn left and drive 1.5 miles to the trailhead and the road's end.

Contact: Mount Hood National Forest, Clackamas River Ranger District, Estacada Ranger Station, 595 Northwest Industrial Way, Estacada, OR 97023, 503/630-6861.

55 PHANTOM BRIDGE
5.2 mi/2.5 hrs

north of Detroit in Willamette National Forest

Map 9.4, page 396

Ready for your close-up? Then bring your camera (and a friend) and head to this natural archway that you can peek through. Traveling along French Creek Ridge Trail, you'll pass by Dog Tooth Rock one mile up on your left, squeeze past tiny Cedar Lake, and then climb for another mile to a natural bridge you just have to see to believe. The beauty of it all? Unlike many other attractions in the state, it's not right off the highway, and there's no tram or paved walkway leading to a platform. Translation: You may just have the scenery all to yourself. The total elevation gain is about 400 feet.

User Groups: Hikers, dogs, horses, and mountain bikes. No wheelchair access.

Permits: Permits are not required. Parking and access are free.

Maps: For a map of Willamette National Forest, contact Nature of the Northwest Information Center. For a topographic map, contact Green Trails, Inc. (ask for Battle Ax, map number 524), 206/546-MAPS (206/546-6277), www.greentrails.com; or ask the USGS for Battle Ax.

Directions: From the west end of Detroit on Highway 22, turn north onto French Creek

Road. Drive 4.1 miles to Forest Service Road 2207, and turn right. Continue 3.6 miles to the parking area on the right. The trail is confusing here, because the French Creek Ridge passes through here. Don't take the trail leading from the parking lot. Instead, cross the road from the parking lot to the other French Creek Ridge trail marker.

Contact: Willamette National Forest, Detroit Ranger District, HC 73, Mill City, OR 97360, 503/854-3366.

56 RHODODENDRON RIDGE TO HAWK MOUNTAIN
10.0 mi/5.0 hrs

on Rhododendron Ridge in the southern portion of Mount Hood National Forest

Map 9.4, page 396

For a little something different, try the more remote Hawk Mountain, where an old fire lookout cabin commands views of Mount Jefferson and Mount Washington. But you don't need to walk far in order to capture some scenery, thanks to the new-growth pine trees: Their little heads just aren't tall enough to obstruct your view of Mount Hood or of the rhododendrons lining the way. Lest you think this is a walk in the park, take note: It's strongly encouraged that you get a map of the area before setting out, because the trail stops at an abandoned road after about a mile, and you have to walk for roughly a mile before continuing through the trail. After five miles total, veer left at an unmarked trail to climb up about .5 mile to Hawk Mountain. It's worth the trip to see the cabin and its scenic neighborhood, and you're likely to have it all to yourself, but take a map along to guide your way.

User Groups: Hikers, dogs, mountain bikes, and horses. No wheelchair access.

Permits: Permits are not required. Parking and access are free.

Maps: For a map of Mount Hood National Forest, contact Nature of the Northwest Information Center. For a topographic map, contact Green Trails, Inc. (ask for Breitenbush, map number 525), 206/546-MAPS (206/546-6277), www.greentrails.com; or ask the USGS for Mount Lowe and Breitenbush Hot Springs.

Directions: From Estacada, drive southeast on Highway 224 for 27 miles. When it turns into Forest Service Road 46, continue another 3.5 miles to Forest Service Road 63. Turn right and drive 8.9 miles to Forest Service Road 6350. Turn left and drive 1.2 miles to a fork, veering right at the fork and continuing another 4.5 miles on the gravel road. Turn left at the fork and drive one mile to the trailhead and small parking area on the right.

Contact: Mount Hood National Forest, Clackamas River Ranger District, Estacada Ranger Station, 595 Northwest Industrial Way, Estacada, OR 97023, 503/630-6861.

57 STAHLMAN POINT
5.0 mi/2.5 hrs

on the south side of Detroit Reservoir in Willamette National Forest

Map 9.4, page 396

For a convenient hike near the Detroit Reservoir camping areas, try this climb through younger Douglas fir forest to a former lookout site. It gains 1,300 feet in 2.5 miles, the last 200 of which are rocky, so watch your step. From the top you can look 3,000 feet over the towns of Detroit and Idanha, Detroit Lake, and Mount Jefferson (hey, it wouldn't be a former lookout site if it didn't have any views, after all). The lake, actually a man-made reservoir created in 1955, has been a popular fishing, boating, and camping spot ever since. After gazing out and pondering how different Detroit, Oregon is from Detroit, Michigan, start your descent to enjoy all the area has to offer.

User Groups: Hikers and dogs. No mountain bikes or horses are allowed. No wheelchair access.

Permits: Permits are not required. Parking and access are free.

Maps: For a map of the Willamette National Forest, contact Nature of the Northwest In-

formation Center. For a topographic map, contact Green Trails, Inc. (ask for Detroit, map number 556), 206/546-MAPS (206/546-6277), www.greentrails.com; or ask the USGS for Detroit.

Directions: From the east end of Detroit (50 miles east of Salem on Highway 22), turn right on Blowout Road and drive 3.5 miles. The well-marked trailhead and large parking area are on the left side of the road.

Contact: Willamette National Forest, Detroit Ranger District, HC 73, P.O. Box 320, Mill City, OR 97360, 503/854-3366.

58 COFFIN MOUNTAIN
3.0 mi/2.0 hrs

south of Highway 22 in Willamette National Forest

Map 9.4, page 396

It's an unfortunate but strangely fitting name, as you sometimes feel like you're on a death march on this hot, exposed trail. There's a reason for that: You're starting at 4,800 feet elevation and climbing 1,000 feet, so pack plenty o' H20 for this. Gorgeous views on both sides will serve to distract you—Mount Jefferson and Three Fingered Jack to the north and the southern Cascade range to the south. As you creep up the unrelenting switchbacks along the exposed and wildflower-filled mountain, a rocky overhang makes you think it's your destination, which is the ultimate psych-out; you can't see Coffin Mountain until you round the final bend and see the lookout tower. A viewing platform awaits you on the top of the 5,771-foot peak, and here, Mount Hood joins the view gang. Head back the way you came for the return trip.

User Groups: Hikers, dogs, mountain bikes, and horses. No wheelchair access.

Permits: Permits are not required. Parking and access are free.

Maps: For a map of the Willamette National Forest, contact Nature of the Northwest Information Center. For a topographic map, contact Green Trails, Inc. (ask for Detroit, map number 556), 206/546-MAPS (206/546-6277), www.greentrails.com; or ask the USGS for Coffin Mountain.

Directions: From Salem, drive 50 miles east on Highway 22 to Detroit and continue another 18.9 miles to Straight Creek Road/Forest Service Road 11. Turn right and drive 4.2 miles to Forest Service Road 1168 (don't turn at the first 1168 sign). Turn right and drive 3.8 miles to Forest Service Road 450. Turn left and drive less than .1 mile to the parking area and the trailhead on your right.

Contact: Willamette National Forest, Detroit Ranger District, HC 73, P.O. Box 320, Mill City, OR 97360, 503/854-3366.

59 BACHELOR MOUNTAIN
3.8 mi/2.5 hrs

south of Highway 22 in Willamette National Forest

Map 9.4, page 396

Interesting name choices—Bachelor and neighboring Coffin Mountain. Both definitely convey the sense of aloneness you'll get when you hike these trails. Bachelor is not a long trail, but since you start at 4,800 feet you may get a sudden case of the "are we there yet" (funny how altitude is the great equalizer, no?). The Douglas fir forest trail gains 900 feet in elevation, and the last .5 mile is a steep and rocky climb. You'll come to a junction with Bruno Meadows Trail at the 1.5 mile mark, but just keep on trucking straight to the top. When you reach the former lookout site, you can take a gander at the panoramic view, or snap a shot of it if you have one of them thar newfangled cameras that offer that feature. Once you've impressed your friends with your zoom lens and put away all your equipment, head back down the way you came.

User Groups: Hikers, dogs, horses, and mountain bikes. No wheelchair access.

Permits: A federal Northwest Forest pass is required to park here. The cost is $5 for a day pass or $30 for an annual pass. You can buy a day pass at ranger stations, from private vendors, or through Nature of the Northwest Information Center.

Maps: For a map of the Willamette National Forest, contact Nature of the Northwest Information Center. For a topographic map, contact Green Trails, Inc. (ask for Detroit, map number 556), 206/546-MAPS (206/546-6277), www.greentrails.com; or ask the USGS for Coffin Mountain.

Directions: From Salem, drive 50 miles east on Highway 22 to Detroit and continue another 18.9 miles to Straight Creek Road/Forest Service Road 11. Turn right and drive 4.2 miles to Forest Service Road 1168 (don't turn at the first 1168 sign). Turn right and drive 4.4 miles to Forest Service Road 430. Turn left and continue .5 mile to the end of the road and the parking area and trailhead.

Contact: Willamette National Forest, Detroit Ranger District, HC 73, P.O. Box 320, Mill City, OR 97360, 503/854-3366.

60 RED LAKE TRAIL TO POTATO BUTTE
7.2 mi/3.5 hrs

north of Mount Jefferson in the Olallie Lake Scenic Area

Map 9.5, page 397

There are actually many lakes along this trail, but Red Lake gets top billing because it's the first you pass. There are hundreds of lakes in the Olallie Lake Scenic Area, and here is a great way to get a sample platter of them (pass the salt). At 1.5 miles, you'll pass Red Lake herself, and then all lined up in a nice orderly fashion for you are Averill, Wall, and Sheep Lakes within one more mile. At Sheep Lake, turn left to head up to 5,310-foot Potato Butte for scenic views of Mount Hood all the way up the steep climb. Turn back the way you came, turning right at Sheep Lake and return the way you came. Red Lake Trail also extends to the Olallie Lake area.

User Groups: Hikers, dogs, mountain bikes, and horses. No wheelchair access.

Permits: Permits are not required. Parking and access are free.

Maps: For a map of Mount Hood National

Forest and the Olallie Lake Scenic Area, contact Nature of the Northwest Information Center. For a topographic map, contact Green Trails, Inc. (ask for Breitenbush, map number 525), 206/546-MAPS (206/546-6277), www.greentrails.com; or ask the USGS for Olallie Butte.

Directions: From Estacada, drive 27 miles southeast on Highway 224 to Forest Service Road 46. Continue straight on Forest Service Road 46, and drive 26.5 miles to the sign for Red Lake Trail (gravel Forest Service Road 380, which is unmarked). Park in a small pullout on the side of the road .9 mile up; the trailhead is on the left.

Contact: Mount Hood National Forest, Clackamas River Ranger District, Estacada Ranger Station, 595 Northwest Industrial Way, Estacada, OR 97023, 503/630-6861.

61 SOUTH BREITENBUSH GORGE
4.9 mi one-way/2.5 hrs

on the northwest side of Mount Jefferson in Willamette National Forest

Map 9.5, page 397

There are several things to enjoy along this easy riverside trail. For starters, there's the gorge, where the river passes through a 300-foot basalt narrow (a short, marked side trail leads down to the view). Then there's the soothing sound of the river itself, rushing along as a backdrop through this dense Douglas fir and western hemlock forest. There are a few spots to access this trail as a shuttle hike, but it's short and flat enough to do the whole shebang if you have the urge. Don't miss the log footbridge over Roaring Creek for a good photo-snapping spot.

User Groups: Hikers and dogs. No horses or mountain bikes are allowed. No wheelchair access.

Permits: A federal Northwest Forest pass is required to park here. The cost is $5 for a day pass or $30 for an annual pass. You can buy a day pass at ranger stations, from private vendors, or through Nature of the Northwest Information Center.

Maps: For a map of Willamette National For-

est, contact Nature of the Northwest Information Center. For a topographic map, ask the USGS for Breitenbush Hot Springs.

Directions: From Salem, drive 50 miles east on Highway 22 to Detroit, and turn left (north) onto paved Forest Service Road 46. Drive 11 miles and turn right onto gravel Forest Service Road 4685. To reach the main trailhead, ignore the first two signs (at .5 mile and 1.5 miles) and drive 2.2 miles to the pullout and trailhead on the right.

Contact: Willamette National Forest, Detroit Ranger District, HC 73, P.O. Box 320, Mill City, OR 97360, 503/854-3366.

62 TRIANGULATION PEAK
4.2 mi/2.5 hrs

northwest of Mount Jefferson in the Mount Jefferson Wilderness of Willamette National Forest

Map 9.5, page 397

If you're the type who likes a nice warm-up before hitting the heavy-duty climbing, this hike is for you. The first 1.5 miles are easy hiking through Douglas fir and western hemlock, with wildflowers and plenty of views through clearings of Mount Hood to the north. You'll see a rocky protrusion jutting up in the distance, a false alarm that's not your destination: Instead, it's Spire Rock, and you'll come face to face with it after 1.5 miles. Warmed up yet? Good, but you'll need some reserves in your tank to climb the switchbacks up to the 5,400-foot peak, where great views of the Mount Jefferson Wilderness are yours for the taking. Keep in mind that since you're starting at well over 4,000 feet of elevation, this trail can still be snowy through July, so save it for later in the season.

User Groups: Hikers, dogs, and horses. No mountain bikes are allowed. No wheelchair access.

Permits: A free wilderness permit is required to hike here and is available at the trailhead. No Northwest Forest pass is required.

Maps: For a map of the Mount Jefferson Wilderness, contact Nature of the Northwest Information Center. For a topographic map, contact Green Trails, Inc. (ask for Mount Jefferson, map number 557), 206/546-MAPS (206/546-6277), www.greentrails.com; or ask the USGS for Mount Bruno and Mount Jefferson.

Directions: From Salem, drive 50 miles east on Highway 22 to Detroit, and continue another 6 miles to McCoy Road/Forest Service Road 2233. Turn left and drive eight miles to a junction, and turn right to continue for another 1.2 miles. Turn right onto Forest Service Road 635; the trailhead and small parking area are on the right side of the road, just past the junction.

Contact: Willamette National Forest, Detroit Ranger District, HC 73, P.O. Box 320, Mill City, OR 97360, 503/854-3366.

63 WHITEWATER TO JEFFERSON PARK
10.2 mi/6.0 hrs

on the north side of Mount Jefferson in the Mount Jefferson Wilderness in Willamette National Forest

Map 9.5, page 397

You don't have to walk far to get good views of Mount Jefferson—thar she blows as soon as you step on the trail. This is the easiest route to the popular Mount Jefferson Wilderness, and the area is already showing signs of overuse. Mount Jefferson came in a close second in the competition for tallest mountain in the state, edged out by 742 feet by Mount Hood. You start off by entering the cool old-growth Douglas fir forest for 1.5 miles before you reach a trail junction. Turn right to climb the ridgeline for another mile before leveling out. Continue a few more miles, and turn left at the junction with Pacific Crest Trail to come upon the alpine lakes and open wildflower-filled meadows of Jefferson Park. Everyone seems to know about this trail, so it's guaranteed to be filled to the max on sunny weekends. The trail can be snow-covered through July, so either come early in the season if you don't mind some snow (and missing out on the wildflowers) or wait until fall to have a little elbow room.

User Groups: Hikers, dogs, and horses. No mountain bikes are allowed. No wheelchair access.

Permits: Free wilderness permits are required, available at the trailhead. In addition, a federal Northwest Forest pass is required to park here. The cost is $5 for a day pass or $30 for an annual pass. You can buy a day pass at ranger stations, from private vendors, or through Nature of the Northwest Information Center.

Maps: For a map of the Mount Jefferson Wilderness, contact Nature of the Northwest Information Center. For a topographic map, contact Green Trails, Inc. (ask for Mount Jefferson, map number 557), 206/546-MAPS (206/546-6277), www.greentrails.com; or ask the USGS for Mount Bruno and Mount Jefferson.

Directions: From Salem, drive 50 miles east on Highway 22 to Detroit, and continue another 10.3 miles to Whitewater Road/Forest Service Road 2243. Turn left and drive 7.5 miles to the parking area at the end of the road and the well-marked trailhead.

Contact: Willamette National Forest, Detroit Ranger District, HC 73, P.O. Box 320, Mill City, OR 97360, 503/854-3366.

64 PAMELIA LAKE/GRIZZLY PEAK
10.2 mi/6.5 hrs

on the southwest side of Mount Jefferson in the Mount Jefferson Wilderness of Willamette National Forest

Map 9.5, page 397

This is a prime overnight spot, but as there are few campsites in the lake area, other people have the same idea, so you probably won't be solo-ing it. Whether you choose to do this as a day hike or a two-day trek, two things are guaranteed: You're in for a killer workout and some knockout views of Mount Jefferson. Start off through the cool, refreshing old-growth Douglas fir, hemlock, and western red cedar forest along rushing Pamelia Creek, a pretty and peaceful 2.3-mile stroll that gains 800 feet in elevation. That was just a warm-up: Once you hit the lake, take a right to the junction with 2.8-mile Grizzly Peak Trail for a nearly 2,000-

foot climb to the 5,800-foot summit. Turn around here and camp near Pamelia Lake, or return the way you came if you prefer to call it a day.
User Groups: Hikers, dogs, and horses. No mountain bikes are allowed. No wheelchair access.
Permits: An free overnight wilderness permit is required to camp here. Contact the Detroit Ranger District, HC 73, P.O. Box 320, Mill City, OR 97360, 503/854-3366. In addition, a federal Northwest Forest pass is required to park here. The cost is $5 for a day pass or $30 for an annual pass. You can buy a day pass at ranger stations, from private vendors, or through Nature of the Northwest Information Center.
Maps: For a map of the Mount Jefferson Wilderness, contact Nature of the Northwest Information Center. For a topographic map, contact Green Trails, Inc. (ask for Mount Jefferson, map number 557), 206/546-MAPS (206/546-6277), www.greentrails.com; or ask the USGS for Mount Jefferson.
Directions: From Salem, drive 50 miles east on Highway 22 to Detroit and continue another 11.9 miles to Forest Service Road 2246. Turn left and drive 3.7 miles to the parking area at the end of the road and the well-marked trailhead.
Contact: Willamette National Forest, Detroit Ranger District, HC 73, P.O. Box 320, Mill City, OR 97360, 503/854-3366.

65 INDEPENDENCE ROCK LOOP
1.7 mi/1.5 hrs
east of Marion Forks off Highway 22 in Willamette National Forest

Map 9.5, page 397

Unlike neighboring Marion Lake, this trail doesn't attract hordes of people, which means it's overgrown in parts, but the overgrown ground plants make a nice contrast to the tall old-growth trunks. The sweet smell of gorgeous pink rhododendrons also contrasts well to the pine scent, making this easy trail a feast for the senses. A small side trail leads up to Independence Rock itself in all its glory (those scared of heights

may not share the love, because footing can be a little sketchy). Turn back the way you came, or continue on the trail for a 1.7-mile loop. If you choose the loop, you'll have to walk more than .5 mile on the road back to your car.
User Groups: Hikers, dogs, mountain bikes, and horses. No wheelchair access.
Permits: Permits are not required. Parking and access are free.
Maps: For a map of Willamette National Forest, contact Nature of the Northwest Information Center. For a topographic map, contact Green Trails, Inc. (ask for Mount Jefferson, map number 557), 206/546-MAPS (206/546-6277), www.greentrails.com; or ask the USGS for Marion Forks.
Directions: From Salem, drive 50 miles east on Highway 22 to Detroit, and continue another 16.8 miles to Forest Service Road 2255 (at Marion Forks). Turn left and drive .1 mile to a small turnout on the side of the road to the right. The trailhead is across the road, on the left side as you're driving in.
Contact: Willamette National Forest, Detroit Ranger District, HC 73, P.O. Box 320, Mill City, OR 97360, 503/854-3366.

66 MARION LAKE LOOP
5.4 mi/2.5 hrs
on the southwest side of Mount Jefferson in the Mount Jefferson Wilderness of Willamette National Forest

Map 9.5, page 397

You need only to pull up to the parking lot to get a sense that this is a popular trail. Families flock to this lake because it's an easy two miles in to its shores. The well-maintained, wooded trail doesn't actually circle the lake itself, but you can make a little loop of your own by going right at the junction about .5 mile after passing by Lake Ann, and making another right to view Marion Falls. Return to the trail, then keep left at the junction to travel past the northwest lakeshore, then turn left again to head back the way you came. If you want more solitude and views of Mount Jefferson, head up to Marion Mountain: Instead of turning left to reach the lakeshore, turn right onto Blue Ridge Trail for 1.8 miles, then turn left at Pine Ridge Trail for one mile, turning left again to climb .8 mile to the 5,400-foot peak of Marion Mountain. The trail also connects to the Eight Lakes Basin trail system for an eight-mile loop. As with many of this area's trails, there are endless possibilities if you want to backpack.

User Groups: Hikers, dogs, and horses. Mountain bikes are not allowed. No wheelchair access.

Permits: A free wilderness permit is required to hike here and is available at the trailhead. In addition, a federal Northwest Forest pass is required to park here. The cost is $5 for a day pass or $30 for an annual pass. You can buy a day pass at ranger stations, from private vendors, or through Nature of the Northwest Information Center.

Maps: For a map of the Mount Jefferson Wilderness and Willamette National Forest, contact Nature of the Northwest Information Center. For a topographic map, contact Green Trails, Inc. (ask for Mount Jefferson, map number 557), 206/546-MAPS (206/546-6277), www.greentrails.com; or ask the USGS for Marion Forks and Marion Lake.

Directions: From Salem, drive 50 miles east on Highway 22 to Detroit and continue another 16.8 miles to Forest Service 2255 (at Marion Forks). Turn left and drive 4.5 miles to the end of the road and the trailhead.

Contact: Willamette National Forest, Detroit Ranger District, HC 73, P.O. Box 320, Mill City, OR 97360, 503/854-3366.

67 METOLIUS RIVER TRAIL
5.0–11.5 mi/2.5–5.5 hrs

northwest of Sisters in Deschutes National Forest

Map 9.5, page 397

One of the largest spring-fed rivers in the country, the Metolius is a popular camping area. In such a hot and dry area, it's also refreshing—if you're camping nearby, enjoy a soak in the river. The dusty and flat path is good for both running and meandering. From the trailhead at Canyon Creek campground, hike 2.5 miles to the Wizard Falls Hatchery, where you can take a self-guided tour and see why this is a hot spot for fly-fishing: rainbow, brook, brown and trophy trout, as well as kokanee and Atlantic salmon, mingle with the three million other fish here. (Kids Day is the second Saturday of June, so plan accordingly.) You can either turn back here or continue past the hatchery for three more miles to the Lower Bridge Campground, where you can cross the bridge and continue on the other side (crossing again when you hit the hatchery) for an additional 6.5-mile loop.

User Groups: Hikers and dogs. No mountain bikes or horses are allowed. No wheelchair access.

Permits: Permits are not required. Parking and access are free.

Maps: For a map of the Deschutes National Forest, contact Nature of the Northwest Information Center. For a topographic map, contact Green Trails, Inc. (ask for Whitewater River, map number 558), 206/546-MAPS (206/546-6277), www.greentrails.com; or ask the USGS for Black Butte, Candle Creek, and Prairie Farm Spring.

Directions: From Sisters, drive nine miles west on Highway 20 to paved Forest Service Road 14. Turn right and drive 2.6 miles to a right fork. Keep going straight at this point, continuing on Forest Service Road 1419 for 2.2 miles, and keep going straight as it changes to paved Forest Service Road 1420. Drive 3.3 miles, and turn right on Forest Service Road 400. Drive .8 mile to the Canyon Creek Campground. The parking area and trailhead are on the far side of the campground.

Contact: Deschutes National Forest, Sisters Ranger District, Highway 20/Pine Street, P.O. Box 249, Sisters, OR 97759, 541/549-7700.

Chapter 10

© MEGAN MCMORRIS

Northeast Oregon

Northeast Oregon

Pop quiz: What's the deepest canyon in North America? Wrong. It's actually Hells Canyon, which plummets 7,900 feet between Seven Devil's Mountain in western Idaho and Wallowa Mountain in northeastern Oregon. (Your likely first guess, the Grand Canyon, is actually 2,600 feet shy of this.) Snaking through it all is, well, the Snake River (popular with white-water rafters), which you can walk along on several of this chapter's shorter hikes or arrange a longer backpacking trip along its shores. One of the short hikes in Hells Canyon, Stud Creek, is only accessible from the Idaho border, and getting there is one of the most scenic drives in this book.

Probably the best hiking in the region is in the Wallowa-Whitman National Forest and Eagle Cap Wilderness, just west of the Idaho/Oregon border. The Wallowas (as the locals call it) are known as the Alps of Oregon, with nearly 20 peaks that stand over 8,000 feet. The area is famous for its Lakes Basin Loop, high-alpine lakes surrounded by wildflower meadows, as well as for many other backpacking trips. Keep your head up here, because black bears, elk, and deer proliferate in these parts. (The cute town of Joseph, nearby, is home to the World's Best Ice Cream, at Joe's Place, on the main drag, but you won't find that in any reference book except this one.) Scenic Wallowa Lake, from where Lakes Basin Trail and other high-alpine lake trailheads start, is a popular destination, with camping, cabins, boating, horseback riding, restaurants, and even a wedding chapel. The entire Wallowa-Whitman forest offers plenty of other high-alpine lake trailheads, too, if you prefer to avoid the circuslike (but cool) atmosphere at Wallowa Lake.

Its neighbor to the northwest is the remote Umatilla National Forest (pronounced YOU-ma-TILL-a) and North Fork John Day Wilderness, known for wildlife like deer and Rocky Mountain elk, as well as for the popular and scenic South Fork Walla Walla Trail. If solitude is your goal, you're likely to find it in this forest.

Umatilla National Forest also extends south, cutting across the Blue mountain range. Lining the Blue Mountain Scenic Byway are trails galore right off the highway and surrounding the Anthony Lakes Ski Area, from long easy strolls along North Fork John Day River to intense climbs leading to high alpine lakes and mountain meadows.

Farther south, we come to the drier, dustier Strawberry Mountain Wilderness, in Malheur National Forest, which is packed with miles of trails both remote and not-so-remote, and even a climb up to the summit of 9,039-foot Strawberry Mountain. The Strawberry Lakes Basin is an especially big hit among the crowds, who come here for short loops around the lake with a backdrop of Strawberry Mountain looking over the proceedings.

Finally, for some short and sweet trips, you need to take in the scene that is the John Day Painted Desert Area, and the Fossil Monument Areas, where you can see colorful layers of volcanic ash and preserved fossils on a trip that will take you back in time (well before your time, that is). To the west is Ochoco National Forest, where you can get up-close and personal with red rock Twin Pillars and Stein's Pillar, jutting up 200 feet in the air.

So, to recap: In this chapter you'll find the Alps of Oregon, the deepest gorge in North America, short history-filled strolls through volcanic ash formations, scenic white-water river hikes, and a couple of red-rock pillars thrown in for good measure. From remote excursions to filled-to-the-gill hot spots, you'll find everything you ever wanted in this diverse part of the state. And more.

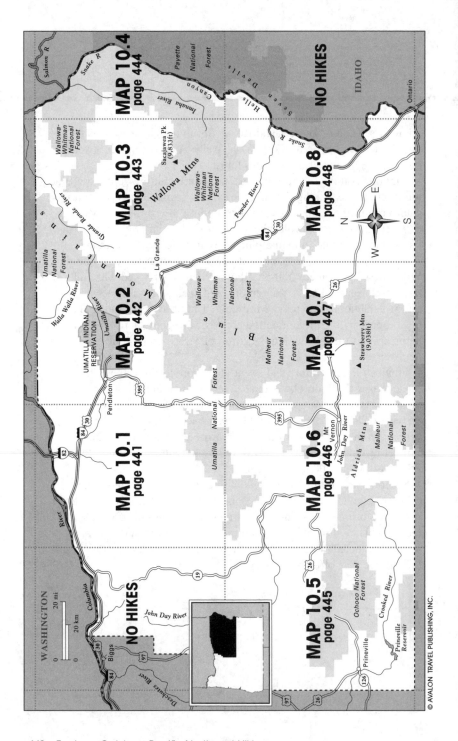

© AVALON TRAVEL PUBLISHING, INC.

Map 10.1

Hikes 1–4
Pages 449–450

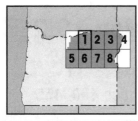

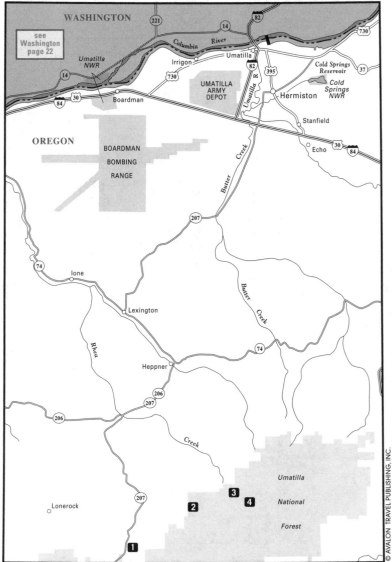

Map 10.2

Hikes 5–14
Pages 450–455

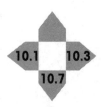

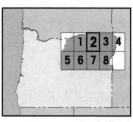

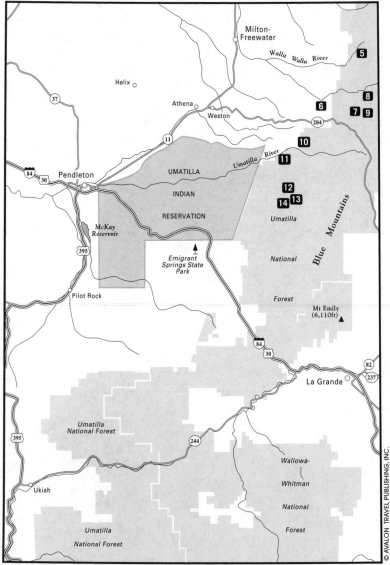

Map 10.3

Hikes 15–30
Pages 456–465

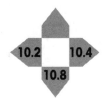

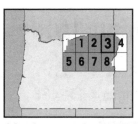

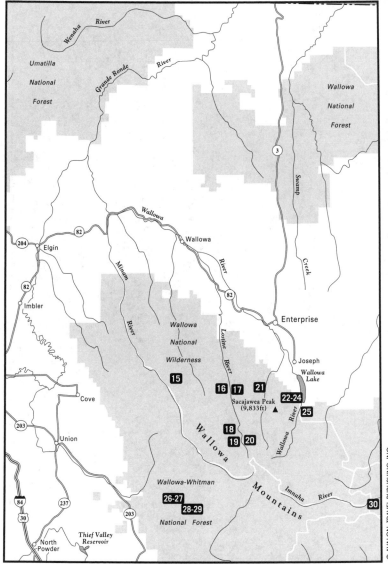

Map 10.4

Hikes 31–33
Pages 465–466

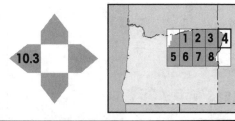

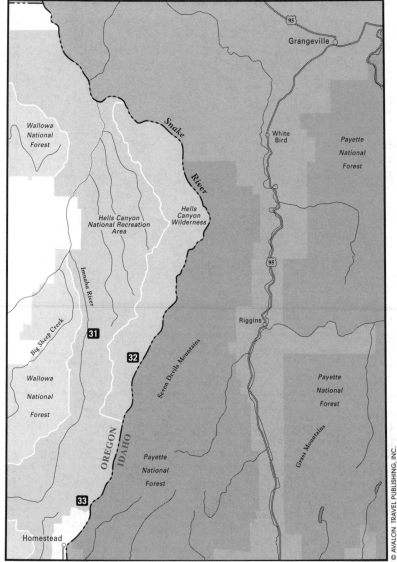

© AVALON TRAVEL PUBLISHING, INC.

Map 10.5

Hikes 34–37
Pages 467–468

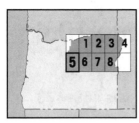

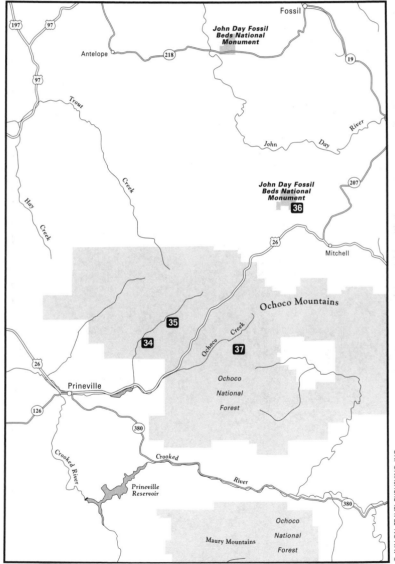

Map 10.6

Hikes 38–41
Pages 469–470

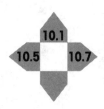

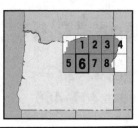

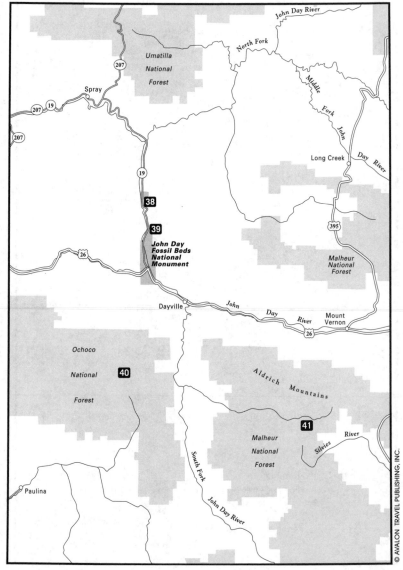

Map 10.7

Hikes 42–68
Pages 471–483

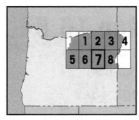

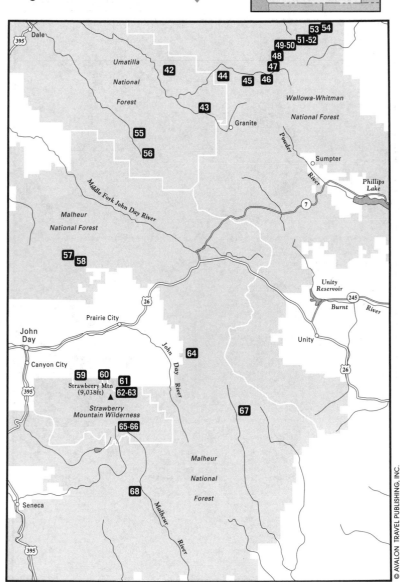

Map 10.8

Hike 69
Page 484

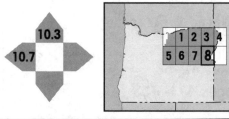

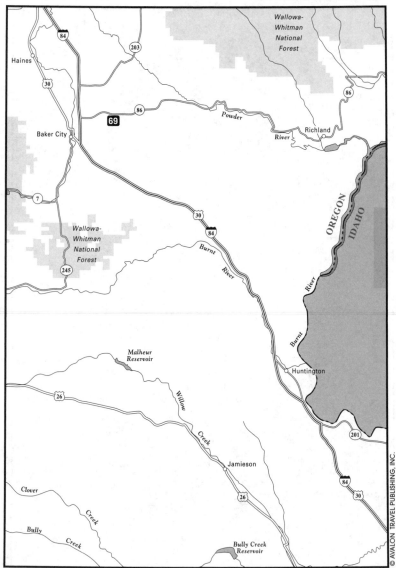

❶ BULL PRAIRIE LAKE
0.5 mi/0.5 hr

south of Heppner off Highway 207 in Umatilla National Forest

Map 10.1, page 441

In the remote and wild Umatilla Forest, you sometimes may wonder where everyone is. Well, wonder no more: They're all packed into this pretty and popular lake. (Okay, not everyone, but still.) Surrounded by willows and wildflowers, Bull Prairie Lake is all the rage as a prime trout fishing spot, complete with floating piers. The flat .5-mile gravel path is fine for families who want to add in a leg-stretcher while camping nearby or fishing at the lake.

User Groups: Hikers and dogs. No mountain bikes or horses are allowed. No wheelchair access.

Permits: Permits are not required. Parking and access are free.

Maps: For a map of Umatilla National Forest, contact Nature of the Northwest Information Center. For a topographic map, ask the USGS for Whitetail Butte.

Directions: From Heppner, drive 40 miles south on Highway 207. At the sign for Bull Prairie Recreation Area, turn left (east) onto Forest Service Road 2039. Drive one mile to the recreation area on the right. There is no official trailhead, but there are many access points around the lake.

Contact: Umatilla National Forest, Heppner Ranger District, P.O. Box 7, Heppner, OR 97836, 541/676-9187.

❷ MADISON BUTTE LOOKOUT TRAIL TO TUPPER BUTTE
2.0 mi/1.0 hr

south of Heppner in Umatilla National Forest

Map 10.1, page 441

For a one-mile jaunt to a knockout view all to yourself, head up to Tupper Butte. And we're talking up: The trail can't be bothered with gentle switchbacks; instead, it climbs straight up an old jeep trail 1,800 feet to the 5,184-foot summit of Tupper Butte. Near the top, the trail forks; take the left fork to reach a meadow packed with flowers such as daisies and Indian paintbrush, to mention just a few. (The path straight ahead to Madison Butte is not passable at this writing.) Stick around and check out the view of Umatilla National Forest, as well as a healthy chunk of northeastern Oregon.

User Groups: Hikers, dogs, and horses. No mountain bikes are allowed. No wheelchair access.

Permits: Permits are not required. Parking and access are free.

Maps: For a map of Umatilla National Forest, contact Nature of the Northwest Information Center. For a topographic map, ask the USGS for Madison Butte.

Directions: From Heppner, drive 26 miles south on Highway 207, .25 mile past Anson Wright Park, and turn left (east) onto Sunflower Flat Road/Forest Service Road 22. Drive four miles and turn left onto Forest Service Road 2119. Continue 3.5 miles and turn left onto Forest Service Road 21. Drive .7 mile to the trailhead on the left (park at the side of the road), starting from the locked gate on the abandoned road.

Contact: Umatilla National Forest, Heppner Ranger District, P.O. Box 7, Heppner, OR 97836, 541/676-9187.

❸ SKOOKUM TRAIL
5.0 mi/2.5 hrs

south of Heppner in Umatilla National Forest

Map 10.1, page 441

Following an old jeep road at the beginning, Skookum Trail climbs steeply up to Madison Butte, gaining a cool 1,000 feet in elevation in just one mile. Up for it? Well, that's not all . . . This trail is not currently maintained, which is good news for solitude-seekers and not-so-good news for those who like a well-marked trail with a plaque thrown in every once in a while. It's best to pick up a map if you want to check out this area, because there are a few junctions that begin to look the same after awhile, and they tend to be unmarked.

Here's a quick peek at the trail: After climbing, you'll head left (west) at Copple Butte Trail to Madison Butte for great views of the valley below. After enjoying the vista laid out before you, retrace your steps. You can combine this trail with Alder Creek for a 5.5-mile loop (and a gentler descent your knees will thank you for).

User Groups: Hikers, dogs, and horses. No mountain bikes are allowed. No wheelchair access.

Permits: Permits are not required. Parking and access are free.

Maps: For a map of Umatilla National Forest, contact Nature of the Northwest Information Center. For a topographic map, ask the USGS for Madison Butte.

Directions: From Heppner, drive 26 miles south on Highway 207, .25 mile past Anson Wright Park, and turn left (east) onto Sunflower Flat Road/Forest Service Road 22. Drive four miles and turn left onto Forest Service Road 2119. Continue 3.5 miles and turn left onto Forest Service Road 21, continuing for 5.8 miles to Forest Service Road 140. Turn left and drive for .5 mile to the road's end and the trailhead.

Contact: Umatilla National Forest, Heppner Ranger District, P.O. Box 7, Heppner, OR 97836, 541/676-9187.

❹ ALDER CREEK
6.0 mi/3.0 hrs

south of Heppner in Umatilla National Forest

Map 10.1, page 441

If you love to whip out a map to blaze your own trail, try this guy. When last visited, it was in need of some sprucing up and trimming around the edges. The good news, oh, map lover, is that you are roughly 99.7 percent guaranteed not to run into another soul out here. The trail starts out as a cool and shaded path along its namesake, Alder Creek, crossing over the creek twice before heading up for a long but relatively gentle climb, gaining 800 feet in the final two miles. Although there are steep

sections, the challenge on this trail is due more to the obstacles along the way, as there are a few logs and branches to hop over, around, and sometimes even scoot under. The trail is also overgrown in parts, but luckily (or unluckily, depending on your take) a barbed wire fence runs along the right side of the trail for the entire time, which comes in handy, although barbed wire does tend to detract from the scenery a smidge. Once at the top, enjoy the view of the valleys below before returning the way you came, or bushwhack and scramble to the top of Madison Butte for a better glimpse. The trail also connects with Skookum Trail (see listing in this chapter for that loop option), but it's easier to navigate from the other direction, as there are no signs and it's easy to get disoriented in this remote area.

User Groups: Hikers, dogs, and horses. No mountain bikes are allowed. No wheelchair access.

Permits: Permits are not required. Parking and access are free.

Maps: For a map of Umatilla National Forest, contact Nature of the Northwest Information Center. For a topographic map, ask the USGS for Madison Butte.

Directions: From Heppner, drive 26 miles south on Highway 207, .25 mile past Anson Wright Park, and turn left (east) onto Sunflower Flat Road/Forest Service Road 22. Drive four miles and turn left onto Forest Service Road 2119. Continue 3.5 miles and turn left onto Forest Service Road 21, continuing for 5.8 miles to Forest Service Road 140. Turn left and drive for .5 mile to the road's end and the trailhead.

Contact: Umatilla National Forest, Heppner Ranger District, P.O. Box 7, Heppner, OR 97836, 541/676-9187.

❺ NORTH FORK WALLA WALLA
11.0 mi one-way/
1.0 to 2.0 days

southeast of Walla Walla, Washington, in Umatilla National Forest

Map 10.2, page 442

This is the more remote side to the Walla Walla

River, mainly because of the hard-to-find trail-head and the long, dramatic (one might even say death-defying) drive on the twisty, dusty road in. You'll feel like you've arrived at a true adventure before you've even left your car, so if that's your bag, dive on in, because the Walla Walla awaits (how can you resist repeating that name? It means "place of many waters," in case you were wondering). Once you've arrived, the trail doesn't even make it easy for you, dropping quickly through thick forest to a small stream crossing and then an open meadow (when you reach a junction with an old jeep road, keep going straight). You won't likely encounter many hikers, but it is a popular mountain and dirt-biking area. It's probably best to get a map of the area before you venture out, not only for the drive in but for the hike itself, as it comes to junctions with roads at times, and it's not the most well-marked trail in the area. Still, there are places to fish and camp along the way, so if you want to take a walk on the wilder side of the Walla Walla (there it is again!), you might just find what you're looking for here.

User Groups: Hikers, dogs, horses, and mountain bikes. No wheelchair access.

Permits: Permits are not required. Parking and access are free.

Maps: For a map of Umatilla National Forest, contact Nature of the Northwest Information Center. For a topographic map, ask the USGS for Big Meadows.

Directions: From Walla Walla, Washington, drive 14 miles east on Mill Creek Road to the junction with Forest Service Road 65. Turn right and drive 9.2 miles to the junction with unmarked Forest Service Road 65-040. The trailhead is on the right, about 50 yards from the junction.

Contact: Umatilla National Forest, Walla Walla Ranger District, 1415 West Rose Street, Walla Walla, WA 99362, 509/522-6290.

6 SOUTH FORK WALLA WALLA
**19.0 mi one-way/
1.0–2.0 days**

southeast of Milton-Freewater in Umatilla National Forest

Map 10.2, page 442

The Walla Walla is not only fun to say, but fun to hike. And bike. And camp. And fish. And even motorbike. Yep, it gets a mite crowded in these parts on a sunny day, and it's not hard to see why it wins the popularity contest. The trail hugs the riverbank for several miles and climbs up the valley walls occasionally to give you a glimpse of the river and valley below before dropping back to the shaded riverside. There are plenty of prime camping and fishing spots along the way, so you can explore the trail at your leisure. (Unfortunately, along with the easy access to this hot spot is the bane of every outdoor-lover's existence: litter!) About 1.5 miles in, look for the old foundation and chimney of Demaris Cabin, and continue on, exploring the volcanic cliffs forming the canyon walls. Keep your ears open for rattling and buzzing, as the trail is also popular with rattlesnakes and yellowjackets. Shuttle hikers can access the trail from the upper trailhead for a 19-mile hike one-way.

User Groups: Hikers, dogs, mountain bikes, and horses. No wheelchair access.

Permits: Permits are not required. Parking and access are free.

Maps: For a map of Umatilla National Forest, contact Nature of the Northwest Information Center. For a topographic map, ask the USGS for Bone Springs, Tollgate, and Jubilee Lake.

Directions: From the south end of Milton-Freewater, turn east onto 14th Street (which quickly runs into 15th Street) and follow signs to Harris County Park. Drive for 13 miles (the road turns into Walla Walla River Road). Just past Harris County Park, you'll arrive at the parking lot and the trailhead at the road's end. To reach the upper trailhead, follow directions to the North Fork Walla Walla, turning left to continue on Forest Service Road 65 at the road junction and North Fork trailhead. Continue another three miles to Deduct Pond and the trailhead, on the right side of the road.

Contact: Umatilla National Forest, Walla Walla Ranger District, 1415 West Rose Street, Walla Walla, WA 99362, 509/522-6290.

⁊ BURNT CABIN
8.0 mi/4.0 hrs

north of Tollgate in Umatilla National Forest

Map 10.2, page 442

Sometimes it's the simple rules of life that are so easy to forget when you're caught up in an outdoors adventure, so this bears repeating: What goes up must come down. Simple, yes, but you'll want to keep this in mind when you descend the four steep switchbacking miles down (2,300 feet, to be exact), because you'll need to conserve your energy for the hike back up. Just enjoy the scenery while you still have the strength for it—the views of the steep brown cliffs of the valley make it worth your while. Be on the lookout for rattlesnakes in this area, and bring plenty of water, as it can get scorching here. The narrow and often rocky trail finally lets up near the end of the trail and spits you out at the South Fork Walla Walla River (see listing in this chapter); you can explore the river before you start your climb up. Once you're back at the trailhead, stick around for a history lesson: The trail starts near the Target Meadow Campground, which was used as a camp and target range for soldiers from Old Fort Walla Walla from the late 1800s to 1906. You can still see damage to the trees, and the target mound itself.

User Groups: Hikers, dogs, mountain bikes, and horses. No wheelchair access.

Permits: A federal Northwest Forest pass is required to park here. The cost is $5 for a day pass or $30 for an annual pass. You can buy a day pass at the trailhead, at ranger stations, from private vendors, or through Nature of the Northwest Information Center.

Maps: For a map of Umatilla National For-est, contact Nature of the Northwest Information Center. For a topographic map, ask the USGS for Tollgate.

Directions: From Tollgate, turn left (north) onto Forest Service Road 64. Drive .2 mile to a junction with the Target Meadow Camp Road/Forest Service Road 6401. Turn left at the junction and drive 1.5 miles to Forest Service Road 6401-050. Turn right and continue one mile to the Target Meadow campground. At the campground, the road forks—stay to the left and drive another .5 mile until the road's end, the parking area, and the trailhead. The trail starts about 50 yards from the trail marker (it can be hard to find). Note: The road can be closed through mid-June due to snow, so check ahead before you venture out.

Contact: Umatilla National Forest, Walla Walla Ranger District, 1415 West Rose Street, Walla Walla, WA 99362, 509/522-6290.

⁸ ROUGH FORK
6.4 mi/3.5 hrs

northeast of Tollgate in Umatilla National Forest

Map 10.2, page 442

If you want to dip straight down into the South Fork Walla Walla River and ditch the crowds near the river trailhead, try this steep descent. You'll plunk down about 13 miles from the lower river trailhead and about 6 miles from the upper trailhead, so chances are you'll be on your own—except for the deer and rattlesnakes, that is (keep your eye out for the latter). Also, remember to bring water with you, because it's a hot and dusty trail. Oh yeah, and don't forget about the 1,780-foot climb back to your car after you reach the river. It's a speedy descent to the river, with views of the brown and green valley walls, and the rushing river itself. The Mottet Campground is a cute and remote site, so stick around if you want to make a weekend out of the trip (or if you need to rest after the steep climb up).

User Groups: Hikers, dogs, mountain bikes, and horses. No wheelchair access.

Permits: A federal Northwest Forest pass is

required to park here. The cost is $5 for a day pass or $30 for an annual pass. You can buy a day pass at the trailhead, at ranger stations, from private vendors, or through Nature of the Northwest Information Center.

Maps: For a map of Umatilla National Forest, contact Nature of the Northwest Information Center. For a topographic map, ask the USGS for Tollgate.

Directions: From Tollgate, drive 12 miles north on dirt Forest Road 64 to the junction with Jubilee Lake. After the lake junction, drive another 3.5 miles to a sign for Rough Fork. Turn left onto Forest Service Road 6411 (which is a rough road) and drive 1.3 miles to an unmarked fork just before Mottet Campground. Turn right onto unmarked Forest Service Road 6403 and drive less than .1 mile (keeping to the left at another unmarked fork) to the trailhead. Note: The road in is often closed to snow through mid-June, so call ahead to make sure it's open before heading out.

Contact: Umatilla National Forest, Walla Walla Ranger District, 1415 West Rose Street, Walla Walla, WA 99362, 509/522-6290.

9 JUBILEE LAKE NATIONAL RECREATION TRAIL
2.6 mi/1.5 hrs

northeast of Tollgate in Umatilla National Forest

Map 10.2, page 442

For a relatively flat lake loop, you can't go wrong with Jubilee Lake (you also can't go wrong with the name, which is all about fun). Although it can be a popular lake, with a large campground, it's surprisingly solitary, since most people prefer to hit the great fishing spots rather than take a stroll. Well, they're missing out. It's a trail for taking it easy and enjoying the scenery without putting in too much effort, and plenty of benches line the route so you can do just that. On the north shore, there are private nooks for casting in the stocked lake. Note to spring trail-seekers: Jubilee Lake is closed through June due to snow, so call ahead before you arrive.

User Groups: Hikers and dogs. No mountain bikes or horses are allowed. The south shore of the lake is paved and wheelchair accessible. **Permits:** A $3 day-use fee is collected at the entrance.

Maps: For a map of Umatilla National Forest, contact Nature of the Northwest Information Center. For a topographic map, ask the USGS for Jubilee Lake.

Directions: From Tollgate, drive 12 miles north on dirt Forest Road 64 to the Jubilee Lake Campground. The trailhead leaves from the boat ramp.

Contact: Umatilla National Forest, Walla Walla Ranger District, 1415 West Rose Street, Walla Walla, WA 99362, 509/522-6290.

10 LICK CREEK/ GROUSE MOUNTAIN
7.0 mi/3.5 hrs

southeast of Tollgate in the North Fork Umatilla Wilderness of Umatilla National Forest

Map 10.2, page 442

Starting at 4,050 feet in elevation, the upper trailhead offers unobstructed insta-views of the North Fork Umatilla Valley and sprawling grassy wildflower meadows and hills. It can be hot, dry, and exposed at first, so remember to bring water and sunscreen. After about a mile, you'll start to descend through forest, where it gets cooler and shadier with each step, as the trail leads down to the North Fork Umatilla River. It's a remote trail, and the only people you're likely to encounter are morel mushroom seekers, who flock to the area in the summer. The trail passes through Grouse Mountain saddle, where a faint trail leads up to the peak. If you're interested in this more adventurous feat, pick up a map before you go, because the route is not well marked or maintained. You can also access the trail from the lower trailhead if you'd rather climb to the top.

User Groups: Hikers, dogs, and horses. No mountain bikes are allowed. No wheelchair access. **Permits:** Permits are not required. Parking and access are free.

Maps: For a map of the North Fork Umatilla Wilderness and Umatilla National Forest, contact Nature of the Northwest Information Center. For a topographic map, ask the USGS for Bingham Springs and Blalock Mountain.

Directions: From Weston, drive 14.8 miles east on Highway 402 and turn right on McDougall Camp Road/Forest Service Road 3715. Drive three miles to the end of the road and the small parking pullout. To reach the lower trailhead, drive seven miles east from Pendleton on I-84 to Exit 216. Turn left (north) toward Walla Walla for 2.1 miles, then turn right on Mission Road. Drive 1.6 miles, then turn left on Cayuse Road for 10.8 miles. Turn right onto Bingham Road (which turns into Forest Service Road 32), and continue for 15.5 miles to the Corporation Guard Station and the parking area, to the left.

Contact: Umatilla National Forest, Walla Walla Ranger District, 1415 West Rose Street, Walla Walla, WA 99362, 509/522-6290.

11 NORTH FORK UMATILLA
9.8 mi one-way/
5.0 hrs-2.0 days

east of Pendleton in the North Fork Umatilla Wilderness of Umatilla National Forest

Map 10.2, page 442

As you can see above, it's tricky to gauge just how long it will take the average hiker to explore this area, because that's up to you. For a peaceful stroll along the river, check out the first four miles of this trail. This section gains just 450 feet in elevation and saunters along the rushing water on a narrow dirt path filled with flitting butterflies and the sounds of chirping birds. The trail leaves the river to climb Coyote Ridge for the last five miles, gaining 2,000 feet in elevation to views of the river below and the Umatilla wilderness area. So take your pick: You can either turn around before the climb for a pleasant eight-mile roundtrip, or continue on for the steep trip up the ridge for a shuttle hike to the upper trailhead, or do it as an out-and-back backpacking trip.

User Groups: Hikers, dogs, and horses. No mountain bikes are allowed. No wheelchair access.

Permits: A federal Northwest Forest pass is required to park here. The cost is $5 for a day pass or $30 for an annual pass. You can buy a day pass at ranger stations, from private vendors, or through Nature of the Northwest Information Center.

Maps: For a map of the North Fork Umatilla Wilderness and Umatilla National Forest, contact Nature of the Northwest Information Center. For a topographic map, ask the USGS for Bingham Springs and Andies Prairie.

Directions: From Pendleton, drive seven miles east to Exit 216. Turn left (north) toward Walla Walla for 2.1 miles, then turn right on Mission Road. Drive 1.6 miles, then turn left on Cayuse Road for 10.8 miles. Turn right onto Bingham Road (which turns into Forest Service Road 32), and continue for 15.6 miles, turning left into the Umatilla Forks day-use pullout and parking area. The trailhead is to the left of the sign. To reach the upper trailhead from Tollgate, drive one mile east on Highway 204 and turn south onto Forest Service Road 3719. Drive two miles and turn right onto Forest Service Road 041, continuing another two miles to the end of the road and the trailhead at Coyote Ridge.

Contact: Umatilla National Forest, Walla Walla Ranger District, 1415 West Rose Street, Walla Walla, WA 99362, 509/522-6290.

12 NINE MILE RIDGE
13.6 mi/7.0 hrs

east of Pendleton in the North Fork Umatilla Wilderness of Umatilla National Forest

Map 10.2, page 442

Okay, so it's called the Nine Mile Ridge, and the length is actually 6.8 miles one-way, but who's to quibble? Climbing up this first section will make it seem like it's nine miles anyway, as it gains 1,800 feet in the first two miles. The trail is overgrown in parts, so true adventurers will love it (while those who prefer a well-maintained trail may not be sharing the joy). After the first two strenuous miles, the trail levels off to the ridgecrest, where you can enjoy views of the Umatilla wilderness valley below, and maybe some local wildlife like elk, deer, black bears, and cougars. It's best to bring along a detailed map for this one, because sometimes trail signs are missing in this area.

User Groups: Hikers, dogs, and horses. No mountain bikes are allowed. No wheelchair access.

Permits: Permits are not required. Parking and access are free.

Maps: For a map of the North Fork Umatilla Wilderness and Umatilla National Forest, contact Nature of the Northwest Information Center. For a topographic map, ask the USGS for Bingham Springs and Andies Prairie.

Directions: From Pendleton, drive seven miles east to Exit 216. Turn left (north) toward Walla Walla for 2.1 miles, then turn right on Mission Road. Drive 1.6 miles, then turn left on Cayuse Road for 10.8 miles. Turn right onto Bingham Road (which turns into Forest Service Road 32), and continue for 16.1 miles. Turn left at the junction, .25 mile past the Umatilla Forks Campground, before the South Fork Umatilla bridge, and drive .1 mile up a rough side road to a small parking area on the left. (To the right is a short access road to the Kiwanis clubhouse; the gate is sometimes locked.) The trail begins to the left as you're driving in (in front of the parking turnout). When you come to a trail junction shortly after entering, take the left junction (the sign may be missing).

Contact: Umatilla National Forest, Walla Walla Ranger District, 1415 West Rose Street, Walla Walla, WA 99362, 509/522-6290.

13 BUCK CREEK
7.0 mi/3.5 hrs

east of Pendleton in the North Fork Umatilla Wilderness of Umatilla National Forest

Map 10.2, page 442

This lightly used trail meanders down Buck Creek for 3.5 miles, crossing it several times. Since it gains only 800 feet in elevation, it's a good choice for those who want to explore the

wilderness without having to hoof it up nearby Buck Mountain (see listing in this chapter). It can be overgrown in parts, but it's a simple trail to follow. If you like to feel as if you're in the middle of the deep wilds, this is worth checking out. Locals in this part of the Umatilla Forest include coyotes, elk, black bears, and deer, so you may have a chance to see a few natives while you explore.

User Groups: Hikers, dogs, and horses. No mountain bikes are allowed. No wheelchair access.

Permits: Permits are not required. Parking and access are free.

Maps: For a map of the North Fork Umatilla Wilderness and Umatilla National Forest, contact Nature of the Northwest Information Center. For a topographic map, ask the USGS for Bingham Springs.

Directions: From Pendleton, drive seven miles east to Exit 216. Turn left (north) toward Walla Walla for 2.1 miles, then turn right on Mission Road. Drive 1.6 miles, then turn left on Cayuse Road for 10.8 miles. Turn right onto Bingham Road (which turns into Forest Service Road 32), and continue for 16.1 miles. Turn left at the junction, .25 mile past the Umatilla Forks Campground, before the South Fork Umatilla bridge, and drive .1 mile up a rough side road to a small parking area, on the left. (To the right is a short access road to the Kiwanis clubhouse; the gate is sometimes locked.) The trail begins to the left as you're driving in (in front of the parking turnout). When you come to a trail junction shortly after entering, stay on the trail straight ahead that travels along the creek.

Contact: Umatilla National Forest, Walla Walla Ranger District, 1415 West Rose Street, Walla Walla, WA 99362, 509/522-6290.

14 BUCK MOUNTAIN
7.0 mi/3.5 hrs

east of Pendleton in the North Fork Umatilla Wilderness of Umatilla National Forest

Map 10.2, page 442

This lightly used trail doesn't give you time to

warm up. Instead, it shoots straight uphill for almost 2,000 feet for the first 1.5 miles. Then you catch a break, gaining only 300 feet in elevation to reach the summit, surrounded by meadows. The trail continues for a total of 7.5 miles, ending at a junction with Lake Creek Trail, where you can do a 12-mile loop to Buck Creek to return to the trailhead. Otherwise, if the view is your goal, head back when you reach the summit about 3.5 miles down the trail. Word of warning before you set out: You'll be lucky if the signs are still in place, as some of them look like they've been used as target practice or are missing altogether. Also, the trail can be overgrown and faint in parts, so you'd be smart to get a map before you set out. Even the trailhead is tricky to find. But if you like the challenge of route-finding and setting off into parts unknown to many, this may be your ticket.

User Groups: Hikers, dogs, and horses. No mountain bikes are allowed. No wheelchair access.

Permits: Permits are not required. Parking and access are free.

Maps: For a map of the North Fork Umatilla Wilderness and Umatilla National Forest, contact Nature of the Northwest Information Center. For a topographic map, ask the USGS for Bingham Springs.

Directions: From Pendleton, drive seven miles east to Exit 216. Turn left (north) toward Walla Walla for 2.1 miles, then turn right on Mission Road. Drive 1.6 miles, then turn left on Cayuse Road for 10.8 miles. Turn right onto Bingham Road (which turns into Forest Service Road 32), and continue for 16.1 miles. Turn left at the junction, .25 mile past the Umatilla Forks Campground, before the South Fork Umatilla bridge, and drive .1 mile up a rough side road to a small parking area on the left. (To the right is a short access road to the Kiwanis clubhouse; the gate is sometimes locked.) The trail begins to the left as you're driving in (in front of the parking turnout). Take the right fork of the trail to Buck Mountain (the sign may be missing).

Contact: Umatilla National Forest, Walla Walla

Ranger District, 1415 West Rose Street, Walla Walla, WA 99362, 509/522-6290.

15 BEARWALLOW TO STANDLEY CABIN
9.6 mi/5.0 hrs

south of Minam in Eagle Cap Wilderness of Wallowa-Whitman National Forest

Map 10.3, page 443

Starting at over 6,000 feet in elevation sure has its advantages: You get great views right off the bat of the Wallowa mountain range and the valley below with little exertion on your part. Since you're so far off the beaten path, this is prime time for wildlife viewing—give my regards to my bear friend there, and tell him next time I'm in the area, we'll do berries. Bears are quite common in the Wallowa Mountains, as are deer, elk, cougars, and woodpeckers. The trail starts along a forested ridgeline as you travel nearly 1,000 feet up to the 7,200-foot Standley Cabin, an old cabin from the early 1900s. You probably won't see anyone else while you're here, since the road in is long and rough. For this reason, it can be handy to bring a friend along to hop out and remove any obstacles in the road, and to unclench your fingers from the steering wheel after you've arrived at the trailhead. The road tends to be blocked through June due to snow, so make sure all is clear before you head out.

User Groups: Hikers, dogs, and horses. Mountain bikes are not allowed. No wheelchair access.

Permits: A free wilderness permit is required to hike here and is available at the trailhead. A federal Northwest Forest pass is also required to park here. The cost is $5 for a day pass or $30 for an annual pass. You can buy a day pass at the trailhead, at ranger stations, from private vendors, or through Nature of the Northwest Information Center.

Maps: For a map of Eagle Cap Wilderness and Wallowa-Whitman National Forest, contact Nature of the Northwest Information Center. For a topographic map, ask the USGS for Mount Moriah.

Directions: From Wallowa, drive about 17 miles west on Highway 82 to mile marker 35. Turn left (south) onto Big Canyon Road and drive 10 miles. Turn left and drive another six miles on Forest Service Road 050 to the end of the road and the trailhead.

Contact: Wallowa-Whitman National Forest, Wallowa Valley Ranger District, 88401 Highway 82, Enterprise, Oregon 97828, 541/ 426-4978.

16 BOWMAN TRAIL TO CHIMNEY/WOOD LAKES
14.8 mi/1.0–2.0 days

south of Wallowa in Eagle Cap Wilderness of Wallowa-Whitman National Forest

Map 10.3, page 443

 This trail is a feast for the senses: For the ears, you have the Lostine River whitewater rapids. For the eyes, you have the snow-capped Wallowa Mountains behind you as you hike, which you will want to rest and take a look at here and there on the steep climb. And for the nose, a pine scent fills the air. It's hard to talk about this neck of the woods without lapsing into superlatives. The trailhead starts at 5,200 feet, so take it easy as you start the ascent, which starts gradually but quickly becomes steeper as you climb 2,000 feet in 3.5 miles, when you'll come upon a junction. Turn right for another 1.5 miles, passing Laverty Lakes (or stopping there if you like) to Chimney Lake, a perfect place to stop and rest, with the Wallowa Mountains as the backdrop. It's just a taste of the mountain lakes, though, because in another .5 mile is Hobo Lake, followed by Wood Lake another two miles down. The total mileage from the trailhead to Wood Lake is 7.4 miles. Return the way you came after drinking in the view, or camp here for the night. The trail also continues past the junction with Chimney Lake to cross alpine meadows to the North Minam River (total trip is 20 miles round-trip). Whichever route you take, you should bring a map and water along for this area, as the many intersecting trails can be confusing (although they tend to be well marked).

User Groups: Hikers, dogs, and horses. No mountain bikes are allowed. No wheelchair access.

Permits: A free wilderness permit is required to hike here and is available at the trailhead. A federal Northwest Forest pass is also required to park here. The cost is $5 for a day pass or $30 for an annual pass. You can buy a day pass at the trailhead, at ranger stations, from private vendors, or through Nature of the Northwest Information Center.

Maps: For a map of the Eagle Cap Wilderness and Wallowa-Whitman National Forest, contact Nature of the Northwest Information Center. For a topographic map, ask the USGS for North Minam Meadows.

Directions: From Wallowa, drive 7.6 miles south on Highway 82 to Lostine, and turn right on Lostine River Road (a paved two-lane road). Drive for 14.7 miles (after seven miles it turns into good gravel and dirt road), and park in the well-marked Bowman trailhead parking area to the left. The well-marked trailhead is to your right as you're walking from the parking lot back to the road.

Contact: Wallowa Mountains Visitor Center, Eagle Cap Ranger District, 88401 Highway 82, Enterprise, OR 97828, 541/426-5546.

17 FRANCES LAKE
18.2 mi/1.0–2.0 days

south of Wallowa in Eagle Cap Wilderness of Wallowa-Whitman National Forest

Map 10.3, page 443

If you plan to head to Frances Lake, be warned right off the bat: It's long. It's uphill. It gains 3,300 feet in elevation. And considering you're already starting from 5,200 feet, you will definitely be feeling the altitude (unless you've climbed Everest recently, in which case this will be a breeze). But it's also worth it, with views of the Eagle Cap peaks and Chimney Lake (see listing in this chapter) across the Lostine River canyon, brook trout fishing, and camping spots around the lake. Along the way, look out for deer, elk, black bears, and mountain goats. Although it's do-able in one day, it's a good trail for an overnight backpacking trip, because it would be a long haul back to your car in one day. At the very least, start off first thing in the morning, if you're not planning to camp, to give yourself plenty of time. This trail is maintained, but heavy storms sometimes make it hard to pass by the many felled trees (more so than on other trails). Make sure you check beforehand that all is well before you head out.

User Groups: Hikers, dogs, and horses. No mountain bikes are allowed. No wheelchair access.

Permits: A free wilderness permit is required to hike here and is available at the trailhead. A federal Northwest Forest pass is also required to park here. The cost is $5 for a day pass or $30 for an annual pass. You can buy a day pass at the trailhead, at ranger stations, from private vendors, or through Nature of the Northwest Information Center.

Maps: For a map of the Eagle Cap Wilderness and Wallowa-Whitman National Forest, contact Nature of the Northwest Information Center. For a topographic map, ask the USGS for North Minam Meadows and Chief Joseph Mountain.

Directions: From Wallowa, drive 7.6 miles south on Highway 82 to Lostine, and turn right on Lostine River Road (a paved two-lane road). Drive for 14.7 miles (after seven miles it turns into good gravel and dirt road), and park in the well-marked Bowman trailhead parking area to the left. The trail starts to the left as you're walking back from the parking area to the road, crossing a meadow before it hits the true trailhead.

Contact: Wallowa Mountains Visitor Center, Eagle Cap Ranger District, 88401 Highway 82, Enterprise, OR 97828, 541/426-5546.

18 MAXWELL LAKE
8.0 mi/4.5 hrs

south of Wallowa in Eagle Cap Wilderness of Wallowa-Whitman National Forest

Map 10.3, page 443

If you want to check out one of the many Wallowa mountain lakes but don't feel like hauling up a 10-mile trail to get there, you'll like Maxwell

Lake. The trail starts out on a gentle switch-backing, but the climb steepens later on (total elevation gain: 2,300 feet). You'll want to keep your head up, because sometimes the trail can be hard to follow after a bad storm before it's been maintained. But you'll want to keep your head up anyway, to let the views sink in. Before you turn on the first switchback, turn around to view the snowcapped Wallowa peaks behind you for the first good photo op. Save some camera film, though, there's more to come. The small lake sits at 7,729 feet, which means more views ahead—and all that for a four-mile price of admission.

User Groups: Hikers, dogs, and horses. No mountain bikes are allowed. No wheelchair access.

Permits: A free wilderness permit is required to hike here and is available at the trailhead. A federal Northwest Forest pass is also required to park here. The cost is $5 for a day pass or $30 for an annual pass. You can buy a day pass at the trailhead, at ranger stations, from private vendors, or through Nature of the Northwest Information Center.

Maps: For a map of the Eagle Cap Wilderness and Wallowa-Whitman National Forest, contact Nature of the Northwest Information Center. For a topographic map, ask the USGS for North Minam Meadows.

Directions: From Wallowa, drive 7.6 miles south on Highway 82 to Lostine, and turn right on Lostine River Road (a paved two-lane road). Drive for 17.4 miles (after seven miles it turns into good gravel and dirt road) to the parking area on the left. The trail starts across the road in Shady Campground.

Contact: Wallowa Mountains Visitor Center, Eagle Cap Ranger District, 88401 Highway 82, Enterprise, OR 97828, 541/426-5546.

19 WEST FORK LOSTINE TO MINAM/BLUE LAKES
14.2 mi/7.5 hrs to 2.0 days

south of Wallowa in Eagle Cap Wilderness of Wallowa-Whitman National Forest

Map 10.3, page 443

Blue Lake sits apart from the other Lakes Basin

trails, so it doesn't always get the attention it deserves—which is a good thing for hikers craving solitude. Shortly after the trailhead, the trail comes to a well-marked junction. Take the right fork to travel along and over the West Fork Lostine River, heading through the Douglas fir forest for a gentle ascent (total elevation gain is 2,200 feet for the entire 7.1-mile trip). Views of 9,595-foot Eagle Cap and the Lostine Valley get better with every step, and you'll arrive at Minam Lake at 6.1 miles. You can stay here or travel another one mile to Blue Lake, which is the smaller and more remote of the two sister lakes. Camping spots are limited at Blue Lake but more numerous at Minam Lake (and at the trailhead) if you want to stay overnight. As with all the trails in the Lakes Basin area, although the trails tend to be well marked, there are a lot of options for longer loops, so get a map before you set out.

User Groups: Hikers, dogs, and horses. No mountain bikes are allowed. No wheelchair access.

Permits: A free wilderness permit is required to hike here and is available at the trailhead. A federal Northwest Forest pass is also required to park here. The cost is $5 for a day pass or $30 for an annual pass. You can buy a day pass at the trailhead, at ranger stations, from private vendors, or through Nature of the Northwest Information Center.

Maps: For a map of the Eagle Cap Wilderness and Wallowa-Whitman National Forest, contact Nature of the Northwest Information Center. For a topographic map, ask the USGS for Steamboat Lake and Eagle Cap.

Directions: From Wallowa, drive 7.6 miles south on Highway 82 to Lostine, and turn right on Lostine River Road (a paved two-lane road). Drive for 18.1 miles (after seven miles it turns into good gravel and dirt road) to the end of the road and the large parking area at Two Pan trailhead. The trail starts at the end of the parking area, to the left of the Two Pan trailhead sign.

Contact: Wallowa Mountains Visitor Center, Eagle Cap Ranger District, 88401 Highway 82, Enterprise, OR 97828, 541/426-5546.

20 EAST LOSTINE RIVER TO MIRROR LAKE
14.6 mi/7.5 hrs

south of Wallowa in Eagle Cap Wilderness of Wallowa-Whitman National Forest

Map 10.3, page 443

One of many access routes to the Lakes Basin area, this one isn't as populated as other trailheads. It does tend to be snowed in later than its surrounding cousins, though, so check to make sure the white stuff is out of there before deciding on this route. The river sounds like a highway, but the only traffic jams here are of the elk, deer, and bears that populate the area. At the marked junction shortly after the trailhead, take the left fork to lead up to short switchbacks through the forest before entering a lush meadow filled with wildflowers and a sneak peek at Eagle Cap itself, standing at a majestic 9,595 feet. There are places to camp at Mirror Lake, along the way, and at the trailhead if you want to stick around (which you will). Pick up a map before you go, because although the trails tend to be well marked in this area, there are plenty of intersecting trails and longer loop possibilities.

User Groups: Hikers, dogs, and horses. No mountain bikes are allowed. No wheelchair access.

Permits: A free wilderness permit is required to hike here and is available at the trailhead. A federal Northwest Forest pass is also required to park here. The cost is $5 for a day pass or $30 for an annual pass. You can buy a day pass at the trailhead, at ranger stations, from private vendors, or through Nature of the Northwest Information Center.

Maps: For a map of the Eagle Cap Wilderness and Wallowa-Whitman National Forest, contact Nature of the Northwest Information Center. For a topographic map, ask the USGS for Steamboat Lake and Eagle Cap.

Directions: From Wallowa, drive 7.6 miles south on Highway 82 to Lostine, and turn right on Lostine River Road (a paved two-lane road). Drive for 18.1 miles (after seven miles it turns into good gravel and dirt road) to the end of the road and the large parking area at Two Pan trailhead. The trail starts at the end of the parking area, to the left of the Two Pan trailhead sign.

Contact: Wallowa Mountains Visitor Center, Eagle Cap Ranger District, 88401 Highway 82, Enterprise, OR 97828, 541/426-5546.

21 HURRICANE CREEK TO ECHO LAKE
16.0 mi/2.0 days

south of Enterprise in Eagle Cap Wilderness of Wallowa-Whitman National Forest

Map 10.3, page 443

A popular access trail to the Lakes Basin area, the crowds thin out as you head up to Echo Lake, and there's a reason for that: It's a steep, rocky, and sometimes unmaintained climb up to the lake. Start off early if you plan to make this a day hike; if you want to stay overnight, there are plenty of places to camp along the trail and at the lake. After five miles, you come to the junction with Echo Lake Trail and then climb another 2,400 feet in three miles. While you're walking along the creek, you'll have views of the two highest peaks in the Eagle Cap Wilderness to your left across the valley: 9,839-foot Sacajawea and 9,832-foot Matterhorn peaks, followed by the 9,595-foot Eagle Cap. Although the trail tends to be free of snow earlier than others in the area, it's a flash food area, and mountain runoff makes some creeks uncrossable, so it's best to hit this later in the season or at least check ahead before you head out.

User Groups: Hikers, dogs, and horses. No mountain bikes are allowed. No wheelchair access.

Permits: A free wilderness permit is required to hike here and is available at the trailhead. A federal Northwest Forest pass is also required to park here. The cost is $5 for a day pass or $30 for an annual pass. You can buy a day pass at the trailhead, at ranger stations, from private vendors, or through Nature of the Northwest Information Center.

Maps: For a map of the Eagle Cap Wilderness and Wallowa-Whitman National Forest,

contact Nature of the Northwest Information Center. For a topographic map, ask the USGS for Chief Joseph Mountain and Eagle Cap.

Directions: From Enterprise, drive south on Hurricane Creek Road for 8.8 miles (it's a paved two-lane road for the first five miles, then turns into a gravel road for 1.5 miles, then a one-lane paved road). Park at the entrance to Hurricane Creek trailhead and the parking area. The well-marked trail is to the left of the parking lot as you're driving in from the road.

Contact: Wallowa Mountains Visitor Center, Eagle Cap Ranger District, 88401 Highway 82, Enterprise, OR 97828, 541/426-5546.

22 ICE LAKE
15.8 mi/9.0 hrs to 2.0 days

south of Joseph in Eagle Cap Wilderness of Wallowa-Whitman National Forest

Map 10.3, page 443

Starting from the popular West Fork Wallowa trailhead to the high alpine lake, the trail is a long but beautiful climb up. After 2.8 miles, the trail forks to the left to start Ice Lake Trail. It's another 5.1 miles up to Ice Lake, with views of the Matterhorn and surrounding 9,000-foot Wallowa peaks, plus the wildflower meadows and of course Ice Lake itself, sitting pretty at a cool 7,920 feet. You can also hit the Matterhorn summit from here if you're really aching for adventure (but get a detailed map before you go, because it's not as heavily used as the lower trails). Before you get all hot and bothered around the collar and decide to jump in, remember two things: As with all trails in this scenic area, the area can be crowded, especially on holiday weekends. It's also at high altitude, so you should expect snow at least through June (check ahead to make sure trails are clear). For both of those reasons, shoot for later in the season, preferably midweek (yeah, yeah, the job gets in the way, I know). Also, keep in mind that camping is limited at Ice Lake, so if you plan to stay overnight, please make sure you check the Eagle Cap Wilderness regulations.

User Groups: Hikers, dogs, and horses. No mountain bikes are allowed. No wheelchair access.

Permits: A free wilderness permit is required to hike here, available at the trailhead. Parking and access are free.

Maps: For a map of the Eagle Cap Wilderness and Wallowa-Whitman National Forest, contact Nature of the Northwest Information Center. For a topographic map, ask the USGS for Joseph, Aneroid Lake, and Eagle Cap.

Directions: From Enterprise, drive 12.4 miles south on Highway 82 to Wallowa Lake State Park. Continue past Wallowa Lake and head straight (passing the campground entrance sign to the right) to the end of the road. Park at the parking area on the right side of the road, and walk across the street to the trailhead, forking to the right after the trailhead sign.

Contact: Wallowa Mountains Visitor Center, Eagle Cap Ranger District, 88401 Highway 82, Enterprise, OR 97828, 541/426-5546.

23 LAKES BASIN LOOP
22.7 mi/2.0 days

south of Joseph in Eagle Cap Wilderness of Wallowa-Whitman National Forest

 Map 10.3, page 443

Welcome to the ultimate experience. The Lakes Basin is one of the most popular destinations in the state, where people flock to hit the high alpine lakes surrounded by snow-capped peaks, where you can see why the Wallowa Mountains are often referred to as the Alps of Oregon. The trail can be packed at the start, where horseback riders and hikers from the nearby campground hit the trailhead for shorter hikes. Only the true adventure-seekers make it to the top, though (and a surprising amount actually do just that). The trail starts out along the West Fork Wallowa River, up through the valley meadows, climbing almost 4,000 feet, where an 11-mile loop starts around the alpine lakes with backdrops of 9,000-plus-foot Eagle Cap, Sentinel Peak, East Peak (and the list goes on), and plenty of camping spots along the way. Keeping in mind that this area

is often snowed in through June, so check ahead to make sure the trails are snow-free. The Lakes Basin is also accessible from Hurricane Creek and the East Fork Lostine River (see listings in this chapter), and shorter loop possibilities are endless. Or at least they seem that way.

User Groups: Hikers, dogs, and horses. No mountain bikes are allowed. No wheelchair access.

Permits: A free wilderness permit is required to hike here and is available at the trailhead. Parking and access are free.

Maps: For a map of the Eagle Cap Wilderness and Wallowa-Whitman National Forest, contact Nature of the Northwest Information Center. For a topographic map, ask the USGS for Joseph, Aneroid Lake, and Eagle Cap.

Directions: From Enterprise, drive 12.4 miles south on Highway 82 to Wallowa Lake State Park. Continue past Wallowa Lake and head straight (passing the campground entrance sign to the right) to the end of the road. Park at the parking area on the right side of the road, and walk across the street to the trailhead, forking to the right after the trailhead sign.

Contact: Wallowa Mountains Visitor Center, Eagle Cap Ranger District, 88401 Highway 82, Enterprise, OR 97828, 541/426-5546.

24 HAWKINS PASS
24.0 mi/2.0 days

south of Joseph in Eagle Cap Wilderness of Wallowa-Whitman National Forest

Map 10.3, page 443

The Lakes Basin is a popular area, and one way to go right through it without passing Go is to follow the West Fork Wallowa River right to its end, 8,330-foot Hawkins Pass. Of course, in order to get there you need to invest a healthy climb of 4,685 feet. But no need to do it all in one swoop—you have a good 12 miles to get there. Climbing up the West Fork Wallowa River, you'll pass the Lakes Basin in all its wildflower-meadow and alpine-lake glory; continue straight when the loop forks to the right, passing scenic Frazier Lake before climbing straight up to Hawkins Pass. Camping spots abound in this area, but realize that it can get a smidge crowded, especially on a holiday weekend. Also, you should always check ahead to make sure these high-altitude trails are snow-free, as they can be blocked through June.

User Groups: Hikers, dogs, and horses. No mountain bikes are allowed. No wheelchair access.

Permits: A free wilderness permit is required to hike here and is available at the trailhead. Parking and access are free.

Maps: For a map of the Eagle Cap Wilderness and Wallowa-Whitman National Forest, contact Nature of the Northwest Information Center. For a topographic map, ask the USGS for Joseph, Aneroid Lake, and Eagle Cap.

Directions: From Enterprise, drive 12.4 miles south on Highway 82 to Wallowa Lake State Park. Continue past Wallowa Lake and head straight (passing the campground entrance sign to the right) to the end of the road. Park at the parking area on the right side of the road, and walk across the street to the trailhead, forking to the right after the trailhead sign.

Contact: Wallowa Mountains Visitor Center, Eagle Cap Ranger District, 88401 Highway 82, Enterprise, OR 97828, 541/426-5546.

25 EAST FORK WALLOWA
14.0 mi/8.0 hrs to 2 days

south of Joseph in Eagle Cap Wilderness of Wallowa-Whitman National Forest

Map 10.3, page 443

Popular and right off Wallowa Lake, this trail is shared by hikers and horses at the start (watch your step), not to mention the buzzing of a hydroelectric plant. Be patient, because soon you'll leave the ruckus behind and start your ascent. After the trailhead sign, fork left to head up the East Fork Wallowa, which flows along the entire route. You'll pass through wildflower meadows with views of the 9,000-plus-foot Wallowa peaks as you climb up the nearly 4,000 feet to Tenderfoot Pass, where the trail ends. Aneroid Lake, sitting in the basin surrounded by the high alpine peaks, is six miles from the trailhead, where you can camp for the night if

you want to make it an overnight trip. But first, continue past the lakes to 8,500-foot Tenderfoot Pass and the trail's end for even better views from above. Like many of this area's trails, there are plenty of loop options here, and the trails tend to be well marked; get a map to explore your options in this cool area. Also, the trails can be snowbound through June, so check ahead to make sure the paths are snow-free.

User Groups: Hikers, dogs, and horses. No mountain bikes are allowed. No wheelchair access.

Permits: A free wilderness permit is required to hike here, available at the trailhead. Parking and access are free.

Maps: For a map of the Eagle Cap Wilderness and Wallowa-Whitman National Forest, contact Nature of the Northwest Information Center. For a topographic map, ask the USGS for Joseph and Aneroid Mountain.

Directions: From Enterprise, drive 12.4 miles south on Highway 82 to Wallowa Lake State Park. Continue past Wallowa Lake and head straight (passing the campground entrance sign to the right) to the end of the road. Park at the parking area on the right side of the road, and walk across the street to the trailhead, forking to the left after the trailhead sign.

Contact: Wallowa Mountains Visitor Center, Eagle Cap Ranger District, 88401 Highway 82, Enterprise, OR 97828, 541/426-5546.

26 EAGLE CREEK TO DIAMOND LAKE
18.0 mi/2.0 days

northeast of Baker City in Eagle Cap Wilderness of Wallowa-Whitman National Forest

Map 10.3, page 443

Following West Fork Eagle Creek for the first couple of miles, the trail gets off to a slow start and holds no hint of the good things to come. Horses share the trail for the first portion, so it can be dusty and muddy in parts as you pass by an open meadow. Creek crossings can be difficult when the runoff is high, so you should probably plan to hit this one later in the season. Just when you started to get the hang of things, the trail changes gears on you, climbing up switchbacks almost 2,000 feet. The trail forks to the left before hitting Echo Lake (see following listing), when you'll turn left and head straight up to higher ground, climbing about 3,000 feet in elevation when all is said and done. You'll probably have the alpine lake all to yourself, as most people visiting the area head to the Lakes Basin area.

User Groups: Hikers, dogs, and horses. No mountain bikes are allowed. No wheelchair access.

Permits: A federal Northwest Forest pass is required to park here. The cost is $5 for a day pass or $30 for an annual pass. You can buy a day pass at the trailhead, at ranger stations, from private vendors, or through Nature of the Northwest Information Center.

Maps: For a map of the Eagle Cap Wilderness and Wallowa-Whitman National Forest, contact Nature of the Northwest Information Center. For a topographic map, ask the USGS for Steamboat Lake and Bennet Peak.

Directions: From Medical Springs, drive 1.6 miles south on Forest Service Road 70. Turn left onto Forest Service Road 67 and drive 13.9 miles to Forest Service Road 77. Turn left and continue 5.1 miles to Forest Service Road 77-500. Turn right, and the trailhead and parking area are on the left. Note: The last few miles of this are rough but passable road.

Contact: Wallowa Mountains Visitor Center, Eagle Cap Ranger District, 88401 Highway 82, Enterprise, OR 97828, 541/426-5546.

27 EAGLE CREEK TO ECHO/ TRAVERSE LAKE
13.0 mi/7.0 hrs to 2.0 days

northeast of Baker City in Eagle Cap Wilderness of Wallowa-Whitman National Forest

Map 10.3, page 443

Traveling along West Fork Eagle Creek, this trail starts off with several stream crossings that can be tricky in the early summer, so it's best to visit when the runoff has calmed down. The trail starts off on a dusty and often muddy path (you can thank the horses for that) crossing through an open meadow—watch for deer, at least when the horses aren't around—before starting the switchback routine. It's five uphill miles to Echo Lake, which sits at 7,220 feet, where you can camp for the night or continue another 1.5 miles to Traverse Lake. Either way, you'll be likely to have the digs to yourself, as the crowds tend to descend upon the nearby Lakes Basin area. This trail also accesses Diamond Lake (see Eagle Creek to Diamond Lake listing in this chapter) at a junction before you reach Echo Lake. Total elevation gain is about 3,000 feet, and the fact that the trailhead already starts at 5,451 feet means you'll be feeling every step of the way.

User Groups: Hikers, dogs, and horses. No mountain bikes are allowed. No wheelchair access.

Permits: A federal Northwest Forest pass is required to park here. The cost is $5 for a day pass or $30 for an annual pass. You can buy a day pass at the trailhead, at ranger stations, from private vendors, or through Nature of the Northwest Information Center.

Maps: For a map of the Eagle Cap Wilderness and Wallowa-Whitman National Forest, contact Nature of the Northwest Information Center. For a topographic map, ask the USGS for Bennet Peak.

Directions: From Medical Springs, drive 1.6 miles south on Forest Service Road 70. Turn left onto Forest Service Road 67 and drive 13.9 miles to Forest Service Road 77. Turn left and continue 5.1 miles to Forest Service Road 77-500. Turn right, and the trailhead and parking area are on the left. Note: The last few miles of this are rough but passable.

Contact: Wallowa Mountains Visitor Center, Eagle Cap Ranger District, 88401 Highway 82, Enterprise, OR 97828, 541/426-5546.

28 EAGLE LAKE
14.0 mi/7.0 hrs to 2.0 days

northeast of Baker City in Eagle Cap Wilderness of Wallowa-Whitman National Forest

Map 10.3, page 443

Starting on a sandy trail shared by horses, Main Eagle Trail eases you into things by starting out flat so you can warm up before climbing almost 2,500 feet to Eagle Lake. It travels along Eagle Creek for its entire length, through meadows and across footbridges, to reach a trail junction at 5.8 miles. Turn right to continue just over a mile to the lake. Trail junctions tend to be well marked in this area, but as there are so many intersecting trails (such as Lookingglass Lake Trail, covered in this chapter, which shares the first four miles with Eagle Lake), it's a good idea to bring along a map. While you're at it, bring along your camera, because the 9,000-plus-foot tall Wallowas reign supreme in this area, always mugging for the camera. You can camp along the trail and at the lake if you want to make this an overnight stop.

User Groups: Hikers, dogs, and horses. No mountain bikes are allowed. No wheelchair access.

Permits: A federal Northwest Forest pass is required to park here. The cost is $5 for a day pass or $30 for an annual pass. You can buy a day pass at the trailhead, at ranger stations, from private vendors, or through Nature of the Northwest Information Center.

Maps: For a map of the Eagle Cap Wilderness and Wallowa-Whitman National Forest, contact Nature of the Northwest Information Center. For a topographic map, ask the USGS for Bennet Peak and Krag Peak.

Directions: From Medical Springs, drive 1.6 miles south on Forest Service Road 70. Turn left onto Forest Service Road 67 and drive 13.9 miles to Forest Service Road 77. Turn left, continue .7 miles, and keep straight to continue onto Forest Service Road 7755. Drive 3.6 miles to the road's end and the trailhead.

Contact: Wallowa Mountains Visitor Center, Eagle Cap Ranger District, 88401 Highway 82, Enterprise, OR 97828, 541/426-5546.

29 LOOKINGGLASS LAKE
14.0 mi/7.0 hrs to 2.0 days

northeast of Baker City in Eagle Cap Wilderness of Wallowa-Whitman National Forest

Map 10.3, page 443

Starting off as a hot, sandy path, the trail soon heads into the cool confines of Eagle Creek. It's a gentle path that will give you energy to enjoy the scenery of waterfalls and meadows before the real climbing begins. At 4.1 miles, you'll reach a junction with Lookingglass Lake Trail. Take a right here to travel almost three miles to the lake, where you'll see that it's called Lookingglass because of the constant view it enjoys (okay, I just made that up, but still). This area is crawling with hot campsites, so you can make it an overnight trip if you want, and you'll probably have it all to yourself because it's not as highly traveled as other parts of this scenic area. This trail shares the first four miles with Eagle Lake Trail (see listing in this chapter).

User Groups: Hikers, dogs, and horses. No mountain bikes are allowed. No wheelchair access.

Permits: A federal Northwest Forest pass is required to park here. The cost is $5 for a day pass or $30 for an annual pass. You can buy a day pass at the trailhead, at ranger stations, from private vendors, or through Nature of the Northwest Information Center.

Maps: For a map of the Eagle Cap Wilderness and Wallowa-Whitman National Forest, contact Nature of the Northwest Information Center. For a topographic map, ask the USGS for Bennet Peak and Krag Peak.

Directions: From Medical Springs, drive 1.6 miles south on Forest Service Road 70. Turn left onto Forest Service Road 67, and drive 13.9 miles to Forest Service Road 77. Turn left, continue .7 mile, and keep straight to continue onto Forest Service Road 7755. Drive 3.6 miles to the road's end and the trailhead.

Contact: Wallowa Mountains Visitor Center, Eagle Cap Ranger District, 88401 Highway 82, Enterprise, OR 97828, 541/426-5546.

30 SOUTH FORK IMNAHA
34.6 mi/3.0 days

north of Richland in Eagle Cap Wilderness of Wallowa-Whitman National Forest

Map 10.3, page 443

The mileage may look daunting at first glance, but you don't need to travel far to reach great views, and then you can turn around where you started. Following the South Fork Imnaha River, the easy path starts off as a wide, dusty, flat trail. If a scenic and flat trip is what you're after, you can head just two miles in to Blue Hole, where the river shoots through the rocky gorge. If a strenuous backpacking trip is what you're after, keep on going, because the trail gets steeper at the end, gaining 4,000 feet in elevation up to 8,330-foot Hawkins Pass, in the Lakes Basin. Camp here for views of the 9,000-plus-foot Wallowa peaks.

User Groups: Hikers, dogs, and horses. No mountain bikes are allowed. No wheelchair access.

Permits: A federal Northwest Forest pass is required to park here. The cost is $5 for a day pass or $30 for an annual pass. You can buy a day pass at ranger stations, from private vendors, or through Nature of the Northwest Information Center.

Maps: For a map of the Eagle Cap Wilderness and Wallowa-Whitman National Forest, contact Nature of the Northwest Information Center. For a topographic map, ask the USGS for Deadman Point, Cornucopia, Krag Peak, Eagle Cap, and Aneroid Mountain.

Directions: From Richland, drive east on Highway 86 to the junction with Wallowa Mountain Loop Road/Forest Service Road 39. Turn left and drive 23.1 miles, then turn left on Imnaha River Road/Forest Service Road 3960. Drive 8.6 miles to the road's end and the trailhead (the road turns to gravel for last .2 mile, but otherwise, the whole route is paved).

Contact: Wallowa Mountains Visitor Center,

Eagle Cap Ranger District, 88401 Highway 82, Enterprise, OR 97828, 541/426-5546.

31 SADDLE CREEK TO FREEZEOUT SADDLE/ SNAKE RIVER
4.0–22.0 mi/ 2.5 hrs–2.0 days

east of Joseph in Hells Canyon National Recreation Area of Wallowa-Whitman National Forest

Map 10.4, page 444

This is the trail of many names and many routes. Saddle Creek Trail leads two miles up to Freezeout Saddle via a grassy mountain, where you can see the switchbacks ahead and behind you (remember to keep looking behind you for the views down, because you quickly gain 3,000 feet in elevation). Reaching a rock cairn marking the saddle, the trail then continues another nine miles to Snake River. If you're turning back here, cross the summit ridge (turning right) for some even better views of the Hells Canyon gorges and Wallowa peaks. No offense to trees, but there's something to be said for crisscrossing up a treeless domain, because, well, there's nothing to get in the way of the glorious views. From the saddle, the trail also continues straight for nine miles, plunging a healthy 5,000 feet to Snake River, so you can also extend this trip into a two-day affair and camp at the river. And then we come to option number three, taking the high road (or trail as the case may be): Continuing on Saddle Creek Trail after reaching the summit, you'll come across the High Trail junction after another two miles, which is a daunting 36.6 miles one-way, with views of the spectacular canyon and Seven Devil's peaks across the border in Idaho. The fourth and final option is to continue across the ridgeline to do a loop back to the right fork at the trailhead, but it's not recommended, because the trail can be sparse at times; if you choose this route, you should have your bearings. Whatever route you take will be lined with views the entire time in this sparse area, so you can't go wrong.

User Groups: Hikers, dogs, and horses. No mountain bikes are allowed. No wheelchair access.

Permits: A federal Northwest Forest pass is required to park here. The cost is $5 for a day pass or $30 for an annual pass. You can buy a day pass at ranger stations, from private vendors, or through Nature of the Northwest Information Center.

Maps: For a map of the Hells Canyon National Recreation Area and Wallowa-Whitman National Forest, contact Nature of the Northwest Information Center. For a topographic map, ask the USGS for Sheep Creek Divide, Hat Point, and Old Timer Mountain.

Directions: From Joseph, drive 40 miles east on Highway 350 to Imnaha. Turn south on Imnaha River Road/County Road 727 and drive 12.5 miles to Forest Service Road 4230. Turn left and drive 2.7 miles to the end of the road and the trailhead.

Contact: Wallowa Mountains Visitor Center, Hells Canyon National Recreation Center, 88401 Highway 82, Enterprise, OR 97828, 541/426-5546.

32 STUD CREEK
2.0 mi/1.5 hrs

along the Snake River in Hells Canyon National Recreation Area in Wallowa-Whitman National Forest

> Map 10.4, page 444

Many trails in the Hells Canyon area seem to go on forever, but you don't need to spend an entire day to explore America's deepest canyon: This trail is short and sweet (although rather rocky), traveling along the Snake River for two miles to a pebble beach. It starts near the Hells Canyon Visitors Center and the dam itself, which offers guided tours and is a popular launching point for white-water rafting trips. (One cool thing about the dam is you can only reach it via the Idaho side, so you get to slip into another state for a beautiful drive in.) Though the area is hot, you should absolutely, positively wear long pants, because if the desert brush doesn't kill you, the poison oak

that cloaks the area sure will. The trail travels along a rocky cliff for views that will make you want to throw yourself over said cliff if you didn't bring along a camera. Once you've hit the rocky beach, turn back the way you came and spend some time at the visitors center, getting to know your canyon. Hey, you just trekked through its lovely territory, you owe it a favor.

User Groups: Hikers, dogs, and horses. No mountain bikes are allowed. No wheelchair access.

Permits: Permits are not required. Parking and access are free.

Maps: For a map of the Hells Canyon National Recreation Center and Wallowa-Whitman National Forest, contact Nature of the Northwest Information Center. For a topographic map, ask the USGS for Squirrel Prairie.

Directions: From Richland, drive 30 miles east on Highway 86 to Copperfield. Drive across the Snake River Bridge to Idaho and turn left (north) onto Forest Service Road 454. Drive 21.9 miles to Hells Canyon Dam. Turn left and cross the dam into Oregon, and turn right (north). Drive .9 mile to the visitors center parking. The trailhead starts just west of the boat ramp.

Contact: Wallowa Mountains Visitor Center, Hells Canyon National Recreation Center, 88401 Highway 82, Enterprise, OR 97828, 541/426-5546.

33 HELLS CANYON RESERVOIR
9.6 mi/9.5 hrs

north of Copperfield in Hells Canyon National Recreation Area of Wallowa-Whitman National Forest

> Map 10.4, page 444

Scooting along the Snake River (which, incidentally, is aptly named—look out for rattlers), this trail is a walk on the wild side. First off the bat, you need to find the trail, which is across a small rock field at the parking lot. Then you need to skirt some nasty poison oak that thrives here, so bring long pants. Finally, you have to do all of that and soak in the scenery of the purple-hued rocks and wild sunflowers and the deep gorge, viewing Idaho's fine contribution to Hells

Canyon across the white-water river. Although trails tend to be well marked in this area, and the trail is rather straightforward (along the river, followed by along the river), the path is overgrown toward the end and may be a little faint because it's lightly used, so turn back when the trail ends.

User Groups: Hikers, dogs, and horses. No mountain bikes are allowed. No wheelchair access.

Permits: Permits are not required. Parking and access are free.

Maps: For a map of the Hells Canyon National Recreation Area and Wallowa-Whitman National Forest, contact Nature of the Northwest Information Center. For a topographic map, ask the USGS for Homestead.

Directions: From Richland, drive 30 miles east on Highway 86 to Copperfield. Turn left (north) on Homestead Road and drive 9.1 miles to the road's end and the parking area. Note: The trailhead is tricky to find. It starts to the north of the road's end, across a small rock field.

Contact: Wallowa Mountains Visitor Center, Hells Canyon National Recreation Center, 88401 Highway 82, Enterprise, OR 97828, 541/426-5546.

34 STEIN'S PILLAR
4.0 mi/2.0 hrs

northeast of Prineville in Mill Creek Wilderness of Ochoco National Forest

Map 10.5, page 445

Poor Stein's doesn't have a twin pillar to keep it company, unlike its neighbor Twin Pillars, but then again, it doesn't have to share all the attention, which it basks in quite a bit, as it's a popular destination. The trail starts off as a hot and dusty route, with the smell of juniper to keep you company, and slips in and out of desert terrain and cool forest for a change of pace at almost every step. A viewpoint of the spindly and rather slender pillar arrives shortly before the end of the trail, where you can stop here or continue on for a rocky scramble to bring you face to face with the 200-foot red rock pillar. It's just one of many attractions in

the unique and rugged Ochoco Mountains and is worth the quick trip in to see it.

User Groups: Hikers, dogs, and horses. No mountain bikes are allowed. No wheelchair access.

Permits: Permits are not required. Parking and access are free.

Maps: For a map of Ochoco National Forest, contact Nature of the Northwest Information Center. For a topographic map, ask the USGS for Stein's Pillar.

Directions: From Prineville, drive nine miles east on U.S. 26 to Mill Creek Road/Forest Service Road 33 and turn left (north). Drive 6.7 miles and turn right over a bridge to Forest Service Road 3300-500. Drive two miles (exactly, check your odometer) to the unmarked gravel parking circle, on the left. It can be tricky to find—if you miss it, you'll soon come to the end of the road. The trailhead is on far end (east side) of the pullout.

Contact: Ochoco National Forest, P.O. Box 490, Prineville, OR 97754, 541/416-6500.

35 TWIN PILLARS
11.0 mi/6.0 hrs

northeast of Prineville in Mill Creek Wilderness of Ochoco National Forest

Map 10.5, page 445

Jutting 200 sheer cliff feet in the air, the Twin Pillars are a sight to see, and it's even better when you can hike to visit them, so you can enjoy the view as you rest from the nearly 2,000-foot climb. The trail starts off relatively easy for the first mile but then shifts into high gear as you climb to views of the Mill Creek Valley. Several stream crossings may be dicey in the spring, so check ahead to make sure all is well in the area before setting off.

User Groups: Hikers, dogs, and horses. No mountain bikes are allowed. No wheelchair access.

Permits: Permits are not required. Parking and access are free.

Maps: For a map of Ochoco National Forest, contact Nature of the Northwest Information Center. For a topographic map, ask the USGS for Stein's Pillar.

Directions: From Prineville, drive nine miles east on U.S. 26 to Mill Creek Road/Forest Service Road 33. Turn left (north) and drive 10.7 miles to the Wildcat Campground parking area on the right. The trail begins on the north side of the parking area, just to the left of the trailhead sign.

Contact: Ochoco National Forest, P.O. Box 490, Prineville, OR 97754, 541/416-6500.

36 JOHN DAY PAINTED HILLS
2.5 mi/1.5 hrs

in John Day Fossil Beds National Monument west of Mitchell off Highway 26

Map 10.5, page 445

If you really want to feel like a spring chicken, take a stroll through the Painted Hills trails, which have you beat by a good 39 million years (give or take). Four mini-trails lead through this area. Even if you snored through geology class, you can't help but be fascinated by the colorful hills, whose hues constantly change depending on the time of day and weather. Plants steer clear of the hills because of their poor nutrient makeup, which leaves the hills bald and beautiful, perfect for your viewing pleasure. The first trail is 1.5-mile Carroll Rim Trail, a gentle climb to a viewing bench. Next up is Painted Hills Overlook Trail, lined with benches and another vantage point of the colorful hills. The highlight of the trip is coming up, the .25-mile loop through Painted Cove, where you can actually walk on a footbridge right through the red hill, lined with interpretive signs to fill your head with all the geology facts to dazzle your friends with over dinner. The last stop is the .25-mile Leaf Fossil Loop, which may not be visually interesting upon first glance until you notice the fossils on display at the trailhead and the fossils littering the hill (respect the fossils—they are your elders, remember—and don't pick one up). So, let's recap: Climb to two viewpoints to get a feel for the situation, loop around and through a brilliant rust-colored hill, and then take a peek at some fossil collections. You won't ex-

actly get a workout on these hikes, but it's a perfect place to bring kids if they're starting to yawn through their science classes. This place can be packed with families from all over on a sunny day.

User Groups: Hikers and dogs (remember to keep them leashed). No mountain bikes or horses are allowed. No wheelchair access.

Permits: Permits are not required. Parking and access are free.

Maps: A free trail brochure is available at the Painted Hills Overlook trailhead. For a topographic map, ask the USGS for Painted Hills.

Directions: From Mitchell, drive three miles west on U.S. 26 (about 50 miles east of Prineville) and turn north on Burnt Ranch Road. Drive 5.6 miles, then turn left on Bear Creek Road and drive 1.1 miles. To reach Painted Hills Overlook Trail, turn left to the large parking lot and well-marked trailhead on the west side of the lot. Carroll Rim Trail starts across the street from the parking lot. To reach Painted Cove Trail, continue down Bear Creek Road for another .6 mile, turn right at the fork, and drive .4 mile to the well-marked trailhead and parking area to the left. To reach Leaf Hill Fossil Loop, backtrack to Bear Creek Road, and turn right at the fork for one mile. The well-marked trailhead and parking area are on the right.

Contact: John Day Fossil Beds National Monument, 32651 Highway 19, Kimberly, OR 97848, 541/987-2333.

37 LOOKOUT MOUNTAIN
16.0 mi/8.0 hrs

east of Prineville in Ochoco National Forest

Map 10.5, page 445

With a name like Lookout, it better be good, right? Well, it is, in more than one way. First, it's a good sweat-inducing climb of nearly 3,000 feet before reaching the 6,900-foot summit, where you'll encounter the second good thing: the view of the Cascade Range. Along the way, don't get so bogged down with the climb that you miss out on the wildflower meadows and the four-footed locals, like deer and elk. Remember to bring water and sunscreen, as it can get scorching in this area.

User Groups: Hikers, dogs, mountain bikes, and horses. No wheelchair access.

Permits: Permits are not required. Parking and access are free.

Maps: For a map of Ochoco National Forest, contact Nature of the Northwest Information Center. For a topographic map, ask the USGS for Ochoco Butte and Lookout Mountain.

Directions: From Prineville, drive east on U.S. 26 for 16 miles, and fork right onto Forest Service Road 22. Drive eight miles, and park in the small pullout to the right (just past the Ochoco ranger station, on your left).

Contact: Ochoco National Forest, P.O. Box 490, Prineville, OR 97754, 541/416-6500.

38 FLOOD OF FIRE/ STORY IN STONE

1.0 mi/0.5 hr

northwest of Dayville in the John Day Fossil Beds National Monument

Map 10.6, page 446

Talk about your identity crisis: The John Day Valley has seen it all in its years, playing host to a subtropical forest, massive lava flows, and hardwood forests—not to mention the locals (including rhinos, camel, and early elephants) trampling through its delicate earth. After all that prehistoric rolling with the punches, it's come out on the flip side to reveal dramatic red and white cliffs against gray valley walls, and you can walk right through them (just don't trample the earth like those inconsiderate rhinos used to). The .25-mile Flood of Fire Trail extends to cliffside views of the John Day River, while the Story in Stone Trail's .25 mile offers up a touch exhibit with replica fossils. Though the area is a magnet for tourists, who flock from all over to visit, even native Oregonians—or those who never thought they would get excited about a couple of fossils—will be gawking at this sight (just don't em-

barrass yourself; keep your mouth firmly shut at all times). Blue Basin and Island of Time Trails (see listings in this chapter) are nearby, so you can stick around for the day to get the full picture—and more pictures.

User Groups: Hikers and dogs (remember to keep them leashed). No mountain bikes or horses are allowed. No wheelchair access.

Permits: Permits are not required. Parking and access are free.

Maps: Trail brochures are available at the trailhead. For a topographic map, ask the USGS for Mount Misery.

Directions: From Dayville, drive five miles west on U.S. 26 to Highway 19. Turn right (north) and drive 12.5 miles to the "John Day Fossil Beds National Monument" sign (passing the first sign). Turn right and drive a short distance to the parking area and both trailheads.

Contact: John Day Fossil Beds National Monument, 32651 Highway 19, Kimberly, OR 97848, 541/987-2333.

39 BLUE BASIN OVERLOOK/ ISLAND OF TIME

4.0 mi/2.0 hrs

northwest of Dayville in the John Day Fossil Beds National Monument

Map 10.6, page 446

Who needs South Dakota when we have the Badlands of Oregon right in our backyard? Colorful cliffs of blue, green, red, and white line this dramatic valley, and you can see it all on these relatively short trails. Get ready for an information overload, because everything you ever wanted to know about the area is available at the trail signs. A somewhat steep climb starts off the three-mile Blue Basin Overlook loop, where you can check out the multilayered cliffs and examine the fossil beds (just remember to keep your grubby paws off of them). After you've looped back, climb up the .5-mile Island of Time, which jets out to beat Overlook Trail at its game, peering over the middle of the trail. The John Day Fossil Beds area is a plethora of geology lessons, and even the most jaded will find themselves in awe. Bring a camera, because even if you've never felt compelled to snap a shot, you will here. Also bring water, because the area is hot and dry. These trails are near Flood of Fire and Story in Stone Trails (see listings in this chapter); don't go away until you've tried them all, because you'll want as many different perspectives on this unique area as possible.

User Groups: Hikers and dogs (remember to keep them leashed). No mountain bikes or horses are allowed. No wheelchair access.

Permits: Permits are not required. Parking and access are free.

Maps: Trail brochures are available at the trailhead. For a topographic map, ask the USGS for Picture Gorge West.

Directions: From Dayville, drive five miles west on U.S. 26 to Highway 19. Turn right (north) and drive six miles to the "John Day Fossil Beds National Monument" sign. Turn right and drive a short distance to the parking area and both trailheads.

Contact: John Day Fossil Beds National Monument, 32651 Highway 19, Kimberly, OR 97848, 541/987-2333.

40 BLACK CANYON
25.0 mi/2.0 days

south of Highway 26 in the Black Canyon Wilderness of Ochoco National Forest

Map 10.6, page 446

Snaking for 14.5 miles through the Black Canyon Wilderness, Black Canyon Trail is wilderness at its best—which often means dealing with the elements. In this case, the elements include a grand total of 12 creek crossings, so come prepared. Just getting into the wilderness can be tricky: You'll need to cross the John Day River to start on the trail, and you may find other area trails are not well marked or maintained, or the road in is rough. Here's the best access route: Start from Boeing Field Trail, which plops you .5 mile into the canyon roughly two miles from the trailhead and lets you explore the 6,000-foot canyon

cliffs and the wildlife of this remote area, including elk, black bears, cougars, and deer. Watch out for rattlesnakes. If you're not up for the full length of the trail, or if the creek crossings are getting to you, there are plenty of spots to camp for the night, or you can turn around and make it as long or as short of a hike as you want. A bonus about the tricky entrances is that you're bound to have it all to yourself, so you may want to plan for an overnight trip while you're there.

User Groups: Hikers, dogs, and horses. No mountain bikes are allowed. No wheelchair access.

Permits: Permits are not required. Parking and access are free.

Maps: For a map of Ochoco National Forest, contact Nature of the Northwest Information Center. For a topographic map, ask the USGS for Wolf Mountain and Aldrich Gulch.

Directions: From John Day, drive about 40 miles west on U.S. 26 to Forest Service Road 12. Turn left and drive 19 miles (the first 6.9 are paved) and turn left on Forest Service Road 38. After 8.3 miles, turn right onto Forest Service Road 5810. The Boeing Field trailhead is one mile down on the left side, starting in a meadow. Park at the side of the road.

Contact: Ochoco National Forest, Paulina Ranger District, 7803 Beaver Creek Road, Paulina, OR 97751, 541/477-6900.

41 MYRTLE CREEK
15.8 mi/8.0 hrs

north of Burns in Malheur National Forest

Map 10.6, page 446

Following its namesake, this 7.9-mile trail through ponderosa pine forest is relatively gentle, climbing less than 1,000 feet along its course. Why the higher rating for difficulty, you ask? Because it's not exactly a snap to find, and light use in the area makes for light trails in spots. If you do venture out, make sure to bring along a map of the area, because side trails do take off from here, and the markings aren't always in place. Even the Forest Service signs are sometimes missing. But you're guaranteed some peace and quiet, and if you want an adventure, Myrtle is your ticket.

User Groups: Hikers, dogs, mountain bikes, and horses. No wheelchair access.

Permits: Permits are not required. Parking and access are free.

Maps: For a map of Malheur National Forest, contact Nature of the Northwest Information Center. For a topographic map, ask the USGS for Myrtle Park Meadows.

Directions: From Burns, drive 17.9 miles north on U.S. 395 to the unmarked junction with Forest Service Road 31 (just north of Devine Summit). Turn left (west) and drive 13.1 miles to Forest Service Road 3100-226. Turn left and drive to the road's end and the trailhead.

Contact: Malheur National Forest, Emigrant Creek Ranger District, 265 Highway 20 South, Hines, OR 97738, 541/573-4300.

42 SOUTH WINOM TRAIL
8.0 mi/4.0 hrs

southeast of Ukiah in the North Fork John Day Wilderness of Umatilla National Forest
Map 10.7, page 447

This trail sits front and center of the OHV trail system, but they're not allowed on this trail, so you can have it all to yourself. And you probably will: It travels through a burned area from the '90s, with the bare, slender tree trunks giving you a clear view of the Winom Creek Valley you're hiking through. It's a pleasant and gentle walk along South Winom Creek and a chance to view the burned sections up close. The trail is better maintained than some of its neighbors that didn't fare so well in the fire, and it's a pretty straightforward route, but be aware that it may be faint in parts. Keep your eyes peeled for the locals who wander through the John Day wilderness area, like mule deer and Rocky Mountain elk.

User Groups: Hikers, dogs, and horses. No mountain bikes are allowed. No wheelchair access.

Permits: Permits are not required. Parking and access are free.

Maps: For a map of North Fork John Day Wilderness and Umatilla National Forest, contact Nature of the Northwest Information Center. For a topographic map, ask the USGS for Pearson Ridge and Kelsay Butte.

Directions: From Ukiah, drive 22.6 miles southeast on the Blue Mountain Scenic Byway/Forest Service Road 52 to the junction with Forest Service Road 440. Turn right and drive .7 mile. At the fork leading to the South Winom Campground, turn left and continue .2 mile to the parking pullout on the right. The trailhead is across the road on the left.

Contact: Umatilla National Forest, North Fork John Day Ranger District, P.O. Box 158, Ukiah, OR 97880, 541/427-3231.

43 GRANITE CREEK
6.8 mi/3.5 hrs

northwest of Granite in the North Fork John Day Wilderness of Umatilla National Forest
Map 10.7, page 447

Descending along Granite Creek to the North Fork John Day River, this relatively gentle trail is a great spot to escape the more popular riverside crowds while still accessing the river itself. The trail loses only 400 feet in its 3.4-mile length, so it's an easy jaunt along a scenic creek before hitting the river. Since you'll reach the river at the trail's halfway point, you're likely to see fewer people than if you started at the North Fork John Day trailhead. When you arrive at the trailhead, there are two forks: The one to the left goes down an old mining road, and you can use this as a return trip for a loop. The decaying mining operations here are evidence of the once-booming gold mines in the area, so if that kind of stuff does it for you, it's worth the trip in—just remember to leave any objects that you see behind.

User Groups: Hikers, dogs, and horses. No mountain bikes are allowed. No wheelchair access.

Permits: Permits are not required. Parking and access are free.

Maps: For a map of the North Fork John Day

Wilderness and Umatilla National Forest, contact Nature of the Northwest Information Center. For a topographic map, ask the USGS for Desolation Butte.

Directions: From Granite, drive 1.5 miles west on Forest Service Road 10. Turn right onto Granite Creek Road/Forest Service Road 1035. Drive 4.3 miles, then turn left onto a spur road for .2 mile, to the parking area and trailhead, straight ahead at the road's end. (Start on the trailhead to the right.)

Contact: Umatilla National Forest, North Fork John Day Ranger District, P.O. Box 158, Ukiah, OR 97880, 541/427-3231.

44 NORTH FORK JOHN DAY RIVER

22.9 mi one-way/ 2.0 days

at the junction of Highways 52 and 73 in the North Fork John Day Wilderness of Umatilla National Forest

Map 10.7, page 447

There's something to be said for meandering trails along scenic rivers. You don't have to think too much about whether you're on the right trail, you just keep the river at your side and enjoy the scenery. Wildflower meadows start the peaceful walk, and good ol' John Day himself keeps you company along the way. The river's quite the spot for fishing, camping, and picnicking, as well as for natives like elk, deer, black bears, and bald eagles. Evidence of the area's 1860s gold-mining boom pops up along the trail, so keep an eye out (just leave everything you see behind). It's a long haul down the river, but it's worth it. One option is to leave a car at Granite Creek, a closer trailhead than the lower trailhead, which intersects the trail about halfway.

User Groups: Hikers, dogs, and horses. No mountain bikes are allowed. No wheelchair access.

Permits: A federal Northwest Forest pass is required to park here. The cost is $5 for a day pass or $30 for an annual pass. You can buy a day pass at ranger stations, from private vendors, or through Nature of the Northwest Information Center.

Maps: For a map of the North Fork John Day Wilderness and Umatilla National Forest, contact Nature of the Northwest Information Center. For a topographic map, ask the USGS for Desolation Butte and Olive Lake.

Directions: From Ukiah, drive about 43 miles southeast on the Blue Mountain Scenic Byway/Forest Service Road 52 to the North Fork John Day campground. Drive .1 mile and park in the trailhead parking area to the right. The well-marked trailhead is to the right as you're driving in.

Contact: Umatilla National Forest, North Fork John Day Ranger District, P.O. Box 158, Ukiah, OR 97880, 541/427-3231.

45 BALDY LAKE

14.0 mi/7.0 hrs

west of Baker City in the North Fork John Day Wilderness of Wallowa-Whitman National Forest

Map 10.7, page 447

Traveling through the Baldy Creek drainage, the seven-mile Baldy Creek Trail climbs almost 2,000 feet through spruce, fir, and pine forest before hitting the lake, which rests in a basin below Mount Ireland. Just before you reach the lake, take a short detour on an abandoned road for a view of the historic Cable Cove mining area and the valley below. Keep in mind that, like many trails in this area, the road in is often closed through July, so hit this one later in the season.

User Groups: Hikers, dogs, and horses. No mountain bikes are allowed. No wheelchair access.

Permits: A federal Northwest Forest pass is required to park here. The cost is $5 for a day pass or $30 for an annual pass. You can buy a day pass at ranger stations, from private vendors, or through Nature of the Northwest Information Center.

Maps: For a map of the North Fork John Day Wilderness and Wallowa-Whitman National Forest, contact Nature of the Northwest Information Center. For a topographic map, ask the USGS for Crawfish Lake and Mount Ireland.

Directions: From Baker City, drive north on U.S.

30 about 10 miles to Haines and turn left (west) onto Elkhorn Scenic Highway (which becomes Anthony Lakes Highway after 1.8 miles and Forest Service Road 73 after 14.8 miles). Drive for a total of 35.7 miles to Forest Service Road 395. Turn left and drive .1 mile to the end of the road and the parking area. The trailhead is on the left side of the road as you're driving in.

Contact: Wallowa-Whitman National Forest, Baker City Ranger District, 3165 10th Street, Baker City, OR 97814, 541/523-4476.

46 PEAVY TRAIL
8.0 mi/4.0 hrs

west of Baker City in the North Fork John Day Wilderness of Wallowa-Whitman National Forest

Map 10.7, page 447

Driving in can be a little rough, so you would think you'd have the place all to yourself. Surprisingly, there are a fair number of solitude-seekers camping along the meadows of this remote area. Part of the reason is that nearby Peavy Cabin is available for rent, which you'll pass on the way to the trail. Once you hit the trail, you're likely to have it all to yourself, though. The path travels through a 1996 fire zone, which at times makes the trail a little faint; on the way, you'll pass Cunningham Cove Trail, which at this writing was too faint to follow through the sparse forest. But if you want a little something different—or if you plan to rent the cabin for an overnight stay—try this trail, which follows the North Fork John Day River drainage along an abandoned road. After two miles, the trail climbs about 1,500 feet to a meadow, where you can camp for the night to escape the campers nearby. Keep in mind that the road in is often snowy through July, so check conditions before you head out.

User Groups: Hikers, dogs, and horses. No mountain bikes are allowed. No wheelchair access.

Permits: A federal Northwest Forest pass is required to park here. The cost is $5 for a day pass or $30 for an annual pass. You can buy a day pass at ranger stations, from private vendors, or through Nature of the Northwest Information Center.

Maps: For a map of the North Fork John Day Wilderness and Wallowa-Whitman National Forest, contact Nature of the Northwest Information Center. For a topographic map, ask the USGS for Crawfish Lake and Anthony Lakes.

Directions: From Baker City, drive north on U.S. 30 about 10 miles to Haines and turn left (west) onto Elkhorn Scenic Highway (which becomes Anthony Lakes Highway after 1.8 miles and Forest Service Road 73 after 14.8 miles). Drive for a total of 35.4 miles to Forest Service Road 380. Turn left and drive three miles to the road's end and the parking area. (Note: This road is rough, and a sign says it's not recommended for passenger cars. It's passable, but slow-going.) The trail starts directly in front of you as you're driving in.

Contact: Wallowa-Whitman National Forest, Baker City Ranger District, 3165 10th Street, Baker City, Oregon 97814, 541/523-4476.

47 CRAWFISH LAKE
3.0 mi/1.5 hrs

west of Baker City in Wallowa-Whitman National Forest

Map 10.7, page 447

There are actually two ways to get to Crawfish Lake. They're both roughly the same distance, but the lower trailhead is slightly shorter and steeper. Either way, it's a three-mile round-trip trek through fir, spruce, and pine forest, traveling through a burned section from a 1986 fire, where you can still see bare trunks and scorched bark. For the shorter and steeper route, take the lower trailhead, which starts on an old rocky road before the trail narrows and enters the forest. Even though you're gaining only 300 feet in elevation, keep in mind you're starting at 6,800 feet, so don't be surprised (and don't let your ego get bruised) if you break a sweat on the trip up. Finally it levels out near the lake and arrives at a rock field on the left (thankfully, there's no need to pass through that; the trail is rocky enough as it is). Pack your bug repellent, because mosquitoes thrive in the lake area. This area is often snowed in through July, so it's a good idea to check ahead to see if the roads are clear.

User Groups: Hikers, dogs, and horses. No mountain bikes are allowed. No wheelchair access.

Permits: A federal Northwest Forest pass is required to park here. The cost is $5 for a day pass or $30 for an annual pass. You can buy a day pass at ranger stations, from private vendors, or through Nature of the Northwest Information Center.

Maps: For a map of the Wallowa-Whitman National Forest, contact Nature of the Northwest Information Center. For a topographic map, ask the USGS for Crawfish Lake.

Directions: From Baker City, drive north on U.S. 30 about 10 miles to Haines and turn left (west) onto Elkhorn Scenic Highway (which becomes Anthony Lakes Highway after 1.8 miles and Forest Service Road 73 after 14.8 miles). Drive for a total of 33.4 miles, and turn left less than .1 mile to the large parking area. Trailhead is at the end of the parking area, to the right of the sign along an abandoned road.

Contact: Wallowa-Whitman National Forest, Baker City Ranger District, 3165 10th Street, Baker City, OR 97814, 541/523-4476.

48 LAKES LOOKOUT
1.4 mi/1.5 hrs

west of Baker City in Wallowa-Whitman National Forest

Map 10.7, page 447

It may be short, but don't discount this little guy, because he's also tough. It's a quad-killer that leaves you reaching for the oxygen tank, because you begin at no less than 7,800 feet of elevation. The trail starts up an abandoned road then quickly narrows, leveling out so you can catch your breath before the final push to the top (nice of it, don't you think?). You'll have to scramble over boulders at the top of the trail before you reach the summit, where the wall is etched with wilderness graffiti, as people took it upon themselves to stake claim with "I was

here" signs and "Betty loves Tommy." Pass that by for the view from the 8,552-foot old fire lookout (used in the early 1900s), where you can see where it got its name. It's an incredible view that seems to stretch forever (okay, maybe just into the neighboring counties), where you can see the many lakes and peaks of the Anthony Lakes area. Like many trails in this area, it's often snowed in through July, so check on road conditions beforehand.

User Groups: Hikers, dogs, and horses. No mountain bikes are allowed. No wheelchair access.

Permits: No passes are required. Parking and access are free.

Maps: For a map of the Wallowa-Whitman National Forest, contact Nature of the Northwest Information Center. For a topographic map, ask the USGS for Anthony Lakes.

Directions: From Baker City, drive north on U.S. 30 about 10 miles to Haines and turn left (west) onto Elkhorn Scenic Highway (which becomes Anthony Lakes Highway after 1.8 miles and Forest Service Road 73 after 14.8 miles). Drive for a total of 27.5 miles to Forest Service Road 210. Turn left and drive 1.6 miles, then turn right at the T-junction for .3 mile. Park to the left in a pullout, and the trail starts to the right along an old road. (It can be tricky to find since the trailhead sign is near the parking area. As you're facing the summit, the trail starts to the right—south—of you.) Note: Road 210 is rough along a steep cliff, but passable for passenger cars.

Contact: Wallowa-Whitman National Forest, Baker City Ranger District, 3165 10th Street, Baker City, OR 97814, 541/523-4476.

49 ANTHONY LAKE SHORELINE/ HOFFER LAKES
3.0 mi/1.5 hrs

west of Baker City in Wallowa-Whitman National Forest

Map 10.7, page 447

You can stroll along the gravel path of Anthony Lakes with interpretive signs introducing you to locals like Jacob's Ladder and Jeffrey's

Shooting Star, but why not hit two lakes for the price of one? Make that three lakes, since Hoffer Lakes is actually now divided into two lakes by a meadow, due to sediment creeping up. Start along the Anthony Lake shoreline, with 8,000-plus-foot Gunsight Butte and Angell Peak as backdrops. Then hit the well-marked Hoffer Lakes Trail on the south shore, taking a right if you're touring the lake counterclockwise to extend your trip another two miles round-trip, heading back after viewing the lakes to continue the lakeshore loop. It's an easy stroll with views, and camping is available at nearby Anthony Lakes Campground. The trail is usually snowed in through July, so unless you want to make this a snowshoe trek, it's best to wait until late in the season.

User Groups: Hikers, dogs, and horses. No mountain bikes are allowed. No wheelchair access.

Permits: No passes are required. Parking and access are free.

Maps: For a map of the Wallowa-Whitman National Forest, contact Nature of the Northwest Information Center. For a topographic map, ask the USGS for Anthony Lakes.

Directions: From Baker City, drive north on U.S. 30 about 10 miles to Haines and turn left (west) onto Elkhorn Scenic Highway (which becomes Anthony Lakes Highway after 1.8 miles and Forest Service Road 73 after 14.8 miles). Drive for a total of 23.8 miles to Forest Service Road 170 at the well-marked Anthony Lakes Campground. Before hitting the campground, turn right to the parking area on the left across from the guard station (which is not marked as such; just look for the cabin). There's no official trailhead, but this is a good spot to start your loop, traveling counterclockwise to reach Hoffer Lakes Trail, on the other side of the lake.

Contact: Wallowa-Whitman National Forest, Baker City Ranger District, 3165 10th Street, Baker City, OR 97814, 541/523-4476.

50 BLACK LAKE
2.0 mi/1.0 hr

west of Baker City in Wallowa-Whitman National Forest

Map 10.7, page 447

You can reach Black Lake via Elkhorn Crest Trail (see listing in this chapter) because the trails intersect halfway up the one-mile gentle ascent, but then you'd be missing out on Lilypad Lake, which is covered in yellow waterlily blossoms all summer. The trail passes Lilypad Lake after only .25 mile and then connects with Elkhorn Crest Trail before veering off to Black Lake, which sits at 7,344 feet. It's a good way to enjoy some of the many lakes in the area without spending all day to get there (but this does mean it could attract more crowds). Hit this hike after June, because the road up to the trail tends to be snowed in before then.

User Groups: Hikers, dogs, and horses. No mountain bikes are allowed. No wheelchair access.

Permits: Permits are not required. Parking and access are free.

Maps: For a map of the Wallowa-Whitman National Forest, contact Nature of the Northwest Information Center. For a topographic map, ask the USGS for Anthony Lakes.

Directions: From Baker City, drive north on U.S. 30 about 10 miles to Haines and turn left (west) onto Elkhorn Scenic Highway (which becomes Anthony Lakes Highway after 1.8 miles and Forest Service Road 73 after 14.8 miles). Drive for a total of 23.8 miles to Anthony Lakes Campground. Turn left, and just before you reach the campground, turn left into the parking area and the well-marked trailhead.

Contact: Wallowa-Whitman National Forest, Baker City Ranger District, 3165 10th Street, Baker City, Oregon 97814, 541/523-4476.

51 SUMMIT LAKE
25.0 mi/2.0 days

west of Baker City in Wallowa-Whitman National Forest

Map 10.7, page 447

Traveling along Elkhorn Crest National Recreation Trail, the path quickly ascends 1,000 feet in the first two miles to reach Elkhorn Ridge and views of the Blue and Wallowa Mountains and the Baker Valley below. The trail itself is 22.6 miles one-way, but one good choice for an overnight stop is Summit Lake, which sits surrounded by sheer cliff walls on three sides. Deer, elk, and mountain goats aren't dummies, either; they know this is a great spot to catch some views, so you may see some along the way. After 5.5 miles, the trail leads to an old road, which you cross to pick up Summit Lake Trail for another 1.5 miles to the lake. Keep in mind that this trail is often blocked by snow through July, so check ahead before you set out.

User Groups: Hikers, dogs, and horses. No mountain bikes are allowed. No wheelchair access.

Permits: A federal Northwest Forest pass is required to park here. The cost is $5 for a day pass or $30 for an annual pass. You can buy a day pass at ranger stations, from private vendors, or through Nature of the Northwest Information Center.

Maps: For a map of the Wallowa-Whitman National Forest, contact Nature of the Northwest Information Center. For a topographic map, ask the USGS for Anthony Lakes and Bourne.

Directions: From Baker City, drive north on U.S. 30 about 10 miles to Haines and turn left (west) onto Elkhorn Scenic Highway (which becomes Anthony Lakes Highway after 1.8 miles and Forest Service Road 73 after 14.8 miles). Drive for a total of 23.8 miles to the trailhead just before you reach Anthony Lakes Campground. The large parking area and Elkhorn Crest trailhead are on the left side of the highway.

Contact: Wallowa-Whitman National Forest, Baker City Ranger District, 3165 10th Street, Baker City, OR 97814, 541/523-4476.

52 ELKHORN CREST NATIONAL RECREATION TRAIL TO LOST LAKE
14.0 mi/7.0 hrs

west of Baker City in Wallowa-Whitman National Forest

Map 10.7, page 447

The highest trail in the Blue Mountains, the 22.6-mile Elkhorn Crest National Recreation Trail climbs 1,000 feet in the first two miles for views of the Wallowa and Blue Mountains and the Baker Valley. But you don't need to walk 43-some-odd miles (unless you feel compelled, in which case there are plenty of campsites along the way). You may have company along the way, as deer, elk, and mountain goats like the views too and often travel through the path. The trail hits six lakes along its course, including a side trail (trails tend to be well marked in this area) to Lost Lake, surrounded by wildflower meadows. This is a good turn-around point for a day hike (for an overnight option on this trail, see the Summit Lake listing in this chapter). Plan this hike for later in the season: Although the road in tends to open earlier than others in the area, the high altitude (up to 8,000 feet on the trail) means it's often snowy through July.

User Groups: Hikers, dogs, and horses. No mountain bikes are allowed. No wheelchair access.

Permits: A federal Northwest Forest pass is required to park here. The cost is $5 for a day pass or $30 for an annual pass. You can buy a day pass at ranger stations, from private vendors, or through Nature of the Northwest Information Center.

Maps: For a map of the Wallowa-Whitman National Forest, contact Nature of the Northwest Information Center. For a topographic map, ask the USGS for Anthony Lakes.

Directions: From Baker City, drive north on U.S. 30 about 10 miles to Haines and turn left (west) onto Elkhorn Scenic Highway (which becomes Anthony Lakes Highway after 1.8 miles and Forest Service Road 73 after 14.8 miles). Drive for a total of 23.8 miles to the trailhead just before you reach Anthony Lakes Campground. The large parking area and trailhead are on the left side of the highway.

Contact: Wallowa-Whitman National Forest, Baker City Ranger District, 3165 10th Street, Baker City, OR 97814, 541/523-4476.

53 VAN PATTEN LAKE
3.0 mi/1.5 hrs

west of Baker City in Wallowa-Whitman National Forest

Map 10.7, page 447

The trail is only .5 mile each way to the lake, so you'd think it would be packed. But then you have to consider the drive in: The mile-long road to the top is so steep, rough, and rutted that unless you have a monster truck, there's no way you'll want to hazard driving it. It's recommended that you start instead one mile down on foot and begin a slow climb up the rough road to the actual trailhead. You'll feel as if you're in the middle of nowhere and think there's no way a trail actually exists, when suddenly there's a sign announcing that you've arrived. The trail itself gains 1,000 feet in elevation in just .5 mile (!), another way that it weeds out the crowds. The panoramic view of the Wallowa Mountains will be yours, all yours. Although the road up to this trail tends to be clear of snow earlier than others in the area, you should check ahead of time before heading out.

User Groups: Hikers, dogs, and horses. No mountain bikes are allowed. No wheelchair access.

Permits: Permits are not required. Parking and access are free.

Maps: For a map of the Wallowa-Whitman National Forest, contact Nature of the Northwest Information Center. For a topographic map, ask the USGS for Anthony Lakes.

Directions: From Baker City, drive north on U.S. 30 about 10 miles to Haines and turn left (west) onto Elkhorn Scenic Highway (which becomes Anthony Lakes Highway after 1.8

miles and Forest Service Road 73 after 14.8 miles). Drive for a total of 20.9 miles and turn left onto Forest Service Road 130. Park at the side of the road (there's plenty of room) and walk up the rough road for one mile to the trailhead; you'll want to take the road that leads up and to the left as you're driving in.

Contact: Wallowa-Whitman National Forest, Baker City Ranger District, 3165 10th Street, Baker City, Oregon 97814, 541/523-4476.

54 DUTCH FLAT
16.8 mi/8.0 hrs to 2.0 days

west of Baker City in Wallowa-Whitman National Forest

Map 10.7, page 447

Climbing through a forest of spruce, larch, ponderosa pine, and lodgepole pine, you'll catch glimpses of the meadows right off the bat through clearings. The trail climbs steadily, gaining 3,200 of elevation on its way to Dutch Flat Meadows (a great camping spot if you want to stay overnight) and Dutch Flat Lake before the final steep and rocky push to Dutch Flat Saddle. The beauty of gaining elevation is that the views only get better with every step.

User Groups: Hikers, dogs, and horses. No mountain bikes are allowed. No wheelchair access.

Permits: A federal Northwest Forest pass is required to park here. The cost is $5 for a day pass or $30 for an annual pass. You can buy a day pass at ranger stations, from private vendors, or through Nature of the Northwest Information Center.

Maps: For a map of the Wallowa-Whitman National Forest, contact Nature of the Northwest Information Center. For a topographic map, ask the USGS for Anthony Lakes and Rock Creek.

Directions: From Baker City, drive north on U.S. 30 about 10 miles to Haines, and turn left (west) onto Elkhorn Scenic Highway (which becomes Anthony Lakes Highway after 1.8 miles and Forest Service Road 73 after 14.8 miles). Drive for a total of 17.7 miles and turn left onto Forest Service Road 7307. Drive 1.2 miles to the end of the road and the well-marked trailhead straight ahead, behind the restroom as you're driving in.

Contact: Wallowa-Whitman National Forest, Baker City Ranger District, 3165 10th Street, Baker City, OR 97814, 541/523-4476.

55 SOUTH FORK DESOLATION
16.2 mi/8.0 hrs

southeast of Dale in Umatilla National Forest

Map 10.7, page 447

Starting through a sparse forest, this trail climbs up to 7,400 feet (gaining almost 2,000 feet in elevation) as it follows Desolation Creek. Views of the Umatilla mountain range and valleys await you at the top. Its name may be desolate, which is fitting in some way considering that you're escaping the crowds who flock to nearby Olive Lake, but you won't be missing any company when you have the views to yourself. Like many of this area's trails, the path can be faint at times, so you should definitely bring a map along for this one.

User Groups: Hikers, dogs, horses, and mountain bikes. No wheelchair access.

Permits: Permits are not required. Parking and access are free.

Maps: For a map of Umatilla National Forest, contact Nature of the Northwest Information Center. For a topographic map, ask the USGS for Desolation Butte.

Directions: From Dale, drive 21.1 miles east on Forest Service Road 10, and turn right on Forest Service Road 45. Drive one mile and park in the pullout to the right; the trailhead begins to the left.

Contact: Umatilla National Forest, North Fork John Day Ranger District, P.O. Box 158, Ukiah, OR 97880, 541/427-3231.

56 OLIVE LAKE
2.5 mi/1.5 hrs

southeast of Dale in Umatilla National Forest

Map 10.7, page 447

Olive Lake is better known for its campground,

but there's also a gentle wooded trail surrounding it that is surprisingly uncrowded (if you don't count the people fishing on the banks here and there). A few gentle hills allow you to gain a better glimpse of the shimmering water below, and you cross a footbridge to head into an overgrown portion of the trail nearly at the end. It's simple to follow, gets you away from the campsite, is easy enough for kids, and offers plenty of spots to plop down and dip your feet in the water. It's not exactly a wilderness excursion, but if you're already camping in the area and want to walk off some of those s'mores, this is a great lakeshore loop.

User Groups: Hikers, dogs, mountain bikes, and horses. No wheelchair access.

Permits: Permits are not required. Parking and access are free.

Maps: For a map of Umatilla National Forest, contact Nature of the Northwest Information Center. For a topographic map, ask the USGS for Olive Lake.

Directions: From Dale, drive 26.9 miles east on Forest Service Road 10, then turn right into the Olive Lake Campground onto Forest Service Road 430 for .3 mile. Turn left into the day-use parking area near the lake. The trail starts at the lake (there's no official trailhead).

Contact: Umatilla National Forest, North Fork John Day Ranger District, P.O. Box 158, Ukiah, OR 97880, 541/427-3231.

57 MAGONE SLIDE
1.5 mi/1.0 hr

north of John Day in Malheur National Forest

Map 10.7, page 447

Is it just me, or does the Magone (pronounced ma-GO-nee) Slide sound like a popular dance step? The lake is a popular spot for fishing and picnicking, but to escape the action try this nearby trail. Along the way, you'll walk past ponderosa pines that look like they've been doing a little sliding recently themselves, growing at odd angles and sometimes even just lying in the path (the nerve). Nearby Magone Lake was formed by a landslide in the 1860s, and this is a great spot to check out where it all happened; you can see evidence of the slide where terraces were formed by all that sliding around. Wildflowers line the area, and you'll end up climbing 300 feet to reach two viewpoints along cliffs, where you can see the lake below, the Strawberry Mountains, and the John Day Valley. Feel free to dance at the top.

User Groups: Hikers and dogs. No mountain bikes or horses are allowed. No wheelchair access.

Permits: Permits are not required. Parking and access are free.

Maps: For a map of Malheur National Forest, contact Nature of the Northwest Information Center. For a topographic map, ask the USGS for Magone Lake.

Directions: From John Day, drive nine miles east on U.S. 26 and turn left (north) onto County Road 18. Drive 12.4 miles to Forest Service Road 3620, a one-lane paved road, and turn left to drive 1.3 miles to Forest Service Road 3618. Turn right and drive 1.2 miles to a small parking pullout and the trailhead on the right (it can be tricky to find, but there is a sign).

Contact: Malheur National Forest, Blue Mountain Ranger District, 431 Patterson Bridge Road, P.O. Box 909, John Day, OR 97845, 541/575-3000.

58 MAGONE LAKE
1.5 mi/1.0 hr

north of John Day in Malheur National Forest

Map 10.7, page 447

Back in the 1880s, former Civil War officer Major Joseph Magone (pronounced ma-GO-nee, so you don't embarrass yourself) was known for his BYOF (bring your own fish) policy: He'd haul bucketfuls of his own fish and dump 'em in the lake so he could fish in his favorite spot. Today, those fish are long gone, but their descendants remain, and many people take advantage of the bounty of rainbow and brook trout. It's a veritable zoo of

creatures, with beavers, mule deer, woodpeckers, chipmunks, and mallards among the locals. The simple, partly paved trail loops the 5,000-foot in elevation lake, and a campground is nearby if you want to spend some time partaking in ol' Magone's favorite pastime.

User Groups: Hikers and dogs. No mountain bikes or horses are allowed. Wheelchair accessible.

Permits: Permits are not required. Parking and access are free.

Maps: For a map of Malheur National Forest, contact Nature of the Northwest Information Center. For a topographic map, ask the USGS for Magone Lake.

Directions: From John Day, drive nine miles east on U.S. 26 and turn left (north) onto County Road 18. Drive 12.4 miles to Forest Service Road 3620, a one-lane paved road, and turn left and drive 1.3 miles to Forest Service Road 3618. Turn right and drive one mile to the Magone Lake day-use area, on the left, and the trail (there is no official trailhead).

Contact: Malheur National Forest, Blue Mountain Ranger District, 431 Patterson Bridge Road, P.O. Box 909, John Day, OR 97845, 541/575-3000.

59 PINE CREEK
21.0 mi/1.0–2.0 days

southeast of John Day in the Strawberry Mountain Wilderness of Malheur National Forest

Map 10.7, page 447

Getting into the remote Strawberry Mountains is no easy task. Here's a back-door route: Traversing the spiny backbone of the Strawberry mountain range, this trail switchbacks up to cross over Bald Mountain (total elevation gain is 800 feet) and comes to an end at a three-way junction with Onion Creek and Buckhorn Meadows Trails (see listings in this chapter); you can camp along the trail if you want to make this a two-day trip. Like many of the Strawberry Mountain Wilderness trails, this one can be hot and dry, so bring plenty of water. Trails are also not always marked in this area, so come prepared with a map.

User Groups: Hikers, dogs, and horses. No mountain bikes are allowed. No wheelchair access.

Permits: Permits are not required. Parking and access are free.

Maps: For a map of the Strawberry Mountain Wilderness and Malheur National Forest, contact Nature of the Northwest Information Center. For a topographic map, ask the USGS for Pine Creek Mountain.

Directions: From Prairie City, drive 6.5 miles west on U.S. 26 and turn left (south) onto Pine Creek Road/County Road 54. Follow Pine Creek Road for 8.5 miles to the end of the road and the trailhead (the road may be gated at the trailhead; the trail starts here).

Contact: Malheur National Forest, Blue Mountain Ranger District, 431 Patterson Bridge Road, P.O. Box 909, John Day, OR 97845, 541/575-3000.

60 INDIAN CREEK
12.8 mi/6.5 hrs

south of Prairie City in the Strawberry Mountain Wilderness of Malheur National Forest

Map 10.7, page 447

Want an up-close view of Strawberry Mountain without having to hike all day (or camp overnight)? Try Indian Creek Trail, which climbs through alpine meadows and wild onion fields (gaining 2,600 feet in elevation along the entire trail) to get a closer peak at the namesake of this wilderness area. Turn back whenever you want, because the trail then ends at a junction with Pine Creek (see listing in this chapter), so you can add mileage to the trip if you're not ready to head back into civilization yet. If you do decide to add on to the trip, you should definitely bring a map, because trail signs may be missing in this area (road signs too, for that matter, so add a road atlas to that list).

User Groups: Hikers, dogs, and horses. No mountain bikes are allowed. No wheelchair access.

Permits: Permits are not required. Parking and access are free.

Maps: For a map of the Strawberry Mountain Wilderness and Malheur National Forest, contact Nature of the Northwest Information Center. For a topographic map, ask the USGS for Strawberry Mountain.

Directions: From Prairie City, drive 4.5 miles west on U.S. 26 to Indian Creek Road/County Road 55. Turn left (south) and follow Indian Creek Road eight miles to the trailhead on the right. Park at the side of the road.

Contact: Malheur National Forest, Prairie City Ranger District, P.O. Box 337, Prairie City, OR 97869, 541/820-3311.

61 ONION CREEK TO STRAWBERRY MOUNTAIN
9.0 mi/5.5 hrs

south of Prairie City in the Strawberry Mountain Wilderness of Malheur National Forest

Map 10.7, page 447

Most of the crowds descend upon nearby Strawberry Lake area, but not many try the summit of the mountain itself. Following Onion Creek Trail, the path climbs 3,600 feet, with the final push to the summit topping the total off at an even 4,000. As if that's not hard enough, the trail gets a little faint at times once it hits the open alpine meadows, so look for rock cairns along the way. Stand on top of the 9,039-foot peak and take in the views of the Eagle Cap and Elkhorn Mountains. Keep in mind that because of the high elevation, the trail can be snowy through July, so check ahead to make sure it's clear. Onion Creek Trail continues another two miles, passing by Strawberry Basin Trail to end at Pine Creek (see listings in this chapter).

User Groups: Hikers, dogs, and horses. No mountain bikes are allowed. No wheelchair access.

Permits: Permits are not required. Parking and access are free.

Maps: For a map of the Strawberry Mountain Wilderness and Malheur National Forest, contact Nature of the Northwest Information

Center. For a topographic map, ask the USGS for Strawberry Mountain.

Directions: From Prairie City, drive south on County Road 60 for 12 miles to the trailhead on the right.

Contact: Malheur National Forest, Prairie City Ranger District, P.O. Box 337, Prairie City, OR 97869, 541/820-3311.

62 STRAWBERRY LAKE/ LITTLE STRAWBERRY LAKE
6.4 mi/3.0 hrs

south of Prairie City in the Strawberry Mountain Wilderness of Malheur National Forest

Map 10.7, page 447

Just when you were wondering where all the people are in the remote Strawberry wilderness, you suddenly find out as you enter Strawberry Campground (read: avoid this place on a holiday weekend if you prefer a little elbow room). The trail starts on Strawberry Basin Trail from the campground, leading one mile to a junction with Slide Basin Trail. Keep to the right to pass along the western shore of Strawberry Lake for .8 mile, then continue along another .8 mile to visit Strawberry's little sis, passing by Strawberry Falls on the way before forking to the left for .6-mile Little Strawberry Lake Trail. You can't loop around her (she's too little and dainty), but you can stand and admire the Lake with the Cutest Name on Earth, which is surrounded by meadows and onion fields (what, no strawberry fields?). Retrace your steps, completing the loop of Strawberry Lake by turning right to trace the eastern shore. The total elevation gain is 1,200 feet, with views of Strawberry peak nearby. Strawberry Basin Trail extends three more miles to end at Onion Creek Trail (see listing in this chapter).

User Groups: Hikers, dogs, and horses. No mountain bikes are allowed. No wheelchair access.

Permits: Permits are not required. Parking and access are free.

Maps: For a map of the Strawberry Mountain Wilderness and Malheur National Forest, contact Nature of the Northwest Information Center. For a topographic map, ask the USGS for Strawberry Mountain.

Directions: From Prairie City, drive south on County Road 60 for 12 miles to the road's end and Strawberry Campground. Park in the day-use area, where the trail begins.

Contact: Malheur National Forest, Prairie City Ranger District, P.O. Box 337, Prairie City, OR 97869, 541/820-3311.

63 SLIDE LAKE
7.6 mi/4.0 hrs

south of Prairie City in the Strawberry Mountain Wilderness of Malheur National Forest

Map 10.7, page 447

Starting for the first mile on the popular Strawberry Basin Trail, Slide Basin Trail then veers to the left (east), traveling through the forest and climbing up almost 2,000 feet to open views of Strawberry Mountain, Slide Creek Basin, and the John Day Valley. The trail then passes Slide Falls and connects with Skyline Trail and Slide Lake Trail to slide down (sorry, can't resist) to the lake itself. The wildflowers are especially brilliant in mid-July, which is when you should plan a visit, because the trails tend to be snowed in through June.

User Groups: Hikers, dogs, and horses. No mountain bikes are allowed. No wheelchair access.

Permits: Permits are not required. Parking and access are free.

Maps: For a map of the Strawberry Mountain Wilderness and Malheur National Forest, contact Nature of the Northwest Information Center. For a topographic map, ask the USGS for Strawberry Mountain.

Directions: From Prairie City, drive south on County Road 60 for 12 miles to Strawberry Campground and park in the day-use area, where Strawberry Basin Trail begins.

Contact: Malheur National Forest, Prairie City Ranger District, P.O. Box 337, Prairie City, OR 97869, 541/820-3311.

64 REYNOLDS CREEK
3.0 mi/1.5 hrs

southeast of Prairie City in the Strawberry Mountain Wilderness of Malheur National Forest

Map 10.7, page 447

While waiting for the other trails in the area to open up already, try some spring training on Reynolds Creek Trail. It starts at 4,300 feet, so it's usually open earlier than its neighbors standing on a higher ground. Plus, it's short and sweet, with a gentle ascent of 600 feet, so you can break yourself into summer shape gently. It travels along Reynolds Creek through the Baldy Mountain area and through old-growth forest, just a taste of what lies ahead when the area's longer trails are snow-free.

User Groups: Hikers and dogs. No mountain bikes or horses are allowed. No wheelchair access.

Permits: Permits are not required. Parking and access are free.

Maps: For a map of the Malheur National Forest, contact Nature of the Northwest Information Center. For a topographic map, ask the USGS for Isham Creek and Deardorff Mountain.

Directions: From Prairie City, drive 7.5 miles west on County Road 62/Forest Service Road 14. Turn left onto Forest Service Road 2635 and drive four miles to the trailhead.

Contact: Malheur National Forest, Prairie City Ranger District, P.O. Box 337, Prairie City, OR 97869, 541/820-3311.

65 MUD LAKE
7.0 mi/3.5 hrs

south of Prairie City in the Strawberry Mountain Wilderness of Malheur National Forest

Map 10.7, page 447

It's easy to see how this one got its name, as it can get a touch soggy in parts. It's best to hit this one later in the season, when everything has had a chance to dry off. Whenever you go, you're practically guaranteed solitude, because it's a re-

mote area. If you're looking for a relatively short day hike with a little climbing involved (elevation gain is 1,700 feet) and a lakeside view, check this one out. Just be warned: The drive in is rough, which seals the promise of solitude.

User Groups: Hikers, dogs, and horses. No mountain bikes are allowed. No wheelchair access.

Permits: Permits are not required. Parking and access are free.

Maps: For a map of the Malheur National Forest, contact Nature of the Northwest Information Center. For a topographic map, ask the USGS for Strawberry Mountain.

Directions: From Prairie City, drive 22 miles south on County Road 62/Forest Service Road 14 to Summit Prairie. Turn right (west) onto Forest Service Road 16 and continue five miles to Forest Service Road 1648. Turn right (north) and drive 2.5 miles to Forest Service Road 924-021. Turn right and drive 1.4 miles, then turn left onto Forest Service Road 039 for .8 mile to the trailhead.

Contact: Malheur National Forest, Prairie City Ranger District, P.O. Box 337, Prairie City, OR 97869, 541/820-3311.

66 MEADOW FORK
9.2 mi/4.5 hrs

south of Prairie City in the Strawberry Mountain Wilderness of Malheur National Forest

Map 10.7, page 447

Climbing through old-growth pine and fir forest, you'll get a chance to reflect without hearing other people yammering away, because this is a lightly used trail (and better maintained than its neighbors). You won't have views to distract you from your inner thoughts until the upper part of the trail, when you're tired of your own inner voice anyway and just want to soak in the scenery of the Strawberry mountain range and the valleys below. The trail gains 1,300 feet in elevation, and it's a hot and dry area, so bring some water for the road.

User Groups: Hikers, dogs, and horses. No mountain bikes are allowed. No wheelchair access.

Permits: Permits are not required. Parking and access are free.

Maps: For a map of Malheur National Forest, contact Nature of the Northwest Information Center. For a topographic map, ask the USGS for Strawberry Mountain and Logan Valley West.

Directions: From Prairie City, drive 22 miles south on County Road 62/Forest Service Road 14 to Summit Prairie. Turn right (west) onto Forest Service Road 16, and continue five miles to Forest Service Road 1648. Turn right (north) and drive 2.5 miles to Forest Service Road 924-021. Turn right and drive 1.4 miles, then turn left onto Forest Service Road 039 for .8 mile to the trailhead.

Contact: Malheur National Forest, Prairie City Ranger District, P.O. Box 337, Prairie City, OR 97869, 541/820-3311.

67 NORTH FORK MALHEUR
12.4 mi one-way/2.0 days
southeast of Prairie City in the Strawberry Mountain Wilderness of Malheur National Forest

Map 10.7, page 447

Crossing a footbridge over the North Fork Malheur River at the trailhead, this ambling riverside stroll is like many of the trails in this area: lightly used. But it's maintained better than many in the area (which have been left out of this book due to fire damage or overgrowth), so you'll have a good shot at seeing no one except for the bighorn sheep, mule deer, and Rocky Mountain elk that roam the region. You may choose to turn back halfway for a day hike, or to camp along the river. There's also a sweet camping spot at North Fork Campground, one mile before the trailhead, off the road.

User Groups: Hikers, dogs, horses, and mountain bikes. No wheelchair access.

Permits: Permits are not required. Parking and access are free.

Maps: For a map of Malheur National Forest, contact Nature of the Northwest Information Center. For a topographic map, ask the USGS for Flag Prairie and Buck Trough Spring.

Directions: From Prairie City, drive south on County Road 62/Forest Service Road 14 to Deardorff Creek. Turn left onto Forest Service Road 13 and drive 16.4 miles. Turn right at a T-intersection onto Forest Service 16 and drive 2.2 miles, then turn left onto Forest Service Road 1675. Drive 3.5 miles to the trailhead (note: this last road is rough), one mile past North Fork Campground.

Contact: Malheur National Forest, Prairie City Ranger District, P.O. Box 337, Prairie City, OR 97869, 541/820-3311.

68 MALHEUR RIVER NATIONAL RECREATION TRAIL
15.2 mi/7.5 hrs
southeast of Seneca in Malheur National Forest

Map 10.7, page 447

Deer, bighorn sheep, and elk roam this national recreation trail (okay, they don't exactly follow the trail, but they're entitled to take shortcuts), which travels along the scenic Malheur River, with great fishing spots along the banks. Though it attracts a few more visitors than other area trails, you'll still feel far, far away from the "real world" as you travel through the ponderosa pine forest along the riverbank.

User Groups: Hikers, dogs, and horses. No mountain bikes are allowed. No wheelchair access.

Permits: Permits are not required. Parking and access are free.

Maps: For a map of Malheur National Forest, contact Nature of the Northwest Information Center. For a topographic map, ask the USGS for Dollar Basin.

Directions: From Seneca, drive 16.5 miles east on Logan Valley Road/Forest Service Road 16 to Forest Service Road 1643. Turn right (south) and continue 10 miles to Dollar Basin. Turn left to continue on Forest Service Road 1643 and drive one mile to the Malheur River and the trailhead.

Contact: Malheur National Forest, Emigrant Creek Ranger District, 265 Highway 20 South, Hines, OR 97738, 541/573-4300.

69 HISTORIC OREGON TRAIL
4.2 mi/2.0 hrs

east of Baker City off Highway 86

Map 10.8, page 448

Back in the 1800s, the Oregon Trail served as a gateway to the west for farmers, missionaries, and people seeking a better life in this fine state. By 1852, so many people had used the corridor that it had turned from a faint path to a real-life wagon road, and an industrious soul by the name of Ezra Meeker sought to place markers along the trail. Way to go, Ezra, because the government saw what he was doing and decided to get in on the action themselves. Poor Ezra was long gone by the time they really got down to business, though; it wasn't until 1978 that the trail was dubbed the Oregon National Historic Trail. While much of the trail has been swallowed by superhighways and maybe a couple of McDonald's, there are still 300 miles of wagon ruts that exist to this day. Check out this interpretive trail for a stroll back in time.

User Groups: Hikers and dogs. No horses or mountain bikes are allowed. Wheelchair accessible.

Permits: Permits are not required. A $5 fee is charged at the entrance.

Maps: Free trail maps are available at the entrance and online at www.oregontrail.blm.gov. For a topographic map, ask the USGS for Virtue Flat.

Directions: From Baker City, drive six miles east on Highway 86 to the National Historic Oregon Trails Interpretive Center. The trail begins behind the center.

Contact: National Historic Oregon Trail Interpretive Center, 22267 Oregon Highway 86, P.O. Box 987, Baker City, OR 97814, 541/523-1843.

Chapter 11

© KEVIN FOREMAN

The Southern Cascades

The Southern Cascades

While Portland has Mount Hood knocking on its door asking for it to come out and play, Bend residents have a similar temptation, times three: The Three Sisters, standing tall at over 10,000 feet, come in just behind Mount Jefferson and Mount Hood in the tallest-peak category, rounding out the top five in the state. They're the centerpiece to the Southern Cascade region and within an easy 20-minute drive of the outdoors mecca and mountain-biking hub Bend. South Sister, standing next to the Mount Bachelor Ski Area, is one of the highest peaks you can climb without any equipment (besides good hiking boots).

But you don't have to tackle a summit to get in a good hike around here. In the surrounding Three Sisters Wilderness of Deschutes National Forest, there are plenty of shorter hikes to viewpoints of the imposing triplets, plus backpacking treks to alpine lakes at their basin.

Crater Lake National Park, in the southern region, is another must-see. The deepest lake in the country, Crater Lake has gotten a clean bill of health as one of the clearest lakes in the world. Go anytime but winter, when the park is closed. The Pacific Crest Trail (PCT) winds through the park, and the most noteworthy PCT hikes are covered in this chapter. From half-mile treks up to viewpoints to backpacking trips into the forest on the PCT, you can do it all in this park, and all within viewing range of the clear, blue lake. The unofficial Most Unusual Hike also exists in this park: You can hike down to the lakeshore, take a boat across to Wizard Island, then hike up to the volcanic peak for a view from inside this massive crater.

Coming in a close second to Crater Lake is Waldo Lake, one of the largest natural bodies of water in the state and the second deepest.

Scientists took their clear-lake detection devices down to Waldo Lake in Willamette National Forest and—voilà! It's also one of the clearest lakes in the world. You can do a 22-mile loop around the whole lake if you're looking for a great backpacking adventure.

The northern section covered in this chapter is filled with interesting geological formations, like cinder cone peaks, craters, and rocky cliffs, and peaks that attract climbers from all over. The distinct prominent points of Smith Rock State Park and Three Fingered Jack are omnipresent at viewpoints near and far (that Jack, he tends to hog the attention with his jaunty wave).

Surrounding the west side of Crater Lake is the Rogue River National Forest, where the Rogue River National Recreation Trail extends for a whopping 49 miles down the scenic rushing waters. There are plenty of places to access the river and its surrounding hikes right off Highway 62. The 26.5-mile McKenzie River and 9.1-mile Deschutes River Trails are also popular riverside paths, with many access points along the way. Other water adventures include the second-highest waterfall in Oregon—Salt Creek Falls, in Willamette National Forest—and lake hikes galore, from short trails right off the highway to the more remote Sky Lakes and Mountain Lakes Wilderness Areas of Winema National Forest.

It's hard to pinpoint one cool thing about a region filled with so many adventures, but one noteworthy aspect here is trail accessibility. Unlike other wilderness areas that require a long haul through rough Forest Service roads, most of the hikes in this chapter are just a short drive from the highway, if not right off the highway itself. This only adds to their popularity (read: crowds), but the sights in this interesting area make up for the lack of elbow room.

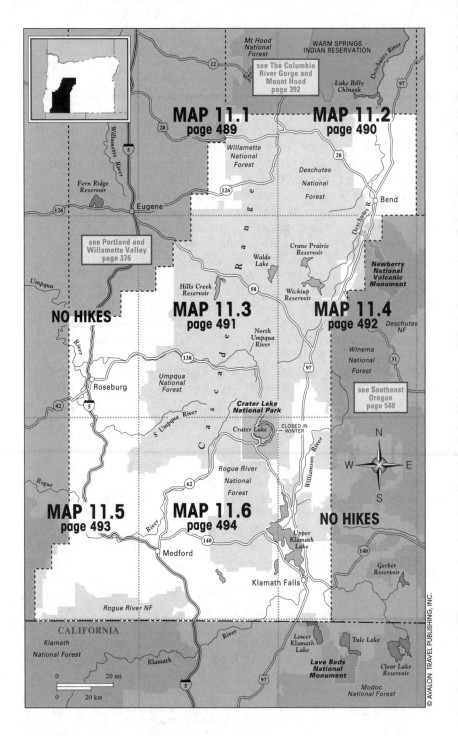

MAP 11.1
page 489

MAP 11.2
page 490

see The Columbia
River Gorge and
Mount Hood
page 392

Mt Hood
National
Forest

WARM SPRINGS
INDIAN RESERVATION

Deschutes River

Lake Billy
Chinook

Willamette
National
Forest

Deschutes

National

Forest

Bend

see Portland and
Willamette Valley
page 376

Fern Ridge
Reservoir

Eugene

Willamette River

Umpqua

NO HIKES

Waldo
Lake

Crane Prairie
Reservoir

Newberry
National
Volcanic
Monument

Hills Creek
Reservoir

Wickiup
Reservoir

MAP 11.3
page 491

MAP 11.4
page 492

Deschutes
NF

River

North
Umpqua
River

Winema
National
Forest

Roseburg

Umpqua
National
Forest

see Southeast
Oregon
page 540

Crater Lake
National Park

CLOSED IN
WINTER

Cascade Range

S Umpqua River

Crater Lake

Rogue

Rogue River
National
Forest

Williamson River

MAP 11.5
page 493

MAP 11.6
page 494

NO HIKES

River

Medford

Upper
Klamath
Lake

Gerber
Reservoir

Rogue River NF

Klamath Falls

CALIFORNIA

Klamath
National Forest

Klamath

River

Lower
Klamath
Lake

Tule Lake

Clear Lake
Reservoir

Lava Beds
National
Monument

0   20 mi

0   20 km

Modoc
National Forest

© AVALON TRAVEL PUBLISHING, INC.

Map 11.1

Hikes 1–8
Pages 495–498

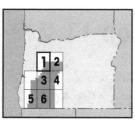

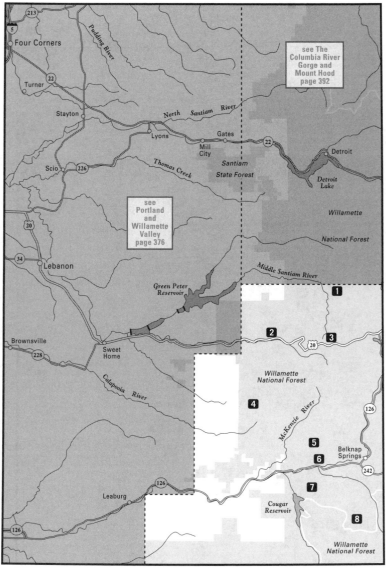

213

5

Four Corners

Pudding River

Turner 22

Stayton

North Santiam River

Lyons Gates

Mill City

Scio 226

Thomas Creek

Santiam State Forest

22 Detroit

Detroit Lake

see The Columbia River Gorge and Mount Hood page 392

Willamette

National Forest

see Portland and Willamette Valley page 376

20

34

Lebanon

Middle Santiam River

Green Peter Reservoir

1

Brownsville 228

Sweet Home

2

20 **3**

Calapooia River

Willamette National Forest

4

McKenzie River

126

5

Belknap Springs

6

242

Leaburg 126

7

Cougar Reservoir

8

126

Willamette National Forest

Map 11.2

Hikes 9–27
Pages 499–508

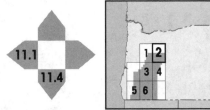

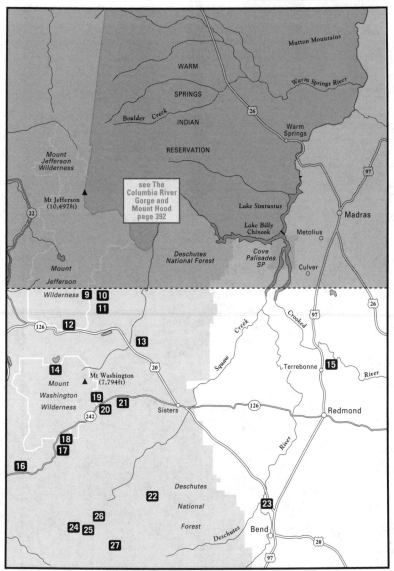

© AVALON TRAVEL PUBLISHING, INC.

Map 11.3

Hikes 28–45
Pages 509–517

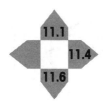

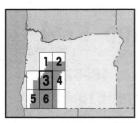

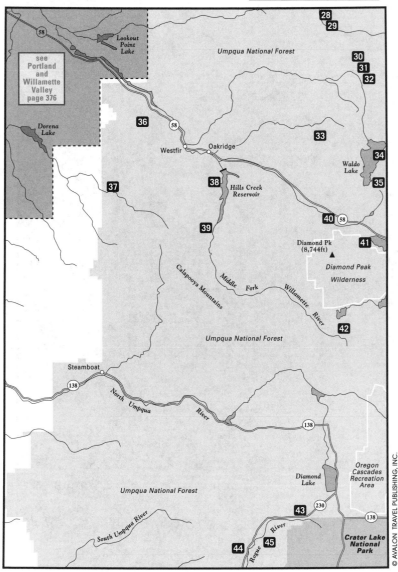

Map 11.4

Hikes 46–52
Pages 518–521

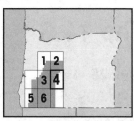

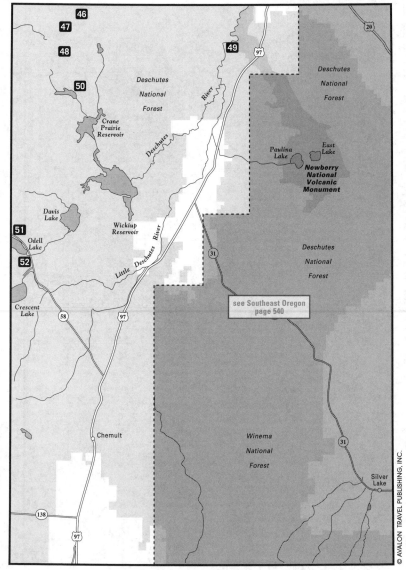

Map 11.5

Hikes 53–60
Pages 521–524

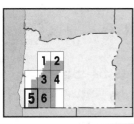

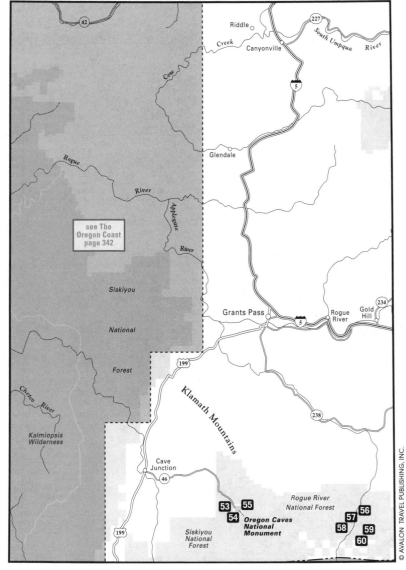

© AVALON TRAVEL PUBLISHING, INC.

Map 11.6

Hikes 61–85
Pages 525–536

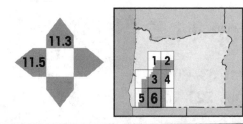

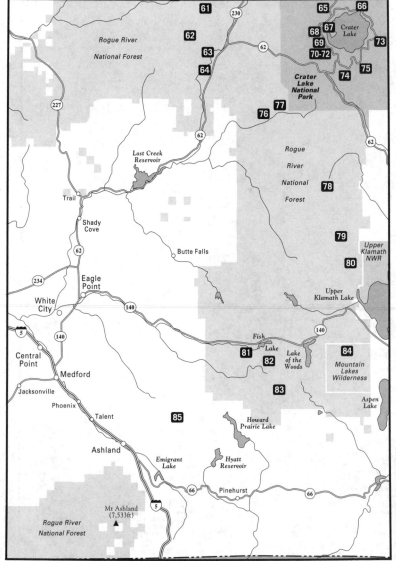

1 PYRAMIDS

4.2 mi/2.0 hrs

west of Highway 22 in Willamette National Forest

Map 11.1, page 489

Sure, the Three Sisters may get most of the fame and fortune, but there is another triple-threat here, with a view that stops traffic. The Three Pyramids stand right in a row, and you can climb up to the remains of their 1934 lookout for panoramic views of the Cascades. The trail gains 1,600 feet in elevation on the climb up to the 5,618-foot lookout. It's a heavily wooded trail that pops out into broad open meadows, adding to your viewing pleasure. South Pyramid Trail also connects to this, but it's not as well maintained as this one, so it's best to stick to the path of least resistance here and head back from the lookout.

User Groups: Hikers and dogs. No horses or mountain bikes are allowed. No wheelchair access.

Permits: A federal Northwest Forest pass is required to park here. The cost is $5 for a day pass or $30 for an annual pass. You can buy a day pass at ranger stations, from private vendors, or through Nature of the Northwest Information Center.

Maps: For a map of Willamette National Forest, contact Nature of the Northwest Information Center. For a topographic map, ask the USGS for Coffin Mountain and Echo Mountain.

Directions: From Salem, drive 52 miles east on Highway 22 to Detroit, continuing for another 28 miles. Turn right (south) on Lava Lake Meadow Road, following signs to Old Cascade Crest trails. Continue down the road, turning right at a fork 1.9 miles down. Drive 3.5 miles to the trailhead on the left.

Contact: Willamette National Forest, Sweet Home Ranger District, 3225 Highway 20, Sweet Home, OR 97386, 541/367-5168.

2 ROOSTER ROCK

6.8 mi/4.0 hrs

north of U.S. 20 in the Menagerie Wilderness of Willamette National Forest

Map 11.1, page 489

The trail up to Rooster Rock walks to the beat of a different drummer. Instead of switchbacking up to a peak, it just keeps going straight. And up. Just when you're getting the hang of the uphill climb, the trail takes it up a notch. It's like an outdoors stair-climber whose ramp level keeps increasing one level at a time. You might also feel like your destination is unknown until you round a bend almost two miles in and you can see the rocky, roosterlike formation through a clearing to the right. The trail is actually called Trout Creek Trail—the actual Rooster Rock Trail starts three miles down the highway, but it gains the same 2,300 feet in just 2.1 miles. Trust one who's been there, you'll want that extra .7 mile to get there, because it's steep enough as it is. You'll hit Rooster Rock Trail .5 mile from the base of the rock, but hold your high-fiving and back-slapping, because the trail must go on. It's just a short (steep) climb to a viewpoint that rocks, so it's worth it. The pillar is also popular with rock climbers, so don't be surprised if you see someone popping their head over the edge from the base itself.

User Groups: Hikers and dogs. No mountain bikes or horses are allowed. No wheelchair access.

Permits: A federal Northwest Forest pass is required to park here. The cost is $5 for a day pass or $30 for an annual pass. You can buy a day pass at ranger stations, from private vendors, or through Nature of the Northwest Information Center.

Maps: For a map of Willamette National Forest and the Menagerie Wilderness, contact Nature of the Northwest Information Center. For a topographic map, ask the USGS for Upper Soda.

Directions: From Sweet Home, drive 17.4 miles east on U.S. 20 to the Trout Creek trailhead and the parking area on the left side of the highway.

Contact: Willamette National Forest, Sweet Home Ranger District, 3225 Highway 20, Sweet Home, OR 97386, 541/367-5168.

❸ IRON MOUNTAIN
3.4 mi/2.0 hrs

north of U.S. 20 in Willamette National Forest

Map 11.1, page 489

The trail up to Iron Mountain starts off gently through wildflower meadows (and all the bugs that go with them). In fact, it starts off so gently you may wonder if you're on the right trail. You are, and you'll start to climb soon enough, so enjoy the stroll while it lasts. After crossing the highway from the short trail leading from the parking lot and entering the meadow, you'll see Iron Mountain to your right, like a castle of rock with proud majestic spires—and even a little white marker on the 5,455 summit. Then leave the meadow behind to dip into the forest for the switchbacks up for views of Mount Jefferson, Three Fingered Jack, and the Three Sisters. A stone bench sits at a viewpoint along the way, so you can rest before the final climb. You'll come to a couple of junctions along this trail, and if you take the 3.5-mile Cone Peak Trail, you'll be in nature heaven as it passes through a nature museum of the 300 species of flowering plants that live on the volcanic slope of Cone Peak. You can also combine the two trails for a 5.5-mile loop—when you return to the Cone Peak trailhead, take Santiam Wagon Trail heading west back to your car. The total elevation gain for both trails is 1,455 feet.

User Groups: Hikers and dogs. No mountain bikes or horses are allowed. No wheelchair access.

Permits: A federal Northwest Forest pass is required to park here. The cost is $5 for a day pass or $30 for an annual pass. You can buy a day pass at ranger stations, from private vendors, or through Nature of the Northwest Information Center.

Maps: For a map of the Willamette National Forest, contact Nature of the Northwest Information Center. For a topographic map, ask the USGS for Harter Mountain.

Directions: From Sweet Home, drive 31.8 miles east on U.S. 20 to Forest Service Road 15. Turn right at the Iron Mountain sign, and drive a short distance to the parking area, on the right side of the road. The trail starts on the east side of the parking area.

Contact: Willamette National Forest, Sweet Home Ranger District, 3225 Highway 20, Sweet Home, OR 97386, 541/367-5168.

❹ TIDBITS MOUNTAIN
3.9 mi/2.0 hrs

north of Blue River Lake in Willamette National Forest

Map 11.1, page 489

Only tidbits remain of Ye Ol' Tidbits Lookout, but the views haven't gone anywhere. A short hike through old-growth forest, with a rocky scramble up to the top, will give you access to a glimpse of the Cascade Range from the 5,185-foot summit (the total elevation gain is 1,200 feet). You'll come to several junctions along the way, so when in doubt, turn left to reach the top (the trails tend to be well marked in this region, but signs can always go AWOL when you least expect it). Retrace your steps, this time turning right at both junctions, to return to your car.

User Groups: Hikers, dogs, and mountain bikes. No horses are allowed. No wheelchair access.

Permits: Permits are not required. Parking and access are free.

Maps: For a map of Willamette National Forest, contact Nature of the Northwest Information Center. For a topographic map, ask the USGS for Tidbits Mountain.

Directions: From Eugene, drive 40 miles east on McKenzie Highway/Highway 126 to Blue River. Continue three miles to Forest Service Road 15. Turn left (north) and drive 4.7 miles to Forest Service Road 1509. Drive eight miles to the trailhead parking area on the left. The trail starts a short distance up Spur Road 877.

Contact: Willamette National Forest, McKenzie River Ranger District, 57600 McKenzie Highway, McKenzie Bridge, OR 97413, 541/822-3381.

5 LOOKOUT CREEK OLD-GROWTH TRAIL
7.0 mi/3.5 hrs

north of McKenzie Bridge in H. J. Andrews Experimental Forest of Willamette National Forest

Map 11.1, page 489

If you go ga-ga over old-growth trees, this is your ticket. The 3.5-mile trail gains just 400 feet through, yes, old-growth Douglas fir forest along a scenic wooded trail, with Lookout Creek to keep you company. It's located in the H. J. Andrews Experimental Forest, a living laboratory of ancient forest (don't let the term "laboratory" fool you—no white smocks are required).

User Groups: Hikers and dogs. No mountain bikes or horses are allowed. No wheelchair access.

Permits: Permits are not required. Parking and access are free.

Maps: For a free brochure, contact Willamette National Forest, McKenzie River Ranger District, 57600 McKenzie Highway, McKenzie Bridge, OR 97413, 541/822-3381. For a topographic map, ask the USGS for McKenzie Bridge.

Directions: From Eugene, drive 40 miles east on McKenzie Highway/Highway 126 to Blue River. Continue three miles to Forest Service Road 15. Turn left (north) and drive four miles to Forest Service Road 1506. Turn right and drive seven miles to the trailhead and parking area.

Contact: Willamette National Forest, McKenzie River Ranger District, 57600 McKenzie Highway, McKenzie Bridge, OR 97413, 541/822-3381.

6 MCKENZIE RIVER NATIONAL RECREATION TRAIL
26.5 mi one-way/2.0 days

on the McKenzie River between McKenzie Bridge and Clear Lake

Map 11.1, page 489

This is a perfect spring fling to get you ready for all the other trails to shake off their white stuff and open up. The trail follows the white-water McKenzie River the entire length, but hold on to your hat—there's more. Lots more. The trail passes by several waterfalls, reservoirs, lava flows, old-growth forest, and even hot springs—plus plenty of campgrounds along the way, so you can turn the trip into an overnight excursion. There are also a couple of loop options: three-mile Waterfall Loop and five-mile Clear Lake Loop, both of them near the upper trailhead, so you may want to do those for a day hike (although that area tends to be more crowded). Another option is to do the entire length and arrange a car shuttle at the upper trailhead. Unlike some wilderness trails, where you have to drive forever to get from one trail to the other, there are many access points along the route that are right off the highway. The total elevation gain is just 800 feet, just the thing to get your sea (um, river) legs back for hiking again.

User Groups: Hikers, dogs, and mountain bikes. No horses are allowed. No wheelchair access.

Permits: Permits are not required. Parking and access are free.

Maps: For a map of Willamette National Forest, contact Nature of the Northwest Information Center. For a topographic map, ask the USGS for McKenzie Bridge, Belknap Springs, Tamolitch Falls, and Clear Lake.

Directions: The trail can be accessed at many places along McKenzie Highway/Highway 126. To reach the lower trailhead from Eugene, drive 50 miles on the McKenzie Highway past the McKenzie Bridge to the trailhead, on the left (north) side of the road, one mile past the McKenzie Bridge Ranger Station. Other marked access points are along the highway. The upper trailhead is another 25 miles down, at Clear Lake.

Contact: Willamette National Forest, Sweet Home Ranger District, 3225 Highway 20, Sweet Home, OR 97386, 541/367-5168.

7 CASTLE ROCK
2.0 mi/1.0 hrs

south of McKenzie Bridge in Willamette National Forest

Map 11.1, page 489

Lording over the Willamette River Valley, 3,808-foot Castle Rock is easy to get to if you choose the path of least resistance. If you want the red-carpet treatment straight to views of the valley, this trail is perfect for a short leg-stretcher or a warm-up for another hike nearby. Remember not to cackle at those who have chosen the longer path—the locals don't take kindly to that sort of thing. You'll pass the lower trailhead on the route in, which is a 9.2-mile round-trip to the top, so take your pick. The peak is also accessible via the royal King-Castle Trail, which is 15 miles round-trip.

User Groups: Hikers, dogs, and mountain bikes. No horses are allowed except on King-Castle Trail. No wheelchair access.

Permits: Permits are not required. Parking and access are free.

Maps: For a map of Willamette National Forest, contact Nature of the Northwest Information Center. For a topographic map, ask the USGS for McKenzie Bridge.

Directions: From Eugene, drive about 42 miles east on McKenzie Highway/Highway 126 to Forest Service Road 19, about five miles west of the McKenzie River Bridge. Turn right (south) and drive one mile, keeping straight to continue on Forest Service Roads 19 and 410 to Forest Service Road 2639. Turn left (east) and drive .5 mile to Forest Service Road 480. Drive six miles to the trailhead at the end of the road. Note: The last miles of this road are rough. To reach the longer lower trailhead, follow the directions above, driving on Forest Service Roads 19 and 410 for two miles, then turn left onto

Forest Service Road 411 and drive 2.7 miles to the parking area on the left side of the road.

Contact: Willamette National Forest, McKenzie River Ranger District, 57600 McKenzie Highway, McKenzie Bridge, OR 97413, 541/822-3381.

8 OLALLIE RIDGE/ OLALLIE MOUNTAIN
9.7 mi one-way/
1.0 to 2.0 days

south of McKenzie Bridge on the northern border of the Three Sisters Wilderness in Willamette National Forest

Map 11.1, page 489

So many choices, so little time. It's hard to pick one over another here, so here are all your options. For a shorter trip up to a view, start from the Horsepasture trailhead, and climb 1,400 feet in 1.2 miles up to Horsepasture Mountain for views of the Three Sisters, Mount Washington, Mount Jefferson, Diamond Peak, and Mount Hood. Then return the way you came for a 2.5-mile round-trip. If you're just getting started, continue instead along Olallie Ridge, where wildflowers are at their best in late June. The whole ridgeline is filled with viewpoints, passing Taylor Castle peak in another three miles and continuing to 5,700-foot Olallie Mountain (which is also accessible via another trailhead along the way, which brings you to the mountain in a three-mile round-trip). It's worth it to do the whole ridge, camping overnight along the way, or arrange a shuttle at the Pat Saddle trailhead near Olallie Mountain.

User Groups: Hikers, dogs, mountain bikes, and horses. No wheelchair access.

Permits: Permits are not required. Parking and access are free.

Maps: For a map of Willamette National Forest, contact Nature of the Northwest Information Center. For a topographic map, ask the USGS for French Mountain and Chucksney Mountain.

Directions: From Eugene, drive 50 miles east on McKenzie Highway/Highway 126 to Horse

Creek Road/Forest Service Road 2638 at McKenzie Bridge. Turn right (south) and drive two miles to Wapiti Road/Forest Service Road 1993. Turn right and continue 8.5 miles to the Horsepasture Saddle trailhead on the right side of the road. To reach the trailhead near Olallie Mountain: From Eugene, drive 40 miles east on McKenzie Highway/Highway 126 to Blue River. Continue past Blue River, following Cougar Reservoir signs for Forest Service Road 19. Turn right (south) and drive to Cougar Dam. Turn left onto Forest Service Road 1993 across Cougar Dam and continue 15 miles to Pat Saddle Trail on the right side of the road.

Contact: Willamette National Forest, McKenzie River Ranger District, 57600 McKenzie Highway, McKenzie Bridge, OR 97413, 541/822-3381.

9 DUFFY AND MOWICH LAKES
9.0 mi/4.5 hrs

west of Three Fingered Jack in the Mount Jefferson Wilderness

Map 11.2, page 490

Why hit just one lake when you can reach two? You'll pay only two more miles to reach Mowich Lake after Duffy. And it's worth the trip to see both alpine lakes (elevation: 5,000 feet). Since it's a relatively easy jaunt, and since there are so many routes that lead off from here and go deeper into the Jefferson Wilderness, it can be a little crowded at times. But if you want a perfect picnic spot where you can feel like you earned your lunch, this is a good choice. After lunch, you can also add a view to your day by continuing up another 1.5 miles and another 800 feet up to 5,843-foot Red Butte for a view of the Mount Jefferson area and Three Fingered Jack. In August 2003, this area was closed due to the Booth and Bear fires. Check trail conditions before you head out.

User Groups: Hikers, dogs, and horses. No mountain bikes are allowed. No wheelchair access.

Permits: A federal Northwest Forest pass is required to park here. The cost is $5 for a day pass or $30 for an annual pass. You can buy a day pass at ranger stations, from private ven-

dors, or through Nature of the Northwest Information Center.

Maps: For a map of the Mount Jefferson Wilderness and Willamette National Forest, contact Nature of the Northwest Information Center. For a topographic map, ask the USGS for Santiam Junction, Three Fingered Jack, and Marion Lake.

Directions: From Salem, drive 52 miles east on Highway 22 to Detroit, and continue another 27 miles to Big Meadows Road/Forest Service Road 2267. Turn left (east) and drive three miles to the trailhead and parking area at the end of the road.

Contact: Willamette National Forest, Detroit Ranger Station, HC73, P.O. Box 320, Mill City, OR 97360, 503/854-3366.

10 ROCKPILE LAKE
10.0 mi/5.0 hrs

north of Three Fingered Jack in the Mount Jefferson Wilderness

Map 11.2, page 490

Yet another route through the Mount Jefferson Wilderness, this trail accesses the Pacific Crest Trail for countless options (pick up a map of this area before you go; you'll be glad you did). For a day trip to cute Rockpile Lake, nestled at 6,300 feet, try this trail that leads five miles and gains 2,300 feet in elevation to hit the Pacific Crest Trail and the lake itself. From here, you can turn back the way you came or turn left (south) on the PCT to make a loop, keeping left at all junctions and passing by equally tiny Minto Lake to return to the trailhead for a 13.5-mile loop. As with many trails in this area, the choices go on from the trailhead—you can also access the Marion Lake trail system to the west and North Cinder Peaks to the north for backpacking trips. In August 2003, this area was closed and possibly damaged due to the Booth and Bear fires. Check conditions before you head out.

User Groups: Hikers, dogs, and horses. No mountain bikes are allowed. No wheelchair access.

Permits: A free wilderness permit is required to

hike here and is available at the trailhead. A federal Northwest Forest pass is also required to park here. The cost is $5 for a day pass or $30 for an annual pass. You can buy a day pass at ranger stations, from private vendors, or through Nature of the Northwest Information Center.

Maps: For a map of the Mount Jefferson Wilderness and Deschutes National Forest, contact Nature of the Northwest Information Center. For a topographic map, contact Green Trails, Inc. (ask for Mount Jefferson, map number 557), 206/546-MAPS (206/546-6277), www.greentrails.com, or ask the USGS for Marion Lake.

Directions: From U.S. 20 at Santiam Pass (about 85 miles east of Salem and 22 miles west of Sisters), drive eight miles east to Jack Lake Road/Forest Service Road 12. Turn left (north) and drive four miles to Forest Service Road 1230. Continue straight for 1.7 miles to Forest Service Road 1234, then turn left and drive one mile to Forest Service Road 1235. Turn right and drive four miles to Bear Valley trailhead and the parking area at the end of the road.

Contact: Deschutes National Forest, Sisters Ranger District, Highway 20/Pine Street, P.O. Box 249, Sisters, OR 97759, 541/549-7700.

11 CANYON CREEK MEADOWS LOOP

8.1 mi/4.0 hrs

east of Three Fingered Jack in the Mount Hood Wilderness

Map 11.2, page 490

Traveling through the Canyon Creek Meadows with an up-close view of Three Fingered Jack, this popular loop gives you access to the good stuff without having to hike forever to get there. The well-marked loop is 4.5 miles, unless you want to continue another 1.8 miles (and why not?) straight up the wildflower meadows for the grand finale at the base of 7,841-foot Three Fingered Jack. An extinct volcano with a funny-sounding name and an even funnier look, Three Fingered Jack features three distinct protrusions that are landmarks from viewpoints around the state. Returning back,

turn right to complete the loop, keeping left at all junctions to return to the trailhead. In August 2003, this area was closed and possibly damaged due to the Booth and Bear fires. Check conditions before you head out.

User Groups: Hikers, dogs, and horses. No mountain bikes are allowed. No wheelchair access.

Permits: A free wilderness permit is required to hike here and is available at the trailhead. A federal Northwest Forest pass is also required to park here. The cost is $5 for a day pass or $30 for an annual pass. You can buy a day pass at ranger stations, from private vendors, or through Nature of the Northwest Information Center.

Maps: For a map of the Mount Jefferson Wilderness and Deschutes National Forest, contact Nature of the Northwest Information Center. For a topographic map, contact Green Trails, Inc. (ask for Whitewater River, map number 558), 206/546-MAPS (206/546-6277), www.greentrails.com, or ask the USGS for Three Fingered Jack.

Directions: From U.S. 20 at Santiam Pass (about 85 miles east of Salem and 22 miles west of Sisters), drive eight miles east to Jack Lake Road/Forest Service Road 12. Turn left (north) and drive four miles to Forest Service Road 1230. Continue straight for 1.7 miles, then turn left onto Forest Service Road 1234 and drive five miles to the trailhead and parking at Jack Lake Campground.

Contact: Deschutes National Forest, Sisters Ranger District, Highway 20/Pine Street, P.O. Box 249, Sisters, OR 97759, 541/549-7700.

12 PACIFIC CREST TRAIL TO THREE FINGERED JACK

10.5 mi/5.5 hrs

on the southern slope of Three Fingered Jack in the Mount Jefferson Wilderness

Map 11.2, page 490

The extinct volcano Three Fingered Jack is a beacon to climbers, who flock to scale its 7,841-foot height. You can get pretty close to the action on a stellar viewpoint by accessing the Pacific Crest Trail right off the highway.

It's a dry, dusty path, so bring water—as well as your camera to snap some shots of this unusual guy. It's a strenuous and sometimes rocky route to a viewpoint right next to Jack himself. You can also do a loop by heading straight to Square Lake, then turning left at all junctions to add another mile to your route. If you're hiking with others who aren't quite as into sweat as you are, they can take an easy stroll to Square and Round Lakes (four miles round-trip) from the same trailhead. In August 2003, this trail was closed and possibly damaged due to the Booth and Bear fires. Check conditions before you try this route.

User Groups: Hikers, dogs, and horses. No mountain bikes are allowed. No wheelchair access.

Permits: A federal Northwest Forest pass is required to park here. The cost is $5 for a day pass or $30 for an annual pass. You can buy a day pass at ranger stations, from private vendors, or through Nature of the Northwest Information Center.

Maps: For a map of the Mount Jefferson Wilderness and Deschutes National Forest, contact Nature of the Northwest Information Center. For a topographic map, contact Green Trails, Inc. (ask for Whitewater River, map number 558), 206/546-MAPS (206/546-6277), www.greentrails.com, or ask the USGS for Three Fingered Jack.

Directions: From Salem, drive 52 miles east on Highway 22 to Detroit and continue 36 miles to Santiam Pass (22 miles west of Sisters). Follow signs to the Pacific Crest Trail parking lot on the left (north) side of the road.

Contact: Deschutes National Forest, Sisters Ranger District, Highway 20/Pine Street, P.O. Box 249, Sisters, OR 97759, 541/549-7700.

🔳 BLACK BUTTE

4.0 mi/2.0 hrs

north of Sisters in Deschutes National Forest

Map 11.2, page 490

The Black Butte volcano has enjoyed quite a bit of attention in the fire lookout station de-

partment. Whereas other lookout stations atop fine viewpoints have long since gone by the wayside, 6,436-foot Black Butte has kept Forest Service workers busy for years, making sure she has a nice little lookout on top. In 1910, a platform was built between two trees, where rangers perched to survey the area. The platform endured for 12 years, until a cupola structure was completed in 1922, where it waited to be outdone in 1934 by a bigger, flashier 83-foot lookout tower. The cute cupola got its revenge when the tower collapsed in 2001—but not before an even flashier, shinier tower was built in 1995 and flown in specially to be placed gently on the butte. Got all that? The whole point is, Black Butte is an important lookout site, which means the view can't be beat, from that attention-hogging Three Fingered Jack to the Cascade mountain range. The hike up to the summit gains 1,600 feet in elevation, starting in a ponderosa pine forest and ending up on a hot exposed area.

User Groups: Hikers, dogs, and horses. No mountain bikes are allowed. No wheelchair access.

Permits: A federal Northwest Forest pass is also required to park here. The cost is $5 for a day pass or $30 for an annual pass. You can buy a day pass at ranger stations, from private vendors, or through Nature of the Northwest Information Center.

Maps: For a map of Deschutes National Forest, contact Nature of the Northwest Information Center. For a topographic map, ask the USGS for Black Butte.

Directions: From Sisters, drive 6.3 miles northwest on U.S. 20 to Green Ridge Road/Forest Service Road 11. Turn right (north) and continue 3.9 miles to Forest Service Road 1110. Turn left and drive 5.5 miles to the end of the road and the trailhead.

Contact: Deschutes National Forest, Sisters Ranger District, Highway 20/Pine Street, P.O. Box 249, Sisters, OR 97759, 541/549-7700.

14 PATJENS LAKE LOOP
5.5 mi/2.5 hrs

at Big Lake in the northern Mount Washington Wilderness

Map 11.2, page 490

Accessing three small lakes, the Patjens Lake Loop is a chance to take a dip (literally) in the remote Mount Washington wilderness. Meandering through lodgepole pine, western hemlock, and alpine fir forest, the trail is a relatively easy stroll to these small alpine lakes, which are a perfect setting for a picnic, reflection, or an impromptu dip.

User Groups: Hikers, dogs, and horses. No mountain bikes are allowed. No wheelchair access.

Permits: A free wilderness permit is required to hike here and is available at the trailhead.

Maps: For a map of the Mount Washington Wilderness and Willamette National Forest, contact Nature of the Northwest Information Center. For a topographic map, ask the USGS for Clear Lake and Mount Washington.

Directions: From U.S. 20 at Santiam Pass (about 85 miles east of Salem and 22 miles west of Sisters), turn south on Big Lake Road/Forest Service Road 2690 at the sign for Hoodoo Ski Area. Drive one mile past Big Lake Campground to the trailhead on the right side of the road.

Contact: Willamette National Forest, McKenzie River Ranger District, 57600 McKenzie Highway, McKenzie Bridge, OR 97413, 541/822-3381.

15 SMITH ROCK STATE PARK LOOP
4.0 mi/2.0 hrs

northeast of Redmond on the Crooked River off Highway 97

Map 11.2, page 490

How Smith Rock got its name still stymies historians. The optimist side of the camp proclaims that it was named after the pioneer and Oregon legislator John Smith, who discovered the formations in 1867. The pessimist side says it was actually named for a soldier who fell to his death from the highest peak in the 1860s while camping with his company (yikes!). Either way, there were two Smiths involved in some way in the 1860s, so we'll just leave it at that. Two things are clear, though: The park is a sight to behold, and Smith Rock has probably the blandest name in the whole park, what with walls like the Christian Brothers, Morning Glory, Monkey Face, and Misery Ridge (wonder how they got their names?). The park is renowned among climbers, who come from all over to scale the walls. But you don't need to know your way around a carabiner to witness the scene—you can keep both feet firmly planted on the ground and travel along the trail system through the state park. The main drag is a pleasant four-mile loop that brings you up close to the walls and most likely a few climbers.

User Groups: Hikers, dogs, horses, and mountain bikes. No wheelchair access.

Permits: A $3 day-use fee is collected at the park entrance, or you can get an annual Oregon Parks and Recreation pass for $25; contact Oregon Parks and Recreation, 800/551-6949.

Maps: For a free park brochure and map, contact Oregon Parks and Recreation Department, 800/551-6949, www.oregonstateparks.org. For a topographic map, ask the USGS for Redmond.

Directions: From Redmond, drive about five miles north on U.S. 97 to Terrebone and turn right (east) on Smith Rock Way, following signs for three miles to the park entrance.

Contact: Oregon Parks and Recreation Department, 1115 Commercial Street Northeast, Salem, OR 97301, 800/551-6949, www.oregon state parks.org.

16 PROXY FALLS/LINTON LAKE
4.2 mi/2.5 hrs

south of McKenzie Pass Highway in the Three Sisters Wilderness of Willamette National Forest

Map 11.2, page 490

These trails are actually two separate entities altogether, but who's to get technical? They're so close together off Highway 242 that it's simple to do them both. And you'll want to: Start off with a 1.25-mile warm-up to Proxy Falls, where you'll walk through open lava fields and forest on your way to two different falls, each waiting to show off for you. Then head back on the highway to visit Linton Lake in a quick three-mile trip; this is a popular fishing hole for the locals (or for you, if you're into that kind of thing). Two falls, one lake, one lava field, one forest, one small drive, and one picnic later, you can call it a day. Since the trails are right off the highway, they can be a little crowded, but that's the price you pay for convenience. Keep in mind that Highway 242 is often closed until July.

User Groups: Hikers and dogs. No horses or mountain bikes are allowed. No wheelchair access.

Permits: A free wilderness permit is required to hike at Linton Lake and is available at the trailhead. A federal Northwest Forest pass is also required to park at both trails. The cost is $5 for a day pass or $30 for an annual pass. You can buy a day pass at ranger stations, from private vendors, or through Nature of the Northwest Information Center.

Maps: For a map of the Three Sisters Wilderness and Willamette National Forest, contact Nature of the Northwest Information Center. For a topographic map, ask the USGS for Linton Lake.

Directions: From Eugene, drive 55 miles east on McKenzie Pass Highway/Highway 126, five miles past the town of McKenzie Bridge, to the junction with Highway 242. Continue east on Highway 242 for nine miles to Proxy Falls Trail on the right (south) side of the road. Linton Lake Trail is 1.5 miles down the road from Proxy Falls.

Contact: Willamette National Forest, McKenzie River Ranger District, 57600 McKenzie Highway, McKenzie Bridge, OR 97413, 541/822-3381.

17 OBSIDIAN TRAIL LOOP
11.0 mi/4.5 hrs

south of McKenzie Pass Highway in the Three Sisters Wilderness of Willamette National Forest

Map 11.2, page 490

Warning: If you want to hike in this area, you need to get a permit before you enter, because it's now a limited-use area (see information below). Okay, now that we have that out of the way, here's the deal: Gaining 1,200 feet in elevation throughout the hike, you'll pass through a lava field and over the Obsidian Cliffs before hitting a junction with the Pacific Crest Trail. Turn left to pass by the Obsidian Falls, turning left again at the next junction to complete the loop. Remember to bring your camera along; since you were so special to see this cool area, you'll want to show it off to your friends. Keep in mind that Highway 242 is often closed until July, so plan ahead. Restrictions, restrictions.

User Groups: Hikers, dogs, and horses. No mountain bikes are allowed. No wheelchair access.

Permits: A free limited-use wilderness permit is required to hike here and is available from Willamette National Forest, McKenzie River Ranger District, 57600 McKenzie Highway, McKenzie Bridge, OR 97413, 541/822-3381. A federal Northwest Forest pass is also required to park here. The cost is $5 for a day pass or $30 for an annual pass. You can buy a day pass at ranger stations, from private vendors, or through Nature of the Northwest Information Center.

Maps: For a map of the Three Sisters Wilderness and Willamette National Forest, contact Nature of the Northwest Information Center. For a topographic map, ask the USGS for North Sister and Linton Lake.

Directions: From Eugene, drive 55 miles east on McKenzie Pass Highway/Highway 126, five miles past the town of McKenzie Bridge, to the junction with Highway 242. Continue east on Highway 242 for six miles to the Obsidian Trail sign on the right (south) side of the road.

Contact: Willamette National Forest, McKenzie River Ranger District, 57600 McKenzie Highway, McKenzie Bridge, OR 97413, 541/822-3381.

18 SCOTT TRAIL TO FOUR-IN-ONE CONE

10.0 mi/5.0 hrs

west of Sisters in the Three Sisters Wilderness of Willamette National Forest

Map 11.2, page 490

Like Scott Trail's neighbor, Obsidian Trail, this is a fascinating walk through lava flows and alpine meadows. Unlike its neighbor, it doesn't require limited-use permits. Yet. So take a stroll down Scott Trail, named for Felix Scott (hey, at least the trail isn't called Felix), a true trailblazer in his day who led 50 men through the Cascade Mountains in 1862. The trail follows part of his route, and what a route it is—a tough walk through a lava field. No wonder he ended up bagging it to find a new, wagon-friendly course, which became the approximate path of the Willamette Pass Highway. The trail ends at the junction with the Pacific Crest Trail, but remember that to travel south into the Obsidian area, you'll need a permit. Before the end of the trail, though, you'll come across Four-in-One Cone on your right, which you can scramble to the top of for a cool view. Either way, it's best to leave your sandals at home for this one—your ankles will thank you. Keep in mind that Highway 242 is often closed until July.

User Groups: Hikers, dogs, and horses. No mountain bikes are allowed. No wheelchair access.

Permits: A free wilderness permit is required to hike here and is available at the trailhead. A federal Northwest Forest pass is also required to park here. The cost is $5 for a day pass or $30 for an annual pass. You can buy a day pass at ranger stations, from private vendors, or through Nature of the Northwest Information Center.

Maps: For a map of the Three Sisters Wilderness and Willamette National Forest, contact Nature of the Northwest Information Center. For a topographic map, ask the USGS for North Sister.

Directions: From Eugene, drive 55 miles east on McKenzie Pass Highway/Highway 126, five miles past the town of McKenzie Bridge, to the junction with Highway 242. Continue east on Highway 242 to the Scott Lake turnoff on the left (north) side of the road. The trail starts across the road.

Contact: Willamette National Forest, McKenzie River Ranger District, 57600 McKenzie Highway, McKenzie Bridge, OR 97413, 541/822-3381.

19 PACIFIC CREST TRAIL TO LITTLE BELKNAP CRATER

4.0 mi/2.0 hrs

west of Sisters in the Mount Washington Wilderness

Map 11.2, page 490

Someday, we'll probably all get a chance to walk on the moon, but why wait another millennium? You'll feel as if you're walking on the moon here when you make your way across the lava field on the Pacific Crest Trail to Little Belknap Crater. The nearby Dee Observatory offers a glimpse through its stone shelter windows of the lava fields and craters in the distance, but they're not so distant that you can't walk to them. It's about two miles to reach the crater summit, and it's unlike any hike around. Thin scraggles of trees struggle to poke up out of the lava surface (you have to admire their determination). The trail is sometimes hard to follow since you're walking right through the lava field, so use the 6,872-foot cinder-and-ash volcanic cone as your beacon, along with its bigger neighbor, the Belknap Crater. From the summit, and actually all throughout the hike, you can see views of the Three Sisters. Just refrain from doing the moon-walk on the crater itself, because it's not the best surface on which to break out the dance moves. If you don't want to risk a twisted ankle on this route, you can also try the paved one-mile Lava River Interpretive Trail, just east of the Dee Observatory.

User Groups: Hikers, dogs, and horses. No mountain bikes are allowed. No wheelchair access.

Permits: Permits are not required. Parking and access are free.

Maps: For a map of the Mount Washington Wilderness and Willamette National Forest, contact Nature of the Northwest Information Center. For a topographic map, ask the USGS for Mount Washington.

Directions: From Eugene, drive 50 miles east on McKenzie Highway/Highway 126 to the town of McKenzie Bridge. Continue five miles east to the junction with Highway 242. (From Sisters, drive west about 15 miles on Highway 242.) Continue east on Highway 242 to McKenzie Pass and the Pacific Crest Trail marker on the left (north) side of the road, just before the Dee Wright Observatory. Note: Highway 242 is often closed until July.

Contact: Willamette National Forest, McKenzie River Ranger District, 57600 McKenzie Highway, McKenzie Bridge, OR 97413, 541/822-3381.

20 PACIFIC CREST TRAIL/ MATTHIEU LAKES
6.0 mi/3.0 hrs

west of Sisters in the Three Sisters Wilderness of Deschutes National Forest

Map 11.2, page 490

Traveling along the old Oregon Skyline Trail, which has been replaced by the good ol' PCT, this loop goes to two shimmering lakes with great views of the Sisters peaks, all lined up for your viewing pleasure—although North Sister is closer, so she kind of hogs the spotlight. You may be sharing the glory with some PC-Ters and their horses, so just nod and smile and you'll be fine. You'll start from Lava Camp (yes, more lava) and come to a junction with the PCT. Head left to start the loop, keeping straight at the loop junction to continue to

North Matthieu Lake, the big bro' of the two lakes. Stick around here to soak in the scenery before continuing the loop to visit the little guy, South Matthieu. Complete the loop by returning to the junction at South Matty, and this time turn right to head back to your car (and some lava walls on the way).

User Groups: Hikers, dogs, and horses. No mountain bikes are allowed. No wheelchair access.

Permits: A free wilderness permit is required to hike here and is available at the trailhead. Parking and access are free.

Maps: For a map of the Three Sisters Wilderness and Deschutes National Forest, contact Nature of the Northwest Information Center. For a topographic map, ask the USGS for Mount Washington and North Sister.

Directions: From Eugene, drive 55 miles east on McKenzie Pass Highway/Highway 126, five miles past the town of McKenzie Bridge, to the junction with Highway 242. Continue east for one mile on Highway 242 to Forest Service Road 900 at the sign for Lava Camp Lake. Turn right (south) and drive .3 mile to the Pacific Crest Trail parking area on the right.

Contact: Deschutes National Forest, Sisters Ranger District, Highway 20/Pine Street, P.O. Box 249, Sisters, OR 97759, 541/549-7700.

21 BLACK CRATER
7.6 mi/5.0 hrs

west of Sisters in the Three Sisters Wilderness of Deschutes National Forest

Map 11.2, page 490

Need to break into a hike gently? Then do some jumping jacks at the parking lot, because this trail cuts you no breaks from the get-go. Instead, it just sails on up 2,351 feet (and you'll feel that last foot, too) through thick mountain hemlock forest to reach the 7,251-foot summit, where you can view North Sister, Mount Washington, and a special bird's-eye view of the McKenzie Pass lava flows. In fact, you can even see as far north as Mount Adams on a clear day—just don't pick a day that's scorching, because this area is renowned for hot, dry weather. The only problem is that Highway 242 doesn't tend to open its pearly gates until July 1, so that leaves the hot summer months or the fall. Choose wisely.

User Groups: Hikers, dogs, and horses. No mountain bikes are allowed. No wheelchair access.

Permits: A free wilderness permit is required to hike here and is available at the trailhead. A federal Northwest Forest pass is also required to park here. The cost is $5 for a day pass or $30 for an annual pass. You can buy a day pass at ranger stations, from private vendors, or through Nature of the Northwest Information Center.

Maps: For a map of the Three Sisters Wilderness and Deschutes National Forest, contact Nature of the Northwest Information Center. For a topographic map, ask the USGS for Mount Washington and Black Crater.

Directions: From Sisters, drive 11.5 miles west on Highway 242 to the trailhead parking lot on the left (south) side of the road (3.5 miles east of the McKenzie Pass).

Contact: Deschutes National Forest, Sisters Ranger District, Highway 20/Pine Street, P.O. Box 249, Sisters, OR 97759, 541/549-7700.

22 CAMP LAKE/CHAMBERS LAKE BASIN
14.0 mi/7.0 hrs to 2.0 days

between the South and Middle Sisters in the Three Sisters Wilderness of Deschutes National Forest

Map 11.2, page 490

Nestled between the South and Middle Sisters (you can still wave at North Sister, but she gets left out of the picture for the most part), the Chambers Lake Basin is a perfect place to overnight and to wipe the sweat off your brow from a handy water source. Traveling from the Pole Creek trailhead, you'll hike for two miles to catch up to Camp Lake Trail, then turn right to lead five more miles to the lakes. Plan a camping trip here if you can, because unless you actually climb the peaks (more on that later in this chapter), this is the clos-

est you'll come to them. The total elevation gain on the trail is 1,200 feet. Keep in mind Highway 242 is usually closed until July, which makes for a perfect summer getaway.

User Groups: Hikers, dogs, and horses. No mountain bikes are allowed. No wheelchair access.

Permits: A free wilderness permit is required to hike here and is available at the trailhead. A federal Northwest Forest pass is also required to park here. The cost is $5 for a day pass or $30 for an annual pass. You can buy a day pass at ranger stations, from private vendors, or through Nature of the Northwest Information Center.

Maps: For a map of the Three Sisters Wilderness and Deschutes National Forest, contact Nature of the Northwest Information Center. For a topographic map, ask the USGS for Trout Creek Butte, Broken Top, and South Sister.

Directions: From Sisters, drive 1.5 miles west on Highway 242 to the junction with Forest Service Road 15. Follow signs to the Pole Creek Trail, 10.5 miles from the junction.

Contact: Deschutes National Forest, Sisters Ranger District, Highway 20/Pine Street, P.O. Box 249, Sisters, OR 97759, 541/549-7700.

23 SHEVLIN PARK LOOP
5.0 mi/2.5 hrs

in Bend's Shevlin Park

Map 11.2, page 490

You're just a javelin's throw away from Bend (well, actually three miles), but you'd never know it. Like many of Oregon's city parks, Shevlin redefines the term "urban" park. If you want to hit some trails and still make it back in time for dinner at the Deschutes Brewery, try the five-mile loop that will take you past and over Tumalo Creek, through Bend's oldest and largest natural park. It's a popular trail with mountain bikers, especially since a paved bike path connects right to the heart of the city.

User Groups: Hikers, dogs, and mountain bikes. No wheelchair access.

Permits: Permits are not required. Parking and access are free.

Maps: For a topographic map, ask the USGS for Shevlin Park.

Directions: From downtown Bend, follow Newport Avenue west, which turns into Shevlin Park Road for four miles. Drive across Tumalo Creek to the parking area. Cross the log bridge over Tumalo Creek to start the trail.

Contact: Bend Metro Park and Recreation Department, 200 Northwest Pacific Park Lane, Bend, OR 97701, 541/389-7275.

24 SOUTH SISTER SUMMIT
11.0 mi/1.0 day

the South Sister Summit in Three Sisters Wilderness of Deschutes National Forest

Map 11.2, page 490

Hovering over the little people and its two other sister peaks, 10,538-foot South Sister is the third-tallest peak in the state. It's also The Peak to Climb, because you don't need any shiny equipment to scale her (except some good hiking boots, water, trail treats, and maybe a tune to hum to distract yourself from the brutal climb). Bring warm clothes, because weather conditions can change at any moment. A dormant volcano, South Sister last blew 2,000 years ago, but after the 5.5-mile climb of 4,758 feet, you may feel like you're about to erupt. A gentler option is Moraine Lake Trail (four miles round-trip), which you'll hit before the climbing really gets under way. This is your last chance to back out—or a good option for those saner souls with you who wish to wave at you from the comfort of the trailhead. The trail is usually not clear of snow until July, so plan accordingly—you'll need the summer to get into shape for it, anyway.

User Groups: Hikers and dogs. No mountain bikes or horses are allowed. No wheelchair access.

Permits: A free wilderness permit is required to hike here and is available at the trailhead. A federal Northwest Forest pass is also required to park here. The cost is $5 for a day

pass or $30 for an annual pass. You can buy a day pass at ranger stations, from private vendors, or through Nature of the Northwest Information Center.

Maps: For a map of the Three Sisters Wilderness and Deschutes National Forest, contact Nature of the Northwest Information Center. For a topographic map, ask the USGS for South Sister.

Directions: From U.S. 97 in Bend, follow signs for Mount Bachelor Ski Area on Cascade Lakes Highway/Highway 46. Drive 33 miles on Cascade Lakes Highway to Devil's Lake Campground on the left side of the highway, at the sign for Devil's Lake Trail.

Contact: Deschutes National Forest, Bend-Fort Rock Ranger District, 1230 Northeast 3rd Street, Suite A-262, Bend, OR 97701, 541/ 383-4000.

25 GREEN LAKES LOOP
13.2 mi/7.0 hrs to 2.0 days

between Broken Top and South Sister in the Three Sisters Wilderness of Deschutes National Forest

Map 11.2, page 490

You don't need to scale a summit to enjoy the scenery near the Three Sisters. Green Lakes Trail gains only 1,300 feet in elevation (a paltry amount compared to the South Sister haul), yet you get more bang for your buck here: Green Lake, a lava field, and a pass where you can squeeze right in between South Sister and Broken Top and still have energy to spare. Be warned that this trail is heavily used, and you'd be wise to wait until the summer crowds have gone back to their real lives and you can slip out on a September weekday. The loop starts on Fall Creek Trail for six miles to Green Lake, which sits snugly between South Sister and Broken Top. Take a short loop around the lake to get all perspectives of the view before completing the loop by turning left after the lake and keeping to the right at all junctions back to the trailhead. If you want to camp here, keep in mind that camping spots fill up quickly and are restricted to designated campsites only.

User Groups: Hikers, dogs, and horses. No mountain bikes are allowed. No wheelchair access.

Permits: A free wilderness permit is required to hike here and is available at the trailhead. A federal Northwest Forest pass is also required to park here. The cost is $5 for a day pass or $30 for an annual pass. You can buy a day pass at ranger stations, from private vendors, or through Nature of the Northwest Information Center.

Maps: For a map of the Three Sisters Wilderness and Deschutes National Forest, contact Nature of the Northwest Information Center. For a topographic map, ask the USGS for Broken Top.

Directions: From U.S. 97 in Bend, follow signs for Mount Bachelor Ski Area on Cascade Lakes Highway/Highway 46, driving 35 miles to the Green Lakes trailhead on the right side of the highway.

Contact: Deschutes National Forest, Bend-Fort Rock Ranger District, 1230 Northeast 3rd Street, Suite A-262, Bend, OR 97701, 541/ 383-4000.

26 TAM MCARTHUR RIM
5.2 mi/3.0 hrs

west of Bend in the Three Sisters Wilderness in Deschutes National Forest

Map 11.2, page 490

Hey, no need to climb up to a top-notch view here. This trail starts high and stays high, starting at 6,500 feet in elevation and moseying up 1,200 feet along its 2.6-mile length. Don't discount the distance, though, because the altitude can make it feel twice as long, slowing your progress to a crawl. But that just gives you more time to check out the view: From the rim, you'll peer down at Three Creek Lake and peer over at Broken Top and South Sister, among the countless other sidekicks of the Sisters area. (Yes, that rascal Three Fingered Jack always seems to make it into the equation; give him a wave.) Keep in mind that the trail may be snowy through July, so save this one for later in the season.

User Groups: Hikers, dogs, and horses. No mountain bikes are allowed. No wheelchair access.

Permits: A free wilderness permit is required to hike here and is available at the trailhead. A federal Northwest Forest pass is also required to park here. The cost is $5 for a day pass or $30 for an annual pass. You can buy a day pass at ranger stations, from private vendors, or through Nature of the Northwest Information Center.

Maps: For a map of the Three Sisters Wilderness and Deschutes National Forest, contact Nature of the Northwest Information Center. For a topographic map, ask the USGS for Tumalo Falls and Broken Top.

Directions: From downtown Sisters, turn south on Elm Street, following signs for Three Creek Lake. Drive 17 miles on Three Creek Road/Forest Service Road 16. The trailhead parking area is to the right shortly down the entrance road to Driftwood Campground.

Contact: Deschutes National Forest, Sisters Ranger District, Highway 20/Pine Street, P.O. Box 249, Sisters, OR 97759, 541/549-7700.

27 TUMALO MOUNTAIN
3.0 mi/2.0 hrs

north of Mount Bachelor in Deschutes National Forest

Map 11.2, page 490

Climb up to 7,775-foot Tumalo Mountain, and let us count the views: Mount Bachelor, Broken Top, and the Three Sisters. Although the trail is a mere 1.5 miles long, which would be a piece of cake on a flat surface, the trailhead begins at 6,350 feet, so if you're feeling a little loopy as soon as you get out of the car, you'll know why. Add in a 1,200-foot climb, and you have yourself a challenge, unless you happen to be spending your nights in an oxygen-deprivation chamber, in which case this will be breeze. Take it slowly and enjoy the scenery on the way up. Keep in mind that the trail can be snowy through July.

User Groups: Hikers and dogs. No mountain bikes or horses are allowed. No wheelchair access.

Permits: A federal Northwest Forest pass is required to park here. The cost is $5 for a day pass or $30 for an annual pass. You can buy a day pass at ranger stations, from private vendors, or through Nature of the Northwest Information Center.

Maps: For a map of Deschutes National Forest, contact Nature of the Northwest Information Center. For a topographic map, ask the USGS for Tumalo Falls and Wanoga Butte.

Directions: From U.S. 97 in Bend, drive on Cascade Lakes Highway/Highway 46 for 27 miles to the Dutchman Sno-Park on the right (north) side of the road.

Contact: Deschutes National Forest, Bend-Fort Rock Ranger District, 1230 Northeast 3rd Street, Suite A-262, Bend, OR 97701, 541/383-4000.

28 FRENCH PETE CREEK
6.0 mi/3.0 hrs

in the South Fork McKenzie River area of Willamette National Forest

Map 11.3, page 491

While the trail actually extends 10 miles one-way, there is a bridgeless creek crossing. Unless you just love to trudge through water, in which case feel free, it's better to turn back at the three-mile mark (you'll know it when you come face-to-face with the river), because the trail isn't maintained after that mark. No worries, though, because you still get to travel through old-growth Douglas fir forest along the rushing French Pete, which makes for a scenic stroll. The total elevation gain is less than 200 feet, so it's just the warm-up you need before hitting other area hikes later in the season. Since you're at low elevation, this trail tends to open earlier than others in the area, which makes for a perfect antidote to spring fever.

User Groups: Hikers and dogs. No mountain bikes or horses are allowed. No wheelchair access.

Permits: A free wilderness permit is required to hike here and is available at the trailhead. A federal Northwest Forest pass is also re-

quired to park here. The cost is $5 for a day pass or $30 for an annual pass. You can buy a day pass at ranger stations, from private vendors, or through Nature of the Northwest Information Center.

Maps: For a map of the Three Sisters Wilderness and Willamette National Forest, contact Nature of the Northwest Information Center. For a topographic map, ask the USGS for Cougar Reservoir and French Mountain.

Directions: From Eugene, drive 40 miles on McKenzie Pass Highway/Highway 126 to Blue River. Continue five miles east past Blue River, and turn right (south) onto Forest Service Road 19. Drive 11 miles south to the French Pete Creek trailhead on the left (east) side of the road.

Contact: Willamette National Forest, McKenzie River Ranger District, 57600 McKenzie Highway, McKenzie Bridge, OR 97413, 541/822-3381.

29 REBEL CREEK/
REBEL ROCK LOOP
11.0 mi/6.0 hrs

in the South Fork McKenzie River area of Willamette National Forest

Map 11.3, page 491

Rebel Rock may sound like the new rage in music, but it's also a pleasant jaunt through old-growth forest. But don't set off for a simple creekside stroll just yet: It also gains a smoking 3,000 feet along the way, adding some ridgetop views to the combination platter. Climbing along the forest and out through a meadow, you'll have unobstructed vistas of the Three Sisters and Mount Jefferson. Combine the Rebel Creek and Rebel Rock Trails for an 11-mile loop by following Rebel Rock Trail to its junction with Rebel Creek, then turn left for the return trip along the creek. Simple? Nope. Worth it? Yep.

User Groups: Hikers, dogs, and horses. No mountain bikes are allowed. No wheelchair access.

Permits: A free wilderness permit is required to hike here and is available at the trailhead.

A federal Northwest Forest pass is also required to park here. The cost is $5 for a day pass or $30 for an annual pass. You can buy a day pass at ranger stations, from private vendors, or through Nature of the Northwest Information Center.

Maps: For a map of Three Sisters Wilderness and Willamette National Forest, contact Nature of the Northwest Information Center. For a topographic map, ask the USGS for Cougar Reservoir, French Mountain, Grasshopper Mountain, and Chucksney Mountain.

Directions: From Eugene, drive 40 miles on McKenzie Pass Highway/Highway 126 to Blue River. Continue five miles east past Blue River, and turn right (south) onto Forest Service Road 19. Drive 14.5 miles to the Rebel Rock trailhead on the left (east) side of the road.

Contact: Willamette National Forest, McKenzie River Ranger District, 57600 McKenzie Highway, McKenzie Bridge, OR 97413, 541/822-3381.

30 CHUCKSNEY MOUNTAIN LOOP
10.5 mi/5.5 hrs

between the Waldo Lake and Three Sisters Wilderness Areas in Willamette National Forest

Map 11.3, page 491

While other, tougher hikes in the area are blanketed in snow, Chucksney Mountain Trail is ready to go. Gaining 2,000 feet in elevation, the trail connects with Grasshopper Trail for a loop that takes you up to 5,760-foot Chucksney Mountain through forests and meadows for views of the Three Sisters and the South Fork McKenzie River below. Start for .25 mile on Grasshopper Trail, then fork right to start your loop. After descending the mountain, hang a left to meet up with Grasshopper again for a 3.5-mile gentle cool-down back to the trailhead.

User Groups: Hikers, dogs, horses, and mountain bikes. No wheelchair access.

Permits: A federal Northwest Forest pass is

required to park here. The cost is $5 for a day pass or $30 for an annual pass. You can buy a day pass at ranger stations, from private vendors, or through Nature of the Northwest Information Center.

Maps: For a map of Willamette National Forest, contact Nature of the Northwest Information Center. For a topographic map, ask the USGS for Chucksney Mountain.

Directions: From Eugene, drive 40 miles on McKenzie Pass Highway/Highway 126 to Blue River. Continue five miles east past Blue River, and turn right (south) onto Forest Service Road 19. Drive 26 miles to Box Canyon Horse Camp on the right side of the road.

Contact: Willamette National Forest, McKenzie River Ranger District, 57600 McKenzie Highway, McKenzie Bridge, OR 97413, 541/822-3381.

31 ERMA BELL LAKES
8.5 mi/4.5 hrs

north of Waldo Lake in Willamette National Forest

Map 11.3, page 491

Erma Bell sure is the Belle of the Ball in these parts. Make that Erma Bells, because you'll pass by three lakes on this gentle path through Douglas fir forest. It's a popular haunt due to the easy path and the three lakes to choose from. First up is Lower Erma Lake, just two miles down. Pass her by if you want to hit a more secluded spot, stopping to check out the waterfall first that separates Lower and Middle Erma Lakes. Then continue another 1.5 miles past Upper Erma to a junction with Williams Lake Trail. Turn left here to hit the lake on your right and another easy five miles back to the trailhead, most likely without the crowds on the return trip.

User Groups: Hikers, dogs, and horses. No mountain bikes are allowed. The first portion of the trail is wheelchair accessible.

Permits: A free wilderness permit is required to hike here and is available at the trailhead. A federal Northwest Forest pass is also required to park here. The cost is $5 for a day pass or $30 for an annual pass. You can buy a day pass at ranger stations, from private vendors, or through Nature of the Northwest Information Center.

Maps: For a map of Willamette National Forest, contact Nature of the Northwest Information Center. For a topographic map, ask the USGS for Waldo Mountain.

Directions: From Eugene, drive 40 miles on McKenzie Pass Highway/Highway 126 to Blue River. Continue five miles east past Blue River, and turn right (south) onto Forest Service Road 19. Drive 25.5 miles to the junction with Forest Service Road 1957. Turn left and drive 3.5 miles to the trailhead in Skookum Campground.

Contact: Willamette National Forest, Middle Fork Ranger District, 46375 Highway 58, Westfir, OR 97492, 541/782-2283.

32 RIGDON LAKES
8.0 mi/4.0 hrs

north of Waldo Lake in the Waldo Wilderness of Willamette National Forest

Map 11.3, page 491

Waldo Lake may bask in the spotlight with a wilderness to call its own, but there are plenty of smaller lakes worth visiting in the Waldo Lake Wilderness, too. A 1996 fire swept through here, and you can get an up-close view of the blackened trees. This easy loop takes you on a tour of three smaller lakes just a short walk away. Starting along the north shore of Waldo, take a right at the junction with Rigdon Lakes Trail to pass by the Upper and Lower Rigdon and Kiwa Lakes. Keep left at all junctions to complete the simple loop back to your car, and then stick around to check out Waldo, the second-largest natural lake in Oregon.

User Groups: Hikers, dogs, and horses. No mountain bikes are allowed. No wheelchair access.

Permits: A free wilderness permit is required to hike here and is available at the trailhead. A federal Northwest Forest pass is also re-

quired to park here. The cost is $5 for a day pass or $30 for an annual pass. You can buy a day pass at ranger stations, from private vendors, or through Nature of the Northwest Information Center.

Maps: For a map of Waldo Lakes Wilderness and Willamette National Forest, contact Nature of the Northwest Information Center. For a topographic map, ask the USGS for Waldo Mountain.

Directions: From Highway 58, three miles west of Willamette Pass, turn north on Waldo Lake Road/Forest Service Road 5897. Drive 12.5 miles, following signs to North Waldo Campground, on Forest Service Roads 5897 and 5898 to the campground. The trail starts near the campground's boat-launch parking area.

Contact: Willamette National Forest, Middle Fork Ranger District, 46375 Highway 58, Westfir, OR 97492, 541/782-2283.

33 WALDO MOUNTAIN
6.0 mi/3.0 hrs

northwest of Waldo Lake in the Waldo Wilderness of Willamette National Forest

Map 11.3, page 491

It's almost a 2,000-foot elevation gain up to 6,357-foot Waldo Mountain Lookout, and it's worth the effort, as you can bear witness to Waldo Lake and its many smaller brothers in the wilderness, as well as its Three Sisters. The trail prefers to save the best for last, so you can concentrate on your climb here, because the views don't start until you get to the top. Retrace your steps here, or if you're feeling particularly energetic, you can add two miles on a loop, taking a right down the east side to hit Waldo Meadows Trail for a return trip.

User Groups: Hikers, dogs, and horses. No mountain bikes are allowed. No wheelchair access.

Permits: A free wilderness permit is required to hike here and is available at the trailhead. A federal Northwest Forest pass is also required to park here. The cost is $5 for a day pass or $30 for an annual pass. You can buy a day pass at ranger stations, from private vendors, or through Nature of the Northwest Information Center.

Maps: For a map of the Waldo Lake Wilderness and Willamette National Forest, contact Nature of the Northwest Information Center. For a topographic map, ask the USGS for Blair Lake and Waldo Mountain.

Directions: From Willamette Pass Highway/Highway 58 at Oakridge, turn east on Salmon Creek Road/Forest Service Road 24. Drive 11 miles to a fork in the road, and veer left onto Forest Service Road 2417. Continue six miles to Forest Service Road 2424. Turn right and follow the road four miles to the trailhead on the right side of the road.

Contact: Willamette National Forest, Middle Fork Ranger District, 46375 Highway 58, Westfir, OR 97492, 541/782-2283.

34 WALDO LAKE LOOP
19.6 mi/1.0–2.0 days

around Waldo Lake in Willamette National Forest

Map 11.3, page 491

The only bummer about this trail is that a large chunk is actually out of view of the lake, and this is a lake you'll want to see. It's the second-deepest natural lake in the state (Crater Lake gets top billing for that prize) and, upon scientific scrutiny, it has been bestowed the honor of being one of the clearest lakes in the world, with water chemistry similar to distilled water's. Cool. But the loop around the lake is still a fabulous one and is quite popular with mountain bikers and runners (many of them training for the Where's Waldo 100K course, which runs in the area, no doubt). It's also relatively gentle, so it's possible as an all-day excursion if you really want to go for it. Short side trails lead to great views of this pristine water, as well as to views of Mount Bachelor, Broken Top, and the Middle and South Sisters. The trail is part of a large trail system, where you can reach Fuji Mountain, Betty Lake, and others. If you want to break it into a two-day trip, you can camp along the route.

User Groups: Hikers, dogs, horses, and mountain bikes. No wheelchair access.

Permits: A federal Northwest Forest pass is required to park here. The cost is $5 for a day pass or $30 for an annual pass. You can buy a day pass at ranger stations, from private vendors, or through Nature of the Northwest Information Center.

Maps: For a map of Willamette National Forest, contact Nature of the Northwest Information Center. For a topographic map, ask the USGS for Waldo Lake.

Directions: From Highway 58, three miles west of Willamette Pass, turn north on Waldo Lake Road/Forest Service Road 5897. Drive 12.5 miles on Forest Service Roads 5897 and 5898, following signs to North Waldo Campground. The trailhead starts from the campground's boat-launch parking area.

Contact: Willamette National Forest, Middle Fork Ranger District, 46375 Highway 58, Westfir, OR 97492, 541/782-2283.

35 THE TWINS
6.6 mi/3.5 hrs

east of Waldo Lake in Willamette National Forest

Map 11.3, page 491

The Twins' cinder cone peaks stand with a view of the Waldo Lake Wilderness, whispering to each other about the local gossip (you know how twins can be), keeping one eye on Waldo and another on the Three Sisters. You can get in on the action yourself by climbing up to the 7,350-foot summit, gaining about 1,500 feet of elevation on the way up this dusty, dry path. From there, you can see their fine view of this interesting wilderness. Take water along, as it can be a hot, dry route.

User Groups: Hikers, dogs, and horses. No mountain bikes are allowed. No wheelchair access.

Permits: A free wilderness permit is required to hike here and is available at the trailhead. A federal Northwest Forest pass is also required to park here. The cost is $5 for a day pass or $30 for an annual pass. You can buy a day pass at ranger stations, from private vendors, or through Nature of the Northwest Information Center.

Maps: For a map of Willamette National Forest, contact Nature of the Northwest Information Center. For a topographic map, ask the USGS for Waldo Lake and The Twins.

Directions: From Willamette Pass Highway/Highway 58, three miles west of Willamette Pass, turn north on Waldo Lake Road/Forest Service Road 5897. Drive six miles to the trailhead, on the right side of the road.

Contact: Willamette National Forest, Middle Fork Ranger District, 46375 Highway 58, Westfir, OR 97492, 541/782-2283.

36 MOUNT JUNE/ HARDESTY MOUNTAIN
9.5 mi/5.0 hrs

south of Lookout Point Reservoir in Umpqua National Forest

Map 11.3, page 491

Imagine climbing up almost 4,000 feet to the top of a summit, only to have your view blocked by a bunch of pesky trees. Well, that's kinda what it's like to hike up Hardesty Mountain these days. The better route is a quick, yet sometimes rocky 1.1-mile trip almost 1,000 feet up to its neighbor, Mount June, who welcomes visitors with open arms and open views of the Willamette Valley and Cascade Range. If you want to feel like you've really earned the views, you can continue on Sawtooth Trail on a ridgeline up to Hardesty Mountain just for the workout, if not for the occasional viewpoints along the way. Retrace your steps for a round-trip of 9.5 miles.

User Groups: Hikers and dogs. No mountain bikes or horses are allowed. No wheelchair access.

Permits: Permits are not required. Parking and access are free.

Maps: For a map of Umpqua National Forest, contact Nature of the Northwest Information Center. For a topographic map, ask the USGS for Mount June.

Directions: From Cottage Grove Ranger Station, drive 17 miles east on Row River Road/Forest Service Road 2400 to Laying Creek Road/Forest Service Road 17. Turn left and continue five miles to Forest Service Road 1751. Turn left and drive 6.4 miles to Forest Service Road 1721. Turn right and drive two miles to Forest Service Road 941. Turn right, continuing a short distance to the trailhead on the right side of the road.

Contact: Umpqua National Forest, Cottage Grove Ranger District, 78405 Cedar Parks Road, Cottage Grove, OR 97424, 541/942-5591.

37 BRICE CREEK
5.5 mi one-way/3.5 hrs

east of Cottage Grove in Umpqua National Forest

Map 11.3, page 491

Traveling past waterfalls and pools and over footbridges, this easy hike is a great way to spend a summer afternoon. Or spring. Or winter, for that matter, since it's a low-elevation trail that gains only 500 feet along its length. Brice Creek Trail follows in the footsteps of Frank Brice Trail, which accessed the Bohemia Mining District in the early 1900s, way before you were born (unless you're a centenarian). Tunnels and mine shafts still line the trail, but keep those hands to yourself if you please. The last mile follows a ditch. Now, ditches aren't known for their scenic beauty, but this one has an interesting history; it used to carry water to generate electricity for a tram at the mill site. An easy amble, some waterfalls, and some mining history thrown in, and you have reason to stick around.

User Groups: Hikers, dogs, mountain bikes, and horses. No wheelchair access.

Permits: Permits are not required. Parking and access are free.

Maps: For a map of Umpqua National Forest, contact Nature of the Northwest Information Center. For a topographic map, ask the USGS for Rose Hill.

Directions: From Cottage Grove Ranger Station, drive 19 miles east on Row River Road/Forest Service Road 2400. Turn right onto Brice

Creek Road/Forest Service Road 2470, and drive 3.3 miles to the West trailhead. Other access points along the road include the Cedar Creek Campground, Lund Park trailhead, and Champion Lake trailhead, all within eight miles of the first trailhead parking area.

Contact: Umpqua National Forest, Cottage Grove Ranger District, 78405 Cedar Parks Road, Cottage Grove, OR 97424, 541/ 942-5591.

38 LARISON CREEK
6.0 mi one-way/3.0 hrs

south of Oakridge in Willamette National Forest

Map 11.3, page 491

Starting from Larison Cove, the creekside stroll gains only 500 feet in elevation along the way, so it's yet another good trail for all types. Stop halfway in to view a clear pool and prime picnic spot (you have to bushwhack a ways, but it's worth the hassle). The path starts to climb from here, so this is a good stopping point if you want a super-simple hike for a six-mile round-trip. If you're planning to enjoy Larison Cove's water, best to steer clear in August, when many of the lakes in the region are closed to all water use during the height of the blue-green algae blooms. Check on conditions before you set out.

User Groups: Hikers, dogs, mountain bikes, and horses. No wheelchair access.

Permits: Permits are not required. Parking and access are free.

Maps: For a map of Willamette National Forest, contact Nature of the Northwest Information Center. For a topographic map, ask the USGS for Oakridge and Holland Point.

Directions: From Oakridge, drive 1.2 miles east on Willamette Pass Highway/Highway 58 to Kitson Springs Road/Forest Service Road 23 at the sign for Hills Creek Reservoir. Turn right and drive .5 mile, forking right onto Forest Service Road 21. The trailhead is 3.3 miles on the right side of the road, near Larison Cove.

Contact: Willamette National Forest, Middle Fork Ranger District, 46375 Highway 58, Westfir, OR 97492, 541/782-2283.

39 MIDDLE FORK WILLAMETTE RIVER
27.0 mi/1.0 day

south of Oakridge in Willamette National Forest

Map 11.3, page 491

Extending for 27 miles along the river, a hefty day trip for many (okay, most), this trail can be accessed from many points along the way. You can choose your distance, or choose a slice from the lower trailhead, which tends to open earlier in the year than the snowy-through-June upper stretches. From the lower trailhead, you'll start through a mixed-growth forest of bigleaf maple and cottonwood, traveling along portions of the old Oregon Central Military Wagon Road. Turn back when you've seen what you want to see, and call it a day.

User Groups: Hikers, dogs, mountain bikes, and horses. No wheelchair access.

Permits: A federal Northwest Forest pass is required to park here. The cost is $5 for a day pass or $30 for an annual pass. You can buy a day pass at ranger stations, from private vendors, or through Nature of the Northwest Information Center.

Maps: For a map of Willamette National Forest, contact Nature of the Northwest Information Center. For a topographic map, ask the USGS for Warner Mountain, Rigdon Point, Emigrant Butte, and Cowhorn Mountain.

Directions: From Oakridge, drive 1.2 miles east on Willamette Pass Highway/Highway 58 to Kitson Springs Road/Forest Service Road 23 at the sign for Hills Creek Reservoir. Turn right and drive .5 mile, forking right onto Forest Service Road 21. Drive 10 miles to Sand Prairie Campground and the junction with Forest Service Road 134. Turn right and follow it through the campground to the parking lot at the picnic area near the river. There are several more access points along Forest Service Road 21, and the lower trailhead is located at Indigo Lake Trail (see listing in this chapter).

Contact: Willamette National Forest, Middle

Fork Ranger District, 46375 Highway 58, West-fir, OR 97492, 541/782-2283.

40 VIVIAN LAKE/ SALT CREEK FALLS

8.0 mi/4.0 hrs

south of Highway 58 in the Diamond Peak Wilderness of Willamette National Forest

Map 11.3, page 491

Think quick: What's the second-highest waterfall in Oregon? Give up? Roll out the red carpet for 286-foot Salt Creek Falls, which you can see on a short .5-mile trip from the trailhead. It may not be as flashy or get as much attention as certain other falls, but it does get its own observation platform. The most powerful waterfall in Southern Oregon, Salt Creek Falls churns out an average yearly flow of about 50,000 gallons per minute (enough water to supply a town of 180,000 people—take that, Multnomah!). After paying your respects and taking a picture, continue on Diamond Falls Loop, passing Diamond Falls before picking up the junction to Vivian Lake, where you'll pass a series of smaller falls. Got your fill of falls? Then continue to the pretty lake for a prime picnic spot.

User Groups: Hikers, dogs, and horses. No mountain bikes are allowed. No wheelchair access.

Permits: A free wilderness permit is required to hike here and is available at the trailhead. A federal Northwest Forest pass is also required to park here. The cost is $5 for a day pass or $30 for an annual pass. You can buy a day pass at ranger stations, from private vendors, or through Nature of the Northwest Information Center.

Maps: For a map of Diamond Peak Wilderness and Willamette National Forest, contact Nature of the Northwest Information Center. For a topographic map, ask the USGS for Diamond Peak.

Directions: From Willamette Pass Highway/Highway 58, five miles west of Willamette Pass, turn south into the parking lot and trailhead for Salt Creek Falls.

Contact: Willamette National Forest, Middle Fork Ranger District, 46375 Highway 58, West-fir, OR 97492, 541/782-2283.

41 YORAN LAKE

10.6 mi/5.5 hrs

south of Highway 58 in the Diamond Peak Wilderness of Deschutes National Forest

Map 11.3, page 491

While many of the area's lakes are within an easy strolling distance of the trailhead, Yoran Lake plays hard to get, requiring a 5.3-mile walk. You won't mind a bit though, because for one it's not as crowded as other trails (although it does receive its fair share of visitors) and for two, it's a pleasant walk through spruce and fir forest, climbing steadily almost 1,150 feet. Yoran Lake sits with a front-and-center view of Diamond Peak, so it's worth the trip in. Keep in mind that this area's lakes have been plagued with blue-green algae blooms and may be closed to water use during August, so check ahead.

User Groups: Hikers, dogs, and horses. No mountain bikes are allowed. No wheelchair access.

Permits: A free wilderness permit is required to hike here and is available at the trailhead. A federal Northwest Forest pass is also required to park here. The cost is $5 for a day pass or $30 for an annual pass. You can buy a day pass at ranger stations, from private vendors, or through Nature of the Northwest Information Center.

Maps: For a map of Diamond Peak Wilderness and Deschutes National Forest, contact Nature of the Northwest Information Center. For a topographic map, ask the USGS for Willamette Pass.

Directions: From Oakridge, drive southeast on Willamette Pass Highway/Highway 58 to Willamette Pass. Drive just beyond the summit to Forest Service Road 5810. Turn right (south) and drive around Odell Lake to the trailhead parking lot on the right side of the road.

Contact: Deschutes National Forest, Crescent Ranger District, 136471 Highway 97 North,

P.O. Box 208, Crescent, OR 97733, 541/433-3200.

42 INDIGO LAKE/ SAWTOOTH MOUNTAIN
9.0 mi/5.5 hrs

southeast of Odell and Crescent Lakes in the Oregon Cascades Recreation Area of Willamette National Forest

Map 11.3, page 491

Check it out: Indigo Lake was named for its color. Intrigued? You should be. It's an easy two-mile walk through fir forest and mountain meadows to the lake itself, plus a mile-long loop around the shores. With Sawtooth Mountain as the backdrop, it's a perfect place to sit and enjoy the water (now would not be the time to try out your black-and-white film; you'll want to capture the intense blue of this pretty lake). But that's not all, folks. If you're up for a climb, pick up Indigo Extension Trail from the north shore, and make your way up for two miles to reach Windy Pass Trail, climbing a steep ridge and 1,400 feet to reach the summit. After getting a view and pictures of the vibrant lake from the top, return via Sawtooth Mountain Trail for a nine-mile loop.

User Groups: Hikers, dogs, horses, and mountain bikes. No wheelchair access.

Permits: A federal Northwest Forest pass is required to park here. The cost is $5 for a day pass or $30 for an annual pass. You can buy a day pass at ranger stations, from private vendors, or through Nature of the Northwest Information Center.

Maps: For a map of Willamette National Forest, contact Nature of the Northwest Information Center. For a topographic map, ask the USGS for Cowhorn Mountain.

Directions: From Oakridge, drive southeast on Willamette Pass Highway/Highway 58 to Willamette Pass. Continue 1.2 miles east to Kitson Springs Road/Forest Service Road 23 at the sign for Hills Creek Reservoir. Turn right (south) and drive .5 mile to a fork, veering right onto Forest Service Road 21. Drive 32 miles to Forest Service Road 2154. Turn left and follow signs to Timpanogas Campground and the trailhead in the day-use parking area.

Contact: Willamette National Forest, Middle Fork Ranger District, 46375 Highway 58, Westfir, OR 97492, 541/782-2283.

43 UPPER ROGUE RIVER/ CRATER RIM VIEWPOINT
18.6 mi/1.0 day

parallel to Highway 230 in Rogue River National Forest

Map 11.3, page 491

Upper Rogue River Trail extends for 49 miles one-way past waterfalls, through the Rogue Gorge (see listing in this chapter), and past campgrounds, all the while sticking near the mighty, rushing river that is the Rogue. But let's be realistic here, are you really going to do 49 miles in one day, and then retrace your steps? Not. Here's an option that accesses the most scenic parts of the trail and gets you away from the campground crowds that tend to frequent the lower sections. Starting from the upper trailhead at the Crater Rim Viewpoint, you'll pass by the Boundary Springs trailhead (see listing in this chapter). Keep right at this junction to continue on Rogue River Trail for four scenic miles of clifftop viewpoints and waterfalls, then dip into the woods for the rest of the trip to Hamaker Campground. As always, you have your options here of retracing your steps or arranging for a personal chauffeur to whisk you from the trailhead in style. Of course, you can always continue on. And on. The trail ends near the Prospect Ranger Station, but it's incredibly difficult to find and not nearly as scenic as this upper half. (While you're there, though, stop in for their helpful advice and detailed trail descriptions.)

User Groups: Hikers and dogs. No mountain bikes are allowed. Horses are allowed only on certain sections of the trail. No wheelchair access.

Permits: Permits are not required. Parking and access are free.

Maps: For a map of Rogue River National Forest, contact Nature of the Northwest Information Center. For a topographic map, ask the USGS for Pumice Desert West, Hamaker Butte, Union Creek, Prospect North, and Whetstone Point.

Directions: From Prospect, drive 12.2 miles north on Highway 62 to the junction with Highway 230. Stay to the left to drive on Highway 230 and continue 18.6 miles north to the Crater Rim Viewpoint and the trailhead on the right. The trail can also be accessed at the Hamaker Campground, Natural Bridge Campground, and River Bridge Campground, all conveniently lined up off of Highway 230.

Contact: Rogue River National Forest, Prospect Ranger District, 47201 Highway 62, Prospect, OR 97536, 541/560-3400.

44 MUIR CREEK
7.8 mi/3.5 hrs

north of Prospect in Rogue River National Forest

Map 11.3, page 491

A berry buffet of huckleberries, blackberries, and strawberries lines this easy path, as do plenty of picnic spots so you can munch on them. Maybe you'll have an unexpected lunch guest, too—deer and elk roam these parts, and you stand a good chance of bumping into one (just say "on your left" and they'll move right on over). Traveling through a fir and pine forest, the trail begins where the Rogue River and Muir Creek meet, and winds past mountain meadows filled with tiger lilies and scarlet gilia.

User Groups: Hikers, dogs, and horses. No mountain bikes are allowed. No wheelchair access.

Permits: Permits are not required. Parking and access are free.

Maps: For a map of Rogue River National Forest, contact Nature of the Northwest Information Center. For a topographic map, ask the USGS for Hamaker Butte.

Directions: From Prospect, drive 12 miles north on Highway 62 to the junction with Highway 230. Stay left and continue 10.3 miles north

on Highway 230. Turn left into the parking area before crossing Muir Creek Bridge. The trailhead is on the north side of the parking area, to the right as you're driving in.

Contact: Rogue River National Forest, Prospect Ranger District, 47201 Highway 62, Prospect, OR 97536, 541/560-3400.

45 MINNEHAHA
6.2 mi/3.0 hrs

north of Prospect in Rogue River National Forest

Map 11.3, page 491

If you hear that an OHV convention is planning to hit the Rogue River area, you'd be wise to steer clear of this trail, which is part of a network of OHV trails in the vicinity. It's also open to bikes, horses, dogs, scooters—just kidding about the last one, but you get the point: It's used by all, and you can see the tracks as evidence that someone was here. Still, it's a level, flat walk along Minnehaha Creek, an old route used in the 1860s by miners and stockmen on their way to the gold mines in the John Day Valley. It passes through a Douglas fir and pine forest and meadows before a climb overlooking the creek and waterfalls below. Check out the lava rock that still remains from the Mount Mazama ash that covered the area 6,800 years ago.

User Groups: Hikers, dogs, horses, and mountain bikes. No wheelchair access.

Permits: Permits are not required. Parking and access are free.

Maps: For a map of Rogue River National Forest, contact Nature of the Northwest Information Center. For a topographic map, ask the USGS for Hamaker Butte.

Directions: From Prospect, drive 12 miles north on Highway 62 to the junction with Highway 230. Stay left and continue 12.2 miles north on Highway 230 to the junction with Forest Service Road 6530 at the sign for Hamaker Campground. Turn right and drive one mile (right after you cross a bridge), then turn right onto Forest Service Road 6530-800. Drive .1

mile to the parking area on the right. The trailhead is on your left, shortly before the parking area.

Contact: Rogue River National Forest, Prospect Ranger District, 47201 Highway 62, Prospect, OR 97536, 541/560-3400.

46 MIRROR LAKES
7.0 mi/3.5 hrs

west of Mount Bachelor in the Three Sisters Wilderness of Deschutes National Forest

Map 11.4, page 492

Passing through small streams and lava features, Mirror Lakes Trail gains just 600 feet in elevation along its 3.5-mile tour. It ends at the Pacific Crest Trail; just turn left to hit the lake, which sits at 5,950 feet elevation with a solitary view of South Sister. You ambitious types can continue another three miles to Nash Lake from the PCT, returning the way you came. It's a slightly lesser-used trail than others in the area, so you may have a little elbow room en route.

User Groups: Hikers, dogs, and horses. No mountain bikes are allowed. No wheelchair access.

Permits: A free wilderness permit is required to hike here and is available at the trailhead. A federal Northwest Forest pass is also required to park here. The cost is $5 for a day pass or $30 for an annual pass. You can buy a day pass at ranger stations, from private vendors, or through Nature of the Northwest Information Center.

Maps: For a map of the Three Sisters Wilderness and Deschutes National Forest, contact Nature of the Northwest Information Center. For a topographic map, ask the USGS for South Sister.

Directions: From U.S. 97 in Bend, follow signs west to Mount Bachelor Ski Area, driving 27 miles on Cascade Lakes Highway/Highway 46. Drive past Mount Bachelor to the Sisters Mirror trailhead on the right (west) side of the road, three miles past the Devil's Lake Campground.

Contact: Deschutes National Forest, Bend-Fort Rock Ranger District, 1230 Northeast 3rd Street, Suite A-262, Bend, OR 97701, 541/383-4000.

47 HORSE LAKE
8.0 mi/4.0 hrs

west of Mount Bachelor in the Three Sisters Wilderness of Deschutes National Forest

Map 11.4, page 492

Mosquito Lake is probably a better name for this lake, as they descend upon you, rubbing their little wings together in anticipation of some fresh blood. And since there aren't a whole lot of other hikers upon which to descend, you'll be a good target. Bring the bug juice, or avoid this place altogether in the buggy early-summer months. Gaining 700 feet in elevation, it's a gentle path to the lake through old-growth mountain hemlock forest. The trail also connects to the Pacific Crest Trail, and you know what that means: loops galore. Since some of the area's trails are not marked, if you try the loop back to the car via the PCT, bring a map along to make sure you're still on course. This route involves taking a left past Colt and Sunset Lakes for a little swap of scenery on the return trip. Otherwise, return the way you came for an easy eight-mile round-trip.

User Groups: Hikers, dogs, and horses. No mountain bikes are allowed.

Permits: A free wilderness permit is required to hike here and is available at the trailhead. A federal Northwest Forest pass is also required to park here. The cost is $5 for a day pass or $30 for an annual pass. You can buy a day pass at ranger stations, from private vendors, or through Nature of the Northwest Information Center.

Maps: For a map of the Three Sisters Wilderness and Deschutes National Forest, contact Nature of the Northwest Information Center. For a topographic map, ask the USGS for Elk Lake.

Directions: From U.S. 97 in Bend, drive 32 miles west on Cascade Lakes Highway/Highway 46, following signs to Mount Bachelor Ski Area, to the Elk Lake trailhead on the left (west) side of the road across from Elk Lake Resort.

Contact: Deschutes National Forest, Bend-Fort Rock Ranger District, 1230 Northeast 3rd Street, Suite A-262, Bend, OR 97701, 541/383-4000.

48 SIX LAKES
5.0 mi/2.5 hrs

southwest of Mount Bachelor in the Three Sisters Wilderness of Deschutes National Forest

Map 11.4, page 492

This is really the Land of Many Lakes, and Six Lakes Trail fits right in. You'll reach Blow Lake in just one mile, then Doris Lake after another easy 1.5-mile hike. Needless to say, it's a hit with families, because you can't beat the simple stroll to two lakes. If you feel ripped off by the trail name, don't worry, you can continue on to smaller lakes. Continue on for six miles total, where the trail ends and you can pick up the PCT (turning left) to reach the more remote Mink Lake. The total elevation gain along the trail is just under 1,000 feet.

User Groups: Hikers, dogs, and horses. No mountain bikes are allowed.

Permits: A free wilderness permit is required to hike here and is available at the trailhead. A federal Northwest Forest pass is also required to park here. The cost is $5 for a day pass or $30 for an annual pass. You can buy a day pass at ranger stations, from private vendors, or through Nature of the Northwest Information Center.

Maps: For a map of the Three Sisters Wilderness and Deschutes National Forest, contact Nature of the Northwest Information Center. For a topographic map, ask the USGS for Elk Lake.

Directions: From U.S. 97 in Bend, drive 34.5 miles west on Cascade Lakes Highway/Highway 46, following signs to Mount Bachelor Ski Area, to the Six Lakes trailhead on the right (west) side of the highway.

Contact: Deschutes National Forest, Bend-Fort

Rock Ranger District, 1230 Northeast 3rd Street, Suite A-262, Bend, OR 97701, 541/383-4000.

49 DESCHUTES RIVER/ DILLON AND BENHAM FALLS
7.0 mi/3.5 hrs

southwest of Bend along the Deschutes River

Map 11.4, page 492

Deschutes River Trail is popular with mountain bikers, white-water rafters, horses, and, well, really just about anyone. So popular, in fact, that separate trails were created for each user (dogs don't get their own trail, though; they have to walk with you, leashed if you please). The riverside trail travels 9.1 miles one-way, passing through Big Eddy Rapids, Dillon Falls, and Benham Falls. You can take your pick, but the most popular sight is near Benham Falls, which has six degrees of separation from a lava flow. The lava spilled, a dam was created, the lake spilled over, and voilà, a scenic falls. In any case, it's a good place to start a walk down Deschutes River Trail, heading north to Dillon Falls for a seven-mile round-trip hike.

User Groups: Hikers, dogs, horses, and mountain bikes. There is wheelchair access at Benham Falls.

Permits: A federal Northwest Forest pass is required to park here. The cost is $5 for a day pass or $30 for an annual pass. You can buy a day pass at ranger stations, from private vendors, or through Nature of the Northwest Information Center.

Maps: For a map of Deschutes National Forest, contact Nature of the Northwest Information Center. For a topographic map, ask the USGS for Benham Falls.

Directions: There are many places to access Deschutes River Trail. To reach the hike suggested above, drive 14.8 miles south from Bend on Highway 97. Turn right (west) onto Forest Service Road 9702 and drive four miles past the Lava Lands Visitor Center to the Benham Falls picnic area and trailhead.

Contact: Deschutes National Forest, Bend-Fort Rock Ranger District, 1230 Northeast 3rd Street, Suite A-262, Bend, OR 97701, 541/383-4000.

50 CULTUS LAKE
10.0 mi/5.0 hrs

southwest of Sunriver in the Three Sisters Wilderness of Deschutes National Forest

Map 11.4, page 492

Starting from the north shore of Cultus Lake, Winopee Trail extends 10 miles to reach the ever-present PCT. Along the way, you'll pass by Teddy Lakes (accessible on a side trail), Muskrat Lake, and the larger Winopee Lake. Day-trippers, pick your pleasure and head back when you can—a good stop is the small Muskrat Lake, where a shelter still stands, for a 10-mile round-trip. Or continue on to Winopee Lake, about three miles down the trail, to add six miles to your trip, which makes for a more remote experience than the popular Cultus Lake. Whatever you do, remember to bring bug juice because the lakes are also quite popular summer retreats for mosquitoes.

User Groups: Hikers, dogs, and horses. No mountain bikes are allowed.

Permits: A free wilderness permit is required to hike here and is available at the trailhead. A federal Northwest Forest pass is also required to park here. The cost is $5 for a day pass or $30 for an annual pass. You can buy a day pass at ranger stations, from private vendors, or through Nature of the Northwest Information Center.

Maps: For a map of the Three Sisters Wilderness and Deschutes National Forest, contact Nature of the Northwest Information Center. For a topographic map, ask the USGS for Crane Prairie Reservoir, Irish Mountain, and Packsaddle Mountain.

Directions: From U.S. 97 in Bend, drive 44 miles west on Cascade Lakes Highway/Highway 46, following signs for Mount Bachelor Ski Area, to the sign for Cultus Lake Resort. Turn right onto Forest Service Road 4635 and drive 1.8 miles, forking right toward the campground, then keep to the right again on a dead-

end gravel road for .5 mile. The trailhead is on the left side of the road.

Contact: Deschutes National Forest, Bend-Fort Rock Ranger District, 1230 Northeast 3rd Street, Suite A-262, Bend, OR 97701, 541/383-4000.

51 PACIFIC CREST TRAIL TO ROSARY LAKES
6.0 mi/3.0 hrs

from Willamette Pass Ski Area to Rosary Lakes in Deschutes National Forest

Map 11.4, page 492

Accessing the Pacific Crest Trail from Willamette Pass, this easy hike travels 600 feet in elevation in three miles to Lower, Middle, and Upper Rosary Lakes. You'll hit Lower Rosary Lake first, the largest of three and a good place to stop for a picnic. Or continue up to the two smaller lakes and save your lunch for the trip back down. Either way, you'll be guaranteed a gentle walk, some views of Pulpit Rock and Maiden Peak on either side, and probably a few PCT hikers along the way, as Willamette Pass is a popular starting and ending point for long-distance hikers.

User Groups: Hikers, dogs, horses, and mountain bikes. No wheelchair access.

Permits: A federal Northwest Forest pass is required to park here. The cost is $5 for a day pass or $30 for an annual pass. You can buy a day pass at ranger stations, from private vendors, or through Nature of the Northwest Information Center.

Maps: For a map of Deschutes National Forest, contact Nature of the Northwest Information Center. For a topographic map, ask the USGS for Willamette Pass and Odell Lake.

Directions: From Oakridge, drive southeast on Willamette Pass Highway/Highway 58 to Willamette Pass. The trailhead is on the left (north) side of the road just past the Willamette Pass Ski Area.

Contact: Deschutes National Forest, Crescent Ranger District, 136471 Highway 97 North, P.O. Box 208, Crescent, OR 97733, 541/433-3200.

52 FAWN LAKE
7.0 mi/3.5 hrs

south of Odell Lake in the Diamond Peak Wilderness of Deschutes National Forest

Map 11.4, page 492

This dusty trail shared by horses travels 750 feet up through fir and hemlock forest to reach Fawn Lake and the junction with Crater Butte Trail. You'll see views of the Redtop and Lakeview Mountains, a perfect setting to set up a picnic on the shores. It's a popular haunt in the Diamond Peak Wilderness, so try to hit this gem in the fall if you can (the trail is generally free of snow from June through November).

User Groups: Hikers, dogs, and horses. No mountain bikes are allowed. No wheelchair access.

Permits: A federal Northwest Forest pass is required to park here. The cost is $5 for a day pass or $30 for an annual pass. You can buy a day pass at ranger stations, from private vendors, or through Nature of the Northwest Information Center.

Maps: For a map of Deschutes National Forest, contact Nature of the Northwest Information Center. For a topographic map, ask the USGS for Willamette Pass and Odell Lake.

Directions: From Bend, drive 50 miles south on Highway 97 to the junction with Highway 58. Turn right (west) and follow signs to Crescent Lake. Turn left onto Forest Service Road 60, and drive 2.2 miles to park in the boat ramp parking area. The trailhead starts from the Crescent Lake Campground.

Contact: Deschutes National Forest, Crescent Ranger District, 136471 Highway 97 North, P.O. Box 208, Crescent, OR 97733, 541/433-3200.

53 NO NAME
1.3 mi/0.5 hr

east of Cave Junction in the Oregon Caves National Monument area of Siskiyou National Forest

Map 11.5, page 493

You have to wonder what happened when the naming committee met with furrowed brows, trying to brainstorm a brilliant adjective to describe this gentle trail. The furrowing is understandable—it's a pretty nondescript trail, though pleasant. If you're already in the area visiting Oregon Caves National Monument, this is your best chance at ditching the crowds. Keep to the left at all junctions (to the right are a couple of dead-ends) along the peaceful path, which goes along a stream and through mixed forest. It's a one-way route, and you'll pop out at the Oregon Caves entrance and the paved road. Just mosey on down the road, back to the parking area, your car, and maybe your awaiting dog, who isn't allowed to take part in the action here (so avoid it on a sweltering day if you're with furry company).

User Groups: Hikers only. No dogs, horses, or mountain bikes are allowed. No wheelchair access.

Permits: Permits are not required. Parking and access to the trails are free; the cave entrance fee is $7.50.

Maps: For a trail map, visit www.nps.gov/orca. For a topographic map, ask the USGS for Oregon Caves.

Directions: From Grants Pass, drive south on Highway 199 for 30 miles to Cave Junction. Turn left (east) onto Highway 46 and drive 19.3 miles to the end of the road at the Oregon Caves National Monument Visitor Center. The trailhead is to the right of the parking lot as you're driving in.

Contact: Siskiyou National Forest, Oregon Caves National Monument, 19000 Caves Highway, Cave Junction, OR 97523, 541/592-2100.

54 CLIFF NATURE INTERPRETIVE TRAIL
1.5 mi/1.0 hr

east of Cave Junction in the Oregon Caves National Monument area of Siskiyou National Forest

Map 11.5, page 493

For a little more of a challenge than No Name, and a great viewpoint to boot, climb 350 feet up this interesting interpretive trail that starts by looping around the cave wall. Those who aced geology will love the little plaques that line the route. Look for curious deer along the trail. As you climb, you reach a bench on top for views of the Siskiyou mountain range below.

User Groups: Hikers only. No dogs, horses, or mountain bikes are allowed. No wheelchair access.

Permits: Permits are not required. Parking and access to the trails are free; the cave entrance fee is $7.50.

Maps: For a trail map, visit www.nps.gov/orca. For a topographic map, ask the USGS for Oregon Caves.

Directions: From Grants Pass, drive south on Highway 199 for 30 miles to Cave Junction. Turn left (east) onto Highway 46 and drive 19.3 miles to the end of the road at the Oregon Caves National Monument Visitor Center entrance. Walk through the visitors center Cave Tour entrance and turn right on Big Tree Trail to connect with Cliff Nature Trail near the cave entrance.

Contact: Siskiyou National Forest, Oregon Caves National Monument, 19000 Caves Highway, Cave Junction, OR 97523, 541/592-2100.

55 BIG TREE LOOP
3.3 mi/2.0 hrs

east of Cave Junction in the Oregon Caves National Monument area of Siskiyou National Forest

Map 11.5, page 493

It's a state of many Big Tree trails, but this guy is one of the largest of the Douglas fir bunch. You'll climb 1,120 feet up on this 3.3-mile loop, traveling through mountain meadows and smaller trees. You'll be glad for the concession stand in the nearby Chateau, because of all the hikes in this area, this is by far the toughest—which means you can lose the rush-hour traffic in and out of the nearby caves.

User Groups: Hikers only. No dogs, horses, or mountain bikes are allowed. No wheelchair access.

Permits: Permits are not required. Parking and access to the trails are free; the cave entrance fee is $7.50.

Maps: For a trail map, visit www.nps.gov/orca. For a topographic map, ask the USGS for Oregon Caves.

Directions: From Grants Pass, drive south on Highway 199 for 30 miles to Cave Junction. Turn left (east) onto Highway 46 and drive 19.3 miles to the end of the road at the Oregon Caves National Monument Visitor Center entrance. Walk through the visitors center Cave Tour entrance to the trailhead.

Contact: Siskiyou National Forest, Oregon Caves National Monument, 19000 Caves Highway, Cave Junction, OR 97523, 541/592-2100.

56 DA-KU-BE-TE-DE
4.8 mi one-way/2.5 hrs

south of Applegate in Rogue River National Forest

Map 11.5, page 493

Let the alarms sound, we have a winner for coolest trail name, which gives a nod to the small Indian tribe who used to live in Applegate Valley. It's an easy, if not the most peaceful, hike along the western shore of pretty Applegate Lake. The trail itself isn't necessarily packed, but here's the rub: You end up passing Hart-tish boat ramp in just .5 mile, and that's when you hit the crowds. It can get a touch confusing, because you have to continue through the parking lot and along a paved walkway on the lake, and then through an open meadow to reach the trail again. (If you get turned around, the helpful guy at the boat-ramp store will steer you right.) The trail ends at Watkins Campground, so this is probably a good hike to do if you're camping there, having a friendly fellow camper drop you off at the trailhead, rather than doing an out-and-back. But you're the boss, so hike it as you wish.

User Groups: Hikers, dogs, horses, and mountain bikes. No wheelchair access.

Permits: Permits are not required. Parking and access are free.

Maps: For a map of Rogue River National Forest, contact Nature of the Northwest Information Center. For a topographic map, ask the USGS for Carberry Creek and Squaw Lakes.

Directions: From Applegate, drive eight miles east on Highway 238 and turn right on Applegate Road. Drive 15 miles to Swayne Viewpoint. Turn into the viewpoint on the left to the parking area. The trailhead starts directly behind the restroom on the right side of the parking lot as you're looking at the lake. Note: Dogs are not allowed in Hart-tish Park, but you can continue through on the trail.

Contact: Rogue River National Forest, Applegate Ranger District, 6941 Upper Applegate Road, Jacksonville, OR 97530, 541/899-3800.

57 GROUSE LOOP
2.8 mi/1.5 hrs

south of Applegate in Rogue River National Forest

Map 11.5, page 493

If you're not up to the challenging Collings Mountain hike (see listing in this chapter) but want a quick quad stretch after sitting around the campground all day, try this short and sweet version. Reaching a fork, take either one (it's a loop, remember?). In the first mile, it gains 700 feet in elevation through old-growth fir and pine forest, to reach the ridgeline for a view of Red Butte and Applegate Lake before descending back to the Grouse Creek Valley and the trailhead.

User Groups: Hikers, dogs, horses, and mountain bikes. No wheelchair access.

Permits: A federal Northwest Forest pass is required to park here. The cost is $5 for a day pass or $30 for an annual pass. You can buy a day pass at ranger stations, from private vendors, or through Nature of the Northwest Information Center.

Maps: For a map of Rogue River National Forest, contact Nature of the Northwest Information Center. For a topographic map, ask the USGS for Carberry Creek.

Directions: From Applegate, drive eight miles east on Highway 238 and turn right on Applegate Road. Drive 15.6 miles to Hart-tish Park, then turn left and park in the day-use area. The trailhead can be tricky to find: You have to walk back up to Applegate Road from the parking area and cross the street to the trailhead. Note: Dogs are not allowed in Hart-tish Park, but are allowed on the trail.

Contact: Rogue River National Forest, Applegate Ranger District, 6941 Upper Applegate Road, Jacksonville, OR 97530, 541/899-3800.

58 COLLINGS MOUNTAIN
14.0 mi/7.0 hrs

south of Applegate in Rogue River National Forest

Map 11.5, page 493

In case you were wondering, and even if you weren't, Collings Mountain was named for two brothers who mined here in the 1850s and '60s. After a gentle start along the Grouse Creek Valley, it's a steep climb up to the ridgetop, gaining 1,000 feet in elevation in the first mile, but then you get all that climbing stuff out of the way and let the views begin. Traveling along the ridge, you can check out the Siskiyou mountain range and Applegate Lake. The trail passes an abandoned miner's cabin, old tunnels, and even an inactive Bigfoot trap (!) along the way. Think it would be cool to saunter into an old mining tunnel? Think twice, because they can be dangerous and the Forest Service has asked us nicely to stay out of 'em. The trail ends at Watkins Campground, passing through the 1981 Watkins fire zone.

User Groups: Hikers, dogs, horses, and mountain bikes. No wheelchair access.

Permits: A federal Northwest Forest pass is required to park here. The cost is $5 for a day pass or $30 for an annual pass. You can buy a day pass at ranger stations, from private vendors, or through Nature of the Northwest Information Center.

Maps: For a map of Rogue River National Forest, contact Nature of the Northwest Information Center. For a topographic map, ask the USGS for Carberry Creek.

Directions: From Applegate, drive eight miles east on Highway 238 and turn right on Applegate Road. Drive 15.6 miles to Hart-tish Park, then turn left and park in the day-use area. The trailhead can be tricky to find: You have to walk back up to Applegate Road from the parking area, cross the street, and turn left; the trailhead sign is on the right as you walk down the road a short distance. Note: Dogs are not allowed in Hart-tish Park, but are allowed on the trail.

Contact: Rogue River National Forest, Applegate Ranger District, 6941 Upper Applegate Road, Jacksonville, OR 97530, 541/899-3800.

59 PAYETTE TRAIL
9.2 mi one-way/5.0 hrs

south of Applegate in Rogue River National Forest

Map 11.5, page 493

If you're camping in the Applegate Lake area and want a longer hike without a lot of effort, you can't go wrong with Payette Trail. Beginning at the French Gulch Campground, the flat trail parallels the eastern shoreline of Applegate Lake for great views of the lake and nearby Collings Mountain. You can either camp overnight along the way in one of the walk-in campsites off the trail, or arrange for a friendly face to meet you on the other side at Manzanita trailhead; it's your choice. Look out for poison oak and ticks along the way.

User Groups: Hikers, dogs, and mountain bikes. No horses are allowed. No wheelchair access.

Permits: Permits are not required. Parking and access are free.

Maps: For a map of Rogue River National Forest, contact Nature of the Northwest Information Center. For a topographic map, ask the USGS for Squaw Lakes.

Directions: From Applegate, drive eight miles east on Highway 238 and turn right on Applegate Road. Drive 12 miles and turn left on Squaw Creek Road over the dam. Drive one mile to the French Gulch parking area and the trailhead on the right. To reach the upper trail-head, continue six miles down Applegate Road from the Squaw Creek Road junction, and turn left at the T-junction onto Carberry Creek Road. Drive one mile to Manzanita Creek Road/Forest Service Road 1041. Turn left and drive two miles to the trailhead and parking area at the end of the cul-de-sac.

Contact: Rogue River National Forest, Applegate Ranger District, 6941 Upper Applegate Road, Jacksonville, OR 97530, 541/899-3800.

60 STEIN BUTTE
9.8 mi/5.0 hrs

south of Applegate in Rogue River National Forest

Map 11.5, page 493

Are you the type who likes to place one foot in one state and one in another? You'll get your chance on Stein Butte Trail, but you'll have to climb to do it (and there's no "Welcome to California" sign on the trail either, so you'll just have to go by feel). Named for one of the many gold prospectors who mined the area in the 1850s and 1860s, the trail takes a brief trip south of the border along the way, gaining 1,400 feet in elevation for 2.5 miles up to 4,400-foot Elliott Ridge. Along the ridge, you can look down at Applegate Lake and across to the Siskiyou mountain range. The trail ends at a junction with Elliott Ridge, where you can turn right to reach the Elliott Ridge trailhead, but you have to walk three miles back to your car along the road, so this is better as an out-and-back hike.

User Groups: Hikers, dogs, mountain bikes, and horses. No wheelchair access.

Permits: Permits are not required. Parking and access are free.

Maps: For a map of Rogue River National Forest, contact Nature of the Northwest Information Center. For a topographic map, ask the USGS for Carberry Creek and Squaw Lakes.

Directions: From Applegate, drive eight miles east on Highway 238 and turn right on Applegate Road. Drive 18.9 miles down Applegate Road to a T-junction. Turn left onto Carberry Creek Road and drive .8 mile to the parking area on the left, across the street from the Seattle Bar sign. From your car, walk a short distance down the gravel road leading from the parking area; the trailhead is on your right. It can be easy to miss since it's hidden from the parking area, but it's well marked once you actually find it.

Contact: Rogue River National Forest, Applegate Ranger District, 6941 Upper Applegate Road, Jacksonville, OR 97530, 541/899-3800.

61 ANDERSON CAMP
1.5 mi/1.0 hr

north of Prospect in Rogue River National Forest

Map 11.6, page 494

If you're the type who likes to feel as if you're on an adventure, and you don't like or need everything mapped out for you, this is for you. But please bring a map along, because it's quite easy to get disoriented out here. The trail is slightly overgrown, which gives it a solitude bonus, and it almost seems to peter out when it hits a couple meadows, so be warned. Switchbacking up to just below the summit of Anderson Mountain (elevation gain on the trail is 1,100 feet), the trail ends at a junction with Rogue-Umpqua Divide Trail and Anderson Camp, a turn-of-the-century sheepherder's camp, where you'll be rewarded with amazing views of the Rogue and Umpqua valleys. You'll be glad you brought along your camera (you did bring one, right?). It's a good idea to memorize exactly which way you came up through the two meadows, because it's easy to get lost. (Ahem.) Also, there's a tricky switchback on the way down that if you miss you'll continue straight into another meadow, creating even more confusion. On the way up, it's an obvious switchback with a sign on a tree pointing to Anderson Camp to the right. On the way down, though, you can easily continue straight without seeing the sign if you don't have your head up. All in all, though, this is a great place

to bring a friend along and enjoy the peaceful scenery for a quick trip that will feel like an adventure.

User Groups: Hikers, dogs, and horses. No mountain bikes are allowed. No wheelchair access.

Permits: Permits are not required. Parking and access are free.

Maps: For a map of Rogue River National Forest, contact Nature of the Northwest Information Center. For a topographic map, ask the USGS for Union Creek.

Directions: From Prospect, drive 6.1 miles north on Highway 62 to Forest Service Road 68. Turn left and drive 2.7 miles, then turn right onto Forest Service Road 6510 (gravel) for 5.8 miles to Forest Service Road 6515. Turn left and drive 6.3 miles to the trailhead on the left. There's no parking at the trailhead, but there are two small turnouts to the right, a short distance both before and after the trailhead.

Contact: Rogue River National Forest, Prospect Ranger District, 47201 Highway 62, Prospect, OR 97536, 541/560-3400.

62 GOLDEN STAIRS
8.6 mi/4.0 hrs

north of Prospect in Rogue River National Forest

Map 11.6, page 494

The name conjures up a "Stairway to Heaven" feeling, gliding up on an enchanted path to an enlightened and breathtaking view. Well, it does start in a stairlike fashion but quickly evens out, and it's decidedly run of the mill for such a fancy-schmancy name, which it got from an alleged gold mine in the area back in the 1860s. Still, it is a good trail for solitude as it ventures into the fir forest and then switchbacks to 5,350 feet up the rocky southern ridge of Falcon Butte (total elevation gain is 1,600 feet). Views include Abbott Butte and Elephant Head, and, after another gentle uphill, the Crater Lake rim.

User Groups: Hikers, dogs, and horses. No mountain bikes are allowed. No wheelchair access.

Permits: Permits are not required. Parking and access are free.

Maps: For a map of Rogue River National Forest, contact Nature of the Northwest Information Center. For a topographic map, ask the USGS for Abbott Butte.

Directions: From Prospect, drive 6.1 miles north on Highway 62 to Forest Service Road 68. Turn left and drive five miles, then turn right onto Forest Service Road 550 for 2.1 miles. Park in a small pullout to the left just past the trailhead marker, which is on the right side of the road.

Contact: Rogue River National Forest, Prospect Ranger District, 47201 Highway 62, Prospect, OR 97536, 541/560-3400.

63 UNION CREEK
8.8 mi/4.0 hrs

north of Prospect in Rogue River National Forest

Map 11.6, page 494

Union Creek is a pretty, flat creekside stroll, but as with many trails that are near campgrounds, it can get a little crowded. Traveling along Union Creek, the trail starts near the day-use area. A sign leads you to the amphitheater over a footbridge, but turn left instead to saunter down the path. It leads past Farewell Bend Campground and right on through Union Creek Campground before turning to leave the tent world behind. The best part of the trail is the upper portion, which is a more peaceful saunter through Douglas fir forest, because you can see Union Falls just .5 mile from the end of the trail.

User Groups: Hikers and dogs. No horses or mountain bikes are allowed. No wheelchair access.

Permits: Permits are not required. Parking and access are free.

Maps: For a map of Rogue River National Forest, contact Nature of the Northwest Information Center. For a topographic map, ask the USGS for Union Creek.

Directions: From Prospect, drive 10.7 miles north on Highway 62 to Union Creek Campground. Turn left and park at the visitors center (there's

no day-use parking at the Campground), to the right immediately after turning from the highway.

Contact: Rogue River National Forest, Prospect Ranger District, 47201 Highway 62, Prospect, OR 97536, 541/560-3400.

64 ROGUE GORGE
7.0 mi/3.5 hrs

north of Prospect in Rogue River National Forest

Map 11.6, page 494

The first part of this trail, traveling along the Rogue River, is nothing to write home about. It's sandy, crowded with people fishing and frolicking in the river, and passes right by and sometimes almost through campsites, so you feel as if you're invading someone's space. But the best things come to those who wait. Soon you'll lose the crowds and gain the view. It's 3.5 miles to Rogue Gorge, where the river rushes through a lava chute. After retracing your steps to the trailhead, take the short trail to Natural Bridge, which was formed by basaltic lava bubbling through the earth and moving through tubes, eventually to be replaced by a river of water. Indians and early settlers used the bridge to cross the river, but you can't. What you can do, though, is head up to a great viewpoint just a short distance up the popular trail, and this time, the view is worth the crowds.

User Groups: Hikers and dogs. No horses or mountain bikes are allowed. No wheelchair access.

Permits: Permits are not required. Parking and access are free.

Maps: For a map of Rogue River National Forest, contact Nature of the Northwest Information Center. For a topographic map, ask the USGS for Union Creek.

Directions: From Prospect, drive 9.7 miles north on Highway 62 to Natural Bridge Campground. Turn left and drive past the campground for .7 mile (turning left at the fork) to the end of the road and the parking area for

Natural Bridge Viewpoint. The trailhead starts to the right as you're looking at the river.

Contact: Rogue River National Forest, Prospect Ranger District, 47201 Highway 62, Prospect, OR 97536, 541/560-3400.

65 PACIFIC CREST TRAIL TO BALD CRATER/BOUNDARY SPRINGS

18.0 mi/2.0 days

north of Fort Klamath in Crater Lake National Park

Map 11.6, page 494

It's possible to do this hike in one day, but you'll want to stick around longer because there are some great camp spots along the way. Starting on the Pacific Crest Trail, you'll walk for 3.2 miles to the junction with Boundary Springs (Red Cone Springs camping spot is a cozy area on a small spring just .5 mile past this junction). On your left you'll pass by the aptly named Red Cone, a red cinder-cone volcano, and see views of Mount Thielsen. Speaking of volcanoes, you'll definitely notice that you're walking on one, as the soft pumice has a way of creeping into your boots no matter how tightly laced they are. Continuing on the gentle downhill hike, you'll pass the small Bald Crater on your six-mile trek to the small, cold Boundary Springs. (If you're overnighting, you'll need to camp .25 mile from the springs.) You can also combine this trail with Spheghum Bog for a loop back to the PCT and your car. As with all the trails in this park, all junctions are clearly marked so it's nearly impossible to make a wrong turn.

User Groups: Hikers only. No dogs, horses, or bikes are allowed. No wheelchair access.

Permits: There is a $10 entrance fee to the park. A wilderness permit is also required for overnight visits as is available at the park entrance.

Maps: A trail map is available at the park entrance. For a map of Crater Lake National Park, contact Nature of the Northwest Information Center. For a topographic map, ask the USGS for Pumice Desert West and Crater Lake West.

Directions: From Fort Klamath, drive 15 miles north on Highway 62 to the West Crater Lake Park entrance. Turn right onto Munson Valley Road, and drive six miles east to Rim Village and the junction with Rim Drive. Turn left (north) onto Rim Drive and continue to North Entrance Road. Turn left and drive three miles north to the Pacific Crest trailhead on the left (west) side of the road. From the north entrance, it's 6.5 miles down the North Entrance Road for the trailhead on the right. Note: The park is usually open from June through November, depending on snow conditions.

Contact: Crater Lake National Park, P.O. Box 7, Crater Lake, OR 97604, 541/594-3100.

66 CLEETWOOD COVE/ WIZARD ISLAND

4.0 mi/1.5 hrs

north of Fort Klamath in Crater Lake National Park

Map 11.6, page 494

Want to get a closer look at Crater Lake's clear, blue water? Cleetwood Cove Trail is the only way to do it. It's a short yet steep drop to the cove, losing 700 feet in elevation, but just remember that you have to climb back up at the end. Also keep in mind that the cove starts at 6,176 feet of elevation, so that combination of steep climb and altitude makes for a tough (but worth it) hike. If you want to get an even closer look at the lake, hop on a boat (the fee is $19.25 for adults) for a tour to Wizard Island, a 1.8-mile round-trip hike up 800 feet to the summit of the cinder-cone volcano, for a panoramic view of the caldera from a different perspective. The boat also cruises around the whole lake for a 1.75-hour guided tour, so you can glide along inside the caldera and see it from all angles. Note: As of this writing, they have added new, environmentally friendly boats, and so the price may be increasing. Also, the boats do not always run on a set schedule, so check before you go if you want to try this hike.

User Groups: Hikers only. No dogs, horses, or bikes are allowed. No wheelchair access.

Permits: There is a $10 entrance fee to the park. A wilderness permit is also required for overnight visits and is available at the park entrance.

Maps: A trail map is available at the park entrance. For a map of Crater Lake National Park, contact Nature of the Northwest Information Center. For a topographic map, ask the USGS for Crater Lake East.

Directions: From Fort Klamath, drive 15 miles north on Highway 62 to the West Crater Lake Park entrance. Turn right onto Munson Valley Road and drive six miles east to Rim Village and the junction with Rim Drive. Turn left (north) onto Rim Drive and continue 4.5 miles past North Entrance Road, to the Cleetwood Cove trailhead, on the right. Note: The park is usually open from June through November, depending on snow conditions.

Contact: Crater Lake National Park, P.O. Box 7, Crater Lake, OR 97604, 541/594-3100.

67 WATCHMAN PEAK
1.4 mi/1.0 hr

north of Fort Klamath in Crater Lake National Park

Map 11.6, page 494

It would be a perfect 10 were it not for the large crowds streaming up the Watchman. But let them look, because the scenery is the best around, in a park packed with views. You'll start on the Rim Trail/PCT Bypass for .25 mile, then turn left and climb up 500 feet to a view from 8,025-foot Watchman Peak that takes in Wizard Island below—plus 360-degree vistas of the clear, blue lake and the omnipresent cinder cone peaks that seem to follow you around the park. It's worth battling the throngs to make it up to this one.

User Groups: Hikers only. No dogs, horses, or bikes are allowed. No wheelchair access.

Permits: A $10 fee is collected at the park entrance. A wilderness permit is also required for over-night visits and is available at the park entrance.

Maps: A trail map is available at the park entrance. For a map of Crater Lake National

Park, contact Nature of the Northwest Information Center. For a topographic map, ask the USGS for Crater Lake West.

Directions: From Fort Klamath, drive 15 miles north on Highway 62 to the West Crater Lake Park entrance. Turn right onto Munson Valley Road and drive six miles east to Rim Village and the junction with Rim Drive. Turn right onto Rim Drive and drive for three miles to the trailhead on the right. Note: The park is usually open from June through November, depending on snow conditions.

Contact: Crater Lake National Park, P.O. Box 7, Crater Lake, OR 97604, 541/594-3100.

68 PACIFIC CREST TRAIL BYPASS/RIM TRAIL
16.0 mi/8.0 hrs

north of Fort Klamath in Crater Lake National Park

Map 11.6, page 494

For viewpoints that the average car tourist who four-wheels it through Crater Lake will never see, check out the Rim Trail. You'll climb steeply up to the west rim of Crater Lake for a secluded view of the clear, blue lake, plus you'll get on a first-name basis with the Devil's Backbone and Hillman Peak along the way. But don't get carried away with the views, because there are truly ankle-twisting climbs and sandy spots. Walking and gawking at the same time can be hazardous to your health. The Pacific Crest Trail didn't pass through these parts until 1995, when the trail was rerouted so long-distance hikers could see the sights too (they'd earned it, after all). Starting from the trailhead, start up the Pacific Crest Trail a short distance to a junction. Turn right as the trail leaves the PCT (give it a wave) then quickly climbs up the crater of Mount Mazama. Enjoy your first viewpoint at Merrian Point, and then begin the seclusion part of the competition, as you continue the climb and leave those flatlanders behind. You can do the hike one-way or connect with any of the other trails in the northwest section of the park to create a big loop.

The trail does meet the road at times, so hikers can also choose to access just part of the trail. At the entrance, you can get a handy trail map for all your options, because the list really does go on. The trails are incredibly well maintained and well marked, so you should never have problems finding your way. After a day of hiking, drop down to the Rim Village, where a burger and cold suds are tapping their toes waiting for you to get done already with this hiking business.

User Groups: Hikers only. No dogs, horses, or bikes are allowed. No wheelchair access.

Permits: A $10 fee is collected at the park entrance. A wilderness permit is also required for overnight visits and is available at the park entrance.

Maps: A trail map is available at the park entrance. For a map of Crater Lake National Park, contact Nature of the Northwest Information Center. For a topographic map, ask the USGS for Crater Lake West.

Directions: From Fort Klamath, drive 15 miles north on Highway 62 to the West Crater Lake Park entrance. Turn right onto Munson Valley Road and drive six miles east to Rim Village and the junction with Rim Drive. Turn left on Rim Drive and continue to the Pacific Crest Trail parking lot on the left side of the road. The trail is on the right (east) side of the road. Note: The park is usually open from June through November, depending on snow conditions.

Contact: Crater Lake National Park, P.O. Box 7, Crater Lake, OR 97604, 541/594-3100.

69 LIGHTNING SPRING
8.0 mi/4.0 hrs

north of Fort Klamath in Crater Lake National Park

Map 11.6, page 494

Crater Lake is one of the clearest lakes in the world. Scientists even came in and measured it with their clear-lake devices and discovered, on June 25, 1997, that they could see down to 142 feet. Whoa. It's also the deepest lake in the country and the seventh-deepest in the world—1,943 feet at its deepest point. It's also the bluest lake in the world. Okay, that last one isn't scientifically proven, but you will definitely think the same when you see it. Crater Lake is simply something you have to see. Now on to the hike: Starting near the rim of the lake, the well-marked Lightning Spring Trail leads four miles to the Pacific Crest Trail. After one mile, you'll hit Lightning Spring itself, which is a small cold spring with a backcountry camping spot. After passing the spring, the path travels down an easy hill along Lightning Spring Creek to the PCT. If you're just getting warmed up, you can turn right (north) on the PCT for a mile to Bybee Creek camping spot, a cozy site near a small cold stream. Continue on to connect with Spheghum Bog, Boundary Springs, and the Red Cone Springs Campground. Or just retrace your steps for some more lake views. The only reason this hike was not given a higher scenery rating is because it doesn't actually give you many views of the lake itself, except at the beginning. But it is good for accessing backcountry campsites, and the view at the start will make your camera start snapping shots by itself.

User Groups: Hikers only. No dogs, horses, or bikes are allowed. No wheelchair access.

Permits: There is a $10 entrance fee to the park. A wilderness permit is also required for overnight visits and is available at the park entrance.

Maps: A trail map is available at the park entrance. For a map of Crater Lake National Park, contact Nature of the Northwest Information Center. For a topographic map, ask the USGS for Crater Lake West.

Directions: From Fort Klamath, drive 15 miles north on Highway 62 to the West Crater Lake entrance. Turn right onto Munson Valley Road and drive six miles east to Rim Village. The Lightning Spring trailhead is on the west end of the parking lot. Note: The park is usually open from June through November, depending on snow conditions.

Contact: Crater Lake National Park, P.O. Box 7, Crater Lake, OR 97604, 541/594-3100.

70 DISCOVERY POINT
2.6 mi/1.5 hrs

north of Fort Klamath in Crater Lake National Park

Map 11.6, page 494

Imagine walking along, lost in your own thoughts—maybe even having a conversation with yourself, anything's possible—when suddenly you come across a massive, clear-blue lake five miles in diameter and surrounded by steep 2,000-foot rock walls. Well, this is where it all happened, oh, about 150 years ago when 21-year-old John Wesley Hillman and his party were out mucking about, trying to find the Lost Gold Mine. Little did they realize they would happen upon a gold mine in a different form. Peering down at the lake, they declared it the bluest lake they'd ever seen. A hundred years later, it would also be declared one of the clearest lakes in the world. So check it all out up this path gaining just 100 feet in elevation to Discovery Point, where you can imagine discovering this amazing phenomenon.

User Groups: Hikers only. No dogs, horses, or bikes are allowed. No wheelchair access.

Permits: There is a $10 entrance fee to the park. A wilderness permit is also required for overnight visits and is available at the park entrance.

Maps: A trail map is available at the park entrance. For a map of Crater Lake National Park, contact Nature of the Northwest Information Center. For a topographic map, ask the USGS for Crater Lake West.

Directions: From Fort Klamath, drive 15 miles north on Highway 62 to the West Crater Lake Park entrance. Turn right onto Munson Valley Road and drive six miles east to Rim Village. The Discovery Point trailhead is at the west end of the Rim Village parking lot. Note: The park is usually open from June through November, depending on snow conditions.

Contact: Crater Lake National Park, P.O. Box 7, Crater Lake, OR 97604, 541/594-3100.

71 DUTTON CREEK
4.8 mi/2.5 hrs

north of Fort Klamath in Crater Lake National Park

Map 11.6, page 494

Traveling from Crater Rim to the Pacific Crest Trail, this path isn't the best for views of the lake but is a good chance to check out the cool old-growth mountain hemlock and pine forest, and maybe even some Crater Lake natives, like black-tailed deer, red fox, coyotes, elk, and porcupines. The trail ends at the PCT junction and the Dutton Creek camp. The forest often gets overshadowed by the clear, blue lake, but it's scenic itself and worth checking out.

User Groups: Hikers only. No dogs, horses, or bikes are allowed. No wheelchair access.

Permits: There is a $10 entrance fee to the park. A wilderness permit is also required for overnight visits and is available at the park entrance.

Maps: A trail map is available at the park entrance. For a map of Crater Lake National Park, contact Nature of the Northwest Information Center. For a topographic map, ask the USGS for Crater Lake West.

Directions: From Fort Klamath, drive 15 miles north on Highway 62 to the West Crater Lake Park entrance. Turn right onto Munson Valley Road and drive six miles east to Rim Village. The Dutton Creek trailhead is at the south end of Rim Village. Note: The park is usually open from June through November, depending on snow conditions.

Contact: Crater Lake National Park, P.O. Box 7, Crater Lake, OR 97604, 541/594-3100.

72 GARFIELD PEAK
3.4 mi/1.5 hrs

north of Fort Klamath in Crater Lake National Park

Map 11.6, page 494

Although it's a short trip, you do gain 1,000 feet in elevation, and when you're already starting at 7,000 feet, that can translate to high marks in the heavy-breathing department. The trail leads up to Garfield Peak for a panoramic view of the lake, and of Phantom Ship, a ship-shaped island that protrudes 169 feet above the water. As with all hikes in the Crater Lake area, you'll want to bring your camera along to capture the crystal-clear and deep-blue waters of this cool area.

User Groups: Hikers only. No dogs, horses, or bikes are allowed. No wheelchair access.

Permits: There is a $10 entrance fee to the park. A wilderness permit is also required for overnight visits and is available at the park entrance.

Maps: A trail map is available at the park entrance. For a map of Crater Lake National Park, contact Nature of the Northwest Information Center. For a topographic map, ask the USGS for Crater Lake West and Crater Lake East.

Directions: From Fort Klamath, drive 15 miles north on Highway 62 to the West Crater Lake Park entrance. Turn right onto Munson Valley Road and drive six miles east to Rim Village. The Garfield Peak trailhead is on the east side of the Crater Lake Lodge. Note: The park is usually open from June through November, depending on snow conditions.

Contact: Crater Lake National Park, P.O. Box 7, Crater Lake, OR 97604, 541/594-3100.

73 MOUNT SCOTT
5.0 mi/2.5 hrs

north of Fort Klamath in Crater Lake National Park

Map 11.6, page 494

It seems that every hike in the Crater Lake area has a different claim to fame. Mount Scott, at 8,929 feet, holds the prize for the tallest peak in the park and for the best views of the park's cinder cones, the lake below, and neighboring peaks (and the most strenuous climb to get there, gaining 1,500 feet in elevation). Keep in mind that you're starting at high elevation to begin with, so you may wheeze on this hike more than you would at sea level.

User Groups: Hikers only. No dogs, horses, or bikes are allowed. No wheelchair access.

Permits: There is a $10 entrance fee to the park.

A wilderness permit is also required for overnight visits and is available at the park entrance.

Maps: A trail map is available at the park entrance. For a map of Crater Lake National Park, contact Nature of the Northwest Information Center. For a topographic map, ask the USGS for Crater Lake East.

Directions: From Fort Klamath, drive 15 miles north on Highway 62 to the West Crater Lake Park entrance. Turn right onto Munson Valley Road and drive six miles east to Rim Village and the junction with Rim Drive. Turn right onto Rim Drive and drive for 14 miles around the east side of the crater to the Mount Scott trailhead on the right side of the road. Note: The park is usually open from June through November, depending on snow conditions.

Contact: Crater Lake National Park, P.O. Box 7, Crater Lake, OR 97604, 541/594-3100.

74 CASTLE CREST WILDFLOWER GARDEN
1.0 mi/0.5 hr

north of Fort Klamath in Crater Lake National Park

Map 11.6, page 494

If you're a fool for flowers, mark this one high on your list. Save it for July or August, and then tune in to the must-see meadows. The easy one-mile loop gains 500 feet in elevation to tour right through wildflower blooms. It's a perfect ending or warm-up for a day at Crater Lake, and since it's so short, you can combine it with several other trails in the park for a full day of hiking.

User Groups: Hikers only. No dogs, horses, or bikes are allowed. No wheelchair access.

Permits: There is a $10 entrance fee to the park. A wilderness permit is also required for overnight visits and is available at the park entrance.

Maps: A trail map is available at the park entrance. For a map of Crater Lake National Park, contact Nature of the Northwest Information Center. For a topographic map, ask the USGS for Crater Lake West and Crater Lake East.

Directions: From Fort Klamath, drive 15 miles north on Highway 62 to the West Crater Lake Park entrance. Turn right onto Munson Valley Road and drive six miles east to Rim Village. The trailhead starts opposite the park headquarters. Note: The park is usually open from June through November, depending on snow conditions.

Contact: Crater Lake National Park, P.O. Box 7, Crater Lake, OR 97604, 541/594-3100.

75 CRATER PEAK
6.4 mi/3.5 hrs

north of Fort Klamath in Crater Lake National Park

Map 11.6, page 494

For views of Crater Lake itself, you'll need to hit the other viewpoints listed in this chapter. But for views of the surrounding cinder-cone volcanoes and peaks, not to mention the forest itself plus a 1,000-foot climb, take a walk up the crater itself to its 7,265-foot views of the southern crater rim—as well as surrounding peaks like Goose Nest and Union Peak. It's a tough haul, considering you're already starting out at 6,500 feet, so take it slow and take in the scenery on the way.

User Groups: Hikers only. No dogs, horses, or bikes are allowed. No wheelchair access.

Permits: A $10 fee is collected at the park entrance. A wilderness permit is also required for overnight visits and is available at the park entrance.

Maps: A trail map is available at the park entrance. For a map of Crater Lake National Park, contact Nature of the Northwest Information Center. For a topographic map, ask the USGS for Crater Lake East and Maklaks Crater.

Directions: From Fort Klamath, drive 15 miles north on Highway 62 to the West Crater Lake Park entrance. Turn right onto Munson Valley Road and drive six miles east to Rim Village and the junction with Rim Drive. Turn right onto Rim Drive to the trailhead on the right side of the road. Note: The park is usu-

ally open from June through November, depending on snow conditions.

Contact: Crater Lake National Park, P.O. Box 7, Crater Lake, OR 97604, 541/594-3100.

76 COLD SPRINGS
5.2 mi/2.5 hrs

east of Prospect in Rogue River National Forest

Map 11.6, page 494

This is an incredibly simple trail to follow—thanks to the OHV tracks, it's wide enough to walk hand in hand with your hiking partner if that's what you feel like. At first you almost feel as if you're in a museum rather than a forest, because for once you can actually see what you're walking through, unlike other hikes, where you're so in the thick of things you have no perspective on the situation. Sure, some true wilderness folk may sniff at this trail because of its gentle course and OHV tracks, but it's surprisingly peaceful, and there's plenty to gawk at. After two miles, you'll come to a meadow clearing, with views across the valley to Bald Top. Wildflowers like Indian paintbrush, dwarf lupine, and larkspur are out in the early summer, and since the road in tends to be open in May, you'll have a good shot at seeing them. The trail ends at the unremarkable springs, so don't expect much there. The beauty is really just a walk down the peaceful path with wildflower meadows and a view you'll most likely have all to yourself. Word has it that Paul Bunyan's grave is also on this spot, but good luck finding it (and if you do, give me a call, because we searched for hours).

User Groups: Hikers, dogs, mountain bikes and horses. No wheelchair access.

Permits: Permits are not required. Parking and access are free.

Maps: For a map of Rogue River National Forest, contact Nature of the Northwest Information Center. For a topographic map, ask the USGS for Red Blanket Mountain.

Directions: From Prospect, drive one mile east on Prospect-Butte Falls Highway and turn left on Red Blanket Road. Drive .3 mile and turn left onto gravel Forest Service Road 6205. Drive four miles and turn left onto Forest Service Road 6205-100. Continue 7.3 miles to the parking pullout on the left. The trailhead is on the right across the road.

Contact: Rogue River National Forest, Prospect Ranger District, 47201 Highway 62, Prospect, OR 97536, 541/560-3400.

77 VARMINT CAMP
6.2 mi/3.0 hrs

east of Prospect in Rogue River National Forest

Map 11.6, page 494

To beat the heat, head to Varmint Camp. It tours past Varmint Creek along a thick and shady forest of bigleaf maple and Shasta red fir. It crosses the creek, which doesn't have bridges, so if you really want to cool off, now's your chance (although it's best to steer clear when the water levels are high). The trail then passes along a mountain meadow filled with wildflowers and wild onion in the summer. When it hits the road at mile 3.1, hit the road back home, retracing your steps.

User Groups: Hikers, dogs, mountain bikes, and horses. No wheelchair access.

Permits: Permits are not required. Parking and access are free.

Maps: For a map of Rogue River National Forest, contact Nature of the Northwest Information Center. For a topographic map, ask the USGS for Red Blanket Mountain.

Directions: From Prospect, drive one mile east on Prospect-Butte Falls Highway and turn left on Red Blanket Road. Drive .3 mile and turn left onto gravel Forest Service Road 6205. Drive 3.1 miles to Forest Service Road 830 and continue 10 miles to the trailhead on the left, parking at the side of the road.

Contact: Rogue River National Forest, Prospect Ranger District, 47201 Highway 62, Prospect, OR 97536, 541/560-3400.

78 SEVENMILE
3.5 mi/1.5 hrs

northwest of Klamath Falls in Winema National Forest

Map 11.6, page 494

Like the name suggests, the trail follows Sevenmile Creek. Unlike the name suggests, it's 1.75 miles one-way. Well, if you're really a stickler for numbers, you can tack on some miles when you access the Pacific Crest Trail. But that part comes later. The relatively flat trail gains less than 500 feet as it travels along the creek through lodgepole pine forest before leaving it behind to climb along the slopes of the Sevenmile Marsh. It ends at a junction with the Pacific Crest Trail, where you can turn left and continue three miles to Sevenmile Lakes Basin, part of the Sky Lakes Basin.

User Groups: Hikers and dogs. No horses or mountain bikes are allowed. No wheelchair access.

Permits: No passes are required. Parking and access are free.

Maps: For a map of Winema National Forest, contact Nature of the Northwest Information Center. For a topographic map, ask the USGS for Devil's Peak.

Directions: From Klamath Falls, drive 25.3 miles west on Highway 140 and turn right on Westside Road. Drive 6.8 miles and turn left onto Forest Service Road 3330. Drive 2.9 miles on gravel Forest Service Road 3330, then turn left onto 3334. Go 5.5 miles to the end of road, the parking area, and the trailhead.

Contact: Winema National Forest, Klamath Ranger District, 1936 California Avenue, Klamath Falls, OR 97601, 541/885-3400.

79 NANNIE CREEK TRAIL TO SNOW LAKES
13.2 mi/6.5 hrs to 2.0 days

northwest of Klamath Falls in the Sky Lakes Wilderness of Winema National Forest

Map 11.6, page 494

Your heart will be racing the moment you step out of the car, not only from the high elevation (starting at 6,000 feet), but also from the long switchbacks that begin as soon as you set a hiking boot on this rocky trail. Soon you'll enter the cool forest to refresh you as your body temperature rises a couple degrees. Nannie Creek Trail travels up the slope of Lather Mountain and then levels out to pass Puck Lake and to join up with Snow Lakes Trail. This climbs past clear alpine lakes (where you can camp overnight if you want) and heads up steep rocky ridges for viewpoints on both sides before gaining nearly 1,000 feet in just under a mile to end at the Pacific Crest Trail. Keep in mind that trails are not always marked in this area, so you should bring a map along if you want to try this route.

User Groups: Hikers and dogs. No horses or mountain bikes are allowed. No wheelchair access.

Permits: No passes are required. Parking and access are free.

Maps: For a map of Winema National Forest, contact Nature of the Northwest Information Center. For a topographic map, ask the USGS for Devil's Peak and Pelican Butte.

Directions: From Klamath Falls, drive 25.3 miles west on Highway 140 and turn right on Westside Road. Drive 2.3 miles to gravel Forest Service Road 3484. Turn left and drive 5.3 miles to the road's end and the trailhead, which starts just to the right of the trailhead sign.

Contact: Winema National Forest, Klamath Ranger District, 1936 California Avenue, Klamath Falls, OR 97601, 541/885-3400.

80 CHERRY CREEK TRAIL TO SKY LAKES BASIN
11.0 mi/5.5 hrs to 2.0 days
northwest of Klamath Falls in the Sky Lakes Wilderness of Winema National Forest

Map 11.6, page 494

You'll be greeted right off the bat by the sting of pesky mosquitoes who have come to personally welcome you to Cherry Creek. (Bring your bug juice.) Traveling through the Cherry Creek Natural Research Area, which was carved by glaciers, you'll also be greeted with a gradual climb you'll barely notice at first, one of those creeping-up-on-you climbs where you wonder why you're suddenly out of breath. Then the real climb begins about three miles in before popping out at the scenic Sky Lakes basin (with plenty of campsites) and to Trapper Lake. Keep in mind that this trail has some creek crossings, so save it for later in the summer, when the water level is lower. The total elevation gain on the hike is 1,400 feet.

User Groups: Hikers and dogs. No horses or mountain bikes are allowed. No wheelchair access.

Permits: No passes are required. Parking and access are free.

Maps: For a map of Winema National Forest, contact Nature of the Northwest Information Center. For a topographic map, ask the USGS for Pelican Butte and Crystal Spring.

Directions: From Klamath Falls, drive 25.3 miles west on Highway 140 and turn right on Westside Road. Drive one mile to gravel Forest Service Road 3450. Turn left and drive 1.8 miles to the road's end and the trailhead.

Contact: Winema National Forest, Klamath Ranger District, 1936 California Avenue, Klamath Falls, OR 97601, 541/885-3400.

81 FISH LAKE
10.0 mi/5.0 hrs
northeast of Ashland in Rogue River National Forest

Map 11.6, page 494

Traveling along the North Fork of Little Butte Creek, you'll pass through old-growth forest and small meadows. But the biggest hits on this trail are the lava features: About .5 mile from the trail's end at High Lakes Trail, the path crosses Cascade Canal, an 11-mile canal built in the 1900s to carry water from Fourmile Lake to Fish Lake. Water runs through the lava tube for one mile before ending at Fish Lake. You'll also get a glimpse of the Brown Mountain lava flows near the trail's end. And probably the best part about it, halfway up, is Fish Lake, which is a good place to grab some grub at the store there for a picnic. (As with

any trail that leads through a campground, you'll have company for stretches of the trail.)
User Groups: Hikers, dogs, and mountain bikes. No horses are allowed. No wheelchair access.
Permits: Permits are not required. Parking and access are free.
Maps: For a map of Rogue River National Forest, contact Nature of the Northwest Information Center. For a topographic map, ask the USGS for Mount McLoughlin.
Directions: From Ashland, drive two miles east to Dead Indian Memorial Highway. Turn left and drive for 21.8 miles, then turn left onto Highway 37. Continue 7.6 miles to the trailhead on the right, just before North Fork Campground.
Contact: Rogue River National Forest, Ashland Ranger District, 645 Washington Street, Ashland, OR 97520, 541/552-2900.

82 BROWN MOUNTAIN
10.6 mi/7.5 hrs

northeast of Ashland in Rogue River National Forest

Map 11.6, page 494

Huckleberry and wild-mushroom pickers get serious about searching through forests to find these sometimes-hidden treasures. They'll love this trail, which is lined with the little guys. Following the South Fork of Little Butte Creek, the path scoots around the edge of Brown Mountain, but you can't really get a glimpse of it until you hit about 3.5 miles. The trail gains 800 feet on the dot, ending at the Pacific Crest Trail.
User Groups: Hikers, dogs, mountain bikes, and horses. No wheelchair access.
Permits: A federal Northwest Forest pass is required to park here. The cost is $5 for a day pass or $30 for an annual pass. You can buy a day pass at ranger stations, from private vendors, or through Nature of the Northwest Information Center.
Maps: For a map of Rogue River National Forest, contact Nature of the Northwest Information Center. For a topographic map, ask the USGS for Brown Mountain.

Directions: From Ashland, drive two miles east to Dead Indian Memorial Highway. Turn left and drive 21.8 miles to Forest Service Road 37. Turn left and drive six miles to Forest Service Road 3705 (a paved, one-lane road). Turn right and drive 3.2 miles to the trailhead and small parking turnout at the side of the road.
Contact: Rogue River National Forest, Ashland Ranger District, 645 Washington Street, Ashland, OR 97520, 541/522-2900.

83 BEAVER DAM
4.2 mi/2.0 hrs

northeast of Ashland in Rogue River National Forest

Map 11.6, page 494

A convention of creeks meets at Beaver Dam Trail: Beaver Dam itself is the ringleader of the operation, followed by Daley and Deadwood Creeks, which meet to travel through willows and beaver ponds. The path connects Beaver Dam and Daley Creek trails to form a partial loop through fir and pine forest. A particularly industrious plant that thrives in this area is the pacific yew, with red, peeling bark and short, dark-green needles (don't go gnawing at it, it's poisonous). Native Americans used it for archery bows and canoe paddles, and it has even come in handy in cancer research. Also look out for beaver-gnawed branches and woodpeckers along the peaceful path.
User Groups: Hikers and dogs. No mountain bikes or horses are allowed. No wheelchair access.
Permits: Permits are not required. Parking and access are free.
Maps: For a map of Rogue River National Forest, contact Nature of the Northwest Information Center. For a topographic map, ask the USGS for Brown Mountain.
Directions: From Ashland, drive two miles east to Dead Indian Memorial Highway. Turn left and drive 21.8 miles to Forest Service Road 37. Turn left and drive 1.5 miles to the trailhead on the right, just before Daley Creek Campground.
Contact: Rogue River National Forest, Ashland

Ranger District, 645 Washington Street, Ashland, OR 97520, 541/522-2900.

84 VARNEY CREEK TRAIL TO MOUNTAIN LAKES LOOP

17.0 mi/2.0 days

northwest of Klamath Falls in the Mountain Lakes Wilderness of Winema National Forest

Map 11.6, page 494

Crater Lake and Newberry Crater may get more attention because they're so easy to get to by car, but this unique caldera is reachable only by hiking in, which means you lose the crowds, gain the solitude. Eight peaks form the rim of the Mountain Lakes caldera, surrounding many smaller lakes that you can loop around on this 8.2-mile tour. Two backpacking musts: a camera and bug repellent, because it's thick with mosquitoes. Camp in this surreal setting for the night, but remember to set up tent away from water sources. Mountain Lakes Loop Trail is 4.5 miles down Varney Creek Trail, which is a peaceful path through dense forest and over footbridges across the creek. The trail is also accessible from Clover Creek Trail, which comes to the Mountain Lakes Loop junction at 3.3 miles.

User Groups: Hikers, dogs, and horses. No mountain bikes are allowed. No wheelchair access.

Permits: Permits are not required. Parking and access are free.

Maps: For a map of Winema National Forest, contact Nature of the Northwest Information Center. For a topographic map, ask the USGS for Pelican Bay and Aspen Lake.

Directions: From Klamath Falls, drive 21.2 miles west on Highway 140 and turn left on gravel Forest Service Road 3637. Drive 1.7 miles and turn left on Forest Service Road 3664. Continue two miles to the end of the road and the parking area. The trailhead is to the right as you're driving in. To reach Clover Creek Trail from Ashland, drive two miles east to Dead Indian Memorial Highway. Turn left and drive 28.8 miles, then turn right onto Clover Creek Road. Drive 5.8 miles

and turn left onto gravel Forest Service Road 3852. Drive 3.2 miles and park in the pullout to the right. The trailhead is to the right as you walk down the road past the pullout.

Contact: Winema National Forest, Klamath Ranger District, 1936 California Avenue, Klamath Falls, OR 97601, 541/885-3400.

85 GRIZZLY PEAK

6.0 mi/3.0 hrs

northeast of Ashland and west of Dead Indian Memorial Highway

Map 11.6, page 494

Passing through mixed fir and pine forest, you'll start climbing right away, three miles up to the 5,922-foot summit of Grizzly Peak. Only about 10 miles north of Ashland, the peak is a popular trail for a view to see how things are faring a little south of the border. If you've ever wanted to be a fly on the wall and peer down at a city, you'll have a great vantage point of Ashland below, plus the Rogue River Valley, Mount McLoughlin, Diamond Peak, and Mount Shasta. Along the way, don't be surprised to see elk and deer (alas, no grizzlies). In August 2003, this trail was closed due to the East Antelope fire; it was reopened in May 2004.

User Groups: Hikers, dogs, mountain bikes, and horses. No wheelchair access.

Permits: Permits are not required. Parking and access are free.

Maps: For a topographic map, ask the USGS for Grizzly Peak.

Directions: From Ashland, drive two miles east to Dead Indian Memorial Highway. Turn left and drive 6.7 miles to Shale City Road. Turn left onto Shale City Road and drive three miles, then turn left on unmarked road 38-2E-9.2 (there are signs to Grizzly Peak). Drive .8 mile, then fork left for .8 mile and drive up to the end of the road and the parking area. The trailhead starts just south of the parking area, up a short hill.

Contact: Bureau of Land Management, Medford District Office, 3040 Biddle Road, Medford, OR 97504, 541/618-2200.

Chapter 12

© KEVIN FOREMAN

Southeast Oregon

Southeast Oregon

Take a gander at the surface area covered in the Southeast Oregon chapter map. Now count how many hikes are in this area. Get the point? There's not a lot by way of trails in the whole region. So if you crave solitude, if you crave the true wilderness experience, if you crave looking out on a vast expanse of desert and screaming at the top of your lungs, here's your chance.

Rewind . . . Desert? That's right. Although Oregon is probably (okay, definitely) known for the wet stuff, the state is actually mostly desert, most of which lies in the southeast region. This region includes Fremont-Winema National Forest, Gearhart Wilderness, and Steens Mountain, and also dips into the southeast portion of the Deschutes to bring Newberry Crater National Monument and Paulina Peak into the picture.

First off the bat, and right off the main drag of Highway 97, are the Newberry Lava Caves, which come courtesy of their neighbor to the south, Newberry Volcano. Four short and sweet walks are the perfect antidotes to the area's notoriously hot, dry summer days.

Just to the south, in the southeast corner of Deschutes National Forest, Newberry Crater National Monument and Paulina Peak offer short trips to Paulina Falls, a loop around Paulina Lake, and a steep climb up to 7,985-foot Paulina Peak. The Newberry Volcano erupted 1,300 years ago, resulting in lava—and lots of it. You can walk through it, including all 170 million cubic yards of the Obsidian Flow.

If it's solitude you're after, you can't find a better place in the state to be all by yourself than Gearhart Wilderness, in Fremont-Winema National Forest, located in the southwestern part of this region. Only three trails slice through this 22,823-acre wilderness area known as the

"Oregon Outback." Over 300 species of fish and wildlife call the Fremont-Winema forest home, including mule deer, Rocky Mountain elk, and antelope.

And then there's the ever-expansive desert. Driving through this barren land, don't be surprised to see a tumbleweed cross your path (hey, they have to get to the other side, too). Steens Mountain is right in the heart of High Desert Country, in the southeastern corner of this region, and you don't have to climb far to see the sights. You can drive straight up the scenic road to just a quarter mile shy of the 9,733-foot summit itself, with viewpoints along the way of the deep green Kiger Gorge, the steep canyon and the desert valley below, and Wildhorse Lake, sitting pretty 1,000 feet below the summit.

Above all, what you'll notice driving through this area is the lack of people. Although the southeast region comprises roughly one-fourth of the state, it's remarkably unpopulated. The largest town is Burns, in the north-central part of the region, with a head count of just 3,064. Small towns dot the region, and they move at a different pace. Quick illustration of my point: While researching hikes in this area, I was buying trail food with my ATM card, and the lovely lady behind the desk just wrote down my number on a piece of paper, drew a long line underneath with an X, and handed me a pen carved out of wood to sign. I grasped the cumbersome pen and looked at her. "That's a new one," I laughed. "Honey, you're in the middle of nowhere," she replied. I couldn't have said it better myself. After all, with lava flows, caves, volcanoes, desert valleys, deep gorges, and remote wilderness, there's no room left for many people.

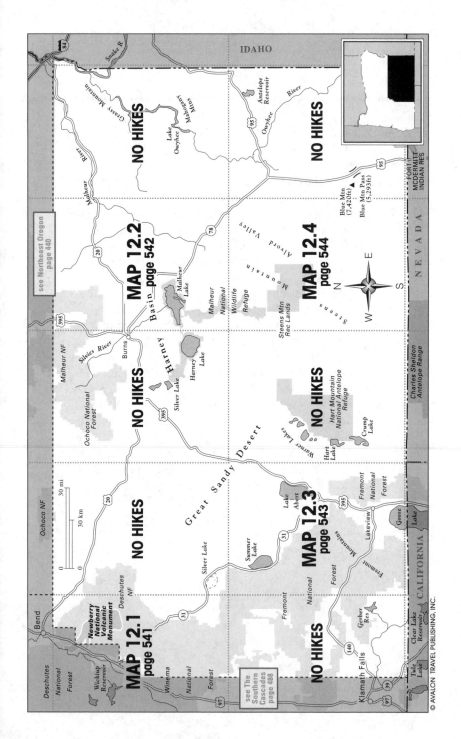

Map 12.1

Hikes 1–6
Pages 545–547

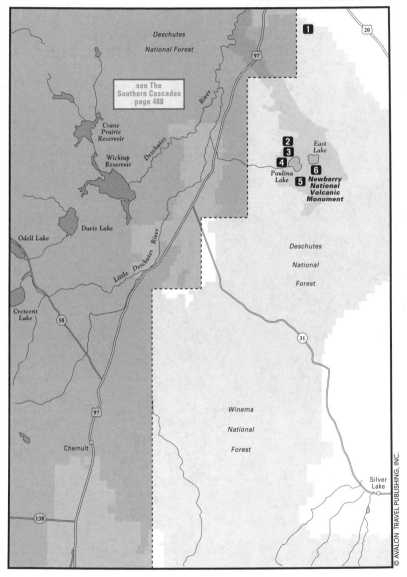

Map 12.2

Hike 7
Page 548

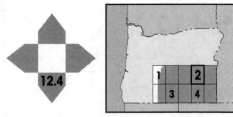

12.4

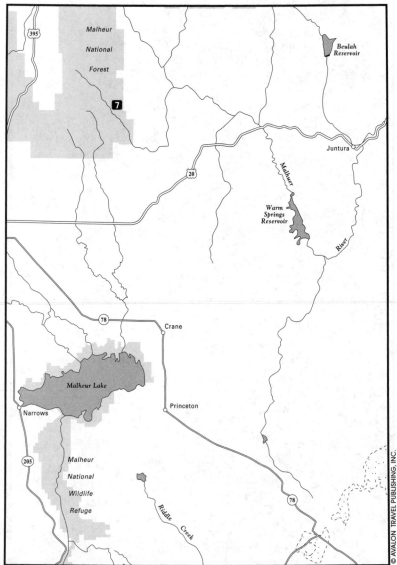

Malheur National Forest

395

7

Beulah Reservoir

Juntura

20

Malheur

Warm Springs Reservoir

River

78

Crane

Malheur Lake

Princeton

Narrows

205

Malheur National Wildlife Refuge

Riddle Creek

78

© AVALON TRAVEL PUBLISHING, INC.

Map 12.3

Hikes 8–12
Pages 548–550

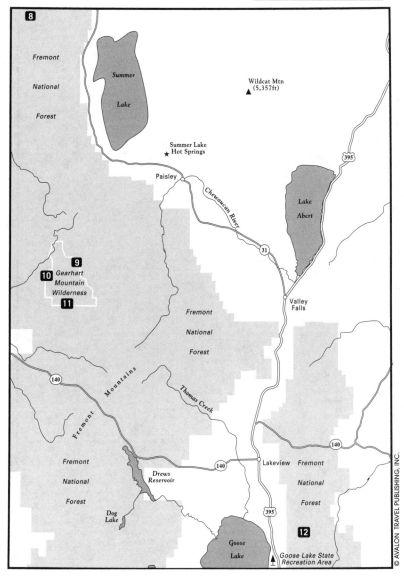

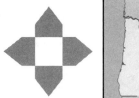

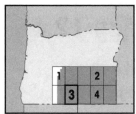

Map 12.4

Hike 13
Page 551

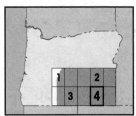

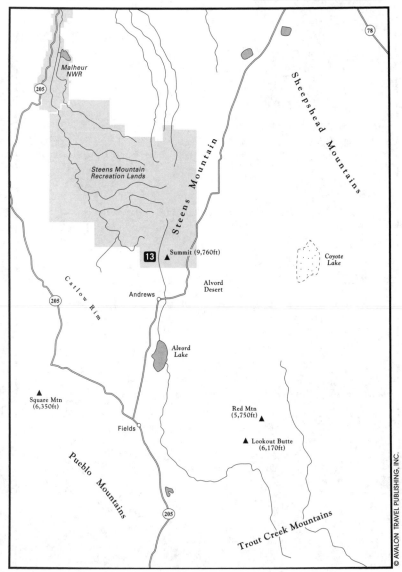

■ NEWBERRY LAVA CAVES
3.4 mi/1.5 hrs

south of Bend in Deschutes National Forest

Map 12.1, page 541

Who needs air conditioning when you can explore the icy depths of lava caves? Not to be confused with the Newberry Lava Monument to the south, these three super-short trails lead to caves right off the highway and are just the ticket to refreshment on one of the Bend area's infamous hot and dry days. The lava tubes were created courtesy of their neighbor to the south, volcano Mount Newberry, and the lava flows formed tunnels that you can explore. First stop: Boyd Cave, a .2-mile descent into the chilly cavern. Next up: Skeleton Cave, a .2-mile trip to two lava tunnels. Not to be left out in the um, dark, is the .5-mile journey down Wind Cave, which features a natural skylight. (Caution: It's hard to keep your footing on the huge rocky mess on the floor.) But those were just a warm-up for the main attraction: A 10-mile trip south on Highway 97 will bring you to Lava River Cave, which is the longest and spookiest of them all, extending one mile into the lava tube. Bring along warm clothes, gloves, a flashlight, and some rock-hopping shoes. Be warned, though: If you are claustrophobic, you may not enjoy these caves as much as the next person, so enter at your own risk. Lava River Cave and Wind Cave are closed between November 1 and April 15 to protect hibernating bats (not that you'd want to go there in the winter anyway; word has it that bears also slumber in these cozy caves). **User Groups:** Hikers, dogs, mountain bikes, and horses (no mountain bikes or horses allowed at Lava River Cave). No wheelchair access. **Permits:** Permits are not required. Parking and access are free for Boyd, Wind, and Skeleton Caves; there is a $3 entrance fee for Lava River Cave. **Maps:** For a map of Deschutes National Forest, contact Nature of the Northwest Information Center. For a topographic map, ask the USGS for Kelsey Butte and Lava Butte.

Directions: From Bend, drive four miles south on U.S. 97 to China Hat Road/Forest Service Road 18. Boyd Cave is nine miles down on the left side of the road; Skeleton Cave is .5 mile east of Boyd Cave; and Wind Cave is another two miles down Forest Service Road 18 from Skeleton Cave.

Contact: Deschutes National Forest, Bend-Fort Rock Ranger District, 1230 Northeast 3rd Street, Suite A-262, Bend, OR 97701, 541/383-4000.

■ NEWBERRY CRATER RIM
21.0 mi/2.0 days

between Bend and La Pine in Newberry Crater National Monument

Map 12.1, page 541

If you want to be a stickler about things, Newberry Crater is actually made of several overlapping calderas, so it should properly be called Newberry Caldera. But whatever you call it, you should check out this amazing sight. Sitting on the top of Newberry Volcano, the four-mile-diameter caldera was formed during a series of eruptions over a period of a half million years. The whole shebang is a 21-mile journey (backpackers should note that there's no water on the trail), but you can easily shorten the trip by taking one of the many access points, such as Paulina Peak Trail (see listing in this chapter). **User Groups:** Hikers, dogs, mountain bikes, and horse. No wheelchair access. **Permits:** A federal Northwest Forest pass is required to park here. The cost is $5 for a day pass or $30 for an annual pass. You can buy a day pass at the trailhead, at ranger stations, from private vendors, or through Nature of the Northwest Information Center. **Maps:** For a map of Deschutes National Forest, contact Nature of the Northwest Information Center. For a topographic map, ask the USGS for Paulina Peak and East Lake. **Directions:** From Bend, drive 22 miles south on U.S. 97 to Forest Service Road 21, about seven miles north of La Pine. Turn left and drive 12 miles to park at Paulina Lake Lodge.

The trail is also accessible at Little Crater Campground on the south side of the park.

Contact: Deschutes National Forest, Bend-Fort Rock Ranger District, 1230 Northeast 3rd Street, Suite A-262, Bend, OR 97701, 541/383-4000.

🔟 PAULINA LAKESHORE LOOP
7.0 mi/3.5 hrs 🔟 🔟

between Bend and La Pine in Newberry Crater National Monument

Map 12.1, page 541

Ⓕ Paulina Lake sits in Newberry Crater, which was created by a series of eruptions over a half-million year span. It's connected by an obsidian flow with sister lake East Lake, but bigger and grander Paulina hogs all the attention. Underground springs and snowmelt feed the lake, which can reach 250 feet in depth. Exploring the seven-mile rim of the lake, you'll come across lava, hidden beaches, hot springs, developed campgrounds, and even an old hand pump in Little Crater Campground that used to churn out 97-degree water (check out campsite 49 to see it). Nearby Paulina Peak looks out over the proceedings from its 7,985-foot summit.

User Groups: Hikers and dogs. No horses or mountain bikes allowed. No wheelchair access.

Permits: A federal Northwest Forest pass is required to park here. The cost is $5 for a day pass or $30 for an annual pass. You can buy a day pass at the trailhead, at ranger stations, from private vendors, or through Nature of the Northwest Information Center.

Maps: For a map of Deschutes National Forest, contact Nature of the Northwest Information Center. For a topographic map, ask the USGS for Paulina Peak and East Lake.

Directions: From Bend, drive 22 miles south on U.S. 97 to Forest Service Road 21, about seven miles north of La Pine. Turn left and drive 12 miles to park at Paulina Lake Lodge. The trail is also accessible at Little Crater Campground on the south side of the park.

Contact: Deschutes National Forest, Bend-Fort

Rock Ranger District, 1230 Northeast 3rd Street, Suite A-262, Bend, OR 97701, 541/383-4000.

🔟 PAULINA CREEK/PAULINA FALLS
6 mi/3.0 hrs 🔟 🔟

between Bend and La Pine in Newberry Crater National Monument

Map 12.1, page 541

Are you an uphill or a downhill person? If you like a longer hike and don't mind a 2,000-foot gentle ascent, try the Peter Skene Ogden trailhead. Traveling along Paulina Creek, the trail hits several waterfalls along the way, but you'll have to walk nearly the whole distance to get to the big enchilada itself, the twin Paulina Falls. A better way to see the sights is to start from Paulina Lake Lodge, where you'll hit the falls after just .25 mile and continue another three miles along Paulina Creek to another falls, turning around for a six-mile round-trip. While you're there, explore Paulina Lake, Paulina Peak, and the Obsidian Flow (see listings in this chapter).

User Groups: Hikers, dogs, and horses. Mountain bikes are allowed only on the uphill portion of the trail. No wheelchair access.

Permits: A federal Northwest Forest pass is required to park here. The cost is $5 for a day pass or $30 for an annual pass. You can buy a day pass at the trailhead, at ranger stations, from private vendors, or through Nature of the Northwest Information Center.

Maps: For a map of Deschutes National Forest, contact Nature of the Northwest Information Center. For a topographic map, ask the USGS for Finley Butte and Paulina Peak.

Directions: To the Peter Ogden trailhead: From Bend, drive 22 miles south on U.S. 97 to Forest Service Road 21, about seven miles north of La Pine. Turn left at the sign for Ogden Group Camp to the large parking area and the well-marked trailhead. To the Paulina Falls trailhead: From Bend, drive 22 miles south on U.S. 97 to Forest Service Road 21, about seven miles north of La Pine. Turn left and drive 12 miles, turning left to the Paulina Creek Falls picnic area, the parking area, and the well-marked trailhead.

Contact: Deschutes National Forest, Bend-Fort Rock Ranger District, 1230 Northeast 3rd Street, Suite A-262, Bend, OR 97701, 541/383-4000.

5 BIG OBSIDIAN FLOW TRAIL
0.8 mi/0.5 hr

between Bend and La Pine in Newberry Crater National Monument
Map 12.1, page 541

It may be the youngest lava flow in Oregon, at a spring-chicken age of 1,300 years, but don't underestimate the power of the Obsidian Flow: Surgical knives made from obsidian are sharper than steel. An interpretive trail with eight signs point out the sights on this magical area, where the black-glass flow extends for 170 million cubic yards, enough rock to pave roads that circle the globe three times. The trail is close to the other Newberry Crater and Paulina Lake hikes, so you can use this as a worthwhile warm-up.

User Groups: Hikers and dogs. Mountain bikes and horses are not allowed. No wheelchair access.

Permits: A federal Northwest Forest pass is required to park here. The cost is $5 for a day pass or $30 for an annual pass. You can buy a day pass at the trailhead, at ranger stations, from private vendors, or through Nature of the Northwest Information Center.

Maps: For a map of Deschutes National Forest, contact Nature of the Northwest Information Center. For a topographic map, ask the USGS for East Lake.

Directions: From Bend, drive 22 miles south on U.S. 97 to Forest Service Road 21, about seven miles north of La Pine. Turn left and drive 12 miles, past Paulina Lake Lodge to the south side of the lake. The trailhead and parking are on the right side of the road between Paulina and East Lakes.

Contact: Deschutes National Forest, Bend-Fort Rock Ranger District, 1230 Northeast 3rd Street, Suite A-262, Bend, OR 97701, 541/383-4000.

6 PAULINA PEAK
4.2 mi/2.5 hrs

between Bend and La Pine in Newberry Crater National Monument
Map 12.1, page 541

The 7,985-foot summit of Paulina Peak (pronounced paul-EYE-nah) is the highest point on Newberry Volcano, and you'll feel every step. It's an unrelenting two-mile climb to the summit (elevation gain is 1,500 feet), where on a clear day you can bear witness to more than eight peaks in three states—Mount Adams in Washington and Mount Shasta in California, along with the neighboring Cascade peaks. And since you'll be chugging water all the way up the steep ascent (or at least you should be), you'll be pleased to note there's a handy toilet up top, rumored to be the highest public toilet in Oregon. How's that for a claim to fame? It's because you can drive to the top, which means after all your effort, you'll arrive to find camera-toting visitors fresh from their cars. The trail also arrives at a junction with Crater Rim Trail, so you can extend your hike if you like. Best to start with the peak first to see if your legs can handle any more miles, though, because although it's not a long climb, it's tough.

User Groups: Hikers, dogs, and horses. No mountain bikes allowed. No wheelchair access.

Permits: A federal Northwest Forest pass is required to park here. The cost is $5 for a day pass or $30 for an annual pass. You can buy a day pass at the trailhead, at ranger stations, from private vendors, or through Nature of the Northwest Information Center.

Maps: For a map of Deschutes National Forest, contact Nature of the Northwest Information Center. For a topographic map, ask the USGS for Paulina Peak.

Directions: From Bend, drive 22 miles south on U.S. 97 to Forest Service Road 21, about seven miles north of La Pine. Turn left and drive 12 miles to Paulina Lake Lodge. Follow signs to the Paulina Lake campground, and turn right on the gravel road. Continue .2 mile to the gravel turnout on the left side of road.

Contact: Deschutes National Forest, Bend-Fort Rock Ranger District, 1230 Northeast 3rd Street, Suite A-262, Bend, OR 97701, 541/383-4000.

▣ CRAFT CABIN
15.2 mi/7.0 hrs

northeast of Burns in Malheur National Forest

Map 12.2, page 542

This trail wins the prize for the most mystifying name: No cabin is on this trail, although supposedly there used to be long ago. Craft Point is nearby, but you don't actually reach it. But hey, it's all just semantics, right? No matter its name, this is a pleasant creekside trail that everyone can enjoy—horses, mountain bikers, hikers, dogs, even cows. Especially cows, come to think of it. You'll most likely encounter plenty of these four-legged friends, or at least see evidence of them (watch your step!). Following Pine Creek, a slow-moving mere ribbon of water at the start of the trail, which widens out eventually, this is a peaceful stroll through steep canyon terrain. You'll have to cross the stream a couple times, but there are handy stepping stones to guide you. Now if only they could do something about the name. . . .

User Groups: Hikers, dogs, mountain bikes, and horses. No wheelchair access.

Permits: Permits are not required. Parking and access are free.

Maps: For a map of Malheur National Forest, contact Nature of the Northwest Information Center. For a topographic map, ask the USGS for Craft Point.

Directions: From Burns, drive 12.3 miles east on U.S. 20 and turn left (north) onto Rattlesnake Road, which turns into Forest Service Road 28. Drive 12.1 miles and turn right onto Forest Service Road 2850. Travel 2.2 miles and turn right on Forest Service Road 2855. Drive 2.2 miles and turn left at a fork, drive another .9 mile, then turn right on Forest Service Road 125 for 1.1 miles to the end of the road and the trailhead parking area.

Contact: Malheur National Forest, Emigrant Creek Ranger District, 265 Highway 20 South, Hines, OR 97738, 541/573-4300.

▣ FREMONT TRAIL TO HAGER MOUNTAIN
8.0 mi/4.0 hrs

in Fremont National Forest south of Silver Lake

map 12.3, page 543

If you like to take pictures of majestic peaks to say, "Hey, I climbed that," you'll like this trail, because there are plenty of viewpoints of this lonesome lookout (which is available for rental). You'll start off in a dense forest for four miles up to the peak. It's a desolate area, so you're likely to have it to yourself, but don't be surprised if you have some company after hoofing it to the 7,200-foot summit, because visitors can also drive straight to the top. The pleasant, well-marked trail starts off flat to warm you up for the climb ahead. Once on top, you'll have views of the High Desert Country, the Cascades, and Mount Shasta.

User Groups: Hikers, dogs, mountain bikes, and horses. No wheelchair access.

Permits: Permits are not required. Parking and access are free.

Maps: For a map of Fremont National Forest, contact Nature of the Northwest Information Center. For a topographic map, ask the USGS for Hager Mountain.

Directions: From La Pine, drive southeast on Highway 31 for 47.5 miles and turn right on East Bay Road/Highway 28. Continue 8.9 miles and turn into a small parking pullout and the trailhead on the left.

Contact: Fremont National Forest, Silver Lake Ranger District, Highway 31, P.O. Box 129, Silver Lake, OR 97638, 541/576-2107.

▣ BLUE LAKE
6.0 mi/3.0 hrs

north of Bly in the Gearhart Mountain Wilderness within Fremont National Forest

Map 12.3, page 543

Meandering through the remote Gearhart

Wilderness (which sees only about 500 visitors each year, during the summer), this trail travels on Gearhart Mountain Trail for three scenic miles to 7,031-foot Blue Lake. Before hitting the lake, you'll pass through wildflower meadows and forests of lodgepole pine and white fir, with vistas of Gearhart Mountain in the distance. A .5-mile loop surrounds the lake, or you can simply rest here and return the way you came. This trail continues another 10 miles over the Gearhart Mountain summit, and can also be done as a shuttle hike for 13.5 miles total (see Gearhart Mountain listing for directions for shuttle parking).

User Groups: Hikers, dogs, and horses. No mountain bikes are allowed. No wheelchair access.

Permits: Permits are not required. Parking and access are free.

Maps: For a map of Fremont National Forest, contact Nature of the Northwest Information Center. For a topographic map, ask the USGS for Lee Thomas Crossing.

Directions: From Bly, drive 1.2 miles east on Highway 140 and turn left on Campbell Road. Go .4 mile and turn right onto paved Forest Service Road 34. Drive 18.9 miles and turn left onto gravel Forest Service Road 3372. Drive 8.2 miles and turn left onto gravel Forest Service Road 015, and continue 1.2 miles to the road's end and the trailhead.

Contact: Fremont National Forest, Bly Ranger District, Highway 140, P.O. Box 25, Bly, OR 97622, 541/353-2427.

🔟 DEMING CREEK TO BOULDER SPRINGS

13.5 mi/7.0 hrs to 2.0 days

north of Bly in the Gearhart Mountain Wilderness within Fremont National Forest

Map 12.3, page 543

It used to be a whole lot easier to access this part of the Gearhart Wilderness, but the bulltrout in Deming Creek didn't care for the old access road—apparently, the silt erosion was threatening their precious little gills. "Let them

walk, that's what they have feet for!" sniffed the head bulltrout, and the Forest Service heeded the advice: In 1999, the old access road to this trail was done away with, lengthening the trail by six miles. Today, trout and trekkers happily exist side by side. Well, not exactly side by side, because while you can hear the creek while you walk, it's a tease on a hot day, because you never really come up to it. Instead, it ventures along a wide trail at first, with views of Gearhart Mountain, before climbing steadily (total elevation gain is 2,500 feet), entering 3.2 miles later into the Gearhart Wilderness. You'll pass through wildflower–dotted Boulder Meadow and pass Boulder Creek before the trail ends at the junction with Gearhart Trail (turn left to continue several more miles to Blue Lake for overnight camping spots). Look out for wildlife like cougars and deer.

User Groups: Hikers, dogs, and horses. No mountain bikes are allowed. No wheelchair access.

Permits: Permits are not required. Parking and access are free.

Maps: For a map of the Fremont National Forest, contact Nature of the Northwest Information Center. For a topographic map, ask the USGS for Campbell Reservoir and Gearhart Mountain.

Directions: From Bly, drive 1.2 miles east on Highway 140 and turn left on Campbell Road. Drive .4 mile and turn right onto paved Forest Service Road 34. Continue 3.9 miles and turn left onto dirt Forest Service Road 335. Go 1.3 miles and turn right onto dirt Forest Service Road 018. Continue 2.8 miles to the end of the road and the trailhead straight ahead as you drive in.

Contact: Fremont National Forest, Bly Ranger District, Highway 140, P.O. Box 25, Bly, OR 97622, 541/353-2427.

11 GEARHART MOUNTAIN
12.0 mi/7.0 hrs to 2.0 days

north of Bly in the Gearhart Mountain Wilderness within Fremont National Forest

Map 12.3, page 543

The word "remote" was created in the 22,823-acre Gearhart Wilderness. There are only two trails (which are categorized as three hikes in this book) that slice through this area, and there's plenty to witness along the way. Have a hankering for some rocks? Check it out: Only .75 mile in from the trailhead, you'll come across the Palisades, a 10-acre display of interesting rock formations and walls. Continue on a couple miles to witness the Dome, a 300-foot bare rock plunked down in the middle of the forest. Then climb farther to amazing views and The Notch, a ridgeline pass of the 8,120-foot Gearhart Mountain summit. The trail continues from here for seven more miles, passing Blue Lake along the way (see Blue Lake listing for trailhead access if you want to arrange a shuttle hike). You can either camp there for the night (adding another eight miles total to your journey) or return once you reach the summit for a 12-mile round-trip day hike.

User Groups: Hikers, dogs, and horses. No mountain bikes are allowed. No wheelchair access.

Permits: Permits are not required. Parking and access are free.

Maps: For a map of Fremont National Forest, contact Nature of the Northwest Information Center. For a topographic map, ask the USGS for Gearhart Mountain.

Directions: From Bly, drive 1.2 miles east on Highway 140 and turn left on Campbell Road. Go .4 mile and turn right onto paved Forest Service Road 34. Drive 14.7 miles and turn left onto Forest Service Road 34-012 (a rocky road) for 1.4 miles to the road's end, past the Corral Creek Campground. Trailhead is to the left beside the welcome sign. (Note: The trailhead on the Forest Service map is referred to as the Lookout Rock Trailhead, although the trail itself is named Gearhart Mountain Trail. Don't ask.)

Contact: Fremont National Forest, Bly Ranger District, Highway 140, P.O. Box 25, Bly, OR 97622, 541/353-2427.

12 CRANE MOUNTAIN
16.0 mi/1.0 day

east of Lakeview in Fremont National Forest

Map 12.3, page 543

Jeep owners, this one is calling your name. If you don't mind a bumpy ride to the trail, you can drive directly to the top of Crane Mountain without passing Go, and start from the summit itself. (Those of us who prefer to pass on having our brains jangled around in our heads while driving would be wise to walk the final two miles up the road to reach the summit and trailhead.) Whether you arrive by wheel or foot, you're definitely in for a great view: Crane Mountain stands at 8,357 feet, and from here hikers can take a peek into California and the surrounding vistas and peaks. Crane Mountain National Recreation Trail is actually 36 miles in length total, and from this trailhead it travels eight miles to the California border, so it's up to you and how much muscle power you have in your legs. One option is simply to hike up to the actual trailhead (if you're one of the aforementioned non-four-wheel drivers), take in the view, and head back down to your car, because the actual beauty of it is the summit itself. Another option is to access the trail at Rogger Meadow trailhead, which reaches Crane Mountain in eight miles for a 16-mile round-trip (see driving directions below). Whatever your pleasure, you're guaranteed some solitude and scenery. Since it starts at such high elevation, the trail can be snowbound through July.

User Groups: Hikers, dogs, mountain bikes, and horses. No wheelchair access.

Permits: Permits are not required. Parking and access are free.

Maps: For a map of the Fremont National Forest, contact Nature of the Northwest Information Center. For a topographic map, ask the USGS for Crane Mountain.

Directions: From Lakeview, drive 4.6 miles north on U.S. 395 to Highway 140. Turn right (east) onto Highway 140 and drive 8.1 miles to Warner Road/Forest Service Road 3915. Turn right and drive 12.2 miles (first 6.7 miles are paved, then it turns to gravel) to Forest Service Road 4011. Turn right and go 3.6 miles to the end of 4011. The road now turns into Forest Service Road 015 for 2.5 bumpy miles, so park at the side of the road and walk up here if you wish. To get to Rogger Meadow trailhead, follow directions above to get to Forest Service Road 3915, then drive 5.6 miles on 3915; the trailhead and parking area are on your right.

Contact: Fremont National Forest, Lakeview Ranger District, HC-64, Box 60, Lakeview, OR 97630, 541/947-3334.

⓭ WILDHORSE LAKE
3.0 mi/2.0 hrs

southeast of Burns in the Steens Mountain Wilderness area

Map 12.4, page 544

Ⓕ You don't even need to get out of your car to witness the beauty of 9,700-foot Steens Mountain, because the long and winding road up the mountain gives you glimpses into the deep gorges and desert below. But you'll definitely want to hop out and see Wildhorse Lake, perched 1,000 feet below the summit. It's a steep and rocky descent to this alpine lake, but it's well worth the trip, as it sits surrounded by wildflowers, with a view of the summit. Steens Mountain paintbrush

and thistle are loyal little plants, and they choose to reside only on this mountain. Animals also love to roam this vast expanse, including deer, elk, and bighorn sheep. As you drive up Steens Mountain Loop Road, viewpoints beckon you to hop out to snap a shot or two, such as Kiger Gorge viewpoint, East Rim viewpoint, and the summit itself (which you can climb .5 mile to). Remember, you're already starting at 9,500 feet of elevation, so don't be surprised if you feel like you're moving in slow motion—it's better that way anyway, because then you have more time to take in the views. The best time of year to visit is late July and on, because it's usually snowbound before then; check ahead on road conditions. Also, even if it's a warm day, it can get chilly here, so bring warm clothes.

User Groups: Hikers and dogs. No mountain bikes or horses are allowed. No wheelchair access.

Permits: Permits are not required. Parking and access are free.

Maps: For a map of Steens Mountain, contact Bureau of Land Management, Burns District Office, 541/573-4400. For a topographic map, ask the USGS for Wildhorse Lake.

Directions: From Frenchglen (60 miles south of Burns on Highway 205), drive east on gravel Steens Mountain Loop Road. Drive 2.9 miles to a T-intersection, and turn left. Keep right at all junctions, and continue 24.2 miles to the end of the road and the trailhead. Park at the side of the road.

Contact: Bureau of Land Management, Burns District Office, 28910 Highway 20 West, Hines, OR 97738, 541/573-4400.

Resources

Resources

National Parks

Crater Lake National Park
P.O. Box 7
Crater Lake, OR 97604
541/594-3100

Mount Rainier National Park
Longmire Wilderness Information Center
Tahoma Woods, Star Route
Ashford, WA 98304
360/569-4453

White River Wilderness Information Center
70004 Highway 410 East
Enumclaw, WA 98022
360/569-6030

Wilkeson Wilderness Information Center
P.O. Box 423
Wilkeson, WA 98396
360/569-6020

North Cascades National Park
Golden West Visitor Center
Stehekin, WA
360/856-5700, ext. 340

Marblemount Wilderness Information Center
7280 Ranger Station Road
Marblemount, WA 98267
360/873-4500

Olympic National Park
Olympic Wilderness Information Center
600 East Park Avenue
Port Angeles, WA 98362
360/565-3130

National and State Forests

Colville National Forest
www.fs.fed.us/r6/colville

Newport Ranger District
315 North Warren
Newport, WA 99156
509/447-7300

Republic Ranger District
180 North Jefferson
Republic, WA 99166
509/775-7400

Sullivan Lake Ranger District
12641 Sullivan Lake Road

Metaline Falls, WA 99153
509/446-7500

Three Rivers Ranger District, Colville Ranger Station
755 South Main
Colville, WA 99114
509/684-7000

Three Rivers Ranger District, Kettle Falls Ranger Station
255 West 11th Avenue
Kettle Falls, WA 99141
509/738-7700

Deschutes National Forest
Bend-Fort Rock Ranger District
1230 Northeast 3rd Street, Suite A-262
Bend, OR 97701
541/383-4000

Crescent Ranger District
136471 Highway 97 North
P.O. Box 208
Crescent, OR 97733
541/433-3200

Sisters Ranger District
Highway 20/Pine Street
P.O. Box 249
Sisters, OR 97759
541/549-7700

Gifford Pinchot National Forest
www.fs.fed.us/r6/gpnf

Cowlitz Valley Ranger District
10024 U.S. 12
Randle, WA 98377
360/497-1100

Mount Adams Ranger District
2455 Highway 141
Trout Lake, WA 98650
509/395-3400

Fremont National Forest
Bly Ranger District
Highway 140
P.O. Box 25
Bly, OR 97622
541/353-2427

Lakeview Ranger District
HC-64
Box 60
Lakeview, OR 97630
541/947-3334

Silver Lake Ranger District
Highway 31

P.O. Box 129
Silver Lake, OR 97638
541/576-2107

Malheur National Forest
Blue Mountain Ranger District
431 Patterson Bridge Road
P.O. Box 909
John Day, OR 97845
541/575-3000

Emigrant Creek Ranger District
265 Highway 20 South
Hines, OR 97738
541/573-4300

Prairie City Ranger District
P.O. Box 337
Prairie City, OR 97869
541/820-3311

Mount Baker–Snoqualmie National Forest
www.fs.fed.us/r6/mbs

Glacier Public Service Center
Glacier, WA 98244
360/599-2714

Verlot Public Service Center
33515 Mountain Loop Highway
Granite Falls, WA 98252
360/691-7791

Darrington Ranger District
1405 Emmens Street
Darrington, WA 98241
360/436-1155

Mount Baker Ranger District Office
810 Highway 20
Sedro-Woolley, WA 98284
360/856-5700

Skykomish Ranger District
74920 Northeast Stevens Pass Highway

P.O. Box 305
Skykomish, WA 98288
360/677-2414

**Snoqualmie Ranger District, Enumclaw
Ranger Station**
450 Roosevelt Avenue East
Enumclaw, WA 98022
360/825-6585

**Snoqualmie Ranger District, North Bend
Ranger Station**
42404 Southeast North Bend Way
North Bend, WA 98045
425/888-1421

Mount Hood National Forest
**Mount Hood National Forest Information
Center**
65000 East Highway 26
Welches, OR 97067
503/622-7674

**Barlow Ranger District, Dufur Ranger
Station**
780 Northeast Court Street
Dufur, OR 97021
541/467-2291

**Clackamas River Ranger District, Estacada
Ranger Station**
595 Northwest Industrial Way
Estacada, OR 97023
503/630-6861

Hood River Ranger District
6780 Highway 35
Mount Hood-Parkdale, OR 97041
541/352-6002

Zigzag Ranger District
70220 East Highway 26
Zigzag, OR 97049
503/622-3191

Ochoco National Forest
Lookout Mountain Ranger District
P.O. Box 490
Prineville, OR 97754
541/416-6500

Paulina Ranger District
7803 Beaver Creek Road
Paulina, OR 97751
541/477-6900

Okanogan National Forest
www.fs.fed.us/r6/oka

Methow Valley Ranger District
24 West Chewuch Road
Winthrop, WA 98862
509/996-4003

Tonasket Ranger District
1 West Winesap
Tonasket, WA 98855
509/486-2186

Olympic National Forest
www.fs.fed.us/r6/olympic

Forks Ranger District
437 Tillicum Lane
Forks, WA 98331
360/374-6522

Hoodsport Ranger District
150 North Lake Cushman Road
P.O. Box 68
Hoodsport, WA 98548
360/877-5254

Quilcene Ranger District
295142 U.S. 101 South
P.O. Box 280
Quilcene, WA 98376
360/765-2200

Quinault Ranger District
353 South Shore Road

P.O. Box 9
Quinault, WA 98575
360/288-2525

Rogue River National Forest
Applegate Ranger District
6941 Upper Applegate Road
Jacksonville, OR 97530
541/899-3800

Ashland Ranger District
645 Washington Street
Ashland, OR 97520
541/552-2900

Prospect Ranger District
47201 Highway 62
Prospect, OR 97536
541/560-3400

Siskiyou National Forest
Chetco Ranger District
P.O. Box 4580
539 Chetco Avenue
Brookings, OR 97415
541/412-6000

Galice Ranger District
200 Northeast Greenfield Road
P.O. Box 440
Grants Pass, OR 97526
541/471-6500

Illinois Valley Ranger District
26568 Redwood Highway
Cave Junction, OR 97523
541/592-2166

Powers Ranger District
42861 Highway 242
Powers, OR 97466
541/439-3011

Siuslaw National Forest
Hebo Ranger District
31525 Highway 22

Hebo, OR 97122
503/392-3161

Mapleton Ranger District
4480 Highway 101, Building G
Florence, OR 97439
541/902-8526

Waldport Ranger District
1094 Southwest Pacific Highway
Waldport, OR 97394
541/563-3211

Tillamook State Forest
Forest Grove District Office
801 Gales Creek Road
Forest Grove, OR 97116
503/357-2191

Umatilla National Forest
www.fs.fed.us/r6/uma

Heppner Ranger District
P.O. Box 7
Heppner, OR 97836
541/676-9187

North Fork John Day Ranger District
P.O. Box 158
Ukiah, OR 97880
541/427-3231

Pomeroy Ranger District
Route 1, Box 53-F
Pomeroy, WA 99347
509/843-1891

Walla Walla Ranger District
1415 West Rose Street
Walla Walla, WA 99362
509/522-6290

Umpqua National Forest
Cottage Grove Ranger District
78405 Cedar Parks Road
Cottage Grove, OR 97424
541/942-5591

Wallowa Mountains Visitor Center, Eagle Cap Ranger District
88401 Highway 82
Enterprise, OR 97828
541/426-5546

Wallowa-Whitman National Forest
Baker City Ranger District
3165 10th Street
Baker City, OR 97814
541/523-4476

Wallowa Valley Ranger District
88401 Highway 82
Enterprise, OR 97828
541/426-4978

Wenatchee National Forest
www.fs.fed.us/r6/wenatchee

Chelan Ranger District
428 West Woodin Avenue
Chelan, WA 98816-9724
509/682-2576

Cle Elum Ranger District
803 West 2nd Street
Cle Elum, WA 98922
509/852-1100

Entiat Ranger District
2108 Entiat Way
P.O. Box 476
Entiat, WA 98822
509/784-1511

Lake Wenatchee Ranger District
22976 Highway 207
Leavenworth, WA 98826
509/763-3103

Leavenworth Ranger District
600 Sherbourne
Leavenworth, WA 98826
509/548-6977

Naches Ranger District
10237 Highway 12
Naches, WA 98937
509/653-2205

Willamette National Forest
Detroit Ranger District
HC 73
Mill City, OR 97360
503/854-3366

McKenzie River Ranger District
57600 McKenzie Highway
McKenzie Bridge, OR 97413
541/822-3381

Middle Fork Ranger District
Lowell Office
60 South Pioneer Street
Lowell, OR 97452
541/937-2129

Sweet Home Ranger District
3225 Highway 20
Sweet Home, OR 97386
541/367-5168

Winema National Forest
Klamath Ranger District
1936 California Avenue
Klamath Falls, OR 97601

Parks, Recreation Areas, and Other Resources

Bend Metro Park and Recreation Department
200 Northwest Pacific Park Lane
Bend, OR 97701
541/389-7275

Bureau of Land Management
Burns District Office
28910 Highway 20 West
Hines, OR 97738
541/573-4400

Medford District Office
3040 Biddle Road
Medford, OR 97504
541/618-2200

Salem District Office
1717 Fabry Road Southeast
Salem, OR 97306
503/375-5646

Spokane District Office
1103 North Fancher Street
Spokane, WA 99212-1275
509/536-1200

City of Eugene Parks and Open Space
Recreation Services Division
99 West 10th Avenue, Suite 340
Eugene, OR 97401
541/682-5333

Columbia River Gorge National Scenic Area
902 Wasco Avenue, Suite 200
Hood River, OR 97031
541/386-2333

Hells Canyon National Recreation Center
88401 Highway 82
Enterprise, OR 97828
541/426-5546

John Day Fossil Beds National Monument
32651 Highway 19
Kimberly, OR 97848
541/987-2333

Lane County Parks Division, Armitage Park
90064 Coburg Road
Eugene, OR 97408
541/682-2000

Mount St. Helens National Volcanic Monument
www.fs.fed.us/gpnf/mshnvm
Monument Headquarters
(Gifford Pinchot National Forest)
42218 Northeast Yale Bridge Road
Amboy, WA 98601
360/449-7800
Mount Margaret Backcountry: 360/449-7871
Climbing Info-Line: 360/449-7861

Mount St. Helens–Coldwater Ridge Visitor Center
3029 Spirit Lake Highway
Castle Rock, WA 98611
360/274-2114

Mount St. Helens–Johnston Ridge Observatory
3029 Spirit Lake Highway
Castle Rock, WA 98611
360/274-2140

National Historic Oregon Trail Interpretive Center
22267 Oregon Highway 86
P.O. Box 987
Baker City, OR 97814
541/523-1843

The Nature Conservancy of Oregon
821 Southeast 14th Avenue
Portland, OR 97214
503/230-1221

Nature of the Northwest Information Center
800 Northeast Oregon Street, Suite 177
Portland, OR 97232
800/270-7504 for Northwest Forest permits
503/872-2750 for maps and other products
www.naturenw.org

Oregon Caves National Monument
19000 Caves Highway
Cave Junction, OR 97523
541/592-2100

Oregon Dunes National Recreation Area
855 Highway 101
Reedsport, OR 97467
541/271-3611

Oregon Parks and Recreation Department
1115 Commercial Street Northeast
Salem, OR 97301
800/551-6949
www.oregonstateparks.org

Oregon State University, College of Forestry
8692 Peavy Auditorium Road
Corvallis, OR 97330
www.cof.orts.edu

Portland Parks and Recreation
1120 Southwest 5th Avenue, Suite 1302
Portland, OR 97204
503/823-PLAY (503/823-7529)

Seattle City Parks and Recreation
100 Dexter Avnue North
Seattle, WA 98109
206/684-4075
www.cityofseattle.net/parks

Tryon Creek State Natural Area
11321 Southwest Terwilliger Boulevard
Portland, OR 97219
503/636-9886

Washington Department of Fish and Wildlife
201 North Pearl Street
Ellensburg, WA 98926
509/925-6746

Columbia Basin Fish and Wildlife Authority
6653 Road K Northeast
Moses Lake, WA 98837
509/765-6641

Washington Department of Natural Resources
P.O. Box 47001
Olympia, WA 98504-7001
360/902-1375

Washington State Parks and Recreation Commission
P.O. Box 42650
Olympia, WA 98504-2669
360/902-8844 (information) or 360/902-8500
(State Parks Pass)
www.parks.wa.gov

Map Resources

Green Trails
P.O. Box 77734
Seattle, WA 98177
206/546-MAPS (206/546-6277)
www.greentrails.com

Nature of the Northwest
Information Center
800 Northeast Oregon Street, Suite 177
Portland, OR 97232
503/872-2750 (800/270-7504 for Northwest
Forest permits only)
www.naturenw.org

USGS
Oregon Office
10615 Southeast Cherry Blossom Drive

Portland, OR 97216
503/251-3200
www.usgs.gov

USGS Information Services
Box 25286
Denver, CO 80225
www.store.usgs.gov

Outdoor Recreation Information Center
In the Seattle REI Building
222 Yale Avenue North
Seattle, WA 98109-5429
206/470-4060

Hiking Clubs and Groups

Cascade Chapter of Sierra Club
180 Nickerson Street
Suite 202
Seattle, WA 98109-1631
206/523-2147
www.cascade.sierraclub.org

Cascadians of Yakima, WA
www.cascadians.org

Chemeketans Outdoor Club
www.chemeketans.org

Mazamas
909 Northwest 19th Avenue
Portland, OR 97209
503/227-2345
www.mazamas.org

Mountaineers
300 3rd Avenue West
Seattle, WA 98119
206/284-8484
www.mountaineers.org

Mountains-to-Sound Greenway
1011 Western Avenue
Suite 606
Seattle, WA 98104
206/812-0122
www.mtsgreenway.org

Oregon Trails Club
www.trailsclub.org

Pacific Northwest Trail Association
P.O. Box 1817
Mount Vernon, WA 98273
877/854-9415
www.pnt.org

Washington Trails Association
1305 4th Avenue
Suite 512
Seattle, WA 98101-2401
206/625-1367
www.wta.org

Acknowledgments

From Scott Leonard

Writing a hiking guide that covers the entire state of Washington turned out to be quite an endeavor. Such a monumental task could not have been completed without the assistance of many great people.

Thank you to Robin Clark for imparting her knowledge of the Alpine Lakes. Similar gratitude is due to Professor Doug McKeever for sharing his expertise of the North Cascades, Ray and Sam Warner for recommendations for the South Cascades, and friendly Park Ranger Lizza Demsetz for helping with Mount Rainier National Park.

Many thanks to my friends David Dow, Ben Cate, Andrea Penglase, Erica Capuana, Al Her, Pete Lenaker, Pete Kingham, Andy Kingham, and my step dad Justus Mills for their time on the trail and for taking part in many stories.

Appreciation goes to Liz Westbrook, James Herndon, and Andy Leung for providing a place to stay for a summer. Thanks Victrola Coffee & Art for the office.

The editors at Avalon have been great to work with. Thank you Grace Fujimoto and Marisa Solís. A big thank you to Rebecca Browning for this opportunity.

Washingtonians benefit from a rich history of hiking guides. I would like to thank Harvey Manning and Ira Spring for spreading a passion for wilderness in each of their books while setting a high standard for outdoor writing. Robert L. Wood has written extensively on the Olympics, and his work is indispensable.

I can't say thank you enough to Louise Alexander, who was there for me too many times to count. You are a beautiful woman, without whom I couldn't have written this book. Thank you.

And last, but not least, thanks to Venus the dog, the best trail buddy ever.

From Megan McMorris

Who's kidding who here? You think I did all this myself? Not by a long shot. While I was zipping across the state, others were right there with me, researching trails, giving their two-cents' worth, and adding valuable details. Here's a shout out to everyone who helped and supported me throughout this entire project.

First and foremost, I want to thank Kevin Foreman. Your extensive research helped me add in some cool "insider" tips and scope out the best routes. Your love of researching fun facts on the Internet helped me fill in tidbits. Your cool ideas and our brainstorming summits rounded out the book. And that's only the half of it. Reminding me to fill my car's tires, searching for me in the middle of the night when there was a "miscommunication" about when I was supposed to arrive home (oops!), and showing me how to use your camp stove so it wouldn't blow up kept me safe. Finally, your endless patience and support (not to mention the endless trips to the store for Pepsi One and chocolate!) toward the end of this project—when I suddenly turned into an unrecognizable, mumbling form of myself—kept me sane. Thanks for everything.

Secondly, a hearty high-five to my research team: Kevin "DJ Master Flash Kevie Kev" Dickson and Anne Marie "Queen o' Puns" Moss. Dudes, thanks for your enthusiasm, time, and efforts. Kevin, thanks in particular for becoming the proud owner of Roxie the Jeep, who tirelessly went on back roads through Mount Hood and Umatilla National Forest. One would think that after you got Roxie stuck in the mud, encountered rattlesnakes, searched endlessly for nonexistent trails, and got hopelessly lost, you would have called it quits. But thanks to your insane love of adventure, you were always ready for more—with humor. Thanks to both of you for taking this project and running with it, for your adventurous spirits, and most of all, for never failing to make me double over with laughter.

Also, thanks to my mom, Penny, for keeping me fed with homemade trail mix (and tuna wraps as we drove!) and entertained with talking books, and for braving the elements with me on two weekend hiking trips. I'm officially on a first-name basis with the UPS man because of your many care packages! And to my dad, Fred, thanks for keeping me safe and oriented on the road with your many gifts of Sue the trusty Subaru, maps, and emergency kits (and don't worry, I do have health insurance). Let the Amazon.com wars begin with the McMorris books!

To the countless forest and park service workers and others I met with, called, and emailed, thanks for filling in details and encouraging my many questions without making me feel like a pest. A special nod to wilderness whiz Rene Casteran, of the Chetco Ranger District of the Siskiyou National Forest, for your thorough details on trails in the Kalmiopsis Wilderness. Also thanks to friends Jacki, Ryan, and Heather for personal insights and tips on several trails.

Thanks to my sister Erin and my McBuddies Diane, Heather, and Andy for their support and understanding that I was going to cancel trips and not return emails or phone calls for a while, and for still being on a speaking basis with me when all was said and done.

Of course, thanks to Avalon Travel Publishing for their already stellar Foghorn Outdoors series and for letting me come on board; thanks especially to my ever-enthusiastic editor, Marisa Solís.

Last but certainly not least, thanks to my Hiking Paw-Dah in Crime, Corvus the Dog. Corvie, what can I say? You were always eager to go every weekend, never complained when the drive was bumpy or when we got lost, and painstakingly researched interesting wildlife and plants along the trail. You kept me safe from a bear, let me use your moonlit white tail as a beacon when we got stuck in the dark, kept an ear open for strange sounds outside our tent, and most of all just kept me sane with your sweet company. This one is for you, little buddy.

Index

Notes

Notes

Notes

Notes

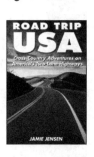

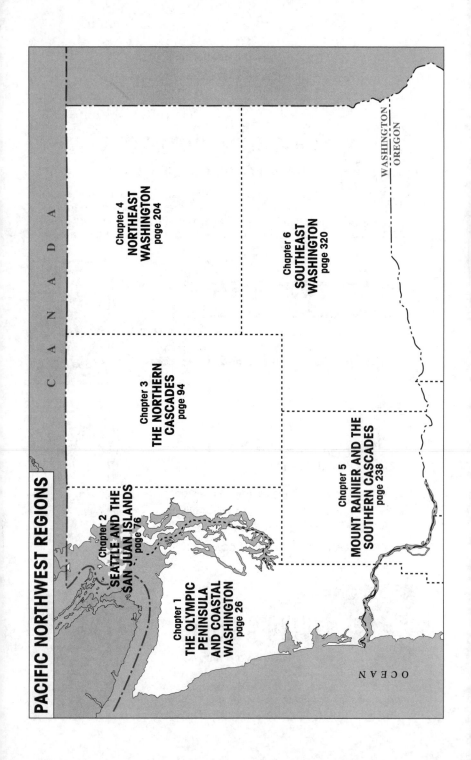

PACIFIC NORTHWEST REGIONS

CANADA

Chapter 2
SEATTLE AND THE SAN JUAN ISLANDS
page 76

Chapter 3
THE NORTHERN CASCADES
page 94

Chapter 4
NORTHEAST WASHINGTON
page 204

Chapter 1
THE OLYMPIC PENINSULA AND COASTAL WASHINGTON
page 26

Chapter 5
MOUNT RAINIER AND THE SOUTHERN CASCADES
page 238

Chapter 6
SOUTHEAST WASHINGTON
page 320

WASHINGTON
OREGON

OCEAN